DATA BASE MANAGEMENT

DATA BASE MANAGEMENT

SECOND EDITION

Fred R. McFadden

Department of Business Information Systems
University of Colorado
Colorado Springs, Colorado

Jeffrey A. Hoffer

School of Business
Indiana University
Bloomington, Indiana

The Benjamin/Cummings Publishing Company, Inc.
Menlo Park, California • Reading, Massachusetts
Don Mills, Ontario • Workingham, U.K. • Amsterdam • Sydney
Singapore • Tokyo • Madrid • Bogota • Santiago • San Juan

To our wives, Evelyn McFadden and Patty Hoffer.

Sponsoring Editor: Jake Warde
Production Supervisor: Betsy Dilernia
Production and Illustration Coordination: George Calmenson, The Book Company
Design Consultant: Wendy Calmenson, The Book Company
Copy Editor: Carol Dondrea
Illustration: Art by AYXA
Cover Design: Juan Vargas
Cover Art: Richard Kharibian
Composition and Camerawork: Graphic Typesetting Service

The basic text of this book was designed using the Modular Design System, as developed by Wendy Earl and Design Office Bruce Kortebein.

Library of Congress Cataloging-in-Publication Data

McFadden, Fred R., 1933–
Data base management / Fred R. McFadden, Jeffrey A. Hoffer.
p. cm.
Includes bibliographies and index.
ISBN 0-8053-6783-7
1. Data base management. I. Hoffer, Jeffrey A. II. Title.
QA76.9.D3M395 1988
005.74--dc19 87-24643
CIP

DEFGHIJ-DO-89

The Benjamin/Cummings Publishing Company, Inc.
2727 Sand Hill Road
Menlo Park, California 94025

Preface

This text is designed for an introductory course in data base management. Such a course is usually required as part of an information systems curriculum in business schools, computer technology programs, and applied computer science departments. The Data Processing Management Association (DPMA) and Association for Computing Machinery (ACM) curriculum guidelines both outline this type of data base management course. This second edition is a major update of the first edition, which has been used successfully at both undergraduate and graduate levels, as well as in management and professional development programs.

The second edition updates and expands material in areas undergoing rapid change due to improved managerial practices, systems design methods, and technological improvements. Sections of the text that have been considerably enhanced because of these changes include those on

- Relational data base technology (including the SQL standard)
- Personal computer data base systems
- The entity-relationship data model
- Fourth-generation languages
- End-user computing
- Data base systems for the Apple Macintosh computer
- Expert system data bases

In addition, the second edition includes many pedagogical improvements in topics that have proven to be especially difficult or time consuming to grasp. More examples, figures, and hints for easier learning have been provided on data structures, network data base processing, distributed data bases, and conceptual data base modeling. New end-of-chapter review questions and exercises have been included to improve the development of basic skills and to reinforce fundamental principles. In addition, a second color has been added to draw attention to critical concepts and parts of illustrations.

Thus, this second edition of *Data Base Management* provides sound, clear, and current coverage of concepts, skills, and issues needed for coping with the expanding organizational data resource. Further, since industry is populated with a wide variety of both mainframe and personal computer data base technologies, the text presents a balanced coverage of these.

ORGANIZATION OF THE BOOK

We encourage instructors to customize their use of the book to meet the needs of both the curriculum and student career plans. The modular nature of the text, its broad coverage, and the inclusion of several sections on advanced topics and emerging issues make customization easy.

Feedback from those who have used the first edition has shown us that several chapter-reading sequences work well. For example, the sections in Chapter 6 on each of the three major data models (hierarchical, network, and relational) can be read separately and grouped with associated implementation chapters (12, 13, and 14 and 15, respectively). Chapter 3 on strategic data planning can be read just prior to Chapters 7 and 8 on data base design (in fact, many instructors prefer to have Chapter 3 read twice: once with Chapters 1 and 2 and then again when discussing data base design). The only firm chapter precedences are Chapter 6 before Chapters 12, 13, 14, or 15; and Chapters 7, 8, and 9 in sequence. It is strongly recommended that Chapters 1 and 2 be read first, since they provide an overview and background for the whole text.

SCOPE OF THE BOOK

Data Base Management was originally developed, and has been enhanced, to meet an unfilled need. Several excellent data base texts and reference books are available today; however, most of these books emphasize issues relevant in a computer science curriculum (basically, the design of data base management system software and operating system file access methods). The goal of this text is to provide adequate technical detail while emphasizing the management and implementation issues relevant in a business information systems curriculum. Thus, the text provides the student with the background necessary to successfully implement a wide variety of data bases in organizations.

The significant updates of the second edition contribute to this original goal by adding *new* coverage of managerial methods and technical issues. This expanded second edition includes:

- Emphasis on the concept of information as a corporate resource and on managers as stewards of this resource.

- A separate chapter on strategic data base planning (Chapter 3), with clear linkage to the process of data base design and development.
- Emphasis on data administration, with extensive discussion of its role and organization placement.
- Emphasis on the role of the data dictionary/directory as a tool in planning and controlling the information resource.
- Complete discussion of data base design, including normalization. Data base design is shown to have a definite link to information systems analysis and design. Design is also clearly separated from implementation.
- Coverage of a wide range of data base technologies, with emphasis on selecting the proper system for the business situation. Particular data base systems covered include SQL/DS and DB2, ORACLE, INGRES, IDMS, IMS, dBASE III Plus, R:base 5000, FOCUS, and REFLEX for the Macintosh.
- Coverage of *both* mainframe and personal computer data base development environments, including screen formatters, report writers, easy query-by-example facilities, menu systems, and PC–mainframe data transfer.
- Use of particular data base systems to demonstrate capabilities, to provide concrete examples, and to facilitate the development of basic skills and concepts. No specific system is covered in depth, since this would both unfairly bias the student and would quickly become obsolete.
- Discussion of distributed data bases, data base computers, and data bases in expert systems.
- Coverage of traditional as well as fourth-generation data base management technology.

LEARNING AIDS AND SUPPLEMENTS

To assist the student and instructor, *Data Base Management* includes the following learning aids:

- Realistic **Case Examples** illustrate important concepts throughout the text. Two running case examples throughout the text highlight concerns from industry: Pine Valley Furniture Company for the manufacturing sector, and Mountain View Community Hospital for the service sector. A third case example, Lakewood College in Chapter 7, emphasizes the needs of public institutions. Case examples are identified by the symbols shown in the margins.
- A **Summary** at the end of each chapter capsulizes the main concepts of the chapter.

- The **Chapter Review** tests students' knowledge. The **Review Questions** check the students' grasp of new terms and important concepts. **Problems and Exercises** require the students to apply their knowledge to realistic situations, and in some cases to extend this knowledge to new problems and situations. Matching questions help the student to distinguish critical terms.
- A **Glossary of Acronyms** (containing about 100 entries) and a **Glossary of Terms** (containing about 300 terms) are included.

The text is part of a complete educational package that is designed to provide a high level of support to the instructor:

- The *Instructor's Manual* is a comprehensive, 400-page guide containing numerous instructional resources. First, for each chapter there are 6 to 10 **Teaching Suggestions**: lecture outlines, teaching hints, and student projects and activities that make use of the chapter content. Second, there are complete **solutions** to both the **Review Questions** and the **Problems and Exercises** in the text. Third, there are 600 **multiple-choice and true-false questions** (approximately 40 per chapter) with answers; these questions have been enhanced in the second edition. Fourth, the *Instructor's Manual* includes a set of over 100 **masters for overhead transparencies** of enlarged illustrations and tables from the text. The *Instructor's Manual* also includes solutions to the cases in the *Case Book*, and each solution is implemented in one popular data base package. (Implementations are provided using dBASE III Plus, R:base 5000, ORACLE, INGRES, and FOCUS.)
- The second edition of the *Case Book for Data Base Management* contains nine realistic cases for course projects, including two cases that emphasize managerial issues: one focuses on data base system selection. Most of these cases are taken from actual company situations. The solutions and implementations can be worked out using either mainframe computers, minicomputers, or personal computers.
- The use of dBASE III PLUS, by Larry Metzelaar and Marianne Fox, provides a comprehensive introduction to this popular microcomputer data base tool. The Limited Use Version of the software is bound into this practical manual.

For more information about the text and to request any of the supplements, please contact your local Sales and Marketing Representative or call toll free (800) 227-1936, or in California (800) 982-6140.

ACKNOWLEDGMENTS

We are grateful to the numerous individuals who contributed to the preparation of the second edition of this textbook. First, we wish to thank our reviewers for their detailed reviews and their many suggestions, characteristic of their thoughtful teaching styles. Those who reviewed the second edition text were George Diehr, University of Washington; Alan Duchan, Canisius College; Ralph Duffy, North Seattle Community College; Dean James, Embry-Riddle Aeronautical University; Bill Korn, University of Wisconsin–Eau Claire; and Charles J. Wertz, Buffalo State College. Valuable guidance on the modifications to be included in the second edition also came from various market research advisors. These advisors were Walter Briggs, University of Alaska–Anchorage; Carol Chrisman, Illinois State University; Bill Courter, Jackson Community College; Richard Epstein, West Chester University; Dimitrios Fotiadis, Wentworth Institute of Technology; Charles F. Fromme, Queensborough College; Clare Hamlet, Pima College; Jan Harrington, Bentley College; Angela Keith, Elizabethtown Community College; Gary Kern, University of Notre Dame; Scott McIntyre, University of Colorado–Colorado Springs; Douglas Mallenry, Creighton University; Bill Mein, Clarkson University; Milton Pine, Cal State University–Dominguez Hills; and Michael G. Sklar, University of Georgia.

Next, we wish to thank our typists, Kathy Abeyta, Kathy Claybaugh, and Patty Hoffer, who were tireless and meticulous in capturing the manuscript on word processing systems so that the inevitable revisions could be accomplished with relative ease. We also benefited from discussions with our colleagues, especially Daniel Couger and Scott McIntyre (University of Colorado) and Ananth Srinivasan (Indiana University). Of special significance are the contributions of material and the writing of sections by Steve Michaele (AT&T), Scott McIntyre (University of Colorado), and Tom Finneran (independent consultant, Princeton, NJ).

We are very grateful to the staff of Benjamin/Cummings for their support throughout the project. In particular, we wish to thank Jake Warde (editor), Devra Lerman (editorial assistant), Sally Elliott (editor-in-chief), and Betsy Dilernia (production supervisor) for their encouragement and guidance. George Calmenson and his staff at The Book Company have provided excellent production, design, and editorial support. Our thanks also go to our many students who helped test the manuscript in its various stages. We would like to thank the following students who assisted in preparing the *Instructor's Manual* and in reviewing the manuscript: Terry Ryan, Kathleen George-Douglas, Cheryl McKay, Edd Joyner, Laurie Kiracofe, Li Cheng, Mary Alexander (Indiana University); and Jackie Gianunzio and Rose Johnston (University of Colorado). To all of these individuals, and to our families, we give our thanks. It hardly needs saying that much of the value of this text is due to their assistance, but we alone bear responsibility for any errors or omissions that remain between the covers.

Fred R. McFadden
Jeffrey A. Hoffer

Brief Contents

Detailed Contents

PART V FUTURE DIRECTIONS 631

Part I

Basic Concepts

The first three chapters of this text present the basic concepts of data base management. In Chapter 1, we introduce the data base environment. Here we contrast the data base approach with conventional file processing, illustrating the potential advantages of the data base approach. We also introduce the major software components of a data base environment, including data base management systems and data dictionary/directory systems.

In Chapter 2, we describe the basic concepts and characteristics of data, introducing the concepts of entities and entity classes. In this chapter, we describe the basic associations between data items and other data entities, as well as the three-level ANSI/SPARC data model, which is the underlying model for most data base management systems today.

Chapter 3 is an introduction to data base planning. We explain the importance of planning to successful data base implementation. We describe the steps in data base planning and introduce a simple top-down model that integrates data base planning with overall business system planning. Also, we introduce a case example of a hospital, which is used extensively throughout the remainder of the text.

Chapter 1

The Data Base Environment

INTRODUCTION

This book is about the data resource of organizations and about the management of that resource. The recognition by management that data (or information) is indeed a resource is a recent development. According to Diebold:

> Information, which in essence is the analysis and synthesis of data, will unquestionably be one of the most vital of corporate resources in the 1980s. It will be structured into models for planning and decision making. It will be incorporated into measurements of performance and profitability. It will be integrated into product design and marketing methods. In other words, information will be recognized and treated as an asset. (1979, 41)

Two important factors demonstrate management's acceptance of data resource management: firm commitment to the data base approach and successful establishment of the data administration function.

A **data base** is a shared collection of interrelated data designed to meet the varied information needs of an organization. A data base has two important properties: It is integrated and it is shared. By *integrated* we mean that previously distinct data files have been logically organized to eliminate (or reduce) redundancy and to facilitate data access. By *shared* we mean that all qualified users in the organization have access to the same data, for use in a variety of activities.

The data base approach offers a number of important and practical advantages to an organization. Reducing redundancy improves the consistency of data while reducing the waste in storage space. Sharing data often permits new data processing applications to be developed without having to create new data files. In general, less redundancy and greater sharing lead to less confusion between organizational units and less time spent resolving errors and inconsistencies in reports. The data base approach also permits centralized control over data standards, security restrictions, and integrity controls. This facilitates the natural evolution and change of information systems *and* organizations. It encourages the use of powerful query languages by users who have no previous programming experience. Finally, the data base approach promotes data independence, which insulates application programs from modifications to the data base itself. All of these advantages are described in the following sections.

DATA AS A RESOURCE

Every organization has a pool of resources it must manage effectively to achieve its objectives. Although their roles differ, all resources—human, financial, and material—share a common characteristic: They all incur cost and are of value to the organization.

It is now recognized that data are also a resource since they, too, incur cost and are of value to an organization. In fact, the value of data is unique in that the entire organization depends on its availability for the management of other resources. Any organization that fails to treat data (or information) as a resource and to manage it effectively will be handicapped in how it manages its human, material, and financial resources.

In this text, we distinguish between data and information. **Data** are facts concerning people, objects, events, or other entities. Data can be financial and quantitative or they can be qualitative and subjective; they can be internal or external; they can be historical or predictive. There are many sources of data in an organization: financial and managerial accounting, production and operations, sales, payroll and personnel, planning, and so on.

Information is data that have been organized or prepared in a form that is suitable for decision making. For example, a list of students and grade point averages in random order is data, but a list of students arranged in order of grade point averages (highest to lowest) represents information to a person responsible for voting an outstanding student award. A pool of carefully organized data can readily be used to produce a variety of information.

To manage their data resources more effectively, many organizations are formally defining their data and placing them into data bases. As we have already said, a data base is an integrated collection of data that is shared by all organizational users. An organization may choose to have a single, large integrated data base; several separate data bases maintained on a central

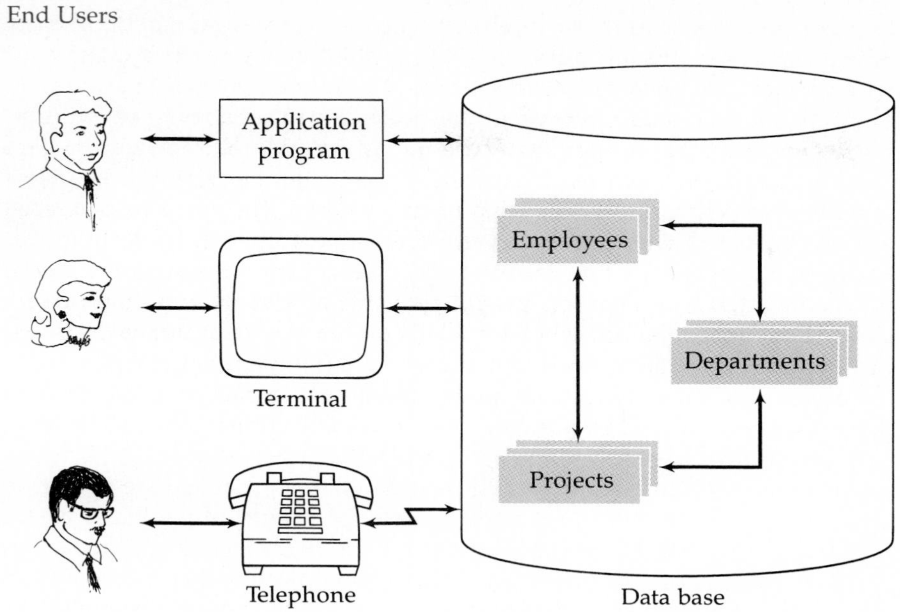

Figure 1-1
A notion of a data base

computer; or separate data bases maintained on separate computers within organizational divisions. We will describe the advantages and disadvantages of each of these approaches in later chapters.

The notion of a data base is shown in Figure 1-1. The data base is conceived as a single entity that consists of a collection of interrelated records. Within the data base are stored records of importance to individual users. There can be numerous users sharing the data base. End users can access the data base in various ways, such as through application programs, display terminals, or perhaps even by means of a telephone.

We describe the data base approach and its advantages and disadvantages by means of a realistic case example. In this example, a small company progresses from manual information systems to a small computer using traditional files and finally to considering the data base approach.

Case Example: Pine Valley Furniture

Pine Valley Furniture Company manufactures high-quality, all-wood furniture and distributes it to stores in a metropolitan area. There are several product lines, including dinette sets, stereo cabinets, wall units, living room furniture, and bedroom furniture. Pine Valley employs about 50 persons at the present time and is experiencing rapid growth.

Pine Valley Furniture was founded about ten years ago by Donald Knotts, its general manager and majority owner. Mr. Knotts had made custom furniture as a hobby and started the business in his own garage. Pine Valley Furniture was operating out of a rented warehouse until five years ago, when it was moved to its present location.

Managing the data resource at Pine Valley Furniture was relatively simple during the first years of its operation. At first, Mr. Knotts kept most of the information needed to run the business in his head, although a few records were kept, mostly for tax purposes. When the business expanded into the rented warehouse, there were about 10 employees. It was then that Mr. Knotts hired a part-time bookkeeper to keep a small set of books. These books included a general ledger and accounts receivable and payable ledgers. The books, in effect, were a small, centralized data base that provided most of the information needed to run the company at that time.

When Pine Valley Furniture moved into its present location, its product line had expanded and its sales volume had doubled in two years. Its work force had grown to over 30 employees. With this organizational growth and complexity, Mr. Knotts found that he could no longer manage the operation by himself. He therefore organized the company into functional areas of responsibility. Manufacturing operations were organized into three main sections: Fabrication, Assembling, and Finishing. Each of these sections had a manager. Also, separate departments were established for several business functions. There was now a Sales Department, an Orders Department, an Accounting Department, and a Purchasing Department. Pine Valley Furniture had emerged from the entrepreneurial mode of operation to a formal organization with functional departments and managers.

When Pine Valley Furniture organized into functional departments, it also changed its approach to managing its data resources. The single set of books that it had used previously was no longer adequate to run the business. Instead, each department now had its own books—files, ledgers, and so on—and informal lines of communication were established to transfer data between departments.

Figure 1-2 shows the manual information system at Pine Valley Furniture. This diagram depicts the flow of data for the mainstream functions—order processing, billing, shipping, and processing work orders. Most customer orders are received in Sales by telephone. The Sales Department refers to a customer file to check the customer's credit and then prepares a sales order. The sales order is then sent to the Orders Department, which checks a products file to determine whether the requested item is in stock. If the item is in stock, the clerk prepares a packing slip. If the item is not in stock (or if the stock level has dropped below a predetermined level), the clerk prepares a work order to manufacture a lot of the item. One copy of the sales order is sent to Accounting, and another copy is filed in the Orders Department. The Accounting Department prices the sales order and prepares an invoice for items shipped to the customer. A packing slip is also included with each customer shipment.

Notice in Figure 1-2 that each department has a separate file (or files) to support its operations and answer its questions. The files shown in Figure

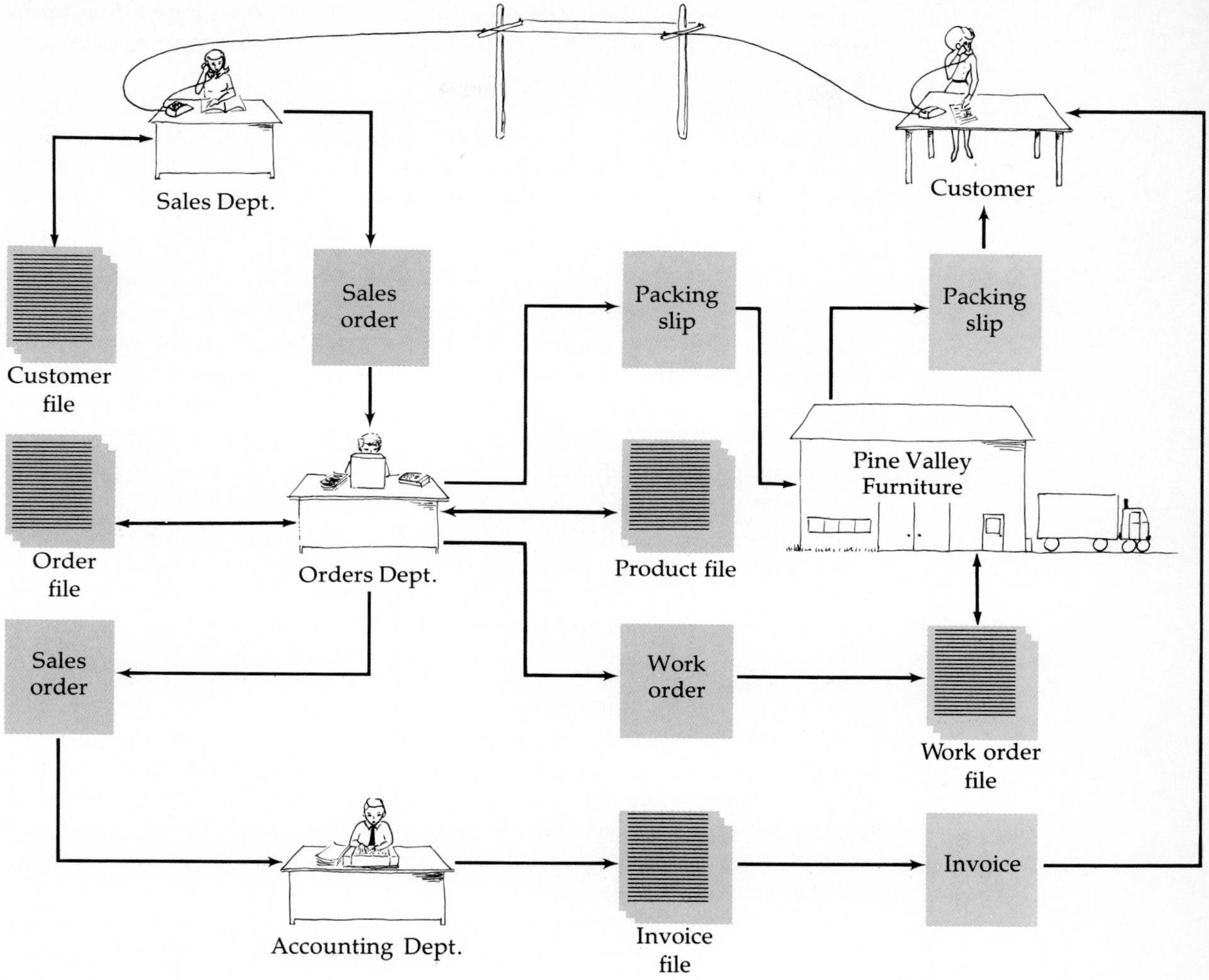

Figure 1-2
Manual information system (Pine Valley Furniture)

1-2, and typical user questions that might be answered by referring to these files, are shown in the following table:

Department	File	Typical Questions
Sales	Customer	What is customer ABC's address and credit limit?
Orders	Product	How many tables (product #123) do we have in stock?
Accounting	Invoice	How much does customer ABC owe us on invoice #567?
Manufacturing	Work Order	How many units of product #123 are we scheduled to build today?

Other departments also have files to support their operations. For example, Purchasing has a file of purchase orders to indicate what materials are currently on order from vendors.

The information system portrayed in Figure 1-2 is a manual system. In this system, the data files are decentralized, and each department works with a portion of the organization's data. Although the system works, it has a number of deficiencies or disadvantages:

1. A constant stream of paperwork (in the form of memos, reports, transactions, and so on) and telephone calls is required to communicate changes and keep the files synchronized.
2. The system cannot easily provide answers to more complex operational questions. For example, to answer the question "What invoices are outstanding for order #123 from customer ABC?" will probably require some research on the part of the Orders Department.
3. Managers cannot easily obtain summary information required for decision making.
4. Duplicate data exist throughout the organization, resulting in lack of consistency and miscommunication. For example, information concerning customer orders is maintained in the Sales, Orders, Accounting, and Shipping departments at Pine Valley Furniture.

It is tempting to assume that a computer would help eliminate many of these typical shortcomings of a manual information system. True, a computer will often permit data to be processed faster and more accurately. However, considering the traditional file processing environment that has prevailed for decades, many of the preceding problems would remain or might even be amplified. This is because in the traditional approach the designer essentially seeks to automate existing manual systems, as we will explain in the following section.

TRADITIONAL FILE PROCESSING SYSTEMS

The traditional approach to information systems design focuses on the data processing needs of individual departments in the organization. The information systems (or IS) group responds to user requests by developing (or acquiring) new computer programs, often one at a time, for individual applications such as accounts receivable, payroll, and inventory control. Each application program or system that is developed is designed to meet the needs of a particular department or user group. That is, there is no overall map, plan, or model to guide the growth of applications.

Each new computer application is typically designed with its own set of data files. Much of the data in these new files may already be present in existing files for other applications. However, to meet the needs of the new

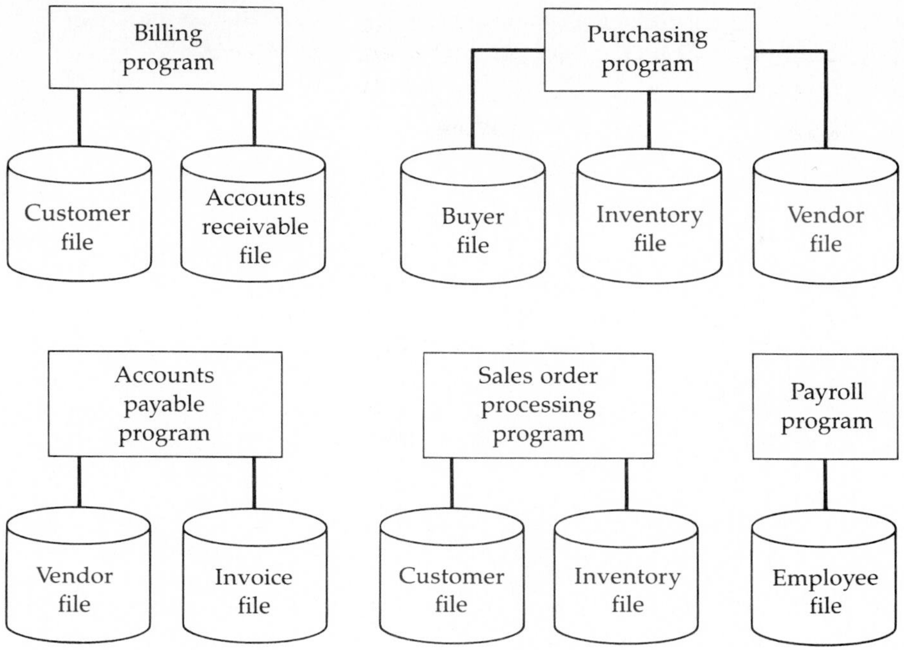

Figure 1-3
Traditional file processing approach

application, the existing files would have to be restructured. This, in turn, would require that existing programs that use these same files be revised or completely rewritten. For this reason, it is often far simpler (and also less risky) to design new files for each application.

The traditional approach to data processing applications is illustrated in Figure 1-3. Notice that the application programs shown in the figure may access one or more data files. A significant factor in the traditional approach is that each application program contains the data definitions for each file that it accesses, as well as the commands for handling the files. For example, the payroll program in Figure 1-3 contains a detailed definition of the employee file. Each application program "owns" its data files, and the program logic is dependent on (or closely interwoven with) the data formats and descriptions.

File Processing Systems at Pine Valley Furniture

Three years ago, Pine Valley Furniture Company acquired a small computer. The company had been experiencing numerous operating problems, including declining customer service and increasing inventory levels. Although the company had grown rapidly, profits had failed to keep pace. Mr. Knotts decided that the manual information system that existed at that time (illustrated in Figure 1-2) was no longer sufficient to manage a fast-growing

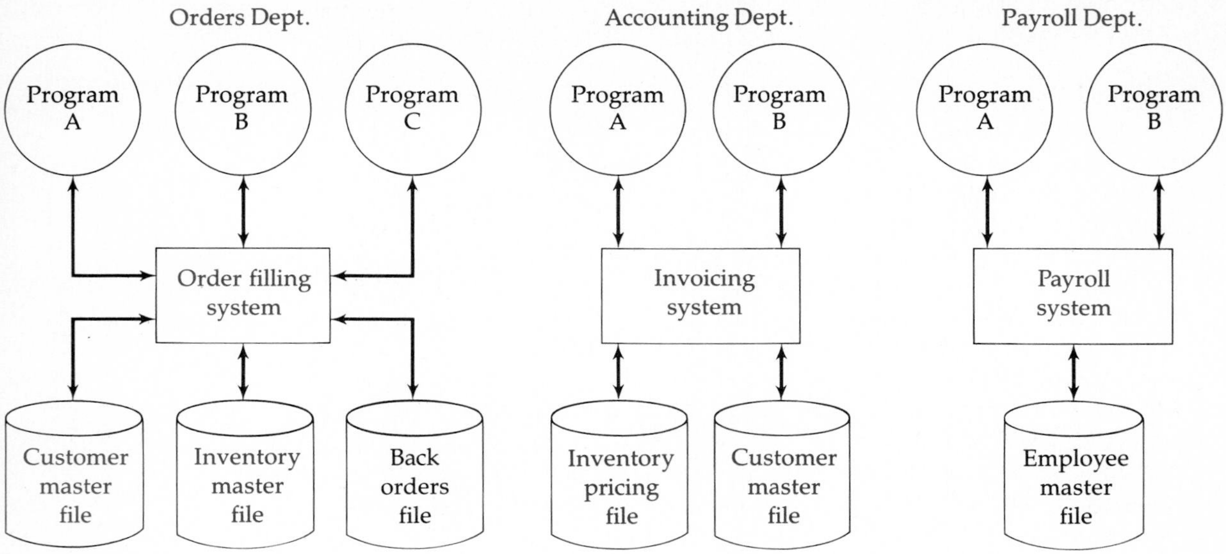

Figure 1-4
Three application systems at Pine Valley Furniture

business. After some evaluation, a small computer was selected and installed at Pine Valley Furniture.

Most of the applications that have subsequently been installed on the computer are in the accounting and financial areas. At the present time, these applications include order filling, invoicing, accounts receivable, inventory control, accounts payable, payroll, and general ledger. Most of these application programs were purchased from a software vendor who modified the programs to meet the requirements of Pine Valley Furniture.

Three of the computer applications at Pine Valley Furniture are depicted in Figure 1-4. The systems illustrated are order filling, invoicing, and payroll. The figure shows the major data files associated with each application system. We will now define each of the terms illustrated in Figure 1-4.

An **application system** is an integrated set of application programs, data files, and procedures that performs a business process or function. For example, the Invoicing System prepares an invoice for each shipment of furniture to a customer of Pine Valley Furniture.

An **application program** performs one task (or a related set of tasks) associated with an application. For example, program B in the invoicing application is a Pricing Program that records a unit price for each item, extends the price for the number of items ordered, and computes a total price for the invoice.

A **data file** (or simply **file**) is a collection of records. The records in a file are often (but not always) of the same type. For example, the Customer Master File contains one record for each of Pine Valley Furniture's customers.

A **logical record** (or simply **record**) is a collection of related data items that describe a particular object or entity. For example, each Customer Master Record contains the following data items: CUSTOMER#, NAME, BILLING ADDRESS, SHIP-TO ADDRESS, CREDIT RATING, and DISCOUNT RATE (we often use # as an abbreviation for NUMBER, as in CUSTOMER#).

A **data item** is a unit fact concerning some object. It is the smallest named unit of data in an information system.

Notice that each application system in Figure 1-4 has its own data files. This is typical of traditional applications. Files for one application may contain data that duplicate data from another application. In some cases, two files within the same application may contain duplicate data. For example, the Inventory Master File used by the Order Filling System and the Inventory Pricing File used in the Invoicing System both contain data describing products sold by Pine Valley Furniture. Also, these two application systems both use a Customer Master File. Is this master file actually one file, or two distinct files with duplicate information? In this case, the two applications happen to share a single Customer Master File. However, there remains a considerable amount of duplicated data in the files used in the various applications at Pine Valley Furniture.

Notice, too, the similarity in design between the computer systems at Pine Valley Furniture and the earlier manual systems they replaced (compare Figures 1-2 and 1-4). In each case, the approach was to develop procedures and associated data files to solve data processing problems for individual functional departments. With the computer systems, the data files are no longer physically located within the individual departments, as in the manual system. However, since they are tailored to the needs of each application or department, they are generally regarded as "belonging" to that department or application, rather than as a resource to be shared by all departments or users.

The computer applications at Pine Valley Furniture have generally been successful. They have allowed the company to reduce its paperwork burden and improve its response to customer orders. They have also provided management with better information concerning costs, sales, and profits. Nevertheless, managers at Pine Valley are dissatisfied with several aspects of the new computer system. While the applications have helped improve the operations management function, they have had little impact on middle management and still less on top management. Mr. Knotts and the other managers at Pine Valley Furniture have come to realize that there are basic limitations to traditional file processing systems. Some of these limitations are described next.

Disadvantages of File Processing Systems

The basic disadvantages of file processing systems are uncontrolled redundancy, inconsistent data, inflexibility, limited data sharing, poor enforcement of standards, low programmer productivity, and excessive program maintenance.

Uncontrolled Redundancy In file processing systems, each application has its own files. This approach inevitably leads to a high level of data redundancy. There are several disadvantages to recording the same data item in multiple files. First, valuable storage space is wasted. Second, the same data may have to be input several times to update all occurrences of a data item. Third, inconsistencies (or various versions) often result, which require time to resolve and correct. As we shall see, some replication of data can be useful but careful control is required.

Inconsistent Data When the same data are stored in multiple locations, inconsistencies in the data are inevitable. For example, several of the files at Pine Valley Furniture contain customer data. Suppose that there is an address change for one of the customers. If the files are to be consistent, this change must be made simultaneously (and correctly) to each of the files containing the customer address data item. Since the files are controlled by different users, however, it is very likely that some files will reflect the old address while others reflect the new address.

Inconsistencies in stored data are one of the most common sources of errors in computer applications. They lead to inconsistent documents and reports and undermine the confidence of users in the integrity of the information system. For example, the outdated customer address just described may lead to a customer invoice being mailed to the wrong location. As a result, the invoice may be returned and the customer payment delayed or lost.

Inflexibility A file processing system resembles a mass production facility. It produces numerous documents and reports routinely and efficiently, provided that these outputs were anticipated in the original design of the system. However, such systems are often quite inflexible and cannot easily respond to requests for a new or redesigned "product." In other words, an application system cannot readily satisfy demands for information in a new format that was not anticipated in the original design. This often leads to considerable frustration on the part of the users, who cannot understand why the computer system cannot give them information in a new format when they know it exists in the application files.

For example, the Order Filling System at Pine Valley Furniture contains three files: Customer Master, Inventory Master, and Back Orders (see Figure 1-4). Suppose that the Orders Department manager wants to obtain a list of back-ordered items for a given customer. Unless this request had been anticipated when the system was designed, it will be difficult to satisfy the request. If the request represents a new requirement, a new application program may be required to extract the required records from each file and produce the desired report.

Limited Data Sharing With the traditional applications approach, each application has its own private files and there is little opportunity for users to share data outside of their own applications. Referring to Figure 1-4, you will notice that users in the Accounting Department have access to the Invoicing System and its files. However, they may not have access to the Order Filling System files, which are used primarily by the Orders Department.

One consequence of limited data sharing is that the same data may have to be entered several times in order to update files with duplicate data. For example, at Pine Valley Furniture, a change in the description for an inventory item would have to be entered separately into the Order filling and Invoicing systems, since each contains its own version of an inventory file.

Another consequence of limited data sharing is that in developing new applications, the designer often cannot (or does not) exploit data contained in existing files. Instead, new files are designed that duplicate much of the existing data. Suppose that the manufacturing manager at Pine Valley Furniture requests a new system for scheduling production orders. Such a system would undoubtedly require an inventory file in order to provide economical order quantities, status of existing orders, and related inventory information. Of course, an Inventory Master File already is being used in the Order Filling System. However, a redesign of this file would be required to meet the requirements of the scheduling application. This, in turn, would probably require a complete rewrite of Programs A, B, and C in the Order Filling System (see Figure 1-4). Instead, the designer would specify a new Inventory File for the Production Scheduling System. In file processing systems, the cycle of limited data sharing and redundancy is perpetuated in this manner.

Poor Enforcement of Standards Every organization requires standard procedures and methods so that it may operate effectively. Within information systems, standards are required for data names, formats, and access restrictions. Unfortunately, data standards are difficult to make known and enforce in a traditional file processing environment, mainly because the responsibility for system design and operation has been decentralized. Two types of inconsistencies may result from poor enforcement of standards: synonyms and homonyms. A **synonym** results when two different names are used for the same data item—for example, student number and matriculation number. A **homonym** is a single name that is used for two different data items. For example, in a bank the term *balance* might be used to designate a checking account balance in one department and a savings account balance in a different department.

Enforcement of standards is particularly difficult in larger organizations with decentralized responsibility and decision making. Without centralized control or coordination, users in various departments may purchase their own computers and develop their own private applications without regard for compatibility or sharing of data. However, even in a small company, the achievement of standards is often difficult in an applications environment. At Pine Valley Furniture, the individual applications that were purchased from the software vendor were of a stand-alone variety and were not really compatible with one another (although all the applications were integrated with the Accounting General Ledger System). The various application programs often used different names and formats for the same data items, which made modifications more difficult and precluded data sharing.

Low Programmer Productivity In traditional file processing systems, the programmer must often design each record and file used by a new application program and then code the data definitions into the program (although this process can sometimes be simplified—by using standard data division descriptions together with copy libraries, for example). The programmer must also select the file access method to be used and write procedural input/output statements in the program. This burden of designing files and records, describing data, and writing procedural input/output statements is repeated for each application program and constitutes a major portion of the system development effort. As such, it is a major contributor to low programmer productivity—a problem that continues to plague the data processing industry. Low programmer productivity, in turn, increases software costs, such as those for the packaged software products purchased by Pine Valley Furniture.

Excessive Program Maintenance In file processing systems, descriptions of files, records, and data items are embedded within individual application programs. Therefore, any modification to a data file (such as a change of data name, format, or method of access) requires that the program (or programs) be modified. To illustrate, suppose that the data item CUSTOMER NAME had to be expanded from a 20-character field to a 25-character field in the Customer Master File at Pine Valley Furniture. As a result of this simple change, several programs in the Order Filling System and Invoicing System would have to be modified.

The process of modifying existing programs is referred to as **program maintenance.** In many organizations today, 80% or more of the programming effort is devoted to this activity. Much of the shortage of computer programmers and the large backlog of new applications can be attributed to the burden of maintaining programs in file processing systems.

The disadvantages discussed here were especially pronounced in first- and second-generation application systems. In third-generation systems, a number of powerful support packages and tools have been introduced to help overcome (or at least minimize) some of the disadvantages. These software support packages include access methods for secondary keys, generalized file management and report writers, on-line query processing, transaction processing systems, data dictionaries, and high-level programming languages. However, even with these facilities, there remain the fundamental deficiencies of file processing systems: redundant data, low sharing of data, lack of standards and control, and low productivity.

Although the impact of many of the disadvantages of the file processing approach can be reduced, doing so requires much costly human intervention and time. A much more desirable solution is to establish standards for data processing and to create a philosophy and automated environment in which these disadvantages can be controlled or eliminated from the start. This is the basis for the data base approach.

DATA BASE APPROACH

The data base approach represents a different concept in information resource management. Data are viewed as an important, shared resource that must be managed like any other asset, such as people, materials, equipment, and money. According to Everest (1976), the data base concept is rooted in an attitude of *sharing* common data resources, *releasing control* of those data resources to a common responsible authority, and *cooperating in the maintenance* of those shared data resources.

A data base is a shared collection of interrelated data, designed to meet the information needs of multiple users. Each user may be provided a unique view of the data base, according to his or her information needs. The data are stored so they are independent of the program that uses them. A common and controlled approach is used in accessing and protecting data, adding new data, and modifying and retrieving existing data.

A data base is illustrated in Figure 1-5. The data base consists of ten files; the lines connecting the files represent interrelationships among the files. Notice that unlike in the file processing approach (Figures 1-3 and 1-4) the files in Figure 1-5 are not directly associated with application programs.

Data Base Approach for Pine Valley Furniture

Pine Valley Furniture Company has not yet attempted to implement any data bases. However, Mr. Knotts is aware of the data base approach and some of its potential advantages. Let's look at how the furniture company's applications system would be designed from a data base approach.

A model of the important data relationships at Pine Valley Furniture is illustrated in Figure 1-6. The model shown in this figure is called a **conceptual model.** Each rectangle in the model represents an entity. An **entity** is a person, place, object, event, or concept about which the organization wishes to record data. Arrows between entities represent relationships between those entities (an arrow with two heads means a "many" relationship—we will explain such relationships in Chapter 2). A **relationship** is a logical association between two entities. For example, the arrow from Customer to Order in Figure 1-6 indicates that a given customer may have several outstanding orders with Pine Valley Furniture at any given time. Also, the arrow from Order to Invoice indicates that each customer order

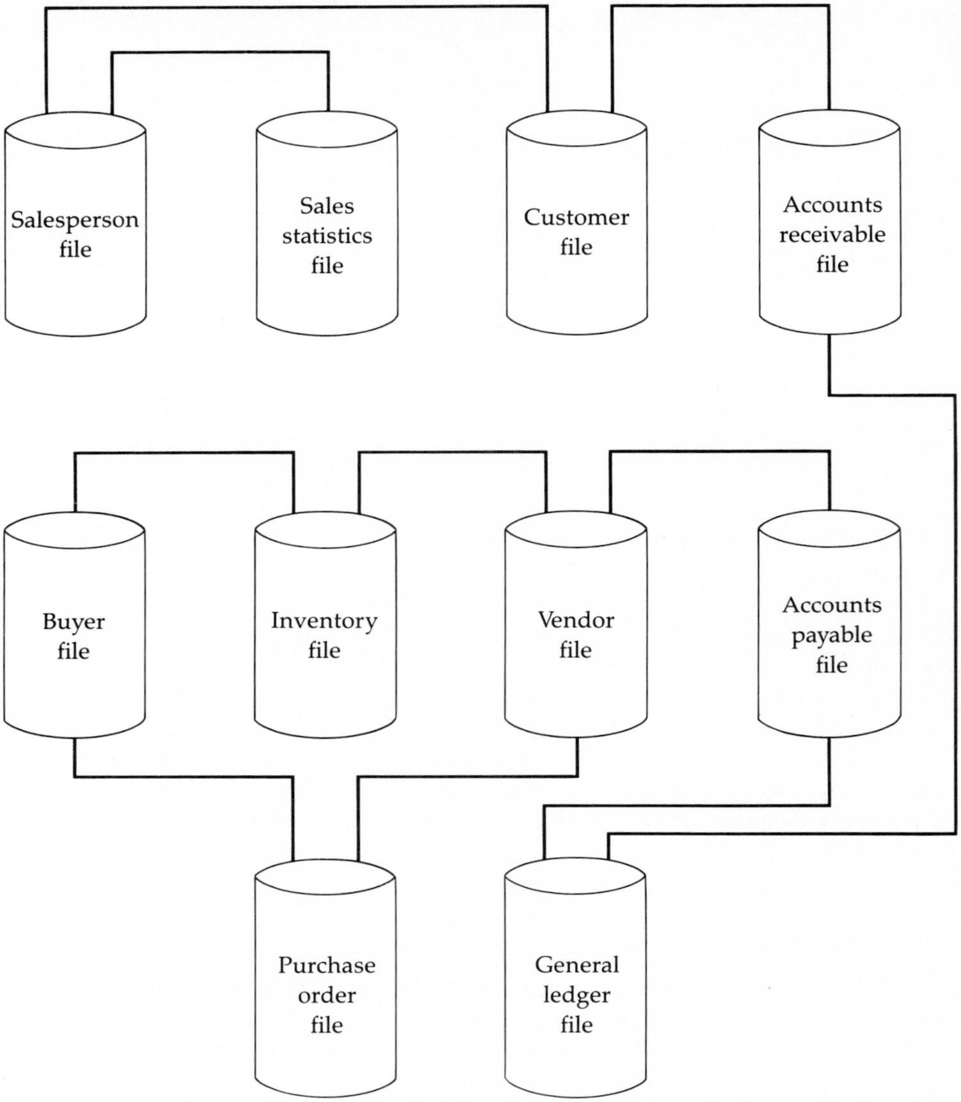

Figure 1-5
Data base as a collection of interrelated files (Source: McLeod 1986. Copyright © 1986 by Science Research Associates, Inc.)

may have one or more invoices, each representing a partial shipment. Depending on the data base management system that is used, the conceptual model shown in Figure 1-6 may be implemented as a collection of interrelated files, such as that shown in Figure 1-5.

At this point, we merely illustrate a conceptual model. In later chapters, we will explain detailed procedures for deriving such models.

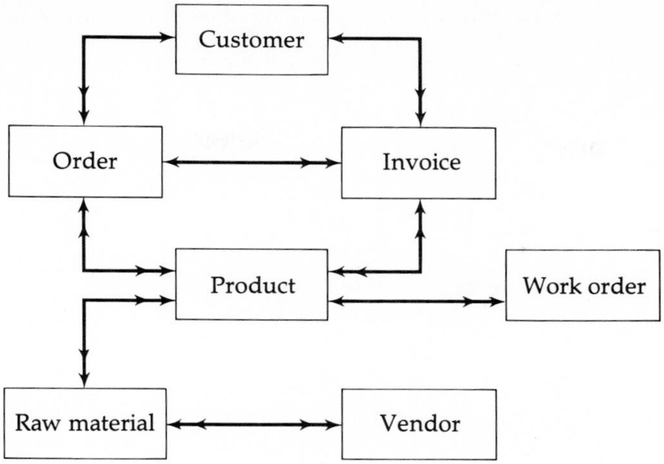

Figure 1-6
Conceptual data model (Pine Valley Furniture)

Benefits of the Data Base Approach

The data base approach offers a number of potential advantages compared to traditional file approaches. These benefits include minimal data redundancy; consistency of data; integration of data; sharing of data; enforcement of standards; ease of application development; uniform security, privacy, and integrity controls; data accessibility and responsiveness; data independence; and reduced program maintenance.

Minimal Data Redundancy With the data base approach, previously separate (and redundant) data files are integrated into a single, logical structure. In addition, each occurrence of a data item is recorded ideally in only one place in the data base. For example, the fact that the SHIP-TO ADDRESS for a specific customer of Pine Valley Furniture is 328 Acacia Street might be recorded in two separate files in a file processing system (see Figure 1-4). In a data base system, however, this fact will normally be recorded only once.

We are not suggesting that *all* redundancy can or should be eliminated. Sometimes there are valid reasons for storing multiple copies of the same data (e.g., data access efficiency, data validation checks). However, in a data base system, redundancy is *controlled*. It is designed into the system to improve performance (or provide some other benefit), and the system is (or should be) aware of the redundancy.

Consistency of Data By eliminating (or controlling) data redundancy, we greatly reduce the opportunities for inconsistency. For example, if each SHIP-TO ADDRESS is stored only once, we cannot have disagreement on the stored values. When controlled redundancy is permitted in the data base, the data base system itself should enforce consistency by updating each

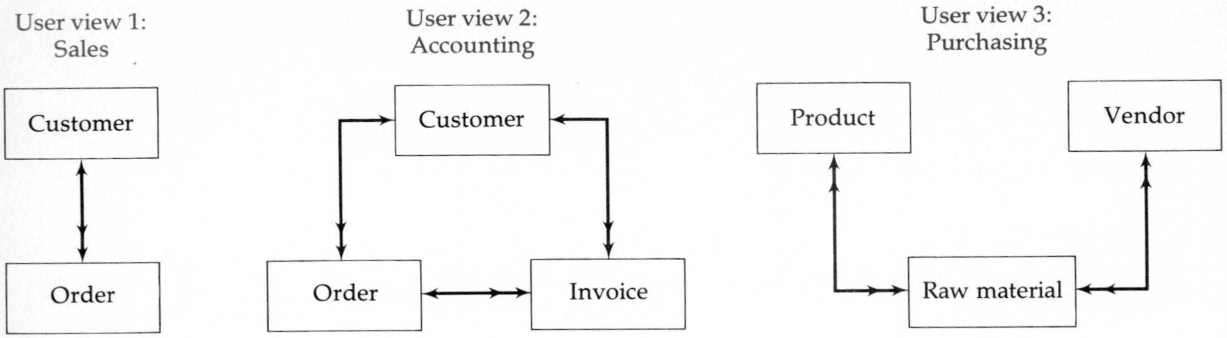

Figure 1-7
Three possible user views (Pine Valley Furniture)

occurrence of a data item when a change occurs. If the data item SHIP-TO ADDRESS is stored in two separate records in the data base, then the data base system should update this data value in both records whenever a change occurs. Unfortunately, many systems today do not enforce data consistency in this manner.

Integration of Data In a data base, data are organized into a single, logical structure, with logical relationships defined between associated data entities. In this way, the user can easily relate one item of data to another related item. For example, take another look at Figure 1-6. Suppose the user identifies a particular Product. Since this entity is logically related to the Raw Material entity, the user can easily determine what raw materials are required to build the product. Also, the user can check to see what raw materials are on order from a vendor, since the Raw Material entity is logically related to the Vendor entity. Data management software (described later) performs the function of associating logically related data items, regardless of the physical organization or location of the items in the data base.

Sharing of Data A data base is intended to be shared by all authorized users in the organization. For example, if Pine Valley Furniture implemented a data base, it would be designed to satisfy the information needs of Accounting, Sales, Manufacturing, Purchasing, and other departments. The company could essentially return to the "single set of books" that it had when it was first founded. Most data base systems today permit multiple users to share a data base concurrently, although certain restrictions are necessary, as described in later chapters.

In a data base system, each functional department is provided with its own view (or views) of the data base. Each such departmental view (or **user view**) is a subset of the conceptual data base model. For example, Figure 1-7 shows three possible user views for Pine Valley Furniture. The first user view is for the Sales Department and shows the relationship between the Customer and Order entities. The second user view is for the Accounting Department and shows the relationships among the Customer, Order, and

Invoice entities. The third user view is for the Purchasing Department and shows the relationships among the Product, Vendor, and Raw Material entities. These user views simplify the sharing of data since they provide each user with the precise view of data required to make a decision or perform some function without making the user aware of the overall complexity of the data base.

Enforcement of Standards Establishing the data base administration function is an important part of the data base approach. This organizational function has the authority to define and enforce data standards. If a data base administration function existed at Pine Valley Furniture, this office would approve all data names and formats, and grant access rights throughout the company. Moreover, all changes to data standards would have to be approved by data base administration. Data base administration is discussed in Chapter 10.

Ease of Application Development A major advantage of the data base approach is that the cost and time for developing new business applications are greatly reduced. Studies show that once the data base has been designed and implemented, a programmer can code and debug a new application at least two to four times faster than with conventional data files (even greater improvements are possible with very high level languages). The reason for this improvement is that the programmer is no longer saddled with the burden of designing, building, and maintaining master files. Thus, the cost of software development is reduced, and new applications are available to the user in a much shorter time span.

Uniform Security, Privacy, and Integrity Controls The data administration function has complete jurisdiction over the data base and is responsible for establishing controls for accessing, updating, and protecting data. Centralized control and standard procedures can improve data protection, compared to that provided by a dispersed data file system. However, if proper controls are not applied, a data base probably will be *more* vulnerable than conventional files, since a larger user community is sharing a common resource. We describe measures for data base security, privacy, and integrity in Chapter 11.

Data Accessibility and Responsiveness A data base system provides multiple retrieval paths to each item of data, giving a user much greater flexibility in locating and retrieving data than with data files. Retrieval of data can cross traditional departmental boundaries. To illustrate, refer to the conceptual model for Pine Valley Furniture (Figure 1-6). Suppose that a customer calls requesting information about several items that have been back-ordered. While on the phone, the salesperson can look up the CUSTOMER record, then display the particular Order in question. The salesperson can then display the PRODUCT record for each item on that order.

Finally, the salesperson can display the Work Order status for each back-ordered item to determine its completion date.

This example represents a routine (planned) sequence of retrievals. But a data base system can also satisfy certain ad hoc (one-time) requests for data without the need for an application program. For example, a manager might request a special summary of sales by size of store or by geographical location. Such requests can often be satisfied through a user-oriented query language or report writer. Although some of these features may be provided in applications systems, data base systems are generally much more responsive to changing information requirements.

Data Independence The separation of data descriptions from the application programs that use the data is called **data independence.** As a result of data independence, an organization's data can change and evolve (within limits) without necessitating a change in the application programs that process the data. Data independence is one of the major objectives of the data base approach.

In traditional systems, the descriptions of the data and the logic for accessing those data are built into each individual application program. Thus, the program is *dependent* on the data files. Any change to the data file requires modifying or rewriting the application program.

With the following example King (1981, 128–129) vividly illustrates the problems of data dependence:

> In a particular organization, data integration is proposed between payroll and personnel departments. Reading the latest literature on data base, the DP manager convinces user management to share their data requirements and the benefits are outlined. Program development progresses for the two application areas, and the development effort results in the successful implementation of both applications with all the expected benefits. Personnel is then asked by management to encourage the employees to carpool. This new function requires that new data elements (map coordinates, carpool request, carpool driver) be added to the data base. After careful consideration of the requirement, it is discovered that 15 bytes of new information will have to be added to the personnel record. Since this increase in record length will be added to the physical record, in conventional systems it must be added to the record length description in each program that accesses the record. The DP manager is now faced with asking the payroll department to fund changes in all the payroll programs, when the payroll department is uninterested in the new data. The personnel department would like to accommodate the new requirement with a minimum of impact as well. In conventional systems, both application areas would have to change all programs that reference that record type. It is standard to encounter resistance on the part of user management when they are asked to accommodate data requirements for departments other than their own.

As this example illustrates, data dependence in a traditional data file environment discourages users from sharing data. Instead, independent data files are established for each new application program. The greater the number of programs and files that exist, the more reluctant the DP department is to respond to the latest needs of end users because of the costs of modifying programs and data.

Reduced Program Maintenance Stored data must be changed frequently for a variety of reasons. New data item types are added, data formats are changed, new storage devices or access methods are introduced, and so on. In a data file environment, these changes require modifying the application programs that access the data. The term *maintenance* refers to modifying or rewriting old programs to make them conform to new data formats, access methods, and so forth.

In a data base system, data are independent of the application programs that use them. Within limits, either the data or the application programs that use the data can be changed without necessitating a change in the other factor. As a result, program maintenance can be significantly reduced in a modern data base environment.

In this section, we have identified ten major potential benefits of the data base approach. However, we must caution the reader that many organizations have been frustrated in attempting to realize some of these benefits. For example, the goal of data independence (and therefore reduced program maintenance) has proven elusive due to the limitations of older data models and data base management software. Fortunately, the newer relational model (described in Chapter 15) provides a significantly better environment for achieving these benefits.

Another reason for failure to achieve the intended benefits is poor organizational planning and data base implementation. Even the best data management software cannot overcome such deficiencies. For this reason, we stress data base planning and implementation in this text.

Risks to the Data Base Approach

As with any business decision, the data base approach is not without risks, and these risks, or costs, must be recognized and handled.

New, Specialized Personnel Frequently, organizations that adopt the data base approach or purchase a data base management system (DBMS) need to hire or train individuals to maintain the new data base software, develop and enforce new programming standards, design data bases to achieve highest possible performance, and manage the staff of new people. Although this personnel increase may be more than offset by other productivity gains, an organization should not minimize the need for these specialized skills, which are needed to obtain the most out of potential benefits. We will discuss these staff requirements for data base management in Chapter 10.

Need for Explicit Backup Minimal data redundancy, with all its associated benefits, also may fail to provide backup copies of data. Such backup or independently produced copies are helpful in restoring damaged data files and in providing validity checks on crucial data. To ensure that data are accurate and available whenever needed, either data base management software or additional procedures have to provide these essential capabilities. A data base management system usually automates many more of the backup and recovery tasks than a file system. Data base security, integrity, and recovery are covered throughout this book.

Interference with Shared Data The concurrent access to shared data via several application programs can lead to some problems. First, when two concurrent users both want to change the same or related data, inaccurate results can occur if access to the data is not properly synchronized. Second, when data are used exclusively for updating, different users can obtain control of different segments of the data base and lock up any use of these data (so-called deadlock). Data base management software must be designed to prevent or detect such interferences in a way that is transparent to the user.

Organizational Conflict A shared data base requires a consensus on data definitions and ownership as well as responsibilities for accurate data maintenance. Experience has shown that conflicts on how to define data, data length and coding, rights to update shared data, and associated issues are frequent and difficult managerial issues to resolve. Organizational commitment to the benefits of the data base approach, organizationally astute data base administrators, and a sound evolutionary schedule for data base development are all needed to handle these organizational issues.

When Can an Organization Justify Data Base?

Implementing the data base approach requires a large investment of organizational resources. An investment in new software products, additional hardware, and new personnel skills is normally required. Management commitment and time are also needed. Other costs include education and training, conversion, and documentation. To justify the conversion to data base, an organization should perform an extended analysis of benefits and costs. McFadden and Suver (1979) describe techniques for analyzing data base costs and benefits.

A quick indication of whether conversion to data base is justified can often be obtained by considering the information system in an organizational context. The following factors favor the data base approach in an organization (U.S. Department of Commerce 1980):

1. Application needs are constantly changing, with considerable uncertainty as to the important data elements, expected update or processing functions, and expected volumes to be handled.
2. Rapid access is frequently required to answer ad hoc questions.

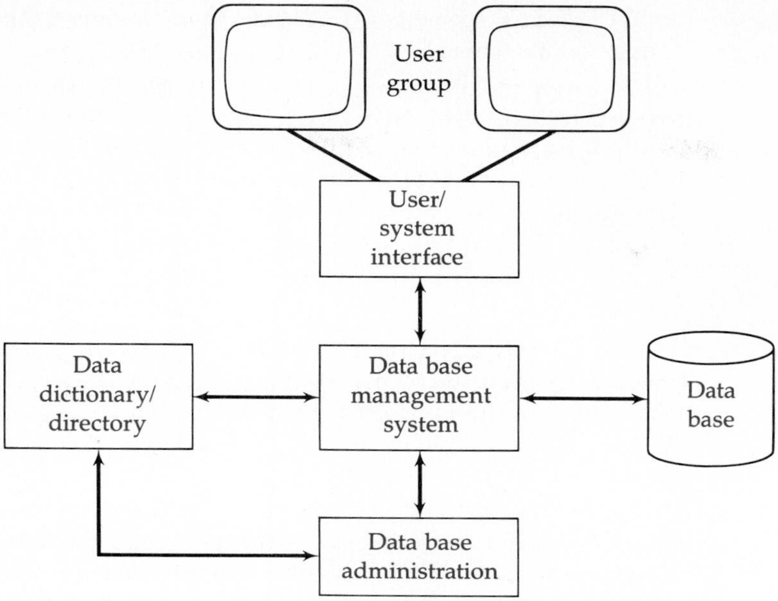

Figure 1-8
Components of a data base environment

3. There is a need to reduce long lead times and high development costs in developing new application systems.
4. Many data elements must be shared by users throughout the organization.
5. There is a need to communicate and relate data across functional and departmental boundaries.
6. There is a need to improve the quality and consistency of the data resource and to control access to that resource.
7. Substantial dedicated programming assistance is not normally available.

COMPONENTS OF THE DATA BASE ENVIRONMENT

The major components of a typical data base environment are shown in Figure 1-8. By studying these components and their relationships, you will gain a better understanding of the data base approach and its advantages. The six components shown in Figure 1-8 are described briefly in the following list. Each component is described in greater detail in subsequent chapters.

1. *User group.* The user group consists of all requesters of data. There are three basic categories of user requests: read only, add/delete, and

modify. All user requests for data are made through the data base management system.

2. *Data base management system, or DBMS.* The DBMS is a software system that receives and satisfies all requests for data. Normally, the DBMS provides concurrent access to multiple data base users. Also, the DBMS must be able to recover or restore a damaged data base from backup copies and logs or audit trails of data base activity.
3. *Data base.* The data base is the physical repository of all user data. For example, student information is contained within a university data base.
4. *Data dictionary/directory, or DD/D.* The DD/D is a repository of all *definitions* of data used by the organization. For example, all data item names, lengths, and representations are stored in the DD/D. As we will see in later chapters, the DD/D is a key tool in managing an organization's data resources.
5. *User/system interface.* The user/system interface consists of the languages and other facilities by which users request data and interact with the data base. Different users require different types of interfaces. For example, a programmer may require a procedural language such as COBOL, whereas a manager would likely prefer a menu-driven system.
6. *Data base administration, or DBA.* This organizational group is responsible for overall direction and control of the data resource. Chapter 10 is devoted to data base administration.

The arrows in Figure 1-8 indicate the interactions among the various data base components. For example, the DBMS interacts with four other components, as follows:

1. *User/system interface.* All requests for data from users, and all transfers of data, are channeled through this interface.
2. *Data base.* The DBMS retrieves, updates, and stores data in the data base in response to user requests.
3. *Data dictionary/directory.* The DBMS obtains data definitions (such as record layouts) from the DD/D.
4. *Data base administration.* The DBA group receives reports such as activity rates, performance, and problems (or exceptions) from the DBMS.

With advances in software, the user/system interface is becoming increasingly user-friendly. Examples of such advances are: menu-driven systems, use of a "mouse," and voice-recognition systems. These systems promote *end user computing*—that is, users who are not computer experts can define their own reports, displays, and simple applications. In fact, some organizations are creating *information centers*—organizational units that can be consulted to assist users in this endeavor. Of course, in such an environment, data base administration must ensure that adequate security measures are enforced to protect the data base.

To simplify the presentation in this first chapter, numerous other components of a typical data base environment are *not* shown in Figure 1-8. These components (including the operating system, teleprocessing monitor, and application programs) are described in detail in Chapter 11.

In summary, the DBMS operational environment shown in Figure 1-8 is an integrated system of hardware, software, and people that is designed to facilitate the storage, retrieval, and control of the information resource (Clark 1980).

RELATIONSHIP OF DATA BASE TO MIS AND DSS

Information systems (and data bases) must satisfy the information needs of all levels of management in an organization—operational, middle, and top management. However, the information needs at the various levels are quite different. In fact, it is often said that an organization requires two types of information systems—operational and management.

Operational information systems support everyday operations of the organization. They provide detailed information such as status reports, action documents, and displays. The primary objectives in operational information systems are accuracy and rapid response.

Management information systems (MIS) provide information required by managers for planning and decision making. They provide summary information to managers (especially at higher levels). In management information systems, the emphasis is on flexibility and ease of use.

Traditional information systems have essentially been operational in their orientation, and attempts to structure these systems to provide management information have met with only limited success. However, the emergence of data bases, high-level languages, personal computers, and other technology has finally made it possible to provide systems that truly support management planning and decision making. In fact, these systems are often called decision support systems.

A **decision support system** (DSS) is a system that supports managerial decision making by providing information and tools for analysis. A DSS will normally include the following components:

1. A terminal (often a personal computer) located in a manager's office or other convenient location.
2. A DBMS for building, accessing, and manipulating local files or data bases.
3. A powerful, high-level language for retrieving and manipulating data.
4. Modeling tools (such as forecasting and simulation) for evaluating various alternative decisions.

Figure 1-9
Example of a simple decision support system (DSS)

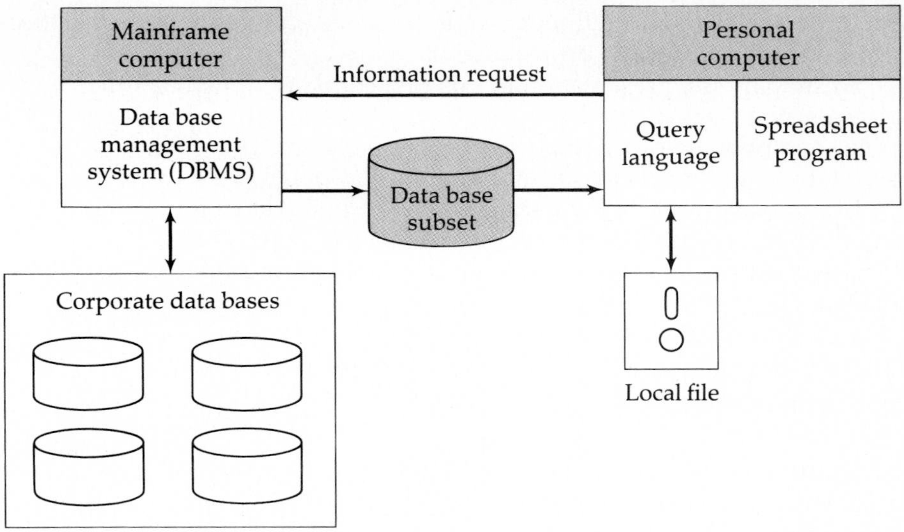

A simple (but very common) example of a DSS is shown in Figure 1-9. In this example, a personal computer (used by a manager) is linked to the organization's mainframe computer. The mainframe computer uses a DBMS to maintain the organization's data bases, which contain operational-level data.

The manager uses the personal computer with a high-level query language to formulate English-language requests for data relevant to a particular decision-making situation. These requests are passed to the mainframe computer, which uses the DBMS to extract the requested data from the data base. These data are passed to the personal computer, where they may then be displayed or summarized and stored as a local file or data base. Also, the manager may use the data in a model (in this case, a financial spreadsheet program) to evaluate various alternatives. In this way the organizational data bases can be used as a source of data for a DSS.

SUMMARY

In this chapter, we have presented data as an important organizational resource, deserving of top management planning and control. The traditional approach to managing this resource—through dispersed data files—often results in redundant and inconsistent data, inflexible systems, and exorbitant maintenance costs. The net result is systems that exceed cost estimates yet are not responsive to management needs.

The data base approach represents a completely different approach to managing data resources. With this approach, the overall information needs of the organization are defined before individual application programs are designed and implemented. Advantages of the data base approach include minimum data redundancy, maximum data sharing, and reduced maintenance costs. Many of these advantages are the result of data independence, which insulates end user views (and application programs) from changes to the data base itself. To achieve these benefits, a number of additional costs must be incurred. These include the costs of new software and hardware, skilled personnel, training, and conversion to data base.

Major components of a data base system include the data base management system (DBMS), which is used to manage the user data base, and the data dictionary/directory. Data base administration is the organizational function primarily responsible for managing the data resource.

Chapter Review

REVIEW QUESTIONS

1. Define each of the following terms:
   a. data
   b. information
   c. data base
   d. application system
   e. application program
   f. data file
   g. record
   h. data item
   i. data independence
   j. data base management system (DBMS)
2. Contrast the following terms:
   a. data dependence; data independence
   b. data base management system; decision support system
   c. user data base; data dictionary/directory
   d. operational information system; management information system
   e. data; information
   f. synonym; homonym
3. List and briefly describe seven disadvantages of many traditional application systems.
4. Explain why data redundancy is so common in traditional application systems.
5. List and briefly describe ten benefits that can often be achieved with the data base approach, compared to traditional application systems.
6. Briefly describe six major components in a data base environment.
7. List seven factors that, if present, would favor the data base approach in an organization.

8. Where are data definitions maintained in each of the following environments:
   a. traditional file processing system
   b. data base system

PROBLEMS AND EXERCISES

1. Match the following terms and definitions:

_____ data item	a. logical association between entities
_____ applications system	b. data organized for decision making
_____ entity	c. collection of records
_____ relationship	d. unit fact
_____ DBMS	e. integrated set of programs
_____ DD/D	f. person, place, object, or event
_____ data base	g. collection of related data items
_____ information	h. stores data definitions
_____ file	i. shared collection of related data
_____ logical record	j. manages the user data base

2. Draw a conceptual model (similar to Figure 1-6) for each of the following:
   a. Football team: entities are Team, Coaches, Agents, Players, Games
   b. Family: entities are Mother, Father, Children, Cars
   c. Bank: entities are Branches, Customers, Tellers, Accounts, Transactions
3. Add the entity Employee to the conceptual model in Figure 1-6. Assume that a given work order may require one or more employees.
4. Pine Valley Furniture wants to create a production scheduling application. Draw a diagram of an application system (see Figure 1-4). Assume that this system requires information about products, work orders, and raw materials. Also assume that three application programs will be required.
5. Show a user view (similar to those in Figure 1-7) for a production scheduling system at Pine Valley Furniture. Assume that the company has implemented a data base using the conceptual model shown in Figure 1-6. This application requires information about products, work orders, and raw materials.
6. Examine Figure 1-5, which illustrates a data base as a collection of interrelated files.
   a. What two files can be easily referenced from the Salesperson file?
   b. What files reference the Vendor file?
7. Visit an organization that has installed a data base system. Talk to the person in data administration and determine each of the following:
   a. Which of the benefits of the data base approach have been realized by the organization?
   b. What major components of a data base system (Figure 1-8) are present in the organization?
   c. Does the organization have a conceptual model? In what form is it represented?

REFERENCES

Auerbach Publishers, eds. 1981. *Practical Data Base Management.* Princeton, N.J.: Auerbach Publishers.

Clark, Jon D. 1980. *Data Base Selection, Design, and Administration.* New York: Praeger Publishers.

Diebold, John. 1979. "IRM: New Directions in Management." *Infosystems* (October).

Everest, Gordon C. 1976. "Database Management Systems Tutorial." In *Readings in Management Information Systems,* edited by Gordon B. Davis and Gordon C. Everest. New York: McGraw-Hill.

Fife, Dennis W., W. Terry Hardgrave, and Donald R. Deutsch. 1986. *Database Concepts.* Cincinnati: Southwestern Publishing.

King, Judy M. 1981. *Evaluating Data Base Management Systems.* New York: Van Nostrand Reinhold.

Martin, James. 1981. *An End-User's Guide to Data Base.* Englewood Cliffs, N.J.: Prentice-Hall.

Martin, James. 1983. *Managing the Data-Base Environment.* Englewood Cliffs, N.J.: Prentice-Hall.

McFadden, Fred R., and James D. Suver. 1979. "Costs and Benefits of a Data Base System." *Harvard Business Review* (January-February): 131–139.

McLeod, Raymond, Jr. 1986. *Management Information Systems.* 3d ed. Chicago: SRA.

Synott, William R., and William H. Gruber. 1981. *Information Resource Management.* New York: Wiley-Interscience.

U.S. Department of Commerce. National Bureau of Standards. 1980. *Guideline for Planning and Management of Database Applications.* FIPS Publication 77. Washington, D.C.: Government Printing Office.

Chapter 2

Data Concepts and Characteristics

INTRODUCTION

In his book *The Third Wave,* Alvin Toffler (1980) describes the emergence of a new era, which he terms the age of the information society. According to Toffler, the information society represents a "third wave" in societal evolution, displacing the earlier agricultural and industrial societies. The information society is bringing about fundamental changes in work patterns, organizational arrangements, and individual life styles.

To most persons in a modern, computerized society, this "third wave" is already becoming a fact of life. We are practically submerged in information at work, at home, and at most places in between. Personal computers are invading our homes as well as our offices and factories. Managers and other professionals are often bombarded by more information than they can assimilate or use effectively.

Despite our first-hand familiarity with data and information, most of us have a rather simplistic and one-dimensional view of these commodities. To understand data as an organizational resource, we must have accurate definitions and understand the concepts and characteristics of data. In this chapter, we describe the nature of data and develop many of the basic definitions. We also describe the views of data required by its various users and the concept of data independence.

DATA VERSUS INFORMATION

The terms *data* and *information* are often used interchangeably. In this section, we distinguish between these two terms.

Data are facts concerning people, places, events, or other objects or concepts. We will assume that data are recorded on some computer-processible medium such as magnetic ink or optical characters, magnetic disk surface, or computer semiconductor memory. Data are often relatively useless to human decision makers until they have been processed or refined in some manner.

Information is data that have been processed and refined and then displayed in a format that is convenient for decision making or other organizational activities. For example, a report listing customers whose credit accounts are past due by 60 days or more contains information that is useful to a credit manager.

In practice, however, the distinction between data and information is often difficult to maintain. Data become information when used in the context of making a specific decision or when applied to the solution of a particular problem. Thus, the definition depends on how the data (or information) are used, rather than on inherent properties of the data. As a result, in the context of information systems, it is common to use the terms interchangeably.

In this text, we use the term *data* when referring to the facts recorded in a data base. However, we often use the term *information* to refer to the overall "information resource" of an organization. Today, organizations frequently extract selected portions of one data base, summarize these, and then store them in a separate data base (often on a personal computer). We will not distinguish this second, derived data base by a separate term.

NATURE OF DATA

In this section, we provide the basic definitions of data. As shown in Figure 2-1, three realms, or levels of abstraction, must be considered in describing data. These realms are reality (the real world), metadata ("information about data"), and the actual data.

Reality

Reality consists of the organization itself, the various components of the organization, and the environment in which the organization operates. Any organization is a collection of people, facilities, and artifacts (or objects) that

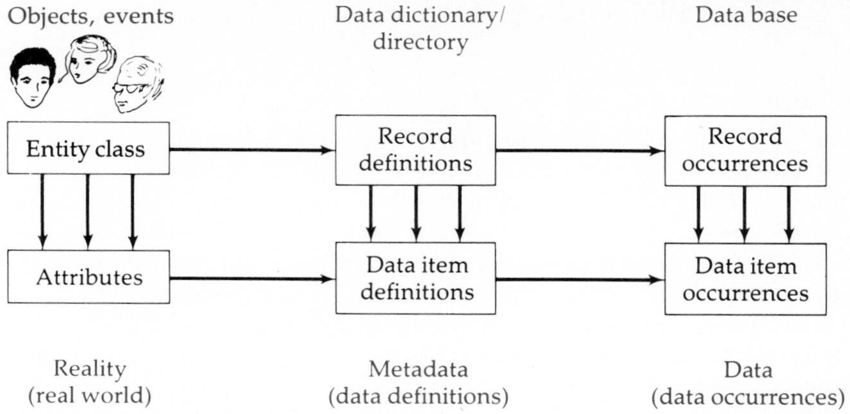

Figure 2-1
Three realms used to describe data

are organized to satisfy certain goals. Each organization interacts with its environment and both influences and is influenced by that environment.

An **entity** is any object or event about which the organization chooses to collect and store data. An entity may be a tangible object, such as an employee, a product, a computer, or a customer, or it may be an intangible item, such as a bank account, a cost center, a part failure, or an airline flight. Examples of entities at Pine Valley Furniture Company include customers, products, sales orders, work centers, and employees.

An **entity class** is a collection of entities that possess similar characteristics. Examples of entity classes are Customers, Students, and Patients. Entity classes are sometimes referred to as entity sets or entity types.

Entities are grouped into entity classes for convenience. In general, each entity is assigned to one, and only one, entity class. However, the definition of entity classes, as well as the assignment of an entity to an entity class, can be somewhat arbitrary. For example, consider the Employee entity class. Does this consist of persons who are full-time employees only, or does it also include part-time employees? And, what entities constitute the entity class Work Center: individual machines, machine groups, or entire departments? Questions such as these must be resolved before appropriate models of organizational data can be developed.

The number of entity classes for an organization depends on the size and complexity of that organization. For example, a medium-sized corporation typically defines several hundred entity classes, whereas a small company such as Pine Valley Furniture would probably have less than a hundred entity classes.

For each entity class, there are a number of attributes of interest to an organization. An **attribute** is a property of an entity that we choose to record. For example, two entity classes at Pine Valley Furniture Company are Customers and Products. Here are some of the attributes for these entities:

Customers	**Products**
Customer number	Product number
Name	Description
Address	Finish
Telephone number	Price
Credit limit	Weight
Balance	

For each entity class, ten or more attributes are typically defined. Therefore, an organization with several hundred entity classes may expect to define several thousand attributes.

Each entity in an entity class must possess at least one attribute (or several in combination) that distinguishes it from other entities in that class. This unique property of an entity is called an **identifier.** For example, a social security number is an identifier for an employee, and a product number is an identifier for a product. In some situations, the identifier will be a combination of two or more attributes—for example, invoice number and product number. The entity identifier must be unique; no two entities in any entity class may have the same value for this attribute.

Attributes are properties of individual entities. Another type of property that we are interested in is the **association,** which is some form of relationship between two (or more) entities. Associations may exist between entities of the same entity class or between entities from two (or more) entity classes. Here is an example of each type of association at Pine Valley Furniture:

1. In the Employee entity class, some employees are managers while the remainder are workers. An association called Manages allows us to determine the workers reporting to a given manager (or the manager of a given worker).
2. There is an entity class called Customers and another called Orders. By defining an association called Open Orders between entities from these two entity classes, we can determine all outstanding orders for a given customer.

The direct representation of associations between entities is one of the main features that distinguishes the data base approach from conventional file applications.

Entities are components of the real world of the organization and its environment. However, it is usually impractical for a manager (or other employee) to make decisions or take actions based on direct observation of these entities. Imagine a manager having to walk to a warehouse and count the items in a bin whenever an inventory action is required, or having to call a customer to obtain the shipping address prior to dispatching each shipment. Instead of direct observation, the organization relies on a model of the entities in the form of data that describe their properties. This brings us to the second realm of data: metadata.

Metadata

Metadata is information about the data in an organization. It is used by data base administrators and others to develop logical models of an organization's entities and the associations between those entities. Metadata is stored and maintained in the organization's data dictionary/directory.

Corresponding to each entity class in the real world, there is normally one record type defined in the metadata realm. Also, corresponding to each attribute, there is a data item type defined in the metadata realm (see Figure 2-1).

A **data item** is a unit fact. It is the smallest named unit of data in a data base and therefore the smallest unit of data that has meaning to a user. Examples of data items are EMPLOYEE-NAME, STUDENT#, and ORDER-DATE (recall that we often use # as an abbreviation for NUMBER, as in STUDENT#). Information that is normally catalogued in the data dictionary/directory for each data item type includes the data item name, length, type (or representation), and a brief narrative description.

Data items are sometimes called data elements, fields, or attributes. However, we prefer to use the term *data item* when referring to a unit of data. *Field* is a physical, rather than logical, term that refers to the column positions within a record where a data item is located. We have already defined *attribute* as a property of a real-world entity rather than as a data-oriented term. However, since there is a data item for each attribute, the two terms are often used interchangeably. In fact, in the relational model (presented in Chapter 6), the term *attribute* is used instead of *data item*. The term *data element* is simply a synonym for *data item*, but is used less frequently.

A **data aggregate** is a collection of data items that is named and referenced as a whole. For example, a data aggregate called NAME might be composed of the data items LAST-NAME, FIRST-NAME, and MIDDLE-INITIAL. Also, a data aggregate called SALES might consist of four data items: SALES-FIRST-QUARTER, SALES-SECOND-QUARTER, SALES-THIRD-QUARTER, and SALES-FOURTH-QUARTER. When data aggregates are used, they must be defined in the data dictionary/directory. Metadata that are recorded for each data aggregate type include the data aggregate name, description, and names of the included data items. In COBOL, data aggregates are referred to as group items.

A **record** is a named collection of data items and/or data aggregates. Most organizations define one record *type* for each entity class. Thus, if there is an entity class called Sales Orders, we might choose to define a record type called SALES-ORDER-RECORD. Metadata defining each record type are catalogued in the data dictionary/directory. These metadata include the record name, description, size (or length), component data items and aggregates, and identification of primary and secondary keys (described shortly).

In addition to records describing entities, some records describe associations (relationships) between entities. Often this type of record (called an **intersection** record) arises when some event has occurred involving the associated entities.

A **key** is a data item used to identify a record. There are two basic types of keys: primary keys and secondary keys.

A **primary key** is a data item that uniquely identifies a record. The primary key of a record corresponds to the identifier of a real-world entity. For example, STUDENT# would normally be the primary key for STUDENT records. As with identifiers, there may be several possible (or candidate) primary keys for the same record. Also, two or more data items may be required to identify a record. Most data systems do not permit a primary key field to have a missing value.

A **secondary key** is a data item that normally does not uniquely identify a record but identifies a number of records in a set that share the same property. For example, the data item MAJOR might be used as a secondary key for STUDENT records. Of course, this data item does not identify a unique record; for example, many students will have business as a major. However, the secondary key does identify a subset of students who are business majors. Secondary keys are useful when data are referenced by categories (this will be explained in Chapter 5).

Data

The third (and last) realm in Figure 2-1 consists of data **occurrences.** For each entity in the real world, there is normally a record occurrence that contains data item values describing that entity. For example, at Pine Valley Furniture, there are 50 employees in the Employee entity class. Thus, there are 50 Employee record occurrences in the data base. However, there is only one definition of this record type in the metadata.

A **file** is a named collection of all occurrences of a given record type. For example, the Employee file at Pine Valley Furniture Company consists of 50 Employee records at the present time.

Notice the important distinction between metadata (data definitions) and data (data occurrences). Metadata (such as data item definitions) are not stored in the data base. Conversely, occurrences of user data are not stored in the data dictionary/directory. Although many modern data management systems permit a user to query the data dictionary with the same language used for data base processing, the distinction between data and metadata is clearly maintained.

A file may be visualized as a two-dimensional array, called a **flat file.** An example of a flat file arrangement of data is shown in Figure 2-2. The table, or two-dimensional array, shown in this figure contains sample product data for Pine Valley Furniture Company. Thus, the data correspond to the Product entity class. Each column of the table contains values for a particular data item. The data item names at the top of the table correspond to product attributes. Each row of the table represents a record occurrence

Figure 2-2
Flat file representation of data (Pine Valley Furniture)

Data items

Data item names →

PRODUCT#	DESCRIPTION	FINISH	ROOM	PRICE
0100	TABLE	OAK	DR	500
0350	TABLE	MAPLE	DR	625
0625	CHAIR	OAK	DR	100
0975	WALL UNIT	PINE	FR	750
1000	DRESSER	CHERRY	BR	800
1250	CHAIR	MAPLE	LR	400
1425	BOOKCASE	PINE	LR	250
1600	STAND	BIRCH	BR	200
1775	DRESSER	PINE	BR	500
2000	WALL UNIT	OAK	LR	1200

Records

Primary key   Secondary keys

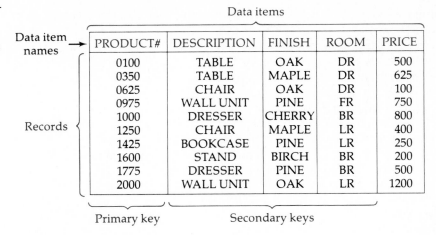

at the intersection of each row and column. This is an important property of flat files.

The primary key for the PRODUCT records is PRODUCT#. A particular value of PRODUCT# (such as 1250) uniquely identifies a record occurrence. The data items DESCRIPTION, FINISH, and ROOM have been designated as secondary keys. A particular value for one of these keys designates a subset of records (rather than a particular record). For example, the description "wall unit" identifies two records (product numbers 0975 and 2000).

To complete the description of the three realms in Figure 2-1, we may define a **data base** as a named collection of interrelated files. Thus, a data base contains data occurrences that describe one or more entity classes and the association between those entity classes.

An Example

The managers of Pine Valley Furniture are interested in finding out more about data bases. Mrs. Griffin, the sales manager, has purchased a copy of dBase III, a popular microcomputer data base management system (see Krumm 1985).

To gain some experience in using this package, Mrs. Griffin has decided to create the file shown in Figure 2-2. After loading dBase III, she responds to the "dot prompt" with the following command:

- create product

This command instructs dBase III to create a new file called Product, with data about entities in this entity class. The system then displays a data entry screen requesting the definition of each field (or data item) appearing in records in the file. Mrs. Griffin responds as follows:

	field name	type	width	dec
	XX X X X X X X X X X X	X X	X X X X	X X
1	PRODUCT_NO	C	4	
2	DESCRIPTION	C	15	
3	FINISH	C	10	
4	ROOM	C	2	
5	PRICE	N	5	0

Thus, Mrs. Griffin has provided the name, type (C = character, N = numeric), maximum width, and number of decimal places for each field in a PRODUCT record. This product file definition (metadata) is now available for use, and is independent of what data on products actually exist. Next, she wishes to enter the actual data. One way to do this is to use the following command:

- append

In response to this command, dBase III displays a data entry screen with blanks to be filled in for the data for each record. For example, Mrs. Griffin enters the highlighted data for the first record:

Record No.	1
PRODUCT_NO	0100
DESCRIPTION	Table
FINISH	Oak
ROOM	DR
PRICE	500

After entering data for all of the records, Mrs. Griffin decides to use the interactive query language to display selected records. For example, to display the record for product number 1000 she enters the following command:

- display for product-no = '1000'

Since PRODUCT NUMBER is the primary key, there is only one record that satisfies this request, and dBase III displays the following:

RECORD#	PRODUCT-NO	DESCRIPTION	FINISH	ROOM	PRICE
5	1000	Dresser	Cherry	BR	800

Finally, Mrs. Griffin decides to display records based on selection using a secondary key. For example, to display all records for WALL UNITS she enters the following:

- display for description = 'wall unit'

The system responds by displaying the following:

RECORD#	PRODUCT-NO	DESCRIPTION	FINISH	ROOM	PRICE
4	0975	wall unit	pine	FR	750
10	2000	wall unit	oak	LR	1200

As expected, more than one record is displayed when selection is based on a secondary key value.

This example has required the use of only a few simple features of dBase III. However, it has helped demonstrate to Mrs. Griffin both the power and the ease of using microcomputer data base management software (we describe dBase III in greater detail in Chapter 15).

ASSOCIATIONS BETWEEN DATA ITEMS

In this section, we describe simple graphical techniques for representing data items and the associations between data items. Later we will show how associations arise between records. Each type of data item is represented by an ellipse (or "bubble") with the data item name enclosed, as follows:

An **association** is a logical, meaningful connection between data items. An association implies that values for the associated data items are in some way dependent on each other.

A data base contains hundreds (or even thousands) of data items, and there are many possible associations among these. Fortunately, many of these possible associations are meaningless and of no interest to the organization. For example, there is no meaningful association between the following two data items:

However, there is an important association between these two data items:

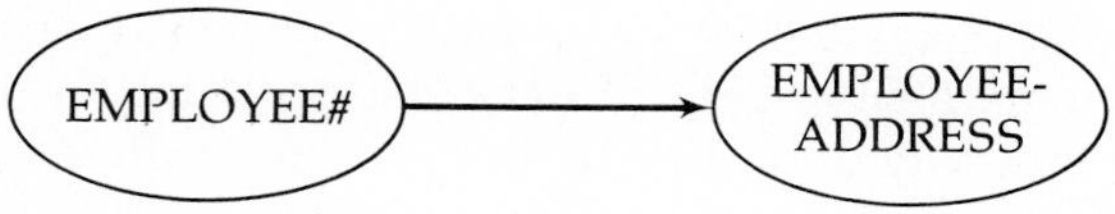

The association results from the observation that each employee has an address. We will represent associations by arrows connecting the data items, as in this illustration.

Types of Associations

Suppose that we have two data items, A and B. From data item A to data item B there are two possible associations, or mappings: a one-association and a many-association. We will represent these two possible associations with the following notation:

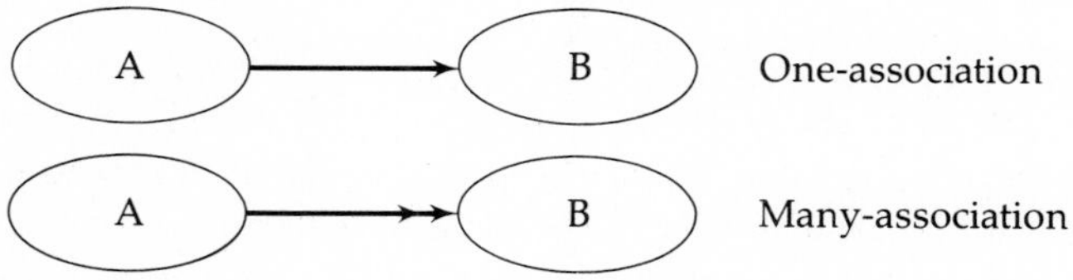

A **one-association** from data item A to data item B means that for a specified period of time, *a given value* of A has one and only one value of B associated with it. That is, if we know the value of A, then the value of B is implicitly known. We represent a one-association with a single-headed arrow. Assuming that at a given period of time each employee has exactly one address, the following mapping is a one-association:

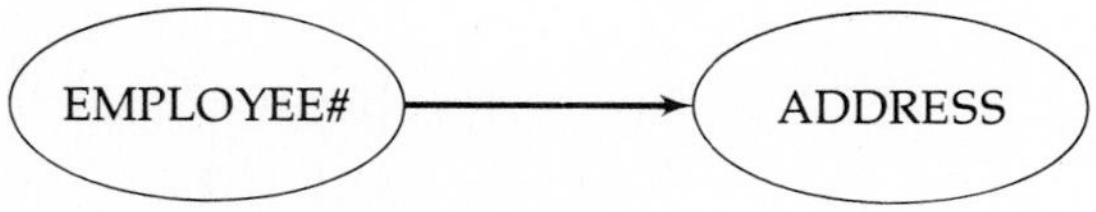

A **many-association** from data item A to data item B means that at each period in time, a given value of A has zero, one, or many values of B associated with it. We represent a many-mapping with a double-headed arrow. Assuming that for a specified period of time each employee may have taken zero, one, or more than one training course, the following mapping is a many-association:

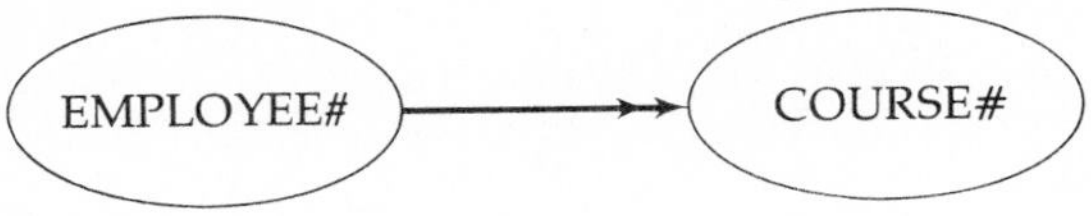

There is another type of association between data items, called a conditional association, which is a variation of those already described. With a **conditional association,** for a given value of data item A there are two possibilities: Either there is exactly one value of data item B, or there is no value of data item B. We diagram a conditional association as a one-association with a zero recorded on the arrow:

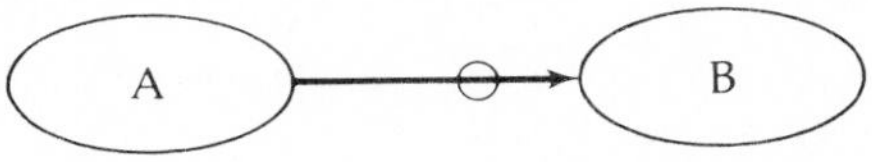

Here is an example of a conditional association in a hospital environment:

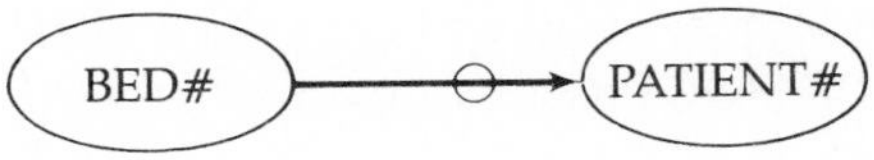

That is, each hospital bed either will be assigned to one patient or, at some instant in time, may be unassigned.

Reverse Associations

If there is an association from data item A to data item B, there is also a reverse association from B to A. This leads to three possible associations between data items: one-to-one, one-to-many, and many-to-many. These associations are diagrammed as follows:

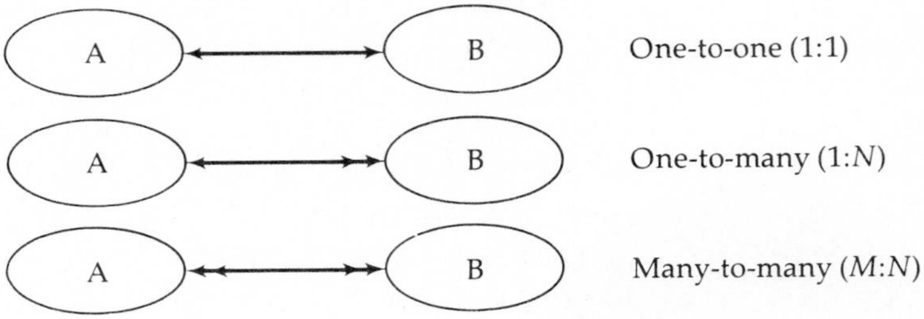

A **one-to-one association** means that for a given period of time, each value of data item A is associated with exactly one value of data item B. Conversely, each value of B is associated with one value of A.

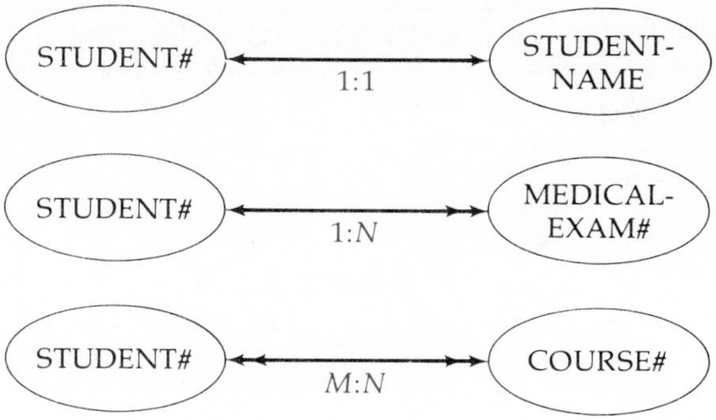

Figure 2-3
Examples of associations between data items

A **one-to-many association** means that for a given period of time, each value of data item A is associated with zero, one, or more than one value of data item B. However, each value of B is associated with exactly one value of A. The mapping from B to A is said to be many-to-one, since there may be many values of B associated with one value of A.

A **many-to-many association** means that for a given period of time, each value of data item A is associated with zero, one, or many values of data item B. Also, each value of B is associated with zero, one, or many values of A.

Examples of these three associations are shown in Figure 2-3. If we assume that no two students have the same name, then the association between STUDENT# and STUDENT-NAME is 1:1 (in reality, duplicate student names must be expected). The association between STUDENT# and MEDICAL-EXAM# is 1:*N* (each student may take several medical exams, but each exam pertains to a particular student). Finally, the association between STUDENT# and COURSE# is *M:N* (each student registers in many courses, and each course has many students registered).

In modeling an organization's data, we are not always interested in a given reverse association. If a particular reverse association is not of interest, the arrowheads are simply omitted in the link from data item B to data item A.

Importance of Associations

You may wonder why we are so careful in defining data and the associations between data items. The reason is that data are a corporate asset, and it is important to represent data associations accurately in order to control data, yet allow the data base to evolve over time. According to Percy (1986):

> The data a company owns differentiates it from its competitors. What uniquely defines data entities, what information can be determined by individual occurrences of those entities, and what rules are associated with attributes and relationships, are largely what makes an enterprise unique and what drives its idiosyncratic success.

Figure 2-4
Bubble chart of PRODUCT record (Pine Valley Furniture)

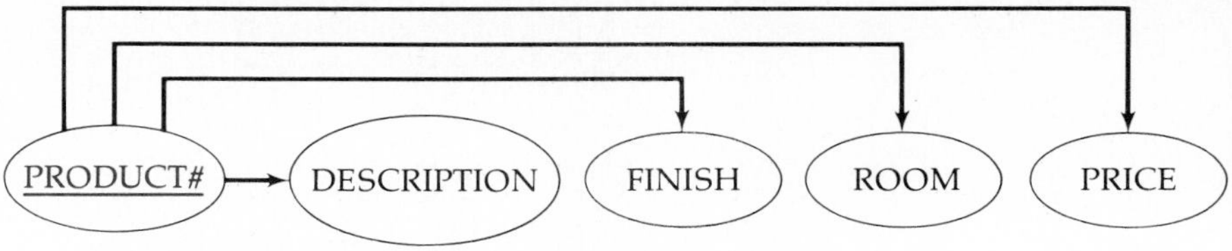

Figure 2-5
Representing record types and occurrences (Pine Valley Furniture)
(a) PRODUCT record type
(b) PRODUCT record occurrence

PRODUCT#	DESCRIPTION	FINISH	ROOM	PRICE

(a)

0975	WALL UNIT	PINE	FR	750

(b)

The association between two data items is defined for a given instant of time, or for a specified period of time. For example, in defining the association between Bed and Patient as 1:1, we are clearly referring to the *current* occupant. If the patient's history is kept, then either we must change this relationship or else define an additional relationship representing the relationship between Bed and Patients over time.

Bubble Charts

The notation we have introduced for representing data items and associations can be used to develop complex data models. We will use the term *bubble charts* to refer to data models that are expressed using this notation. Bubble charts are useful for grouping data items into records and for deriving more complex data models.

Grouping Data Items A record is a collection of data items that represents a particular entity. Each record has a primary key that uniquely identifies the record. Therefore, there is a one-association from the primary key of a record to each of the remaining data items in the record. For example, consider the PRODUCT records for Pine Valley Furniture Company (see Figure 2-2). A bubble chart showing the structure of these records appears in Figure 2-4. The data item PRODUCT# is underlined to indicate that it is the primary key for this record type. Note that reverse associations have been ignored for now.

Data items are grouped into records (such as in Figure 2-4) using a technique called **normalization.** This is a step-by-step procedure for ana-

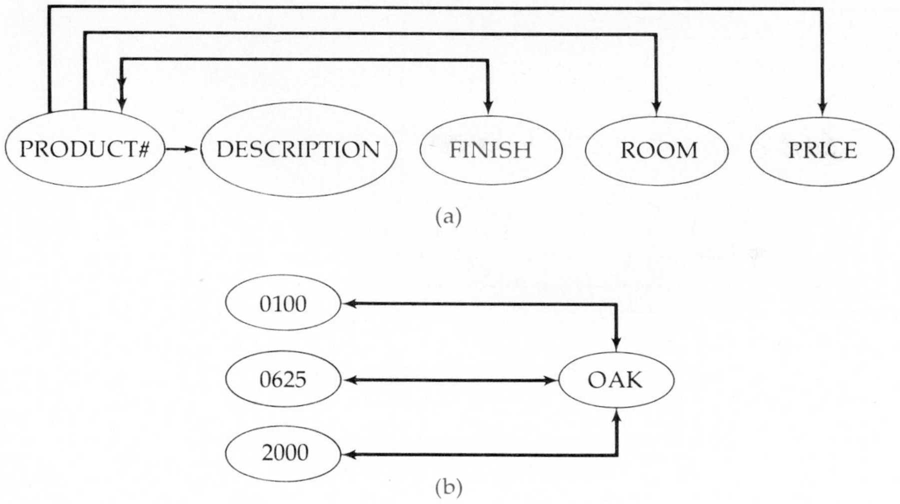

Figure 2-6 Representing secondary keys (Pine Valley Furniture)
(a) Bubble chart with secondary key (finish)
(b) Occurrences for a particular value (oak)

lyzing the associations between data items. We describe normalization in Chapters 6 and 7.

We represent record types by rectangles containing the names of the data items included in the record. Again, the primary key is underlined. A representation of the PRODUCT record type is shown in Figure 2-5a, while Figure 2-5b shows one occurrence of this record type.

Bubble charts also provide insight into the nature of secondary keys. Assume that a secondary key does not uniquely identify a record (the usual case). Therefore, there is a one-to-many association from that secondary key to the primary key of the record, since there may be many primary key values associated with a given value of the secondary key. For example, FINISH is a secondary key for the PRODUCT record type. Therefore, there is a one-to-many association from FINISH to PRODUCT# (see Figure 2-6a). Figure 2-6b shows one occurrence, where the secondary key value is OAK. There are three associated product numbers: 0100, 0625, and 2000.

Secondary keys provide a powerful technique for retrieving selected data records without searching an entire file. In the Product file, we can list all products whose DESCRIPTION is WALL UNIT or whose FINISH is OAK (or a combination of these two factors), as demonstrated in the case example using dBase III.

Modeling Data Structures In addition to grouping data items into records, we can use bubble charts to develop more complex data relationships. We begin with simple user views of data and progressively combine these into more complex data models. For example, Figure 2-7 shows two user views for Pine Valley Furniture. User view 1 contains data for the Customer entity

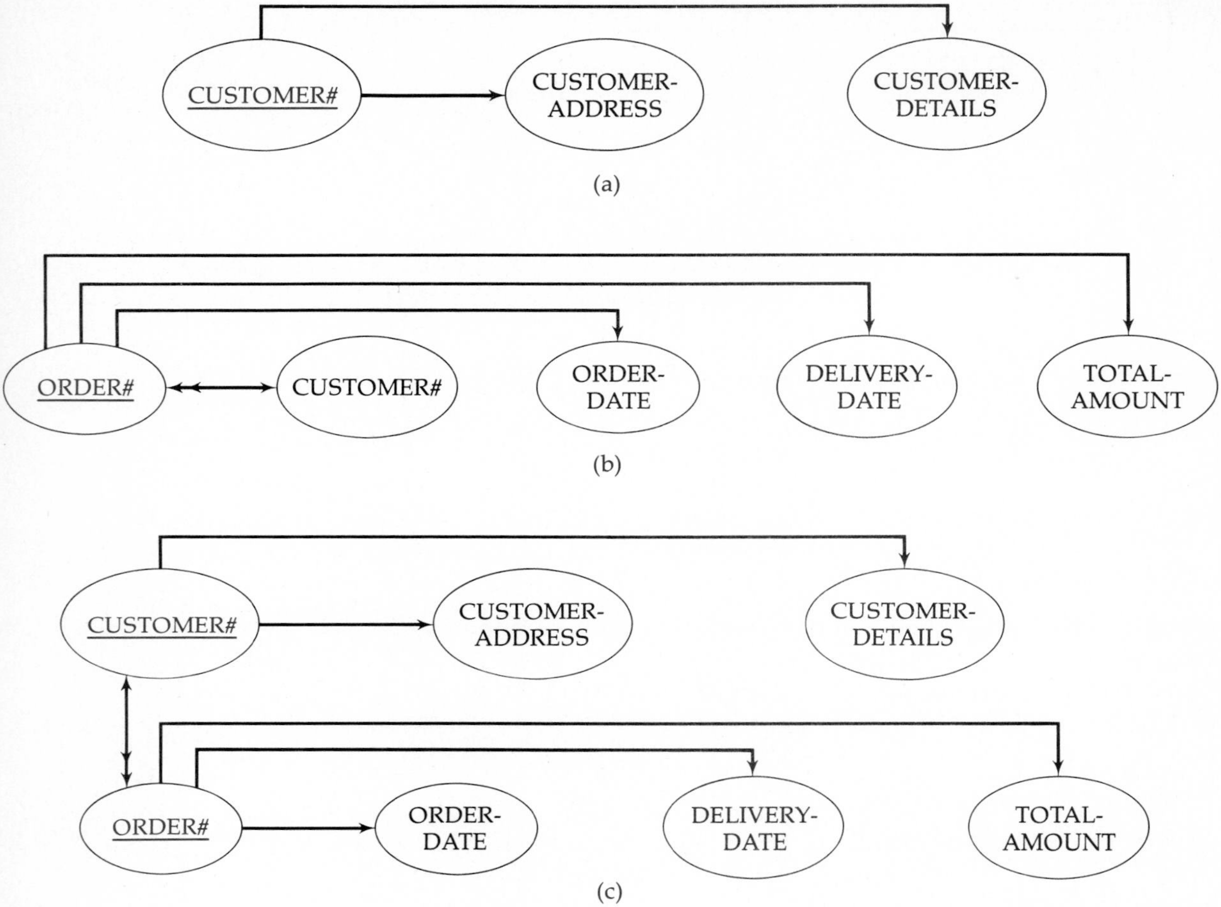

Figure 2-7
Data modeling, combining user views (Pine Valley Furniture)
(a) User view 1: Sales
(b) User view 2: Orders
(c) Combined views

class and is required by the Sales Department to obtain information about individual customers (the data item called CUSTOMER DETAILS actually represents several data items such as SHIP-TO ADDRESS, PHONE#, and so on). User view 2 is required by the Orders Department to look up details of customer orders (ORDER# is the primary key).

Figure 2-7c shows how these two views are combined into a single view. Since CUSTOMER# in user view 2 is already contained in user view 1, it is not repeated in the combined view.

The process of combining user views to obtain an overall data model is described in Chapter 8. Since an organization often must structure a data model with several hundred (or even several thousand) data items, data base design software packages are frequently used to assist this process.

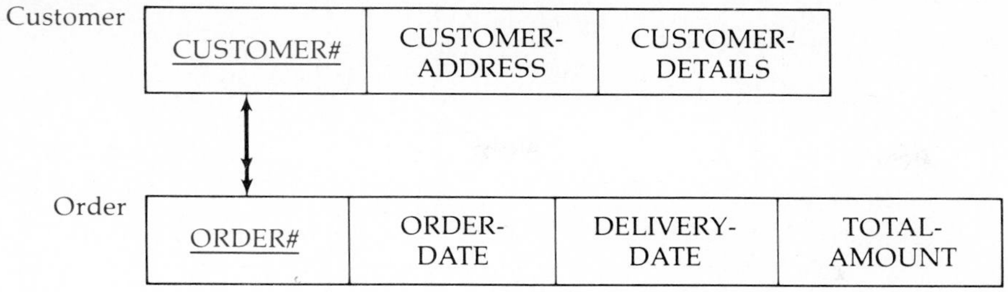

Figure 2-8
Association between two record types (Pine Valley Furniture)

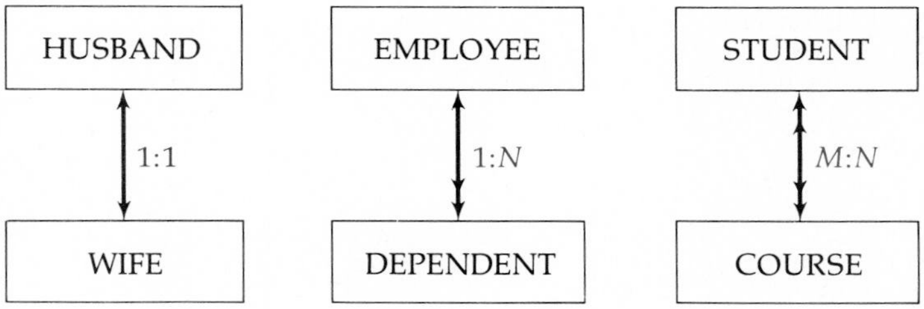

Figure 2-9
Types of associations

ASSOCIATIONS BETWEEN RECORDS

When the data model has been expressed in the form of a bubble chart (as in Figure 2-7), the next step is to group the data items into records. When this is done, the result is a set of record types with associations between them. For example, Figure 2-8 shows the result of grouping the data items in Figure 2-7c into records. There are two resulting record types: CUSTOMER and ORDER. Since the association between the primary keys (CUSTOMER# and ORDER#) is 1:*N*, the association between the record types is also 1:*N*. This reflects the fact that in the real world, at a given instant in time, a customer may have zero, one, or more than one outstanding order, and an order must be associated with exactly one customer.

Types of Associations

Between any two record types there are three possible associations: one-to-one, one-to-many, and many-to-many. Examples of these associations are shown in Figure 2-9. The associations between record types have the same meanings as the associations between data items.

In Figures 2-8 and 2-9 (and other figures in this chapter) the arrows represent associations between *records*—they do not necessarily connect or represent associations between individual data items in those records.

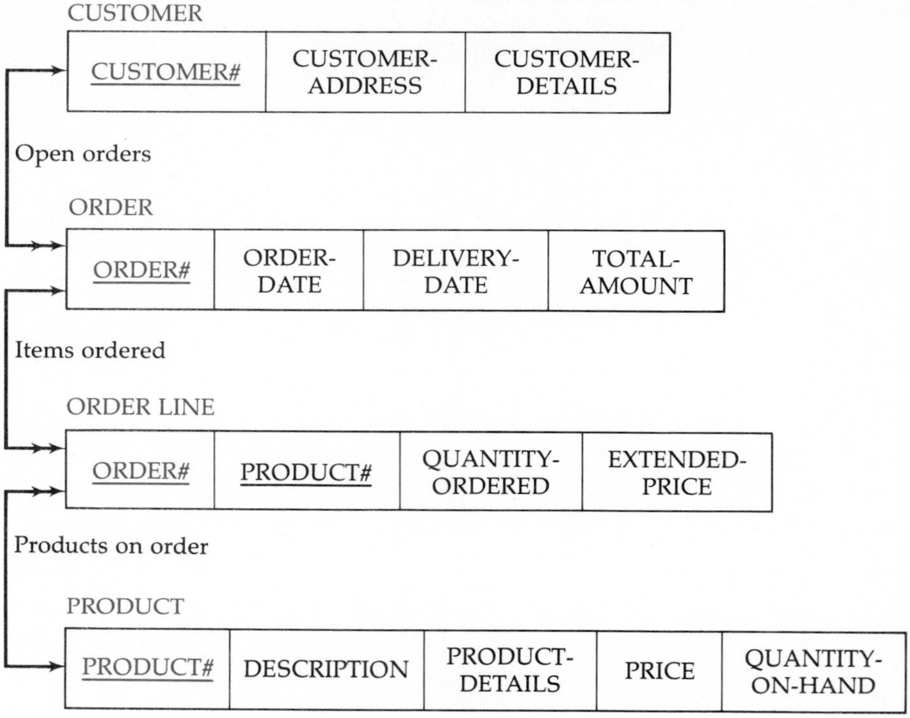

Figure 2-10
Data structure diagram (Pine Valley Furniture)

Data Structure Diagrams

When a data model has been completed, the resulting chart may contain dozens (or hundreds) of record types. The associations between the record types are also shown. We refer to a chart representing a data model as a **data structure diagram** (the term *Bachman diagram* is also used, named after the person who first proposed this technique).

A data structure diagram for a portion of the data base at Pine Valley Furniture Company is shown in Figure 2-10. This diagram contains four record types: CUSTOMER, ORDER, ORDER LINE, and PRODUCT. Three of these record types (CUSTOMER, ORDER, and PRODUCT) represent real-world entities. The ORDER LINE record type represents the association between Orders and Products, as we will see shortly. All the associations shown in the data structure diagram are one-to-many. In large, complex data structure diagrams, it is often useful to label each association arrow with a meaningful name, as illustrated in the figure.

One occurrence of this data structure is shown in Figure 2-11. Customer #B324 has two outstanding orders: #221 and #316. Order #221 is for two dressers (product #1000) and one bookcase (product #1425). The total amount

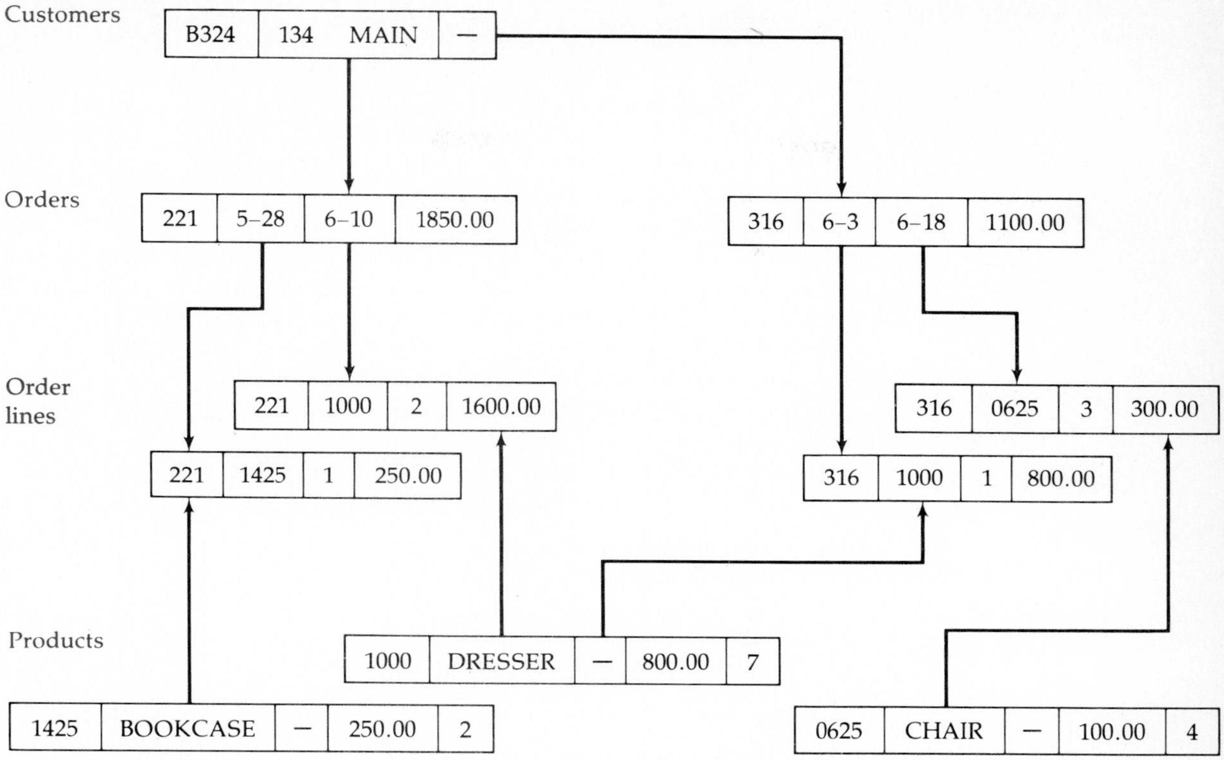

Figure 2-11
An occurrence of a data structure (Pine Valley Furniture)

of this order is $1850. Order #316 is for one dresser (product #1000) and three chairs (product #0625). The total amount of this order is $1100. Notice that product #1000 appears on two separate orders for the same customer.

The data structure diagram in Figure 2-10 provides a logical model of the data required for the "demand side" of business operations at Pine Valley Furniture Company. By providing a primary key value, a user can obtain data about a particular customer, order, or product. Also, by providing a secondary key value, a user can display a group of records that share a certain property (for example, all customers whose credit limit is $5000). Finally, by using the associations between records, a user can obtain much additional information, such as all outstanding orders for a given customer, all products (or line items) on a given order, and all outstanding orders for a given product. Of course, a full data structure diagram for this company would include many more data items, record types, and associations.

The links between records in Figure 2-10 represent logical associations between records (and their associated entities). They do not represent "pointers" or other physical means of implementing associations or relationships. We describe techniques for implementing such associations in Chapter 5.

Concatenated Keys

Some data items cannot be uniquely identified by a simple primary key that consists of one data item. A primary key that consists of two or more data items is required to identify these data items. Such a key is called a **concatenated key** (the term *concatenated* means "joined together"). The term *composite key* is also sometimes used.

In Figure 2-10, the ORDER LINE record type has a concatenated key consisting of ORDER# joined with PRODUCT#. Each occurrence of this record type represents one line on a particular customer order. Both ORDER# and PRODUCT# are required to identify the QUANTITY-ORDERED and therefore the EXTENDED-PRICE. Neither ORDER# nor PRODUCT# by itself is sufficient to identify these items. For example, Figure 2-11 shows that for product #1000, the order quantity on order #221 is 2, while on order #316 it is 1.

On a bubble chart we will show a concatenated key as a single bubble with the data items that compose the key joined by a plus sign, +. Here is an example:

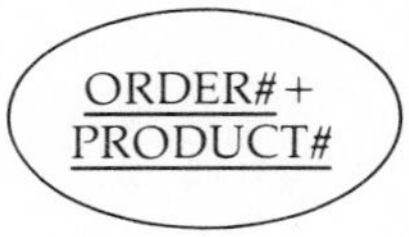

Many-to-Many Associations Actually, the concatenated key in ORDER LINE (ORDER# + PRODUCT#) has a deeper meaning. No many-to-many associations are expressly shown in Figure 2-10; only one-to-many associations are shown. Yet it seems there should be a many-to-many association between Orders and Product: Each customer order may request several products, while at a given instant each product may have zero, one, or many outstanding orders.

The association between the Order entity class and the Product entity class is indeed many-to-many, as shown in Figure 2-12a. However, this association has been resolved into two one-to-many associations by the creation of a third record type called ORDER LINE (Figure 2-12b). The ORDER LINE record type contains data about the association between the ORDER record type and the PRODUCT record type (namely, QUANTITY-ORDERED and EXTENDED-PRICE). A record that contains such data is called an **intersection record.** The primary key of such a record is the concatenation of the associated primary keys (in this case, ORDER# + PRODUCT#).

If a data base has been properly designed, the data structure diagram will contain few many-to-many associations. During the process of normalization (described in Chapters 6 and 7), these associations will be resolved into appropriate 1:*N* associations, as in the preceding example. Notice that the design shown in Figure 2-12b is superior to that shown in Figure 2-12a.

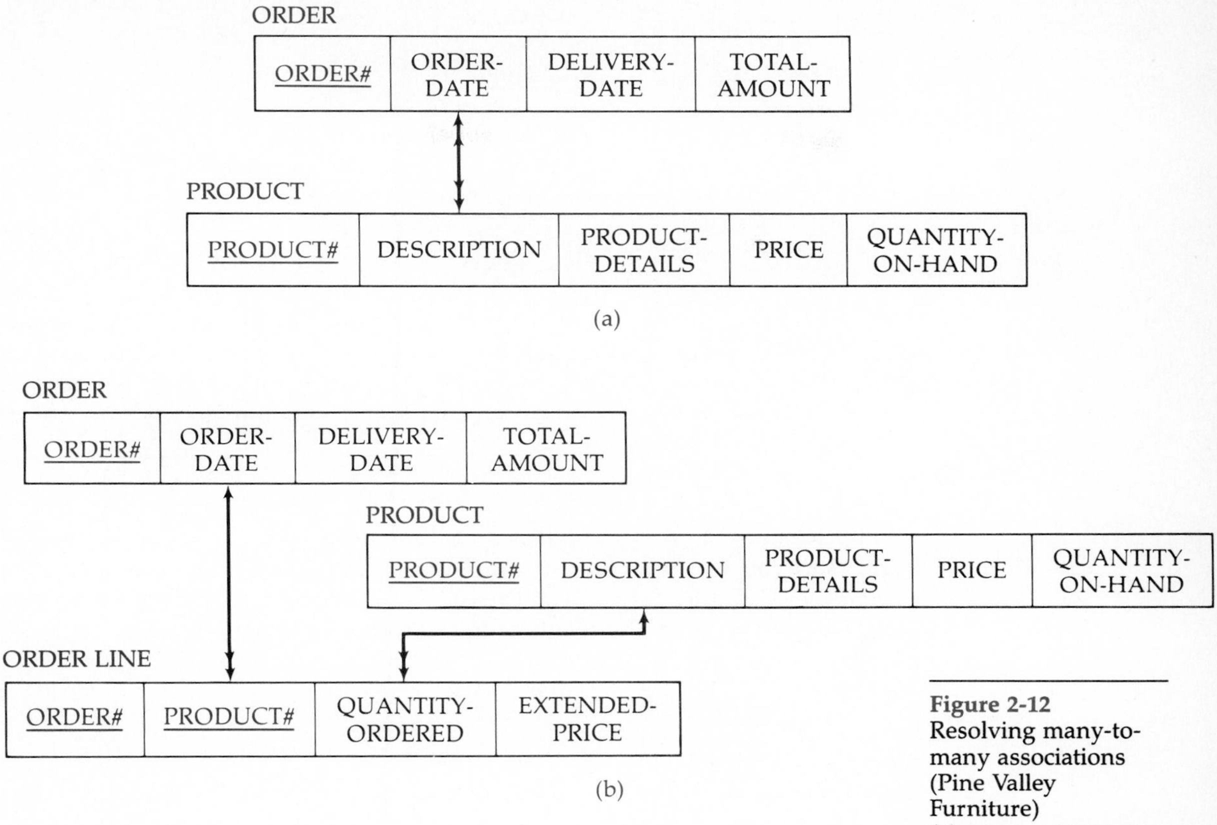

Figure 2-12
Resolving many-to-many associations (Pine Valley Furniture)
(a) a many-to-many association
(b) two one-to-many associations

The intersection data in ORDER LINE is a more natural way for the user to view the data.

It might seem that resolving a many-to-many association is accomplished at the cost of additional redundancy. After all, the data items ORDER# and PRODUCT# are repeated in ORDER LINE. However, we must remember that a data structure diagram is a *logical* (not physical) representation of the data. Separate occurrences of the data items ORDER# and PRODUCT# may or may not be physically stored in the ORDER LINE record occurrences. We describe physical data representations in Chapters 4 and 5.

Deeply Concatenated Keys In the preceding example, the intersection record allowed us to form an association between two entity classes—Orders and Products. Sometimes, however, we wish to form an association between three or more entity classes. Again, we can use an intersection record for this purpose.

Suppose that a company orders parts from several different suppliers. These parts are stocked at several different warehouses. Thus, we have a

Figure 2-13
Associations between multiple record types

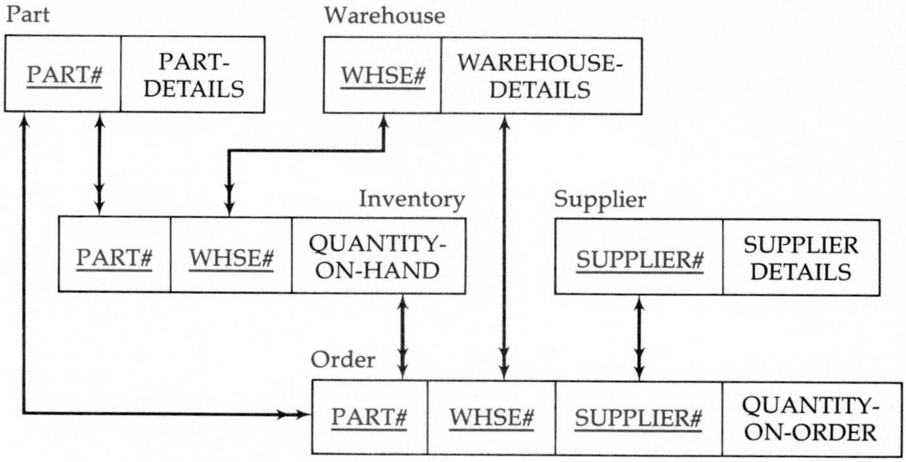

many-to-many association between three entity classes: Suppliers, Parts, and Warehouses. At a given instant in time, the quantity of parts on order (QTY-ON-ORDER) depends on three data items: PART#, SUPPLIER#, and WHSE#. We express the relationship between these data items as follows:

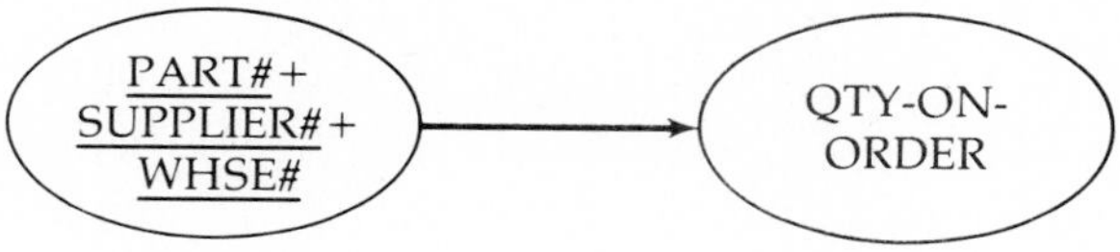

The associations between entity classes are shown in Figure 2-13. There are two intersection records: INVENTORY and ORDER. The INVENTORY record type contains the data item QUANTITY-ON-HAND, which represents the quantity of parts on hand at a particular warehouse (once a part is in inventory, the identity of the supplier is no longer of interest). The ORDER record type contains the QUANTITY-ON-ORDER, which depends on three data items as described earlier. This record type allows us to convert an *M:N* association among three entity classes into three 1:*N* associations.

Multiple Associations Between Two Record Types

In data modeling, it is sometimes appropriate to define two or more associations between the same two record types. For example, Figure 2-14 shows the data structure diagram for a simple accounting application. There are two record types: LEDGER and TRANSACTION. In the Ledger file, there is one record occurrence for each numbered account in the general ledger. The Transaction file contains recent transactions that are posted to the gen-

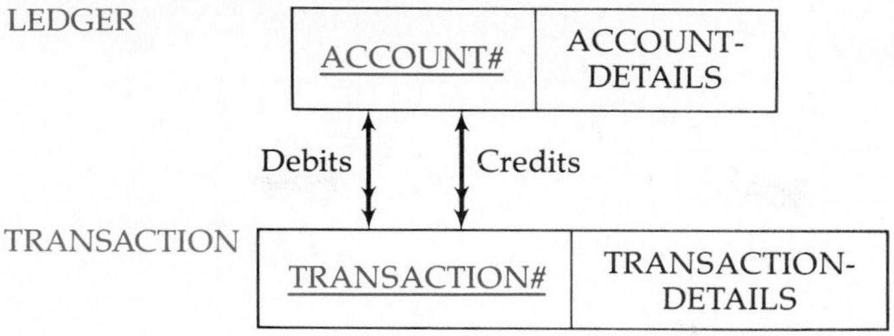

Figure 2-14
Multiple associations between two record types

eral ledger accounts. There are two one-to-many associations between Ledger and Transaction, called DEBIT and CREDIT. At a given instant in time, DEBIT associates all transactions, if any, that cause a debit entry to a particular ledger account. CREDIT provides a similar association between a given ledger account and transactions that result in credit entries. For example, if transaction number 1234 is a payment on account by the customer, Jane Brown, it represents a credit to that customer's accounts receivable ledger account, and a debit to the cash account.

When there are two or more associations between two record types, as in this example, each association must be named or labeled so that the nature of each association is clear to the users. It is often desirable to name single associations between record types in a data structure diagram, since this tends to improve user understanding of the data model.

Recursive Associations (Loops)

So far, we have described associations between two different entity classes (and therefore record types). In data modeling, we frequently need to describe associations between entities in the same entity class (for example, Students or Employees). An association between entities in the same entity class is called a **recursive association** (or **loop**). There are three types of recursive associations: one-to-one, one-to-many, and many-to-many.

One-to-One Pine Valley Furniture Company has an Employee file as part of its data base. Some of its employees are married to other employees, so there is a 1:1 spouse relationship between these employees. We can picture this relationship as follows:

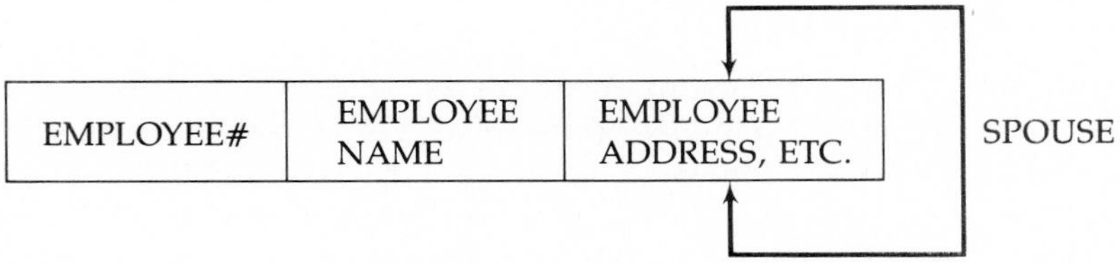

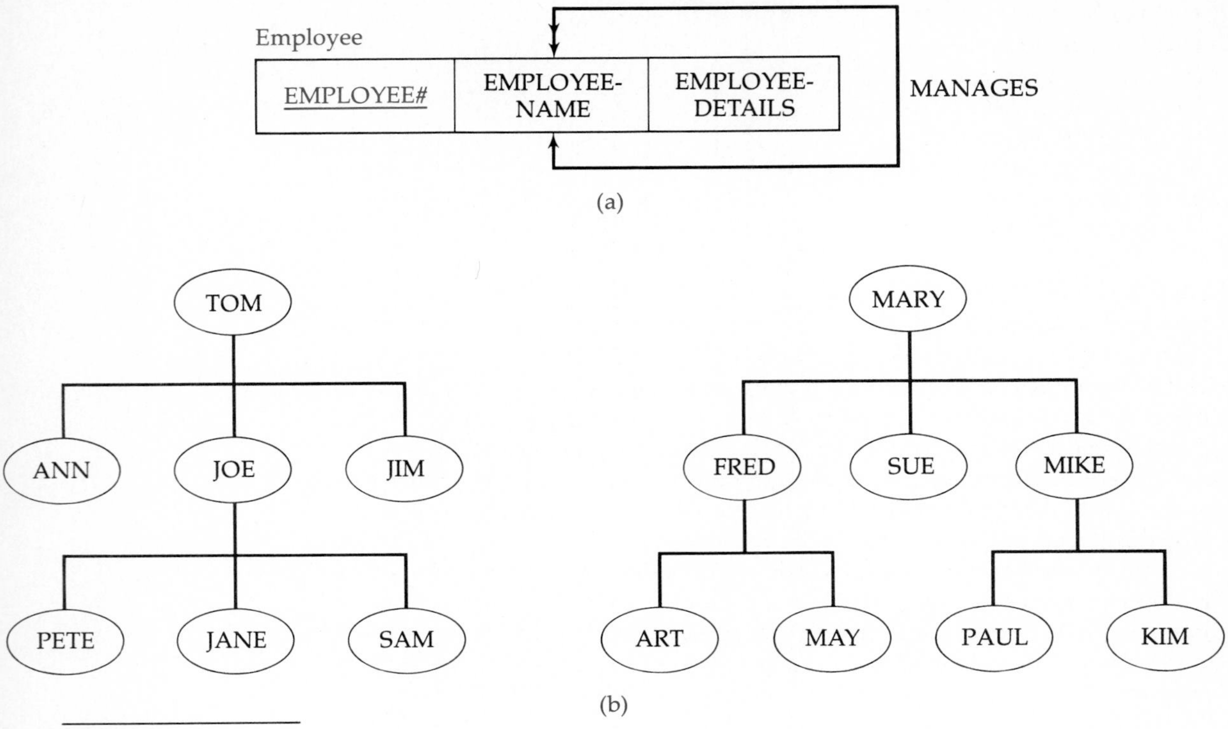

Figure 2-15
Recursive association ($1{:}M$):
(a) data structure
(b) two occurrences

That is, for married employees there is a 1:1 association (called "spouse") between husband and wife. Of course, many employees are not married to other employees. To accurately reflect this fact, we need to change the above to a 1:1 conditional association in both directions:

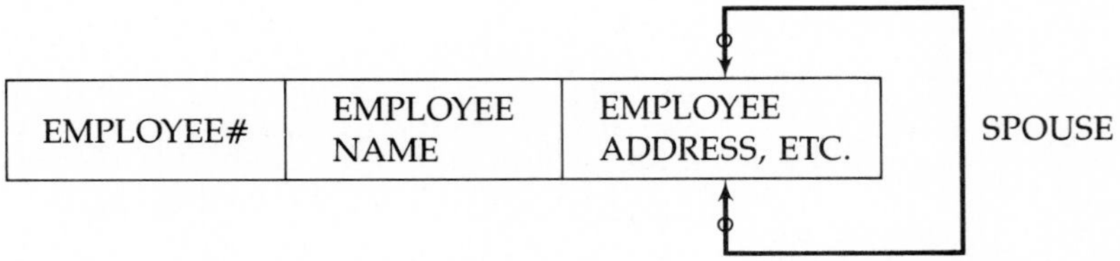

With this association defined, once we have located a particular employee record we can quickly locate the spouse's record (if one exists).

One-to-Many In a one-to-many recursive association, in a specified time period each entity is formally associated with zero, one, or many entities in the same entity class. However, in the reverse association there is a 1:1 relationship. For example, Figure 2-15 shows the usual MANAGES association among employees in the Employee entity class. If we assume that each employee has only one manager, then MANAGES is a $1{:}N$ association. Since there is only one record type, the link appears in the form of a loop (Figure 2-15a). The reverse association is 1:1 since each employee has only one manager.

Two occurrences of this data structure are shown in Figure 2-15b. In a loop, or recursive association, a given entity can be both a "parent" and a "child." For example, the employee MIKE manages two employees (PAUL and KIM) and is managed by another employee (MARY). A recursive relation can encompass an arbitrary depth (number of levels).

Many-to-Many In some organizations, each employee may have more than one manager (this is often referred to as a "matrix" form of organization). In this case, the MANAGES association among employees is *M:N*, since each employee both manages and is managed by several employees. This is an example of a many-to-many recursive association.

The most frequently used many-to-many recursive association in data bases is the bill of materials structure (see Figure 2-16). Many products are made of subassemblies, which in turn are composed of other subassemblies, parts, and so on. As shown in Figure 2-16a, the bill of materials data structure is an *M:N* recursive association between entities we call Items. Two occurrences of such a structure are shown in Figure 2-16b. Each of these diagrams shows the immediate components of each item as well as the quantities of each component. For example, item X consists of item U (quantity 3) and item V (quantity 2).

Notice that the associations in Figure 2-16 are in fact *M:N*. Several of the items have more than one component type (for example, item A has three immediate component types: V, X, and Y). Also, several of the items are used in different higher-level assemblies. For example, item X is used in both item A and item B.

A many-to-many recursive association is usually reduced to one (or more) one-to-many associations by using an intersection record type. In Figure 2-16c, an intersection record type called STRUCTURE is shown. There is one such intersection record for each *immediate* component of an item. The primary key of the STRUCTURE record is the concatenation of ASSEMBLY# (the parent item number) and COMPONENT# (the component item number). The intersection data contained in the record is QUANTITY-USED, the quantity of each component. For example, referring to Figure 2-16b, item X uses item V (quantity 2). The intersection record for this combination appears as follows:

X	V	2

When the association in Figure 2-16c has been defined we can look up a record for a particular item, then (using the association) quickly determine all components of that item.

Figure 2-16
Bill of materials recursive association:
(a) data structure *(M:N)*
(b) two occurrences
(c) data structure (1:*N*)

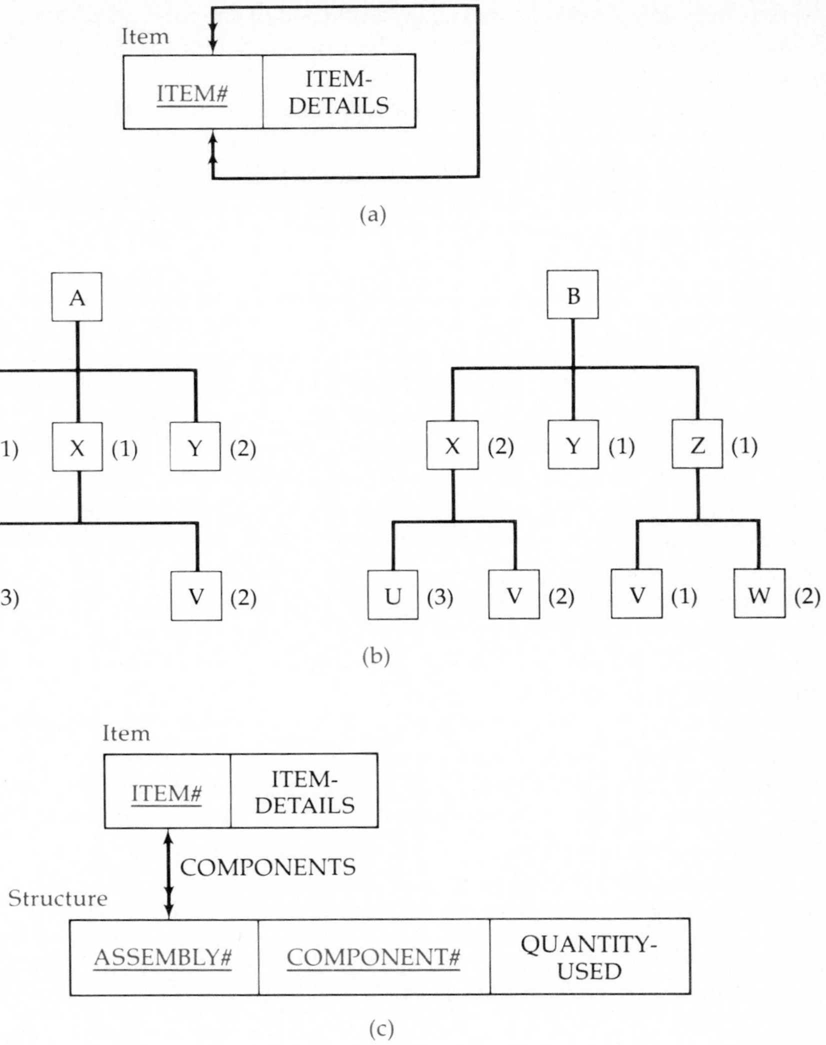

Three-Schema Architecture

Suppose that Pine Valley Furniture Company decides to develop and implement one or more data bases. There will be a need to provide different views of the data for different users. For example, a salesperson will require views of customer and sales data, while an accountant will require views of product and invoice data.

Actually, there is a need for three distinct levels or views of a data base:

1. The *conceptual* level. This is an integrated view of the entire data base. It is the view of the data base administrator. Figure 2-10 is an example

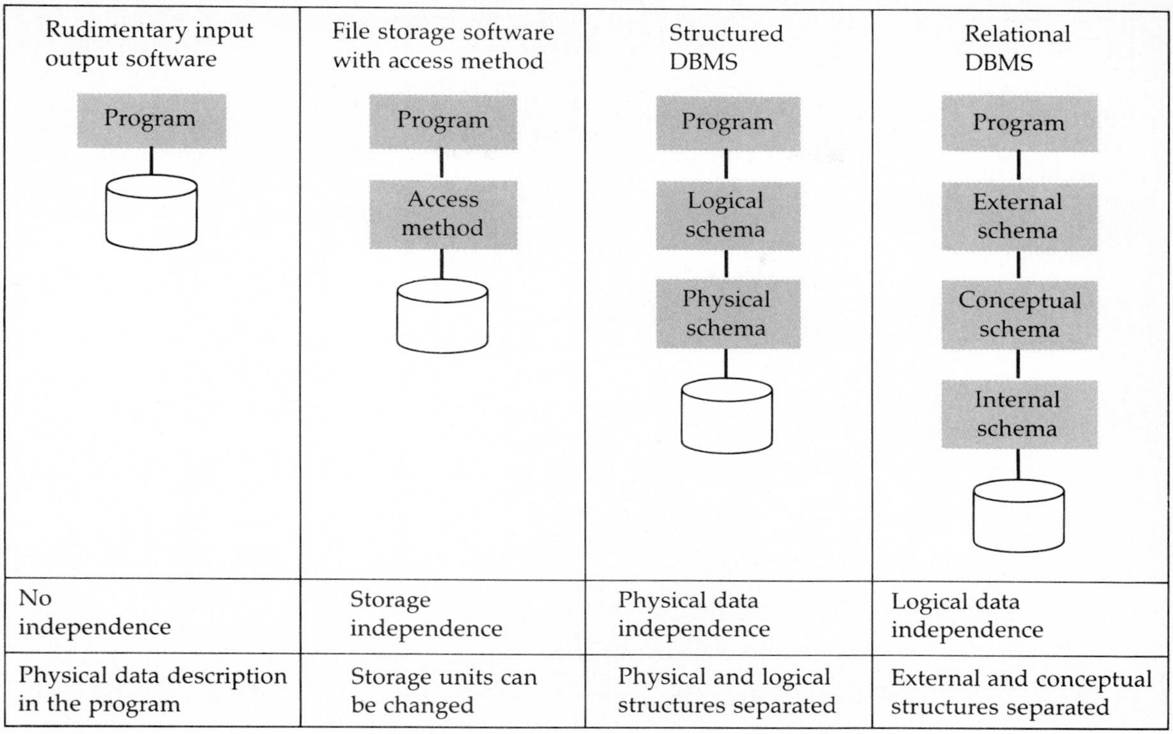

Figure 2-17
Evolution of data management software (Source: Computer Associates International, Inc., Copyright 1986)

of a conceptual level view for Pine Valley Furniture (although it would need to be expanded to be useful).

2. The *external* or *user view* level. This is the view of each individual user (or application program). Figure 2-8 is an external view for a salesperson for Pine Valley Furniture Company.
3. The *internal* or *implementation* view. This view describes how the data base is actually stored and managed on computer secondary storage. The internal model describes records, files, indexes, and other physical storage constructs.

A data base management system that provides these three levels of data is said to follow a *three-schema architecture* (Tsichritzis and Klug 1977). A *schema* is a logical model of a data base. It captures the metadata that describe an organization's data in a language that can be understood by the computer.

Figure 2-17 shows a simplified view of how data management systems have evolved over time. For the earliest data processing applications there was no formal data management software, and all data descriptions and input/output instructions were coded in each application program. Thus, there was no data independence—every change to a data file required modification or rewriting of the application program.

The first formal data management software was referred to as "access

Table 2-1 Important Types of Data Independence

Level of data independence	Examples of changes
	Logical
Data item format	Data item type, length, representation, or unit of measure
Data item usage	How a data item is derived, used, edited, or protected
Logical record structure	How data items are grouped into logical records
Logical data structure	Overall logical structure or conceptual model
	Physical
Physical data organization	How the data are organized into stored records
Access method	What search techniques and access strategies are used
Physical data location	Where data are located on storage devices
Storage device	Characteristics of the physical storage devices used

methods." An access method is a software routine that manages the details of accessing and retrieving records in a file (we describe several access methods in Chapter 4). As shown in Figure 2-17, access methods provide *storage independence.* That is, storage units can be changed (for example, newer storage units can replace older units) without altering or modifying application programs.

Most early data base management systems employed a two-level schema. A *logical* schema corresponds to an external or user view that describes the data as seen by each application program. A *physical* schema corresponds to the internal schema that describes the representation of data in computer facilities. As shown in Figure 2-17, the two-schema architecture added *physical* data independence. That is, the data structures or methods of representing data in secondary storage could be altered without modifying application programs. For example, to achieve greater efficiency, linked lists could be used instead of indexes without changing application programs (we describe both of these techniques in Chapter 5).

The two-level schema was characteristic of structured data base management systems, such as those that use the hierarchical and network data models (introduced in Chapter 6). Although these DBMS represented a step forward, they still did not provide logical data independence.

The three-schema architecture shown in the last column of Figure 2-17 is provided mainly by some contemporary relational DBMS. With this architecture, a third level (called the conceptual schema) is inserted between the internal and external schemas. The conceptual schema provides an integrated view of the data resource for the entire organization. The conceptual schema evolves over time—that is, new data definitions are added to it as the data base grows and matures.

As shown in Figure 2-17, the advantage of the three-schema architecture is that it provides logical (as well as physical) data independence. With *logical* data independence, the conceptual schema can grow and evolve over time without affecting the external schema. As a result, existing application programs need not be modified as the data base evolves.

A summary of logical and physical data independence is shown in Table 2.1. The table shows the typical changes that can be made for each type of independence, without altering application programs. Although data base management systems differ in the amount and level of data independence they provide, only the relational data model provides most of the types of data independence shown in the table.

SUMMARY

In this chapter, we have described the nature of data (or information, which is data that have been processed and displayed for a decision maker). Data exist in three realms: reality (representing entities and their properties), metadata (representing record types and data item types), and data (representing actual stored data values).

We described techniques for representing data. These techniques include bubble charts (for representing associations between data items) and data structure diagrams (for representing associations between record types).

To provide data independence, some data base management systems provide a three-level architecture for visualizing an organization's data base. The three levels in this model (called the ANSI/SPARC model) are the conceptual model, the external models (or views), and the internal model. This model provides two levels of data independence: physical, which insulates a user from changes to the internal model, and logical, which insulates a user from changes to the conceptual model. We provide examples of these levels in subsequent chapters.

Chapter Review

REVIEW QUESTIONS

1. Define each of the following terms:
   a. entity
   b. entity class
   c. association
   d. metadata

e. attribute
f. data item
g. data aggregate
h. record
i. file
j. primary key
k. secondary key

2. Contrast the following items:
   a. physical data independence; logical data independence
   b. primary key; secondary key
   c. conceptual model; external model
   d. attribute; data item
   e. entity, entity class

3. Give at least one synonym for each of the following terms:
   a. data item
   b. association
   c. entity class
   d. data aggregate
   e. data structure diagram
   f. recursive association

4. What is a recursive association? What are the two types of recursive associations?

5. Briefly describe each of the following:
   a. conceptual model
   b. external model
   c. internal model

6. Briefly describe the three realms used in describing data.

PROBLEMS AND EXERCISES

1. Match the following terms and definitions:

_____ metadata	**a.** recursive association
_____ attribute	**b.** object or event
_____ data item	**c.** named collection of data items
_____ data aggregate	**d.** information about data
_____ secondary key	**e.** uniquely identifies a record
_____ loop	**f.** microcomputer DBMS
_____ entity	**g.** property of an entity
_____ dBase III	**h.** collection of similar entities
_____ entity class	**i.** identifies records that share a common property
_____ primary key	**j.** unit fact

2. Consider each of the following changes to a data base. Assuming that an application program is unaffected by the change, indicate whether it is an example of logical or physical data independence.
   a. Move the data to newer, faster storage devices.
   b. Change a data item called ZIP-CODE from a five-digit field to a nine-digit field.
   c. Change from indexed sequential access method (ISAM) to virtual sequential access method (VSAM).

d. Add a new data item called CARPOOL to an existing EMPLOYEE record type.
e. Add a new record type called TEXTBOOK to an instructional data base.

3. Give two examples (other than those in the text) of each of the following associations between two entities:
   a. one-to-one
   b. one-to-many
   c. many-to-many
   d. recursive one-to-many
   e. recursive many-to-many
   f. multiple associations

4. Examine the PRODUCT data in Figure 2-2 and answer the following questions:
   a. What items are designated bedroom (BR) furniture? (Give the item numbers.)
   b. What items have PINE finish?
   c. What items have a PRICE that is $500 or less?
   d. What items of PINE bedroom furniture sell for $500 or less?

5. An EMPLOYEE record type has the following attributes:

   EMPLOYEE# (11 characters)
   NAME (25 characters)
   JOB-TITLE (15 characters)
   DATE-OF-BIRTH (10 characters)
   SALARY (12 numeric, 2 decimal places)

   a. Show typical data for six employees using a flat file representation (similar to Figure 2-2).
   b. Write dBase III commands to CREATE a file named Employee (including data item definitions).
   c. Write a dBase III command to display the record for employee no. 123-45-6789.
   d. Write a dBase III command to display the records for employees whose job title is Programmer.

6. List five attributes for each of the following entity classes:
   a. Patient
   b. Student
   c. Car
   d. Video Game
   e. Textbook

7. List five entity classes for each of the following attributes:
   a. Name
   b. Color
   c. Weight
   d. Price

8. Draw a bubble chart (similar to Figure 2-6b) for the secondary key value ROOM = 'LR' in Figure 2-2.

9. Draw a bubble chart showing the associations between the following data items (make any assumptions that are necessary): STUDENT#, STUDENT-NAME,

TELEPHONE#, COURSE#, COURSE-NAME, UNITS, INSTRUCTOR-NAME, INSTRUCTOR-OFFICE#.

10. Combine the following user views into a single view:

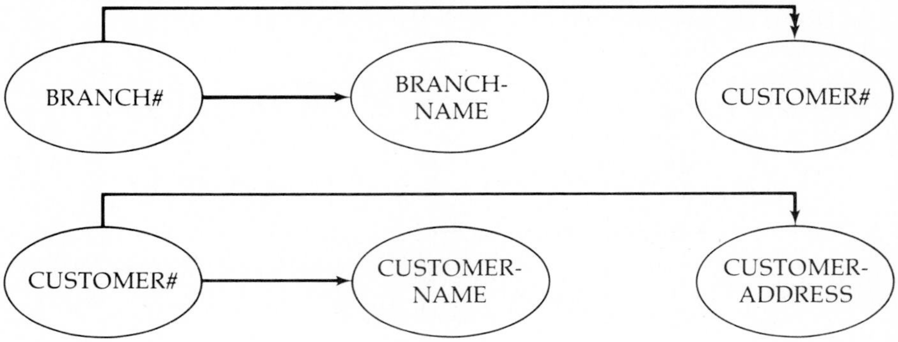

11. Draw an occurrence of each of the following:
    a. data structure diagram in Figure 2-13
    b. data structure diagram in Figure 2-14
    c. data structure diagram in Figure 2-16c

12. Draw a data structure diagram for each of the following associations:
    a. A given course can have several prerequisite courses, and a given course can be a prerequisite for several other courses.
    b. A student can register in several courses, and a course can have many students registered.
    c. A computer can run a number of software packages, and each software package can run on zero, one, or many computers.
    d. A student can have zero, one, or many roommates (who are also students).

REFERENCES

Computer Associates International, Inc. 1986. *CA-Universe: Product Concepts and Facilities Manual.* Los Angeles: CAI.

Date, C. J. 1981. *An Introduction to Data Base Systems.* 3d ed. Reading, Mass.: Addison-Wesley.

Katzan, Harry. 1975. *Computer Data Management and Data Base Technology.* New York: Van Nostrand Reinhold.

Krumm, Rob. 1985. *Understanding and Using dBase II & III.* New York: Brady Communications.

Martin, James. 1983. *Managing the Data-Base Environment.* Englewood Cliffs, N.J.: Prentice-Hall.

Percy, Tony. 1986. "My Data, Right or Wrong." *Datamation* (June 1): 123.

Toffler, Alvin. 1980. *The Third Wave.* New York: William Morrow.

Tsichritzis, D. C., and A. Klug, eds. 1977. "The ANSI/X3/SPARC DBMS Framework: Report of the Study Group on Data Base Management Systems." *Information Systems,* 3.

Chapter 3

Data Base Planning

INTRODUCTION

Data base systems were first installed in business enterprises during the late 1960s. Since that time, thousands of organizations have converted to this approach. Yet today, the promise of data base is largely unrealized in many companies. According to Voell (1980):

> Data base and data administration have, by and large, not lived up to the expectations and promises made in most writings. The corporate data base integrated to reduce redundancy, accessible to multiple applications, protected from the unauthorized, and controlled so that it contains only valid information is a myth. Today, data base is largely just an access method. Similarly, the data administration function is not controlling a global view of information. The real promise and benefits of a corporate data base are valid, but are yet to be realized.

Why have so many enterprises failed to realize the potential of the data base approach? No doubt there are many reasons. However, comparison of successful and unsuccessful organizations reveals that lack of adequate planning for data base is the most common and pervasive shortcoming. Thus, before we address the basic elements of data base technology (Chapters 4–6) and examine a detailed process of how to design and develop a data base (Chapters 7–9), we, like any organization, must deal with data base planning.

IMPORTANCE OF DATA BASE PLANNING

Traditionally, information systems have not really been planned or designed at all, but have evolved in a "bottom-up" fashion as stand-alone systems to solve isolated organizational problems. In effect, traditional information systems ask the question: What procedure (application program) is required to solve this particular problem as it exists today? The problem with this approach is that the required organizational procedures are likely to change over time as the environment changes. For example, a company may decide to change its method of billing customers, or a university may change its procedures for registering students. When such changes occur, it is usually necessary to modify existing application programs.

In contrast, data resource management essentially asks the question: What data base requirements will satisfy the information needs of the enterprise today and well into the future? A major advantage of this approach is that an organization's data are less likely to change (or will change more slowly) than its procedures. For example, unless an organization changes its business fundamentally, its underlying data structure will remain reasonably stable over a ten-year period. However, the procedures used to access and process the data will change many times during that period. Thus, the challenge of data resource management is to design stable data bases that are relatively independent of the languages and programs used to update them.

To benefit from this data base approach, the organization *must* analyze its information needs and plan its data base carefully. If a data base approach is attempted without such planning, the results may well be disastrous. The resulting data base may support individual applications, but will not provide a resource that can be shared by users throughout the enterprise. The DBMS becomes just a costly access method that provides the same structured reports and displays as the previous systems. Program maintenance problems continue to plague the data processing organization.

With the acceptance of data as a valuable organizational resource, an entirely different planning approach is required. The organization must develop strategic plans for its data resources, just as it develops strategic plans for its human, financial, and material resources. The planning process must be "top-down," so that information systems and data base planning are integrated with basic enterprise objectives. The result is a comprehensive data base plan that will provide a road map for data base design and implementation.

This chapter presents a framework for data base planning. Although no single methodology or standard approach is used for this purpose, the techniques presented are representative of those being used by successful organizations. According to Holland (1980): "A very few organizations are superimposing a data model over their business systems plan. These are the electronic organizations of the future that will significantly reduce their maintenance costs, provide program and data independence, add new applications with ease and enjoy an effective user environment."

ORGANIZATIONAL ENVIRONMENT

A major objective of data base planning is to develop a **strategic data model.** This data model should be a model of the information needs of the entire organization, both today and well into the future—say ten years or more.

The data model should be understood and supported by the various functional areas of the organization. A high-level overview of the functions common to most organizations is shown in Figure 3-1. The four functional areas shown in this figure are Marketing, Production/Operations, Management, and Support Services. As the diagram shows, each of the functions has an interface with the others.

Marketing (sometimes referred to as the "demand side" of the organization) is responsible for creating and/or identifying the demand for products and services. Marketing may be further broken down into sales, advertising, market research, distribution, and related activities. Production/Operations (the "supply side") is responsible for providing the products and services. This function may consist of materials management, production scheduling and control, production operations, and so on. Support Services consists of functions such as engineering, accounting, personnel, and maintenance. Management is responsible for the overall planning and direction of the organization.

It is usually not practical for an organization to implement its data base all at once or over a short time span. Instead, the data base is implemented in stages over a period of time—perhaps several years. The end result might be a single large data base or, more likely, several smaller data bases. For

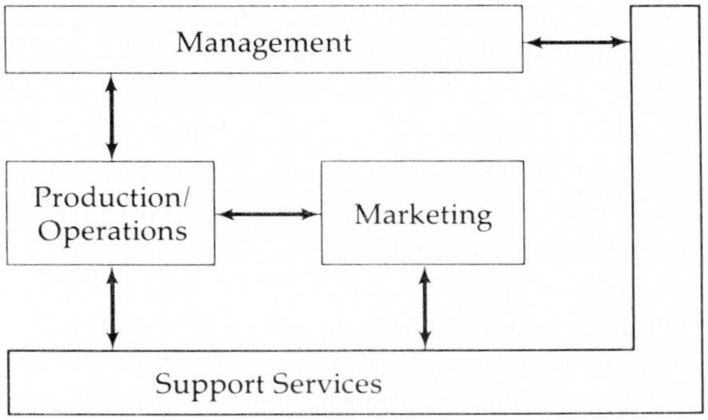

Figure 3-1
Functional overview of a business enterprise (Source: Holland 1981, p. 32. Holland Systems Corporation, Ann Arbor, Michigan.)

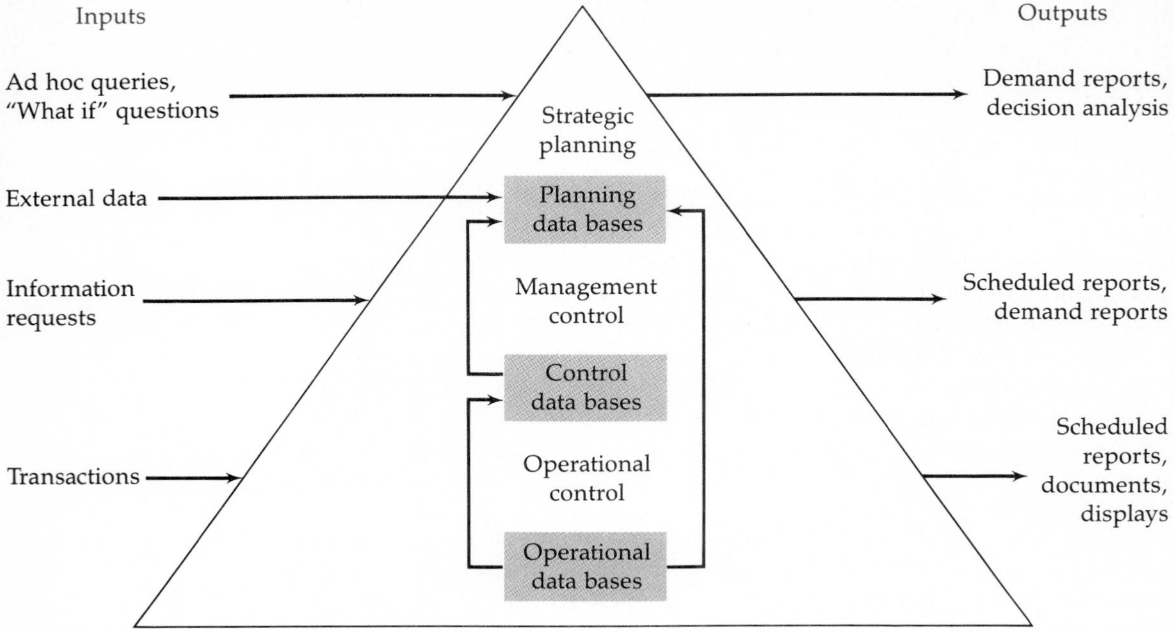

Figure 3-2
Typical information needs by management level

this reason, it is important that the organization have a strategic data base plan and data model to guide the implementation. Without such a plan, the data base will evolve in a haphazard fashion and will fail to yield its intended benefits.

Anthony (1965) has identified three levels of management planning and control in an organization: strategic planning, management control, and operational control. As suggested in Figure 3-2, each of these levels of management has different data base requirements. At each higher level, the data bases are in more summarized form. The arrows in Figure 3-2 represent the aggregation of data from each lower level to each higher level data base.

Operational control focuses on the execution of specific tasks and activities. It is concerned with scheduling and controlling individual jobs, procuring materials, and taking specific personnel actions.

The data base of operational control consists of detailed information describing customers, products, employees, and other entities, and transactions affecting those entities. These data are frequently nonmonetary and are based on transactions such as patient registrations, material receipts, and personnel assignments. The operational control system must produce documents and displays that are immediately useful for operational decision making. Several data bases may exist at this level since one comprehensive operational data base may be too difficult to design or implement.

Management control (or middle management) is concerned with allocating resources and ensuring that resources are obtained and used effectively and efficiently in accomplishing company objectives. Thus, management control is concerned with balancing the use of resources, measuring progress against plans, and taking corrective action when necessary.

The data bases for management control consist largely of summaries of operational data. Typical examples are monthly summaries of performance versus budget, and of categorized sales (e.g., by product line or geographical region). In addition to periodic reports, reports for management control must be made available in response to ad hoc requests. Although most management control data base contents are aggregations of operational-level data, some new data from external sources (e.g., potential customer demographics) may also be introduced.

Strategic planning involves deciding on organizational goals and objectives, determining the resources that will be required, and deciding on the policies to govern the acquisition, use, and disposition of those resources. Strategic managers are responsible for the overall performance of the enterprise.

As shown in Figure 3-2, strategic planning managers need a planning data base to support their decisions. Information in this data base exists in a highly summarized and specialized form. For example, the chief executive officer of a company would most likely be concerned with return on investment or market share growth rather than with the performance of a particular department or product line. A manager at this level often requires a decision support system (described in Chapter 1) that can respond to ad hoc queries for information and simulate various planning alternatives. Also, top managers require considerable external data such as business forecasts, economic data, and competitive information. Thus, the planning data base consists both of external data and internal information summarized from the lower-level data bases.

As we will see later in this text, modern data base management systems permit handling of these three levels of data bases in two different ways. First, they may actually exist as separate data bases, with application programs that produce extracts from lower-level data bases to feed higher-level ones. Many businesses refer to such higher-level data bases as "shadow" or "extract" data bases. The extract data bases may be downloaded and stored on personal computers or workstations. Alternatively, the management control and strategic planning data bases may not physically exist but may simply be "views" defined on the operational data bases. Combinations of these two approaches may also be used in a given organization.

DATA BASE PLANNING PROCESS

The purpose of data base planning is to develop a strategic, or long-range, plan for a data base environment that will support the organization's information needs, both today and in a planned future. The data base plan is a subset of the organization's information systems (IS) plan, which, in turn, is a subset of the overall corporate plan. Thus, we visualize the planning process as hierarchical, or top-down, in nature. An alternative approach is bottom-up, in which the planner extrapolates from existing systems and information needs. However, with this approach, there is no assurance that the data base plan will be in agreement with higher-level plans.

Data base planning should be established as a formal project within the organization. A project team consisting of somewhere between four and eight members (depending on the size and complexity of the organization) seems to work well in practice. Team members should represent a cross section of end users (managers) as well as data processing personnel. The team leader should be chosen carefully and should be a strong candidate for the data administrator position. The project team should report in a staff relationship to the IS director or to a higher-level manager.

An organization will usually conduct a major data base planning effort about every five years. Annual information systems planning will readdress this plan and possibly make minor modifications to it.

Tasks in Data Base Planning

The major tasks in planning for a data base environment are shown in Figure 3-3. The feedback arrows on the left of the figure indicate that data base planning is not strictly a sequential process. Refinements within certain tasks are often necessary as an organization learns more about its data requirements.

Obtain Top Management Commitment (Task 0) Top management should initiate the planning process. Even if they don't, however, the study team must nevertheless obtain a firm commitment by top management. There are several reasons why this commitment is so important. First, it provides authority to initiate the planning process. Also, it ensures that the resources and cooperation needed to develop the plan will be made available. Management commitment sends signals to the rest of the organization that the planning process is important and is to be given high priority. Finally, it helps ensure that the final accepted plan will be implemented. Without the firm commitment of top management the planning process should probably be postponed.

Initiate Study (Task 1) The first task of the project team is to define the goals and objectives of the data base approach in the organization. This requires establishing a scope for the data base in terms of what business areas or functions are to be addressed. First, the project team should identify the problems and limitations of the present environment. Next, the team should identify the benefits to be achieved with the data base environment (we identified the major benefits in Chapter 1). The anticipated benefits are then stated in the form of goals and objectives that mesh with the organization's long-range plans.

Establish the Data Administration Function (Task 2) The functions and responsibilities of data administration (or data base administration) should be defined early in the planning process. The person who is data administrator (or a leading candidate for this position) should assume a leadership role in the subsequent planning steps. Tools, such as a data dictionary/directory system, should be acquired to support the remaining tasks.

Perform Business Systems Analysis (Tasks 3–6) The study team identifies and documents the business functions, processes, activities, and entities. We define and illustrate each of these terms in the next section.

Build Information Model (Task 7) Building an information model is the central step in the entire strategic planning process. This model portrays the major entity classes for the organization and the associations between those entities.

Develop Data Distribution Plan (Task 8) If data will be distributed in several physical data bases, the study team develops a plan for data distribution. (Distributed data bases are described in Chapter 16.)

Develop Implementation Plan (Task 9) The team establishes a timetable and responsibilities for data base implementation. Priorities are established so that the strategic data base plan ties in with overall IS plans.

Conduct Final Review and Evaluation (Task 10) The project team prepares a final report and reviews all components to ensure that they are consistent. The report is presented to top management, and responsibility for updating the plan is assigned.

Top-Down Planning Versus Bottom-Up Design

As shown in Figure 3-4, developing corporate data bases requires both top-down planning and bottom-up design. Top-down planning, which is the topic of this chapter, starts with basic organizational goals and objectives. Using business system planning, we analyze organizational functions, processes, activities, and entities. We then develop an information model in the form of an entity-relationship diagram that portrays the major entities of the organization and the associations between those entities.

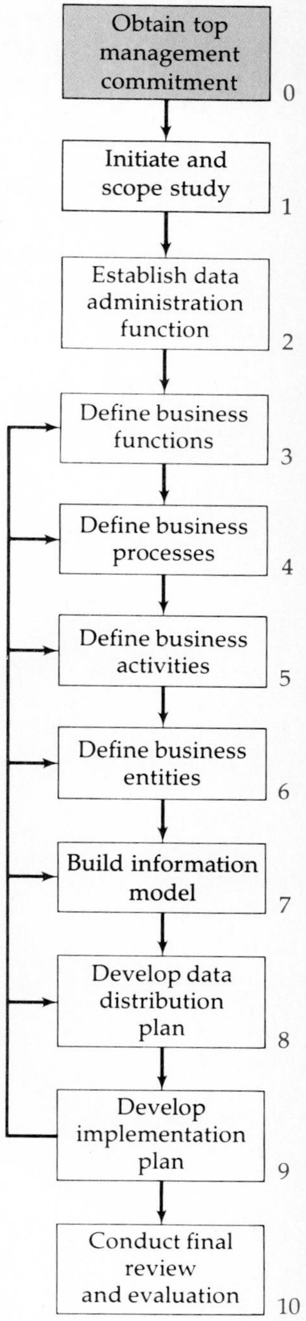

Figure 3-3
Tasks in strategic data base planning

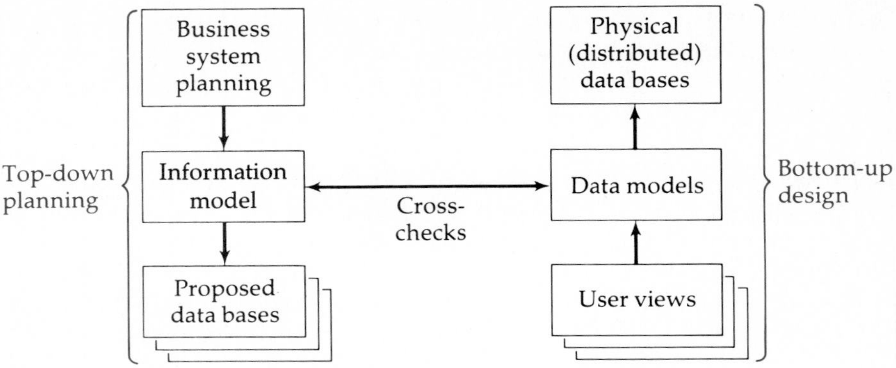

Figure 3-4
Top-down planning versus bottom-up design

Detailed data base design is a bottom-up process (see Figure 3-4). Analysts begin with user views of data and apply normalization techniques to develop detailed data models (data base design is described in Part III). In data base design, the data models are cross-checked against the information model to ensure that they are complete and accurate. Thus, the top-down information model plays three important roles:

1. It provides an overall, integrative view of corporate entities and data.
2. It provides a basis for segmenting the overall corporate data model into a number of manageable data base projects.
3. During detailed data base design, it provides a cross-check and means of integrating individual data bases into the overall corporate framework.

According to Goodhue, Quillard, and Rockart (1986), organizations frequently modify or abbreviate this complete data base planning process. However, drastic reduction of this process can lead to failure of the data base planning effort. The following cautions need to be observed:

- Although commitment from key business managers is often difficult to obtain and the process is very time-consuming, sufficient commitment of time and people is essential.
- Expectations need to be well managed so that all involved realize that this is a long-range planning effort and not one geared to the detailed design of specific applications systems. In fact, a good planning effort designs for business functions not specific applications.
- Strong reliance on purchased applications systems, designed for narrow applications, can force compromises in the coverage of the data base plan. Since organizations are increasingly choosing to purchase application software, those based on data base concepts and technology are more desirable since they can more easily be fit into the overall data base architecture.

- The bottom-up design is especially vulnerable to business changes. Since a typical data base plan can take from 6–12 months, the process must be at a high level (as well as base level) of analysis so that these business changes can be incorporated and their effects clearly seen.

Reducing the effort of data base planning is most effectively done by reducing the *scope* of the data base plan. Goodhue, Quillard, and Rockart have found that this is accomplished by:

1. Targeting each data base planning effort on one part (function) of the business (e.g., marketing) or division (e.g., consumer products). As long as common standards are used for naming and describing data, later cross data base integration is easier.
2. Applying an 80/20 rule to guide data base planning. For example, the firm may focus on Customer, Product/Service, and Facility entities as being the most crucial to the business and, hence, providing 80% of the value of data base process for 20% of the effort (by eliminating most planning for other subjects of the business, such as Employee, Vendor, Inventory, and so on entities).

Data base planning is certainly not a trivial effort. The need for professional data base planners or administrators is very strong, especially in medium to large organizations. User managers must also be involved especially in information modeling since it is driven from a model of the business. Effective data base design not only follows a logical process as outlined in this chapter but also requires a team approach involving business experts, data base specialists, and application system experts. This team should always be guided by the fact that the objective of data base planning is *not* to better manage data (for its own sake), but rather to solve business problems and exploit opportunities to take advantage of data base concepts and technologies.

DATA BASE PLANNING METHODOLOGY

In this section, we describe a methodology for top-down data base planning. This methodology is based on the Business System Planning (BSP) approach developed by IBM to assist organizations in establishing a system architecture plan. Business System Planning is a top-down approach that has as its basic assumption that "an information system plan for a business must be integrated with the business plan and should be developed from the point of view of top management and with their active participation" (*Business System Planning* 1975, 1). The methodology presented here combines some of the features of BSP with other related data base planning approaches. Data base planning is part of overall system planning.

Figure 3-5
Business System Planning process

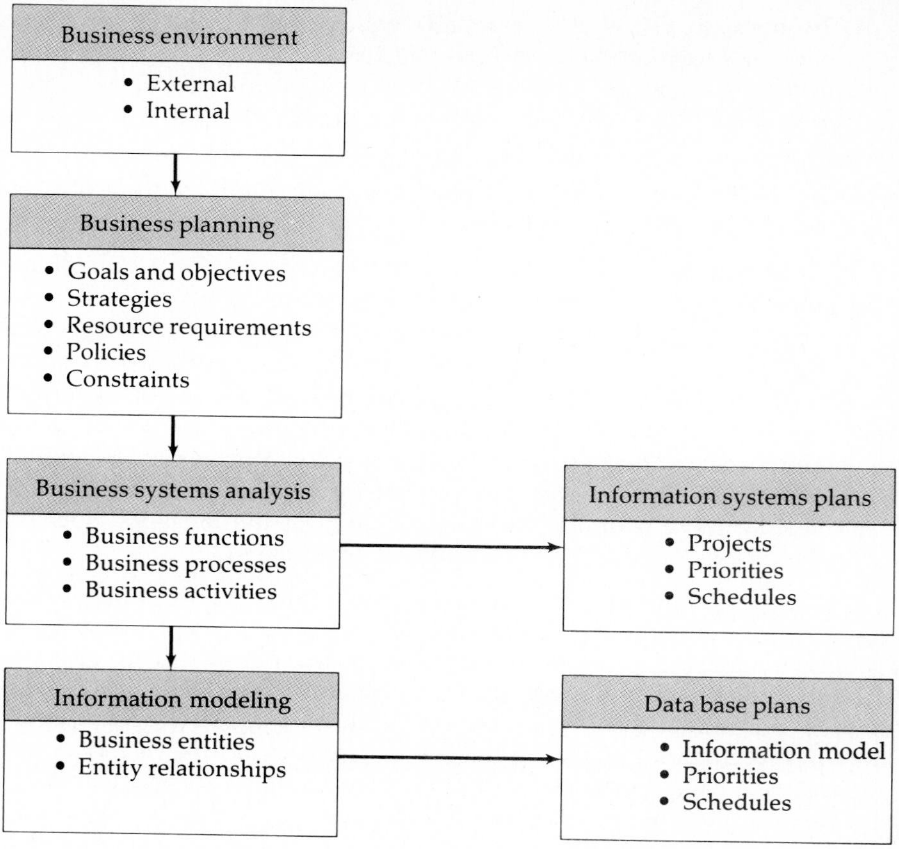

There are four main phases in the planning process. They are: identifying the business environment, business planning, business systems analysis, and information modeling (see Figure 3-5).

Identifying the Business Environment

Identifying the business environment means identifying the internal and external environments in which the firm now exists and will exist over the strategic planning horizon. The external environment includes customers, competitors, suppliers, government, technology, and economic conditions. The internal environment includes policies, practices, and constraints.

Business Planning

Business planning considers the forecasted business environment and develops organizational goals and objectives, strategies (competitive approaches), resource requirements, policies, and constraints. The business plan (sometimes called the master plan) is the fundamental planning document for the organization. It must be carefully documented and communicated to key managers throughout the organization. Also, the business plan must be revised and updated as conditions change.

Business Systems Analysis

The foundation of a comprehensive data base plan is business systems analysis. The goal of this process is to analyze the basic functions and subfunctions of the organization, identifying present and future information needs to support these functions. This analysis of business functions is independent of existing organizational lines. A top-down graphic approach is used to identify organizational functions. First, the major functions of the organization are identified. Each of these functions is then divided into a group of subfunctions, called processes. Each process, in turn, is divided (where appropriate) into a set of elementary subfunctions called activities. Also, the business entities required by each of the processes are identified during the analysis. An example of such an analysis in a manufacturing firm is shown in Figure 3-6 in the form of a simple chart, called a **business chart.**

Business functions are broad groups of closely related activities and decisions that contribute to a product or service life cycle. In Figure 3-6, the functions for the manufacturing firm are identified as follows: planning, materials management, production planning, production operations, and quality assurance. Several additional functions would normally be identified in a manufacturing firm (see Chapter Review exercises). A small company such as Pine Valley Furniture Company may have from 5 to 10 functions, while a large corporation such as IBM might have 20 or more functions.

A business function may correspond to an existing organizational unit, or it may cut across several existing units. For example, the quality assurance business function in Figure 3-6 may actually be spread across several organizational units, such as engineering, purchasing, and quality control. It is far better to relate data base design to basic organizational functions and processes than to organizational units, since the latter are subject to frequent change.

Business processes are decision-related activities that occur within a function and often serve to manage people, money, material, or information. In Figure 3-6, the materials management function has been subdivided into the following processes: requirements planning, purchasing, receiving, inventory accounting, and warehousing. Business processes should again reflect related activity groupings rather than existing departmental functions. Each business function within an organization can often be modeled with some three to ten processes.

Business activities are specific operations or transactions that are required

Figure 3-6
Business chart for a manufacturing company

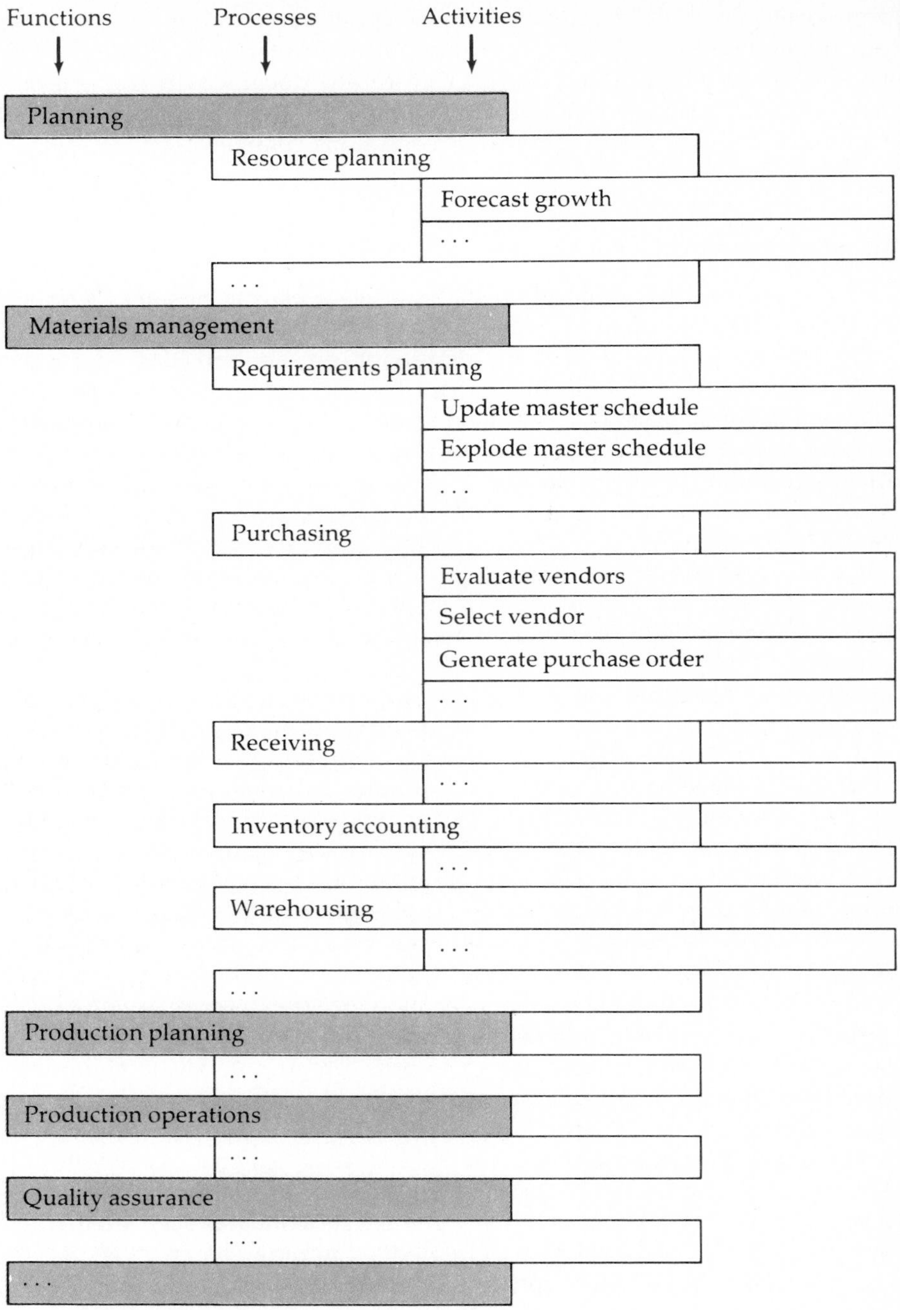

to carry out a process. Each activity is typically performed by some person in the organization. For example, the activity "generate purchase order" is a transaction that is carried out by a buyer, perhaps using an on-line terminal. The business activities that are identified for the purchasing process in Figure 3-6 are the following: evaluate vendors, select vendor, and generate purchase order.

Business entities are persons, objects, or events about which information is recorded in the data base. Many of the entities that are associated with a business process can be identified by reviewing the activities for that process. For example, by reviewing the activities for the purchasing process, we identify the following entities: Vendors, Purchase Orders, and Invoices. In the next section we describe a systematic method for identifying entities and the relationships between entities.

Information Modeling

The company business chart (such as the one in Figure 3-6) identifies the functions, processes, and activities for the organization. However, it does not portray the information architecture or top-down data base design that we require. Information modeling is the process of developing such an information architecture. In carrying out this process we must answer three questions:

1. What are the important business entities for the organization?
2. What are the associations (or relationships) between those entities?
3. How can we best portray the information architecture in graphic form?

Identifying Entities and Relationships To identify all important entities and their relationships, we must fully understand each business process and the "business rules" or practices that govern each activity within the company. To gain this depth of understanding, the data base analyst must work closely with the end users who perform each activity. It is helpful to realize that each activity normally affects one (or more) entities in one (or more) of the following ways:

1. *Creates a new entity occurrence.* For example, the activity "admit student" creates a new occurrence of the Student entity.
2. *Deletes an entity occurrence.* For example, the activity "fire employee" deletes an occurrence of the Employee entity.
3. *Modifies an entity.* For example, the activity "promote employee" modifies an occurrence of the Employee entity.
4. *Establishes a relationship between two (or more) entities.* For example, the activity "enroll student" establishes a relationship between a Student

entity occurrence and a Course entity occurrence (other activities may modify or delete relationships between entities).

5. *Uses an entity without modification.* For example, the activity "evaluate vendors" uses occurrences of the Vendor entity without modifying those occurrences.

We may use these rules to systematically analyze activities and to identify entities and their relationships. Following is the result of applying this technique to the activities in the purchasing process of Figure 3-6:

Activity	**Result**
1. Evaluate vendors	1. Uses the *Vendor* entity without modification.
2. Select vendor	2. Uses the *Vendor* entity without modification.
3. Generate purchase order	3. a. Creates a new occurrence of the *Purchase Order* entity.
	b. Creates an association between the entities *Vendor, Purchase Order, Buyer,* and *Parts.*

Developing Entity-Relationship (E/R) Diagrams After the entities and their relationships have been identified, the next step is to portray this information in the form of a graphic model. In Chapters 1 and 2 we used rectangles to represent entities and arrows to represent associations. For example, the one-to-many association between Customer and Order was represented as follows:

This same notation could be used in this chapter in developing the enterprise information model. However, in order to make the model as understandable as possible to the end user, it is often helpful to use a special symbol (usually a diamond) to represent an association between entities. Also, the association is named, so that the preceding example might appear as follows:

Notice that rather than arrow heads, the nature of the association is explained by symbols such as "1" and "*N*" (which represents "many").

An advantage of this approach is that it allows us to easily represent the association between three (or more) entities. For example, if each vendor supplies multiple customers, each with one or more distinct types of parts, the diagram would appear as follows:

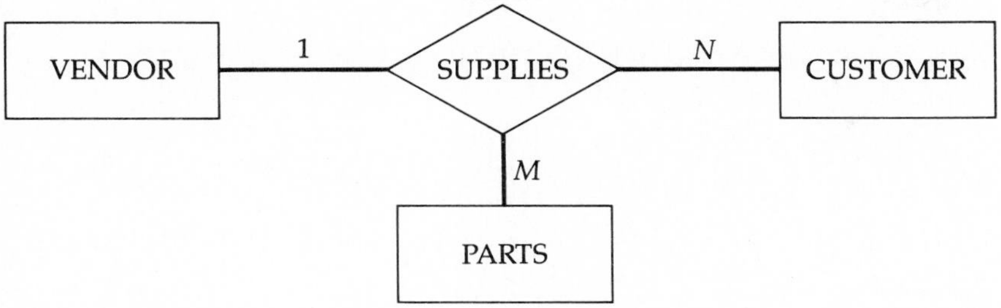

Diagrams that use this notation are referred to as *entity-relationship* (or *E/R*) *diagrams*. An E/R diagram for the purchasing process is shown in Figure 3-7. The business rules that define the relationships shown in this diagram are as follows:

1. A buyer submits one or more purchase orders to a vendor for parts.
2. Each purchase order is the responsibility of one buyer, and is submitted to one vendor.
3. Each purchase order may order multiple parts.

Frequently in top-down information modeling we may identify a particular entity type or class, then become interested in a generalization or abstraction of that entity class. For example, the entity class Computer is a generalization of the entity class Microcomputer. Conversely, we may become interested in specializations of an entity class: Microcomputer, Minicomputer, and Mainframe are individual entity classes that are specializations

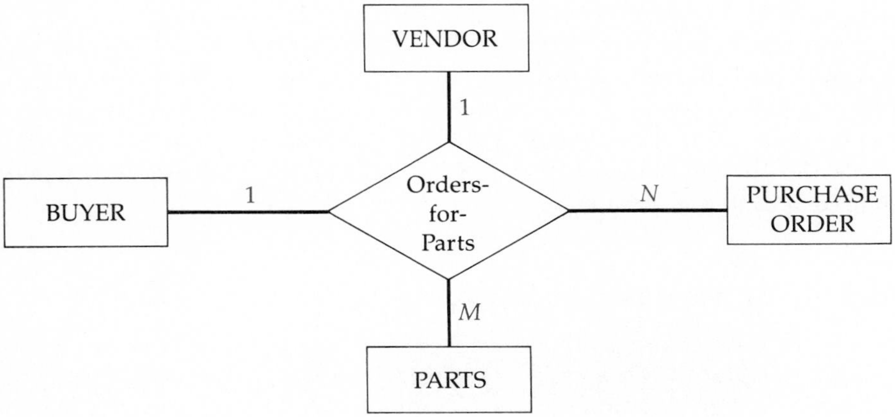

Figure 3-7
Entity-relationship diagram for purchasing

of Computer. In such instances, the generalized entity class is referred to as a *supertype*, while each member class is referred to as a *subtype*. Fortunately, such relationships can easily be represented by entity-relationship diagrams, for example, as follows:

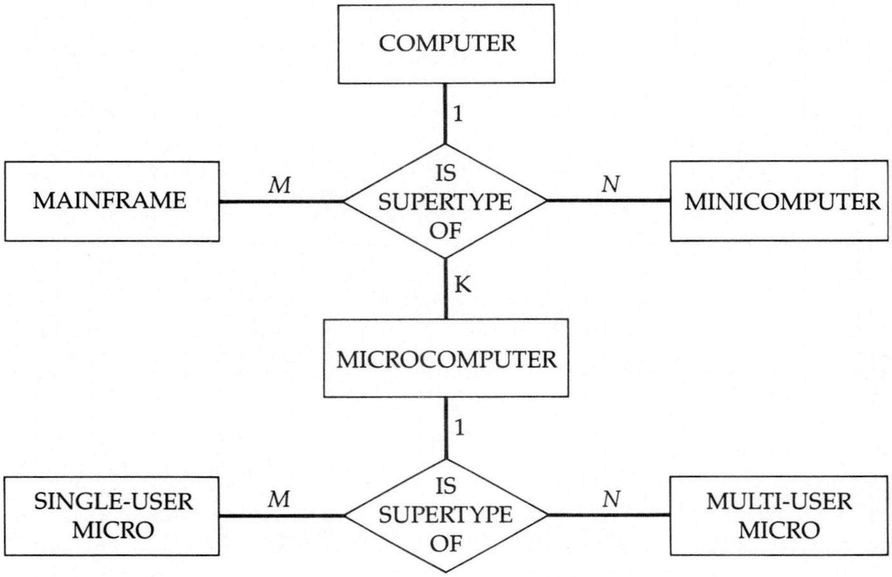

We discuss additional properties of entity-relationship diagrams in Chapter 6. For a rigorous discussion of information modeling using E/R diagrams see Flavin (1981).

Case Example: Mountain View Community Hospital

The principles of data base planning can be illustrated with the case example of a hospital, an organization familiar to most people. Although the example is hypothetical, it does contain many of the elements of a real hospital environment. The same case is used in later chapters to illustrate detailed data base design and implementation.

Identifying the Business Environment

Mountain View Community Hospital is a not-for-profit, short-term, acute general hospital. It is a small to medium-sized hospital, with 100 beds at the present time. Mountain View Community is the only hospital in the

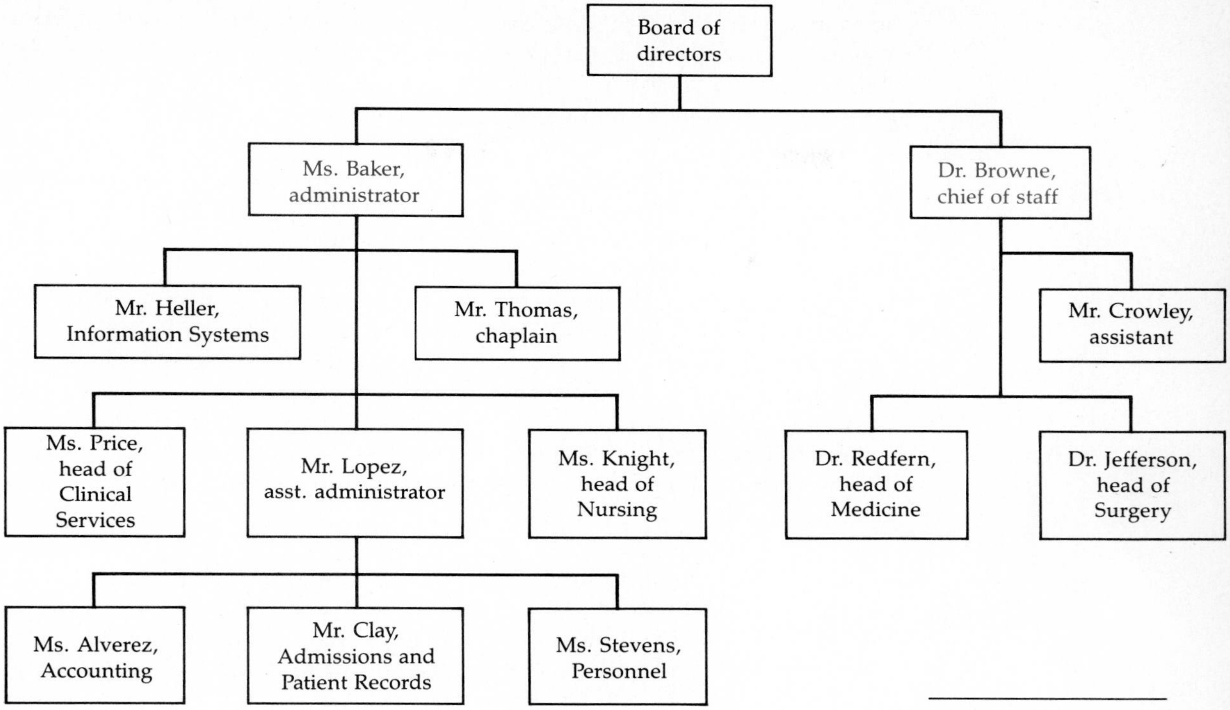

Figure 3-8
Organization chart for Mountain View Community Hospital

city of Mountain View, a rapidly growing city with a population of about 25,000 people in the heart of the Rocky Mountains.

An organizational chart for Mountain View Community Hospital is shown in Figure 3-8. As with most hospitals, Mountain View Community is divided into two organizational groups. The physicians, headed by Dr. Browne (chief of staff) are responsible for the quality of medical care provided their patients. The group headed by Ms. Baker (administrator) provides the nursing, clinical, and administrative support the physicians need to serve their patients.

Business Planning

Mountain View Community has a long-range plan that was prepared with the assistance of a management consulting firm two years ago. The plan, which covers ten years, defines the hospital's service area and its forecasted growth, identifies basic goals and objectives for the hospital, and identifies the capacity and resources that will be required to meet future needs.

Although most admissions to Mountain View Community Hospital are from the city of Mountain View, some patients are also admitted from the surrounding rural areas. As a result, the entire county in which Mountain View is located (Mesa County) was defined as the hospital's service area. The population of Mesa County is about 40,000 at present and has been growing at an annual rate of 8%, a trend that is expected to continue for several years.

The basic goal of Mountain View Community Hospital is to continue to meet the needs of Mountain View and Mesa County for high-quality health care, while containing costs that have been rising in accordance with national trends in recent years.

To support the expected demand for services, the long-range plan calls for expansion and modernization of facilities. These plans include the addition of a new wing in five years, with expansion from the present 100 to 150 beds. Adequate land already exists for this expansion, as well as for additional parking facilities. Also, several existing facilities are to be renovated, including the Admitting and Outpatient registration areas. Two new service facilities are planned over a five-year period: Ultrasound and Occupational Therapy.

Existing Information Systems Mountain View Community has a minicomputer that was leased two years ago. The system has 1 MB central memory and 300 MB on-line disk storage capacity. Plans call for adding a faster processor and additional memory and disk storage capacity during the coming year. However, the extent of these additions has yet to be determined.

Present information systems are batch-oriented and include application programs for patient accounting, billing and accounts receivable, and financial accounting. These application packages were obtained from a software vendor specializing in hospital applications.

Mr. Heller, who was recently appointed manager of Information Systems, identified the following deficiencies with the present systems:

1. The systems do not support the medical staff by recording or reporting the results of laboratory tests and procedures.
2. Since the systems are batch-oriented, they do not support on-line procedures such as patient registration or inquiries regarding billing.
3. The system does not accumulate costs by department or cost center.
4. The system is inflexible and does not respond well to changing management needs or to the frequent changes in reporting requirements of external health agencies.

Management at Mountain View Community had for some time recognized that the present information systems were not responsive to their needs. Mr. Lopez (assistant administrator), who had previous experience with data base systems in a large city hospital, had advocated that Mountain View Community investigate this approach. Mr. Heller was hired as manager of Information Systems partly because of his experience with data base systems. A new systems analyst (Mr. Helms) also was recently hired. Mr. Helms had experience in data base design, and it was expected that he would be a candidate for the data base administrator position if and when it was approved by the board of directors.

At a meeting of the board of directors, Mr. Heller explained the concept of data resource management. Ms. Baker (hospital administrator) proposed that Mountain View Community adopt this approach and that Mr. Helms be appointed data base administrator. The board of directors agreed with the concept, but insisted that a study be conducted to estimate costs and benefits as well as develop an overall data base plan. Ms. Baker formed a study team with the following members: Mr. Lopez, assistant administrator (leader); Ms. Knight, head of nursing; Mr. Crowley, assistant chief of staff; Mr. Heller, manager of Information Systems; and Mr. Helms, systems analyst. An outside consultant was hired to assist them. The consultant spent two days helping the team outline the study approach and establish schedules.

Business Systems Analysis

The study team reviewed Mountain View Community Hospital's long-range plan and proceeded with a business systems analysis. First, the team identified the basic functions of a small general hospital. The functions, which are illustrated in Figure 3-9, consist of the following:

- *Patient care administration,* to manage the logistical and record-keeping aspects of patient care.
- *Clinical services,* to provide laboratory testing and procedures and patient monitoring and screening.
- *Patient care services,* to provide patients with medical care and support services.
- *Financial management,* to manage the financial resources and operations of the hospital.
- *Administrative services,* to provide general management and support services.

Figure 3-9
Hospital business functions (Mountain View Community Hospital)

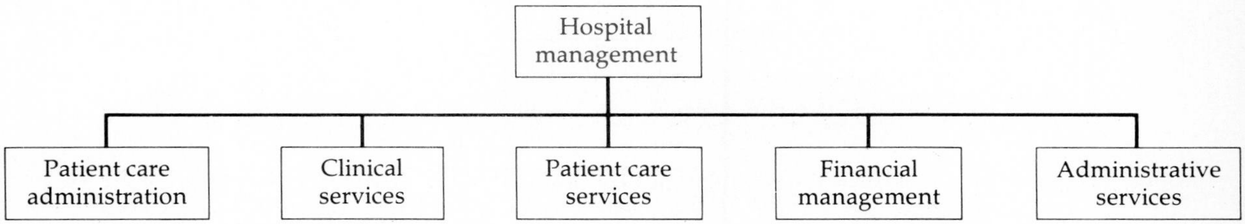

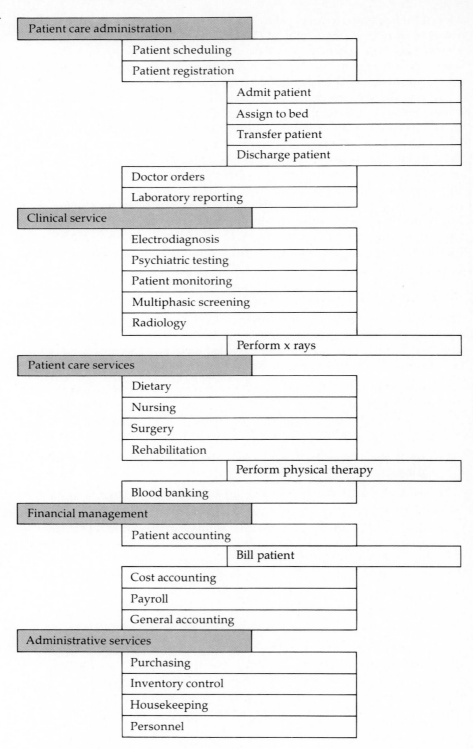

Figure 3-10
Business chart (Mountain View Community Hospital)

- Patient care administration
  - Patient scheduling
  - Patient registration
    - Admit patient
    - Assign to bed
    - Transfer patient
    - Discharge patient
  - Doctor orders
  - Laboratory reporting
- Clinical service
  - Electrodiagnosis
  - Psychiatric testing
  - Patient monitoring
  - Multiphasic screening
  - Radiology
    - Perform x rays
- Patient care services
  - Dietary
  - Nursing
  - Surgery
  - Rehabilitation
    - Perform physical therapy
  - Blood banking
- Financial management
  - Patient accounting
    - Bill patient
  - Cost accounting
  - Payroll
  - General accounting
- Administrative services
  - Purchasing
  - Inventory control
  - Housekeeping
  - Personnel

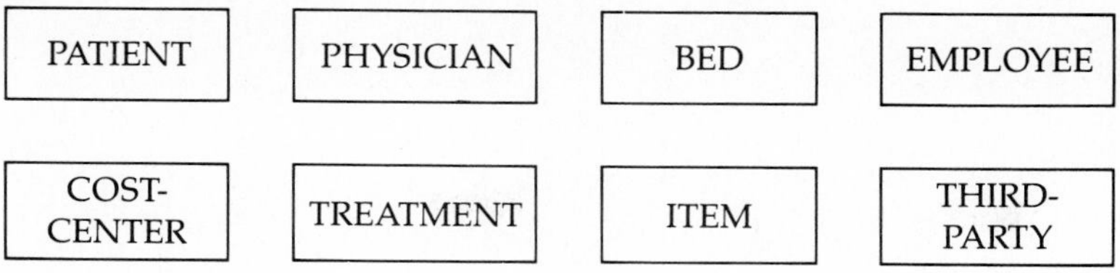

Figure 3-11
Basic entities for Mountain View Community Hospital

Having identified the basic functions, the study team's next step was to define the processes for each function. The project team spent considerable time interviewing other managers to clarify the process definitions. A business chart showing the functions, processes, and some of the activities is shown in Figure 3-10. In total, 22 processes were identified for Mountain View Community Hospital.

As the processes and activities were defined, the study team also identified eight basic business entities required by the processes (see Figure 3-11). The study team recognized that additional entities would be identified during detailed data base design. However, the team felt that these entities define the basic data resources of the hospital.

Information Modeling

The study team reviewed the business entities for the hospital. With some assistance from the outside consultant, they proceeded to develop an entity-relationship diagram (see Figure 3-12). The associations between entities in this diagram are based on the following rules and assumptions.

1. Each patient is assigned to a bed when he or she is admitted to the hospital.
2. One or more physicians may order treatments (physical therapy, X rays, and so on) for a given patient. There may be more than one such treatment ordered by a given physician for the patient.
3. Each treatment is provided by one or more employees and is billed to the patient and/or to one or more third-party insurers of the patient.
4. A patient may be billed for items such as medical supplies, devices, and so on.
5. Each employee and each item that is used is assigned to a unique cost center for accounting purposes.

The study team recognized that the E/R diagram shown in Figure 3-12 is preliminary in nature. Some additional entities that will have to be added to the model in the future include the following: Equipment, Volunteers, Blood Donors, and Benefactors. However, the present model represents an important subset of the information resources for a small hospital.

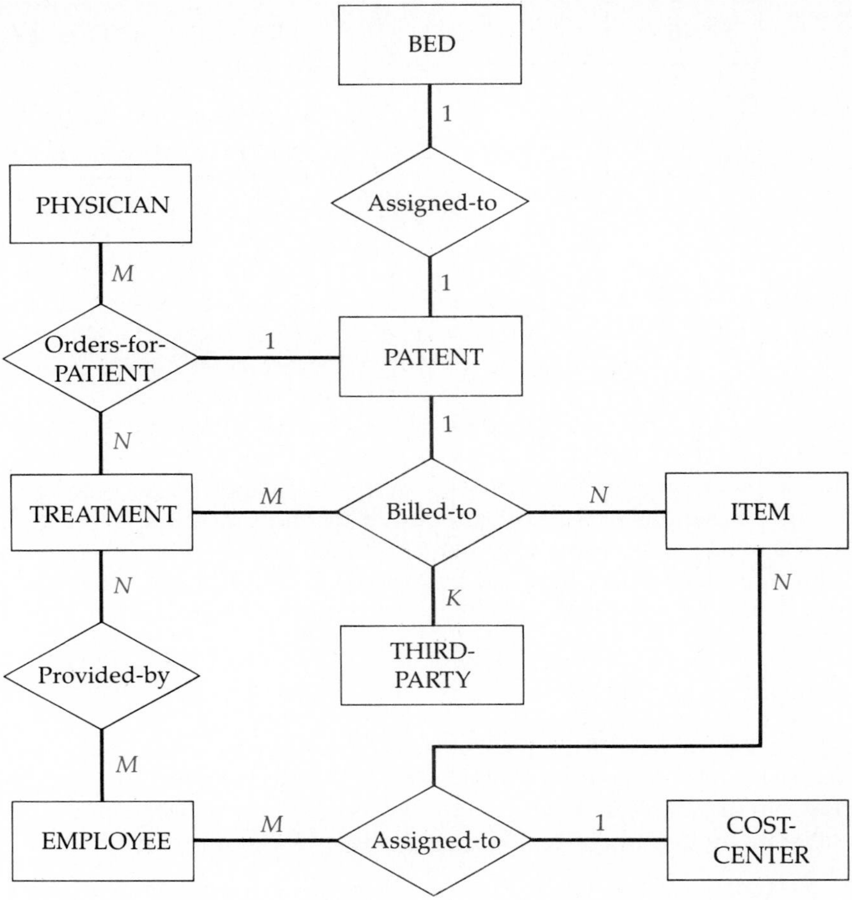

Figure 3-12 Preliminary E/R diagram for Mountain View Community Hospital

Final Report

The study team completed their business systems analysis in about one month. They then prepared a final report summarizing the data base plan for Mountain View Community Hospital. The report included a business chart; a narrative description of hospital functions, processes, activities, and entity classes; an entity-relationship diagram; a list of the benefits and costs of the data base approach; and a two-year plan for data base design and implementation at Mountain View Community Hospital (see Figure 3-13).

The study team presented the data base plan to the board of directors at their regular meeting the following month. The board endorsed the plan and shortly thereafter approved the creation of the data base administrator

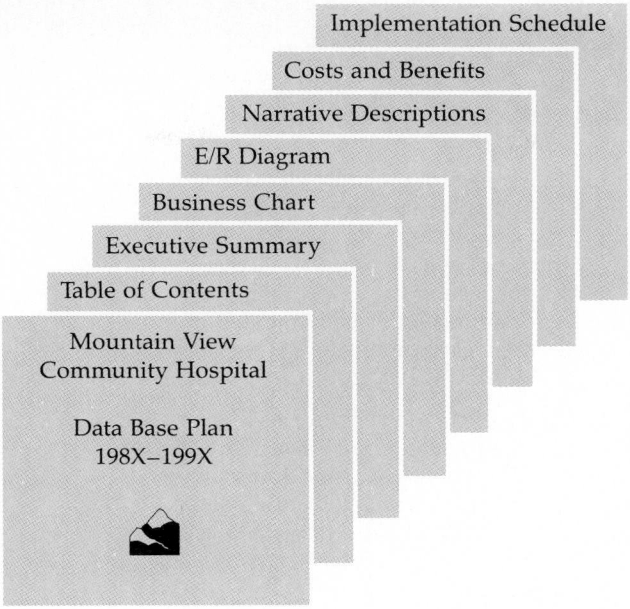

Figure 3-13
Outline of final report for Mountain View Community Hospital

position. Ms. Baker appointed Mr. Helms to this position, to report initially to Mr. Heller.

SUMMARY

Data base planning is essential if the benefits of data resource management are to be realized. The data base plan must support the overall information systems plan as well as basic organizational goals and objectives.

A methodology for data base planning was presented in this chapter. The methodology uses a top-down approach and is performed by a study team sponsored by top management. The basis for the planning effort is the business plan, which is an overall statement of enterprise goals, objectives, policies, and constraints. The methodology presented is patterned after IBM's Business System Planning, which uses a top-down approach to define enterprise functions, processes, activities, and events.

A major objective of data base planning is to develop a preliminary conceptual data model. This model, called the information model, shows the relationships between the important business entities. The data base plan also includes an overall schedule for data base design and implementation. The data base planning process was illustrated with a realistic case example of a hospital.

Chapter Review

REVIEW QUESTIONS

1. Define each of the following terms:
   a. business function
   b. business process
   c. business activity
   d. business entity
   e. enterprise information model
   f. strategic planning
   g. operational control
2. Contrast the following terms:
   a. top-down planning; bottom-up design
   b. business plan; business system plan
   c. strategic planning; tactical management
   d. business processes; business activities
   e. supertype; subtype
3. Briefly describe the ten tasks in data base planning.
4. Define four basic functions common to most enterprises.
5. Describe three levels of management planning and control and the typical inputs and outputs for each level.
6. Why is a data dictionary system valuable during the data base planning process?
7. Describe three uses for the information model.
8. When should the data base administration function be established? Why?
9. Explain how the results of both top-down planning and bottom-up design can be used to develop an enterprise information model.
10. Many organizations attempt to implement data bases without performing the planning described in this chapter. What results would you expect from this approach? Why?

PROBLEMS AND EXERCISES

1. A family can be regarded as a small business organization.
   a. Define the major functions, processes, and activities of a family and draw a business chart.
   b. Define the entities and draw an entity-relationship diagram.
2. Examine the business chart for a manufacturing firm (Figure 3-6).
   a. List three additional functions that would be included in the business chart for a typical manufacturing firm.
   b. List three processes that would be included in the quality assurance function. (*Hint:* Consider various points in a manufacturing firm where quality must be planned or measured.)
   c. List three activities that would be included in the receiving process.

3. Examine the business chart for Mountain View Community Hospital (Figure 3-10). List three activities for each of the following processes:
   a. nursing
   b. payroll
   c. housekeeping
4. List three additional entities that might appear in the E/R model for Mountain View Community Hospital (Figure 3-12).
5. Complete the following table, showing the effect of each business activity at Mountain View Community Hospital on the relevant entities:

Activity	**Result**
Admit patient	Creates a new Patient occurrence
Assign to bed	
Discharge patient	
Perform a treatment	

6. In Chapter 1, the conceptual data model for Pine Valley Furniture was expressed as a network diagram (see Figure 1-6). Redraw this model as an entity-relationship diagram, using meaningful names for associations between entities.
7. Draw a preliminary business chart for Pine Valley Furniture Company. In doing this, perform the following steps:
   a. Review the Pine Valley Furniture case (see Chapter 1).
   b. Review the business chart for a typical manufacturing firm (Figure 3-6).
   c. Make (and state) any assumptions you believe necessary.
8. A professional football team is a business organization.
   a. Define several functions, processes, and activities of a football team and draw a preliminary business chart.
   b. Define several entity classes and draw a tentative E/R diagram.
9. Consider a high school as a business enterprise.
   a. Define several functions, processes, and activities of a high school and draw a business chart.
   b. Define several entity classes and draw an E/R diagram.
10. Examine the business chart for Mountain View Community Hospital (Figure 3-10). List three activities for each of the following processes:
    a. patient accounting
    b. blood banking
    c. rehabilitation
11. Expand the E/R diagram for Mountain View Community Hospital by adding the following entities (and associated relationships): Equipment, Volunteers, Blood Donors.
12. Draw an E/R diagram that expresses the associations among the following entities:
    a. Students, Undergraduate Students, Graduate Students
    b. Bank Customer, Borrower, Depositor, Trust Management User
    c. Vehicle, Air Vehicle, Water Vehicle, Land Vehicle, Road Vehicle, Rail Vehicle, Airplane, Helicopter, Ocean Vessel, River Craft

13. Match the following terms and their definitions:

_____ business function	**a.** abstraction of entity types
_____ business process	**b.** focuses on execution of tasks
_____ business activity	**c.** decision-related activities
_____ business entity	**d.** shows entities and associations
_____ supertype	**e.** focuses on organizational goals
_____ subtype	**f.** broad groups of related activities
_____ E/R diagram	**g.** persons, objects, or events
_____ management control	**h.** specialization of entity types
_____ operational control	**i.** specific operations or transactions
_____ strategic planning	**j.** concerned with resource allocation

14. Visit an organization that is using the data base approach. Evaluate the state of data base planning in that organization—organizational commitment to planning, the methods used, and their effectiveness.

REFERENCES

Anthony, Robert N. 1965. *Planning and Control Systems: A Framework for Analysis.* Cambridge, Mass.: Harvard University Press.

Business System Planning: Information System Planning Guide. 1975. Pub. no. GE20-0527-1. White Plains, N.Y.: IBM Corporation.

Flavin, Matt. 1981. *Fundamental Concepts of Information Modeling.* New York: Yourdon Press.

Goodhue, Dale L., Judith A. Quillard, and John F. Rockart, 1986. "The Management of Data: Preliminary Research Results." Center for Information Systems Research, Sloan School of Management, MIT. Working Paper No. 140 (May).

Haughey, Thomas F., and Robert M. Rollason. 1983. "Refining Information Engineering." *Computerworld* (August 22).

Holland, Robert H. 1980. "Data Base Planning Entails Return to Basics." *Computerworld* (October 27).

———. 1981. "Data Base Stability." *ICP Interface Data Processing Management* (Spring).

Martin, James. 1982. *Strategic Data Planning Methodologies.* Englewood Cliffs, N.J.: Prentice-Hall.

Meurer, Thomas F. 1980. "Solving the Mystery of Data Base Design." *Computerworld* (September 17).

Voell, Ronald F. 1980. "Data Base Planning." In *Advances in Data Base Management.* Vol. 1, edited by Thomas A. Rullo. Philadelphia: Heyden.

Part II

Data Base Architecture

The three chapters in Part II provide a detailed description of the physical and logical data organizations most often used in data base systems.

Chapter 4 is an introduction to physical data organization. We review the characteristics of secondary storage devices, principally magnetic disks. We describe the file organizations used in data base applications, with emphasis on the indexed and hashed organizations. Advantages and disadvantages of each type of physical organization are described.

Chapter 5 describes the data structures used to build and manage data bases. Data structures are used to represent associations between data entities. Some of the important data structures described in this chapter are queues, stacks, sorted lists, rings, multilists, inverted lists, and B-trees. It is essential that you understand the various data structures, since they are building blocks of data management systems.

Chapter 6 introduces data models. Data models are concerned with the way data look to the user, rather than with their physical representations. Three basic data models are described: hierarchical, network, and relational. Also, data manipulation commands are described and illustrated for each of the three models.

Chapter 4

Physical Data Organization

INTRODUCTION

In this chapter, we examine the basic techniques used for storing and accessing data on secondary storage devices. Physical data organization represents the lowest level in the ANSI/SPARC model introduced in Chapter 2 (see Figure 4-1). It is important to realize that this is the only level at which an organization's data base exists in physical form (if we can regard a series of magnetized spots as a physical form!). All the remaining levels in the ANSI/SPARC model are abstract views of the physical data base.

At the physical level, a data base may be viewed as a collection of stored records and files. Here are typical operations we may want to perform on a file:

- Fetch an arbitrary record from the file.
- Insert a record into the file.
- Modify a record in the file.
- Read the entire file.
- Read the next record in the file.

Figure 4-1
ANSI/SPARC architecture

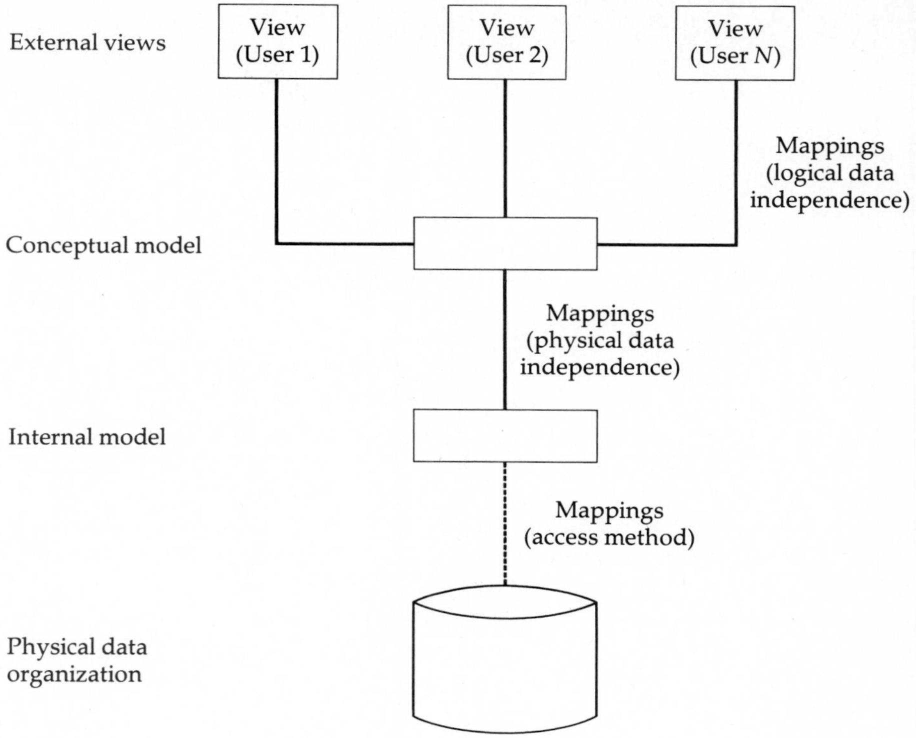

- Delete a record from the file.
- Reorganize the file.

In selecting a physical data organization (or file organization), the system designer must consider a number of important factors, including the physical characteristics of the secondary storage devices to be used, the operating system and file management software (or access methods) available, and the set of criteria that reflect user needs for storing and accessing data.

The criteria that are normally important in selecting a file organization include fast access for retrieval, high throughput for processing transactions, efficient use of storage space, protection from failures or data loss, minimizing need for reorganization, coping with growth, and security from unauthorized use. Often these objectives are conflicting, and the designer must select a physical data organization that provides a reasonable balance among the criteria within the resources available.

In this chapter, we describe only basic file organizations, where storage and retrieval of records are based on a single key (the primary key). In the next chapter, we will describe multiple-key file organizations.

DIRECT ACCESS STORAGE DEVICES

Physical organization of data is strongly influenced by the characteristics of the devices on which the data are stored. In this section, we review the important characteristics of direct access storage devices. We will concentrate on magnetic disk storage, since this is by far the most important type of secondary storage used today. However, most of the concepts described here will also apply to newer storage devices that may emerge in the future.

There are two broad classes of secondary storage devices, or media: sequential devices and direct access devices.

Sequential devices require that records be stored and processed in linear sequence. Individual records are not addressable on these devices. Magnetic tape is the principal type of sequential medium used in computer systems. Tape media range from high-density, reel-mounted tapes used on large computer systems to the small cassettes and cartridges used on micros and personal computers. Magnetic tapes are used primarily to hold backup copies of a data base and logs, and audit trails of data base updates, as protection against system failure, and as a basis for data base recovery.

In a **direct access storage device** (DASD), the entire storage space is divided into a number of discrete locations, much like bins in a warehouse. Each location is individually addressable. As a result, a record can be stored or retrieved directly from a storage location without extensive scanning of other records.

Types of Magnetic Disks

Two types of disk media are frequently used for data base applications: removable media (or disk packs) and fixed media (or Winchester disks).

Removable media refer to disk packs that are designed to be inserted into or removed from a disk drive. A **disk pack** is a set of disks that are mounted together in a stack. The disk pack is placed on a spindle in a disk drive, which rotates the disks at high speed. The major advantage of removable media is that the disk packs can be removed from the disk drive and used to store backup copies of the data or interchanged among disk drives for maximum flexibility.

Figure 4-2
Removable-media disk drive (Courtesy Digital Equipment Corporation)

An example of a disk drive that uses removable media (Digital RA60) is shown in Figure 4-2. The disk pack in the drive shown in this figure has a capacity of 205 million bytes (MB) of user data. There are three drives mounted in a cabinet, with a total capacity of 615 MB.

Fixed media devices are those in which the disks are permanently mounted in the disk drive and cannot normally be removed. These devices are often referred to as **Winchester disks**, after the technology that was initially developed by IBM. With Winchester disks, the magnetic disks and access mechanism are sealed, in a clean-room environment, into a single

Figure 4-3
Fixed-media disk drive (Courtesy IBM)

unit called the **head-disk assembly**, or HDA, that protects the recording media from external contaminants. Although Winchester disks are usually fixed-media devices, there are also removable Winchester disks.

Winchester disks range in size from the standard 14-inch-diameter units used in large computers to the 5¼-inch-diameter units frequently used in personal computers. Even smaller, more compact units (approximately 3 inches in diameter) are being introduced.

Winchester disks offer two important advantages over removable disks: improved data reliability, a result of eliminating contaminants that cause head-disk interference; and higher recording density, which results in higher data transfer rates and lower cost per megabyte of storage. In 1972, a megabyte of disk storage cost about $1,000; ten years later it cost less than $40.

The only disadvantage of fixed-media disks is that since the disks cannot be removed, special provisions must be made to provide backup copies of data. Magnetic tape is often used to copy data files from Winchester disks for this purpose.

A fixed-media disk unit (IBM 3380) is shown in Figure 4-3. Each such disk drive has a total storage capacity of about 1260 MB. We will use this disk unit to illustrate many of the examples in the following sections.

Magnetic Disks for Microcomputers

Both removable and fixed magnetic disk media are commonly used on microcomputers. The most commonly used removable-media type is the familiar floppy disk. Standard floppy disks are 3½ inches and 5¼ inches in diameter. The capacity of contemporary floppy disks ranges from 360 KB bytes to approximately 1.2 MB, depending on disk size and density.

A floppy disk is made out of a thin, flexible plastic material that is coated with magnetic oxide. The disk is surrounded by a protective liner, a sleeve of clothlike material that cleans the disk and traps dust particles. The disk and liner are enclosed in a protective jacket or envelope that adds protection and makes the disk somewhat rigid. This outer jacket has three openings and a notch along one side. The large center opening is used by the disk drive to grip the disk and rotate it. A small circular hole to one side is used for timing purposes, and the long slotted opening is used for access by the read/write head. The notch is called a "write-protect" notch; a tab placed over this notch will prevent writing to the disk.

Most microcomputers are equipped with (or can accommodate) one or more Winchester magnetic disk drives. In some computers the disk drive is enclosed in the system unit; for example, the IBM PC AT is equipped with either 20 or 30 MB of built-in hard-disk storage. The newer Compaq Deskpro 386 computer has available three models with 40, 70, or 130 MB of disk storage, respectively.

Two newer types of magnetic disk storage have been developed especially for microcomputers. These are the removable disk cartridge and the hard-disk-on-a-board.

Removable Disk Cartridge An obvious limitation of the Winchester disk is that it has fixed storage capacity and cannot be removed. An alternative form of storage uses removable disk cartridges; thus, an unlimited amount of data can be made available by inserting new disks. An example of this form, called the Bernoulli Box, is shown in Figure 4-4. This unit is a dual-drive system that accommodates two 20-MB removable cartridges, or a total storage capacity of 40 MB. The performance of this unit equals or exceeds that of most hard-disk drives.

Hard-Disk-on-a-Board This unit typically consists of a 10- or 20-MB miniaturized disk drive that is mounted on an expansion board. The board in turn will fit into a single expansion slot in IBM PC or compatible computers. One version, called the Hardcard, is shown in Figure 4-5. This unit has a 1-inch wide profile and stores 20 MB of data on a 3½-inch disk. To make the drive 1 inch wide, the engineers had to design the motor that drives the disk in this unit ¼ inch thick (other vendors have similar models).

Basic Magnetic Disk Concepts

Whether fixed or removable media are used, certain terms are used to describe disk units and their subdivisions. The major terms of interest are illustrated in Figure 4-6.

A **volume** is a physical storage unit such as a removable disk pack, fixed head-disk assembly, or reel of magnetic tape. Each disk surface in a volume

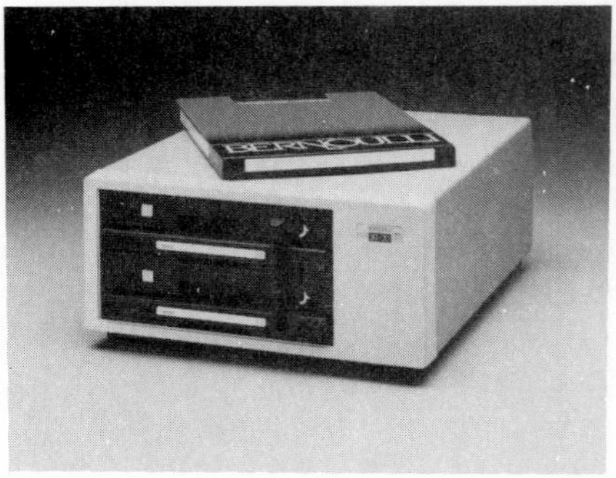

Figure 4-4
Bernoulli Box (Courtesy Iomega Corp.)

Figure 4-5
Hardcard (Courtesy Plus Development Corp.)

is served by one (or more) read/write heads that are attached to access arms (see Figure 4-6). The access mechanism moves the heads in or out (relative to the center of the disks), and positions the heads at a specific track on the recording surface. All the recording heads move in unison, but only one read/write head may actually read or write data at any one time. The disk drive shown in Figure 4-3 uses two independent read/write actuators per disk drive, so that one actuator can be reading data while the other is "seeking" an address.

A **track** is a circular recording position on a disk surface that rotates under a read/write head. All the data recorded on a track may be read by a single read/write head without changing the position of the head.

A **cylinder** consists of the set of tracks that can be read without moving the read/write mechanism. In most disk units, a cylinder consists of the set of tracks from the various surfaces that are in the same radius (thus, the tracks are vertically aligned, as shown in Figure 4-6). In some current disk drives, a cylinder consists of several adjacent tracks on the same surface; however, we will assume a vertical arrangement in the following discussion.

Here are the physical characteristics for the IBM 3380 disk drive shown in Figure 4-3:

Tracks per cylinder: 15

Cylinders per drive: 1770

Track capacity (bytes): 47,476

Thus, the total capacity of each cylinder is 15 tracks × 47,476 bytes per track, or 712,140 bytes. The total capacity of the disk drive is 1770 cylinders × 712,140 bytes per cylinder, or 1,260,487,800 bytes (1.26 gigabytes). This capacity is sufficient to store the text for nearly 1000 textbooks such as this one.

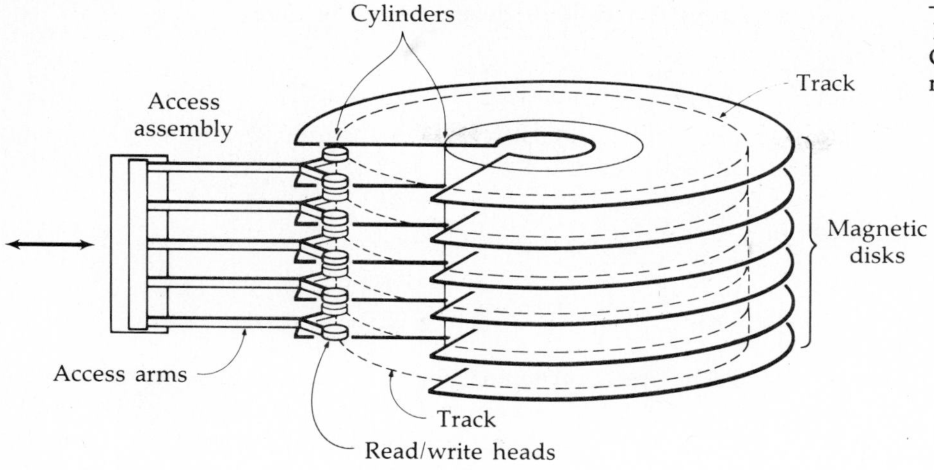

Figure 4-6
Components of a disk module

Disk Performance Factors

The time required to locate and transfer a block of data between disk and main memory depends on three factors: seek time, rotational delay, and transfer time. We will illustrate these factors using the IBM 3380 disk (shown in Figure 4-3) as an example.

Seek time (S) is the time required to move the access arm to a desired cylinder. The seek time may vary from zero (when the arm is already positioned at the correct cylinder) to some maximum value (when the arm must be moved between the first and last cylinders). For timing purposes, the *average* seek time (which is characteristic of the disk model) is usually used. The average seek time for the IBM 3380 disk unit is 16 milliseconds (msec).

Rotational delay is the time required following a seek for the required data block to rotate to a position under a read/write head. The minimum time is zero, while the maximum time is that required for one complete revolution of the disk (R). The *average* rotational delay is $R/2$.

The IBM 3380 disk unit rotates at 3600 revolutions per minute (rpm). Thus, the time required for one complete revolution (R) is $60 \times 1000/3600$, or 16.7 msec. The average rotational delay for this unit is 16.7/2, or about 8.3 msec.

Transfer time is the time required to transmit a block of data between disk and main memory. This factor depends on the data transmission rate (t) and the size of the data block in bytes (B) to be transmitted. The nominal data transmission rate for the IBM 3380 disk is 3 MB per second, or 3000 bytes per millisecond.

Random Access Times The average time (T) required to locate and transmit a random block of data is given by the formula

$$\begin{aligned} T &= \text{seek time} + \text{rotational delay} + \text{transfer time} \\ &= S + \frac{R}{2} + \frac{B}{t} \end{aligned}$$

For example, for the IBM 3380, the average time to randomly locate and transmit a 3000-byte data block is

$$\begin{aligned} T &= 16 + \frac{16.7}{2} + \frac{3000}{3000} \\ &= 16 + 8.3 + 1 \\ &= 25.3 \text{ msec} \end{aligned}$$

Sequential Access Times When data blocks are accessed sequentially (rather than randomly), the access arm is positioned at a given cylinder and all data records on that cylinder are read (or written) without further access arm movement. Thus, for sequential access, the seek time is negligible and may be ignored. The average time to locate and transmit a record in this mode is approximately equal to the average rotational delay. For the IBM 3380, the average sequential access time is 8.3 msec.

Optical Disk Storage

For over 30 years magnetic-based storage devices have been the principal form of DASD in computer applications. However, this technology is now relatively mature and can be improved upon only with increasing difficulty and cost. The use of new peripheral technology, especially optical disks, offers the promise of lower cost and greatly improved performance over magnetic disk.

With optical disk storage, information is recorded on a circular metallic disk by a high-intensity laser beam that inscribes pits (or depressions) on the surface of the disk. A binary 1 is represented by a pit, while the absence of a pit represents a binary 0. A low-intensity laser beam is used to read the binary signals.

At the present time, laser disks can be recorded only once, but not erased. There are two recording technologies: compact disk read-only memory (CD ROM) and write once, read many (WORM) memory. With CD ROM, the vendor records the material on the disk and then distributes it to the user. A CD ROM drive is used to read the material, but it cannot write to the disk. CD ROM disks are used primarily for distributing large data bases such as dictionaries, encyclopedias, and medical references.

In contrast, with WORM technology the user starts with a blank disk and uses the WORM drive to record data one time. The data can then be read repeatedly, but cannot be altered or erased. The primary use of WORM disks and drives is to record large quantities of data for archival purposes. For example, a hospital could permanently store its medical records on WORM disks rather than on microfilm.

Laser disks permit extremely high recording densities. A single 5¼-inch-diameter CD ROM has a capacity of about 550 MB—the equivalent of more than 1500 double-density floppy disks, or nearly 220,000 pages of information. For example, the entire Grolier 20-volume *Electronic Encyclopedia* is available on a single 5¼-inch CD ROM. Also, Microsoft Corporation has developed a *Writer's Bookshelf* that combines ten standard references (*The American Heritage Dictionary, Roget's II Thesaurus,* Bartlett's *Familiar Quotations,* and seven others) on a single CD ROM. Each of the references can be easily accessed from within a word processing program.

According to Polesnak (1984), there are numerous advantages to optical disk technology: large storage capacity, low cost per stored bit, low error rates, the nonerasable nature of recorded data for archival applications, the transportability of the storage medium, and reliability or the ability to recover part of the data base due to damage or loss. Thus, it appears inevitable that optical disks will replace magnetic disks in many applications in the near future, just as compact disks are replacing conventional records. At the present time, there are two barriers to rapid market acceptance of this new medium:

1. Optical disks cannot be erased and rerecorded, as with magnetic media. However, the industry has already developed prototype versions of erasable disks.
2. There is no industrywide standard file format to facilitate storing and accessing data. However, an industry committee is working on such a proposed file standard.

At the present time, random access times are slower for optical disks than for magnetic disks. For example, the average seek time for CD ROM is nearly 1 second, compared to 30 to 70 milliseconds for a contemporary hard disk. For WORM disks, 100-millisecond seek times are typical. Although these times will be improved as technology advances, random access times will probably always be longer for optical disks than for magnetic devices due to the very high intertrack density. However, transfer rates are *higher* for optical disks than for magnetic disks (up to 10 MB/sec).

As the barriers are overcome and technology advances, optical disks will undoubtedly replace magnetic disks for many applications. However, the principles of data organization and management that we discuss throughout the text still apply to this new medium.

DATA STORAGE ON DISKS

A disk volume is essentially a very large electronic filing cabinet. Instead of drawers with dividers, it is subdivided into cylinders, tracks, and blocks. In this section, we examine the techniques for storing data records on disks.

Figure 4-7
Physical storage block on magnetic disk

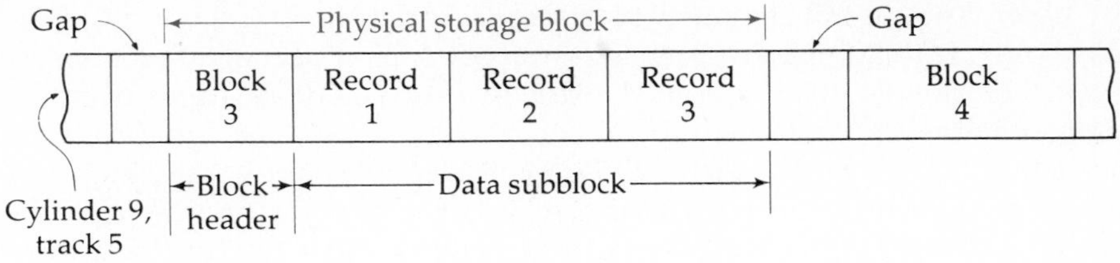

Physical Storage Blocks

A physical storage block is the smallest addressable unit of data on a disk. We will refer to this unit simply as a **block** (the term *physical record* is also sometimes used). Normally, each track contains (or is subdivided into) a number of blocks. In some disk units, the size of a block is fixed by hardware considerations, while in other units, blocks are formatted by software so that the user can choose the block size. In the latter case, the same block size is normally used for an entire file.

A generalized diagram of a physical storage block is shown in Figure 4-7. Notice that the block is divided into two sections—a block header and a data subblock.

The **block header** contains data that allow the system to locate and identify the block. These data usually include a unique block number and the length of the data subblock that follows. (In Figure 4-7 we simply show the block number.) The contents of the block header differ from one disk model to another and also depend on the particular data format chosen by the user. We will illustrate some of the more common formats shortly.

The **data subblock** consists of the stored records that are contained in the block. Each stored record contains user data and may also contain overhead data (such as pointers) that are used to logically relate that particular record to other stored records. The data subblock is the unit of data that is transmitted between computer main memory and the disk volume in response to an input or output command. This means that the block header is *not* transmitted—it is maintained and used by the system to locate and identify data subblocks.

Addressing Storage Blocks

The address of a physical storage block is specified by three factors: cylinder number, track number (which specifies the surface), and block number. Thus, the address of the block shown in Figure 4-7 is as follows:

Cylinder number: 9

Track number: 5

Block number: 3

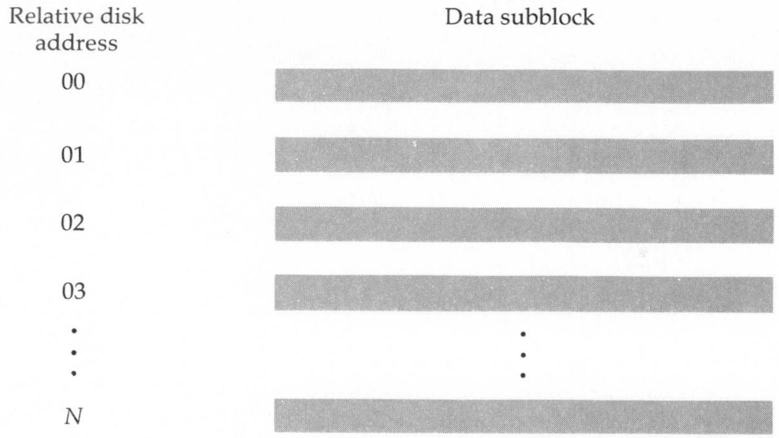

Figure 4-8
Relative disk addressing

Given this block address, the computer can access the block directly. For example, it can execute a command such as the following: "Fetch the data subblock in block 3, track 5, cylinder 9." This command will cause the disk unit to locate that block and read the data subblock into an area of main memory.

The combination of cylinder, track, and block number is referred to as a **physical disk address.** To locate a specific record on magnetic disk, the disk control unit must pass a physical address to the disk unit. However, physical addresses are awkward for purposes of data management. For example, if the data file is reorganized or moved to another area on the disk volume, then the physical addresses of the data blocks must be changed. For this reason, relative (rather than physical) disk addresses are normally used for data management. With **relative disk addresses,** each address specifies a storage block's position relative to the start of the file. Thus, the first block in the file is viewed to have address 0, the second block address 1, and so on (see Figure 4-8).

For the remainder of this text, we will assume that relative disk addresses are used to locate physical storage blocks. That is, we will imagine that for each file stored on disk, the disk volume is organized into a series of physical blocks with relative addresses as shown in Figure 4-8. We will assume that the computer file management system uses the disk directory to convert the relative disk addresses to the necessary physical addresses.

Record Blocking

The number of data records contained in a data subblock is called the **blocking factor.** As shown in Figure 4-9, there are three options: unblocked records, blocked records, and spanned records.

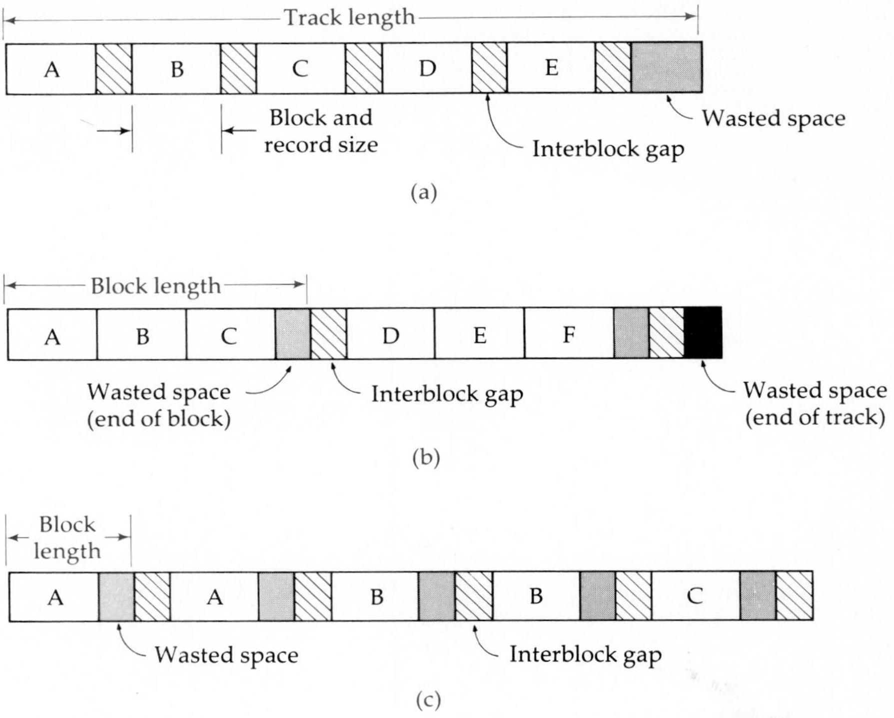

Figure 4-9
Record blocking options:
(a) unblocked records
(b) blocked records
(c) spanned records

Unblocked Records With unblocked records, each data subblock corresponds to one data record. If the length of the data subblock is the same as the length of a data record (as shown in Figure 4-9a), there is no wasted space within each subblock. However, depending on the length of a data subblock compared to the track length, there may be wasted space at the end of each track, as shown in the figure.

Blocked Records With blocked records, several data records are grouped into each data subblock (see Figure 4-9b). Depending on the block length relative to record length, there may or may not be wasted space within each data subblock. Also, there may be wasted space at the end of each track. The designer must choose the block size and blocking factor so as to avoid excess wasted space.

The main advantage of blocked records (compared to unblocked records) is that they speed up input/output operations. This is because a group of records is read or written with each input or output operation. Blocked records also conserve storage space, since there is one block header and interrecord gap for each block of records rather than for each record.

Spanned Records With spanned records, each data record is split into two or more segments. Each segment is stored in a separate data subblock (see

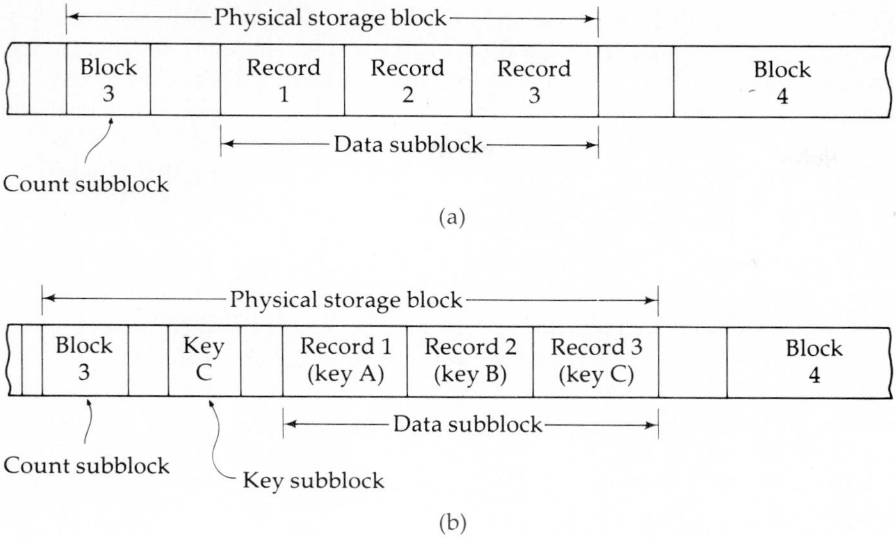

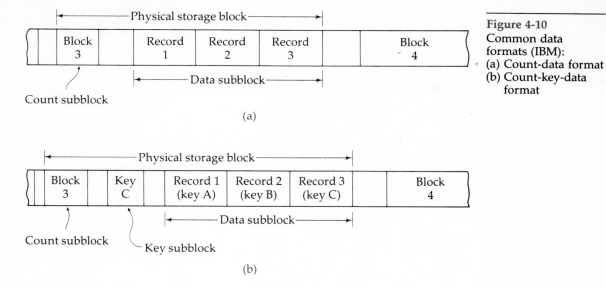

Figure 4-10 Common data formats (IBM): (a) Count-data format (b) Count-key-data format

Figure 4-9c). Spanned records are used only when the length of a record exceeds that of a fixed-length data subblock. Since spanned records complicate input/output operations, they are not widely used in data base applications.

Typical Data Formats

In this section, we briefly describe three data formats frequently used in contemporary disk systems. The first two (count-data and count-key-data formats) are used in IBM (and IBM-compatible) disk drives, including the one shown in Figure 4-3. The third (sector addressing) is used in many other disk systems, including the one shown in Figure 4-2.

IBM Data Formats The two IBM data formats are shown in Figure 4-10. The designer may decide to use either approach, depending on the nature of the application.

The **count-data format** (Figure 4-10a) resembles the format shown in Figure 4-7. The count subblock (which corresponds to the block header) contains the relative address of the physical storage block on the track. The first block on each track has address 0, the second address 1, and so on. This relative address (or block number) is used to locate a specific block. The count-data format is used for sequential files and relative-addressed files.

The **count-key-data format** is shown in Figure 4-10b. With this format, the block header contains two subblocks: a count subblock and a key subblock. The count subblock contains the relative block address on the track (as in the count-data format). The key subblock contains the primary key of the *last* record in the block (that is, the record in that block with the largest primary key value). The count-key-data format allows the system to search a track until a block containing a record with a desired key is located. For example, in Figure 4-10b, the system could determine that block 3 contains the record with key equal to C (or less) before reading that block. The count-key-data format is used with indexed file organizations.

Sector Addressing With the **sector-addressing format,** each track is subdivided into a number of fixed-length sections called **sectors.** A common sector size is 512 bytes (this is the sector length used in the disk unit shown in Figure 4-2). Each sector is addressable. With sector addressing, a physical storage block may consist of one sector or (in some units) two or more sectors linked together.

Throughout this text, we will assume that the IBM data formats are being used, although the principles are much the same when sector addressing is used.

Disk Storage Capacity

A typical problem in file design is to estimate the amount of disk capacity required for each file. This calculation depends on a number of factors: the characteristics of the disk volume, the number of records in the file, the record size, the blocking factor, and the data format to be used. We will illustrate the approach using the IBM 3380 disk unit as an example.

Suppose that an organization wants to create a file of customer records on magnetic disks. This file contains fixed-length records and has the following characteristics:

Number of records: 10,000

Record length: 200 bytes

Blocking factor: 10 records per block

Data format: count-key-data

The number of records that will fit on a track can be calculated using formulas or tables provided by the manufacturer. A track capacity table for the IBM 3380 disk is shown in Table 4-1. If we know the size of each data subblock and the data format to be used, we can look up the number of blocks per track.*

The size of a data subblock is equal to the record size times the blocking factor. In our example, this is 2000 bytes (200 bytes per record times 10 records per block). Referring to the columns for count-key-data format in Table 4-1, this number falls in the range from 1909 to 2068 bytes. According

*In Table 4-1 it is assumed that the length of the primary key in a record is 20 bytes or less, which is the usual case.

Table 4-1 IBM 3380 Track Capacity Table

Count-Data Format		**Count-key Data Format**		**Blocks per Track**
Data Subblock (bytes)		Data Subblock (bytes)		
Min.	Max.	Min.	Max.	
23,477	47,476	23,221	47,220	1
15,477	23,476	15,221	23,220	2
11,477	15,476	11,221	15,220	3
9,077	11,476	8,821	11,220	4
7,477	9,076	7,221	8,820	5
6,357	7,476	6,101	7,220	6
5,493	6,356	5,237	6,100	7
4,821	5,492	4,565	5,236	8
4,277	4,820	4,021	4,564	9
3,861	4,276	3,605	4,020	10
3,477	3,860	3,221	3,604	11
3,189	3,476	2,933	3,220	12
2,933	3,188	2,677	2,932	13
2,677	2,932	2,421	2,676	14
2,485	2,676	2,229	2,420	15
2,325	2,484	2,069	2,228	16
2,165	2,324	1,909	2,068	17
2,005	2,164	1,749	1,908	18
1,877	2,004	1,621	1,748	19
1,781	1,876	1,525	1,620	20
1,685	1,780	1,429	1,524	21
1,589	1,684	1,333	1,428	22
1,493	1,588	1,237	1,332	23
1,397	1,492	1,141	1,236	24
1,333	1,396	1,077	1,140	25
1,269	1,332	1,013	1,076	26
1,205	1,268	949	1,012	27
1,141	1,204	885	948	28
1,077	1,140	820	884	29
1,045	1,076	789	820	30

to the table, the number of blocks per track is 17 (the numbers 1909 and 2068 represent the minimum and maximum data subblock sizes with 17 blocks per track).

The number of records per track in this example will be 170 (since the blocking factor is 10). Thus, the file will require 10,000/170, or 59 tracks (rounded to the nearest integer). Since we stated earlier that for the IBM 3380 disk there are 15 tracks per cylinder, the customer file will require 59/15, or 4 cylinders.

The total capacity of an IBM 3380 disk volume is 1770 cylinders. Thus, the customer file will require 4/1770, or less than one-fourth of 1%, of the capacity of the disk. Clearly, other files will be stored on the disk in addition to the customer file. This leads us to define two additional terms: extent and directory.

An **extent** is a collection of physical storage blocks that are contiguous on a magnetic disk. Normally, a file is allocated to a single extent; however, if enough contiguous blocks are not available, multiple extents may be used. A single extent for the customer file would consist of 1000 blocks and, as we have seen, will require four cylinders.

A disk **directory** is an index to the contents of a disk volume. Since each volume typically contains a number of files, a directory is necessary to identify and locate each file. The directory, which is located at the beginning of a volume, usually consists of two components: a home block and file headers. (Various terms are used in different systems.)

The **home block** contains information concerning the entire volume, including the volume name, a code indicating the owner of the volume, volume protection information, and a master index to the file headers.

Each **file header** identifies one file on the volume. It contains information such as a file name or identifier, file ownership, creation date, and protection factors. Most importantly, the file header contains a list of the extents that make up the file, the number of blocks in each extent, and the physical location of each extent. Thus, the directory provides the file management system with the information required to locate the beginning of each file that is stored on the volume. When a file is created, extended, relocated, or otherwise changed, the system updates the disk directory to reflect these changes.

MANAGEMENT OF INPUT AND OUTPUT

We now describe the hardware and software components used to manage input/output operations. Our purpose is to describe each component in just enough detail to explain its contribution to input/output (I/O) processing.

Hardware Components

The major hardware components of a computer with magnetic disk storage devices are shown in Figure 4-11. The arrows in this diagram represent the flow of both data and control information between the various devices.

The **central processing unit** (CPU) performs all calculations and logical operations and supervises all operations of the remaining computer components.

Main memory consists of a large number of addressable storage loca-

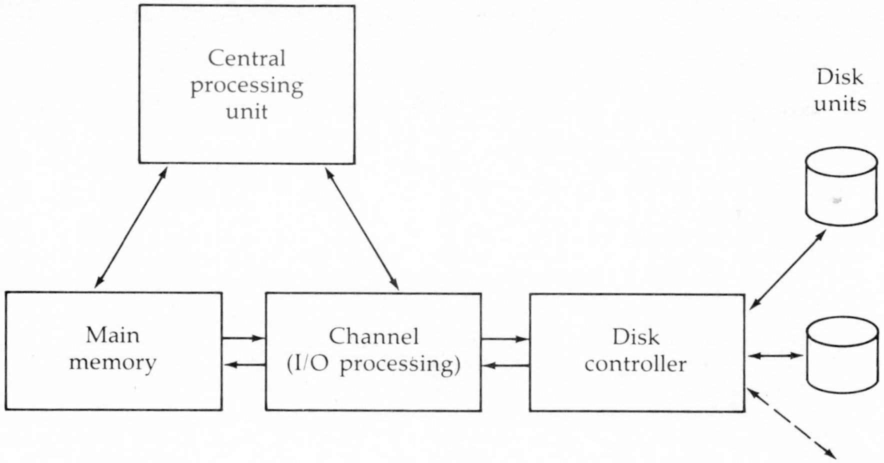

Figure 4-11
Major hardware components

tions that are used to store both program instructions and data items. Data that are stored on magnetic disk must be transferred to main memory before they can be processed by a user program.

An **input/output processor** (or **channel**) is a device that executes input and output instructions under control of the CPU. An I/O processor is essentially a mini- or microcomputer that executes I/O instructions, thereby freeing the CPU for other tasks.

A **disk controller** controls the actual operation of one or more disk units. The disk controller handles all the specific characteristics of each disk unit, such as instructions to read tracks and cylinders. Most disk controllers today are programmable devices that help optimize disk performance and perform error recovery functions.

A microcomputer or personal computer would not contain all the components shown in Figure 4-11. The disk controller is often a chip or card and is normally packaged with the disk drive rather than as a separate unit. Also, most micros do not have channels; instead, the disk and controller are connected to the CPU through a simple port or interface.

Software Components

The major software components in a disk file management system are shown in Figure 4-12.

An **operating system** is the overall supervisory and control program of a computer. The operating system allocates memory, controls the execution of tasks, and provides a variety of utility and support functions.

Most computers today (except some small micros and minis) use a multiprogramming operating system. **Multiprogramming** is a technique whereby several programs are placed in main memory at the same time, *giving the illusion* that they are being executed simultaneously (they are, in fact, being

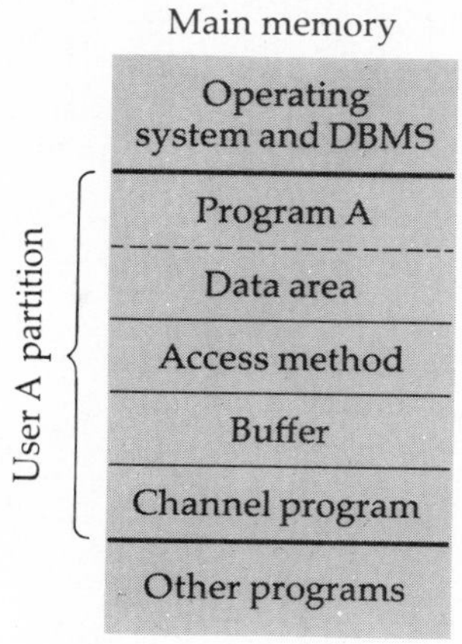

Figure 4-12
Major software components

executed consecutively). When a program requests an input or output operation (such as to read to write a record), the CPU interrupts execution of that program and hands the I/O task to an I/O processor. The CPU then executes another program until it, too, requires an input or output operation. Multiprogramming greatly improves the productivity of a computer, since the slower I/O operations are overlapped with other processing tasks.

A multiprogramming operating system allocates a **partition,** or area of main memory, to each user. The contents of a typical partition (shown in Figure 4-12) are a user application program (with its data area), an access method, a buffer, and a channel program.

An **application program** is a program that performs processing tasks for user functions such as accounts receivable, inventory, and student registration. An application program may insert new records into a data base or may modify or delete existing records. Most application programs are allocated a **data area** for the temporary storage of input and output records and program data.

A **buffer** is an area of memory used to receive a block of stored records from a storage device or used to transmit a block of records to that device. A buffer must be large enough to contain an entire data subblock that is stored on a secondary storage device. In the example using customer records in the previous section, the size of a data subblock (and the corresponding buffer size) is 2000 bytes.

An **access method** is a file management subprogram provided by the operating system. When the CPU is executing an application program and a READ or WRITE instruction is reached, the CPU switches execution to the access method. A copy of the access method being used by a program may be maintained in the user partition or maintained in the system library and linked to user programs.

A **channel program** is a special program provided by the operating system and executed by an I/O processor. Executing a channel program causes a data subblock to be transmitted between secondary storage and a buffer.

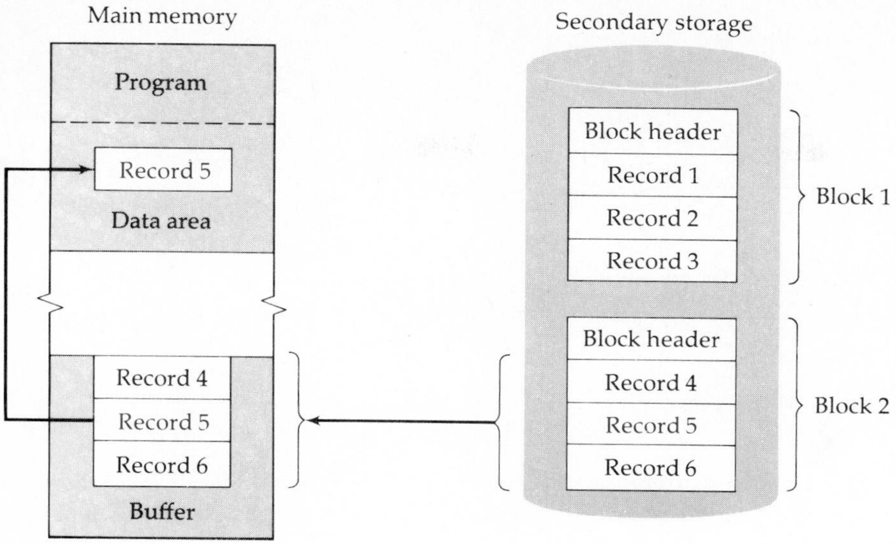

Figure 4-13
Input/output processing

Input/Output Processing

Now let us see how these hardware and software components are coordinated to transmit data records between secondary storage and a user program (see Figure 4-13). Suppose that a user program is being executed in a partition, as shown in the figure. This program accesses data records that are stored on a magnetic disk file (the blocking factor is 3 in this example). When an instruction to READ a record from this file is encountered, the CPU transfers control to the access method. The access method checks to see if the required record is located in the buffer in the program's partition. If the record is located in the buffer, then the access method transfers it from the buffer to the program data area and execution continues. (In Figure 4-13, record 5 has just been transmitted to the program data area.)

If the required record is not in the buffer, the access method passes a request for this record to the operating system. The operating system then builds a channel program to access the required data subblock on magnetic disk. The I/O processor executes this channel program and sends instructions to the disk controller, which activates the disk read/write mechanism as necessary. The required data subblock is read and transmitted to the buffer in main memory. While these input (or output) tasks are being performed, the operating system has transferred control to another user program. The sequence of events for a WRITE instruction is essentially the reverse of those for a READ instruction.

The type of I/O processing just described—where records are moved from a buffer to a program data area before they are processed—is called **move mode** processing. Some systems (and languages) also permit **locate mode** processing, in which records are processed in the buffer without

Figure 4-14
Virtual storage

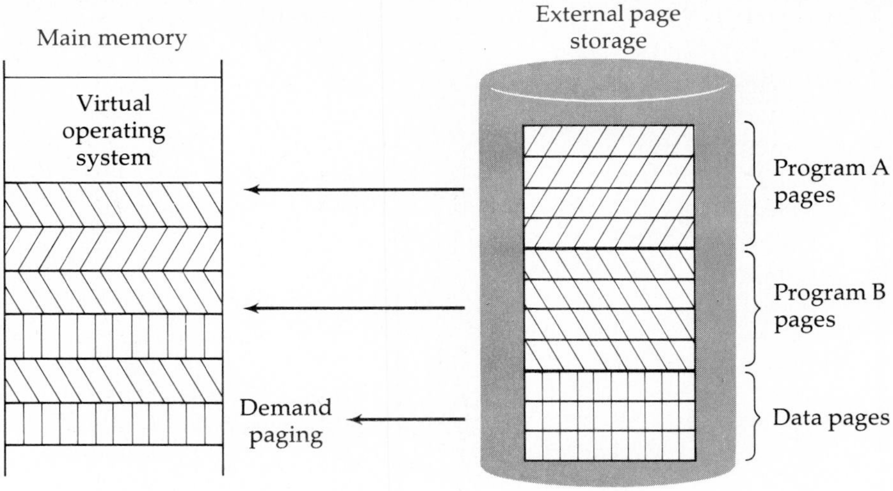

moving them to a program data area. Although locate mode processing is more efficient, it is not available with all systems and is not used as frequently as move mode processing.

From our discussion, we see that the access method (a subprogram of the operating system) is responsible for delivering a single stored record to or from an application program. A program may request a record with a READ command or store a record with a WRITE command. The access method normally provides the following services, which are transparent to the application programmer: blocking and deblocking of records, locating and accessing required data subblocks and transmitting them between main memory and disk storage, and handling exceptions and error conditions. When a data base management system (DBMS) is used, the standard access methods are still normally used to provide these record-handling functions. However, it is the DBMS, acting on behalf of a user program, that initiates the READ or WRITE.

Virtual Storage

Early multiprogramming operating systems assigned a fixed-size memory partition to each user (this is the approach we have assumed in the previous discussion). This approach presented problems of space management and program design. A large program either had to be assigned to a large memory partition or had to be segmented to operate in smaller partitions. To overcome these problems, most multiprogramming operating systems today use an approach called virtual storage (see Figure 4-14).

The term **virtual storage** refers to the fact that an application program's address space may exceed its allocated space (or partition) in main memory. As shown in Figure 4-14, with virtual storage a user program (and its associated access routines and data areas) resides in a partition of external storage (rather than a main memory partition). This storage is called **external page storage** and may be a high-performance disk unit or a mass-storage semiconductor device.

As shown in Figure 4-14, application programs and data files are divided into segments called **pages** (a typical page size is about 4000 bytes). At a given instant, only those pages required for program execution reside in main memory. When the CPU requires a page not in main memory, the virtual operating system causes this page to be read into main memory. This process of transmitting required pages is called **demand paging** and is managed by the virtual operating system. While a new program page is being read from external page storage, the operating system will have the CPU execute a page of another user program.

FILE ORGANIZATION

A **file organization** is a technique for physically arranging the records of a file on a secondary storage device (we will continue to assume the use of magnetic disks). An overview of the basic file organizations is shown in Figure 4-15. Three file organizations are shown: sequential, indexed, and direct. In an indexed organization, the records may be sequential (in which case a block index is used), or nonsequential (in which case a full index is required). We consider only the indexed sequential case in this chapter (indexed nonsequential is described in Chapter 5).

In a direct file organization, two addressing schemes are frequently used: relative addressing and hash addressing. When hash addressing is used, the addressing algorithm usually generates a relative address (this is indicated by an arrow from "hash-addressed" to "relative-addressed" in Figure 4-15).

Figure 4-15
Overview of basic file organizations

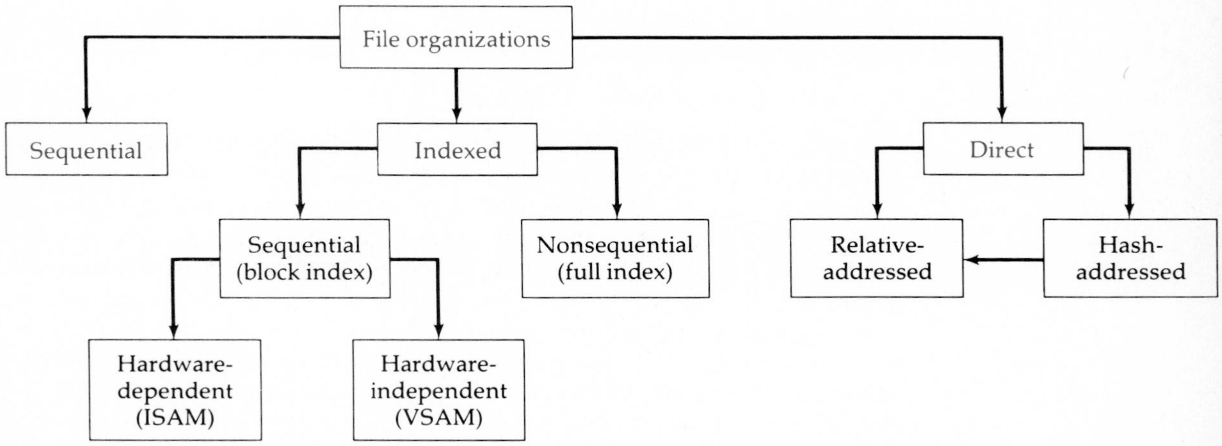

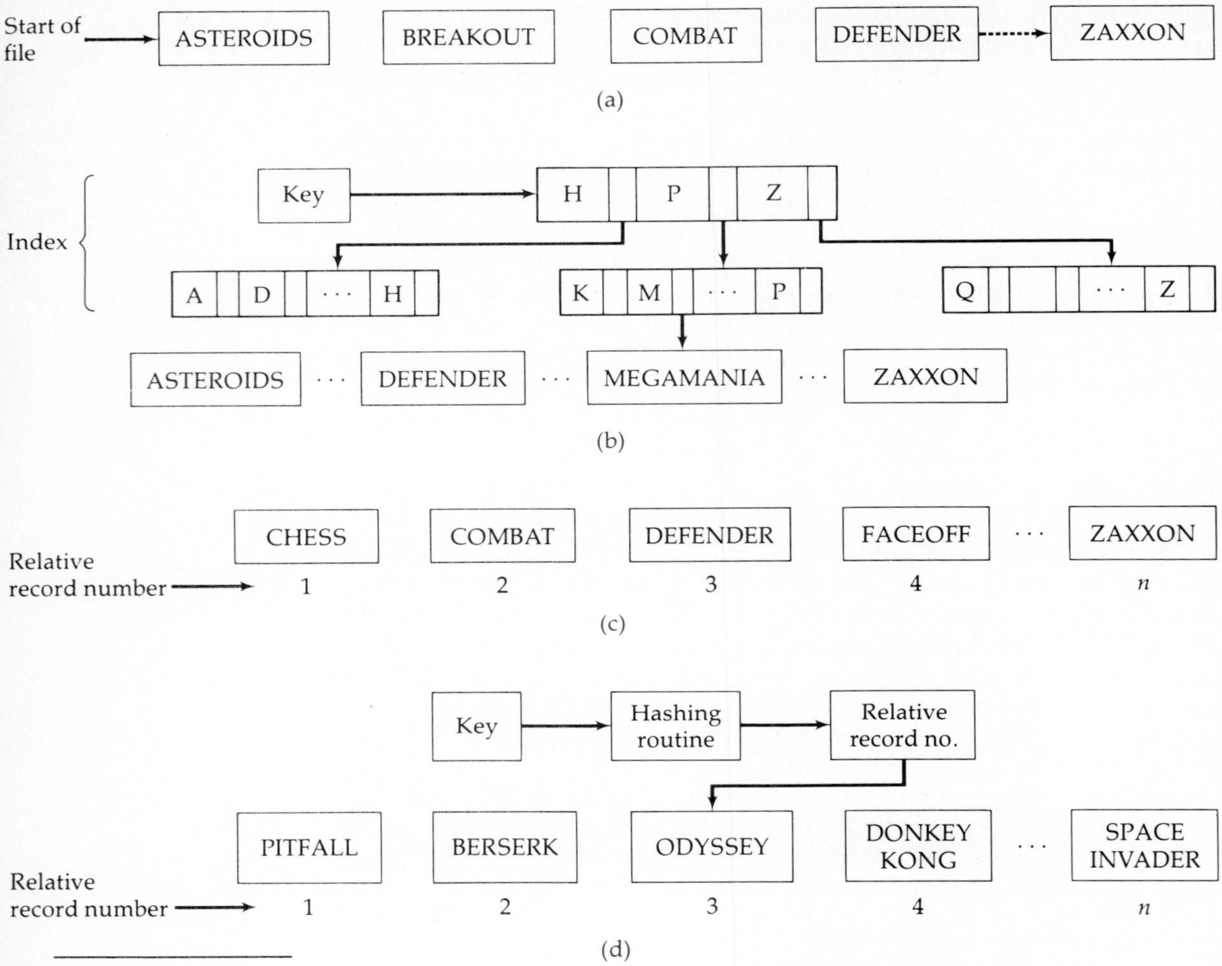

Figure 4-16
Comparison of file organizations:
(a) sequential
(b) indexed sequential
(c) relative
(d) hashed

Comparison of Basic File Organizations

In a **sequential** file organization (Figure 4-16a), the physical order of records in the file is the same as that in which the records were written to the file. Normally, this is in ascending sequence of the primary key (as shown in the example, which consists of the names of popular video games). A given record can be accessed only by first accessing all records that physically precede it.

In an **indexed sequential** organization (Figure 4-16b), the records are also stored in physical sequence according to the primary key. The file management system, or access method, builds an index, separate from the data records, that contains key values together with pointers to the data records themselves. This index permits individual records to be accessed at random without accessing other records. The entire file can also be accessed sequentially in an indexed sequential organization.

We will use the term *relative organization* to refer to a direct file organization in which relative addressing is used. In a *relative* organization (Figure 4-16c), each record can be retrieved by specifying its relative record number. The **relative record number** is a number from 0 to *n* that gives the position of the record relative to the beginning of the file. For example, a program can issue a command such as "read the fourth record in the file." It is the responsibility of the user (or application program) to specify the relative location of a desired record. Records in a relative file are often loaded in primary key sequence (as shown in Figure 4-16c) so that the file may be processed sequentially. However, the records may also be in random sequence, which occurs when the relative file organization is used in conjunction with hash addressing.

The term *hashed organization* is used to refer to a direct file organization in which hash addressing is used. In a **hashed** organization (Figure 4-16d), the primary key value for a record is converted by an algorithm (called a **hashing routine**) into a relative record number. The record is then located by its relative record number, as for a relative organization. The hashing algorithm scatters the records throughout the file, and they are normally not in primary key sequence.

Record Access Modes

You may ask why there is a need for the various file organizations shown in Figure 4-15 (as well as the more complex organizations described in Chapter 5). To answer this, we must review how the records in a file may need to be accessed in different applications. There are two basic modes for accessing records: sequential access and random access.

In **sequential access,** record storage or retrieval starts at a designated point in the file (usually the beginning) and proceeds in linear sequence through the file. Each record can be retrieved only by retrieving all the records that physically precede it. Sequential access is generally used for copying files and for sequential batch processing of records.

In **random access,** a given record is accessed "out of the blue" without referencing other records in the file. Unlike sequential access, random access follows no predefined pattern. Random access is typically used for on-line updating and/or retrieval of records.

A file organization is established when the file is created, and it is rarely changed. However, a record access mode can change each time the file is used. Thus, a file may be processed using the sequential-access mode one time and the random-access mode the next time. (In fact, the access mode may change from one record access to another.) It is therefore important to choose a file organization that permits efficient access according to the record access modes that will be required. Table 4-2 shows the combinations of file organizations and record access modes that are permitted in most systems.

Table 4-2 File Organizations and Record Access Modes

File Organization	Record Access Mode Sequential	Random
Sequential	Yes	No (impractical)
Indexed sequential	Yes	Yes
Direct-relative	Yes	Yes
Direct-hashed	No (impractical)	Yes

As shown in the table, all the file organizations except sequential permit random access. Also, all the organizations except hashed permit sequential access. (Although physical sequential access to a hashed file is technically possible, it is not practical, since the records are not in logical sequential order.) Thus, two of the file organizations—indexed sequential and relative—permit access in both the sequential and random modes.

In the following sections, we will describe the indexed sequential and hashed organizations in greater detail. To illustrate each organization, we will use a portion of the Product file for Pine Valley Furniture (see Table 4-3). To simplify the presentation, only four data items are shown: PRODUCT# (the primary key), DESCRIPTION, FINISH, and ROOM.

Notice that there are gaps in the product number values in Table 4-3. Because of these gaps, it would not be practical to use a relative organization for this file, with product number as the relative record number, since there would be massive gaps in the storage file. (For example, the record for product # 100 would be followed by 24 empty record slots, then the record for product # 125.) This is a typical problem with primary key values, and it indicates why "primary key equals relative address" is not often an acceptable addressing technique for direct files.

INDEXED SEQUENTIAL ORGANIZATION

For several years, the indexed sequential file organization has been the "workhorse" organization for files that are stored on direct access storage devices. The reason is that this organization allows access to records in both the sequential and random modes. Most vendors supply access methods that support indexed sequential organizations and automatically maintain the indexes used to randomly access individual records.

The type of index used in an indexed sequential organization is referred to as a block index. In a **block index,** each index entry refers to a block of

Table 4-3 Product File (Pine Valley Furniture Company)

PRODUCT#	DESCRIPTION	FINISH	ROOM	(Other data)
100	Stereo Cabinet	Maple	LR	
125	Coffee Table	Walnut	LR	
153	Hutch	Maple	DR	
207	Wall Unit	Oak	LR	
221	Stereo Cabinet	Pine	FR	
252	Dining Table	Maple	DR	
286	Desk	Birch	O	
314	Chair	Pine	FR	
363	Room Divider	Walnut	LR	
394	Dining Table	Oak	K	
418	Hutch	Birch	DR	
434	Bookcase	Pine	FR	
488	Lamp Table	Cherry	LR	
500	Computer Desk	Pine	O	
515	Bookcase	Maple	LR	

records (rather than a single record). This simplified index structure is made possible by the fact that the records within each block are in primary key sequence. To locate a specific record, we search the index to locate a block of records, then scan the block until the desired record is found.

If we are willing to maintain a file of records sorted by key values, we can always take advantage of this known order and use a block index to locate a given record quickly. For example, the white pages of an ordinary telephone directory represent an indexed sequential organization. In the upper left-hand corner of each page is the name of the first person listed on that page. By using this block index, we can quickly locate the page that contains a particular name. We then scan the names on that page until the desired name is located.

There are two basic implementations of the indexed sequential organization: hardware-dependent and hardware-independent. In IBM systems, the access methods that support these organizations are called, respectively, indexed sequential access method (ISAM) and virtual sequential access method (VSAM). Most other vendors provide similar access methods or file management systems. The hardware-independent version, or VSAM, is newer and more powerful and has replaced ISAM in many applications.

Hardware-Dependent Implementation (ISAM)

A diagram of an indexed sequential file that uses a single index is shown in Figure 4-17. The product records are stored in ascending product number sequence, three records per track. For simplicity, we assume that the records are unblocked, so that there is one product record per data subblock. The

Figure 4-17
Simple indexed sequential organization

Track index

Track no.	Highest key
1	153
2	252
3	363
4	434
5	515

Track	Key	Record	Key	Record	Key	Record
1	100	Rec 100	125	Rec 125	153	Rec 153
2	207	Rec 207	221	Rec 221	252	Rec 252
3	286	Rec 286	314	Rec 314	363	Rec 363
4	394	Rec 394	418	Rec 418	434	Rec 434
5	488	Rec 488	500	Rec 500	515	Rec 515
6	Overflow area					

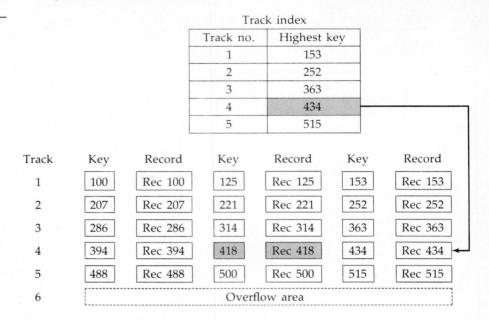

count-key-data format is used for indexed sequential (in Figure 4-17, only the key and data subblocks are shown). An overflow area is shown that will be used to hold new product records that may be added to the file.

A simple track index is shown with the product file in Figure 4-17. For each track, this index contains one entry, the highest key for a product record contained on that track. To locate a specific product record, we search the track index (using "highest key" as the argument) until we find a value that equals or exceeds the target product number. For example, suppose we wish to locate the record for product #418. Searching the track index, we find that this record must be located on track 4. Track 4 may then be scanned to locate record 418 (the count-key-data format allows the computer to search for a record with a specific key).

ISAM Architecture Most files require the use of more than one cylinder of a disk volume. When this occurs, the access method (ISAM) maintains a cylinder index that directs the search for a record to the cylinder on which it is located (see Figure 4-18). For large files, the cylinder index itself is split into several segments and a master index (or index to the index) is maintained. The master index may require one or more levels, depending on the size of the file.

The architecture of an indexed sequential file organization is shown in Figure 4-18. Indexed sequential files are normally composed of three areas:

1. The **prime area,** which contains the data records and the track index. (An index to the tracks of each cylinder is stored at the beginning of each cylinder.)

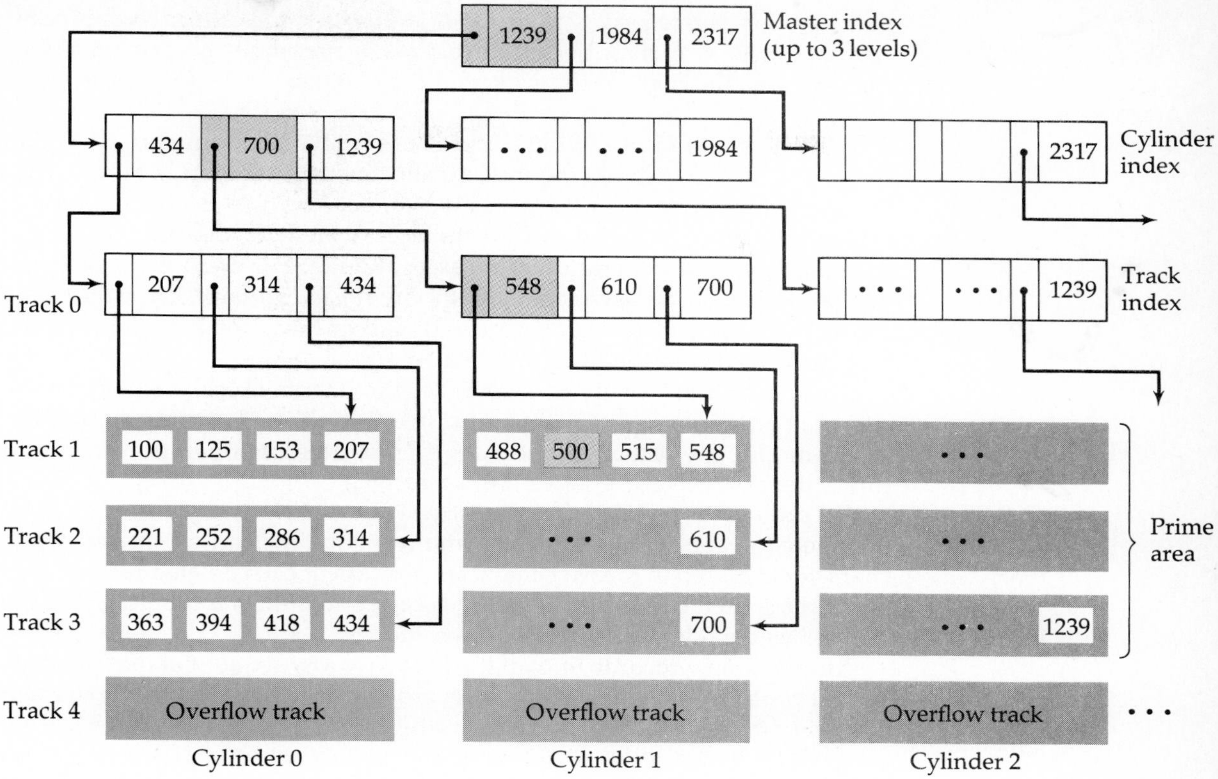

Figure 4-18
Indexed sequential architecture

2. An **overflow area,** used for records that are added to the file but will not fit in the prime area.
3. An **index,** which contains the master index and cylinder indexes.

The use of the multilevel index is illustrated in Figure 4-18. Each arrow in this diagram represents a pointer from one index to a lower-level index. Suppose we wish to locate the record for product #500. Referring first to the master index, we are directed to the first cylinder index. Searching that index, we see that record #500 will be contained on cylinder 1 (if it is in the file). At this point, the disk access mechanism is moved to cylinder 1 (if necessary) and the track index for that cylinder is read into main memory (we assume that the track index is contained on track 0). Searching the track index, we find that the desired record is on track 1 of that cylinder. The target record can then be read by scanning track 1.

In Figure 4-18, the records are unblocked. In most applications, however, it is much more likely that the records would be blocked (several records per data subblock). However, this would not change the index structure or search procedure shown in the figure. Once the track containing a particular record is identified, the track is searched for a physical block that contains that record. The search is straightforward, since in the count-key-data format, each subblock of records is preceded by a key subblock that contains the highest record key in the data subblock (see Figure 4-10).

Processing ISAM Files When records are first loaded onto an ISAM file, the access method creates the indexes such as those shown in Figure 4-18. During subsequent processing of the file, searching and maintenance of this index are also carried out by the access method and are completely transparent to the program that accesses the file. For example, a program can request a particular record by specifying its primary key value. The access method (not the program) searches the indexes and delivers the requested record to the program data area.

To update a record in an ISAM file, the data subblock containing the record is read into main memory using either the sequential- or random-access mode. The record is modified, then written on top of the old record (thus, the new record replaces the old record).

Records to be deleted from an ISAM file are normally not physically removed (or erased) from the file immediately. Instead, a special delete character is placed in the first character position of each deleted record. This character is then used in subsequent accesses to inform a program that the record has been logically deleted from the file.

Inserting new records into an ISAM file (or any sequential file) presents special problems. To maintain the records in key sequence, it might seem necessary to push all the records down beyond the point of insertion. However, this is not a practical solution. Instead, two techniques are used to handle insertions.

With the first technique, some free space is left on each track (not shown in Figure 4-18). This free space will allow occasional insertions but cannot accommodate insertions of clusters of records (e.g., many new product records).

With the second method, overflow areas are reserved for records that overflow tracks in the prime area. Several tracks are usually reserved at the end of each cylinder for this purpose. Also, an independent overflow area may be reserved to receive records that overflow the cylinder overflow areas.

The method of handling overflows in ISAM is illustrated in Figure 4-19. First, record #176 was inserted into the file shown in Figure 4-18. To maintain key sequence, this record was inserted on track 1, replacing record 207, which was moved to the overflow track. A pointer was created from track 1, giving the address of the first overflow record for that track. (In reality, the pointer is placed in the track index, but we will not consider this technical detail.) Next, records numbered 254 and 270 were inserted into the file on track 2. The records they replaced (286 and 314) were moved to the overflow track. These records are chained together, as shown by the arrow from record 286 to record 314. Thus, the records in the prime area are maintained in logical sequence by physical position, while the records in

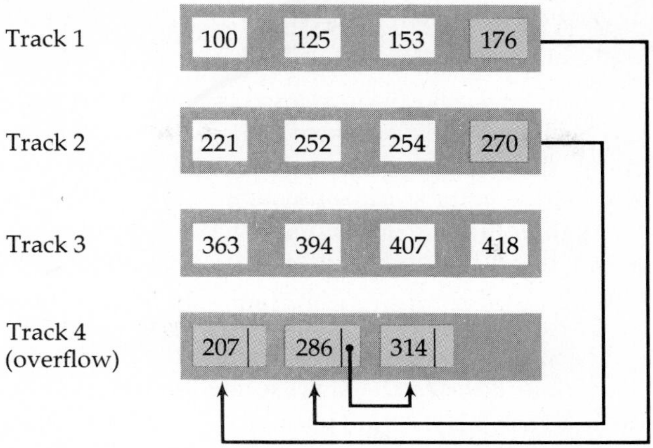

Figure 4-19
Managing overflows in ISAM

the overflow area are maintained in logical sequence by means of pointers.

Over a period of time, the number of records in the overflow areas of an ISAM file will increase. As this occurs, the performance will decline, since more accesses are required on the average to retrieve each record. Thus, an ISAM file needs to be reorganized periodically. In reorganization, the entire file is reloaded and records in the overflow areas are moved to their proper location in the prime area. Also, the indexes are updated as necessary at this time.

Performance Factors A major advantage of indexed sequential files is that they permit rapid sequential access, which is the mode used for sequential retrieval or updating. Since the records are in primary key sequence (or chained in an overflow area), an entire cylinder may be read without moving the access arm. The average access time for sequential processing is therefore equal to the average rotational delay. For the IBM 3380 (or any other disk drive that rotates at 3600 rpm), the average access time for this mode is about 8.3 msec.

In comparison, the average time for random access to an ISAM file is relatively slow. Although the master index to a file is often moved to main memory when the file is opened, the lower levels of a large index normally reside on disk. Thus, two or three disk accesses are required to search the index for random retrieval of a record. Also, when the target track is searched, it may turn out that the search must continue to an overflow area.

As a general rule of thumb, random access to a particular record in ISAM for a large file may be expected to require an average of about three disk accesses. In an earlier section we computed the average access time for the IBM 3380 disk drive as 25.3 msec. Therefore, the average random access time for a given record is about 3×25.3, or 75.9 msec. The maximum rate for random accesses to a large file is about 790 accesses per minute, computed as follows:

$$\frac{60 \text{ sec/min} \times 1000 \text{ msec/sec}}{75.9 \text{ msec/access}} = 790 \text{ accesses/min}$$

In practice, the performance (measured in response time) of a system will decline rapidly well before the access rate reaches this theoretical maximum. We may therefore conclude that indexed sequential files can support a moderate volume of transactions that require random access. However, for high-volume applications (such as airline and other reservation systems), other file organizations (such as direct with hash addressing) are required to provide acceptable performance.

The access times for indexed sequential files (both ISAM and VSAM) can be improved by carefully locating the indexes. As we have already said, the track indexes in ISAM are located in the prime area (usually on the first track of each cylinder). This allows the system to avoid a seek (access arm movement) in going from a track index to the associated data records.

For optimum performance, the cylinder indexes in ISAM should not be interspersed with the data. Ideally, they should be located on a separate disk volume (preferably on a high-performance disk drive). This location permits index searching to proceed on one disk volume in parallel with data searching in the prime areas. However, if the higher-level indexes are located on the same volume as the data, they should *not* be stored on the first cylinder of the file. If the frequency of accesses to the data is fairly evenly distributed across the file, the optimum placement of the cylinder indexes is near the center of the prime data area.

Advantages and Disadvantages of ISAM The major advantages of an ISAM organization are that the file can be processed in both sequential and random modes, new records can be inserted in the middle of the file and processed either randomly or sequentially, and most vendors provide an access method that supports an indexed sequential organization.

The disadvantages of this file organization are that the file must be reorganized periodically to "clean up" overflow records and deleted records, random access to individual records is relatively slow, and the indexes are organized by hardware boundaries (tracks and cylinders). Because of this last item, when a file is transferred to a new disk volume (say with greater track capacity), the indexes must be completely reorganized.

Hardware-Independent Implementation (VSAM)

Virtual sequential access method (VSAM) is a more powerful and flexible access method than ISAM. It supports an indexed sequential organization with multilevel indexes that is similar in concept to ISAM. However, where ISAM organizes records (and therefore indexes) around tracks and cylinders, VSAM is free of these hardware boundaries.

VSAM Architecture The basic architecture of VSAM is shown in Figure 4-20. In an ISAM file, the basic indexed group of records is the collection

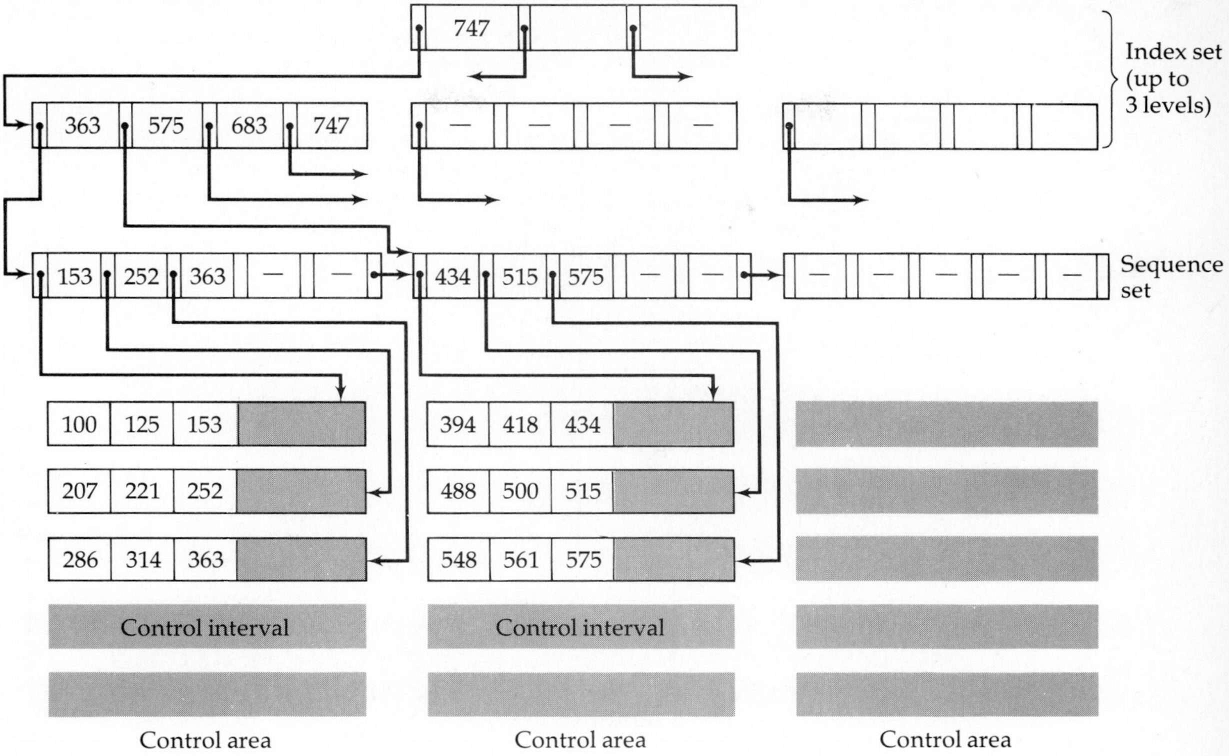

Figure 4-20 Architecture of VSAM

of records on a track (the records may be blocked or unblocked). In a VSAM file, the basic indexed group is called a **control interval** (which may be considered a virtual track). The size of a control interval is chosen by the file designer and may be less than, equal to, or greater than the length of a track. Just as tracks on a disk are grouped into cylinders, control intervals in VSAM are grouped into **control areas** (or virtual cylinders).

Figure 4-20 shows some of the product records loaded on a VSAM file. As with an ISAM file, the records are loaded in primary key sequence in the control intervals. Notice that space for insertion of new records is reserved automatically at the end of each control interval. This is called **distributed free space.** Also, some control intervals in each control area are left empty. The amount of empty space in each control interval and the number of empty control intervals in a control area are specified by the file designer.

The index structure in VSAM is similar to that in ISAM. As shown in Figure 4-20, the index is divided into two components: the index set (up to three levels) and the sequence set. As with ISAM, locating a random record proceeds by starting with the highest level in the index set and progressively searching the index until the target control interval is identified. The control interval is then scanned to locate the desired record.

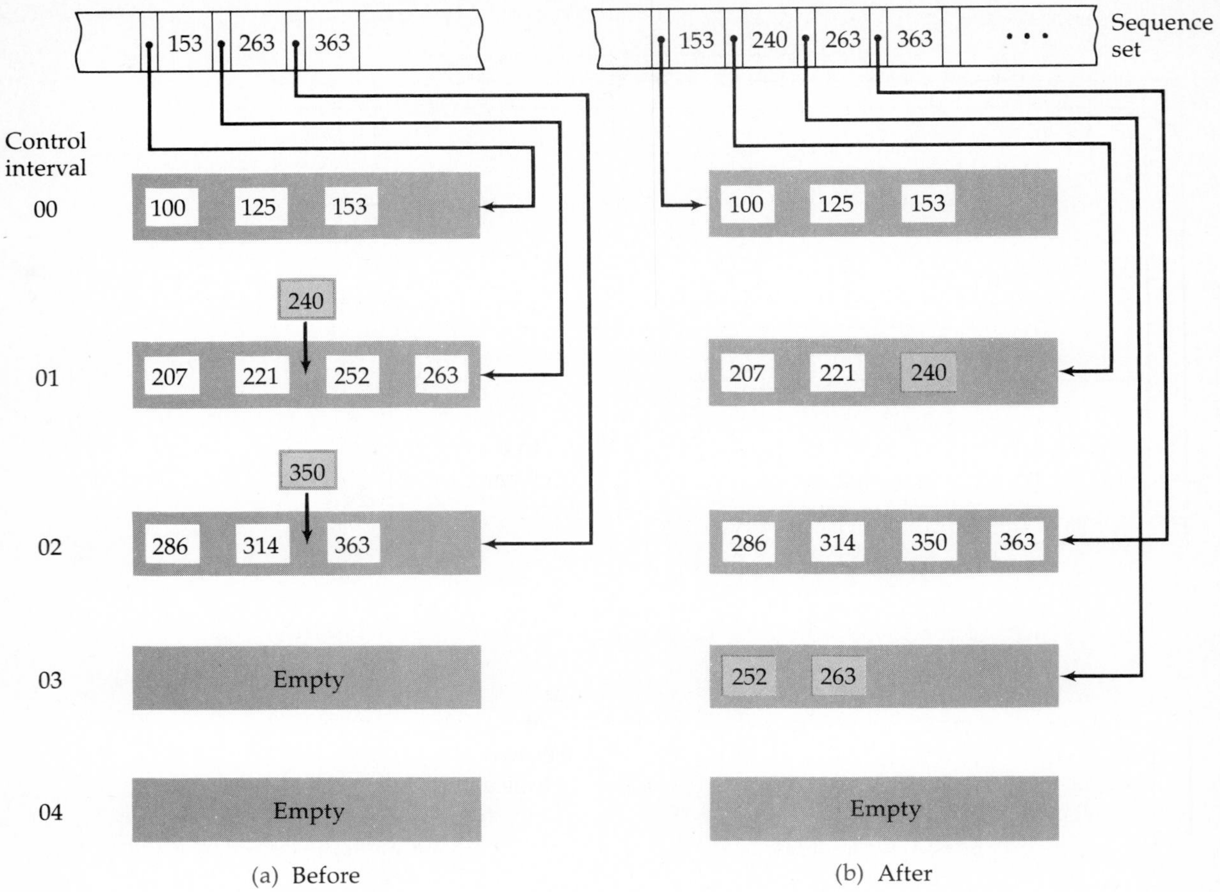

Figure 4-21
Managing record insertions in VSAM

Record Insertions The method of handling record insertions in VSAM is more refined (and efficient) than that in ISAM. When a new record is inserted, if the appropriate control interval is not full, the existing records are moved to the right by the access method and the new record is inserted in key sequence. This is illustrated in Figure 4-21a, where record 350 has been inserted into control interval 02. To make room for this new record, record 363 is moved back in the control interval.

Figure 4-21 also illustrates how insertions are managed when a control interval is full. Suppose we wish to insert record #240 into the file. This record should be placed in control interval 01, between records 221 and 252. However, control interval 01 is already full. Therefore, the access method (VSAM) performs a **control interval split.** About half the records in control interval 01 are placed into an empty control interval. In Figure 4-21b, records 252 and 263 are placed in control interval 03, while records 207, 221, and 240 remain in control interval 01. A new entry is also placed in the sequence set so that this new control interval can be accessed.

Records are always maintained in sequence within each control interval. However, after a control interval split, the records are no longer in sequence within the control area as a whole. In our example, to access the records sequentially after the split, we would have to access the control intervals in the following order: 00, 01, 03, 02. However, notice that the entries in the associated sequence set *are* in sequence. Thus, the sequence set is used to maintain the logical order of records in a control area.

Following a large number of record insertions, a control area may become full. When this happens, it is no longer possible to perform another control interval split for further insertions since all the control intervals are now full. In this case, VSAM performs a **control area split,** allocating a new control area to the file. Approximately half the records in the control area that has become full are moved to the new control area. The indexes are adjusted to reflect the new file structure.

The splitting of control intervals and control areas in an expanding VSAM file resembles the division of cells in a biological organism. No periodic reorganization of the file is required (unlike ISAM), since in essence the file is reorganized incrementally as splits occur.

Processing VSAM Files The sequence set is used for sequential processing of VSAM files. As a result of interval and area splits, the records are not in primary key sequence on the file (except immediately after the file is first loaded). However, the entries in the sequence set are in primary key sequence. Also, the components of the sequence set are chained together horizontally (see Figure 4-20). Therefore, by processing the sequence set from left to right, VSAM can access the records in logical order.

Random access to records in VSAM is similar to that for ISAM. The search begins at the highest level of the index set and proceeds to lower levels until the control interval containing the target record has been located. As with ISAM, the random-access time may be relatively slow owing to the levels of index that must be traversed.

Advantages of VSAM VSAM offers three major advantages over ISAM. First, periodic file reorganization is not required since the file can grow indefinitely by means of the splitting process. Second, the file organization is independent of hardware characteristics. (Thus, a file can be moved to a different volume without restructuring the indexes.) And finally, some versions of VSAM support secondary keys and variable-length records.

HASHED FILES

In many on-line systems, the dominant mode of file access is random. Typical of these are reservation systems (e.g., airline, hotel, and car rental) and information retrieval systems (e.g., library and stock market quotation).

In these systems, both updating and retrieval are accomplished in the random mode, and there is rarely a need for sequential access to the data records.

In such applications, a hashed file organization is often preferred. A hashed file organization provides rapid access to individual records, since it is not necessary to search indexes. The major disadvantage of this organization is that sequential processing is not convenient because the records are not stored in primary key sequence. However, this is not an important consideration for many on-line applications.

Hashed File Principles

The major components and terms associated with hashed files are shown in Figure 4-22. The primary storage area is divided into a number of addressable locations, called **buckets.** Each bucket consists of one or more **slots** where records may be stored. An addressing algorithm transforms each record identifier into a relative address (or bucket number), and the record is stored in that bucket if there is an empty slot. If all slots in the bucket are full, then the record is stored in a bucket in an overflow area.

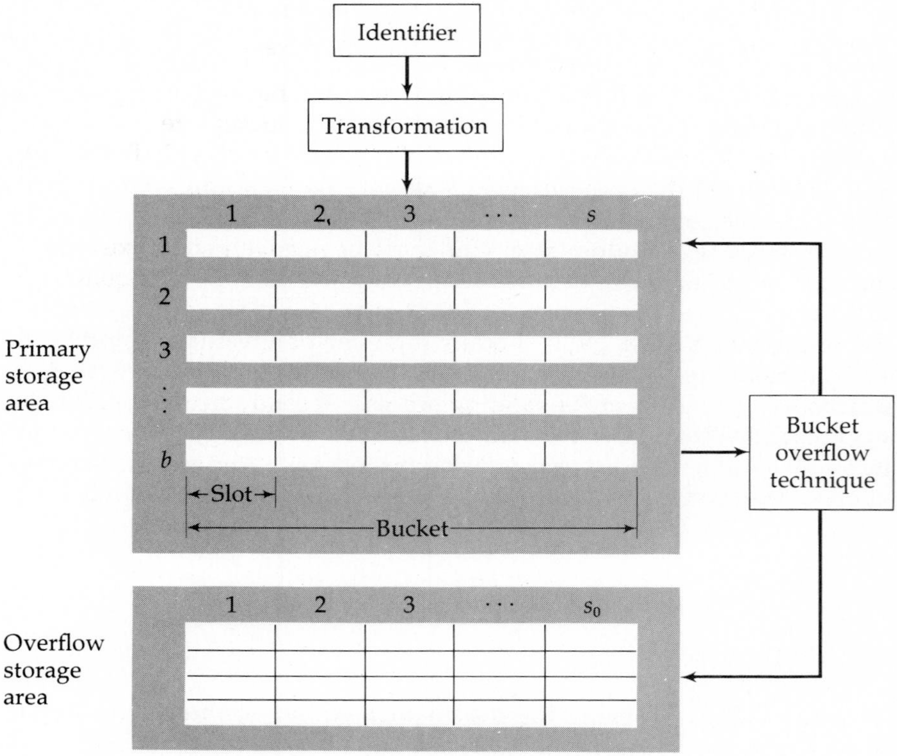

Figure 4-22
Major components of hashed files (Source: Severance and Duhne 1976. Copyright © 1976, Association for Computing Machinery, Inc. Reprinted by permission.)

In terms of the IBM architecture that we have been assuming throughout this chapter, a bucket is simply a physical storage block. The count-data format (shown in Figure 4-10a) is used for hashed files. With this format, the file management system can search for a particular physical storage block (or bucket).

Hashing Routines Records are assigned to buckets by means of a **hashing routine,** or transformation, which is an algorithm that converts each primary key value into a relative disk address. Ideally, the hashing routine that is chosen should distribute the records as uniformly as possible over the address space to be used. This provides two important benefits. First, collisions are minimized. (A **collision** is the assignment of two or more records to the same bucket.) And second, file space is utilized as efficiently as possible.

Of the numerous hashing algorithms that have been proposed (see Martin 1977 for a summary), the one that consistently performs best under most conditions is the **division/remainder method.** The steps used in this procedure are as follows:

1. Determine the number of buckets to be allocated to the file.
2. Select a prime number that is approximately equal to this number.
3. Divide each primary key value by the prime number.
4. Use the remainder as the relative bucket address.

Figure 4-23 shows the results of applying this hashing routine to the product file of Table 4-3. In part (a) of this figure, a bucket size of 1 is used, while in part (b) the bucket size (or record-blocking factor) is 2. To simplify the illustration, only the primary key values (rather than the complete records) are shown in each bucket.

Since there are 15 product records (that is, no more than 15 exist at any one time), with a bucket size of 1, at least 15 buckets will be required. In designing a hashed file, it is best to allow some free space. In this example, 19 buckets (numbered 00 to 18) are allocated. This results in a file-load factor of 15/19, or about 80%. The hashing routine consists of dividing each product number by 19 (a prime number) to generate the address. Note that with this procedure the range of addresses possible is zero up to the divisor minus 1.

The first product number (100) is divided by 19, with the following result:

$$\begin{array}{r} 5 \\ 19\overline{)100} \\ \underline{95} \\ 5 \end{array}$$

Since the remainder is 5, this record is stored in bucket 05. Next, this procedure places record 125 in bucket 11 and record 153 in bucket 01. This

Figure 4-23
Hashed files for product records (Pine Valley Furniture):
(a) bucket size = 1
(b) bucket size = 2

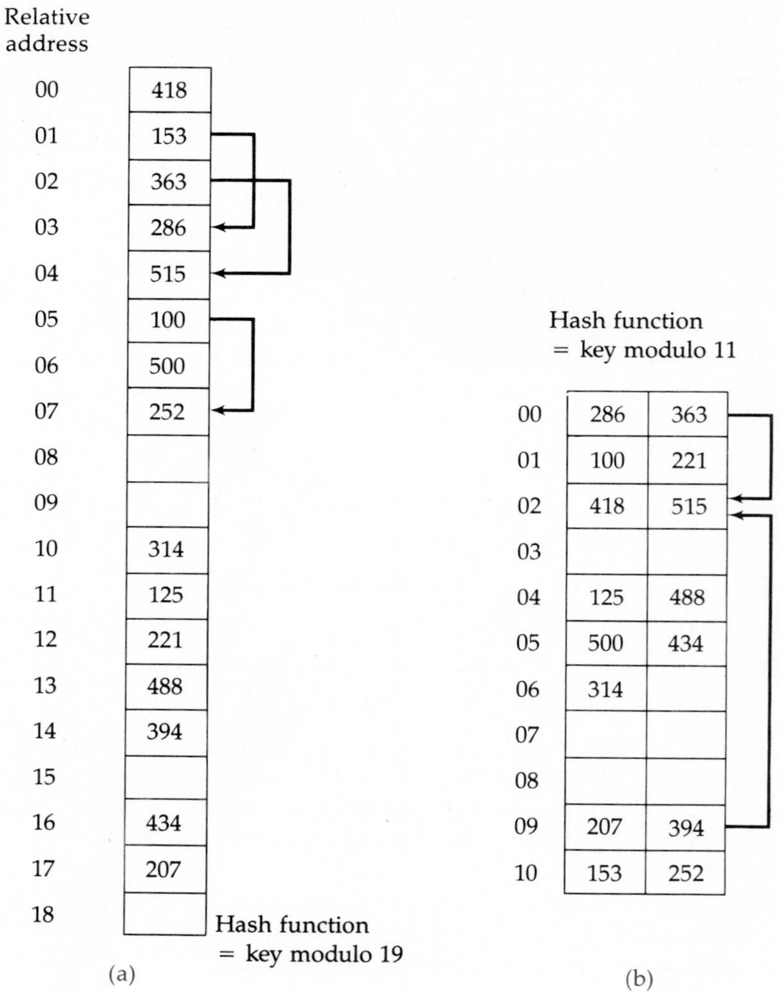

procedure continues until we reach 252. When 252 is divided by 19, the remainder is 5. Since bucket 05 is already full, we have our first collision. A common procedure is to place a record that will not fit in its "home" address into the next available empty bucket (this is called **open overflow**). In this case, record 252 could be placed in bucket 06. However, this might displace another record (yet to be loaded) whose hashed address is 06. To avoid this, record 252 is set aside until all other records have been loaded into their home address.

The result of loading this file is shown in Figure 4-23a. The records were loaded in two passes. In the first pass, all records that fit in their home addresses were stored. In the second pass, the records that created collisions in the first pass were stored in the first available address following their home address. Although the hashing routine distributed the records fairly uniformly throughout the file, there were three collisions: records 252, 286, and 515. For each of these displaced records, a pointer is placed in the home bucket to indicate its overflow location. This technique is called **chained overflow.**

In Figure 4-23b, a hashed file with a bucket capacity of 2 is shown for the same product records. In this case, 11 buckets (numbered 00 to 10) were used. Each product number was hashed by dividing by the prime number 11 and saving the remainder. As in the previous example, the records were loaded in two passes. Two collisions resulted: for records 418 and 515. Since the home address for record 515 is bucket 09, the search for an available space for this record resulted in the record being placed in bucket 02 (in this case, the search "spilled over" to the beginning of the file).

To retrieve a record in a hashed file, the hashing algorithm is applied to the primary key value to calculate the relative bucket address. If the record is located at its home address, then only one disk access is required. If it is in an overflow area, then two (or more) accesses are required. Referring to Figure 4-23a, 12 of the records will require one disk access, while the other 3 records will require two accesses. Assuming that the frequency of accesses to these records is equal, the **average search length** (or number of accesses per record) is 1.2, computed as follows:

$$\text{Average search length} = \frac{(12 \times 1) + (3 \times 2)}{15} = 1.2$$

For an IBM 3380 disk unit, the average access time for this file is 1.2 accesses per record × 25.3 msec (average access time), or 30.36 msec. The theoretical maximum access rate is slightly less than 2000 accesses per minute.

Managing Overflows

As illustrated in the preceding examples, collisions and overflows are inevitable with hashed files. It is therefore necessary to devise methods for storing and retrieving records that exceed a bucket's capacity. Normally, there is a choice as to the chaining technique as well as the type of overflow area that will be used.

Chaining Technique Overflow records may simply be placed in the next available empty slot (open overflow). However, some form of chaining (or use of pointers) is normally used to reduce the number of accesses required to locate an overflow record. As shown in Figure 4-24, there are two types of overflow chaining: coalesced and separate.

With **coalesced chaining,** a record that overflows its home bucket is placed in a free slot in any unfilled bucket. A pointer chain is established for the synonym records. For example, in Figure 4-24a, assume that the home bucket for record D is bucket 1. Since bucket 1 is full, record D is

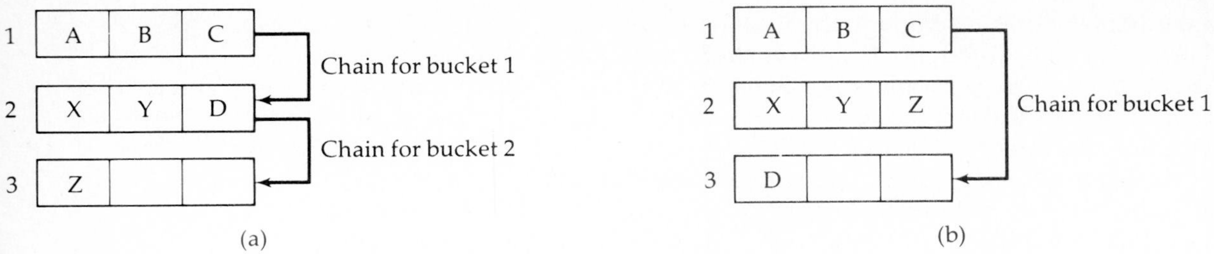

Figure 4-24
Types of overflow chaining:
(a) coalesced chaining
(b) separate chaining

placed in an empty slot in bucket 2. Now an attempt is made to place record Z in bucket 2 (its home address). Since bucket 2 is now full, this record overflows to bucket 3. Notice that with coalesced chaining, overflow from one primary bucket may cause premature overflow in another primary bucket. With coalesced chains, record retrieval times increase as a file-load factor grows.

With **separate chaining,** overflow records are relocated to avoid the merging of synonym chains. For example, in Figure 4-24b, record D is initially placed in bucket 2. However, when an attempt is made to place record Z in bucket 2, record D is relocated to bucket 3. Notice that only one pointer chain is now required, instead of the two chains in the coalesced case. Thus, separate chains have faster retrieval than coalesced chains; however, overhead is required to relocate records.

Separate Overflow Area Overflow records may be placed in empty slots in the primary storage area or in an independent overflow storage area (shown in Figure 4-22). An independent overflow storage area provides three important advantages: It avoids coalesced chains, thereby avoiding an increase in average retrieval times; it avoids the overhead required to relocate overflow records from primary buckets when those buckets are required as home addresses; and it permits orderly and inexpensive file expansion.

In summary, with hashed files, it is usually preferable to place overflow records in buckets in an independent overflow area, with pointers in the home buckets to the overflow buckets.

Hashed File Design

In designing hashed files, use of any of the following three processes will reduce collisions and minimize the average search length:

1. Use a hashing routine that distributes the records as evenly as possible over the available address space (the division/remainder method should normally be used).
2. Select a low load factor (assign more disk capacity than is required for the file).
3. Use a larger bucket capacity (blocking factor).

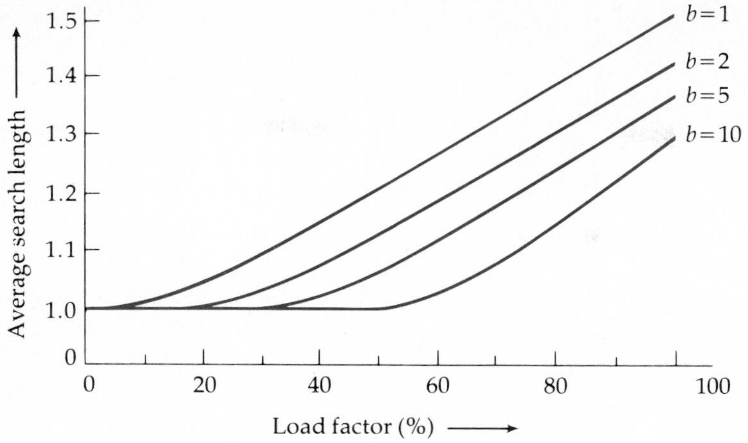

Figure 4-25
Average search length versus load factor (Source: Bradley 1982)

Load Factor The **load factor** is the percentage of space allocated to the file that is taken up by records in the file. For example, the load factor in the file shown in Figure 4-23b is 15/22, or about 68%.

A low load factor reduces the number of records that overflow their home addresses. This, in turn, reduces the average search length. In practice, load factors between 50% and 80% should normally be used. If the file is expected to grow, then a lower load factor should be used initially, since it will increase as insertions occur.

Bucket Capacity Increasing the bucket capacity will also reduce the number of overflows and hence the average search length. This is true because with a bucket capacity greater than 1, some collisions can occur before overflow becomes necessary. Unfortunately, using a bucket capacity greater than 1 can complicate the programming task, as we will soon see.

Given the load factor and bucket capacity, we can use formulas or curves to estimate the average search length. The curves shown in Figure 4-25 show the average search length versus load factor for bucket sizes of 1, 2, 5, and 10 (chained overflow is assumed). For a load factor of 100% and a bucket capacity of 1, the average search length is about 1.5. Notice that for a given load factor (say 80%), we can reduce the average search length by increasing the bucket capacity.

Managing Hashed Files

A comparison of hashed files in a traditional file environment and in a data base environment is shown in Figure 4-26. This figure helps explain why hashed files are more widely used in a data base environment.

File Environment Many access methods (or file management systems) do not directly support hashed files. Instead, the access method supports a

Figure 4-26 Managing hashed files in a traditional file environment versus a data base environment:
(a) traditional file environment
(b) data base environment

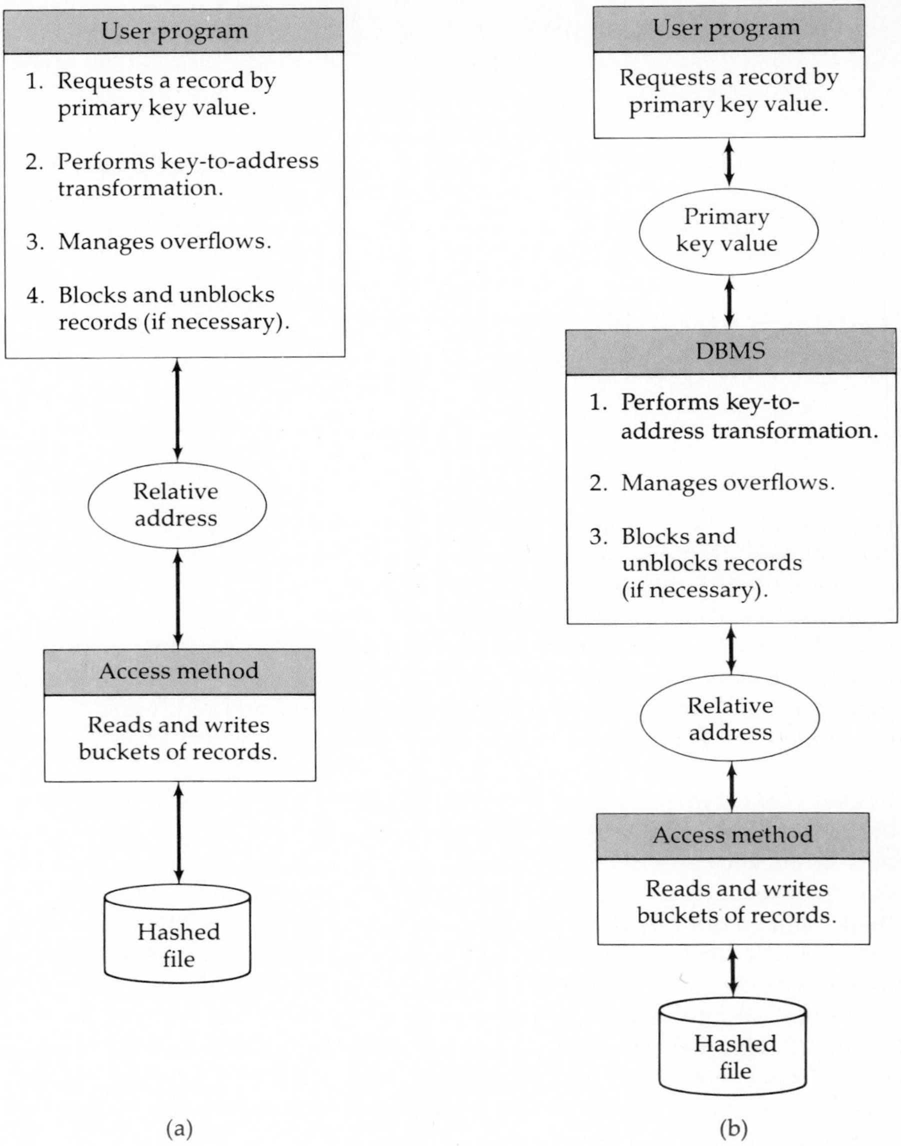

relative file organization. Therefore, as shown in Figure 4-26a, the programmer writing a program that will manipulate hashed files must code many of the file management functions. For example, in writing a COBOL program, the programmer must code the hashing routine (or else cause a routine to be copied from a common library). Also, the programmer is responsible for coding the overflow management routines (such as progressive chained overflow). Finally, if records are blocked (bucket capacity is greater than 1), the programmer may have to write instructions to block and unblock records (although some access methods perform this function). The coding task becomes quite complex, and as a result, hashed files are used only when absolutely necessary.

Data Base Environment Most data base management systems today directly support hashed files. As shown in Figure 4-26b, the file management functions—hashing routines, overflow management, and record management—are built into the DBMS. As a result, the application programmer is relieved of coding these routines and can instead write instructions that request a record by its primary key value. The DBMS transforms this value to a relative address, which is then passed on to the access method. In fact, the ease of using direct hash-addressed file organizations is one of the major advantages of a data base management system.

Advantages and Disadvantages

Hashed files offer two major advantages over indexed sequential organizations: Random access is faster (nearly three times as fast as ISAM), and insertions and deletions are more easily handled.

However, hashed files have four disadvantages: Sequential access is impractical; disk space is not as efficiently utilized (because of lower load factors); periodic reorganization is required; and the programming task may be more complex (not true when a DBMS is used).

SUMMARY

This chapter presented a review of the basic principles and methods of file organization. A file organization is a technique for organizing and accessing records on secondary storage devices.

Throughout the chapter, we have assumed the use of magnetic disk storage devices. We reviewed the basic hardware terms and performance factors associated with magnetic disks—tracks, cylinders, sectors, access times, and so on. Also, basic data formats, such as count-data and count-key-data, were described.

Vendor-supplied access methods insulate the user from many of these hardware details. They allow us to visualize a file extent as a series of storage locations. Each storage location can hold one or more records and can be addressed by specifying its location relative to the beginning of the file. The access method translates this relative address to the necessary hardware address and manages other hardware-dependent details.

Three basic file organizations are frequently used: sequential, indexed, and direct. Indexed sequential organizations (the most common) are used when both sequential and random access to a file are required. Direct files with hashed addressing are frequently employed in on-line data base applications when fast random access to records is required for updating and retrieval. Sequential file organizations are used primarily in making backup copies of data bases.

Chapter Review

REVIEW QUESTIONS

1. Give concise definitions for each of the following terms:
   a. volume
   b. extent
   c. buffer
   d. multiprogramming
   e. virtual storage
   f. hashing routine
   g. block index
   h. control interval
   i. bucket
   j. collision
   k. load factor
2. Contrast the following terms:
   a. removable media; fixed media
   b. physical address; relative address
   c. count-data format; count-key-data format
   d. access method; channel program
   e. ISAM; VSAM
   f. separate chaining; coalesced chaining
3. Prepare a table showing the major advantages of each of the following:
   a. sequential file organization
   b. indexed sequential file organization
   c. hashed file organization
4. Briefly describe three typical magnetic disk data formats.
5. What information is typically contained in each of the following?
   a. home block b. file header
6. What hardware device normally performs the following function?
   a. stores instructions and data at execution time
   b. executes I/O instructions under CPU control
   c. performs calculations and logical operations
   d. optimizes disk performance and performs error recovery
7. Describe three techniques for reducing collisions in hashed files.
8. Give two examples (other than those presented in the text) of everyday occurrences of indexed sequential files.
9. Describe two techniques for managing overflows from a home address in hashed files.
10. With respect to the physical areas of a disk, list in decreasing order of desirability the areas you would use to store overflow from a home address.

PROBLEMS AND EXERCISES

1. Match the following terms to the appropriate definitions.

____ collision	**a.** contains data records and track index
____ multiprogramming	**b.** file management subprogram
____ virtual storage	**c.** virtual track
____ hashing	**d.** removable floppy disk cartridge
____ buffer	**e.** overflow technique in hashed files
____ extent	**f.** several programs appear to execute at same time
____ sector	**g.** two records hash to the same bucket
____ CD ROM	**h.** percent of file space used by records
____ Bernoulli Box	**i.** uses paging to manage memory
____ control interval	**j.** each entry refers to more than one record
____ coalesced chaining	**k.** contiguous physical storage blocks
____ load factor	**l.** subdivision of a track
____ prime area	**m.** optical disk media
____ block index	**n.** area where records are stored
____ access method	**o.** converts a key to an address

2. The inventory file for Apex Manufacturing Company contains 40,000 records. Each record contains 500 bytes (fixed length). The records are to be stored on an IBM 3380 disk volume using the count-key-data format (key length is 15 bytes).
   a. How many cylinders will be required if the blocking factor is 2?
   b. How many cylinders will be required if the blocking factor is 10?
   c. If the records are stored as a VSAM file, what will be the average time to access a record at random (assume that three disk accesses are required)?

3. Redraw the VSAM file in Figure 4-21 to show the effect of inserting the following records:
   a. primary key value 248 b. primary key value 337

4. Redraw the ISAM file in Figure 4-19 to show the effect of inserting the following records (create an additional overflow track if necessary):
   a. primary key value 215 b. primary key value 328

5. A hashed file is to have a capacity of approximately 1000 buckets. The prime number 997 will be used as a divisor in the hashing routine. What addresses will be generated for records with the following key values: 762, 20439, 618472?

6. Redraw the hashed file in Figure 4-23a to show the effect of inserting the following records:

a. primary key value 170
b. primary key value 695
c. primary key value 40

7. What is the average search length for the file shown in Figure 4-23b?
8. The disk unit shown in Figure 4-2 has the following characteristics:
Sector size: 512 bytes
Sectors per track: 42
Tracks per cylinder: 6
Cylinders per disk pack: 1588
Average seek time: 41.7 msec
Rotational speed: 3600 rpm
   a. What is the total capacity (in bytes) for each disk pack?
   b. What is the average access time? (Assume that transfer time is negligible.)
9. Refer to the disk unit described in Problem 8.
   a. What is the average sequential access time to records in an ISAM file?
   b. What is the average random access time to records in an ISAM file?
   c. What is the average random access time to records in a hashed file? Assume that each sector (or bucket) contains one record and that a load factor of 75% is used.
10. Refer to the file described in Problem 2. Suppose that this file is to be loaded on the disk unit described in Problem 8. Assume that records do not span sectors (that is, there will be only one record per sector).
   a. How many cylinders will be required for the data records of this file?
   b. What percent of the total capacity of a disk pack will be required for the data records of this file?
11. The disk unit described in Problem 8 is to be used to store a file containing 10,000 records. A hashed file organization is to be used. The size of each record is 100 bytes. Since the sector size is 512 bytes, five records will be stored per sector (thus, the bucket size is 5).
   a. If an average search length of 1.3 is acceptable, what load factor should be used?
   b. Given your answer to part (a), how many buckets (or sectors) should be allocated to this file?
   c. Given your answer to part (b), how many tracks should be allocated to this file? How many cylinders?
12. Refer to the ISAM file shown in Figure 4-18. On what cylinder and track are each of the following records located?
   a. product #573
   b. product #685
13. A disk drive for a personal computer has the following characteristics:
Bytes per track: 5000
Tracks per cylinder: 8
Cylinders per disk pack: 100
Average rotational delay: 10 msec
Average seek time: 30 msec
   a. What is the total capacity of the disk drive?
   b. A sequential file with 5000 records is placed on this unit. Each track can contain 20 records. How many cylinders are required for this file?

14. Visit a computing center that processes commercial applications.
    a. What access methods are available with this computer and its operating system?
    b. Identify examples of each of the file organizations described in this chapter.
    c. Discuss the factors that are considered in designing files.

REFERENCES

Bohl, Marilyn. 1981. *Introduction to IBM Direct Access Storage Devices.* Chicago: Science Research Associates.

Bradley, James. 1982. *File and Data Base Techniques.* New York: Holt, Rinehart & Winston.

Katzan, Harry, Jr. 1975. *Computer Data Management and Data Base Technology.* New York: Van Nostrand Reinhold.

Martin, James. 1977. *Computer Data Base Organization.* 2d ed. Englewood Cliffs, N.J.: Prentice-Hall.

McManus, Reed. 1986. "CD ROM: The Little Leviathan." *PC World* (October): 272–280. San Francisco: PCW Communications, Inc.

Polesnak, Roman R. 1984. *Optical Disk Storage.* Toronto: Department of Computer Science, University of Toronto.

Severance, Dennis, and Ricardo Duhne. 1976. "A Practitioner's Guide to Addressing Algorithms." *Communications of the ACM* 19 (June): 314–326.

Ullman, Jeffrey D. 1982. *Principles of Database Systems.* 2d ed. Rockville, Md.: Computer Science Press.

Chapter 5

Data Structures

INTRODUCTION

Data structures are the brick, mortar, and glue that hold data bases together. In Figure 5-1 (reproduced from Figure 4-1), data structures are defined in the internal model level and implemented in the physical data organization level of the ANSI/SPARC model introduced earlier. This means that data structures are primarily used by data management technologies [such as data base management systems (DBMSs), operating system access methods, and application development packages] and are often hidden from programmers and end users during systems development and programming.

Although data structures are hidden during the use of most data management functions, there are still several important reasons to study these data base building blocks. First, to achieve the greatest possible performance from DBMSs, we often have to tune data structures to work well with the data and data processing we are using. Second, understanding data structures used by a DBMS will make it easier for us to properly and efficiently program in the DBMS data manipulation languages and to interpret inevitable error messages. Finally, data base designers and programmers need to communicate with DBMS specialists, and an understanding of data structures will aid in this communication.

The efficiency of an application program, such as an Inventory Master File update program for Pine Valley Furniture, depends on the use of a well-

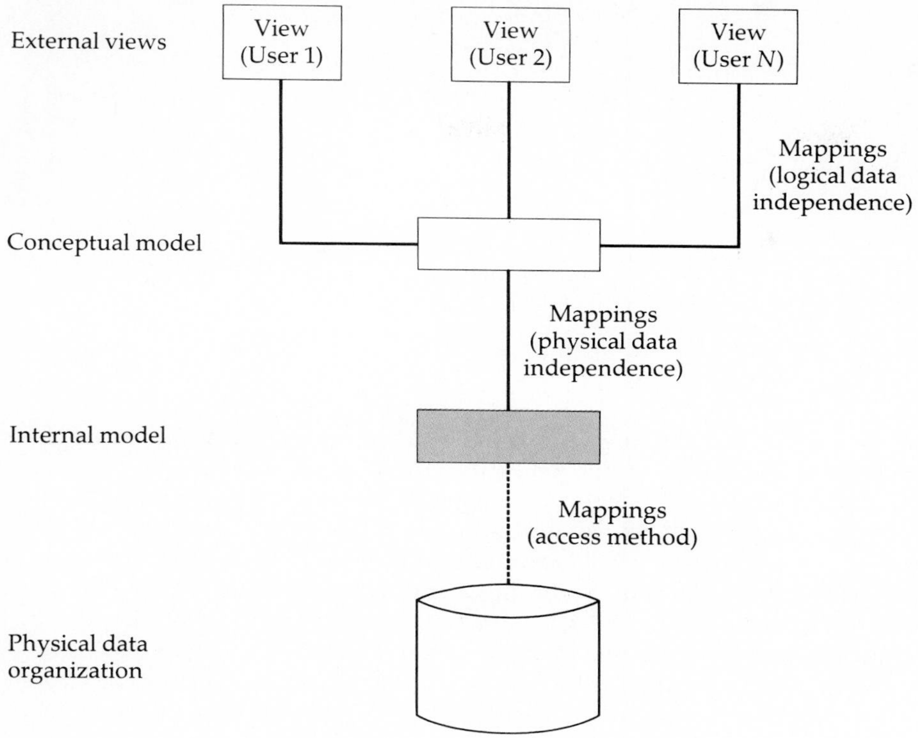

Figure 5-1
Levels of views of data (ANSI/SPARC model)

chosen data management technology. Occasionally, application designers and programmers need to design a new data structure for some specialized requirement; usually, however, the responsibility of the information systems designer is to understand the data processing required and to choose appropriate technologies, including data structures. To make this choice, we need to know how data structures work, which is the purpose of this chapter.

Data structures are used to represent associations between elements of data. These elements could be data items, records, or "data about data," such as the ISAM track index entries in Figure 4-18. For example, data structures can be used to link a Product# to its Description and to connect a Customer record to its associated Open Order records.

In general, data structures connect one element of data to another. This can be viewed in a graphic form, as depicted in Figure 5-2. Here each element of data (data item, record, or overhead data) is a node. Links represent an association between two elements of data. For example, element 1 might stand for a Customer record and element 2 might represent an Order record; then the link between them means that the relationship between a Customer and his or her Orders is represented explicitly in the data structure. The links on the graph give the graph its structure, or architecture. It

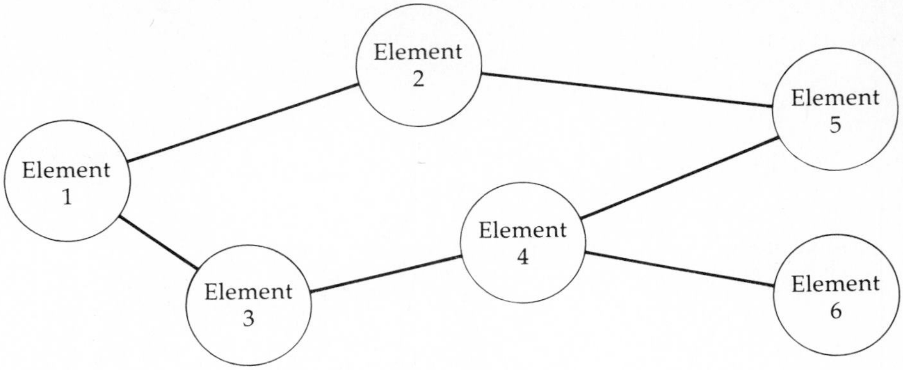

Figure 5-2
Data structures as a graph

is the particular structure of a graph and the way these links are implemented that distinguish one data structure from another.

A data structure is static and "comes to life" only through use. It is as important to discuss how to process (sometimes called "navigate" or "traverse") data structures as it is to discuss their form. Some data structures process updates efficiently with modest data retrieval speed; other structures provide very rapid retrieval, but maintenance is very costly. Both form and process will be covered in this chapter. There is no one best data structure for all data processing needs, so we will introduce a variety of structures frequently used in modern DBMSs for internal and physical data modeling.

Data structures can basically be described by two characteristics: the method used to connect one data element to an associated data element and the architecture of the data structure graph that can be constructed. The first characteristic, called the location method, seems to be more fundamental, and this is where we begin. We will discuss the second characteristic, architecture, later in the chapter.

BASIC DATA STRUCTURES

All data structures assume that data are to be organized so that one element of data precedes another, and so on. Thus, terms like PRIOR/NEXT or PREDECESSOR/SUCCESSOR are frequently used when talking about locating data. That is, finding data is relative to having already found some other piece of data. Data are also assumed to have a natural, logical sequence or sorting rule (such as ascending on part number). Basic location methods are used to connect given data to their predecessors and successors in this sequence. Location methods involve both connection mechanisms and methods for relative placement of actual data. Together, the alternatives for both connection and placement can be used to describe the traditional

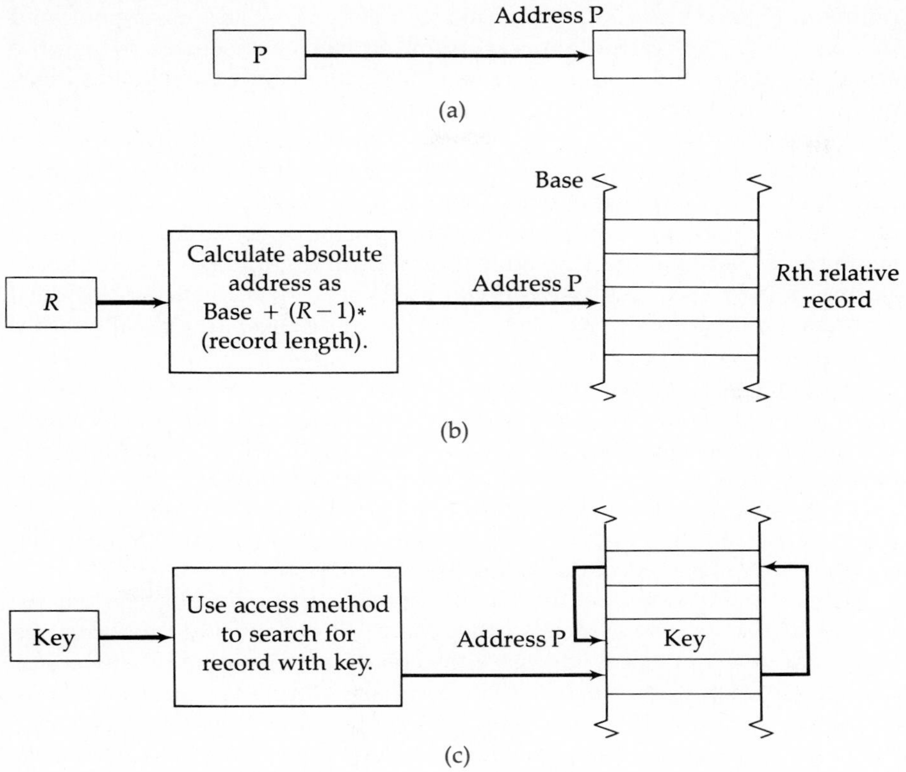

Figure 5-3
Types of pointers:
(a) physical address pointer
(b) relative address pointer for *R*th record in file
(c) logical key pointer for record with key

sequential, linked list, and inverted data structures, as well as various other basic structures and hybrids. Furthermore, it is not uncommon for a given element of data (such as a Customer record) to be a part of multiple data structures (e.g., be sequenced by Customer Number, be related to Customer Order data, and so forth).

Types of Pointers

Fundamental to many data structures is the use of extra data (that is, data without a business use) to connect elements of data. Most often these extra data are called pointers. A **pointer** is a field associated with one piece of data that is used to identify the location of another piece of data. That is, a pointer contains some type of address that can be used to locate associated data. In this section, we introduce the three types of pointers—physical, relative, and logical—and discuss their relative capabilities. Then in the next section we will show how pointers and other constructs are used to build basic data structure building blocks.

Figure 5-3 illustrates the basic differences among the different types of pointers. *Physical* and *relative* refer to the types of disk addressing outlined in Chapter 4. A **physical (address) pointer** resolves absolutely where the associated data reside, since it includes the disk cylinder, track, and block numbers of the data to which we are pointing.

A physical pointer is the fastest type of pointer, since it does not need to be further manipulated to specify data location. It is, however, the most restrictive. If the associated data change location in any way (e.g., because of reorganization of a file), then the pointer must be changed. The pointer value has no alphanumeric relationship to meaningful data base contents, so once a pointer is destroyed, it can be difficult to reconstruct. Physical pointers are of fixed size (the length of disk addresses) and usually rather short (e.g., 4 to 8 bytes).

A **relative (address) pointer** contains the relative position (or "offset") of the associated data with respect to the beginning of the data structure in which the associated data are located. This could indicate a certain byte position within a record, a certain relative record number within a file, or a certain relative block within a file. The reference can be from one file to another. For example, a pointer in a Customer record could connect that record to an associated Order record in the Orders file.

Relative pointers require marginally more computer time (several microseconds) to access the associated data, since the relative address must be translated into a physical address either by data management software or by the operating system access method (disk controllers understand only absolute, physical addresses). This translation process has to "look up" such values as record length and blocking factor to perform this calculation.

The primary advantage of relative pointers is that when the *whole* data structure changes location and all relative data placement within the structure is preserved, relative pointer values into that structure need not change. For the preceding example, the Orders file can be moved from one disk device to another to better distribute disk activity, and the relative pointers in the Customer file need not be modified. Relative pointers are difficult to reconstruct, since they have no alphanumeric relationship to meaningful data. The length of a relative pointer varies between applications but is less than the length of a physical pointer, since a relative address must be no larger than the largest physical address. The length depends on the range of possible relative positions in the data structure. For instance, given a 10,000-record Order file, a relative pointer in the Customer file to link a customer to an associated order would have to be at least 14 bits long (or, more likely, a whole 2 bytes).

A **logical (key) pointer** contains meaningful data (that is, contents of the data base) about the associated element of data. Logical pointers are useful only if the associated data have some additional structure (like an ISAM index) that supports key access on pointer values. Logical pointers are used when very rapid, direct access is not required and meaningful data exist anyhow. For example, an Order file record is likely to contain the Customer# found on the order sales form. This field is included directly in Order file records so that it is readily available to print on shop orders, invoices, status reports, and the like. Occasionally, other customer data (name, address, and so on) are also required. To access these additional data, the Customer# is used to locate the Customer file record via its primary key ISAM index or hashing function on Customer#.

Logical pointers require the most computer time to actually retrieve the associated record because a purely hardware-independent value is used. This value must be transformed into a relative or physical pointer via table lookup, index searching, or a mathematical calculation. In any case, this translation time may include several physical file accesses to retrieve key synonyms or several index blocks. But use of this hardware-independent value means that data can be moved; even relative placement within a structure can be changed, and logical pointers need not change. The cost to accomplish this location independence includes both time and space to maintain the key access method.

Logical pointers tend to be the longest type of pointer. Most data keys are relatively long compared to the length of a relative pointer (which must be capable of holding the value of the number of records in a file) or compared to the length of a disk address (for physical pointers). For example, the Pine Valley Furniture Product Master File in Figure 2-2 has only ten active records with logical pointers (keys) that are, say, 4 bytes long. In this case, a physical pointer might be 8 bytes (depending on the computer addressing scheme), but only a single-byte relative pointer is required. A distinct advantage of logical pointers is that they do have real-world meaning. If destroyed on computer media, they can be readily reconstructed from business documents and other computerized data. Finally, logical pointers can be said to be data that are in common between two nodes (e.g., records). This common data view is inherent (even required) in the relational data model developed in Chapter 6.

Table 5-1 summarizes this comparison of types of pointers. The remainder of this chapter and subsequent chapters will frequently rely on a clear understanding of the different types of pointers and their applications in data management.

Data Structure Building Blocks

All data structures are built from several alternative basic building blocks for connecting and locating data. Connecting methods allow movement between related elements of data. Locating methods allow data within a structure to first be placed or stored and then found.

There are only two basic methods for *connecting* elements of data, as outlined by Severance (1974):

1. An **address sequential** (AS) connection, in which a successor element is placed and located in the physical memory space immediately following the current element (see Figures 5-4a and c).

Table 5-1 Comparison of Types of Pointers

	Type of pointer		
Characteristic	**Physical**	**Relative**	**Logical**
Form	Actual secondary memory (disk) address	Offset from reference point (beginning of file)	Meaningful business data
Speed of access	Fastest	Medium	Slowest
Sensitivity to data movement	Most	Only sensitive to relative position changes	Least
Sensitivity to destruction	Very	Very	Often can be easily reconstructed
Space requirement	Fixed, usually short	Varies, usually shortest	Varies, usually longest

2. A **pointer sequential** (PS) connection, in which some additional data (called a pointer) are explicitly stored in the current element to identify the location of the successor element (see Figures 5-4b and d).

Also, there are only two basic methods for *placement* of data relative to the connection mechanism:

1. **Data direct** (DD) placement, in which the connection mechanism links an item of data directly with its successor (and/or predecessor) item (see Figures 5-4a and b).
2. **Data indirect** (DI) placement, in which the connection mechanism links pointers to the data, not the data themselves (see Figures 5-4c and d).

Address Sequential Connection Address sequential data direct (ASDD, or simply sequential) was described in Figure 4-16a when we were discussing file organizations. It is simple, easy to understand and process, uses no extra storage space above that required for data, and it supports efficient sequential access. Now let's take another look at the list of typical data base operations for record processing introduced at the beginning of Chapter 4 and reproduced below:

- Fetch an arbitrary record from the file.
- Insert a record into the file.

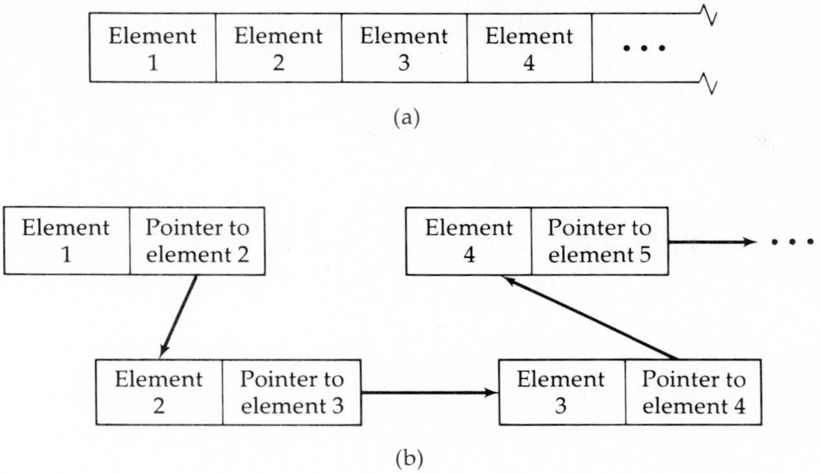

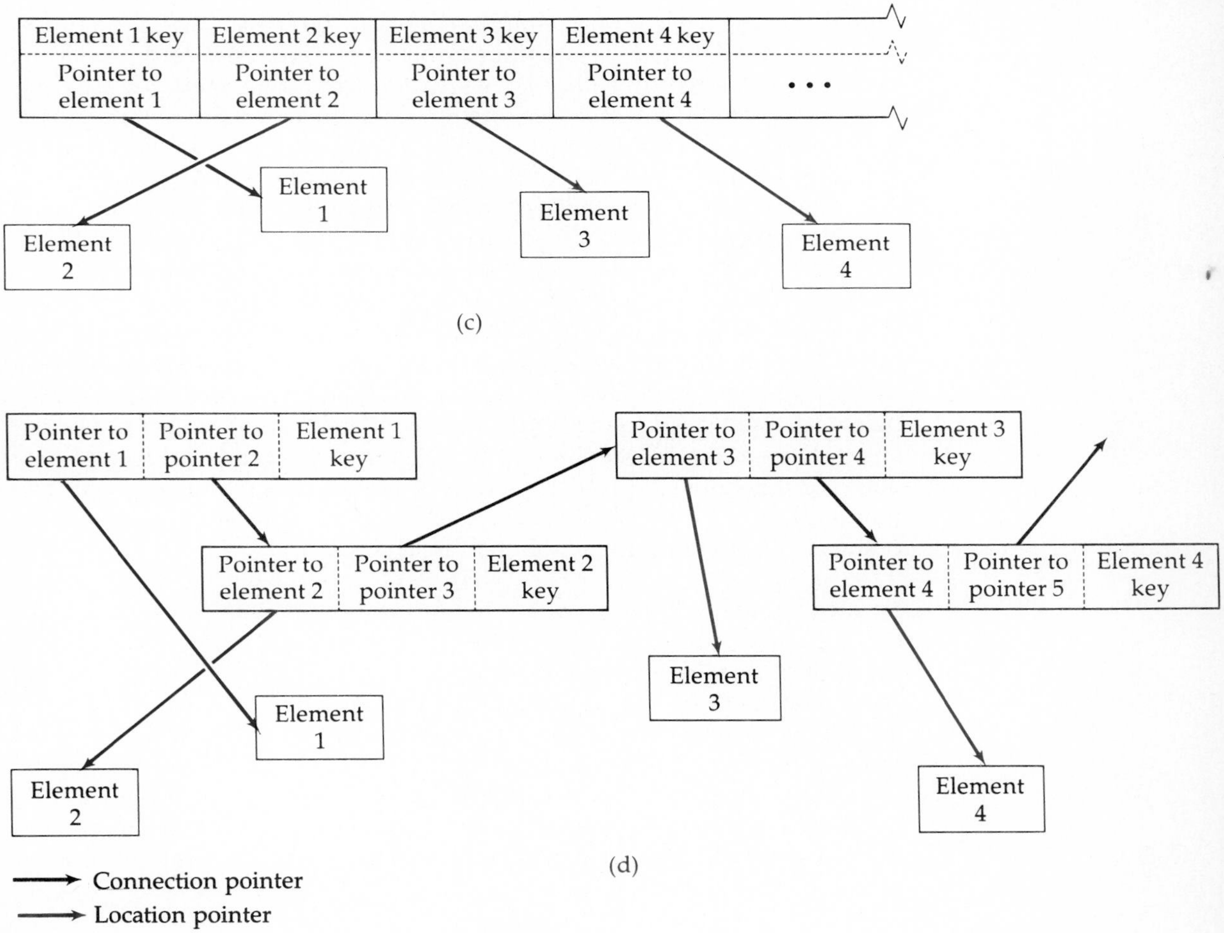

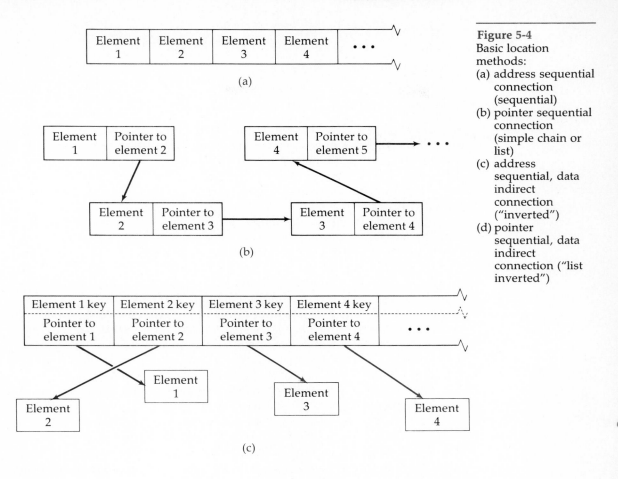

Figure 5-4
Basic location methods:
(a) address sequential connection (sequential)
(b) pointer sequential connection (simple chain or list)
(c) address sequential, data indirect connection ("inverted")
(d) pointer sequential, data indirect connection ("list inverted")

- Modify a record in the file.
- Read the entire file.
- Read the next record in the file.
- Delete a record from the file.
- Reorganize the file.

Sequential performs rather well for the fourth and fifth operations (reading an entire file or the physically next record); it can be economical for the third operation (modifying a record) if the media supports update-in-place, if roughly 10% or more of the file is being modified, and if the amount of storage space does not change; but it is cumbersome, if not impractical, for the other operations.

With ASDD, arbitrary (randomly selected) records cannot be found without possibly extensive scanning of the data structure. For example, consider a typical business file of 100,000 records and sequential access time (conservatively, we will use only average rotational delay) of 8.3 msec (as calculated in Chapter 4 for an IBM 3380 disk drive). We assume for simplicity here that each record access requires a physical file access (that is, no record blocking) and that there is a random application program record processing time between record reads. Access to an arbitrary record (by physical sequential scanning) would be from 8.3 msec (to access the first record) to 830 seconds ($13\frac{5}{6}$ minutes, to access the last physical record), with an average of 6 minutes and 55 seconds (access to middle record of file). These calculations also assume that each access will require a rotational delay and that seeks occur infrequently so that seek time can be ignored.

Insertion of a new element in an ASDD data structure requires that all subsequent elements be moved, which can be time-consuming. Modification is easy if we can simply write the new element values over the old, but sequential data storage media like magnetic tape require the whole set of data to be rewritten. Element deletion itself is simple if we only mark the deleted element as purged and do not immediately recover this now unused space. Depending on the amount of deletion activity, this practice of only marking deletions can lead to excessive wasted space and frequent data reorganizations (called "garbage collection"). Reorganization requires the costly act of rewriting the whole set of elements.

Pointer Sequential Connection Pointer sequential data direct (PSDD, or list) data structures greatly decrease the cost of performing insertion and deletion of new elements; but fetching random elements is usually more costly than with ASDD (since logically adjacent data are not usually physically adjacent). Figures 5-5a and b, respectively, illustrate how new product numbers can be added to and deleted from a PSDD data structure for the Pine Valley Furniture Product Master File. For insertion of product# 200, once space for the new product record is located (which can be *anywhere* in the file where there is an available record slot) and the proper insertion

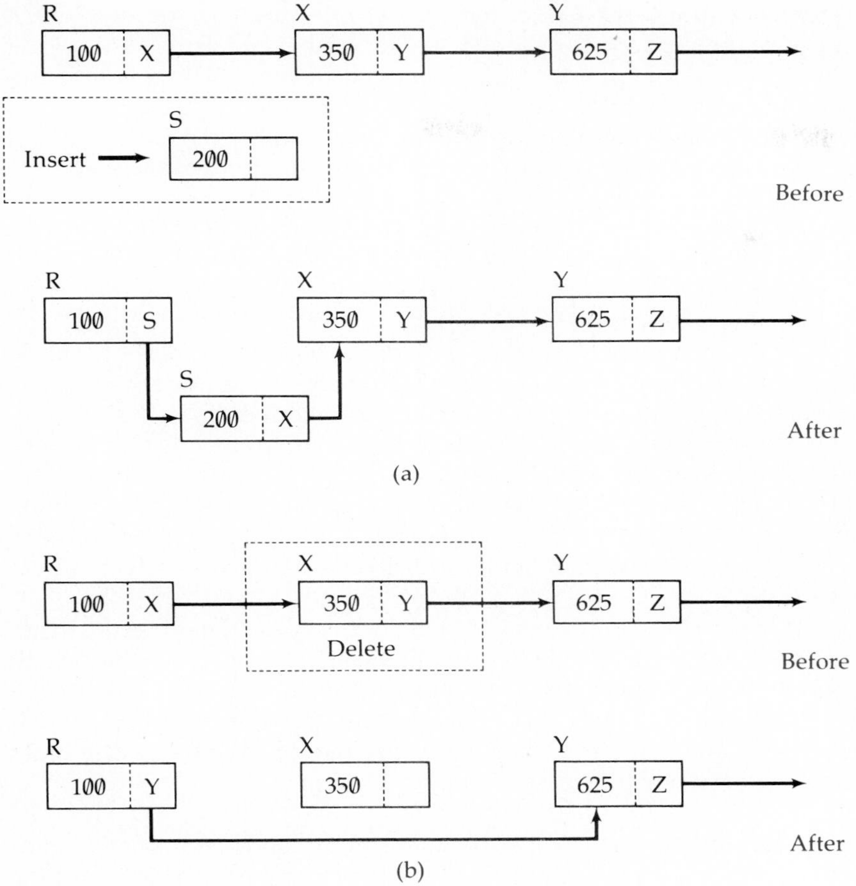

Figure 5-5
Maintaining a pointer sequential data structure:
(a) insertion
(b) deletion

position in the structure is identified (this may involve a scan from the beginning to the proper position, which can be a longer scan than for ASDD), only two pointers need to be changed: the pointer in the predecessor record of product# 200 (100 at location R) and the pointer in the product# 200 record itself (set to location of the successor of 100 prior to the insertion). The remainder of the data structure is independent of this change. This can be viewed as adding a new link to a chain. In a later section ("Linear Interrecord Data Structures"), we will present pseudocode for insertion (and deletion) procedures of several pointer sequential data structures. At this point, concentrate on understanding what has to be done to maintain pointer sequential connections, not *how* (in computer programming terms) to perform such maintenance.

Deletion of an element from a PSDD data structure is even simpler and can be viewed as welding two links of a chain together. In Figure 5-5b, product# 350 at location X is to be deleted. The successor of the element being deleted (product# 625 at location Y) is to become the new direct successor of the predecessor element to the one being deleted (100 at location R). Only the one pointer value has to be changed. The pointer associated with product# 350 does not have to be changed. Special provisions are often necessary when deleting from (or inserting into) an empty pointer sequential data structure. In a later section we will address this issue.

It should be explicitly noted that pointer sequential connection requires "overhead" space beyond meaningful data. This overhead space may seem small, but practice has shown that in total, for all uses of pointers in a data base (in key indexes, record chains, synonym chains, and so on), 100% overhead is not uncommon!

Retrieval of a random record in a pure PSDD data structure is very likely more time-consuming than in an ASDD structure. The same arbitrary record will be in the same relative sequential position in each set. The greater time for PSDD is due to the fact that each movement from node (e.g., record to next record in sequence) will be at least as far physically as the equivalent step for ASDD. With ASDD, this move is to an adjacent physical location of often blocked data (so a physical access is not needed for each record); with PSDD, the move could require the disk head to move in order to access each record.

In summary, PSDD performs very well for the operations of record insertion, record modification, and record deletion if the time to reach the desired position in the list is reasonable (certainly true for short lists), can be acceptable for operations of next record access and file reorganization, and is worse than sequential for reading the entire file. PSDD, like ASDD, does not fetch an arbitrary record very well on average.

Indirect Data Placement Besides connection methods (AS and PS), data structures are also characterized by the relative placement of data and the connection mechanism. Either indirect or direct placement and access to the actual data can be employed.

Indirect placement (see Figures 5-4c and d) usually makes scanning a data structure more efficient (than with data direct), since the connection nodes are often smaller than the actual data being managed and hence can be scanned more quickly and possibly kept in main computer memory for long periods of time.

Consider again the Pine Valley Furniture Product Master File. Each product record may be as much as 300 characters long, which means that only one record will fit in one 300-character data block. If a pointer and a product number are each only 4 characters long, then 37 pointer and key nodes will fit per block in the case of address sequential data indirect (ASDI, or inverted file) implementation. If, as before, we assume 100,000 records in this file, then the average time to scan the pointers will be $1/37$ of what it was when we calculated this earlier, or 11.2 seconds. One more access would be required to retrieve the data (at a cost of an additional random record access time of roughly 25 msec). Because the pointer nodes are so compact compared to the actual data records, many of these pointers can be kept in computer main memory while the file is being used. This means that frequently a physical read of secondary memory to retrieve pointers will not have to be made. Finally, because all the connections are stored in these compact blocks, insertions and deletions are more efficient than with the data direct (DD) counterparts in Figure 5-4.

PSDI (list inverted) provides the greatest flexibility of reorganization. The pointer connections in the index permit record insertions and deletions to occur with minimal movement of index data, which is desirable for very large indexes (which are themselves "files").

The four alternatives of ASDD (sequential), PSDD (chain), ASDI (inverted), and PSDI (list inverted) are all extreme points and "pure" situations. Hybrids, or combinations, frequently occur in one structure. A reexamination of Figure 4-18 on the ISAM structure will demonstrate how ISAM uses address sequential connection within primary data tracks, pointer sequential connection to handle overflows, and data indirect connections via use of multiple indexes. The next section shows how these basic building blocks can be used to arrange the fields of a physical record. Subsequent sections will then address basic data structures for organizing groups of related records.

INTRARECORD DATA STRUCTURES

At the conceptual and external levels of the ANSI/SPARC model (see Figure 5-1), each (logical) record is viewed as one address sequential data direct (ASDD) structure. This is quite adequate, since functional content is what is being designed or understood at these levels. At the internal level, however, efficiency issues of access speed, update time, and storage space become important. This is why many data management technologies choose to compress or split records into forms that are not simple ASDD. The common phenomena of insignificant leading decimal digits, trailing blanks in alphanumeric strings, and missing data can be handled in special ways to make data processing more efficient. Often, one logical record can be broken into several physical records to improve processing that only requires segments of the logical record.

The data structures used to connect fields within a single record are called **intrarecord (data) structures**. Five frequently used intrarecord structures are discussed in the following section, followed by a section on how and why a record may be broken into several parts, even with purposeful duplication of data, to achieve improved data base performance. Later, in Chapter 9, we will illustrate how judicious choice of an intrarecord structure relates to physical data base record design.

Managing Record Space

The five frequently used intrarecord structures are illustrated for the Pine Valley Furniture Product Master File in Figure 5-6. These structures are called positional, relational, indexed, labeled, and fixed-with-overflow (Maxwell and Severance 1973).

Positional Storage The **positional** structure (see Figure 5-6a) has every data item in a fixed, relative location within a record. Each data item has a fixed length, since a fixed amount of space is preestablished for each data item. Each data item is also easily accessed, since it is in a predetermined position. And each data item is allocated space for its longest possible value. This means that wasted space can occur, and will occur frequently for fields with highly variable length (such as narrative descriptions). To counter this, data base designers often force narrative fields to be abbreviated or coded to fit into a reasonably small maximum length.

Space for a new positional record is easily allocated since each is of fixed length. A contiguous pool of record slots will allow deleted record space to be easily recovered because all new records will fit *exactly* into unused space. This process of allocating and deallocating space to records as they are inserted and deleted is called **space management**. The positional structure is by far the most frequently found, owing to its simplicity of field access and ease of space management. Positional storage is a straightforward application of the ASDD basic data structure.

Relational Storage The **relational** structure (see Figure 5-6b) uses a special symbol, called a **delimiter**, to indicate the end of each field. Each field is of variable length, depending on the number of significant alphanumeric characters that exist. Even the maximum allowable length can be changed without requiring reloading of data. Missing fields, such as FINISH and PRICE for product# 1795, are indicated by adjacent delimiters. The relative sequence of data is, however, fixed. Since the sequence is fixed, data items that almost always have a value and for which the length is always the same (e.g., a coded field) can be more efficiently included in the record without a trailing delimiter. For example, the delimiter after the ROOM code in Figure 5-6b is not needed if *this data item* is handled as fixed length.

The total record length is usually variable, as shown in Figure 5-6b; however, this need not be the case (here or in Figures 5-6c or 5-6d as well). If a fixed length for a record can be determined such that it is not possible (or even highly unlikely) that the actual total variable record length (sum of all variable- and fixed-length data) would exceed this value, then fixed-length records are possible. This greatly facilitates space management, since space is easily reused.

A problem with variable-length structures is that space for a small record that is deleted can go unused for a long period until another small record is created (unless the file is reorganized). This effect of blocks of used and unused storage cells is called the **checkerboard effect**. Further, records that

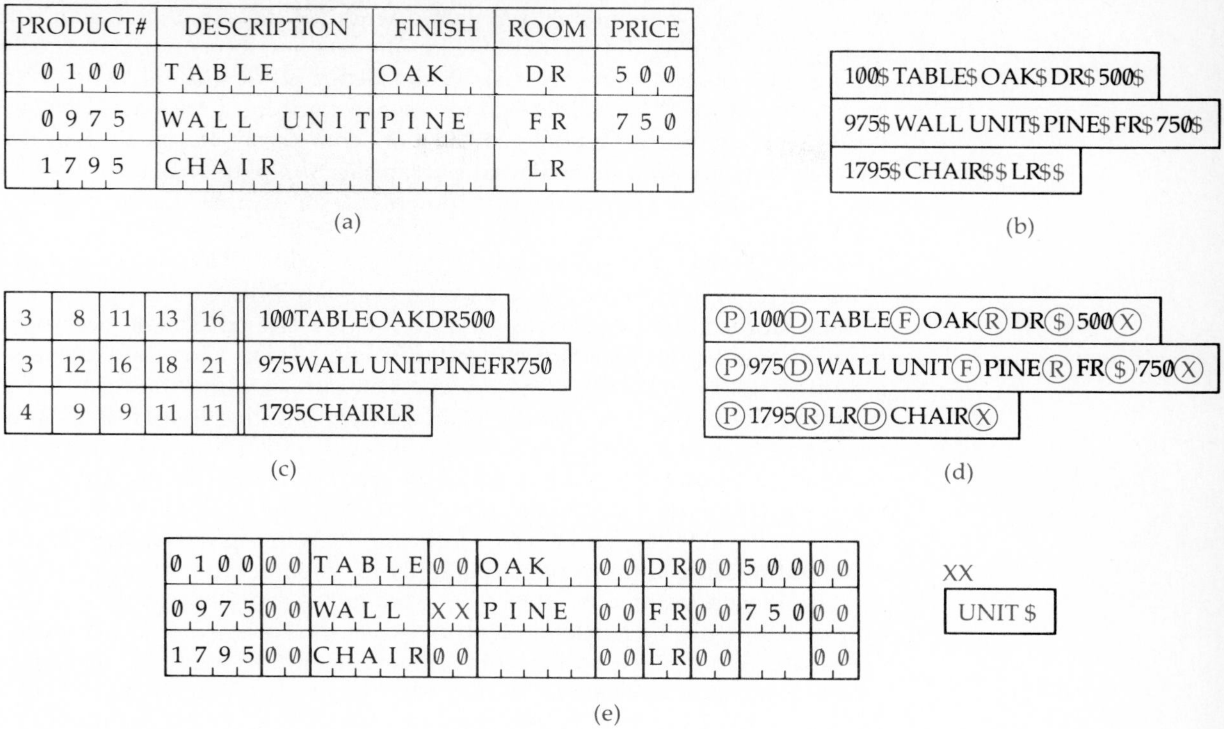
PRODUCT#
DESCRIPTION
FINISH
ROOM
PRICE
0100
TABLE
OAK
DR
500
0975
WALL UNIT
PINE
FR
750
1795
CHAIR
LR
(a)
100$ TABLE$ OAK$ DR$ 500$
975$ WALL UNIT$ PINE$ FR$ 750$
1795$ CHAIR$$ LR$$
(b)
3 8 11 13 16
100TABLEOAKDR500
3 12 16 18 21
975WALL UNITPINEFR750
4 9 9 11 11
1795CHAIRLR
(c)
Ⓟ100Ⓓ TABLEⒻOAKⓇDR$500Ⓧ
Ⓟ975ⒹWALL UNITⒻPINEⓇFR$750Ⓧ
Ⓟ1795ⓇLRⒹCHAIRⓍ
(d)
0100 00 TABLE 00 OAK 00 DR 00 500 00
0975 00 WALL XX PINE 00 FR 00 750 00
1795 00 CHAIR 00 00 LR 00 00
XX
UNIT $
(e)

Figure 5-6
Intrarecord structures (Pine Valley Furniture):
(a) positional
(b) relational
(c) indexed
(d) labeled
(e) fixed-with-overflow

shorten in length can create small, wasted spaces that can remain wasted for long periods owing to the small probability of extremely short records; and records must be removed to a larger space and a "hole" created if the record length expands.

Accessing data within a relational record requires scanning the record and counting delimiters. For example, to retrieve the FINISH of product# 0975 would actually require scanning 14 characters until encountering the second delimiter to find the beginning of PINE. Further scanning is necessary to discover the complete FINISH value (scan until next delimiter). This process can be expedited by using a combination of fixed- and variable-length data and by coding data into fixed lengths whenever possible. Scanning time can also be improved if the delimiter includes the length of the subsequent data item. Then the search routine can skip over unwanted fields.

An additional (potential) penalty with the relational intrarecord structure is the extra space required for delimiters. This space must be traded-off with the possible savings in space from useless characters that are eliminated. If the values of all data items are permitted to have only a typical alphanumeric range, then the delimiter can be eliminated. In this case, one can simply add (or subtract) a constant from the value of the last digit/character of each field, thus taking the representation of the character out of the acceptable range (e.g., 128 would work for the ASCII character set) and, hence, flagging the end of the field. The relational structure is normally used in situations with highly variable data lengths but with relatively fixed length once a value is entered and in cases of significant missing data. The topic of managing missing data will be more completely discussed in Chapter 9. Relational storage is essentially an application of the ASDD basic data structure in which each element is (potentially) of variable length.

Indexed Storage The **indexed** structure (see Figure 5-6c) records the end of each data item (relative character pointer) in an index or directory that is usually stored at the beginning of each record. The advantage here over the relational structure is that this index can be used as a lookup table, and a desired field can be directly retrieved without scanning the record. For example, the index for product# 0975 implies that the FINISH (field 3) of this product is in positions 13–16 (that is, that it starts one position after the end of field 2 and continues until the end of field 3). Missing data are indicated by adjacent index pointers having the same value (see the index for product# 1795 in Figure 5-6c). Data can be missing for numerous reasons, but missing values occur frequently in recently entered records.

An indexed intrarecord structure exhibits the same record space management issues of the relational structure when records are of variable length. The space required for each record, in comparison to relational, depends on the evaluation of delimiter and pointer space. The space required for a delimiter, usually 1 byte, is also sufficient to store any of 256 relative character pointer values. If the record length exceeds 256 bytes, the space for a record index entry will be greater than the overhead space for a delimiter in the relational structure. This evaluation notwithstanding, the indexed structure is used most frequently for long, variable-length records to save scanning costs. Indexed storage is an application of the ASDI basic data structure since the index elements are stored in an address sequential fashion and connect the actual data via pointers.

Labeled Storage The **labeled** structure (see Figure 5-6d) uses unique, short identification codes preceding each data item. These codes, or labels, like delimiters, must not be a legitimate character value in any field. Unlike delimiters, a *different* code is used to label the start of each field.

Labels provide three distinct advantages. First, data item values can be written in any order (e.g., values for previously missing values are simply added to the end of the record). Second, multiple occurrences of data items are easily supported. And third, no space (even for delimiters) is required when data are missing. Disadvantages are that records must be scanned (as with relational) to find individual fields, and label length may be greater than delimiter length if there are many fields in a record. As with delimiters, labels can be augmented with data item length to improve time for scanning through the fields of a record. The labeled structure is most frequently considered for use in those situations where many missing values occur.

Labeled storage is a variation on the basic ASDD data structure and, at a structural level, is very similar to relational storage (although the content of the records in labeled and relational are different).

Fixed-with-Overflow Storage Finally, the **fixed-with-overflow** structure (see Figure 5-6e) combines the concept of fixed-length record with variable-length data. Each data item is allocated a fixed length that is chosen to balance wasted space with frequency of overflow. If the actual data length is no greater than the space allocated, a zero pointer value (called **null**) signifies no overflow on that field. If the actual data are longer than reserved field space (as in the case of WALL UNIT in Figure 5-6e), then the pointer indicates the position of the overflow characters and a delimiter shows the end of the overflow.

With the fixed-with-overflow structure, the start of each data item is known exactly, so data are as easily accessed as in positional and indexed structures. Space requirements are reduced compared to positional structure *if* pointer space is less than the space eliminated (which is *not* the case in Figures 5-6a and 5-6e). Primary data space is easy to manage and reuse since these records are of fixed length. This structure is slightly more complex because of the need to access the separate overflow area, but it combines several advantages of the other structures. Fixed-with-overflow is a hybrid of the ASDD and PSDD basic data structures since most data is connected in physical sequence but overflows are connected via pointers.

Data Item Partitioning and Clustering

What does the phrase "Don't put all your eggs in one basket" mean? It may have been motivated by several factors. First, if all the eggs are in one basket and the basket is lost, stolen, or damaged, then all the eggs can become unusable. That is, we want to protect and secure the investment in eggs. If we divide the eggs into several baskets and one basket is damaged, we still have many useful eggs. Second, since sometimes we want to use large eggs, other times small eggs, sometimes brown eggs, and other times white eggs, all the eggs in one basket would force us to sort through all our eggs each time we wanted to use only a subset. That is, our usage of eggs is selective and we can more quickly find the eggs we want if we divide our supply into separate, categorized baskets.

This egg analogy has direct relevance to intrarecord data structures. By putting data into more usage-oriented physical files, we can improve the performance of a data base and better safeguard the valuable data resource.

The process of dividing a logical record into distinct, noncontiguous physical parts is called **data item clustering** (we are actually clustering together into one physical record data that have some common data processing usage). If these different physical parts are not allowed to have common data items

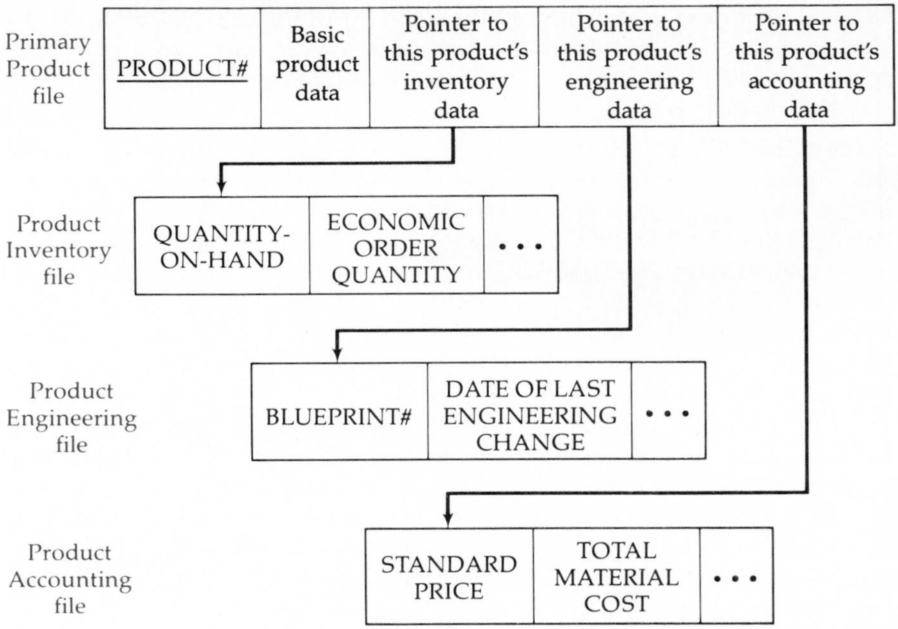

Figure 5-7
Example of data item partitioning (Pine Valley Furniture)

(data redundancy), then this special case is called **data item partitioning.** [See Hoffer and Severance (1975) and Schkolnick (1977) for more detail.]

Figure 5-7 shows one way the total logical PRODUCT record for Pine Valley Furniture could be partitioned into application-oriented segments and separate files. The conceptual PRODUCT record would still be viewed as one comprehensive record. Many external views would conceive of the PRODUCT record as all or even only a subset of the data elements in just one of the partitions. Other external views would see one logical record that was composed of data elements from multiple partitions. The point is that it is only at the internal level that the distinction between partitions needs to be managed. In Chapter 6, we will discuss other human factor reasons why it may be best to break one logical record into clusters. The choice to partition or cluster is made by the data base designer during development of the internal data model from the conceptual data model and information on data usage by application programs.

In Figure 5-7, pointers are used to connect the primary record segment to the other segments. The primary segment contains basic data about a product that are used in many applications. When additional data are required (e.g., on-hand inventory balance or order quantity for inventory control applications), then the appropriate secondary segments are accessed via the pointers from the primary segment or physical record. Alternatives to the structure shown in Figure 5-7 allow direct access into each physical partition via hashing, an ISAM index, or some other file organization on *each* physical file.

LINEAR INTERRECORD DATA STRUCTURES

We present in this section a detailed account of procedures for processing data structures. An understanding of how to process a data structure is important because, with some data base management systems (especially network systems, described in Chapters 6 and 13), we often use procedural language programs written in COBOL. These programs initiate some of the detailed movement from one data record to another. In addition, the more a programmer or data base designer knows about how a DBMS works (e.g., how it inserts new records into a data base), the better prepared these applications people are for (1) selecting data management technologies appropriate for the application at hand, (2) handling errors during program execution, and (3) tuning the data base structures for satisfactory operational efficiency of data base processing.

Interrecord data structures are used to connect different, related records in the same or separate files. Such structures can be used to represent logical orderings of records within the same file (e.g., Product Master Records in Product# numerical order or in Finish alphabetic sequence). These structures can also be used to group together records that have a common characteristic (e.g., all the Product Master Records with a missing price). In addition, these structures can be used to link related records of different types (e.g., a Product Master Record with all the Order records that indicate a customer order for the same product).

A **linear interrecord structure** is one for which there is only one NEXT data element emanating from each element in a given data structure. In some cases, however, there may be *several* linear data structures for the same set of data elements. One example of this, called multilist, is covered later in this section.

Basic Linear Data Structures

Three basic linear data structures are presented here: stacks, queues, and sorted lists/files. Each can be implemented using address sequential or pointer sequential connections. When pointer sequential connections are used, these structures are collectively called linked lists, or more descriptively, chains. Chained, or pointer sequential, versions of these structures will be used for all the illustrations.

Stacks One basic structure is a stack. A **stack** has the property that all insertions (addition of new records) and deletions (removal of no longer needed records) are made at the same end of the data structure. Stacks exhibit a last-in-first-out (LIFO) property. A common example of a stack is a vertical column of plates in a cafeteria line that are in a push-down, pop-up rack. In business data processing, stacklike structures are useful in maintaining a set of unprioritized or unsorted records. For example, Figure 5-8

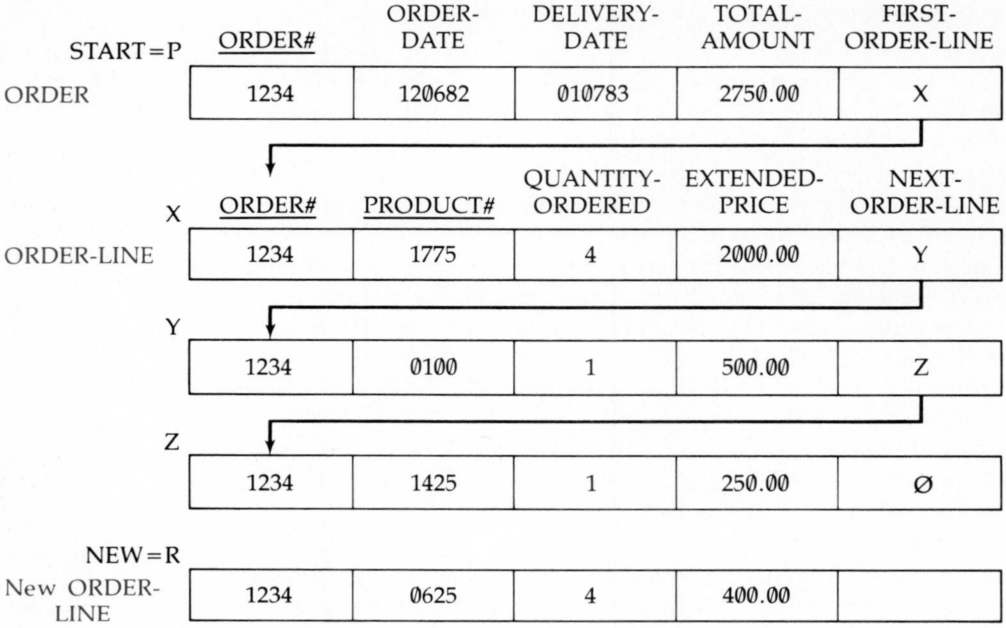
START=P
ORDER
ORDER#
ORDER-DATE
DELIVERY-DATE
TOTAL-AMOUNT
FIRST-ORDER-LINE
1234
120682
010783
2750.00
X
X
ORDER-LINE
ORDER#
PRODUCT#
QUANTITY-ORDERED
EXTENDED-PRICE
NEXT-ORDER-LINE
1234
1775
4
2000.00
Y
Y
1234
0100
1
500.00
Z
Z
1234
1425
1
250.00
Ø
NEW=R
New ORDER-LINE
1234
0625
4
400.00

(a)

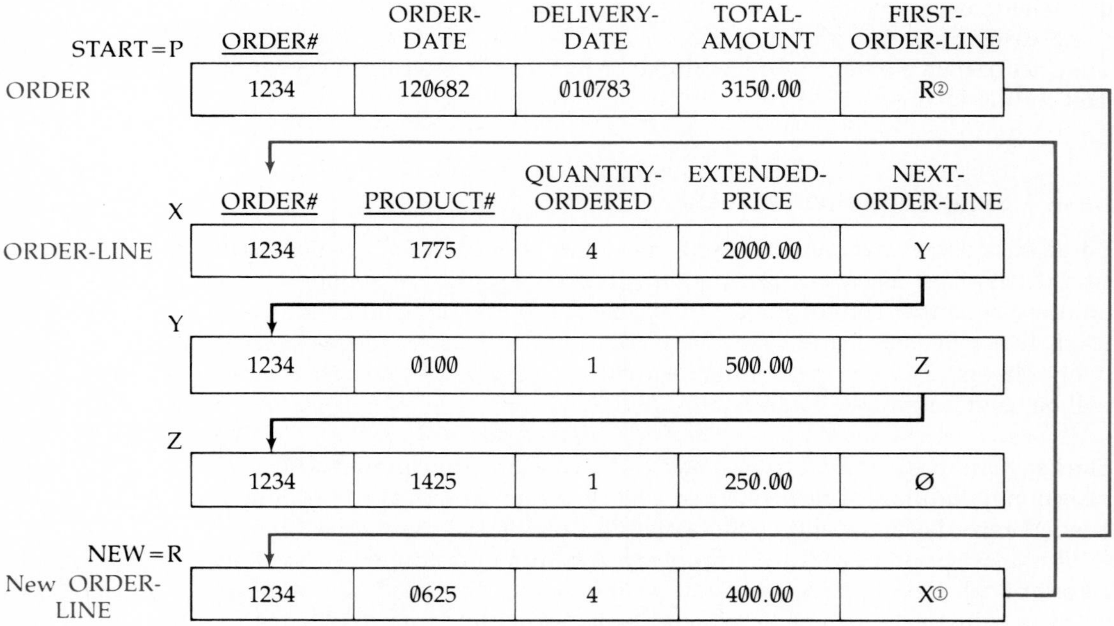
START=P
ORDER
ORDER#
ORDER-DATE
DELIVERY-DATE
TOTAL-AMOUNT
FIRST-ORDER-LINE
1234
120682
010783
3150.00
R②
X
ORDER-LINE
ORDER#
PRODUCT#
QUANTITY-ORDERED
EXTENDED-PRICE
NEXT-ORDER-LINE
1234
1775
4
2000.00
Y
Y
1234
0100
1
500.00
Z
Z
1234
1425
1
250.00
Ø
NEW=R
New ORDER-LINE
1234
0625
4
400.00
X①

(b)

illustrates a pointer sequential or chained stack structure for ORDER-LINE records, all of which are related to a common ORDER record (this example is based on Figure 2-10, which is a data structure diagram for Pine Valley Furniture).

Figure 5-8 (opposite) Example of a stack: (a) before new ORDER-LINE inserted (b) after new ORDER-LINE inserted (Circled numbers next to pointers indicate the step number in the associated maintenance procedure that changes that pointer value.)

In this example, the ORDER record acts as the head-of-chain or start node of the data structure. The value of the FIRST-ORDER-LINE field is a pointer to the first ORDER-LINE record. Here and elsewhere in this chapter we will assume that all pointer fields contain relative record numbers into the file to which they apply. The sequence of ORDER-LINE records is immaterial; consequently, new ORDER-LINE records can most efficiently be inserted at the "top" of the stack. ORDER-LINE records are deleted in LIFO fashion as they are filled for shipment.

The value of Ø in the ORDER-LINE record for PRODUCT# 1425 in Figure 5-8a is called a **null pointer** and signifies the end of the data structure (that is, there are no more ORDER-LINE records for ORDER# 1234). The general notions of chain insertion were illustrated in Figure 5-5a. For the specific data of Figure 5-8a, to insert the new ORDER-LINE record for PRODUCT# 0625, we would simply put the value of X (relative record number pointer) into NEXT-ORDER-LINE for this new record and change FIRST-ORDER-LINE to R. This is shown in Figure 5-8b.

Since insertion and deletion occur at the top of the stack, no scanning or traversing through the stack is necessary for these operations. This makes a stack a very efficient linear data structure. Insertion of a new record can be written in the form of a general insertion procedure or algorithm. If we let NEW be a variable that contains the relative record number of the ORDER-LINE record to be inserted and let START be a variable that contains the relative record number of the ORDER record for this new ORDER-LINE (we will not be concerned with how values for these pointers are discovered), then the following pseudocode procedure accomplishes the insertion:

① NEXT-ORDER-LINE(NEW) ← FIRST-ORDER-LINE(START)
② FIRST-ORDER-LINE(START) ← NEW

In Figure 5-8b the circled numbers next to pointer values indicate which step in this procedure changes which pointer value. This notation will frequently be used in figures in this chapter.

In this procedure (and others to follow), the symbol ← means that the value of the field to the left of the symbol is replaced by the value of the field to the right of the symbol. Field names followed by a variable in parentheses should be read much like an array subscript in many programming languages. For example, NEXT-ORDER-LINE(NEW) should be read as "the value of field NEXT-ORDER-LINE stored in the NEW-th relative record in the ORDER-LINE file," and FIRST-ORDER-LINE(START) should be read as "the value of field FIRST-ORDER-LINE stored in the START-th relative record in the ORDER file."

The reader should note that this procedure will work correctly when we insert the first ORDER-LINE instance for a given ORDER. In this special

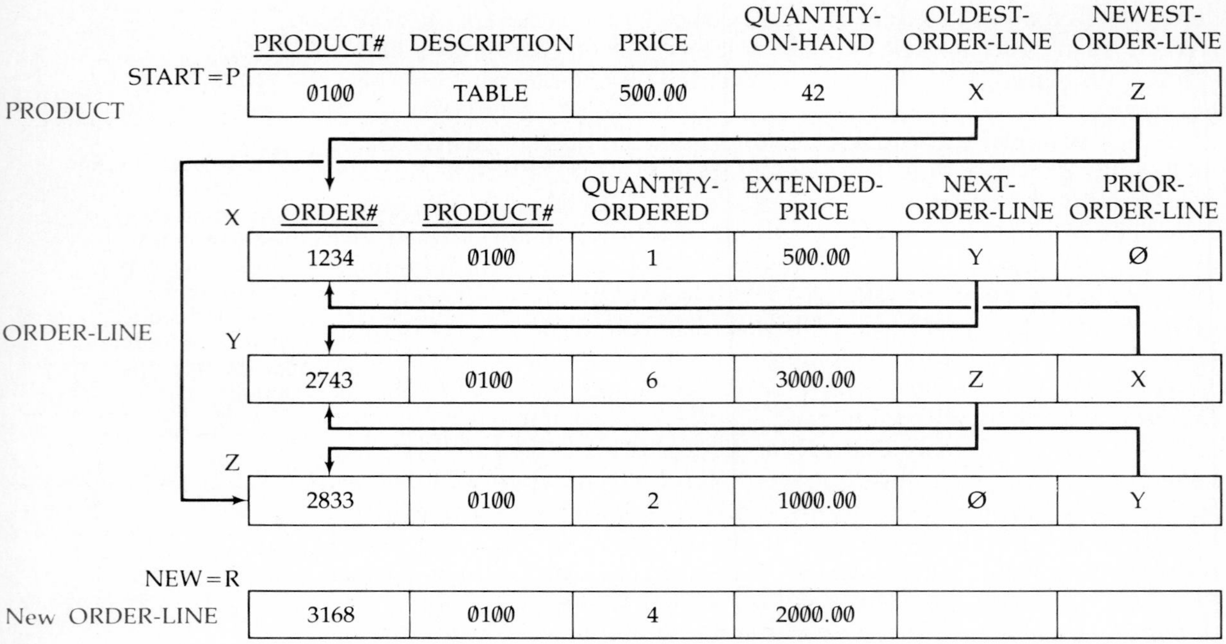
PRODUCT# DESCRIPTION PRICE QUANTITY-ON-HAND OLDEST-ORDER-LINE NEWEST-ORDER-LINE
START=P
PRODUCT
0100 TABLE 500.00 42 X Z
ORDER# PRODUCT# QUANTITY-ORDERED EXTENDED-PRICE NEXT-ORDER-LINE PRIOR-ORDER-LINE
X
1234 0100 1 500.00 Y Ø
ORDER-LINE
Y
2743 0100 6 3000.00 Z X
Z
2833 0100 2 1000.00 Ø Y
NEW=R
New ORDER-LINE
3168 0100 4 2000.00

(a)

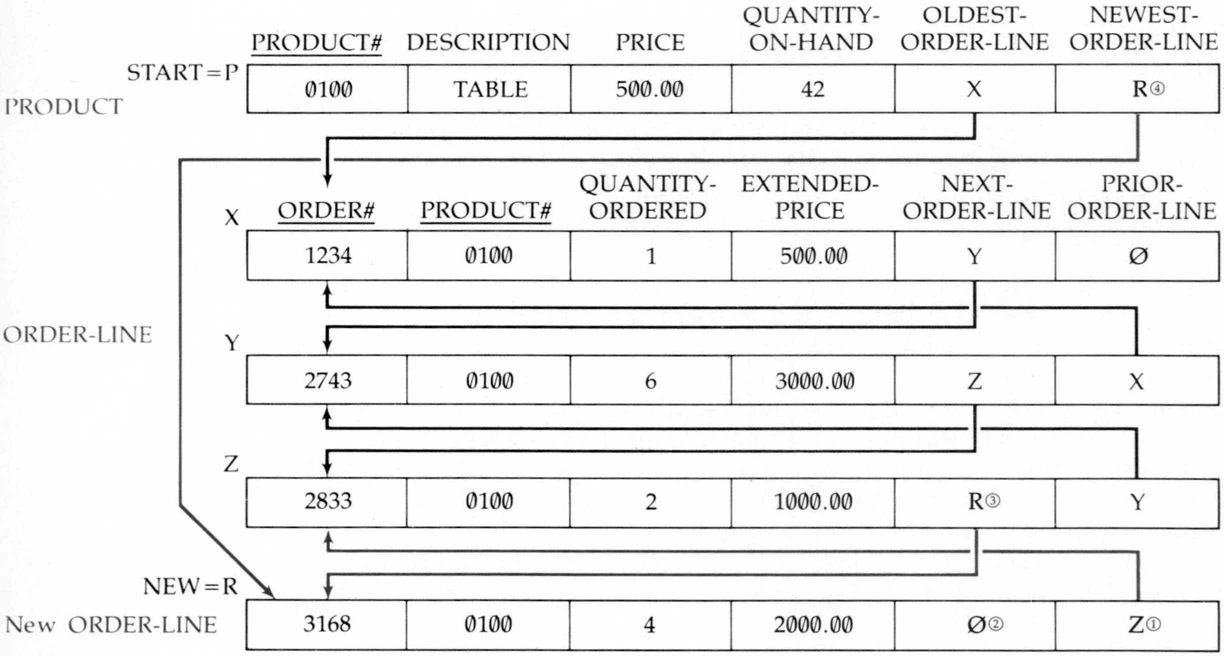
PRODUCT# DESCRIPTION PRICE QUANTITY-ON-HAND OLDEST-ORDER-LINE NEWEST-ORDER-LINE
START=P
PRODUCT
0100 TABLE 500.00 42 X R④
ORDER# PRODUCT# QUANTITY-ORDERED EXTENDED-PRICE NEXT-ORDER-LINE PRIOR-ORDER-LINE
X
1234 0100 1 500.00 Y Ø
ORDER-LINE
Y
2743 0100 6 3000.00 Z X
Z
2833 0100 2 1000.00 R③ Y
NEW=R
New ORDER-LINE
3168 0100 4 2000.00 Ø② Z①

(b)

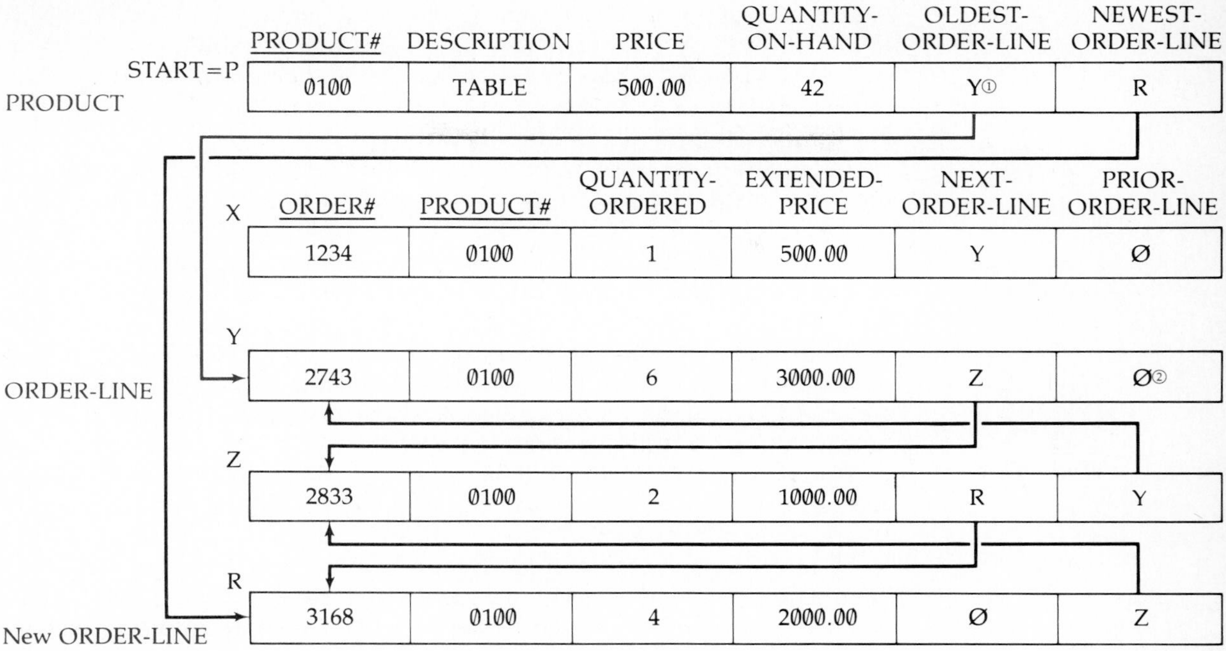

(c)

Figure 5-9 (pp. 154–155) Example of a queue with bidirectional pointers:
(a) before new ORDER-LINE insertion or deletion of OLDEST-ORDER-LINE
(b) after new ORDER-LINE insertion
(c) after both new ORDER-LINE insertion and OLDEST-ORDER-LINE deletion
(Circled numbers next to pointers indicate the step number in the associated maintenance procedure that changes that pointer value.)

case, FIRST-ORDER-LINE(START) will be ø before the insertion and step 1 will properly result in a null pointer for NEXT-ORDER-LINE of the new record. In developing such procedures, the designer should take care to account for all special conditions (such as empty chains). The sequence of steps is important in this procedure (as it is in many data structure maintenance procedures). If step 2 were performed before step 1, for example, then step 1 would not work correctly since the wrong value for FIRST-ORDER-LINE(START) would be used in step 2.

Queues The second basic linear data structure presented here is a queue. A **queue** has the property that all insertions occur at one end and all deletions occur at the other end. A queue exhibits a first-in-first-out (FIFO) property. A common example of a queue is a check-out line at a grocery store. In business data processing, queuelike structures are often used to maintain lists of records in chronological order of insertion. For example, Figure 5-9 illustrates a pointer sequential, or chained, queue of ORDER-LINE records kept in order of arrival (and, hence, filling sequence) for a common PRODUCT record (this example is based on Figure 2-10).

This example also introduces the concept of a bidirectional chain or list structure (to make queue maintenance easier). A **bidirectional chain** has both "forward" and "backward" pointers emanating from each element of data (record in this case). The benefit of having both forward and backward (NEXT/PRIOR) pointers is that when processing a chain in one direction (forward), you do not have to remember or find the immediate predecessor (which often must be updated during insertions and deletions), since it is known directly from the pointer (backward).

In this example, the OLDEST-ORDER-LINE field in the PRODUCT record serves as the head-of-chain pointer for filling orders (deletions), since orders will be filled in first-come-first-served sequence. This NEXT-ORDER-LINE field in the ORDER-LINE record maintains the oldest to newest record order. The NEWEST-ORDER-LINE field serves as the head-of-chain pointer for entering new orders (insertions), since new orders have the lowest priority to be filled. The PRIOR-ORDER-LINE field in the ORDER-LINE record maintains the newest to oldest record sequence. It is assumed that records are inserted as orders are received so that order receipt sequence is the same as the insertion sequence.

Adding a new ORDER-LINE will affect only the NEWEST-ORDER-LINE end of the queue. Since only the end of the chain is involved, insertion is a very efficient operation.

To insert the new ORDER-LINE for ORDER# 3168 (a process similar to the method used with a stack), we put Z into PRIOR-ORDER-LINE for this new record, put ø into the NEXT-ORDER-LINE field of the new ORDER, put R into the NEXT-ORDER-LINE field of the previously newest relative record (Z), and change NEWEST-ORDER-LINE to R. This result is shown in Figure 5-9b. This process can be written into a general insertion procedure as follows (pointers changed by each step are annotated in Figure 5-9b by step number):

① PRIOR-ORDER-LINE(NEW) ← NEWEST-ORDER-LINE(START)
② NEXT-ORDER-LINE(NEW) ← ø
③ NEXT-ORDER-LINE(NEWEST-ORDER-LINE(START)) ← NEW
④ NEWEST-ORDER-LINE(START) ← NEW

This procedure works fine when there is at least one ORDER-LINE record for PRODUCT# 0100. The case of an "empty queue" can be handled by changing only step 3 to be conditionally applied when the queue is nonempty, replacing step 3 with

③ If NEWEST-ORDER-LINE(START) ≠ø then
NEXT-ORDER-LINE(NEWEST-ORDER-LINE(START)) ← NEW

You can verify that the other steps work properly with an empty queue. You can also investigate if the procedure will work properly if the sequence of steps is changed.

Deletion follows a simpler process in which two links are "welded" together. (The general notions of chain deletion were illustrated in Figure 5-5b.) In the example of Figure 5-9, deletion will occur when the oldest order on file for PRODUCT# 0100 can be filled. This will be accomplished in Figure 5-9b by changing OLDEST-ORDER-LINE to Y and indicating that the ORDER-LINE for ORDER# 2743 is now the oldest ORDER-LINE by changing its PRIOR-ORDER-LINE value to ø. The result of these changes is shown in Figure 5-9c. The process can be written into a general deletion procedure:

① OLDEST-ORDER-LINE(START) ←
NEXT-ORDER-LINE(OLDEST-ORDER-LINE(START))

② PRIOR-ORDER-LINE(OLDEST-ORDER-LINE(START)) ← ø

This deletion procedure works fine when deleting the last ORDER-LINE record of an order, so special logic is not required to handle this situation. In general, insertion and deletion (and retrieval) procedures have to be carefully written to consider extreme situations (especially empty chains). Finally, it should be noted that both stacks and queues perform quite efficiently regardless of data structure length (e.g., number of records on a chain). They do so because all activity occurs at the ends, which can be directly accessed from head-of-chain pointers. This efficiency independence from data structure length is not true for the next data structure.

Sorted Lists The last basic linear data structure to be introduced is the sorted list. A **sorted list** has the property that insertions and deletions may occur anywhere within the list; elements of data are maintained in logical order based on a key field value, and elements are inserted or deleted by specifying the key value involved. A common example of a sorted list is a telephone directory. In business data processing, sorted lists occur frequently. For example, Figure 5-10 illustrates a pointer sequential, or chained, sorted list (often referred to as "the" list data structure) of ORDER records related to a CUSTOMER record. The ORDER records are maintained in a single, unidirectional sorted order by DELIVERY-DATE, with the oldest ORDER on the "top" of the list (this example is based on Figure 2-10). Sorted lists are maintained to avoid resorting a set of data (records) each time the oldest, newest, or all in sequence is desired.

In this example, the FIRST-ORDER field serves as the head-of-chain pointer, and it points to the ORDER record for the given CUSTOMER that has the earliest DELIVERY-DATE. The process of inserting the new record for ORDER# 3318 is much more complex than that in prior linear data structures. The greater complexity (and, hence, more processing time) is due to the necessity to scan the chain to find the proper position in which to place the new record. Special logic is required if this place happens to be on either end of the chain or is in an empty chain. To guarantee that insertion (and later deletion) will always be in the interior of the chain, "dummy" first and last records are often included in the chain. This is shown in Figure 5-10b. Although these dummy records require additional space and must be skipped in scanning, the savings in insertion and deletion speed and ease are usually considered more advantageous.

Figure 5-10c shows the result of inserting the record with ORDER# 3318 into the sorted list of Figure 5-10b. The list is scanned starting from the

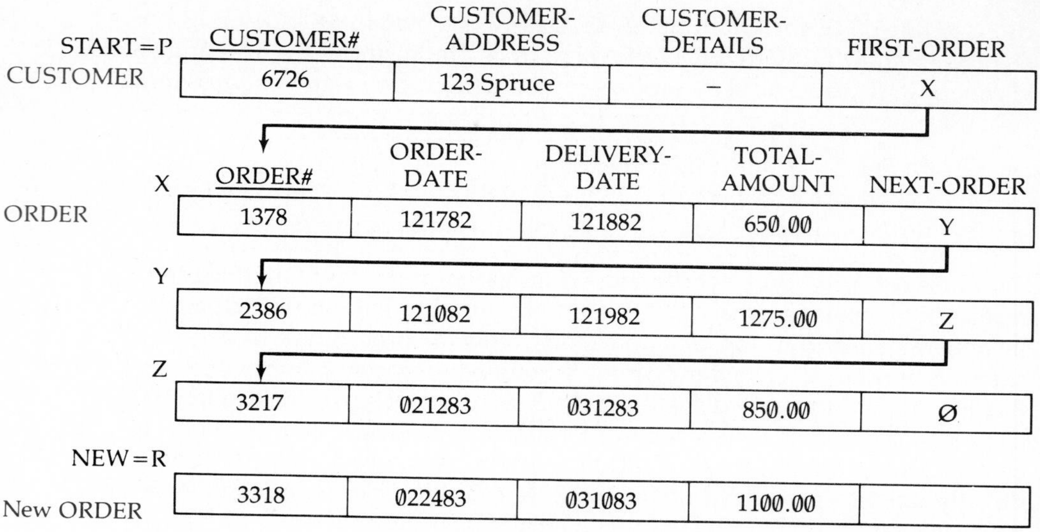
START=P
CUSTOMER
CUSTOMER#
CUSTOMER-ADDRESS
CUSTOMER-DETAILS
FIRST-ORDER
6726
123 Spruce
–
X
X
ORDER
ORDER#
ORDER-DATE
DELIVERY-DATE
TOTAL-AMOUNT
NEXT-ORDER
1378
121782
121882
650.00
Y
Y
2386
121082
121982
1275.00
Z
Z
3217
021283
031283
850.00
Ø
NEW=R
New ORDER
3318
022483
031083
1100.00

(a)

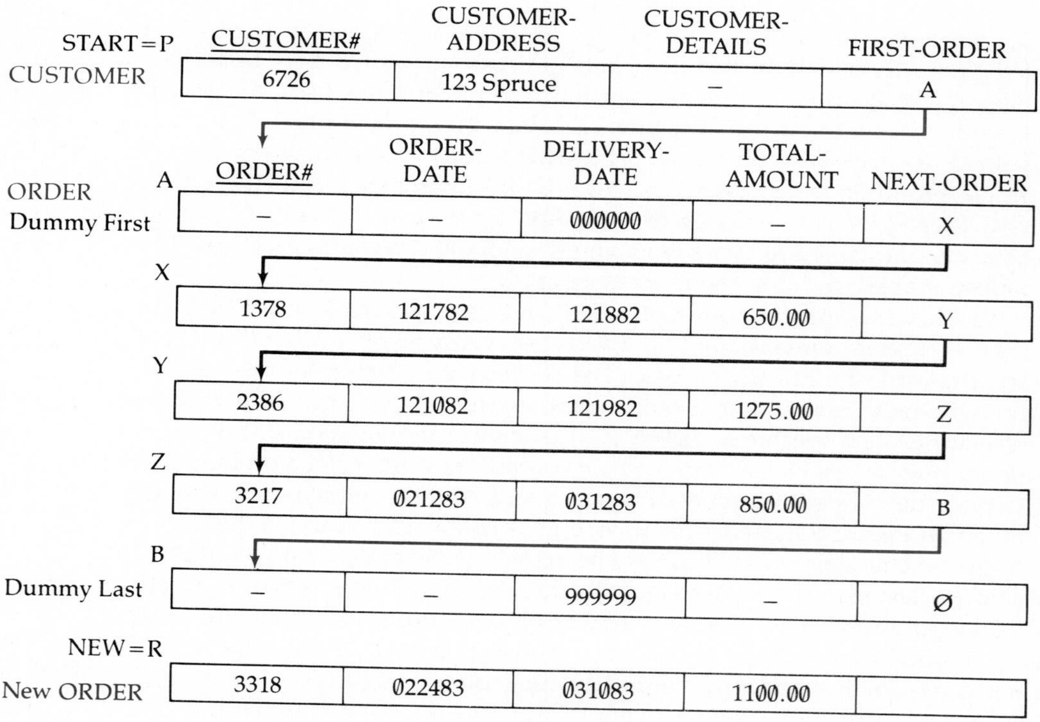
START=P
CUSTOMER
CUSTOMER#
CUSTOMER-ADDRESS
CUSTOMER-DETAILS
FIRST-ORDER
6726
123 Spruce
–
A
A
ORDER
Dummy First
ORDER#
ORDER-DATE
DELIVERY-DATE
TOTAL-AMOUNT
NEXT-ORDER
–
–
000000
–
X
X
1378
121782
121882
650.00
Y
Y
2386
121082
121982
1275.00
Z
Z
3217
021283
031283
850.00
B
B
Dummy Last
–
–
999999
–
Ø
NEW=R
New ORDER
3318
022483
031083
1100.00

(b)

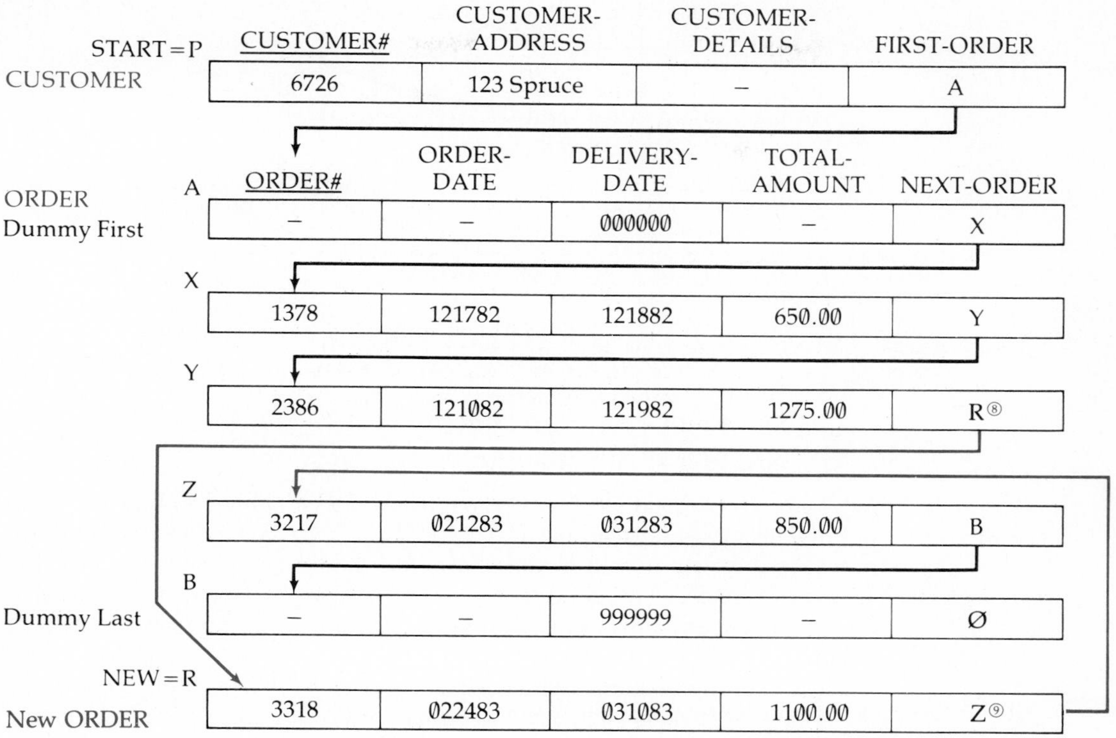

(c)

Figure 5-10 (pp. 158–159) Example of a sorted list:
(a) before new ORDER insertion and without dummy first and dummy last ORDERS
(b) before new ORDER insertion and with dummy first and dummy last ORDERS
(c) after new ORDER insertion
(Circled numbers next to pointers indicate the step number in the associated maintenance procedure that changes that pointer value.)

relative record number in FIRST-ORDER. If duplicate key values are not permitted, then the process must check at each "visit" of an ORDER record that the key there does not match the key for the new ORDER. This type of check is not required in the situation in Figure 5-10, since duplicate key values are allowed (the key is a secondary key).

Since duplicate keys are allowed, we must also decide where to insert a new duplicate: before existing records with same key value, after these duplicate records, or somewhere else. The position that requires the least scanning and, hence, the least time, is before all existing duplicates. If there are no business reasons to do otherwise, the correct position of the record with ORDER# 3318 is found when the first DELIVERY-DATE greater than or equal to 031083 is encountered (this is called the **stopping rule**); it occurs when the scan reaches the record with ORDER# 3217. This ORDER now becomes the successor of the record with ORDER# 3318, so the NEXT-ORDER pointer of the record with ORDER# 3318 is set to value Z. The tricky part is to remember the predecessor (without the aid of backward pointers).

In the following chained sorted list insertion procedure, position variables PRE and AFT are used to hold the values of the predecessor and successor, respectively, of the new ORDER record. Step 7 is included in brackets to indicate where a check for duplicate keys would appear if required. The insertion procedure is:

```
/*  Establish position variables beginning values */
①  PRE ← FIRST-ORDER(START)
②  AFT ← NEXT-ORDER(PRE)
/*  Skip/scan through chain until proper position is found */
③  DO WHILE DELIVERY-DATE(AFT) < DELIVERY-DATE(NEW)
     ④  PRE ← AFT
     ⑤  AFT ← NEXT-ORDER(AFT)
⑥  ENDO
⑦  [If DELIVERY-DATE(AFT) = DELIVERY-DATE(NEW)
       then indicate a Duplicate Error and terminate procedure]
/*  Weld in new chain element */
⑧  NEXT-ORDER(PRE) ← NEW
⑨  NEXT-ORDER(NEW) ← AFT
```

Step 3 says that if we have not yet found a DELIVERY-DATE in the chain that is greater than or equal to the DELIVERY-DATE of the new ORDER, then skip ahead one link in the chain and continue to test for the desired position to insert. The general structure of this procedure is indicated by the three comment lines. These three sections are common to most insertion routines.

Since dummy first and last records were used in this example, we avoided any special steps that might be necessary to handle the circumstances of inserting at the ends of a chain. In general, data structure maintenance routines must be designed to handle a variety of special as well as "normal" conditions. Actually, it is this handling of special conditions that makes writing the routines so complex and why using prewritten functions of a data base management system is so efficient of programmer time and costs. Some of the special conditions that typically need to be handled either by augmentations to the data structure (such as dummy records) or in maintenance routines include: (1) maintenance at the ends of a chain, (2) maintenance of an empty chain, (3) duplicate keys (insertion), (4) missing keys (deletion), (5) records out of sequence, (6) broken chains, (7) deletion of last entry in chain, and (8) insertion into a full structure (if length of chain is limited). Later we will see that a DBMS can properly handle these or provide descriptive error messages to the calling program to indicate the discovery of errors that do not permit processing by the DBMS.

Deletion from a chained sorted list is left as an exercise at the end of the chapter.

Other Linear Structures A variation on basic linear data structures is called a ring. A **ring** is a closed loop data structure in which the end of the chain (and the front, too, in the case of bidirectional chains) points to the head-of-chain element. A ring variation on Figure 5-10a is shown in Figure 5-11. Rings are useful in that they permit us to move to any other chain member from any given chain element. For example, if we had accessed the ORDER

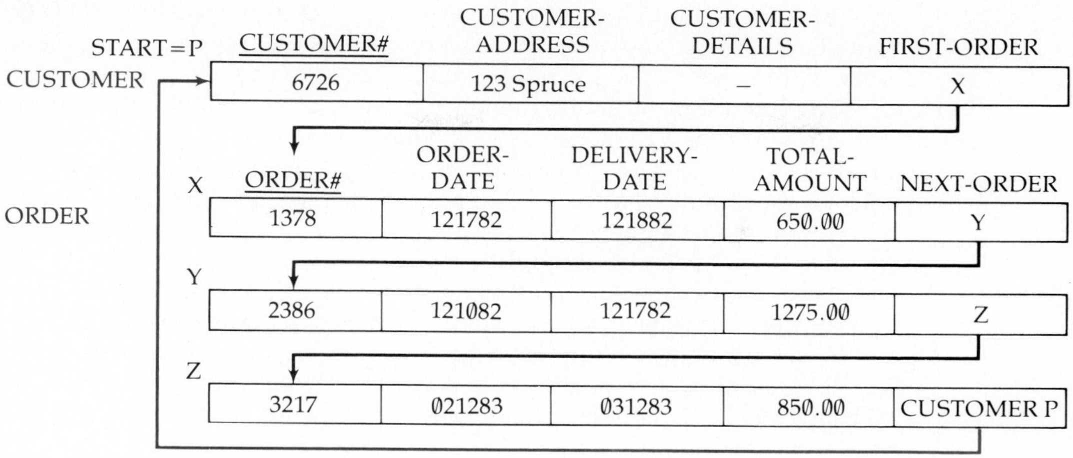

Figure 5-11
Ring data structure

record with ORDER# 2386 via, say, hashing on its primary key of ORDER#, then we could still find all the ORDERs for the customer of the ORDER record with ORDER# 2386. Note that with this ring, the NEXT-ORDER pointer in the last record of the chain must clearly indicate that it points to the CUSTOMER file, not the ORDER file.

As you might expect, many other variations on these basic linear data structures have been invented, and many of these are used in modern data management technologies [see Knuth (1973) for an excellent survey]. Some of these variations will be presented in Chapters 12 and 13. This section should provide the fundamentals necessary to cope with these other structures and to understand how to properly use DBMSs, especially in internal data base specification and procedural language programming.

Multilist Data Structure

An annoying characteristic of address sequential data structures is their inflexibility. Not only must related data follow one another in physical sequence (which causes a lot of work to maintain), but also only *one* sequence (sorted order or association) can be supported with these structures. A chained linear data structure, like those presented in the prior section, avoids the problem of maintaining physical sequential placement. But these basic structures are still limited to representing a *single* logical ordering.

Often in business data processing, and certainly in a data base environment, the same data will be associated in several groups, or several sorted sequences will be desired to support processing of shared data. Consider, for example, the same set of Customer Orders that need to be connected to their associated Customer record, maintained in order date sequence for auditing purposes, and that also need to be grouped together by delivery date for producing reports for the shipping dock. It would be desirable to be able to maintain all these associations without having to duplicate or triplicate the voluminous Order records (a goal of data management). The multilist data structure, among others to be presented later, is a means to achieve this goal.

A **multilist data structure** (better, but not usually, called multichain) is one for which more than one NEXT element of data may emanate from a given element. Thus, multiple pointers (multiple chains) are employed, one each for the different "paths" through the data. Each path links records with a common characteristic or in a different sequence. With multilist, it is possible to be "walking" through one association and in the middle decide to follow another. For example, while accessing the Order records for a given Customer (one chain), we could find all the Orders to be delivered on the same day of one of those Orders (another chain) so as to anticipate possible shipping delays due to a bottleneck (excess work load) on the shipping dock. A multilist data structure for this situation is depicted in Figure 5-12a.

Multilist is a basic building block for implementation of the CODASYL network data model presented in Chapter 13. As a preview of what we will see in that chapter, consider the data structure depicted in Figure 5-12b. In this example, ORDER-LINE records for the same ORDER are linked via one list in PRODUCT# sequence (FIRST-ORDER-LINE and NEXT-ORDER-LINE pointers), and ORDER-LINE records for the same PRODUCT are linked via another list in DUE-DATE sequence (FIRST-LINE-ITEM and NEXT-LINE-ITEM pointers). Thus, the same ORDER-LINE data can be shared by both product management and order processing applications.

Hazards of List Structures

The disadvantage of any list (chain) structure arises with long chains. Scanning a long chain can take an enormous amount of time, since each movement from, say, record to record, may require a disk cylinder change. With single lists, it is often possible to cluster the associated data together into the same cylinder, but with multiple lists, it is very difficult to place each element of data in relatively close proximity to each of its associated data. Long chains also cause a problem when we try to find one or a few records that fall into some category or range of key values. For example, we may want to know what orders to be shipped today were entered one week ago (because data entry errors have been discovered in other orders entered that same day and we wish to take precautions so as to correctly ship today). Answering this question could require scanning a long list of orders (in order date or delivery date sequence) and then checking the other qualification on each record accessed. The next data structure we are going to discuss is designed to handle this so-called multiple-key kind of query more efficiently than multilist.

Also, list data structures are vulnerable to being broken. If an abnormal operating system event occurs in the middle of a list maintenance routine, the list can be partially updated and all links may not be completed. The

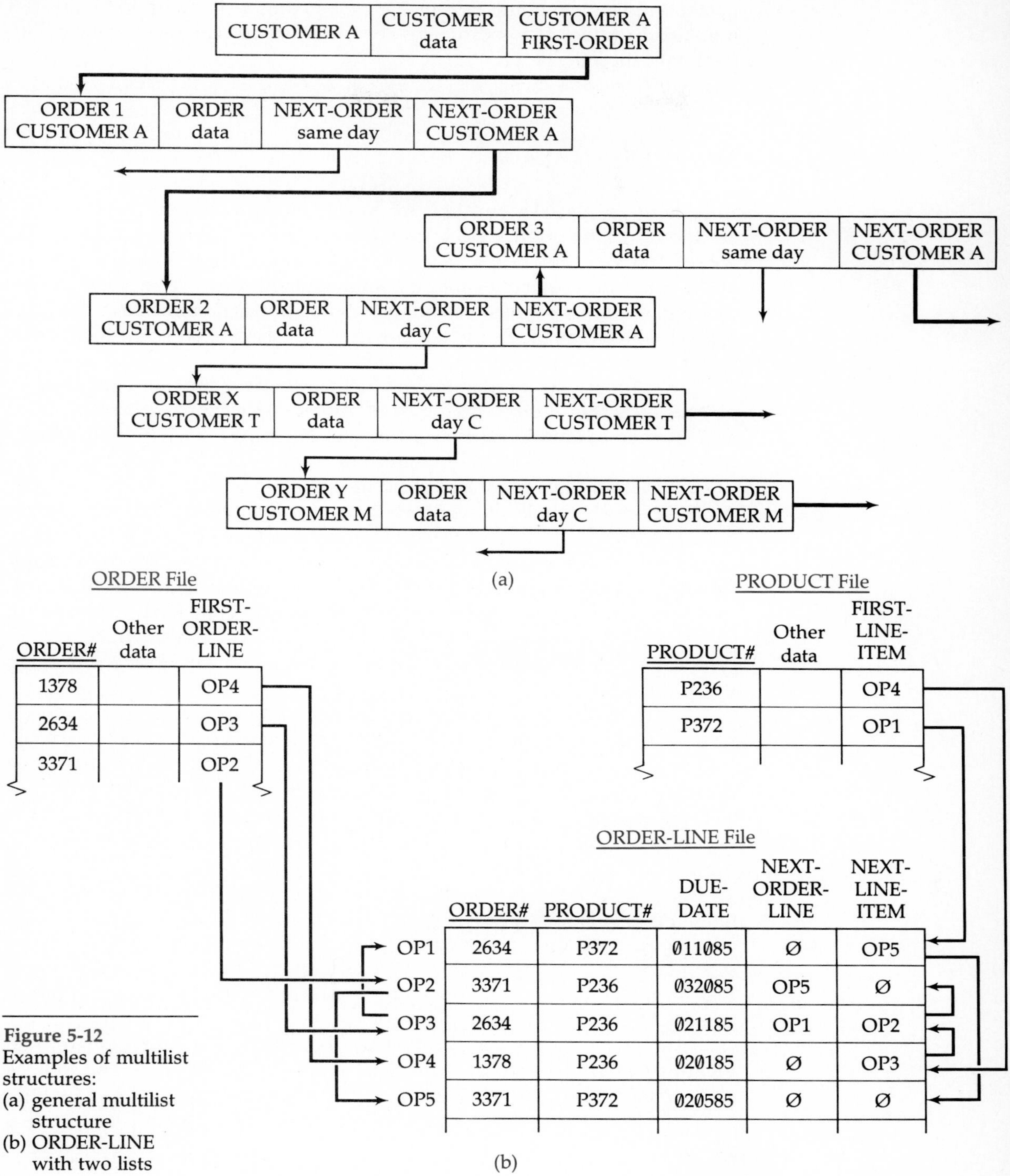

Figure 5-12
Examples of multilist structures:
(a) general multilist structure
(b) ORDER-LINE with two lists

use of bidirectional pointers, storing logical pointers in addition to physical ones, and utilities for finding and repairing broken chains can be used to deal with these hazards.

INVERTED LISTS

A student preparing a term paper for an economics course needs some additional information. She knows that economist Milton Friedman has written on the topic for which she needs information and that she has already found many relevant Friedman publications. From some recent reading, she knows that she needs additional publications related to certain terms that describe (identify, categorize, or are associated with) the kind of information now needed.

The student goes to the university library, where she finds two indexes of periodical literature. One index identifies publications by author name and the second identifies key word topical groupings. Each index identifies (or addresses) a publication by common pieces of data: the periodical name, the publication date, and the page numbers (if you find this analogy helpful, you will see the similarity of these data to a disk address!). The student quickly scans each index and writes down two lists of "addresses": those from the first index for Milton Friedman and those from the second index for the relevant topical key words. She then compares the two lists and finds that only four papers meet both search criteria. Finally, she walks (physically) through the library to retrieve the few relevant publications, having avoided very time-consuming browsing of many publications through the library stacks.

The student in this example has used inverted lists to significantly speed up a multiple-key search of the library. An **inverted list** is a table, list, index, or directory of data addresses that indicates all the data (records) that have a common property. The address sequential data indirect data structure covered earlier in this chapter is a convenient way to view this table. In the next section, we will see that data structures other than ASDI are usually used to manage an index in business applications.

Figure 5-13 views a possible inverted list structure for the PRODUCT file of Pine Valley Furniture (this figure is based on Figure 2-2). Indexes are created to speed processing, usually for qualified access questions that use secondary keys. Secondary keys were defined in Chapter 2 to be data items that normally do not uniquely identify a record, but identify a number of records that share the same property.

Although in Figure 2-2 DESCRIPTION, FINISH, and ROOM were all identified as secondary keys, indexes on only DESCRIPTION and ROOM were created in Figure 5-13. This is because the cost to maintain a FINISH index (which is incurred as new records are added, as old records are deleted,

Figure 5-13
Inverted list structure (Pine Valley Furniture)

PRODUCT# index (primary key)

PRODUCT#	Address
0100	1
0350	2
0625	3
0975	4
1000	5
1250	6
1425	7
1600	8
1775	9
2000	10

DESCRIPTION Index (secondary key)

DESCRIPTION	Addresses
BOOKCASE	7
CHAIR	3, 6
DRESSER	5, 9
STAND	8
TABLE	1, 2
WALL UNIT	4, 10

ROOM index (secondary key)

ROOM	Addresses
BR	5, 8, 9
DR	1, 2, 3
FR	4
LR	6, 7, 10

PRODUCT data file

Address	PRODUCT#	DESCRIPTION	FINISH	ROOM	PRICE
1	0100	TABLE	OAK	DR	500
2	0350	TABLE	MAPLE	DR	625
3	0625	CHAIR	OAK	DR	100
4	0975	WALL UNIT	PINE	FR	750
5	1000	DRESSER	CHERRY	BR	800
6	1250	CHAIR	MAPLE	LR	400
7	1425	BOOKCASE	PINE	LR	250
8	1600	STAND	BIRCH	BR	200
9	1775	DRESSER	PINE	BR	500
10	2000	WALL UNIT	OAK	LR	1200

or as FINISH values are modified) was more than the retrieval savings from use of a FINISH index compared to the alternative of physically *scanning all* PRODUCT records to find those with the specified FINISH. Also, it was observed that questions involving FINISH were not very discriminating; that is, *many* records satisfied queries on FINISH. A rough rule of thumb is that if more than 10% of the records in a file satisfy a key qualification, an index on that key is not very helpful—a complete file scan is equally or more efficient.

Indexes are more compact than the data records they reference. Often, indexes can be kept in computer main memory for extended periods so that secondary memory access costs to retrieve indexes can be reduced. However, indexes for files with a large number of records can also be very large. An index, then, can be viewed as a file itself on which an index can be created, and so on. This is what we saw earlier with ISAM and VSAM.

Not all secondary keys need to be indexed, as noted earlier. But before a data base designer can decide which indexes to create, all secondary keys must be identified. When all data processing is known in advance, then computer program specifications provide an excellent source to identify secondary keys. Before these program specifications are developed or when significant ad hoc data base queries are anticipated, some general guidelines are required to assist in identifying secondary (and even alternative primary) keys. Guidelines for identifying secondary (and primary) keys can be found in Table 5-2. This table summarizes this taxonomy and indicates examples from the Pine Valley Furniture data base for each key type.

Table 5-2 Primary and Secondary Key Taxonomy

Key type	**Description and motivation**	**Example from Pine Valley Furniture**
Simple primary key	This is one data item whose values are unique to each record in a file; frequently required in on-line applications	PRODUCT# for PRODUCT records
Partial value key	A data item with long values may be cumbersome to index. The first *n* characters may be very discriminating, but not unique	PRODUCT-DESCRIPTION for PRODUCT records
Concatenated primary key	Records that contain data about (the relationship between) two entities are identified by a combination of the related entity primary keys	ORDER# and PRODUCT# for ORDER-LINE records

Table 5-2 (continued)

Key type	Description and motivation	Example from Pine Valley Furniture
Concatenated retrieval key	Although lists of addresses from two separate indexes can be intersected to answer queries with AND conditions, a combined key index can avoid this cost	FINISH and ROOM for PRODUCT records
Simple category key	Frequently, records are sought that have a common characteristic (single, nonunique value or range of values)	FINISH for PRODUCT records
Complex category key	Often, queries arise that simply ask which records exist with specified interdata item characteristics	QUANTITY-ON-HAND less than REORDER-POINT for PRODUCT records
Existence/ count key	Some queries ask only if any record exists or how many exist with specified properties; these can be answered from just an index	DELIVERY-DATE of today for ORDER records
Intrafile concatenated key	Complex relationships can exist between records within the same file, such as Bill-of-Materials; a key that is a concatenation of these related record keys can speed access	Parent PRODUCT# and component PRODUCT# for Bill-of-Materials in PRODUCT file
Missing value key	This is a special case of the simple category key in which the characteristic sought is the null value	PRICE for PRODUCT records
Interfile key	This is an inverted list equivalent to a chain structure. Here records are identified by a common characteristic that is also the primary key of another file	PRODUCT# for ORDER-LINE records
Audit/change key	Frequently, data processing audit and control procedures need to know which records have been modified, added, or deleted during the most recent period	PRODUCT# for PRODUCT records (e.g., to tag records with price changes)
Sort key	An index can be used to maintain a sorted order to avoid sorting records before every batch reporting	CUSTOMER-ZIPCODE for CUSTOMER records

TREES

It was observed in the preceding section that an index with a large number of entries can itself present an interesting index data structuring problem. If an index is helpful in storing and searching through data records, then could an index help to organize another index? ISAM, VSAM, and other file organizations, as well as a host of other data structures, all are based on this approach of recursively indexing indexes. This type of hierarchy of data and pointers to data is generalized by the tree data structure. Trees can be used to organize data directly or organize indexes into data.

A **tree data structure** has the property that each element of the structure (except the root) has only one path coming in (that is, there is only one pointer that points to any given element), but there may be zero or many paths coming out of an element (that is, there can be several pointers in any given element pointing to other elements). This set of pointers may be address sequential or pointer sequential connected. A **binary tree** permits at most two paths coming out of an element.

There is a great deal of specialized terminology associated with trees, some of which has already been introduced. Figure 5-14 graphically depicts many of the terms. We may view trees genealogically. The **root** is the element (node) with no parents. All the direct offspring of a common parent are collectively called a **filial set**; each member (node) of a filial set is a **sibling**. All the offspring (both direct descendents and all future generations) form a **subtree**. All terminal elements that have no offspring are called **leaves**. **Level** refers to the distance from the root in terms of number of branches to backtrack to return to the root. In addition, the term **degree** signifies the maximum number of offspring from an element; a binary tree is a tree of degree (or order) 2.

Figure 5-14
Tree terminology

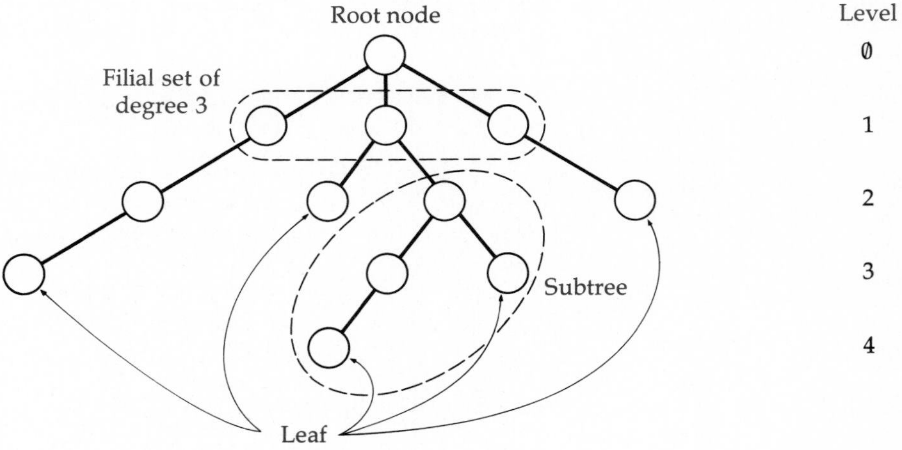

Binary Sequence Trees

Figure 5-15 illustrates one type of binary tree, called a sequence tree, for the PRODUCT file of Pine Valley Furniture. In a **sequence tree**, all the data elements (subtree) accessible, starting from the left pointer (branch) of an element, have key values less than the key for the given element of data, and similarly, the right pointer leads to elements with key values greater than the given element. In box 11 of Figure 5-15, the record for PRODUCT# 1000 is at the root, the element that has no pointers pointing to it. Records for PRODUCT# 0100, 0625, 1425, and 1775 are leaves, those elements that do not point to any other elements. The boxes within Figure 5-15 show the evolution of the sequence tree as each key is inserted in the file. Exercise 10 at the end of the chapter defines a situation for retrieval of records from a sequence tree.

Properties of Trees

Sequence trees, like most trees, are used to provide fast primary key access to records in a file. Sequence trees introduce several important properties that should be considered with *all* trees. These properties are discussed next.

In a sequence tree, some records are closer to the root than others. This means that a different number of comparisons and branches will be required to access different records. If frequently accessed records could be placed close to the root, then overall data base performance could be improved. Most types of trees do build **uniform accessibility** by placing *all* records in leaves and requiring that all leaves be an equal distance from the root (VSAM has this property). This factor of distance from root will be extremely important later when we consider the hierarchical data model in Chapter 6.

The evolution of the tree in Figure 5-15 was dependent on the order in which records were inserted. If, for example, PRODUCT# 1600 had been inserted first, it would have become the root, and the whole structure of the tree would have changed. The worst case here is when the records are loaded in ascending or descending primary key order! Many trees that store data records only in leaves do not exhibit this insertion dependence property. But if the type of tree being used can become pathological in shape with certain insertion sequences, care should be taken in loading records. In general, bushy trees provide the best performance.

Many "varieties" of trees have been developed. Three characteristics are especially useful in distinguishing among trees: branching factor, depth, and sibling connection.

Branching Factor The **branching factor** (or degree) of a tree is the maximum number of children allowed per parent. Large branching factors, in general, create broader, more shallow trees. Since access time in a tree

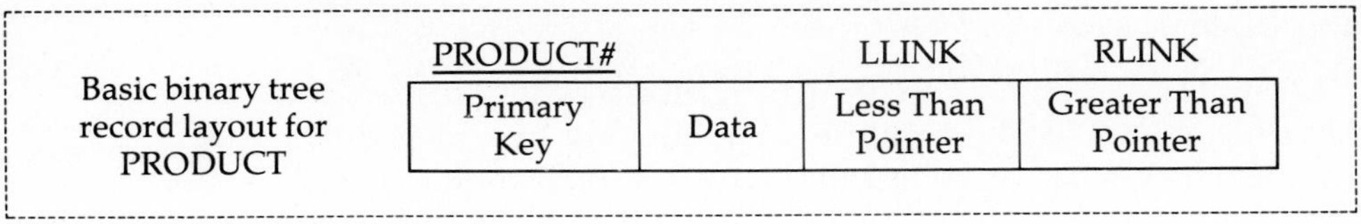
Basic binary tree record layout for PRODUCT
PRODUCT#
LLINK
RLINK
Primary Key
Data
Less Than Pointer
Greater Than Pointer

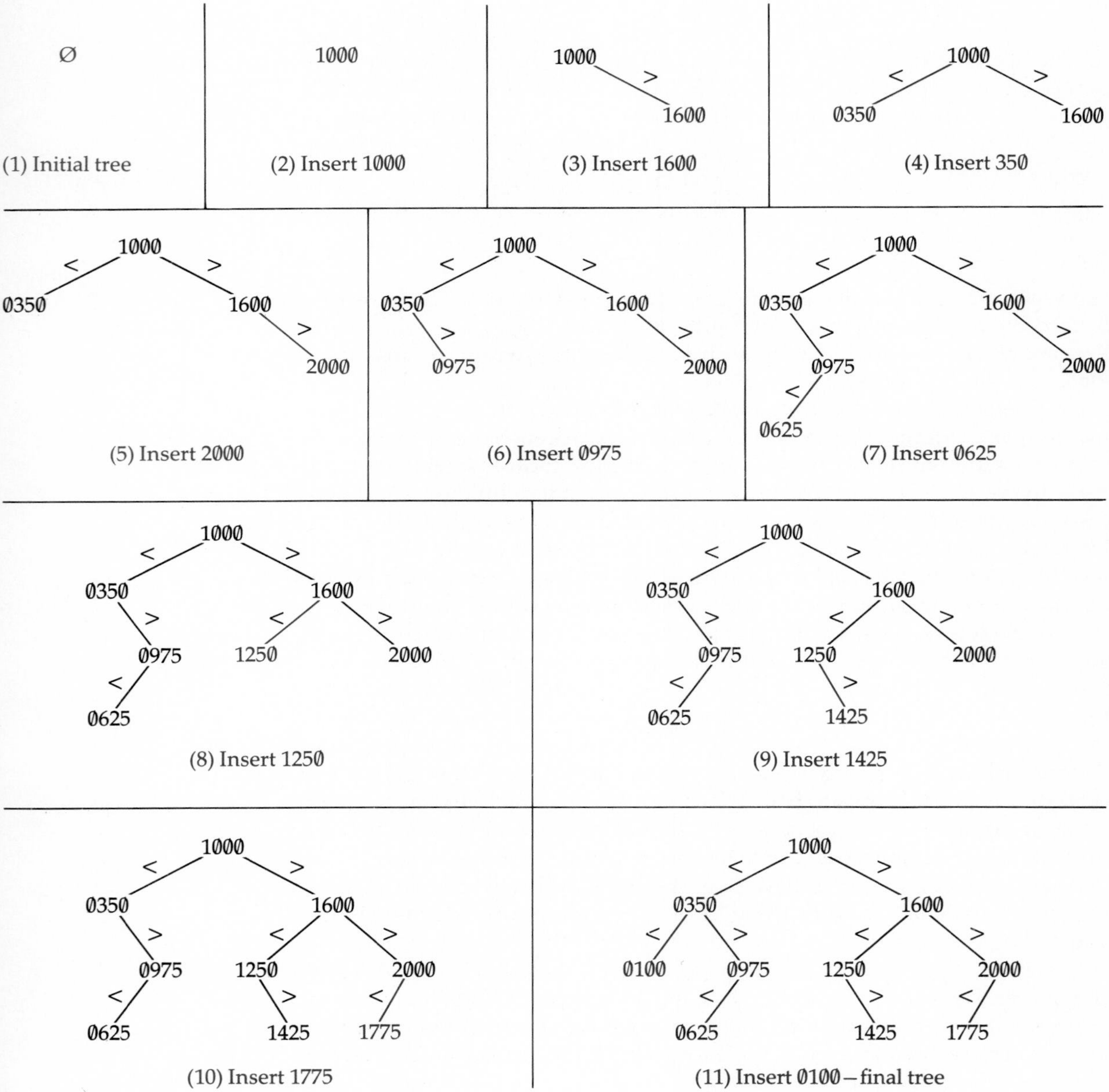
Ø
(1) Initial tree
1000
(2) Insert 1000
1000
1600
(3) Insert 1600
1000
0350
1600
(4) Insert 350
1000
0350
1600
2000
(5) Insert 2000
1000
0350
1600
0975
2000
(6) Insert 0975
1000
0350
1600
0975
2000
0625
(7) Insert 0625
1000
0350
1600
0975
1250
2000
0625
(8) Insert 1250
1000
0350
1600
0975
1250
2000
0625
1425
(9) Insert 1425
1000
0350
1600
0975
1250
2000
0625
1425
1775
(10) Insert 1775
1000
0350
1600
0100
0975
1250
2000
0625
1425
1775
(11) Insert 0100—final tree

depends more often on depth than on breadth, and since movement between levels means a disk access, it is usually advantageous to have bushy, shallow trees.

Figure 5-15 (opposite) Example of a sequence tree (Pine Valley Furniture)

Depth **Depth** is the number of levels between the root and a leaf in the tree. Depth may be the same from root to each node, called a **balanced tree**, or it may vary across different paths. Balanced trees are democratic in that all leaves have approximately the same access costs, but balancing can be costly to maintain as the tree contents are updated. B-trees, to be introduced in the next section, overcome the costly update problems of other types of balanced trees.

Sibling Connection Three general methods exist for connecting members of the same filial set (siblings): parent index, address sequential, and pointer sequential. A **parent index** is a set of pointers in an element, one pointer for each of the offspring. This method provides rapid access to each offspring at the expense of storage space for the pointers. Further, since a pointer to each offspring could lead to various parts of a disk, access to *all* offspring could be time-consuming. A parent index allows easy answering of questions such as: Does a given product have any orders? or How many orders has a given customer placed?

One way to speed up access to the whole filial set is to store the whole set as a block and connect siblings via *address sequential*. In this case, the parent needs only one pointer to the beginning of the block for the filial set. Space is conserved (few pointers) and all siblings are rapidly accessed as a group. The problem is to manage updates (insertions and deletions) to filial sets. When *pointer sequential* connection between siblings is used, space management is easier but access time is slower. The general rule is to use pointer sequential when there is a small filial set, address sequential when the size of the filial set is stable, and parent index otherwise.

B-Trees

The ISAM and VSAM file organizations presented in Chapter 4 are both based on tree data structures. Both use trees to structure an index into records that are stored only at the leaves. Device independence and dynamic index reorganization were the primary distinguishing characteristics of VSAM. VSAM is based on a tree data structure called a B-tree (B, many people believe, stands for "balanced," meaning that all leaves are the same distance from the root). B-trees guarantee a predictable efficiency that many other types of trees do not. For example (according to Knuth 1973, 476), with a B-tree of degree 199, any record in a file as large as 1,999,998 records can be retrieved in three accesses! Although hashing may yield fewer accesses for random record retrieval, hashing does not support sequential retrieval and B-trees do. Not only VSAM, but also many data base management

Figure 5-16
B^+-tree node structure:
(a) nonleaf node
(b) leaf node

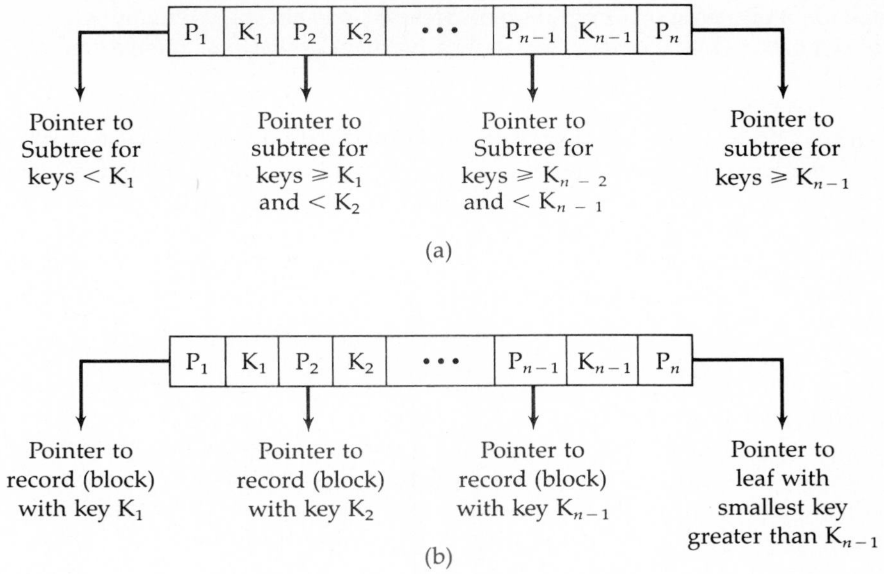

systems now use B-trees as the principal method for primary and secondary key access. B-trees are a hybrid of address and pointer sequential connection along with data indirect location.

There are several varieties of B-trees, with the standard B-tree and the B^+-tree being the most common (see Comer 1979, and Korth and Silberschatz 1986, for more detailed discussions). Since most implementations are of the B^+-tree, it is this variety that we will illustrate.

A **B^+-tree of degree m** has the following properties:

1. Every node has between $\lceil m/2 \rceil$ and m children (m is an integer greater than or equal to 3 and usually odd), except the root, which is not bound by the lower limit.
2. All leaves are at the same level (same depth from root).
3. A nonleaf node that has n children will contain $n - 1$ keys.

Figure 5-16 illustrates the general structure of nonleaf and leaf nodes in a B^+-tree, and Figure 5-17 illustrates a B^+-tree of degree 3 (which is very small, for illustrative purposes only) for the Product Master File of Pine Valley Furniture (developed from Figure 2-2). As with any index, access for each retrieval or maintenance request begins at the root and works through the tree, taking branches associated with a comparison of the desired key with index entries. In a nonleaf node (see Figure 5-16a), each pointer entry addresses the root of a subtree. The $n - 1$ keys in a nonleaf node divide the keys found in that subtree into n subsets or further subtrees. Starting at the root and continuing through one node at each level, if the desired key to retrieve, delete, or insert is greater than or equal to K_i and less than

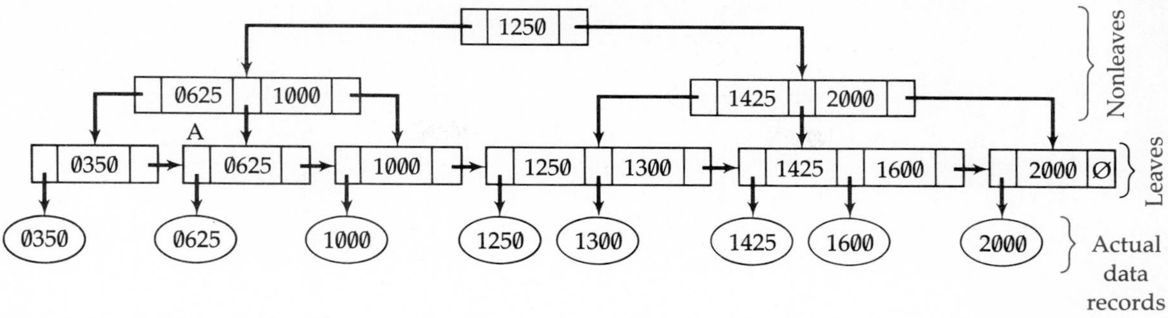

Figure 5-17
Example of B^+-tree

K_{i+1}, then the search continues by accessing the root of the subtree pointed to by P_{i+1}.

The processing at a leaf node (see Figure 5-16b) is somewhat different. First, the pointers address record blocks (usually the case in a primary key index) or may reference individual records (usually the case in a secondary key index). Thus, pointers here are to real data, not index nodes. Note that, because of this fact, each key in nonleaf nodes is repeated in some leaf (see Figure 5-17). Second, the pointer P_n is an exception, in that this pointer addresses the leaf with keys that follow directly in sequence. This permits rapid sequential processing without having to backtrack to nonleaf nodes. In fact, for sequential processing the accessing method could keep track of not only the root but also the address of the leaf with the lowest key, and sequential processing could start directly in the leaves. It should be noted that since real data are referenced indirectly (that is, outside the index itself), then multiple B^+-tree indexes can be maintained on the same data as long as index leaves reference individual data records. As with any index structure, the data records can be stored in any sequence (physical location) since the index maintains the desired sequence. Further, data may be stored without any (or very few) empty record slots.

Maintaining B^+-Trees Insertions and deletions of records from the Product file of Figure 5-17 must preserve the B^+-tree properties. Consider the insertion of PRODUCT# 0800. This key would be logically inserted into node A of Figure 5-17. Figure 5-18a shows the resultant tree. Since the node labeled A still has no more than three children, no restructuring is required. Insertion simply added a new key and pointer to a leaf; the only node affected was the leaf where the key and pointer were inserted. Thus, insertion operations were few and were isolated to a very confined part of the tree.

Now consider insertion of PRODUCT# 1500 into the tree of Figure 5-18a. Node A in Figure 5-18b shows the result of simply inserting this new key into its proper position; however, this node is now "over capacity" with four ($m + 1$) children. The B-tree answer to this is to split node A into two nodes. To split will require choice of a key (PRODUCT#) to be moved to the parent of A (that is, B) to indicate the boundaries for the split of node

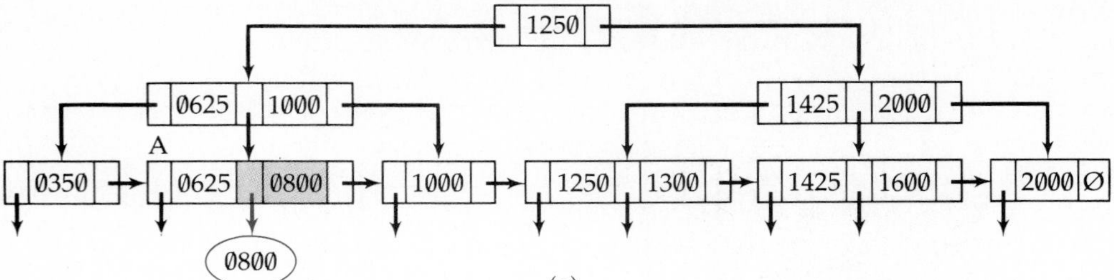
1250
0625 1000
1425 2000
A
0350
0625 0800
1000
1250 1300
1425 1600
2000 Ø
0800

(a)

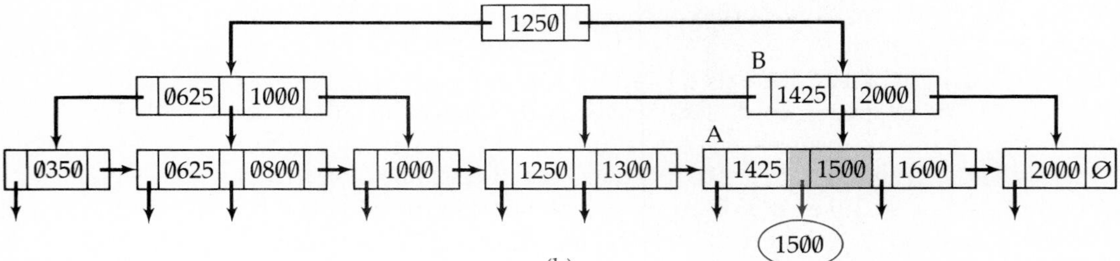
1250
B
0625 1000
1425 2000
A
0350
0625 0800
1000
1250 1300
1425 1500 1600
2000 Ø
1500

(b)

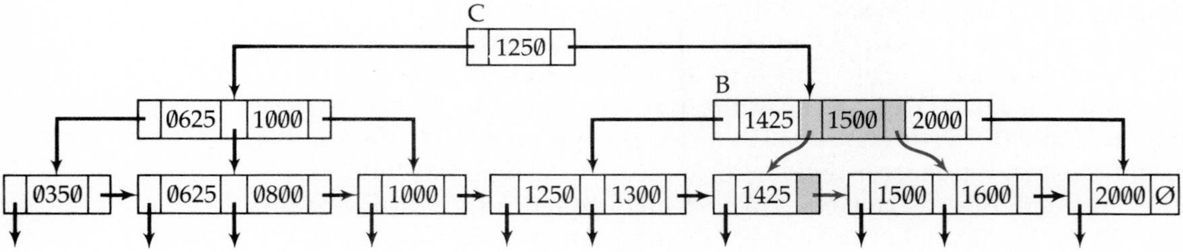
C
1250
B
0625 1000
1425 1500 2000
0350
0625 0800
1000
1250 1300
1425
1500 1600
2000 Ø

(c)

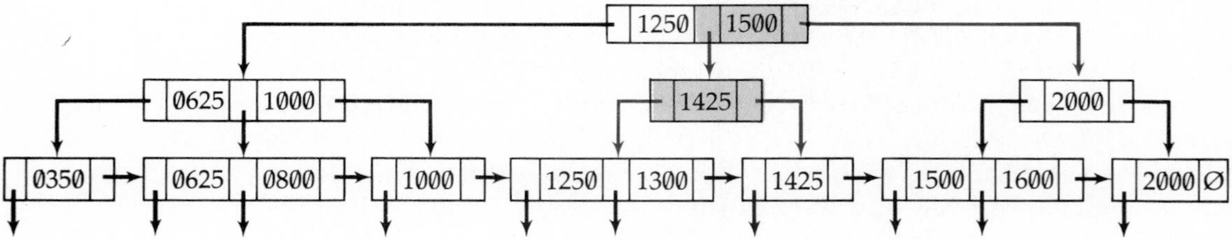
1250 1500
0625 1000
1425
2000
0350
0625 0800
1000
1250 1300
1425
1500 1600
2000 Ø

(d)

A. The result is shown in Figure 5-18c. Since the leaves must contain all keys, key 1500 appears in both node B and a leaf of Figure 5-18c. Now node B is over capacity and must also be split and a key from node B moved to its parent C (the root), as before. The result is shown in Figure 5-18d, where all B^+-tree properties are met and the insertion is complete.

In each insertion case where we had to split a node, we chose the middle key in order to divide nodes as evenly as possible and to permit an equal expansion capacity in all nodes. If insertion results in cascading node splitting all the way to the root, the result is to add a new level to the tree.

Since insertion involves splitting nodes that become too large, not too surprisingly, deletion involves combining a node that becomes too small with some other node. Three situations need to be addressed: (1) deletion of a key that just appears in a leaf, (2) deletion of a key that appears in both a leaf and a nonleaf, and (3) deletion that requires combining nodes. Figure 5-19 contains examples of B^+-tree deletion from each of these three situations. Consider the deletion of PRODUCT# 1600 from Figure 5-18d; this is an example of situation 1 above. Since this situation would leave two pointers in the affected leaf, all that must be done is to eliminate the deleted key and its associated record pointer. The result appears in Figure 5-19a. As with insertion, the effect of deletion is very isolated and inexpensive to perform.

A slightly more involved deletion occurs when PRODUCT# 1250 is deleted from Figure 5-19a, which is an example of situation 2 above. Here not only must key 1250 and its associated record pointer be eliminated from leaf node A in Figure 5-19a, but reference to key 1250 must also be taken out of a nonleaf (in this case, the root). Since key 1300 then becomes the smallest key in the subtree "to the left of" key 1500, key 1300 is moved into the root to replace key 1250. The result is shown in Figure 5-19b. Again, updates to the tree are very isolated and predictable.

An even more extensive type of deletion can be illustrated by deleting PRODUCT# 1500 from the tree of Figure 5-19b; this illustrates situation 3 above since node B in this figure becomes below capacity (less than $\lceil m/2 \rceil$ or two active pointers). Figure 5-19c shows the result of simply deleting this key and its associated record pointer from the leaf and eliminating the key from where it appears in a nonleaf node (in this case, the root). When node underflow occurs, the rule is to combine it with an adjacent sibling. Thus, nodes B and C from Figure 5-19c need to be combined; the result is shown in Figure 5-19d. But now node D underflows, and it is combined with node E; this result is shown in Figure 5-19e. Here the root also reflects the combining of nodes D and E, which means that the "unknown" key in the root, which defines the separation of nodes D and E, is no longer needed. Even with this deletion, much of the tree is unaffected and the nodes that are changed have adjacent keys. Thus, again, maintenance is isolated and the cost is controlled. As noted before, this dynamic reorganization avoids costly, massive, and periodic reorganizations that can force the file to be inaccessible during this work.

Figure 5-18 (opposite)
Examples of B^+-tree insertion:
(a) tree after insertion of PRODUCT# 0800
(b) tree after first step in insertion of PRODUCT# 1500
(c) tree after second step in insertion of PRODUCT# 1500
(d) tree after completion of insertion of PRODUCT# 1500

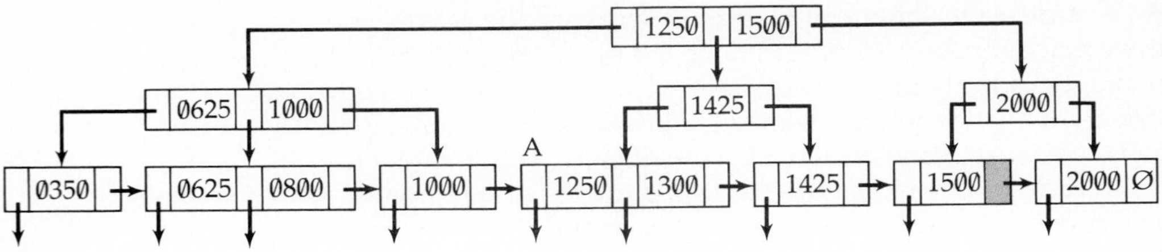
1250 1500
0625 1000
1425
2000
A
0350
0625 0800
1000
1250 1300
1425
1500
2000 Ø

(a)

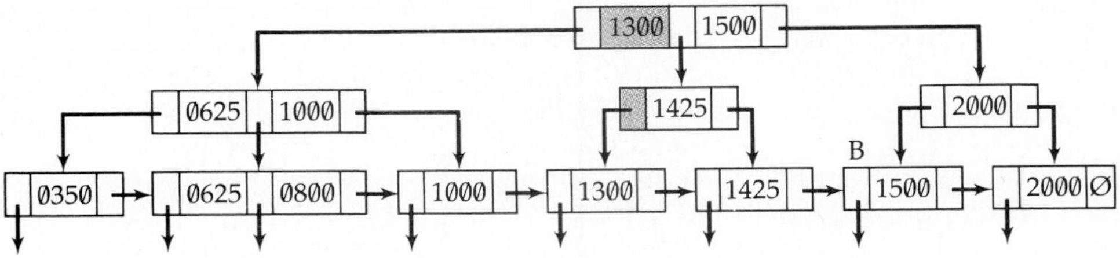
1300 1500
0625 1000
1425
2000
B
0350
0625 0800
1000
1300
1425
1500
2000 Ø

(b)

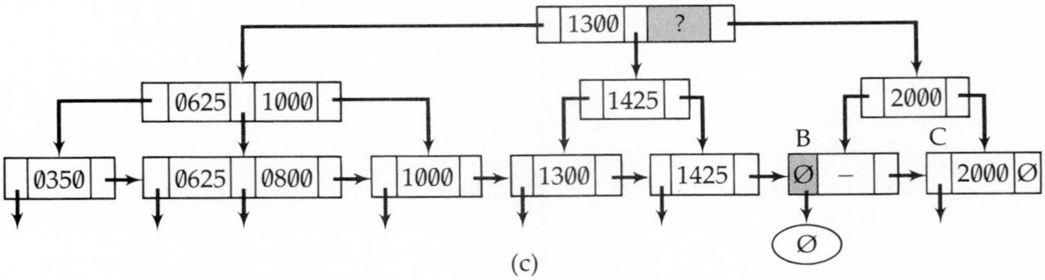
1300 ?
0625 1000
1425
2000
B
C
0350
0625 0800
1000
1300
1425
Ø –
2000 Ø
Ø

(c)

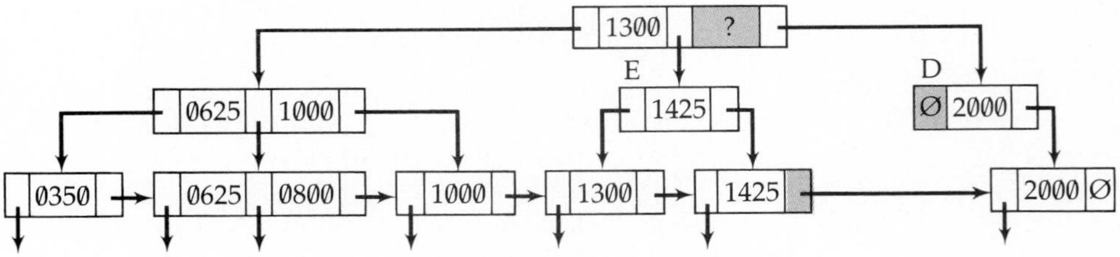
1300 ?
E
D
0625 1000
1425
Ø 2000
0350
0625 0800
1000
1300
1425
2000 Ø

(d)

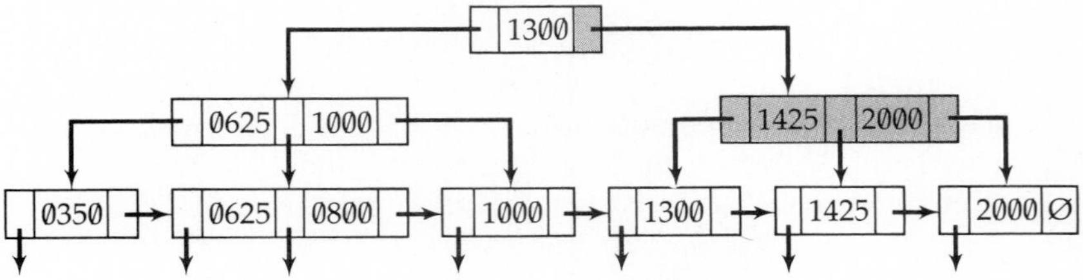
1300
0625 1000
1425 2000
0350
0625 0800
1000
1300
1425
2000 Ø

(e)

A very extensive deletion occurs when the root underflows. When *m*, the degree of the B^+-tree, is greater than or equal to 4, we simply let the root get smaller (since it is not bound by the lower limit according to the tree rules). However, when the last key is eliminated from the root, the tree can be collapsed one level. This type of deletion is left as an exercise at the end of the chapter. Comer (1979) discusses additional B-tree maintenance and the predictable, mathematical properties of B-trees.

Figure 5-19 (opposite) Examples of B^+-tree deletion:
(a) tree after deletion of PRODUCT# 1600
(b) tree after deletion of PRODUCT# 1250
(c) tree after first step in deletion of PRODUCT# 1500
(d) tree after second step in deletion of PRODUCT# 1500
(e) tree after completion of deletion of PRODUCT# 1500

Review of Trees

The preceding discussion of trees has illustrated that they can permit rapid retrieval of data for both random and sequential processing. The examples shown here have all dealt with access to records within one file based on primary keys. The structures illustrated can easily be changed to work with secondary keys. When tree structures are used to connect records in different files, another name is used—the hierarchical data model, which is covered in the next chapter. Trees are special cases of a more general data structure called networks. Since networks are used in data base management primarily to connect records in different files, we will delay consideration of the network data model until the next chapter.

SUMMARY

In this chapter, we presented, as groundwork for understanding data base structures, various data structures. We tried to show the most fundamental components and their impact on data base processing and performance. Address sequential and pointer sequential connection were shown to be basic building blocks of all data structures. File organizations like ISAM and VSAM were explained in terms of their underlying data structure.

We demonstrated that each data structure exhibits its own performance. Some structures manage small sets of data better than large; other structures provide very rapid data retrieval but are costly to maintain. A data base designer must carefully match the characteristics of the data processing to be performed (sequential processing, random record retrieval, quantity of record insertions and deletions, and so on) with an appropriate, efficient data structure. Most of the time this matching is done by selecting operating system access methods and data base management systems that best satisfy the data processing requirements.

We also identified three types of pointers—physical, relative, and logical—and their comparative characteristics. We showed how these pointers and also address sequential connection can be used to build physical records in intrarecord data structures and to represent associations between records in interrecord data structures.

Interrecord data structures were described as basic linear (such as stacks, queues, and sorted lists), multilist (a technique to permit multiple associations to be maintained concurrently among the same data), inverted lists (an indexing technique that supports rapid multiple-key qualification retrieval), and trees (a hierarchical set of indexes and record connections).

The next chapter utilizes these data structures to describe different architectural forms, called data models, for data bases.

Chapter Review

REVIEW QUESTIONS

1. Define each of the following terms:
   a. data structure
   b. successor element of data
   c. address sequential connection
   d. pointer sequential connection
   e. data direct access
   f. data indirect access
   g. pointer
   h. physical pointer
   i. relative pointer
   j. logical pointer
   k. intrarecord data structure
   l. space management
   m. data item partition
   n. linear interrecord structure
   o. stack
   p. queue
   q. sorted list
   r. bidirectional chain
   s. multilist data structure
   t. inverted list data structure
   u. tree data structure
   v. binary tree
   w. root
   x. leaf
   y. B^+-tree
   z. sibling
2. List and explain at least three criteria that could be used to measure the efficiency of data structures.
3. Summarize the relative advantages and disadvantages of the three types of pointers.
4. Explain the data structure(s) used in the ISAM file organization.
5. Define and critically compare the different types of intrarecord data structures.
6. Discuss the relative advantages and disadvantages of multilist and inverted list structures for managing multiple associations and answering multiple-qualification questions.
7. Give at least one example of each type of secondary key from a situation of your choice (but different from Pine Valley Furniture).
8. Explain why it may be beneficial to divide one logical record into several physical records.
9. Explain why a B^+-tree is such an appealing data structure.
10. Discuss how bidirectional pointers can make chain maintenance simpler.
11. What is the purpose of "dummy" nodes at the front and end of a list data structure?

PROBLEMS AND EXERCISES

1. Match the following terms with the most appropriate definition:

_____ binary tree	**a.** field used to reference a piece of data
_____ B^+-tree	**b.** series of pointer sequential connections
_____ queue	**c.** node of a tree with no parents
_____ stack	**d.** all direct offspring of a common parent
_____ sorted list	**e.** insertions may occur anywhere in the list
_____ leaf	**f.** maximum number of children per parent
_____ sibling	**g.** each member of a filial set
_____ pointer	**h.** tree of order two
_____ relative pointer	**i.** LIFO data structure
_____ root	**j.** number of levels between root and leaf
_____ branching factor	**k.** data structure used in VSAM
_____ depth	**l.** element that has no offspring in a tree
_____ filial set	**m.** contains the "offset" of a record
_____ traverse	**n.** FIFO data structure
_____ data indirect	**o.** move through a data structure
_____ intrarecord	**p.** placement of data separate from mechanism to connect data
_____ chain	**q.** within a record

2. Redraw Figure 2-10 to show the use of single directional pointers (chains) to manage the associations in this figure. Show the additional "data about data" (pointers) required in each record type.
3. Consider the following questions processed using the Pine Valley Furniture data base depicted in Figure 2-10.
   a. List all customers with an order due for delivery today.
   b. Count the number of times PRODUCT# 1425 has been ordered in the past year.
   c. List the price of each of the products with a DESCRIPTION of TABLE (Pine Valley makes more varieties of tables than all other types of products combined!).

   Identify the secondary keys used in these queries and for each, explain whether an inverted index would be advantageous.

4. Consider the following data item specifications for a CUSTOMER record at Pine Valley Furniture:

   CUSTOMER: fixed length, always present/known
   CUSTOMER-ADDRESS: highly variable length, always present/known
   DOLLAR-SALES-YTD: fixed length, not present for prospective customers
   CREDIT-LIMIT: fixed length, not present for prospective customers
   SALES-COMMENTS: highly variable length, not present for prospective customers

   Design an intrarecord structure for this CUSTOMER record and justify your design.
5. For the CUSTOMER record defined in Problem 4, discuss a situation that would suggest the need to partition or cluster data items from this record into several physical records.
6. Consider the stack in Figure 5-8. Write a pseudocode record deletion procedure for this stack structure.
7. The queue record insertion procedure of this chapter was facilitated by the use of bidirectional pointers. In Figure 5-9a, delete the head-of-chain pointer NEWEST-ORDER-LINE and the PRIOR-ORDER-LINE pointer and then rewrite the queue insertion procedure. (*Hint:* The null pointer, ø, indicates the end of a chain.)
8. Write a sorted list deletion procedure to delete all ORDER records with key value DELKEY for a given customer using the sorted list depicted in Figure 5-10b. (*Hint:* First list any possible error conditions, similar to duplicate key, that can occur during deletion, and build checks for these errors into your procedure.)
9. Consider the B^+-tree in Figure 5-19e. Modify this B^+-tree to handle the following record updates. Show the cumulative resultant B^+-tree after each modification, and process the changes in the exactly the order given. The updates are:

   Insert 1100
   Insert 1150
   Delete 0625
   Delete 0800
   Delete 2000
   Delete 1300

10. Consider the sequence tree in Figure 5-15. Let LLINK(X) be a pointer to the left subtree of the PRODUCT record at relative address X. Let RLINK(X) be similarly defined for the right subtree. Assume that the address of the root of the tree is stored in variable ROOT. Let PRODUCT#(X) be the product number in the PRODUCT record at relative address X, and let KEY contain the product number to be retrieved. Write a tree search procedure to locate a record with the product number stored in KEY. Your procedure should place the address of the record sought into variable ADDR. Your procedure should be designed to start searching at the root and proceed in the most efficient path. Place a value of ø in ADDR if no record with product number KEY exists.
11. Obtain a copy of Solomon and Bickel (1986) and review the self-assessment questions on file processing as a way to combine your understanding of material in Chapters 4 and 5.

REFERENCES

Comer, D. 1979. "The Ubiquitous B-tree." *ACM Computing Surveys* 11 (June): 121–137.

Hoffer, Jeffrey A., and Dennis G. Severance. 1975. "The Use of Cluster Analysis in Physical Data Base Design." *Proceedings of First Very Large Data Base Conference*, Framingham, Mass., September (available from Association for Computing Machinery), 69–86.

Knuth, Donald. 1973. *The Art of Computer Programming*. Vol. 3, *Sorting and Searching*. Reading, Mass.: Addison-Wesley.

Korth, Henry F., and Abraham Silberschatz. 1986. *Database System Concepts*. New York: McGraw-Hill.

Maxwell, William L., and Dennis G. Severance. 1973. "Comparison of Alternatives for the Representation of Data Item Values in an Information System." Technical report no. 199, September, Dept. of Operations Research, Cornell University.

Schkolnick, Mario. 1977. "A Clustering Algorithm for Hierarchical Structures." *ACM-TODS* 2 (March): 27–44.

Severance, Dennis G. 1974. "Identifier Search Mechanisms: A Survey and Generalized Model." *ACM-Computing Surveys* 6 (September): 175–194.

Solomon, Martin K., and Riva Wenig Bickel. 1986. "Self-Assessment Procedure XV." *Communications of the ACM* 29 (August): 745–750.

Chapter 6

Data Models

INTRODUCTION

A **model** is a representation of real-world objects and events, and their associations. It is an abstraction from reality (that is, in a different form) and, as such, often is simplified for ease of understanding and manipulation. Model airplanes that allow aeronautical engineers to design better airplanes, mathematical models that allow business analysts to improve the operation of an enterprise, and model people (dolls) that allow children to practice the responsibilities of parenthood all suitably represent some real-world situation.

A **data model** is an abstract representation (a description) of the data about entities, events, activities, and their associations within an organization. More liberally, a data model represents (describes) an organization itself, since, for example, it is the association between customers and the orders they submit that leads to associations between Customer records and Order records.

The purpose of a data model is twofold: first, to represent data, and second, to be understandable. If a data model accurately and completely represents required data and is understandable (and easy to use), then it can be used in some application, just as a model airplane can be used in a wind tunnel for testing design features.

Careful thought on the model airplane analogy will suggest that there are three types of airplane models for different applications:

1. Models (or submodels) that each "user" of an airplane conceives. For example, the pilot sees the airplane as a set of instruments and equipment for maneuvering the plane; the aeronautical engineer sees the plane in terms of shapes, lines, and aerodynamics. These are called **external models.**
2. Models that consolidate the aerodynamics, the internal cockpit physical layout, and other views in order to check for inconsistencies (e.g., there may be fine aerodynamic features but not enough passenger capacity to be economical). These models are used by a general design engineer responsible for the overall architecture and objectives of the project (the design engineer in the data base realm is called a data administrator). These are **conceptual models.**
3. Fabrication models that put every part in its place in some abstract form (often a blueprint) so that the airplane can actually be constructed and used. These models are useful to an assembly foreman, construction project manager, and workers responsible for production and daily operations (the blueprint in the data base realm is developed by a data base designer or administrator and is used by programmers and others who build application programs). These are **internal models.**

Figure 6-1 is a version of Figure 5-1 that shows the correspondence between levels of data models in Pine Valley Furniture and the levels of airplane models just presented. There is no direct relationship between examples in the same box other than that they are at the same level of modeling.

At the external level, models or user views are used by systems analysts and users to elicit data requirements. They are used in training to explain to new employees how an information system is used. Here, user understanding is very important, so the model clearly conveys only what a given user wants from a data base. One form of a data model in this level may be flowcharts or data flow diagrams (see DeMarco 1978). Bubble charts, introduced in Chapter 2, can also be helpful here. Data models to be presented in this chapter can also be used to depict user views. End users may interact with a data base by using a query language or problem-oriented language. Thus, external data models are also used to depict, via a specific data processing technology, the data being used by a user. This latter type of external model is often called a **subschema.**

With a conceptual data model, we need to be able to consolidate user views, check for consistency (e.g., do all users refer to the same data item by the same name?), and validate that all data and relationships have been identified. It is important at this level to capture the semantics about data. For example, one user may mean *all* customer orders when she says "orders," but another may use this term only to refer to orders that still have products to be delivered. Further, information about who can do what with data must be captured and represented for subsequent use in developing the

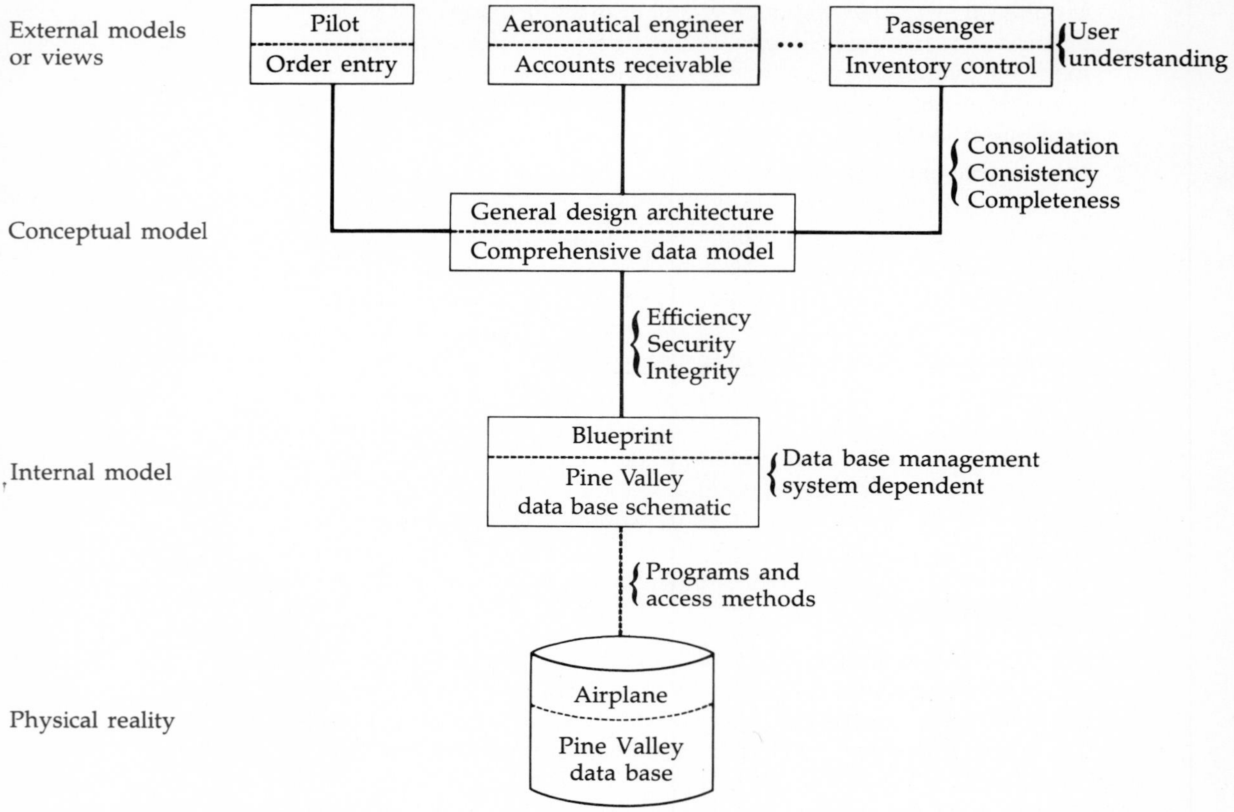

Figure 6-1
Levels of data models compared to airplane models

data base. Finally, the conceptual model, since it is the basis for design of the internal data base, should be supplemented with information about data base usage and maintenance so that an efficient internal structure can be devised.

The final model of data, the internal model (often called a **schema**), provides the interface with computer technologies: data base management systems, operating system access methods, and other programs. This model type uses data structures to build complex architectures for organizing data. Whereas the data structures covered in Chapter 5 dealt primarily with the organization of and access to single files of data, the internal data model (as the other levels did) relates data from different files (e.g., Customer to Order). Because this data model type deals with specific technologies, we will see that each DBMS can have its own unique internal data model or schema architecture.

Thus, we have outlined three categories of data models:

1. External data models, of which there *may* be two subcategories: (a) logical external data models or views used to elicit and describe data

requirements in a technology-independent manner; and (b) subschema data models, which describe only the data required for a given data processing task but which are defined using a technology-dependent style (like a COBOL Data Division, FORTRAN dimension statements, data definition language [DDL] of a DBMS, and so on).

2. Conceptual data models, used to comprehensively define all the data base requirements of all users into a consistent and singular data base description.
3. Internal data models, used to comprehensively define the whole data base using a technology-dependent style—that is, models limited by the capabilities of the technology and that explicitly state how the technology will be used to manage data.

In addition, there is the reality of the objects and events of an organization. We mask out certain characteristics from reality since we determine that these are not necessary in the abstraction. Good data base design depends significantly on a good application area systems analysis to establish the suitable subset for abstraction. This process will be addressed, in part, in Chapters 7 and 8.

The purpose of this chapter is to review various data model architectures that have proved to be appropriate at different levels of abstraction of a data base. We will see that some data models can be applied at several levels, whereas others have been especially designed for specific levels. Chapters 7 and 8 will demonstrate the process of using external and conceptual data models for data base design. As already noted, because the internal data model used to specify the detailed structure of a data base depends on the DBMS being used, this chapter will present only some families of internal data models. Specific implementations of these families are covered in Chapters 12 to 15. This separation of generic data model from implementation emphasizes that any given data model is not the exclusive property of any one DBMS and that a data model can be used to represent data before the appropriate data base technology is selected.

CAPTURING THE MEANING OF DATA IN DATA MODELS

Because data models are abstractions (and, hence, simplifications) of real data, it is difficult, as well as often impractical or unnecessary, to capture all the nuances of the true meaning of data in a data model. Further, arguably the most difficult part of analyzing organizational data is recognizing and capturing the meaning of data and data relationships for all situations in which the data will be used. Each type of data model represents certain aspects of the complete meaning of data fairly well, but may not recognize other aspects at all. The meaning of data is frequently referred to as **data semantics.**

Later, as different models are presented in this chapter, we will examine how these different data models represent different types of data semantics. However, at this point, an overview of many of the important types of semantics will help to put later presentations into the proper perspective.

Many types of semantics deal with relationships between different kinds of data. These types of semantics are, in essence, rules about the integrity of the data base. We have already seen some important semantic concerns in prior chapters—for example, the type of relationship (1:1, and so on) is a very basic data semantic. Some of the most important data semantics that need to be captured when modeling data are: existence dependencies, time, uniqueness, class, and aggregation.

Existence Dependency Semantics

Sometimes an instance of one entity cannot exist without an existence of some other entity. For example, a Customer Order cannot exist without the associated Customer (that is, an order has to be from somebody about whom we already know some characteristics).

Another dimension of existence dependency semantics deals with, for example, whether a Customer entity instance can be eliminated without first eliminating associated Customer Order instances. A special case of an existence dependency occurs when part of the primary key of one entity is the primary key of some other entity. For example, if we do not assign unique Order Numbers to each customer order, then we may choose to use as the Customer Order entity primary key a combination of Customer ID and Date. Here, not only must a Customer entity exist for each Customer Order entity, but also data elements in each entity must have common values. This type of semantic is called **referential integrity** in those data models that place the primary key of one record in associated records. Chen (1977) reviews existence dependency semantics in considerable detail.

Time

Data base contents may or may not be allowed to vary over time. For example, when a shipment of products is formed, it may exist even before it is assigned to some carrier, whereas the shipment cannot be created unless there is one or more associated customer orders. The type of restriction illustrated here—creating a shipment without an order—is called an **insertion restriction** and relates to the time at which data are first stored in a data base.

Once the shipment leaves the warehouse (that is, becomes active), it must always be assigned to some shipper but, because of transshipment, the carrier may change. When the shipment is received, it (and any associated data, such as customer orders being filled by the shipment) must be disassociated from any carrier. Thus, the meaning of the relationship between shipper and shipment must be clear in terms of the time period covered by

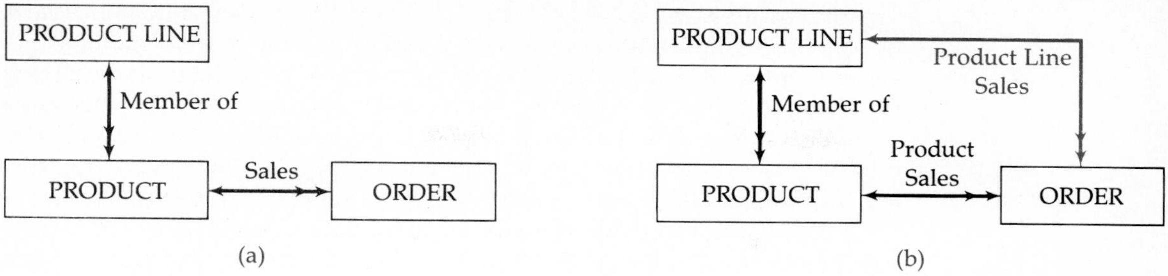

Figure 6-2
Pine Valley Product data base:
(a) data base not recognizing product reassignment
(b) data base recognizing product reassignment

the relationship. The choices for this so-called **retention restriction** on relationships are, in general: (1) fixed—the original association must be maintained; (2) mandatory—some association must always be maintained; and (3) optional—from time to time, no association may occur.

This shipment situation example involves a *current shipper* relationship in which a shipment may exist without an associated carrier and may change associated carrier over time; the association from shipment to carrier is many-to-one. A totally different relationship would maintain the complete history of carriers handling a shipment and, although the shipment may exist without a carrier when it is created, once associated with a shipper it will always be associated with that shipper (and possibly others). When a history is maintained, then explicit reference to time may be required in order to be able to retrieve the actual description of the business situation at any current or past point (or even future if forecasts are included). Now the relationship from shipment to carrier becomes many-to-many.

What is modeled depends on what data processing is to be supported. Although each data value can be time-stamped or tagged to indicate the date the value was entered (transaction time), becomes valid, or stops being valid, time is not used like other pieces of data (as demonstrated in the interpretation of the shipment versus shipment history relationship). Time series data, past versus current versus pending data, and the temporal nature of user data requests (for example, will users want only current snapshot data or might they want historical summary data or the ability to ask for a snapshot for any point in the past) make time a special dimension of organizational data. Time also plays a role in data base recovery, but that use is not addressed here (see Chapter 11).

The following illustrates how data maintenance can effect subtle changes to time-dependent information. Suppose one characteristic of a Product in Pine Valley Furniture is the Product Line or group of products to which it is assigned. Customer orders are processed throughout the year and monthly summaries and trends (which involve comparing current sales to the prior month's sales) are reported by Product Line. Figure 6-2a illustrates the PRODUCT LINE, PRODUCT, and ORDER data and relevant relationships referenced here. In the middle of the year, due to a reorganization of the sales function, PRODUCTs are reassigned to PRODUCT LINEs. Since the Pine Valley data base in Figure 6-2a is not designed to show that PRODUCTs may have different PRODUCT LINEs over different periods of time, all sales reports will show historical sales for a PRODUCT based on a PRODUCT's *current* PRODUCT LINE, not the one at the time of the sale, since current assignment is the only one maintained. We have discussed this problem of time-dependent data with several organizations considered leaders in the use of data base technologies and data modeling. We have discovered that current data models (and data base management systems based on these data models) are so inadequate in handling time that organizations ignore this problem and hope that such inaccuracies balance each other out. Figure 6-2b shows a simple data base design change that accommodates this time-dependent relationship.

It can safely be said that no data model adequately handles time. Clifford and Warren (1983) suggest extensions to the relational model to deal with the time semantic. Time frequently is masked from view when looking at a data model. Auxiliary data and relationship definitions may be necessary to adequately communicate the time dimension in a data model.

Uniqueness

We have already encountered one uniqueness restriction, called a primary key. The value of a primary key distinguishes an instance of one entity from other instances of that entity. A primary key can be composed of one or more data elements. But uniqueness arises in other contexts, as well. For example, each student who is enrolled in a course section (a particular time and place offering of a course) will receive a grade and no single student may receive more than one grade in each section; that is, although multiple grade entity instances will exist for the same section (for multiple students), those associated with the same student will be unique by course section.

Uniqueness of primary keys is handled in almost all data models. However, uniqueness among entity instances related to some other entity instance is really only explicitly recognized in some versions of the network data model.

Another form of uniqueness is called **exclusivity.** Exclusivity means that one of several kinds of data or relationships may be present, but not all. For example, a particular type of task in the production of a product in Pine Valley Furniture may be performed by an hourly worker or a salaried employee, but not both; or, two Pine Valley Furniture employees may be related as supervisor/subordinate, husband/wife, or parent/child, but no two of these relationships may hold for the same pair of employees.

Class–Subclass or Generalization

The term *customer* may not have the same meaning to all people in the organization. For Pine Valley Furniture, some customers are national account furniture store (chain-type store) business customers, some are single-site furniture store businesses, some are individual persons, and some are interior designers. Although all customers have some of the same type of characteristics (name, address, telephone number, and so on), each type of customer may have data elements not ascribed to other types of classes of customers (e.g., national account furniture store customers have a credit limit that other types of customers do not have since all other customers must pay C.O.D.).

Some reports deal with only specific types of customers; other reports summarize data from all customers independent of type. One sales manager may refer to "customer" and mean a different type of entity from another sales manager who uses the same term.

One frequently used way to identify subclasses of an entity is to associate a categorical data element (e.g., type of customer for the above situation) with the entity, for which an instance of the entity must have one and only one value. But this may not be an acceptable method when the set of relevant data elements varies across subclasses (since data models do not allow variable content definitions for different instances in the same class). For example, the subclass of national account customers may have certain characteristics only pertinent to this subclass (such as credit limit, name of assigned national accounts manager, number of outlets); these data elements make the national accounts subclass a (specialized) instance of an entity, Customer. The Customer entity is frequently referred to as an **abstraction** of more specialized entities (such as National Customer, Interior Designer, and so on). As illustrated here, the term *customer* may have different meanings in different contexts and, hence, the Pine Valley Furniture data model may need to represent different but related types of customers and customer classes.

Although most data models can represent generalized entity types, only the entity-relationship and semantic data models reviewed later in the chapter explicitly recognize this type of data semantics. In fact, we briefly introduced the topic of generalization within E/R diagrams in Chapter 3. Smith and Smith (1977) describe the generalization semantic in more detail.

Aggregation

An **aggregation** is a collection of entities. For example, an instance of a Work Order entity for Pine Valley Furniture would actually be the collection of all Raw Materials, Tools, Work Centers, and Factory Workers entity instances needed to produce a certain piece of furniture. A Work Order aggregate will be associated with a particular Customer entity when products are made to order, but changing customer requests may mean that a Work Order is reassigned to different customers while it is active. Besides inheriting the data elements about component entities, an aggregate entity can have data elements not found in component entities. For example, a Work Order might have a Promised Completion Date, as well as Material Descriptions, Tool Codes, and so on from the component entities.

Some Pine Valley Furniture data base users will simply want to refer to

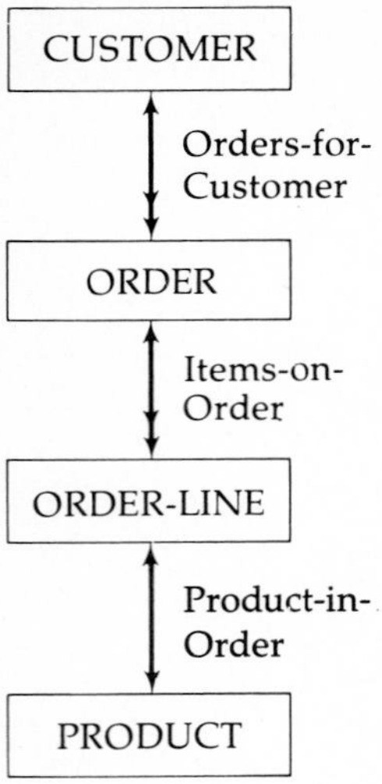

Figure 6-3
Example of hierarchical data model (Pine Valley Furniture)

the Work Order (aggregate) entity as if it were a basic entity. The relational data model (using a concept called a view) and the Semantic Data Model (using an explicit definition of an aggregate entity) are best among the data models reviewed here in dealing with this type of data semantics. Smith and Smith (1977) also discuss the need for this type of data semantics.

Some of these types of data semantics will be considered in more detail as we review the different major data models in the following sections of this chapter. Other semantics types deal more directly with how the types of data models presented here are implemented in technologies, and hence will be discussed later, in Chapters 12 through 15.

A new type of data model, the object-oriented data model, has been evolving from artificial intelligence and actor languages (see Goldberg 1981, and Katz and Lehman 1984). In an **object-oriented data model** an entity is represented as an instance (object) of a class that has a set of properties and operations (methods) applied to the objects. A class, and hence an object, may inherit properties and methods from related classes. Objects and classes are dynamic and can be created at any time, which is typically not possible in most current commercial data base management systems. Early applications of this data model have been in engineering—for example, computer-aided design (CAD), where product components (objects) need to be dynamically created, redefined, and combined into arbitrary higher-order components, and multiple versions, generations, or alternatives of an object maintained.

THE HIERARCHICAL DATA MODEL

A hierarchy is a familiar structure. Organizations have always been viewed as a hierarchy of positions and authority; computer programs have relatively recently been viewed as a hierarchy of control and operating modules; and various taxonomies of animal and plant life view elements in a hierarchical set of relationships.

Definitions

The **hierarchical data model** represents data as a set of nested one-to-many (1:*M*) and one-to-one (1:1) relationships (see "Types of Associations" in Chapter 2 for a review of these terms), as depicted in Figure 6-3 for the Pine Valley Furniture data base from Figure 2-10. There is a single record type, in this case CUSTOMER, that "owns" ORDER, which in turn "owns" ORDER-LINE, which in turn "owns" PRODUCT. No single occurrence of a record type may have more than one "parent" (record type or occurrence) in the hierarchy. Because of the similarity between hierarchies and tree data structures, terms like *root, level,* and *leaf* are also used when discussing hierarchies.

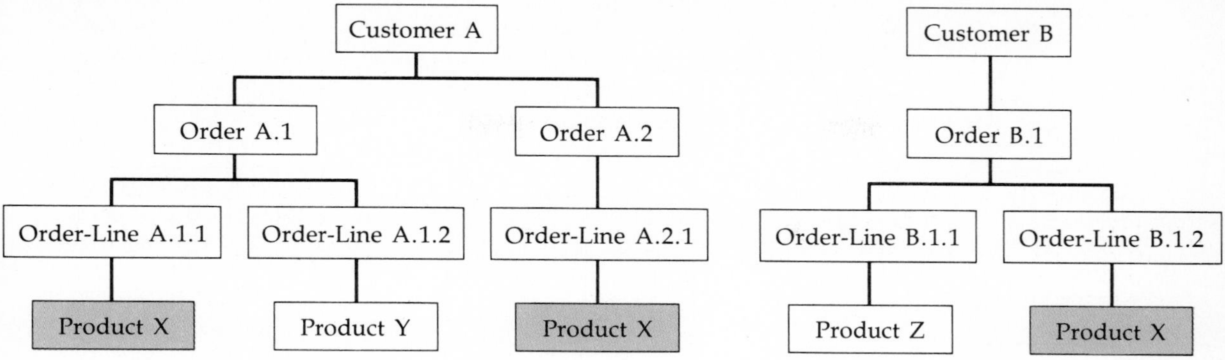

Figure 6-4
Instance diagram for data base in Figure 6-3

Relationships in a Hierarchy

The hierarchical rule of only one parent does not cause a problem as long as relationships are truly 1:*M* from parent to child throughout the hierarchy. A review of Figure 2-10 will indicate that the 1:1 Product-in-Order relationship in Figure 6-3 is a restricted inverse of the 1:*M* Products on Order relationship in Figure 2-10. That is, a given PRODUCT record is associated with many ORDER-LINE records, not just one. But the hierarchical data model rule will not support an *M*:1 relationship.

Figure 6-4 shows via a record instance diagram what must occur to implement the hierarchy rule. The result is *redundancy*. Data concerning PRODUCT# X is associated with three ORDER-LINE records. Since an occurrence of PRODUCT# X can only have one ORDER-LINE parent instance, this PRODUCT# X data must be repeated under each associated ORDER-LINE instance. Each time PRODUCT# X's DESCRIPTION, PRICE, or other data change, application program logic has to guarantee that all copies of these data will be updated (and at approximately the same time in order to prevent potential data base inconsistencies).

Is there any way to avoid this redundancy? Since PRODUCT can also be viewed to "own" all these data, then why not invert the hierarchy? (In fact, Figure 6-3 is the view of the data from the perspective of the customer order processing function; PRODUCT would not be their focus or root; the CUSTOMER would be.)

In Figure 6-5, we show the result of placing PRODUCT as the root of the hierarchy, which might be the perspective of a product sales management function. Now the problem is that the hierarchy rule will force redundancy of *both* ORDER (since different ORDER-LINEs apply to the same ORDER) and CUSTOMER (since different ORDERs are placed by the same CUSTOMER). Without actually comparing the amount of physical data that would be repeated, this hierarchy in Figure 6-5 seems to be less desirable than the one in Figure 6-3.

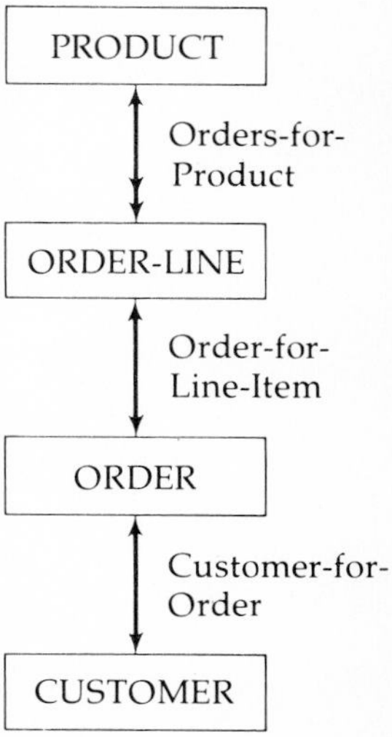

Figure 6-5
Example of product-oriented hierarchy (Pine Valley Furniture)

We can improve the hierarchy of Figure 6-4 slightly if we recognize that 1:1 relationships serve no useful purpose and that no information is lost or

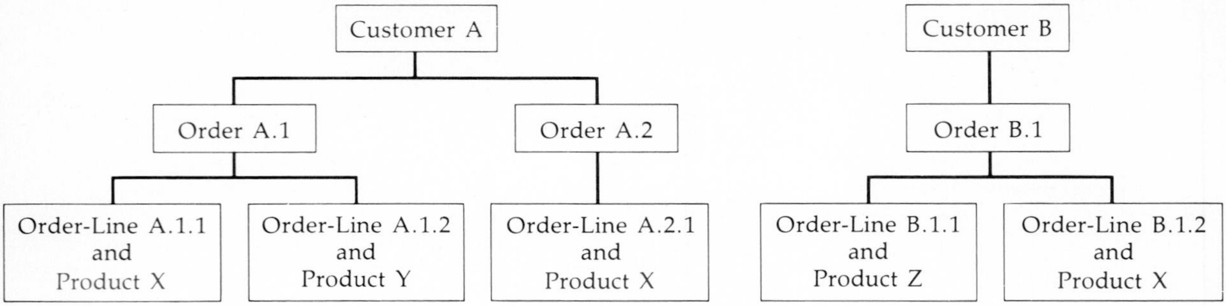

Figure 6-6
Instance diagram for combined ORDER-LINE and PRODUCT from Figure 6-4

further repeated (*or* repeated less) if we combine into *one* record two records that have a 1:1 relationship. Figure 6-6 shows what would happen to Figure 6-4 if we combined ORDER-LINE and PRODUCT record data into one consolidated record type. The result would be to save one level in the hierarchy, which would likely mean one fewer disk access to collect together all the data along one path from a root to a leaf.

Hierarchies are very explicit structures. If one record type is not directly below another in the hierarchy, then no direct relationship (or any direct accessing) between those record types is possible. For example, there clearly is an association between all the ORDER-LINE and PRODUCT records for the same PRODUCT#. But this type of lateral relationship is not possible in a hierarchy.

Multiple subtree hierarchies are also permitted. Figure 6-7 shows what might result from expanding the role of the data base depicted in Figure 6-3 to also support shipping. In this situation, the SHIPMENT-LINE record may contain some data items duplicated from associated ORDER-LINE and PRODUCT records.

Figure 6-7 also suggests another limitation, besides redundancy, of the hierarchical data model. This limitation concerns integrity control and semantics. A SHIPMENT-LINE record should exist *only* when there is an associated ORDER-LINE (we should not ship what has not been ordered). Also, an order cannot be deemed closed until all ORDER-LINEs have been shipped. Because there is no direct relationship between ORDER-LINE and SHIPMENT-LINE in this hierarchy, these integrity constraints cannot be easily enforced by the data model or a DBMS built on the hierarchical data model.

Sometimes in hierarchies, empty relationship record types exist for the sole purpose of relating other record types. Consider Figure 6-7 again and assume that for this data base there is no use for ORDER-DATE, DELIVERY-DATE, and so on, which might be found in the ORDER record. But assume

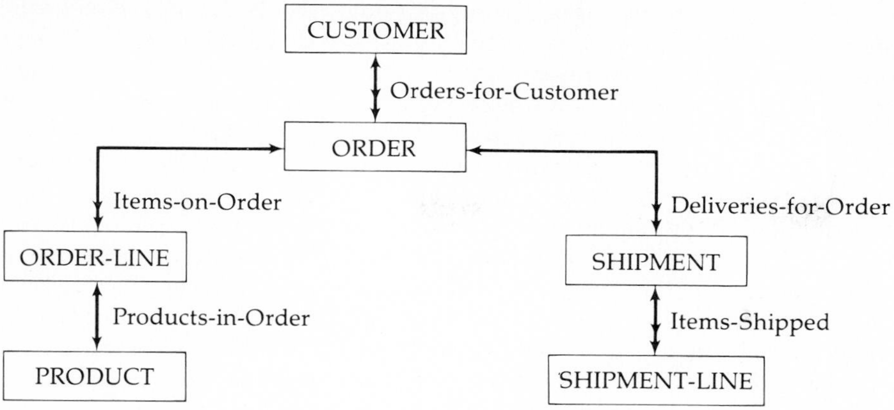

Figure 6-7
Example of hierarchy for order processing and shipping at Pine Valley Furniture

that we do wish to know what was ordered and what has been shipped. In this case, we could still create a relationship ORDER record (sometimes called a dummy record), void of meaningful content, just to link ORDER-LINE records with associated SHIPMENT records.

Data Processing with the Hierarchical Data Model

Hierarchies have the advantage of being familiar structures, and many examples of data and relationships follow such an architecture. Any record occurrence within a hierarchy implicitly contains all the data in record occurrences above it. Hierarchies show "each" relationship explicitly (that is, each relationship is implemented) and require some of the least sophisticated data management technology to manipulate. Any nested relationship present in the hierarchy implies that data can be efficiently retrieved via that relationship.

Hierarchies are, in general, entered at the root, and scanning records to answer questions must begin there. For a query to find all the customers that have ordered PRODUCT# X in the hierarchical data base of Figure 6-3, every CUSTOMER record would have to be retrieved and then, in recursive fashion, each associated ORDER and ORDER-LINE would have to be retrieved (scanning could stop on CUSTOMER-related records as soon as a PRODUCT# X record is found for that customer). The hierarchy of Figure 6-5 would support more efficient retrieval of records for this query, since there, all desired customer data are under one PRODUCT parent; other PRODUCT records and associated ORDERs do not have to be accessed for any purpose to answer this question. This type of sensitivity of hierarchical record placement to data processing requirements will be addressed in more detail in Chapters 8 and 9 on data base design and in Chapter 12 on data base management systems that use the hierarchical data model.

The style of processing a hierarchical data base is distinct. First, with some data base management technologies, a data base is limited to only one hierarchy, so programs cannot be written to report on data directly from two hierarchies. Second, some query programming languages may require special statements or clauses to virtually rearrange the data base hierarchy in order to write a query for certain questions. This virtual rearrangement may be to invert a hierarchy in order to place qualified data items (PRODUCT#) above other data to be retrieved (CUSTOMER-NAME); this rearrangement could also be to move all the data used in the query into a common path from lowest level to highest level referenced. An example of this last requirement can be found in Figure 6-7. Some query languages would require a special phrase to virtually move SHIPMENT data into its associated ORDER record so as to write a program to answer a question such as "What orders for PRODUCT# Y have been shipped in the past week?" (which might be asked in tracing defective goods).

Implementation of the Hierarchical Data Model

Hierarchical data base management systems frequently use inverted indexing as a way to avoid extensive data base scanning (see "Inverted Lists" in Chapter 5). If, in the data base of Figure 6-7, we could index PRODUCT records (a leaf of the hierarchy) on PRODUCT# and then could efficiently find the parent of any record, then the hierarchy of Figure 6-3 could be made to act like the hierarchy of Figure 6-5 to answer the query on the customers of PRODUCT# X. That is, we would enter the hierarchy directly on PRODUCT# X records without having to search for them starting at the root and visiting many immaterial intermediate record instances.

The hierarchy rule of only one parent implicitly means that a record can participate explicitly in only *one* relationship as the target of that relationship. Consider the Orders-for-Customer relationship in Figure 6-3. A Customer could "own" proposed/tentative orders, open orders, and closed orders, to name a few. The hierarchical data model does not permit three relationships in this case. The hierarchical model forces one of two implementations. One approach is to put an additional data item, STATUS, in the ORDER record to distinguish the different types of records. Queries would have to scan all ORDERs to find selected types or a secondary index would have to be created. The second approach is to create three separate record types and have each type below CUSTOMER in the hierarchy. This causes unnecessary and redundant data definitions and may cause significant maintenance work: when an order changes status, we have to move a whole subtree from, say, a proposed subtree to an active subtree, which requires work for subtree removal and reinsertion (possibly reentry of data) with some data base management systems.

Hierarchies are usually implemented using tree type data structures and extensive use of pointers. Each record type in a hierarchy can have any or all of the following pointers:

1. Pointer to the *first* dependent child record for each record type directly below the record (head-of-chain pointer). For example, in Figure 6-3, an ORDER record instance might contain a pointer to the first ORDER-LINE instance for that ORDER.
2. Pointer to the next record of the same type under a common parent (sibling or twin pointer). For example, an ORDER-LINE record instance might have a pointer to the next ORDER-LINE on the same ORDER; a null pointer would be used to signify the end of the list.
3. Pointer to parent record (parent pointer). For example, an ORDER-LINE record instance might have a pointer to the ORDER instance on which it is a line item.
4. Pointer to *each* dependent child record for each record type directly below the record (children pointer array); either this or (1) or (2) above, but usually not both, are implemented. For example, an ORDER record instance might contain *n* pointers, each pointing to each of the ORDER-LINE instances for line items on that ORDER.
5. Pointer to next record of the same type in order by primary key or as part of a primary key access method like a sequence tree (primary key pointer). For example, an ORDER record instance might contain a pointer to the ORDER instance with the next ascending or descending ORDER# key value.

Figure 6-8 illustrates the possible contents of the ORDER record from Figure 6-7 for the types of pointers just given.

A second form of hierarchy implementation uses address sequential connection to cluster together related hierarchical records into one file. This clustering can be viewed logically in Figure 6-9 for the hierarchy of Figure 6-6. This is a logical view, since each record would typically be broken into several fixed-length data blocks owing to the highly variable and long length of this record structure.

Figure 6-8
Example of possible ORDER record contents in a hierarchy with pointer sequential connection

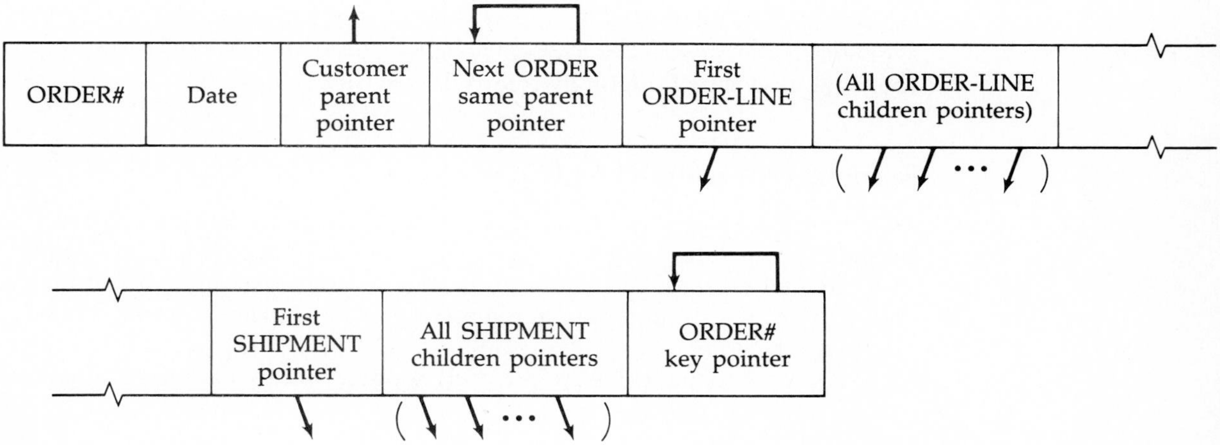

Record 1	Customer A	Order A.1	Order-Line A.1.1 and Product X	Order-Line A.1.2 and Product Y	Order A.2	Order-Line A.2.1 and Product X
Record 2	Customer B	Order B.1	Order-Line B.1.1 and Product Z	Order-Line B.1.2 and Product X		
⋮				⋮		

Figure 6-9
Preorder, depth-first hierarchical record layout

In Figure 6-9, components of the hierarchy are arranged in what is called a preorder, depth-first sequence. That is, we store the data in the record as soon as it is encountered in the hierarchy of Figure 6-6. We proceed to build the record by starting at a root instance (e.g., segment for Customer A) and continue by first taking the leftmost branch from a segment. When we reach a leaf, we pop back up to the prior level (e.g., from Order-Line A.1.1 and Product X we return to Order A.1) and attempt to take the next branch out of the prior level. When we exhaust branches, as with a leaf that has no branches, we return to the prior level. Each time we visit a segment for the *first* time, we append these new data to the record being built. Each root instance defines another record instance.

For hierarchical data base management systems that permit a program to refer to multiple hierarchies, logical or indirect linkages between physical hierarchies may be permitted. For example, if we are permitted to refer to two (physical) hierarchies, then the data base of Figure 6-3 could be redesigned with less redundancy into the two-hierarchy data base of Figure 6-10.

In the data base of Figure 6-10, the actual Order-Line data are stored (using, for example, the storage arrangement of Figure 6-9) in the hierarchy in which they are most frequently used (shown here as the "Customer" tree). The virtual ORD-LINE segment in the "Product" tree points to the associated physical segment in the "Customer" tree. In a pure sense, this two-hierarchy data base would still be hierarchical since data are physically stored to optimize processing in one hierarchy. On the other hand, one can argue that such a data base is no longer hierarchical since the ORDER-LINE segment can be accessed via two entry paths. However, this type of multiple root data base is still popularly referred to as hierarchical.

Summary of Hierarchical Data Model

The hierarchical data model has had a major influence on data management. Its similarity to data structures in programming languages like COBOL and PL/I has made it easy for many programmers to understand. It can be a very efficient structural form when data relationships follow a purely nested 1:*M* pattern.

Existence dependencies are explicitly represented by parent–child rela-

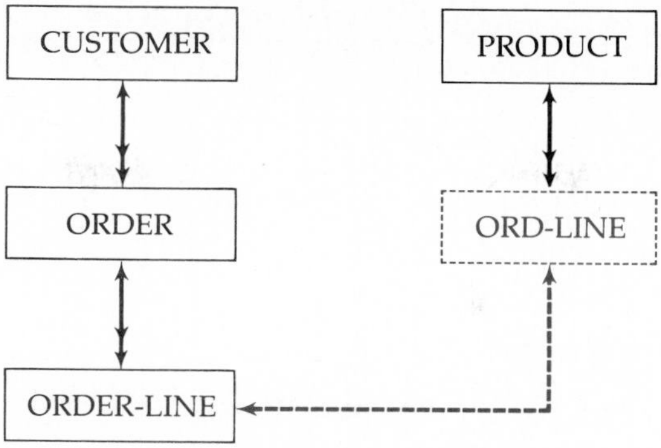

Figure 6-10
Example of a two-root hierarchy

tionships since children may not exist without parents. Because movement of a subtree between different parents is difficult under most hierarchical systems, some types of time-dependent relationships may also be difficult to represent. Most hierarchical implementations permit or even require nested primary key definitions at each node of the hierarchy (the primary key of a node instance is the combination of its parent instance primary key plus one more data item from that node), but uniqueness of a data item across all instances of the parent node may be difficult to represent. Purely hierarchical class-subclass structures can be handled. A subtree can represent an aggregate entity, but hierarchical systems do not usually allow the user to manipulate subtrees as a single entity.

Data base management systems like System 2000 and IMS, based on the hierarchical data model, continue to be popular products (see MRI System Corp. 1981, and IBM 1982). Even considering its limitations, which cause undesirable redundancy, the hierarchical model is well established in practice. However, new DBMSs are being built for network and relational data models, to be covered next.

THE NETWORK DATA MODEL

It was stated in the previous section that the single-parent rule of the hierarchical data model forces redundant and excessive data and structure. When this rule may be violated, we can create a network data model and further eliminate redundancy.

The network model permits as much or as little structure as is desired. We can even create a hierarchy (a special case of a network) if that is what is needed. As with the hierarchical data model, if a certain relationship is not *explicitly* included in the data base definition, then it cannot be used by a DBMS in data base processing.

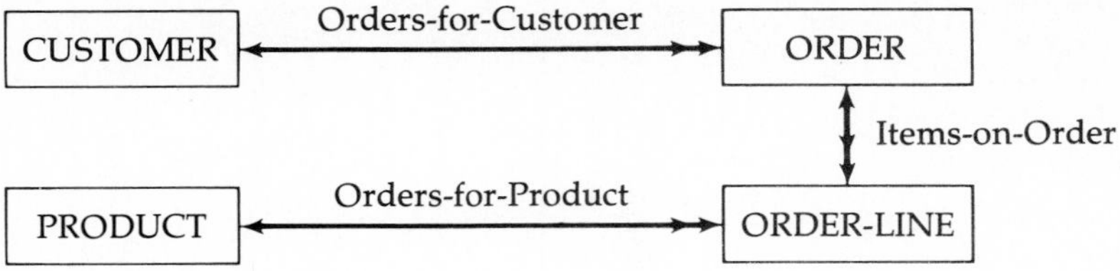

Figure 6-11
Example of a simple network data model (Pine Valley Furniture)

Definitions

The **network data model** represents data as sets of record types and pairwise relationships between record types. Relationships that involve more than two record types (e.g., a relationship among PRODUCT, VENDOR, and WAREHOUSE) are not *directly* permitted (we will return to this point in the next section). Figure 6-11 is a diagram of a network data model for the Pine Valley Furniture data base from Figure 2-10 (you may want to compare Figure 6-11 with Figure 6-3).

There are three types of network data models. The **simple network data model** [the most common because of the efforts of the CODASYL Data Base Task Group (DBTG) in defining a proposed standard for this type of network (CODASYL 1975; CODASYL Data Description Language Committee 1978)] does not permit *M:N* relationships directly in a data base. For example, the simple network model does not permit a direct linkage of ORDER with PRODUCT in Figure 6-11, which would be an *M:N* relationship. The CODASYL network model will be discussed in Chapter 13. In this chapter, we address the general characteristics of network data models without restriction to any particular implementation or standard (such as CODASYL).

The **complex network data model** permits *M:N* relationships to be represented. For example, we could enhance Figure 6-11 to include vendor information on those products that Pine Valley Furniture simply buys and resells under their label. This expanded complex network data base is shown in Figure 6-12a; Figures 6-12b and 6-12c illustrate two alternative equivalent simple network data models.

The PRODUCT-VENDOR-LINK record in Figure 6-12b is called a **link record** and serves only to relate PRODUCTs to VENDORs; it has no meaningful contents. ORDER-LINE, on the other hand, is called an **intersection record** and its meaningful contents are called **intersection data.** In practice, pure link records are rare, since there is usually some data about the relationship to be retained. For example, we probably want to know not only the PRODUCT-VENDOR association, but also the PRODUCT-PRICE from each VENDOR; PRODUCT-PRICE would be stored in the intersection record. Even when no intersection data exists, the link record implementation is advisable so that access paths through the data base stay the same if, in the future, intersection data are identified.

Figure 6-12c shows an approach that will work (if cycles are permitted by the DBMS) when intersection data will never be needed. This cycle

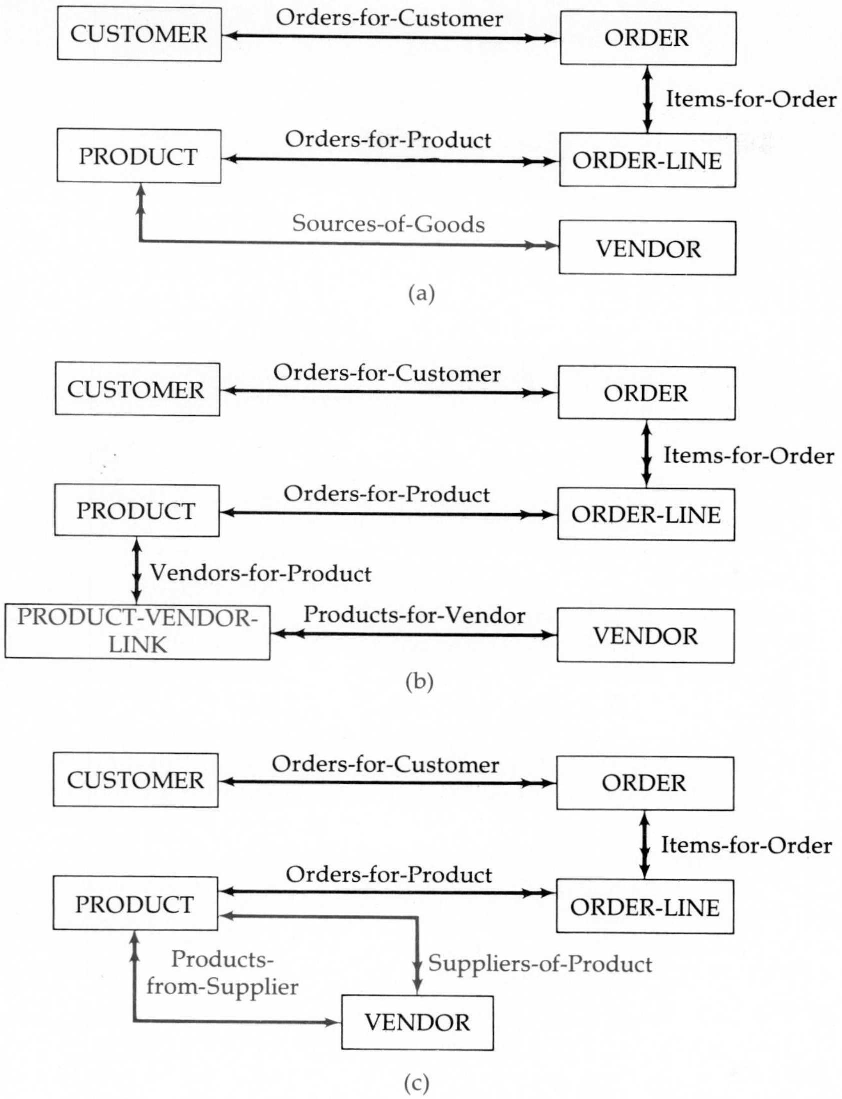

Figure 6-12
Examples of complex and simple network data models (Pine Valley Furniture):
(a) complex network data model
(b) simple network equivalent to the complex network using a link record
(c) simple network equivalent to the complex network using a cycle

approach can present an integrity problem in some data base management systems that control insertion of new records based on existence of current records (see Chapter 13). The link record approach provides greater record independence, since each record type exists on its own.

Very few data base management systems have implemented the complex network data model; one DBMS that has is MDBS III (Micro Data Base Systems, Inc. 1981), which is available on a variety of mini- and microcomputers.

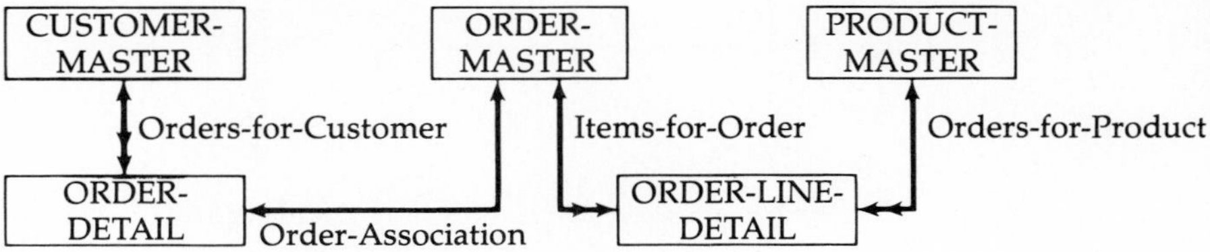

Figure 6-13 Example of a limited network data model (Pine Valley Furniture)

The **limited network data model** divides all record types into two sets: primary or master record type and secondary, detail, or transaction record type. All relationships are from a master to a detail. The data base management systems TOTAL (CINCOM Systems, Inc. 1982) and IMAGE (Hewlett-Packard 1979) are the primary commercial products to adopt this network model. Figure 6-13 illustrates a limited network model for the simple network data base of Figure 6-11. An additional detail record type (called ORDER-DETAIL) is necessary since ORDER cannot be both a child of CUSTOMER and a parent of ORDER-LINE.

A limited network permits the same detail record type to be a detail in two or more relationships (e.g., ORDER-LINE-DETAIL) and the same master record type to be a master for two or more relationships (e.g., ORDER-MASTER). All master record types are accessed via a primary key. To be able to retrieve the ORDER-MASTER in Figure 6-13 once an ORDER-DETAIL is retrieved, we may have to redundantly store the ORDER# in both order record types. The remainder of the ORDER data can be stored in either record. Access from master to detail is assumed to be via a chain.

Relationships in a Network

All network models support the use of multiple 1:*M* relationships between the same pair of record types; with the limited model a given record type may be the master (at head) of all relationships or be the detail (at tail) of all relationships in which it is involved, but not a mixture. Consider, as in the last section, three relationships from CUSTOMER to ORDER for proposed/tentative, open, and closed orders. With a network model, we would simply define three relationships between CUSTOMER and ORDER.

The primary feature of the complex network is its ability to support one record instance (e.g., VENDOR instance) being "owned" by more than one record instance of some other type (e.g., PRODUCT instances). Other network data models do not support multiple parent records of the same type (i.e., *M:N* relationships). In a simple network, we would have to create two 1:*M* relationships, one from PRODUCT to VENDOR (or to a link record) and the other from VENDOR to PRODUCT (or to a link record) to represent

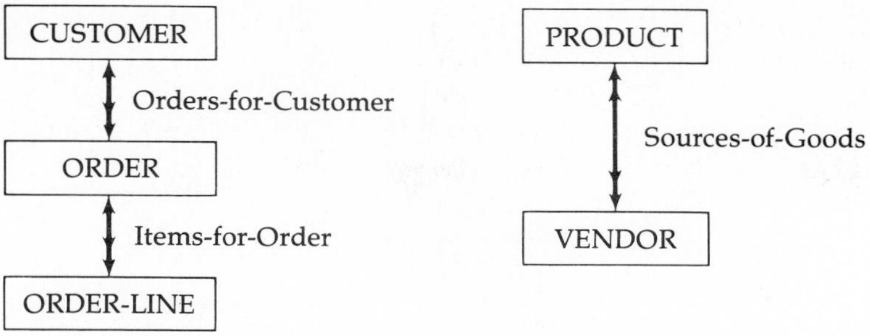

Figure 6-14
Example of a disconnected network data base

such an *M:N* relationship. The problem with this solution is that two relationships have had to be defined, and update of both is the responsibility of the application program, rather than the DBMS. The complex network data model is quite suitable for describing a conceptual data base and for depicting external data bases used for requirements analysis. For the internal data base or for an external subschema data base definition, the relationship capabilities of the DBMS (complex versus simple) must be considered.

It is even possible with networks to create disconnected segments of a data base, as shown in Figure 6-14. In this figure, we have not chosen to implement the relationship from PRODUCT to ORDER-LINE. That is, we will not be able to use a programming language or query language to *simply* retrieve, for example, all the orders for products that are priced greater than $2000 (assuming that PRICE is in the PRODUCT record only). There are, however, ways around this that are not "simple" or not as efficient to program. We could write one program or one program module to find and save the PRODUCT#'s of all PRODUCT records with PRICE greater than $2000. If ORDER-LINE records had a secondary index on PRODUCT#, then another program or module could take the list of PRODUCT#'s, access the ORDER-LINE records for these PRODUCT#'s via the secondary index, and then find the parents of the accessed ORDER-LINE records.

The preceding example emphasizes the true meaning, at the internal data model level, of a relationship. A relationship here really is a direct access path that does not use key access to the target record. In a conceptual or external network data base model, *how* an association is implemented is of no concern. This explicitness is, however, helpful. It clearly informs us what can be economically answered. We will see in a following section that in the case of the relational data model, all relationships are implicit; we will also see that which questions can be answered efficiently and which are very costly to answer cannot be predicted from only the data model.

As was mentioned earlier, the network data model cannot be used to represent *directly* three-way or higher-order relationships. An example of a three-way relationship is what PRODUCTs are supplied to what WAREHOUSEs by what VENDORs. Figure 6-15 illustrates a network structure for *indirectly* representing this three-way relationship, which again uses a link or an intersection record type. A link or intersection record must be created

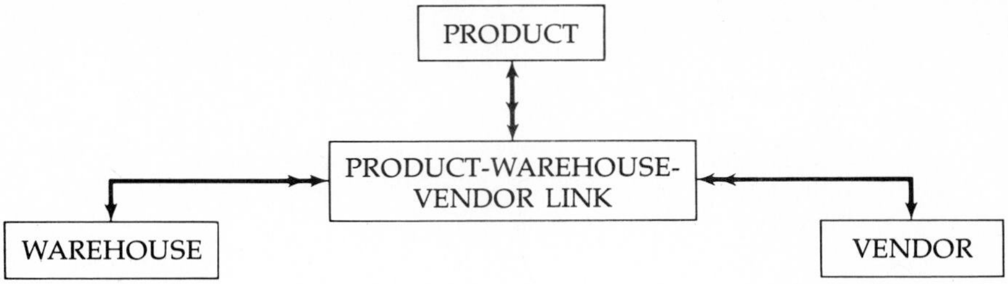

Figure 6-15
Example of a network model structure for a three-way relationship

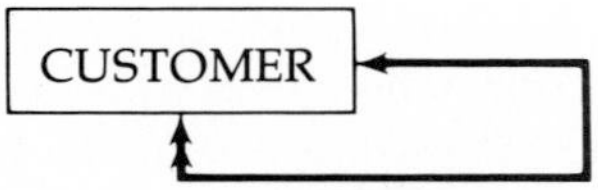

Figure 6-16
Example of a loop relationship in a conceptual or external network data model

for *each* three-way relationship instance. That is, if there were three VENDORs, two PRODUCTs, and four WAREHOUSEs, and each PRODUCT could be shipped to each WAREHOUSE by each VENDOR, there would have to be $3 \times 2 \times 4$ or 24 link or intersection record instances.

Intrafile relationships, sometimes called **loops,** can also arise in data modeling. At the logical external and conceptual data model levels, loops can be shown by a relationship line that exits and enters the same record type, as depicted in Figure 6-16. This example is for a relationship that groups customers together when several customers are subunits of the same organization (e.g., different divisions of General Motors). For the internal network data model, loops can be handled in one of two ways. First, if possible, a secondary index can be created on a PARENT-ORG data item within the CUSTOMER record. A second approach is to create a separate record type, ORGANIZATION, and a 1:*M* relationship from ORGANIZATION to CUSTOMER. Here ORGANIZATION contains parent company records and a parent record owns a set of subunit records.

Another example of an intrafile loop is a **logical sequence** of records within a file. We could illustrate this by substituting CUSTOMER-ZIPCODE sequence for the Same-Organization relationship in Figure 6-16. Such record sorts are only useful in preparing output from data base processing (avoids postretrieval sorting of records or report lines) and hence need to be included only in an internal data model. The typical construct to represent record sequences is called a **singular** or **system relationship.** In this case, the loop relationship is a path that links all the records together in sequence. A pointer chain is usually used to implement this.

Still another type of relationship that can be represented in all but the limited network data model is a **cycle,** or series of relationships that begin and end with the same record type. Cycles can be created to avoid long access paths through a network, and hence are redundant.

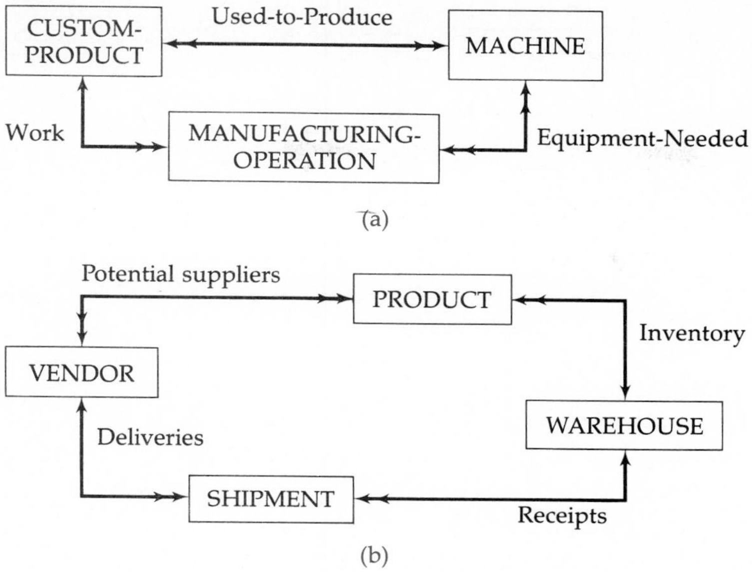

Figure 6-17
Examples of cycles in a network (Pine Valley Furniture):
(a) an efficiency-oriented cycle
(b) a nonimplied cycle

Consider the custom furniture business at Pine Valley Furniture. Figure 6-17a illustrates data relevant for managing the custom furniture projects. In this diagram, a cycle has been used to shorten the path from a MACHINE to the CUSTOM-PRODUCTs it is used to produce. The Used-to-Produce relationship could be used to reduce the cost to find associated CUSTOM-PRODUCT records for a given MACHINE (since intermediate MANUFACTURING-OPERATION records do not have to be accessed). But data base maintenance activities are now redundant (and can be inconsistent); it is possible that a maintenance program would associate a MACHINE with the proper MANUFACTURING-OPERATION, which in turn is associated with the correct CUSTOM-PRODUCT, but the maintenance program could fail to make the proper association from MACHINE to CUSTOM-PRODUCT.

Cycles that are not redundant and not implicit can also occur. In Figure 6-17b the Potential Suppliers relationship is not implied from other data and relationships, since other VENDORs, besides those that *have* shipped products to the firm, could also be possible suppliers.

One additional type of relationship that can occur and can be represented in network data models is called a **class relationship.** Consider the example shown in Figure 6-18, in which ORDERs, INVOICEs, and PAYMENTs for a CUSTOMER are all shown, as well as individual relationships between the record types. The set of all ORDER, INVOICE, and PAYMENT records forms a class of records for CONTACT that Pine Valley Furniture has had with a CUSTOMER. It is possible with some network data base management systems to also define the Contacts-with-Customer relationship, which could be used to produce a chronological history of all customer

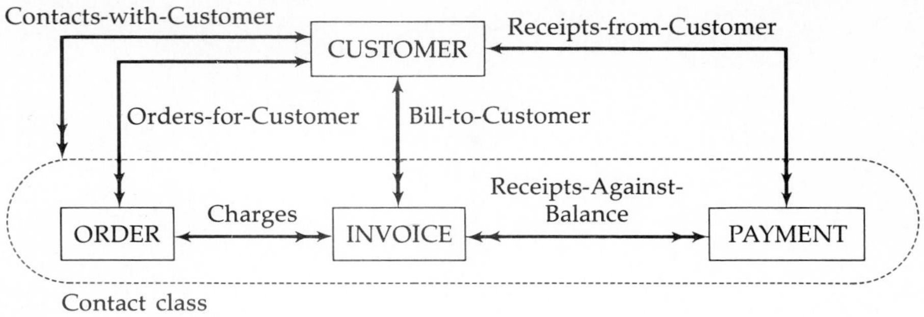

Figure 6-18 Example of a class relationship in a network data model

activities with Pine Valley Furniture. Frequently, class relationships arise when one user does not conceive of different record types (a contact is a contact) and other users conceive of different entities.

Data Processing with the Network Data Model

Network model data bases are often associated with record-level programming languages like COBOL and PL/I, so-called **host languages.** As we will see in Chapter 13, retrieval with most network systems begins by accessing an "owner" record via some entry point (primary key) into the data base. Then the program "walks" through relevant data base records by getting the "first" or "next" record in relationships. Keeping track of where we are in the data base requires diligence. This type of data base processing has been termed **navigation,** since we must maneuver carefully to avoid becoming lost.

The data required for reporting is collected in stages as each related record is retrieved. Records that do not contain required data may have to be accessed in the process. Maintenance of the data base often requires updating of numerous chains, and establishing the proper parent record in each chain for insertion (and deletion) is tedious and prone to subtle mistakes.

Recently, vendors of network-type data base management systems have developed high-level query and maintenance languages that relieve a programmer, especially a nonprofessional, from this kind of detail. Examples of such languages will be presented in Chapter 13 for CODASYL network data base management systems.

Implementation of the Network Data Model

Networks are usually implemented using pointer sequential connections and a multilist-type structure (see Chapter 5). Each record type in a network can have a combination of the following pointers defined (which are similar to those for the hierarchy in Figure 6-8):

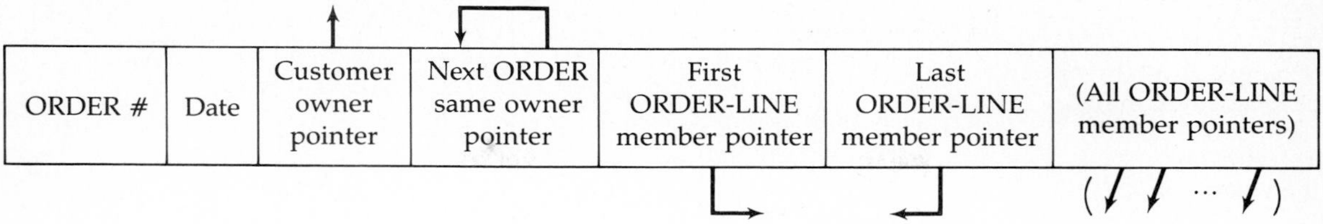

Figure 6-19
Example of possible ORDER record contents in a network data model implementation

1. Pointer to the first (last) record of each target record type (shown by arrowhead), for which the given record is the source or the "owner" (shown by arrow tail) of a relationship [called a head-of-chain (end-of-chain) pointer].
2. Pointer to the next (prior) record or member of the set of records that are all the target of a common source record of a relationship (sibling or twin pointer). This chain of siblings may be kept as a sorted file (see Chapter 5) to reduce the user program logic needed to put output data into proper sequence.
3. Pointer to the source record for each relationship, in which the given record is a target record (parent or owner pointer).
4. Pointer to each target record, for which the given record is the source or owner (children pointer array); pointer types 1 and 2, or this type (but usually not both) is used.

Figure 6-19 illustrates the possible contents of the ORDER record from Figure 6-11 for the types of pointers just described.

A second form of network implementation, especially useful for *M:N* relationships, is a bit map, which is depicted in Figure 6-20 for the Sources-of-Goods relationship from Figure 6-12a. A **bit map** is a matrix created for each relationship. Each row corresponds to the relative record number of a source record, and each column corresponds to the relative record number of a target record of a relationship. A 1 bit in a cell for row X and column Y means that the records corresponding to row X and column Y are associated in this relationship; a zero means no association. For example, Figure 6-20 indicates that PRODUCT with relative record number X is related to VENDOR with relative record numbers 1 and Y (and possibly others not shown). Bit maps are powerful data structures for the following reasons:

1. Any record type(s) can be included in rows or columns.
2. 1:1, 1:*M*, *M:N*, and *M*:1 relationships can all be represented.
3. Rows and columns can be logically manipulated by Boolean operators ("and," "or," "not") to determine records that satisfy complex associations (e.g., any record that has both parent S and parent T).

Figure 6-20
Example of a bit map implementation for a Sources-of-Goods relationship in a network

<u>Sources-of-Goods</u>

PRODUCT \ VENDOR	1	2	···	Y	···
1	1	Ø	···	Ø	···
2	Ø	Ø	···	1	···
⋮	⋮	⋮	⋮	⋮	⋮
X	1	Ø	···	1	···
⋮	⋮	⋮	⋮	⋮	⋮

4. A bit map can be manipulated equally as well in either a row or column access (all the row records for a common column *or* all the column records for a common row) and can be easily extended for *n*-ary relationships.

Summary of the Network Data Model

We have seen that the network data model, in its three forms, can represent a wide variety of data bases. The complex network data model is quite useful for describing an external or conceptual data base because many relationship types can be depicted easily and each relationship and record type is explicitly stated. The simple and limited network models are primarily useful at the internal data base level or with an external data model used for programming (subschema). In both cases, the purpose of the data model is to convey what is *implemented* in the data base.

Some have argued that the network model is complex and difficult to use. Network diagrams, unless thoughtfully arranged, frequently look like an explosion at a spaghetti factory. Networks are also criticized because they have typically been implemented in ways to be consistent with record-at-a-time processing languages, like COBOL; some believe that such data base processing is unnecessarily difficult and unproductive given CPU speed, disk capacity, and transfer rates today.

Since a network is an extension of a hierarchy, the semantic properties of the network model are similar to those of the hierarchical model. Existence dependencies are less clear in a network because of the possibility of multiple parents/owners. As we will see in Chapter 13, network DBMSs, through procedures invoked when data records are loaded into the data base or inserted into relationships, can deal with this semantic. Time, again, is not represented directly in the network data model, but network DBMSs frequently have rules (called relationship retention) that apply to relationships and that can be used to control some aspects of the time semantic. Uniqueness of both primary keys across the data base and keys within relationships are handled. The class-subclass semantic is complex because of multiple parents, but some query languages for network model DBMSs do recognize attribute inheritance; relationships are the construct used to represent this semantic, but relationships are used for other purposes as well. The network model does not have an explicit way to handle the aggregation semantic.

THE RELATIONAL DATA MODEL

The choice of many data base designers and users is the relational data model. As we will see, the relational model is different from network and hierarchical models not only in architecture but also in the following ways:

1. **Implementation independence.** The relational model logically represents all relationships implicitly, and hence, one does not know what associations are or are not *physically* represented by an efficient access path (without looking at the internal data model).
2. **Terminology.** The relational model has been developed with its own terminology, most of which has equivalent terms in other data models.
3. **Logical key pointers.** The relational data model uses primary (and secondary) keys in records to represent the association between two records. Because of this model's implementation independence, however, it is conceivable that the physical data base (totally masked from the user of a relational data base) could use address pointers or one of many other methods.
4. **Normalization theory.** Properties of a data base that make it free of certain maintenance problems have been developed within the context of the relational model (although these properties can also be designed into a network data model data base).
5. **High-level programming languages.** Programming languages have been developed specifically to access data bases defined via the relational data model; these languages permit data to be manipulated as groups or files rather than procedurally, one record at a time.

Definitions

The relational data model uses the concept of a relation to represent what we have previously called a file. A **relation** is viewed as a two-dimensional table. Three examples of relations for Pine Valley Furniture are shown in Figure 6-21. A relation has the following properties:

1. Each column contains values about the same attribute, and each table cell value must be simple (a single value).
2. Each column has a distinct name (attribute name), and the order of columns is immaterial.

Figure 6-21
Example of a relational data model

PRODUCT relation

Attributes

PRODUCT#	DESCRIPTION	PRICE	QUANTITY-ON-HAND	Relative record#
0100	TABLE	500.00	42	1
0975	WALL UNIT	750.00	0	2
1250	CHAIR	400.00	13	3
1775	DRESSER	500.00	8	4

Tuples

Primary key

VENDOR relation

VENDOR#	VENDOR-NAME	VENDOR-CITY
26	MAPLE HILL	DENVER
13	CEDAR CREST	BOULDER
16	OAK PEAK	FRANKLIN
12	CHERRY MTN	LONDON

SUPPLIES relation

VENDOR#	PRODUCT#	VENDOR-PRICE
13	1775	250.00
16	0100	150.00
16	1250	200.00
26	1250	200.00
26	1775	275.00

3. Each row is distinct; that is, one row cannot duplicate another row for selected key attribute columns.
4. The sequence of the rows is immaterial.

As shown in Figure 6-21, a **tuple** is the collection of values that compose one row of a relation. A tuple is equivalent to a record instance. An *n-tuple* is a tuple composed of *n* attribute values, where *n* is called the **degree** of the relation. PRODUCT is an example of a 4-tuple. The number of tuples in a relation is its **cardinality.**

A **domain** is the set of possible values for an attribute. For example, the domain for QUANTITY-ON-HAND in the PRODUCT relation is all integers greater than or equal to zero. The domain for CITY in the VENDOR relation is a set of alphabetic character strings restricted to the names of U.S. cities.

We can use a shorthand notation to abstractly represent relations (or tables). The three relations in Figure 6-21 can be written in this notation as

PRODUCT (PRODUCT#,DESCRIPTION,PRICE,
QUANTITY-ON-HAND)
VENDOR(VENDOR#,VENDOR-NAME,VENDOR-CITY)
SUPPLIES(VENDOR#,PRODUCT#,VENDOR-PRICE)

In this form, the attribute (or attributes in combination) for which no more than one tuple may have the same (combined) value is called the **primary key.** (The primary key attributes are underlined for clarity.) The relational data model requires that a primary key of a tuple (or any component attribute if a combined key) may not contain a null value. Although several different attributes (called **candidate keys**) might serve as the primary key, only one (or one combination) is chosen. These other keys are then called **alternate keys.**

The SUPPLIES relation in Figure 6-21 requires two attributes in combination in order to identify uniquely each tuple. A composite or **concatenated key** is a key that consists of two or more attributes appended together. Concatenated keys appear frequently in a relational data base, since intersection data, like VENDOR-PRICE, may be uniquely identified by a combination of the primary keys of the related entities. Each component of a concatenated key can be used to identify tuples in another relation. In fact, values for all component keys of a concatenated key must be present, although nonkey attribute values may be missing. Further, the relational model has been enhanced by some (e.g., Hammer and McLeod 1978) to indicate that a tuple (e.g., for PRODUCT) logically should exist with its key value (e.g., PRODUCT#) if that value appears in a SUPPLIES tuple; this deals with existence dependencies.

We can relate tuples in the relational model only when there are common attributes in the relations involved. We will expand on this idea in the next section. The SUPPLIES relation also suggests that an *M:N* relationship requires the definition of a third relation, much like a link or intersection record in the simple network model.

Codd (1970) popularized the use of relations and tables as a way to model data. At first glance, this view of data may seem only to be a different perspective on the network data model (all we have done is replace address pointers with logical pointers and eliminate lines from the data base diagram). Several debates have essentially argued this point (see "The Data Base Debate" 1982, and Olle 1975). Codd and many others have shown that relations are actually formal operations on mathematical sets. Further, most data processing operations (e.g., printing of selected records and finding related records) can also be represented by mathematical operators on relations. The result of mathematical operations can be proved to have certain properties. A collection of operations, called normalization, has been shown to result in data bases with desirable maintenance and logical properties. This mathematical elegance and visual simplicity have made the relational data model one of the driving forces in the information systems field.

Relationships in the Relational Data Model

The relational data model is as rich as the complex network model in its ability to represent directly, without much redundancy, a wide variety of relationship types. However, unlike the network model, relationships are implicit; that is, there is no diagrammatic convention (arcs, or links) used to explicitly show a relationship between two relations (i.e., relationship between entities).

The basic construct for representing a relationship in the relational data model is to place a common attribute in each related relation. To see how this works for Pine Valley Furniture, consider the following set of relations that define a relational data base for the complex network of Figure 6-12a:

CUSTOMER(CUSTOMER#,CUSTOMER-ADDRESS,
CUSTOMER-DETAILS)
ORDER(ORDER#,CUSTOMER#,ORDER-DATE,
DELIVERY-DATE,TOTAL-AMOUNT)
PRODUCT(PRODUCT#,DESCRIPTION,PRICE,
QUANTITY-ON-HAND)
ORDER-LINE(ORDER#,PRODUCT#,
QUANTITY-ORDERED,EXTENDED-PRICE)
VENDOR(VENDOR#,VENDOR-NAME,VENDOR-CITY)
SUPPLIES(VENDOR#,PRODUCT#)

In this example, CUSTOMER, PRODUCT, and VENDOR are basic relations that exist independently of all other data. The ORDER relation, too, can exist independently, but one of its attributes, CUSTOMER#, called a **cross-reference key,** implements the Orders-for-Customer relationship from Figure 6-12a. The attribute CUSTOMER# in the ORDER relation could have any name (say, ACCOUNT#). As long as the domain of values and the meaning of CUSTOMER# and ACCOUNT# are the same, then proper linking of related tuples can occur. We will use a dashed underline to denote a cross-reference key. The problem with using different names in different relations for the same attribute is that a "reader" of a relational data base definition may not readily understand that these two attributes can be used to link related data. In most cases, use of a cross-reference key in the relational data model means that, for example, any value of CUSTOMER# found in an ORDER tuple logically should exist as a CUSTOMER# in some unique existing CUSTOMER tuple.

The ORDER relation has its own unique key, ORDER#. An alternate key might be the combination of CUSTOMER# and ORDER-DATE (if customers do not submit two or more orders in a day). If ORDER# was not an essential piece of data for applications of this data base, then the following SALE relation would be sufficient:

SALE(CUSTOMER#,ORDER-DATE,DELIVERY-DATE,
TOTAL-AMOUNT)

Here the CUSTOMER# key appears as (part of) the primary key in each related record (tuple). In this case, CUSTOMER# is referred to as a **foreign key.** The term **referential integrity** applies to both cross-reference and foreign keys, and means that the key value must exist in the associated relation for data base integrity. Thus, a SALE cannot be created unless a CUSTOMER row exists for the referenced customer *and* a CUSTOMER row may not be deleted if this will leave any SALE row without a referenced CUSTOMER. Foreign keys are common in relational data bases due to the way they are designed, as will be seen later.

The ORDER-LINE and SUPPLIES relations exist because of *M:N* relationships. ORDER-LINE is like the intersection record of a network data base where QUANTITY-ORDERED and EXTENDED-PRICE are the intersection data. The concatenated key is composed of the keys of the related relations. The SUPPLIES relation is like the link record of a simple network data base. In this data base, we do not care to know anything about this *M:N* relationship other than the PRODUCT and VENDOR associations themselves.

Three-way and higher-order relationships are represented in a way similar to Figure 6-15 for the network model. The relational version of Figure 6-15 is

PRODUCT(PRODUCT#,DESCRIPTION,PRICE,
QUANTITY-ON-HAND)
VENDOR(VENDOR#,VENDOR-NAME,VENDOR-CITY)
WAREHOUSE(WAREHOUSE#,W-CITY,W-CAPACITY)
P-W-V(PRODUCT#,WAREHOUSE#,VENDOR#,LEAD-TIME)

LEAD-TIME is included to show how intersection data would appear in this case. It is important to note that the relational data model here includes only four relations, whereas the equivalent network model included four record types and three relationships in the representation/definition. The difference, as always, is that relationships are implicit from attributes in different relations that have common domains. Although necessary for relating two relations, having common domains is not a sufficient condition for sensible relating (called joining). For example, QUANTITY-ON-HAND and W-CAPACITY may have the same domain (any positive integer with a specified upper limit), but we would find it difficult to describe a meaningful relationship that relates PRODUCT and VENDOR using this domain and these attributes.

An intrafile loop (intrarelation) relationship is represented in the relational model by including as an additional attribute the relation's primary key. For example, a relationship that groups customers from a common parent organization would be shown with the following modification of the CUSTOMER relation previously given:

CLIENT(CUSTOMER#,CUSTOMER-ADDRESS,
PARENT-CUSTOMER#)

Here both CUSTOMER# and PARENT-CUSTOMER# have the same domain of values.

The properties of a table/relation in the relational data model do prohibit a logical sequence relationship. The relational model assumes that sequence is not a natural characteristic of data but is relevant only when data are manipulated. This emphasizes again the application independence of the relational model. Sequencing will be produced by a data manipulation language during reporting.

Cycles can also be represented in the relational model. In a cycle, relations A and B have a common attribute, relations B and C a common attribute, and so on, until the cycle is completed with relations X and A with a common attribute. Because logical pointers (common attributes) are used to link related tuples, maintenance is not a problem as it was for cycles in the network model. As long as proper logical key values are entered, the correct physical linkages will be made by the DBMS. Referential integrity is, of course, still a concern.

A class relationship can also be depicted in a relational data base. Consider the following relational data model for the class relationship example of Figure 6-18:

CUSTOMER(CUSTOMER#,CUSTOMER-DETAILS)
ORDER(ORDER#,CUSTOMER#,ORDER-DETAILS)
INVOICE(INVOICE#,CUSTOMER#,ORDER#,INVOICE-DETAILS)
PAYMENT(JOURNAL#,CUSTOMER#,PAYMENT-DETAILS)
I-P(INVOICE#,JOURNAL#,AMT-APPLIED, I-P-DETAILS)

The common attribute CUSTOMER# allows a user to deal with all contact entities for the same customer, although a single CONTACT entity (relation) has not been created. Some relational data base management systems support definition of a "view" that could be used to define such a class relation as a merger of attribute values from each of the component CONTACT relations. The JOIN relational operator, to be introduced in the next section, can also be used to create such a merged table.

Any table that satisfies the four properties presented in the previous section can be a relation. In fact, a table with these properties is said to be in **first normal form.** Experience has shown that although sufficient for data processing, first normal form (1NF) relations can still have some undesirable data maintenance properties. In general, these problems are inconsistencies that can occur in a data base after records are inserted, deleted, or modified. The process of ridding a data base definition of these problems or anomalies is called **normalization.** Because it is a process of data base design, normalization will be covered in Chapters 7 and 8. What we will present here are the desirable relationships between *attributes* that are the basis for normalization.

A relationship between attributes is called a **functional dependency.** Attribute B is functionally dependent (or simply dependent) on attribute A if at each point in time, each value of A has only one value of B associated with it. For example,

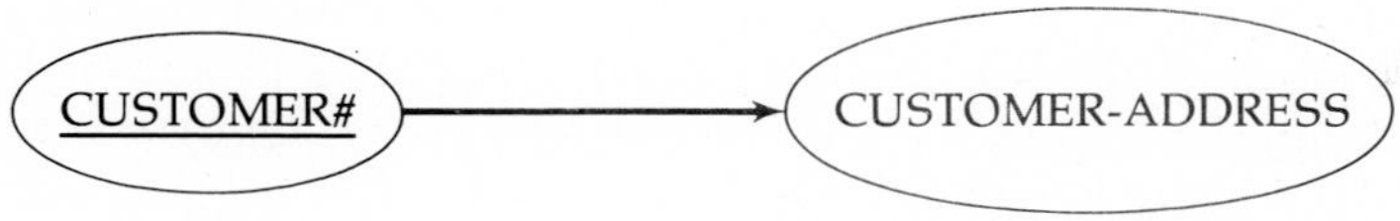

illustrates that CUSTOMER-ADDRESS is dependent on CUSTOMER#.

The primary key (single or concatenated) in a relation uniquely identifies the tuple and hence each of the remaining attributes in the relation. The ORDER and ORDER-LINE relations from the beginning of this section can be illustrated using such a dependency diagram (called a bubble diagram) as follows:

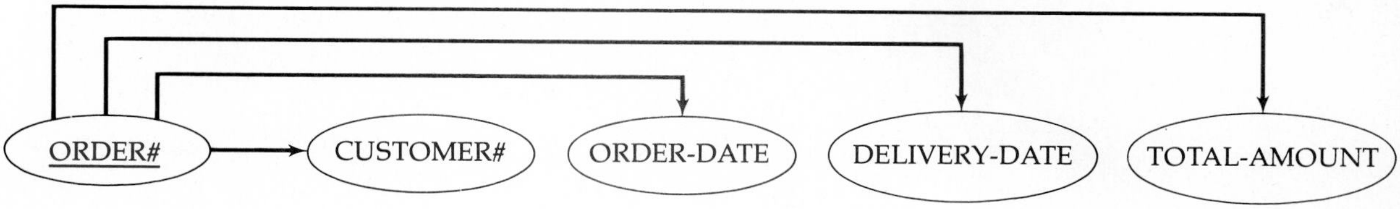

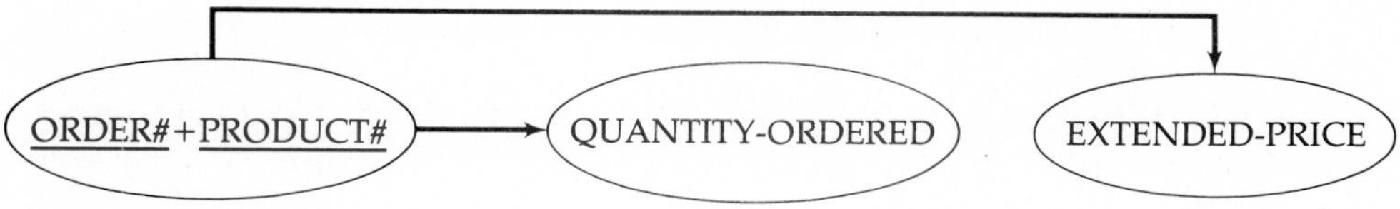

These bubble diagrams indicate that each of the ORDER relation nonkey attributes depends on ORDER# and *only* ORDER#. Further, it is shown that all nonkey attributes of the ORDER-LINE relation depend only on the *whole* concatenated key of ORDER# and PRODUCT#. This example suggests two other relation properties (in addition to the four already given):

5. *All* nonkey attributes should be *fully dependent* on the *whole* key.
6. Each nonkey attribute should be dependent only on the relation's key, not on any other nonkey.

Property (5) is associated with second normal form (2NF) and property (6) with third normal form (3NF). Chapters 7 and 8 demonstrate how to produce relations with these and other properties as part of a data base design process. The purpose here is to introduce the concept of interattribute functional dependencies as an important, practical component of the relational data model. Second, third, and so forth, normal forms are not essential parts of the relational model, but the relational model has been the context for the discovery of these desirable data base design properties. These same properties can be included in a network data base.

Data Processing with the Relational Data Model

The basic component of the relational data model is a relation. Not surprisingly, it is relations, *not* tuples, that are referenced by a programmer or query writer when accessing a data base via a relational DBMS. For this reason, data processing with a relational data base is called file-at-a-time, not record-at-a-time. Whereas programming with the network model involves *repetitively* accessing a record and all its related records, programming with the relational model involves manipulating a series of *groups* (relations) of qualified records, each group as a whole.

Two classes of special-purpose relational data manipulation languages (DMLs) characterize most available methods for processing relational data bases: relational algebra and relational calculus. Chapters 14 and 15 will present detailed examples in each of these classes and examples of a few other unique relational languages. Although some relational data base management systems permit programs written in procedural languages to access a relational data base, the standard practice is to use one of the high-level special-purpose DMLs.

A significant feature of relational languages is that the result of any operation is also a relation. Thus, the result can then be further manipulated by the same operations as so-called base relations.

Relational algebra manipulates one or two relations as operands and produces a new relation as the result. Relational algebra was the first DML proposed for the relational data model. The basic operators were presented in one of Codd's (1970) first publications on the relational model. We will introduce three of these relational algebra operators here (SELECT, PROJECT, and JOIN) to suggest the style of data processing; other operators will be reviewed in Chapter 15.

Figure 6-22a lists examples of the three basic relational algebra operators for the data base of Figure 6-21 (these examples are discussed below).

The first operator, SELECT, retrieves all tuples of a specified relation that satisfy a certain condition and constructs a new table that contains the selected tuples. The qualification in example (a) is an equality restriction on a primary key, so the RESULT relation will contain only one tuple. In example (b), it is possible that many tuples have a value of PRICE less than 550, so RESULT here could contain many tuples. PRICE is a nonunique attribute (potentially a secondary key). It is assumed that a primary key access method has been implemented to make query (a) efficient to process. In the next section, we will see why query (b) may or may not be costly to answer. Example (c) demonstrates that tuple selection conditions may be made complex by connecting basic conditions by Boolean operators ("and," "or," "not").

The SELECT operator constructs a new table by taking a *horizontal* subset

(a) SELECT PRODUCT WHERE PRODUCT# = '0975' GIVING RESULT
(b) SELECT PRODUCT WHERE PRICE < 550.00 GIVING RESULT
(c) SELECT PRODUCT WHERE DESCRIPTION = 'TABLE' AND QUANTITY-ON-HAND > 12 GIVING RESULT
(d) PROJECT SUPPLIES OVER (PRODUCT#, VENDOR-PRICE) GIVING RESULT
(e) PROJECT PRODUCT OVER (DESCRIPTION) WHERE PRICE < 600.00 GIVING RESULT
(f) JOIN VENDOR AND SUPPLIES OVER VENDOR# GIVING RESULT
(g) JOIN VENDOR OVER VENDOR# AND SUPPLIES OVER SUPPLIER# GIVING RESULT

(a)

RESULT relation

PRODUCT#	VENDOR-PRICE
1775	250.00
0100	150.00
1250	200.00
1775	275.00

(b)

RESULT relation

VENDOR#	PRODUCT#	VENDOR-NAME	VENDOR-CITY	VENDOR-PRICE
13	1775	CEDAR CREST	BOULDER	250.00
16	0100	OAK PEAK	FRANKLIN	150.00
16	1250	OAK PEAK	FRANKLIN	200.00
26	1250	MAPLE HILL	DENVER	200.00
26	1775	MAPLE HILL	DENVER	275.00

(c)

Figure 6-22 Relational algebra example:
(a) example relational algebra commands
(b) RESULT table for PROJECT of example (d)
(c) RESULT table for JOIN of example (f)

of an existing table. That is, it selects those whole rows that satisfy a stated condition. In contrast, the PROJECT operator forms a *vertical* subset of an existing table by extracting specified columns (attributes) from all tuples to form a new table. If only some of the key attributes are extracted, the resultant table could contain duplicate rows. Different relational algebra DMLs handle this violation differently. Some automatically eliminate redundancy; some leave elimination of redundant rows as an option for the programmer/user.

Example (d) illustrates the typical form of a command with the PROJECT operator. Figure 6-22 shows the RESULT table of this command for the SUPPLIES relation of Figure 6-21. Note that the RESULT table has one fewer tuple than the SUPPLIES relation, since PROJECTion resulted in duplicate rows. Example (e) demonstrates that PROJECT can include an implicit SELECT by use of a WHERE clause.

The third basic operator, and the one most unique and fundamental to relational algebra, is JOIN. The JOIN operator combines the data from two relations based on values for common attributes (or, more precisely, two attributes with a common domain). As with SELECT and PROJECT, the result of JOIN is also a relation.

Example (f) illustrates the JOIN operator. In this JOIN, the rows of the VENDOR and SUPPLIES relations are scanned. Whenever a tuple from each has the same value for VENDOR#, the two tuples are concatenated to form a new relation tuple. Figure 6-22c is the RESULT relation for this JOIN. Note that there is no RESULT tuple for VENDOR# 12, since this value is *not* in common between the VENDOR and SUPPLIES relations. Tables produced from a JOIN may not have one or more of the six properties discussed previously; the RESULT table for this example violates property (5), which states that all nonkey attributes must be fully dependent on the key. Example (g) shows how each relation in the JOIN can use different names for the same attribute on which the tables are being JOINed. The only requirement is that the two names have the same meaning (domain). In this case, VENDOR# and SUPPLIER# are called **role names.**

The type of JOIN just illustrated is called the **natural join.** The natural join makes all matches for tuples with common values. Chapter 14 will discuss other types of JOINs.

The second major category of relational DMLs is relational calculus. **Relational calculus** manipulates relations implicitly by specifying conditions that can involve attributes from several relations. Relational calculus combines the three algebra operators into one operator, called RETRIEVE, and a WHERE clause for SELECT and JOIN. For example, a relational calculus type of command for example (f) would be

```
RETRIEVE(VENDOR.VENDOR#,SUPPLIES.PRODUCT#,
         VENDOR.VENDOR-NAME,VENDOR.VENDOR-CITY,
         VENDOR.VENDOR-PRICE)
INTO RESULT WHERE VENDOR.VENDOR# = SUPPLIES.VENDOR#
```

Since several relations can be referenced in one query and the same attribute name can be used in each of these, it is necessary to prefix each attribute name with the relation name that applies to the question and that attribute. This example shows how a WHERE clause is used to imply a JOIN. A JOIN literally means that where the common attribute values are equal, create a new tuple. Also, this example shows that PROJECT is replaced in the syntax by listing the attributes that are to be included in the table being created (the INTO table).

Very comprehensive existence statements can be made in relational calculus that essentially combine several JOINs into one statement. Suppose that a snowstorm has made transportation from Denver to Pine Valley Furniture impossible. Pine Valley management realizes that some of its primary suppliers ship from Denver. The Pine Valley purchasing manager poses the following question: "What products supplied by any vendor in Denver have a quantity on hand less than ten units (considered a critically low value)?" Relational calculus would structure the question in the following way:

```
RETRIEVE (PRODUCT.PRODUCT#) INTO RESULT
  WHERE PRODUCT.QUANTITY-ON-HAND<10 AND
        PRODUCT.PRODUCT# = SUPPLIES.PRODUCT# AND
        SUPPLIES.VENDOR# = VENDOR.VENDOR# AND
        VENDOR.VENDOR-CITY = 'DENVER'
```

The WHERE clause provides the equivalent of two JOINs, two attribute value SELECT clauses, and a PROJECT. An equivalent relational algebra would be

```
JOIN PRODUCT AND SUPPLIES OVER PRODUCT# GIVING X
JOIN X AND VENDOR OVER VENDOR# GIVING Y
SELECT Y WHERE QUANTITY-ON-HAND<10 AND
               VENDOR-CITY = 'DENVER' GIVING Z
PROJECT Z OVER(PRODUCT#) GIVING RESULT
```

A relational calculus statement can become very complicated, but it can state in one language command the equivalent of many relational algebra commands (whether written, as here, as separate statements or, as possible in some systems, as nested clauses in one statement).

Other relation-processing languages have been developed. Examples of other unique DMLs will be presented in Chapters 14 and 15.

Implementation of the Relational Data Model

As stated earlier, the relational data model is a purely logical view of data. Unlike the hierarchical and network models, whose structure and diagrammatic conventions imply specific physical linkages, in the relational model, we do not know *what* relationships have been implemented with an efficient access path and we do not know *how* a relationship has been implemented.

We might conclude that, in practice, a wide variety of data structures would be used. Surprisingly, this is not the case.

By far, the most common data structure for implementing a relational data base is the use of tree-structured indexes (often B-trees) on primary and selected secondary keys. Any attribute that is used to select tuples in a PROJECT or WHERE clause is a possible candidate for indexing. Attributes used to JOIN relations can be indexed; frequently, this greatly reduces the cost to perform a JOIN. To JOIN relations VENDOR and SUPPLIES from Figure 6-21 without an index (or without sorting both relations into order by values for the common attribute), we would have to follow this procedure:

1. Do Until end of VENDOR table.
    2. Read next VENDOR tuple.
    3. Scan the *whole* SUPPLIES relation, and if a tuple has the same VENDOR# as the current VENDOR tuple, then create a new RESULT tuple.
4. End Do.
5. Eliminate redundant tuples from relation RESULT.

With an index, step (3) is made much more efficient, since only the SUPPLIES tuples with the same VENDOR#, if any exist, need be retrieved (which is probably a very small percentage for each value of VENDOR#).

Some relational data base management systems use clever schemes to reduce the cost of using key indexes. Each query to be processed is paraphrased into a special form. This form, **disjunctive normal form** (DNF) (see Wong and Chiang 1971), structures the WHERE clauses of a query into a set of conjunctions with only OR operators between conjunctions and only AND and NOT operators within a conjunction. Any query can be rewritten into DNF.

Consider the following WHERE clause:

WHERE (PRICE>700 OR PRICE<520) AND DESCRIPTION = 'TABLE'

This can be rewritten into DNF as

WHERE (PRICE>700 AND DESCRIPTION = 'TABLE') OR
(PRICE<520 AND DESCRIPTION = 'TABLE')

In DNF, each phrase in parentheses is a conjunction. AND operators cause items from two inverted lists to be intersected and OR operators cause items from two inverted lists to be merged. Given the data base of Figure 6-21, the following three lists would be constructed from indexes on PRICE and DESCRIPTION:

LIST 1	LIST 2	LIST 3
PRICE>700	PRICE<520	DESCRIPTION = 'TABLE'
2	1	1
	3	
	4	

This WHERE clause means

```
(LIST 1 AND LIST 3) OR (LIST 2 AND LIST 3)
({2} AND {1})       OR ({1,3,4} AND {1})
   (null)           OR         (1)
                    1
```

The only record (tuple) that satisfies the query is the one in relative record 1, or PRODUCT# 0100.

Some relational data base management systems do not process the AND operators; thus, not all attributes used in WHERE clauses need to be indexed. For example, a DBMS can be designed to recognize that within a conjunction, the result of the ANDing will be a subset of the smallest list. The DBMS will then take the shortest list from each conjunction (*each* conjunction must be processed, since the result will include any record that satisfies any of the conjunctions) and merge the shortest lists together. This avoids the cost of intersecting sets while incurring the cost of accessing additional tuples that fail some qualifications within a conjunction. These extra tuples will have to be eliminated through the evaluation of values within the tuples retrieved. Hopefully, these "false drops" will be few and the extra cost to access these will be less than the cost to access additional indexes and intersect lists.

Indexes appear to be the data structure chosen for relational data bases because of the similarity of Boolean SELECT/WHERE clauses to inverted list intersection and merger. Manipulating index entries is like manipulating the tuples to which the entries point. Trying to determine an efficient pointer sequential network path for a query would cause a lot of overhead. Relational data base management systems are often used for highly interactive on-line information systems, which may have many ad hoc queries. Fast response, at the expense of extra index space, seems to be the popular choice.

Summary of the Relational Data Model

We have described the fundamentals of the relational data model. Because of its independence from the physical data base, the relational model has become an effective tool not only for managing data via a DBMS but also for conceptual and external data modeling. Normal forms, easily checked within the relational model, are often used as rules of data base design. Data manipulation languages based on relational algebra and calculus are often called "user-friendly" and are the model for fourth-generation programming languages (to be discussed in later chapters).

The relational data model does have some caveats. First, the relational model redundantly shows keys as logical pointers for implementing relationships. If these key attribute values are actually represented in all tuples in which they appear, this can lead to considerable redundancy. Further, if key values change, then the data base requires extensive maintenance. For example, if PRODUCT# appears in both the PRODUCT and SUPPLIES relations, then PRODUCT#'s must be carefully changed in two relations when products are recoded. If, on the other hand, a SUPPLIES tuple has an address pointer (physical or relative record number) to its associated PRODUCT tuple, then the SUPPLIES tuples are independent of changes in PRODUCT#'s. Since values of primary relation keys are usually tightly controlled (e.g., they cannot change PRODUCT# without deleting tuples and inserting new ones) and infrequently change value, most practitioners are not concerned with this caveat.

The second caveat is associated with the efficiency of relational data base management systems. The data processing community has found the relational DBMS most attractive for information retrieval applications, characterized by ad hoc multiple-key qualification queries. High-volume transaction processing and data maintenance applications are still frequently performed with hierarchical and network systems, although the performance of relational DBMSs is constantly improving. For those situations that exhibit information processing against a "production" data base, two alternative data base environments have been devised to cope with the lack of sufficient throughput for relational DBMSs. In the first, portions of the transaction/production data base are periodically extracted and loaded into a separate data base managed by a relational DBMS. This solution provides specialized service to two diverse applications and keeps the unstructured information processing from interfering with the main data base. In this way, the main data base performance can be tuned to high-volume applications, where efficiency is crucial. The information processing data base can be used without retarding production performance. More and more, this information processing data base is being placed on a microcomputer to provide even computer independence. Chapter 15 will discuss this development in the data base field.

In the second data base environment for information processing against a production data base, the DBMS used for transaction processing is enhanced to support a relational-like query language. In this way, users can view the data base as a set of flat files and process it at the file level. Many commercial nonrelational data base management systems provide such facilities.

The final caveat, which in some measure has been dealt with by the relational data base management systems, is a lack of semantic quality control in the relational data model. For example, since each table exists on its own, there is no guarantee that a cross-reference or foreign key will reference an existing tuple, since the relational model has no construct or property to force this existence dependency. Consider VENDOR# in the SUPPLIES relation of Figure 6-21. The basic relational model does not state that a value here must correspond to a value of VENDOR# that exists in the VENDOR relation. Many relational data base management systems have included an INTEGRITY clause on relations to specify validation rules on attribute values; for some systems, these rules can include checks on cross-reference keys. Further, the relational data model does not have a way to explicitly handle class-subclass and aggregation semantics. Some relational DBMSs provide a construct called a view that provides for a data base to be logically viewed in multiple ways. The view construct can be used to provide both class-subclass and aggregation capabilities, but explicit definition of these semantics is lacking. Time semantics are not recognized by the relational data model. Each relation must have a nonnull primary key, so uniqueness is handled to some degree.

As has been stated, the relational data model, because of its implementation independence and normalization theory, is used during the process of data base design, even for internal network or hierarchical data bases. To separate conceptual and external data base design totally from the DBMS technology (and not bias the choice of technology to relational), other data models have been developed. The Entity-Relationship Model (see Chen 1976, 1977) and the Semantic Data Model (see Hammer and McLeod 1978) are two such conceptual data models. These models are presented in the next section. This chapter will then conclude with a review of data models, including consideration of human factors of various models (error proneness, understandability, user satisfaction).

TECHNOLOGY-INDEPENDENT DATA MODELS

The hierarchical, network, and relational data models have proved to be effective notations for representing organizational data. With a few limitations (especially for hierarchical), data and a wide variety of relationships can be easily modeled using these architectures. This means that at the internal data model level, we can build data bases to support data processing efficiently for a wide range of data, as well as support query and maintenance processing.

Some people in the data base field, however, have argued that for external and conceptual data modeling, it is better to use data base description conventions that are independent of the particular DBMS that will be or could be used. In this way, a data base designer can specify data base requirements without indicating a bias (albeit subtle) toward use of a particular DBMS. Also, for a truly distributed, multiple data model (and DBMS) data base, a central mapping data model is needed to encompass all distributed components and to be able to translate among all data models used.

Unique data model forms have been developed for external and conceptual levels. Their purpose has been to enhance other data models with additional information particularly relevant at these logical data levels and to provide tools that are independent of technologies used for implementing the conceptual design. Two such data models will be introduced here. They are the Entity-Relationship and Semantic Data models.

Figure 6-23
Example of an Entity-Relationship diagram

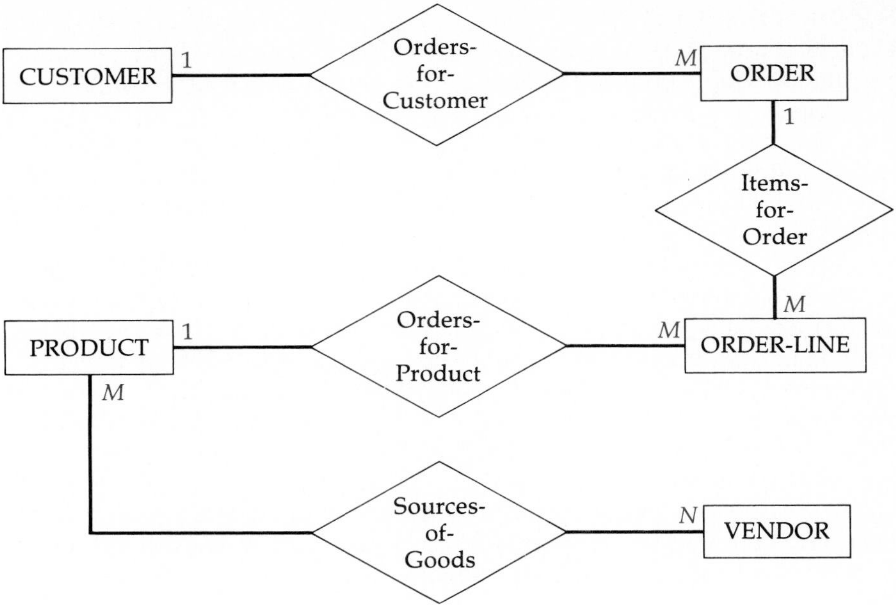

The Entity-Relationship Data Model

Basically, the entity-relationship (E/R) data model (originated by Chen 1976, 1977) augments the network model by introducing a special symbol, the diamond, to explicitly indicate each relationship. Figure 6-23 illustrates this by depicting in E/R notation the complex network data model of Figure 6-12a. Each diamond represents a relationship type; this diamond exists for both 1:*M* and *M:N* relationships between entities (rectangles). Letters on lines between an entity rectangle and a relationship diamond specify the number of entities (e.g., 1 CUSTOMER) associated with each instance of the relationship (e.g., Orders-for-Customer).

Further, a diamond (e.g., Sources-of-Goods) exists whether or not intersection data are present. This means that an E/R diagram does not have to be redrawn, as would a complex network diagram, if such intersection data (e.g., the vendor's price for a product) were recognized. In this way, an E/R diagram acts like a simple network data model (see Figure 6-12b). Thus, it is easy to translate from an E/R data model into a simple network data model for implementation.

An E/R data model can also be supplemented to indicate data elements, as shown in Figure 6-24. Note in this case that both entities and relationships may have data element bubbles associated with them. Data element

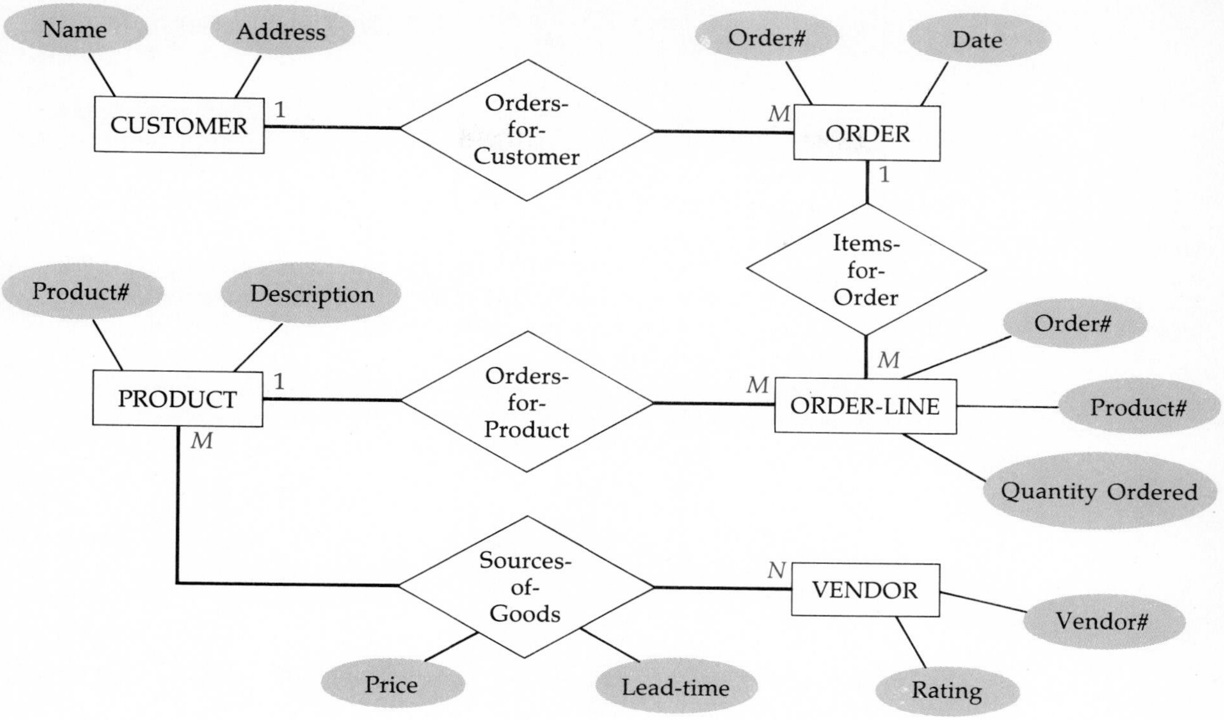

Figure 6-24
Example of an E/R diagram with data elements

bubbles for a relationship are intersection data. When an E/R data model is being implemented, diamonds (relationships) with no associated data bubbles (e.g., Orders-for-Customers) do not have to appear as separate "record" types; a diamond with bubbles requires implementation as a distinct record (relation) type.

Another feature of the E/R data model is the ability to signify special semantic controls on entities and relationships. One such situation is called an **existence dependency,** which is illustrated in Figure 6-25a. Here an ORDER-LINE cannot exist without an associated ORDER. Further, if an ORDER is canceled, then all associated ORDER-LINEs must also be purged. The "E" inside a relationship diamond explicitly indicates an existence dependency. This figure also illustrates a second semantic property, an identifier **(ID) dependency.** Here the ORDER-LINE entity uses the Order# as part of its identifier. If, for some reason, an Order# changes, then the ID dependency explicitly indicates that ORDER-LINE entities associated with such an ORDER also have to be updated. An "ID" in a relationship diamond is used to indicate an ID dependency. Although in this case an existence dependency implies an ID dependency, this is not always true. Figure 6-25b illustrates that an ORDER cannot exist without a CUSTOMER, but each ORDER is identified by an independent primary key (Order#).

Figure 6-26 illustrates the way the E/R data model depicts other types of relationships. Figure 6-26a shows the E/R version of the three-way relationship of Figure 6-15, and Figure 6-26b is the E/R equivalent to the loop relationship of Figure 6-16.

Because relationships can have associated data, the E/R data model poses an interesting dilemma: Is a relationship (diamond) really an entity "in sheep's clothing"? Consider Figure 6-27, which also depicts the complex network data base of Figure 6-12a. Compare Figures 6-24 and 6-27. Note that in Figure 6-24, ORDER-LINE is depicted as an entity, but in Figure 6-27 it is a relationship. Because there is associated data with ORDER-LINE, a relation or record type would appear in an internal implementation, so in this case the distinction between entity and relationship is simply a matter of how one views the data.

Whether or not an entity or relationship results in a record type or relation in an internal implementation basically depends on two factors:

Figure 6-25
Semantic controls in E/R diagrams:
(a) example of existence and ID dependencies
(b) example of an existence dependency only

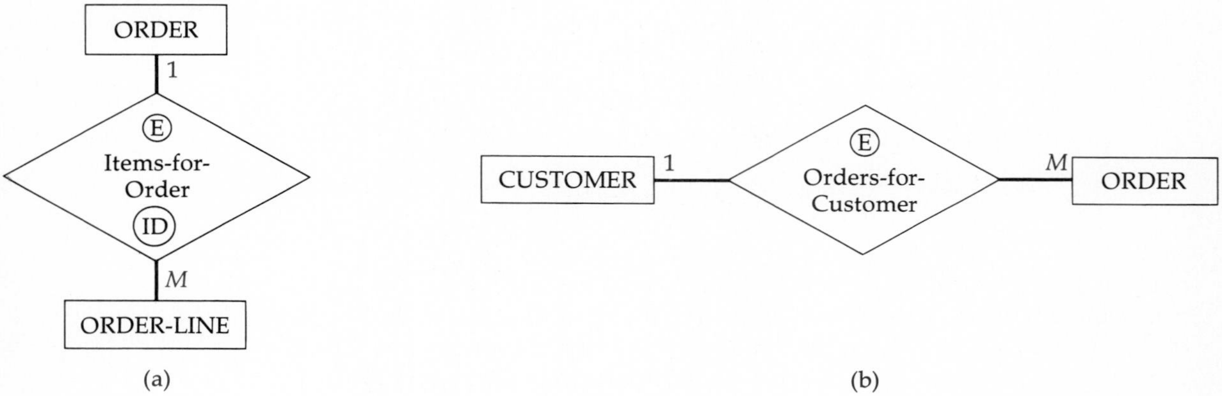

Figure 6-26
Examples of E/R data model:
(a) three-way relationship
(b) loop relationship

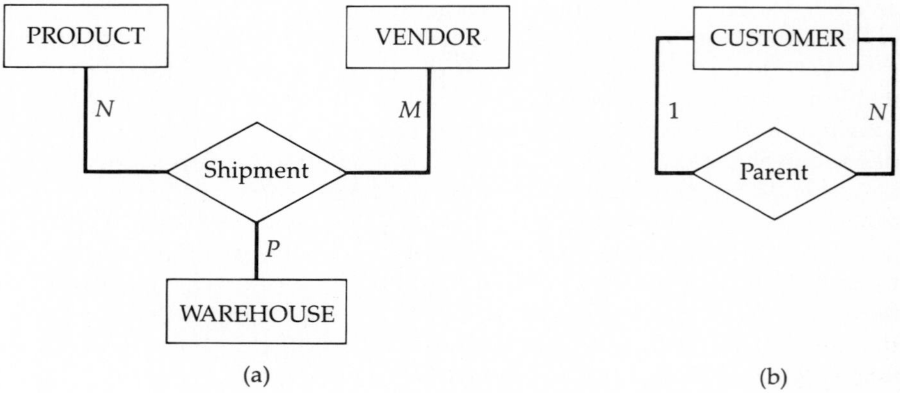

whether there are any data associated with the entity or relationship and the capabilities of the internal data model to be used. For example, in Figure 6-27, since the ORDER-LINE relationship has associated data, it will result in a record or relation. On the other hand, Sources-of-Goods will not require a record type in a complex network internal data model, but will for simple network or relational.

Another interesting situation of implementing an E/R data model is shown in Figure 6-28. Here, since all we know about DEPENDENTs of an EMPLOYEE are their names, network and relational data model implementations are different. A network would simply have two record types associated by a relationship (called a set in Chapter 13), in which the DEPENDENT record would contain Dependent-Name. A relational implementation would not represent DEPENDENTs as a relation, but would only represent essentially the Relatives relationship in which Employee# is a cross-reference to the EMPLOYEE relation. If DEPENDENT were also ID-dependent on EMPLOYEE, then Employee# would also be part of the RELATIVES relation key in the relational implementation.

The exact form and notation for the E/R model is still evolving since, unlike the technology-based data models, the E/R model has not been standardized. Newer, more recent versions of the E/R model have been developed specifically in order to include more semantics into a model of a data

Figure 6-27
E/R diagram with an ORDER-LINE relationship

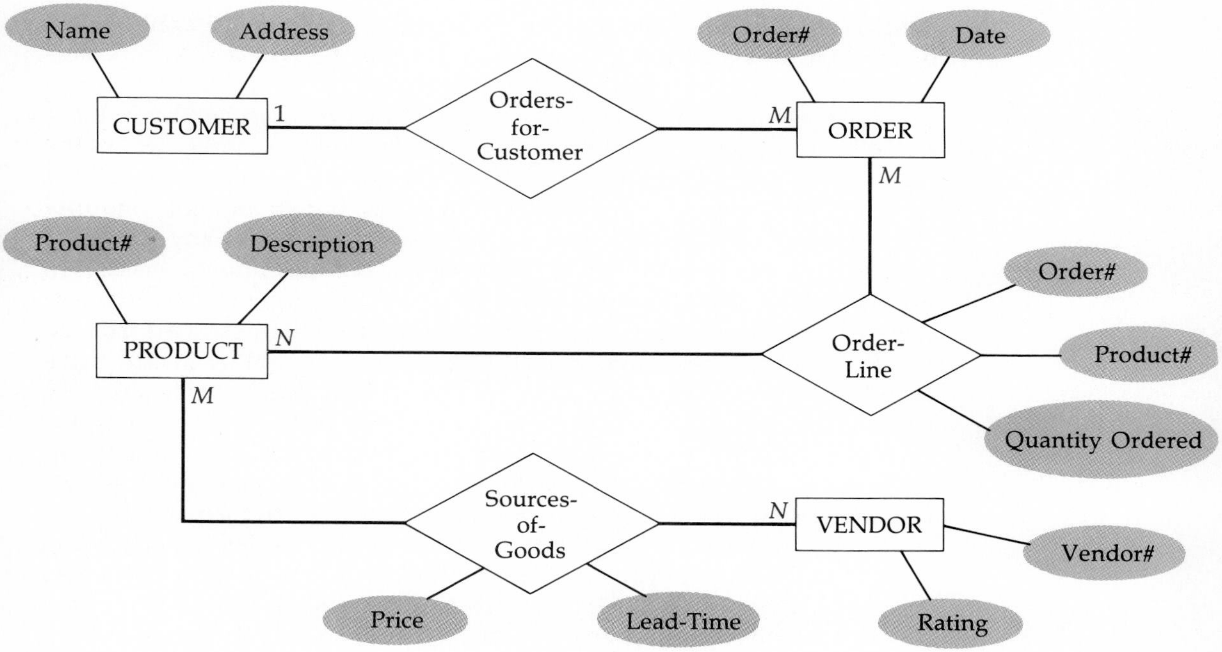

Figure 6-28
Example of implementation of an E/R diagram

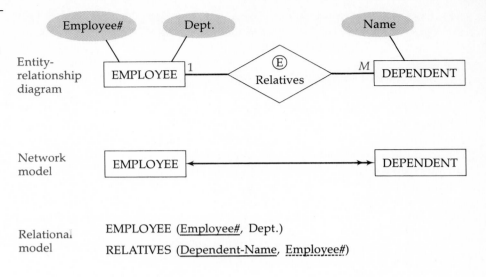

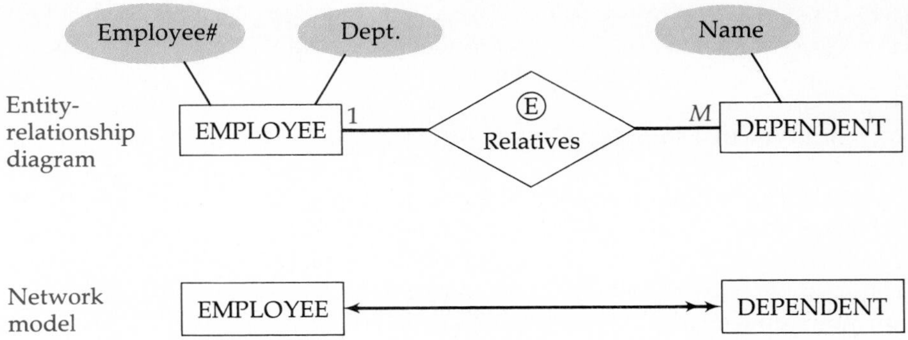

Relational model

EMPLOYEE (Employee#, Dept.)

RELATIVES (Dependent-Name, Employee#)

base. Figure 6-29 is an example of the use of some recent extensions to the E/R model to represent a portion of the Mountain View Community Hospital data base of Figure 3-12. In this example, the Patient, Staff, and Hourly-Staff entities are classes with subclasses of entities, and the Hourly-Staff subclass is itself a subclass of the Staff entity. The Service entity is ID-dependent on keys from the Patient entity and the Nurse or Nonprofessional entities, as indicated by the "performed on" and "performed by" identifying relationships; a service is performed on a patient by either a nurse or a nonprofessional employee, but not both, as indicated by the exclusive arc across the "performed by" relationships. Each patient must have at least one service provided to him or her, but an individual hourly-staff member may never perform a service attributable to any particular patient since the "performed by" relationships indicate optional service. An hourly-staff member may supervise zero, one, or many other hourly-staff members and hourly-staff may be married to each other, but staff married to each other may not supervise each other, as indicated by the exclusive occurrences notation on the "supervises" and "is married to" relationships; such relationships or restrictions involving physicians are of no concern. Each in-patient is assigned to one bed, but a bed may be unoccupied; out-patients are not assigned to a bed. A patient must be treated by at least one physician to be a true patient, but a patient may be treated by many physicians.

The E/R data model is growing in popularity for modeling data during data base planning and conceptual application design. Several automated systems analysis tools now include E/R modeling as one way to display the contents of the data and systems dictionary. The E/R data model is an important contribution to the data base field.

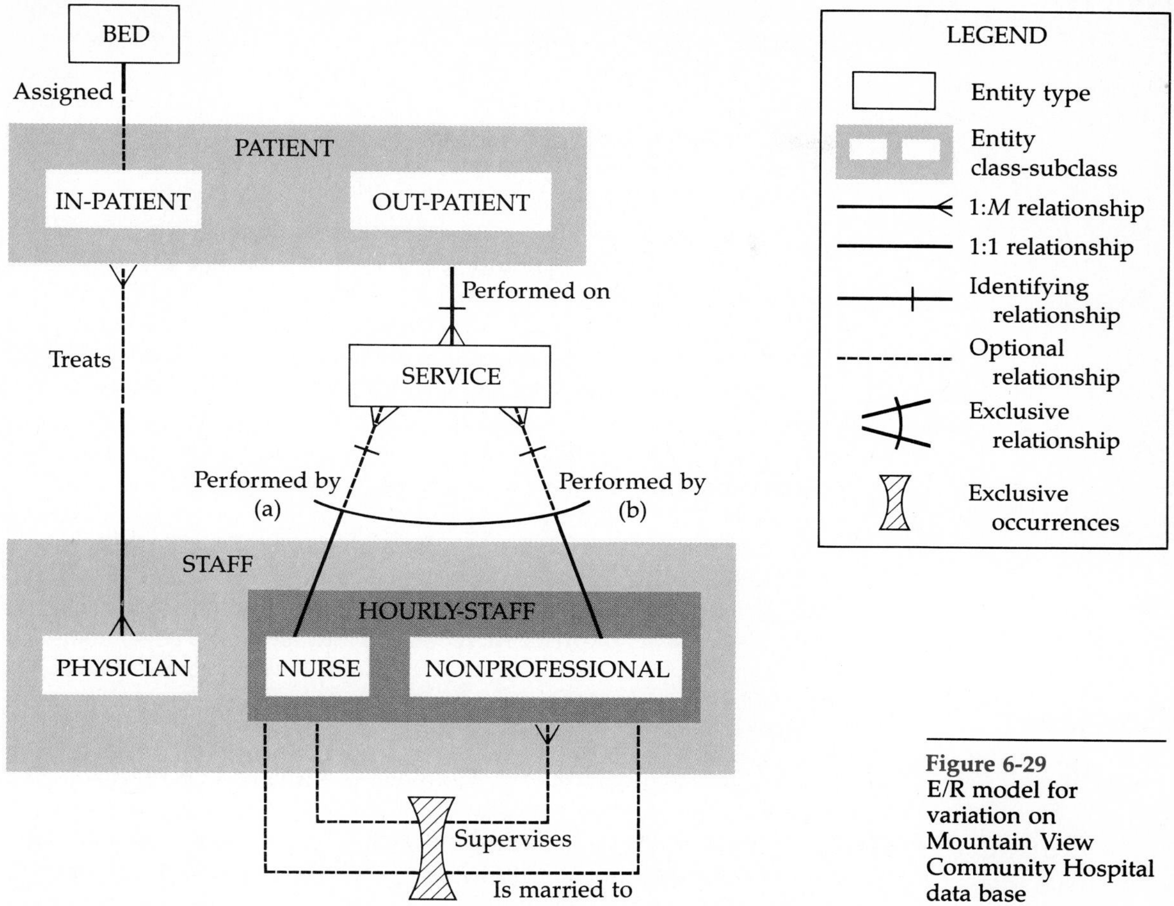

Figure 6-29
E/R model for variation on Mountain View Community Hospital data base

The Semantic Data Model

As was stated earlier, the purpose of data modeling at the external and conceptual levels is to capture an understanding of data in an organization. Emphasis should be on meaning, not structure, so that the data base requirements can be identified. Thus, a data model that concentrates on documenting the meaning of data would incorporate much of the information needed for subsequent structuring of data.

Several sources (Hammer and McLeod 1978; Smith and Smith 1977; Teorey and Fry 1982) suggest information necessary to give meaning to entities and relationships. Some of these items are as follows:

1. **Relationship membership rules.** Each entity may exist independently of the other; the existence of one is dependent on the existence of the other (these two rules were incorporated into the E/R model);

the association is conditional on some criteria (only Customer Orders, not Shop or Build-to-Stock Orders, are linked to Customers); an entity is permanently associated with another entity, and association cannot be switched (an Order is always for a given Customer until the Order is deleted); entity association is temporal (employee assignment to a department); and entities are selectively associated (a warehouse contains products or raw materials, but not both).

2. **Entity abstractions.** This is the class-subclass semantic or generalization-specialization semantic discussed in this chapter. A subclass (such as HOURLY-STAFF from Figure 6-29) may have attributes unique to that entity type (e.g., Hourly-Wage and Skill-Code), but a subclass also inherits the attributes of its superclass (that is, the attributes for any type of Staff, such as Name, Department, and Hire-Date).
3. **Entity aggregations.** This is the same as the aggregation semantic discussed in this chapter. An aggregate entity type may have attributes about the collection of entities in the aggregate. For example, if PRODUCT-LINE is an aggregate entity for which an instance includes all the Product entity instances for a given PRODUCT-LINE, then a PRODUCT-LINE instance might also have attributes such as Product-Line-Manager-Name and Average-Price; or a JOB entity, an instance of which is a set of MATERIAL, WORKER, and ROUTING instances for a particular manufacturing JOB, might have a Promised-Completion-Date. Component entity instances of an aggregate do not inherit properties of the aggregate in which they participate.

With this perspective in mind, Hammer and McLeod (1978) developed the Semantic Data Model to specify this and other descriptive information about entities. The Semantic Data Model (SDM), like the relational model, is not actually a diagrammatic model, but a definitional model. An example of an SDM for part of the data base of Figure 6-12a, with some enhancements to illustrate the extensive descriptive clauses of the SDM, is shown in Figure 6-30. The SDM is extensive, and not all definitional clauses are shown here; only some are included to indicate the richness of this data model.

This figure shows that each entity (class) can be defined by a name (e.g., CUSTOMER), a description, an interclass connection (in the case of entity class, CUST-ORDER), and a set of member attributes. The interclass connection for CUST-ORDER specifies that instances of this entity are a specialization of ORDER entities, specifically those that are Build-to-Stock Orders. The member attributes of an entity (class) are described by a name and a set of clauses that indicate the range of permissible values (e.g., Name of CUSTOMER must come from a set of values called NAMES, defined elsewhere). In addition, attributes can be given a more precise meaning by indicating if values may change, if they may be missing/null, whether they are related to values in other entities (the inverse clause), and if they are nonsimple fields of multiple values (e.g., Contact attribute of CUSTOMER,

Figure 6-30
Example of the Semantic Data Model

CUSTOMER
    Description: all people and organizations that have purchased products from Pine Valley Furniture
    Member attributes:
        Name
            Value class: NAMES
            Not changeable
            May not be null
        Address
            Value class: ADDRESSES
        Contact
            Value class: CUST-ORDER
            Inverse: Client
            Multivalued

ORDER
    Description: all orders for products by customers and orders written to build inventory
    Member attributes:
        Order#
            Value class: ORDER-NUMBERS
            Not changeable
            May not be null
        Date
            Value class: DATES
        Type
            Value class: ORDER-TYPES
        Value
            Value class: MONEY
        Status
            Value class: STATUS-VALUES

CUST-ORDER
    Description: all orders for products by customers
    Interclass connection: subclass of ORDER where Type=CUST
    Member attributes:
        Client
            Value class: NAMES
            Inverse: Contact
            Not changeable
    Class attributes:
        Total-$-Value
            Value class: MONEY
            Derivation: Sum of all Values across all members
        Number-of-Orders-Active
            Value class: INTEGERS
            Derivation: number-of-members of this entity class where Status=Active

which is a list of CUST-ORDER references). An entity class itself, as well as instances of the entity class, may have attributes. For example, the CUST-ORDER class as a whole (that is, as an aggregate entity) is characterized by Total-$-Value, which is a sum of the Value attributes across all instances of this set, and Number-of-Orders-Active, which is a count of the number of active CUST-ORDERs.

As can be seen from this example, the SDM is capable of representing almost any characteristic of data and relationships a data base designer could imagine. In fact, the SDM can be customized to include any descriptive clause desired. An SDM data base description can become quite long because of this richness of information. It is therefore the most complete data model available for defining a data base at external and conceptual levels. When a data base designer requires a method to consolidate various levels of data abstraction, the SDM seems appropriate because of its ability to interconnect the meanings of different entity classes. The SDM is certainly one data modeling tool that should be in the toolbox of any data base designer.

Data base management systems using the so-called object-oriented data model based, in part, on the SDM, are under development. Use of such DBMSs is especially attractive when entity definition is dynamic, such as in engineering applications. For example, as a design engineer develops a new product, a component element will be a dynamic combination (aggregate) of previously defined parts and components. The particular data base structure cannot be anticipated in advance, and engineers need to be able to manipulate the data aggregates to form new components and products.

FACTORS IN SELECTING A DATA MODEL

The diversity of data models presented in this chapter would indicate that the developer of a data base has a difficult choice in selecting an appropriate data model. No single choice is best in all situations; in fact, the evidence suggests that the best choice is to use several data models, each for different purposes.

The choice of an appropriate internal data model should not be made until the conceptual data base is described, since the nature of the data base (types of relationships present, data processing requirements, and so on) will dictate the best internal data model. Basically, this choice is coupled with the selection of a DBMS and will be made primarily based on the adequacy of implementing the conceptual data base, the efficiency of DBMS product, vendor support, price, and various other technical and managerial factors. Chapter 11 will review this choice in more detail. For our purposes here, however, it will be useful to concentrate on one multifaceted factor that could be called "ease of use" as a perspective on evaluating any data model.

For an internal data model and associated DBMS, ease of use primarily relates to the programming interface with a data base. Reisner (1981) has reviewed a wide range of research on data base query languages. These studies have defined ease of use via such precise, quantitative variables as number and severity of errors made during programming, correctness of interpreting the true meaning of a query statement, correctness of specifying the result of a query against a sample data base, training time to reach a specific level of expertise, time to write queries, and confidence that queries written were correct. Most of these studies have been conducted over short time periods, so long-term retention and the effects of prolonged use of query languages or the data models they use are still unknown.

Although these studies reported by Reisner have done much to structure an approach to evaluating query languages and data models, the results have been inconclusive. Some studies have recognized that inexperienced computer users are able to perform better with relational query languages both before and after minimal exposure to such languages than with query languages associated with hierarchical or network data base management systems. More seasoned computer users—those with training in procedural languages—were able to deal with all languages equally well after minimal exposure. Studies have concluded that it is difficult to separate the effects of the query language from the underlying data model; thus, we are not certain whether problems are in the syntax and grammar of query languages or in the internal data models themselves.

One specific study by Brosey and Shneiderman (1978) tried to isolate the effects of the data model by measuring the results of manually using a sample data base. Their results indicated that a hierarchical model was easier for beginners to use, with no difference for more experienced subjects. However, these researchers readily admitted that the data base used in the study had a "natural tree structure." Related, fundamental research in psychology on human information organization has shown similar results. People are able to use a variety of data organizations effectively, as long as they are not forced to use a structure incapable of capturing the true meaning of data. Thus, it would appear that the "natural" structure of data, more than individual, personal preferences, is what matters.

Another study (Hoffer 1982) basically confirms this observation in an environment more akin to conceptual data modeling than programming. In an experiment in which subjects were asked to represent a data base for a situation described in narrative form, a wide variety of data models were used, and often hybrids were developed. Although relational-like architectures were used more frequently than network or hierarchical, the most popular was flow diagrams! Again, more questions were raised than were answered, but several conclusions from this and other work are apparent. First, no one data model dominates others in understandability or any sense of ease of use. Second, since different people with different skills and experience are able to use different data models with various abilities, a data base practitioner must be able to use a variety of data models appropriate for the data base and the user. Finally, data modeling is closely tied to information systems modeling (flowcharts), and the true meaning of data comes from understanding the whole data processing environment. That is, data modeling is part of information systems modeling, and data base design is part of information systems design.

SUMMARY

This chapter has reviewed the major data models that influence the data management field. These models have been reviewed apart from their technological implementations. It is important to recognize that data models are distinct from data base management systems.

Hierarchical, network, and relational data models were defined and discussed as architectures for external, conceptual, and internal data modeling. The Entity-Relationship and Semantic data models were reviewed as tools for external and conceptual data modeling.

These data models were defined, with no bias toward any best alternative. In fact, experience and research suggest that each of these models can be effective as long as their use is not forced into an "unnatural" situation. That is, it is safe to predict that all of these, and probably future models as well, will be used to model data and provide DBMS structure for years to come.

The challenge to data base and data processing professionals is to learn these data models in order to be able to use each as the situation dictates. This chapter addressed the ability of these data models to represent data and relationships. Further, this chapter addressed these data models independently of particular data base management systems (to be covered in Chapters 11 to 15)—thus, these principles can be applied in the use of any DBMS.

Chapter Review

REVIEW QUESTIONS

1. Define each of the following terms:
   a. data model
   b. relationship
   c. external data model
   d. conceptual data model
   e. internal data model
   f. subschema data model

g. hierarchical data model
h. network data model
i. intersection record
j. loop or intrafile relationship
k. system relationship
l. cycle
m. class relationship
n. relational data model
o. relation
p. *n*-tuple
q. normalization
r. functional dependency
s. join
t. disjunctive normal form
u. Entity-Relationship data model
v. existence dependency
w. ID dependency
x. Semantic data model
y. aggregate entity
z. entity specialization

2. Match the terms in each column, which are from the network and relational data models, that are the most similar to each other:

relation	value set
tuple	field
attribute	file
value	data item
role	record
domain	record data name

3. Briefly explain the differences between the simple, complex, and limited network data models.
4. Define a bit map and explain how it can be used to implement relationships.
5. Define first, second, and third normal forms in terms of the data base properties associated with each.
6. Think of a question (query) involving several relations in a university data base. Formulate this question in both relational algebra and relational calculus.
7. Explain why some relational data base management systems do not make use of all indexes that could be used to find the tuples that satisfy a query.
8. Explain why relationships are called explicit in the hierarchical and network data models and implicit in the relational data model.
9. Many people have trouble distinguishing an entity from a relationship. For example, do you regard marriage as a relationship or an entity? Why?
10. Explain why it is desirable to use a technology-independent data model for external or conceptual data modeling.
11. Provide an example of an existence dependency and an example of an ID dependency in a university data base.
12. Explain the purpose of the inverse clause in the semantic data model.

PROBLEMS AND EXERCISES

1. Match each term with the appropriate definition.

______ data model	a. permits *M:N* relationships
______ referential integrity	b. represents only master and detail sets
______ exclusivity	c. intrafile relationships
______ aggregation	d. one row of a relation
______ complex network	e. used to represent record sequences
______ intersection record	f. data elements must have common values
______ limited network	g. collection of related entities
______ loops	h. set of possible values for an attribute
______ system relationship	i. abstract representation of data
______ tuple	j. number of tuples in a relation
______ domain	k. form of uniqueness restriction
______ cardinality	l. contains meaningful data
______ functional dependency	m. class-subclass semantic
______ entity abstraction	n. not chosen as primary key
______ alternate keys	o. relationship between attributes

2. Consider the entities of Vehicle, Buyer, Owner, Sales Invoice, and Service Visit for an automobile dealership. Design a hierarchical, a network (both simple and complex), a relational, and an Entity-Relationship data base model for this situation. Assume any data items you need to give this situation meaning to you.

3. For each of the following relations, determine if there is a violation of a relation property. If not, explain why not. If so, identify which rules are violated and state exactly what part of the relation causes the violation.
   a. MENU(FOOD-ID,FOOD-NAME,PRICE,RECIPE#, NUMBER-OF-PORTIONS)
   b. EMPLOYEE(EMPLOYEE#,SOC-SEC-#,NUMBER-OF-DEPENDENTS)
   c. DAILY-TIPS(DATE,EMPLOYEE#,AMOUNT,EMPLOYEE-NAME)
   d. WORK-SCHEDULE(DATE,SHIFT,EMPLOYEE#)

4. Consider the entities of Agent, Policy, Client, Beneficiary, and Insurance Company in an independent insurance agency. Define two alternative hierarchical data base designs for this situation and compare their relative efficiencies.

5. This chapter described two ways to implement a hierarchy. One of these methods used address sequential connection between records in a common hierarchy instance. Take one of your hierarchies from Problem 4 and show the physical data arrangement for it using this physical hierarchy implementation method.

6. Consider the entities of Project, General Task, and Employee in a project man-

agement or job shop organization. Specify relations with typical attributes to represent these entities and the relationships between them.

7. The Bureau of Motor Vehicles can issue an individual several types of driver's licenses: passenger car, chauffeur, farm vehicle, motor bicycle, and so on. If the bureau ever wanted to consider the LICENSE entity class, what should be done in a relational model for its data base?

8. Consider the relation
   STOCK-TRACE(STOCK-CODE,DATE,HIGH,LOW,CHANGE)
   and the relational calculus statement
   RETRIEVE (STOCK-CODE,CHANGE) INTO RESULT
   WHERE STOCK-TRACE.DATE>831012
   Besides creating a new table RESULT with tuples from STOCK-TRACE and with only STOCK-CODE and CHANGE attributes for recent daily stock activity, will the relational DBMS have to perform any other function to make RESULT a relation with all of its properties?

9. Consider the following two tables:

Airport

LOC-CODE	NUMBER-OF-RUNWAYS	CONTROLLER	RADIO-FREQUENCY
LAX	6	YES	122.65
ORD	8	YES	111.78
ITH	2	NO	130.50
SPR	2	YES	117.55

Schedule

AIRLINE	FLT#	LOC-CODE	ARRIVAL
EA	123	ORD	0923
TW	1173	LAX	1106
BT	6	ORD	1000
CT	12	SPR	1400
EA	123	SPR	1145

   Write a set of relational algebra statements to place FLT# and RADIO-FREQUENCY into a relation called CONTACT, to contact a controller for all scheduled flights. Complete a table with values for the resultant CONTACT relation.

10. Many commercial data processing products claim to use the relational data model. What criteria would you apply to evaluate such a claim? That is, what characteristics must the product have to warrant the relational title?

11. Figure 6-30 shows part of an SDM for the Pine Valley Furniture network data base of Figure 6-12a. Fill in the missing elements of this SDM description.

REFERENCES

Brosey, M., and B. Shneiderman. 1978. "Two Experimental Comparisons of Relational and Hierarchical Database Models." *International Journal of Man-Machine Studies* 10: 625–637.

Chen, Peter P-S. 1977. *The Entity-Relationship Approach to Logical Data Base Design.* Wellesley, Mass.: Q.E.D. Information Sciences, Inc., Data Base Monograph Series No. 6.

———. 1976. "The Entity-Relationship Model—Toward a Unified View of Data." *ACM-TODS* 1 (March): 9–36.

CINCOM Systems, Inc. 1982. *TOTAL Reference Manual.* Cincinnati: CINCOM Systems, Inc.

Clifford, James, and David S. Warren. 1983."Formal Semantics for Time in Databases." *ACM-TODS* 8 (June): 214–245.

CODASYL. 1975. *Data Base Task Group Report, 1971.* Available from the Association for Computing Machinery, New York.

CODASYL Data Description Language Committee. 1978. *DDL Journal of Development.* Hull, Canada: CODASYL.

Codd, E. F. 1970. "A Relational Model of Data for Large Shared Data Bases." *Communications of the ACM.* 13 (June): 77–387.

"The Data Base Debate." 1982. In *Computerworld,* a transcript of part of Data Base '82, a portion of the Wang Institute of Graduate Studies' short summer course.

DeMarco, Thomas. 1978. *Structured Analysis and System Specification.* New York: Yourdon Press.

Goldberg, A. 1981. "Introducing the Smalltalk-80 System." *Byte* 6 (August): 14–26.

Hammer, Michael, and Dennis McLeod. 1978. "The Semantic Data Model: A Modelling Mechanism for Data Base Applications." *Proceedings of ACM-SIGMOD Conference 1978,* Austin, Tex.

Hewlett-Packard. 1979. *IMAGE Data Base Management System Reference Manual: HP3000.* Part no. 32215-90003. Cupertino, Calif.: Hewlett-Packard, September.

Hoffer, Jeffrey A. 1982. "An Empirical Investigation into Individual Differences in Database Models." *Proceedings of Third International Information Systems Conference.* Ann Arbor, Mich., December 1982.

IBM. 1982. *IMS/VS General Information Manual.* Form no. GH20-1260. White Plains, N.Y.: IBM.

Katz, R., and T. Lehman. 1984. "Database Support for Versions and Alternatives of Large Design Files." *IEEE Transactions on Software Engineering* 10 (March): 191–200.

Micro Data Base Systems, Inc. 1981. *Application Program Reference Manual: MDBS-DMS.* Lafayette, Ind.: Micro Data Base Systems.

MRI System Corp. 1981. *System 2000 Reference Manual.* Austin, Tex.: MRI System Corp.

Olle, T. William. 1975. "A Practitioner's View of Relational Data Base Theory." *ACM-SIGMOD FDT-Bulletin 7* (3–4): 29–43.

Reisner, Phyllis. 1981. "Human Factor Studies of Database Query Languages: A Survey and Assessment." *Computing Surveys* 13 (March): 13–31.

Smith, John Miles, and Diane C. P. Smith. 1977. "Database Abstractions: Aggregation and Generalization." *ACM-TODS* 2 (June): 105–133.

Teorey, Toby J., and James P. Fry. 1982. *Design of Database Structures.* Englewood Cliffs, N.J.: Prentice-Hall.

Wong, Eugene, and T. C. Chiang. 1971. "Canonical Structure in Attribute Based File Organization." *Communications of the ACM* 14 (September): 593–597.

Part III

Data Base Design and Administration

Data base design is the process of analyzing the information needs of an organization and developing a conceptual data model that reflects those needs. We describe the process of data base design in Chapters 7 through 9. Chapter 10 then describes the ongoing process of data base administration.

Chapter 7 identifies the four major steps in data base design: requirements analysis, conceptual design, implementation design, and physical design. Requirements analysis is covered in this chapter. Also, the techniques of normalization are introduced in Chapter 7. Normalization is used to construct a conceptual data model from user views of data.

Conceptual design is described in Chapter 8. Conceptual design starts with user requirements for data and produces a data model independent of data base management systems or other physical considerations. We illustrate this process in Chapter 8 by using the hospital case introduced in Chapter 3.

Chapter 9 describes implementation and physical design. Implementation design is concerned with mapping the conceptual data model to a particular DBMS. Physical design deals with selecting record formats, access methods, security design, and related considerations. We describe a number of the trade-offs that must be considered during this process.

Chapter 10 introduces data base administration. We describe functions of data base administration and its importance to success with data base in the organization. Alternatives for organizational placement of data base administration are described.

Chapter 7

Introduction to Data Base Design

INTRODUCTION

This is the first of three chapters devoted to the important topic of data base design. In this chapter, we introduce the basic steps in data base design and describe normalization, which is fundamental to the design process. In Chapter 8, we will describe logical data base design; physical data base design is described in Chapter 9. Data base design is guided by the data base planning process described in Chapter 3.

Data base design is the process of developing data base structures from user requirements for data. It starts with requirements analysis, which identifies user needs (present and future) for data. It then proceeds by translating these user requirements into first a conceptual, then a physical, data base design. The resulting design must satisfy user needs in terms of completeness, integrity, performance constraints, and other factors.

Data base design is a complex and difficult process. It requires the commitment and participation of the entire organization. Also, it requires the use of an organized approach or methodology. Until recently, such methodology did not exist, and data base design was often a haphazard process. However, a number of tools and techniques (including computer-assisted design) are now available to facilitate data base design. We describe a number of such techniques in these chapters.

STEPS IN DATA BASE DESIGN

Teorey and Fry (1982) have developed a general model for data base design, defining four major steps in the design process. These steps, shown in Figure 7-1, are requirements formulation and analysis, conceptual design, implementation design, and physical design. The interconnections (or inputs and outputs) for each of the design phases are also shown in the figure.

Figure 7-1
Major steps in data base design (Adapted from Teorey and Fry 1982)

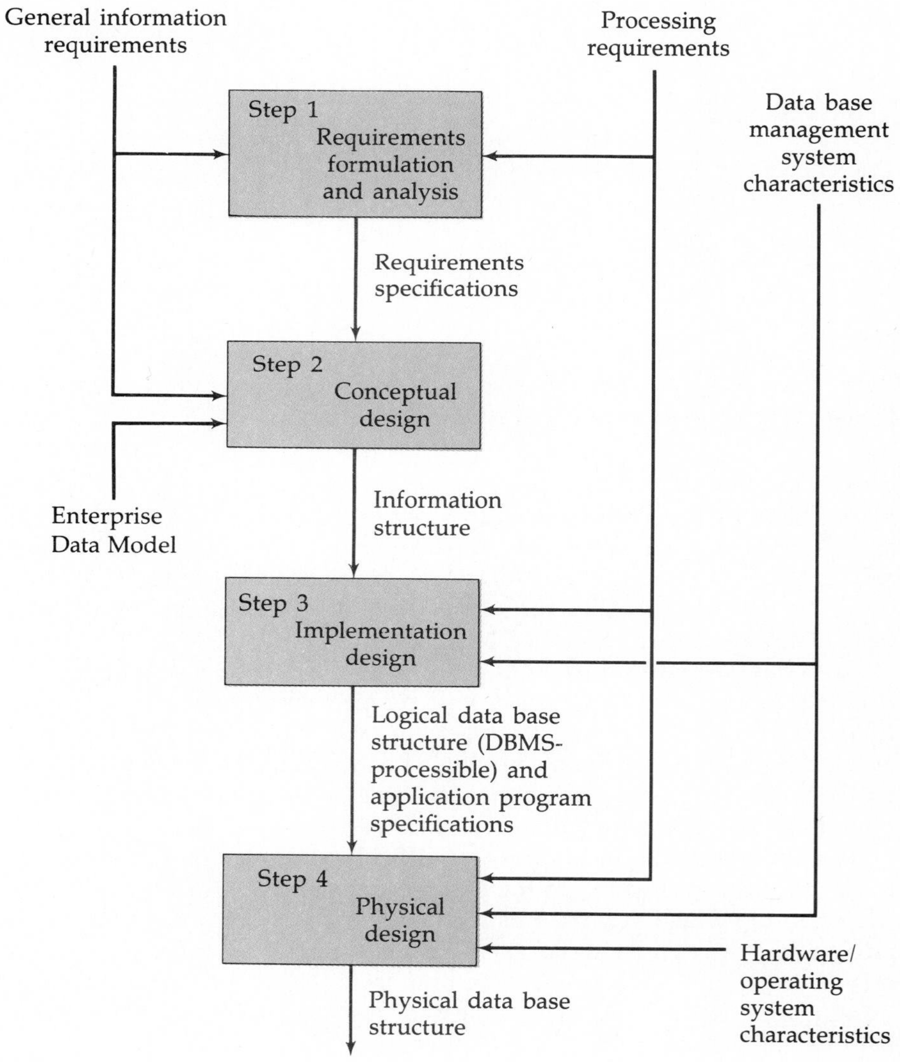

Requirements Formulation and Analysis

The purpose of requirements formulation and analysis is to identify and describe the data that are required by the organization. As shown in Figure 7-1, the major inputs to this process are user information requirements (especially the data items that are used and the associations between those data items) and processing requirements (report frequencies, response-time requirements, and so on). These requirements are identified through interviews with users. As data are defined, the metadata are stored and catalogued in a data dictionary/directory. The output from requirements formulation and analysis (hereafter called requirements analysis) is a set of requirements specifications for conceptual design. We will describe requirements analysis shortly.

Conceptual Design

The purpose of conceptual design is to synthesize the various user views and information requirements into a global data base design. This design is called the conceptual data model (or the conceptual schema) and may be expressed in one of several forms: an entity-relationship diagram, semantic data model, normalized relations, and so on. The conceptual data model describes entities, attributes, and relationships and is independent of specific data models and data base management systems. As the conceptual model is developed, it is cross-checked against the enterprise information model as described in Chapter 3 (see Figure 3-4).

Implementation Design

The purpose of implementation design is to map the conceptual data model into a logical schema that can be processed by a particular DBMS. First, the conceptual data model is mapped into a hierarchical, network, or relational data model. Then DBMS-processible schemas and subschemas are developed using the data description language for the DBMS to be used. Implementation design is considered an intermediate step between logical and physical data base design. We will describe this activity in Chapter 9.

Physical Design

Physical design is the last stage of data base design. It is concerned with designing stored record formats, selecting access methods, and deciding on physical factors such as record blocking. Physical design is also concerned with data base security, integrity, and backup and recovery. We will describe the steps in physical design in Chapter 9.

Stepwise Refinement

The steps in data base design are pictured in Figure 7-1 as proceeding in sequential fashion. In reality, however, there is more repetition between the steps. For example, during conceptual design, it may be discovered that there are gaps in the data definitions, thus pointing out the need for additional requirements formulation and analysis. The entire design process is best viewed as one of stepwise refinement, where the design at each stage is progressively refined through this type of iteration. Design reviews should be performed at the end of each stage before proceeding to the next stage.

REQUIREMENTS ANALYSIS

Requirements analysis is the process of identifying and documenting what data the users require in the data base to meet present and future information needs. During this phase, the data base analyst studies data flows and decision-making processes in the organization and works with users to answer the following questions:

1. What user views of data are required (present and future)?
2. What data elements (or attributes) are required in these user views?
3. What are the primary keys that uniquely identify entities in the organization?
4. What are the relationships among data elements?
5. What are the operational requirements such as security, integrity, and response time?

During requirements analysis, the analyst identifies not only what data are used, but how they are used. For example, in a bank, does the data element CUSTOMER# uniquely identify a customer, even if that customer has accounts at more than one branch of that bank? Is CUSTOMER-NAME an alternate key, or is CUSTOMER# the only candidate key? Who has the authority to update a customer BALANCE? Rules concerning the meaning and usage of data are referred to as **semantic rules**, and they must be identified during requirements analysis.

Steps in Requirements Analysis

In traditional systems, a process-oriented approach is used for requirements analysis, focusing on data flows and processes or transformations. The principal tool of requirements analysis for traditional systems is the data flow diagram.

A quite different approach to requirements analysis is necessary for data base design. This approach, which might be called a data-oriented approach, focuses on the data that must be included in the data base to satisfy user requirements. The principal tools are user view analysis, data definition and description, and normalization.

Actually, both the process-oriented and data-oriented approaches can be used for requirements analysis. The analysts may develop data flow diagrams to help them understand user procedures and data flows and at the same time analyze user views and requirements for information. Together, these two approaches can be used to check for completeness. However, the analysts should be aware that the data flow diagrams reflect existing procedures that are likely to change drastically in a data base environment. We describe structured techniques for developing procedures to access and update data bases in Chapter 9.

Compared to the other steps in data base design, requirements analysis is a relatively unstructured process. The major steps that are normally required are shown in Figure 7-2. They are as follows:

1. Identify the scope of the data base design effort.
2. Develop metadata collection standards and procedures.
3. Identify user views and data requirements.
4. Build a dictionary of data definitions and relationships.
5. Identify data volumes and usage patterns.
6. Establish operational requirements (steps 5 and 6 may be performed after conceptual design is completed).

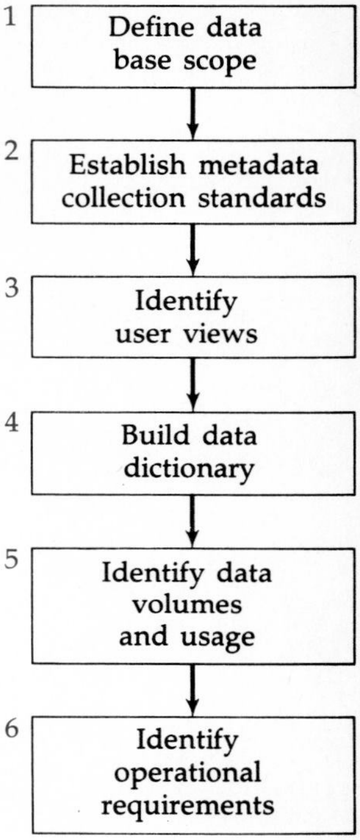

Figure 7-2
Steps in requirements analysis

Define Scope of the Data Base

Ideally, an organization would design and implement a single, global data base that would support all of its functions. However, in most organizations, such a data base would be prohibitively large, complex, and costly to develop. As a result, a better strategy is to design and implement several smaller data bases, all within the context of an overall plan, as described in Chapter 3. This "divide and conquer" strategy must be carefully orchestrated to achieve a confederation of data bases that are reasonably integrated and shareable.

A strategy for partitioning the data base design effort should be part of the overall strategic data base plan. The study team should review the organization's information systems plan before proceeding with the requirements analysis. This plan should include business charts, an enterprise information model, and data base priorities and implementation plans (see Figures 3-10 through 3-13). These plans should be used as an overall framework for data base design.

Establish Data Collection Standards

The major tasks of requirements analysis involve identifying user needs for data, and collecting and recording metadata. The requirements analysis team must interview all managers and key operating personnel in the areas within the scope of the data base design effort. The persons to be interviewed can be determined through discussions with key managers and supervisors. In a larger organization, a questionnaire requesting job titles and descriptions may be sent to each supervisor.

Structured interview techniques should be used during this process, including standardized data collection forms and follow-up procedures. In most cases, at least one follow-up interview with each user is required.

Identify User Views

Data collection initially focuses on user views of data. A **user view** is a subset of data required by a particular user to make a decision or carry out some action. A user view corresponds to an external schema in the ANSI/SPARC model. We identify user views by reviewing tasks that are performed or decisions that are made by users and by reviewing the data required for these tasks and decisions. Existing reports, files, documents, and displays (both input and output) are important sources of information about user views, and the analysts should collect sample copies of all such documents and formal information sources. Also, the analysts must probe to determine the semantic rules that govern the use of data. In addition to formal information sources, informal sources should be identified, such as

Figure 7-3
Example of a user view

LAKEWOOD COLLEGE
GRADE REPORT
FALL SEMESTER 198X

STUDENT#: 38214 MAJOR: INFO. SYSTEMS
STUDENT-NAME: JANE BRIGHT

COURSE#	COURSE-TITLE	INSTRUCTOR-NAME	INSTRUCTOR-LOCATION	GRADE
IS 350	DATA BASE	CODD	B104	A
IS 465	SYSTEMS ANALYSIS	KEMP	B213	C

Data Associations:

STUDENT# ↞──→ STUDENT-NAME, MAJOR
STUDENT# ↞──↠ COURSE-NUMBER
COURSE# ↞──→ COURSE-TITLE, INSTRUCTOR-NAME, INSTRUCTOR-LOCATION
INSTRUCTOR-NAME ↞──→ INSTRUCTOR-LOCATION
(STUDENT#, COURSE#) ↞──→ GRADE

USER VIEW

USERVIEW# 4 NAME Grade Report
DESCRIPTION Mailed to each student at the end of a semester
PRIMARY USER:
NAME LC students LOCATION n/a
ORGANIZATION n/a PHONE n/a
DATA ELEMENTS:

NUMBER	NAME	NUMBER	NAME
1	STUDENT #	4	COURSE #
2	STUDENT-NAME	5	COURSE-TITLE
3	MAJOR	(etc.)	

Figure 7-4
Typical form for describing user views

telephone calls and personal contacts. Also, it is important that future requirements for data be anticipated where possible.

Case Example: Lakewood College

An example of a user view is shown in Figure 7-3. This is a simple grade report that is mailed to the students of Lakewood College at the end of each semester. Semantic rules are summarized by the data associations shown in the figure. We use this view later in the chapter to illustrate the principles of normalization, since it is a view that is familiar to all students.

Data analysts should use a standard form for recording information about user views. A sample form for this purpose is shown in Figure 7-4. Metadata from the student grade report are recorded on the form to illustrate its usage. Each organization will design its own forms for recording information about user views.

In attempting to evaluate future information needs, the analysts must allow for proposed business or organizational changes. When they can be anticipated, it is generally simpler to incorporate future data needs into the data base design. However, not all needs can be anticipated, and so the data base system must be sufficiently flexible to handle growth and change without undermining existing applications.

Build a Data Dictionary

Each data item type that appears in a user view must be defined and described in detail. A standard form should be used for this purpose to ensure uniformity in data collection. A typical form for describing data items (or elements) is shown in Figure 7-5. Some of the attributes (or metadata) that are

Figure 7-5
Typical form for describing data elements

Data element

DATA ELEMENT# 3 NAME MAJOR
DESCRIPTION student's major area of study
SYNONYMS none
SOURCE student record IDENTIFIES n/a
SPECIFICATION:
TYPE Alphanumeric LENGTH 30 characters
ALLOWABLE RANGE n/a
CLASSIFICATION non-sensitive
USAGE:
FREQUENCY 2 times/semester (ave.)
UPDATE AUTHORITY student's advisor only

recorded on this form are data element number (or identification), name, description, type, length, and allowable range. If the data item is an identifier, the name of the entity type that it identifies is also recorded. The form in Figure 7-5 contains entries for the data item STUDENT#, which appears on the Grade Report. Notice that this element is defined as a 30-character alphanumeric data item that can only be updated by the student's advisor.

If an automated data dictionary system is used (which is recommended), forms such as the one shown in Figure 7-5 are furnished by the system vendor. These preprinted forms are used by the analysts to record metadata for entry into the data dictionary. If an automated system is not available during requirements analysis, the organization should design one like this for data collection.

As each data item is defined, it is recorded in the data dictionary. Any inconsistencies that arise are resolved by the analysts. For example, two (or more) names are often found to be used for the same data item (synonyms). In other cases, a single name may be in use for two data items (homonyms). The end result of this effort is a dictionary of standard data definitions and descriptions.

Identify Data Volume and Usage

Information concerning data volumes and usage patterns is required for physical data base design. Collecting these data is another step in requirements analysis. However, it is best performed after a preliminary version of the conceptual data model has been completed, since the analysts and users can then refer to the entities in the data model. We illustrate this step with an example later in the chapter.

Identify Operational Requirements

The analysts must also collect information concerning user operational requirements for data. This includes requirements for each of the following areas:

1. *Security.* Who is authorized to access and modify the data?
2. *Integrity.* What are the editing rules and rules for keeping data items mutually consistent?
3. *Response times.* What are reasonable limits for response times in accessing data?
4. *Backup and recovery.* What are the parameters for backing up and recovering the data base in the event of loss?
5. *Archiving.* How long must data be retained, and in what form?
6. *Growth projections.* How will data bases grow in volume and complexity in the future?

Data Flow Diagrams

Data flow diagrams are widely used in process-oriented systems analysis. They are also useful in supplementing the data-oriented analysis that we describe in this chapter. Data flow diagrams help analysts understand an existing system and provide an excellent tool for communicating with users.

A simple data flow diagram is shown in Figure 7-6. This diagram portrays the data flows for the patient accounting process at Mountain View Community Hospital. Data flows are shown by arrows, while processes (or transformations) are shown by circles. Files (or "data stores") are portrayed by open rectangles (symbols used in data flow diagrams are not yet standardized). For an extended discussion of data flow diagrams and their use, see Weinberg (1979).

NORMALIZATION

In the process of requirements analysis, we identify and describe a number of user views (present and planned) like the one in Figure 7-3. Depending on the scope of the data base, there may be several dozen, or even several hundred, user views such as this one. Each user view, in turn, is typically composed of a number of data items or types. For example, the Grade-Report view contains eight data item types: STUDENT#, STUDENT-NAME, MAJOR, COURSE#, COURSE-TITLE, INSTRUCTOR-NAME, INSTRUCTOR-LOCATION, and GRADE. These data items pertain to several entity classes such as Students, Courses, and Instructors.

The basic problem of logical data base design can be stated as follows:

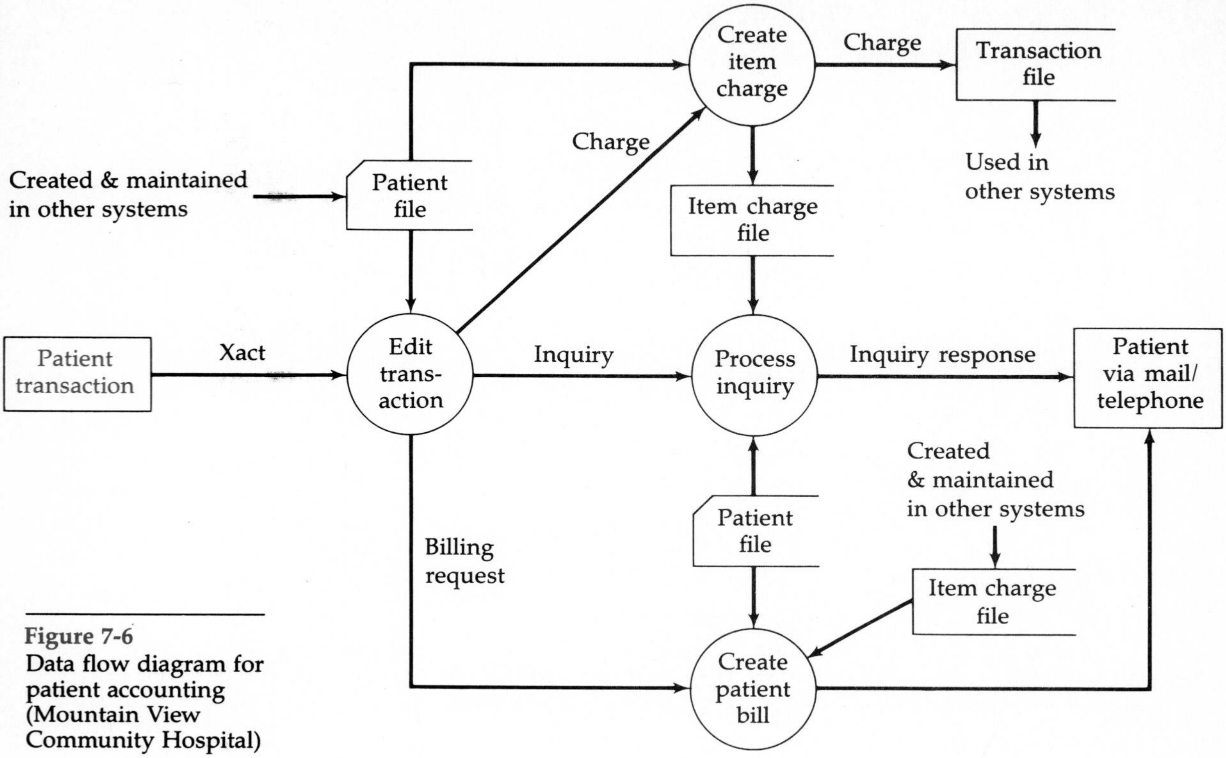

Figure 7-6
Data flow diagram for patient accounting (Mountain View Community Hospital)

Given the mass of metadata that has been collected and organized by requirements analysis, how do we design a conceptual data model that represents these metadata naturally and completely in simplest, least redundant form? In other words, how should the data item types be combined to form relations (or record types) that describe entities and the relationships between entities?

Until recently, data base specialists have lacked a comprehensive technique for logical data base design. As a result, data base design has historically been an intuitive and often haphazard process. However, the techniques of normalization now provide a foundation for logical data base design. Normalization is the analysis of functional dependencies between attributes (or data items). The purpose of normalization is to reduce complex user views to a set of small, stable data structures. Experience clearly shows that normalized data structures are more flexible, stable, and easier to maintain than unnormalized structures.

Steps in Normalization

The basic steps in the normalization process are shown in Figure 7-7. First, user views are identified. Next, each user view is converted to the form of an unnormalized relation. Any repeating groups are then removed from

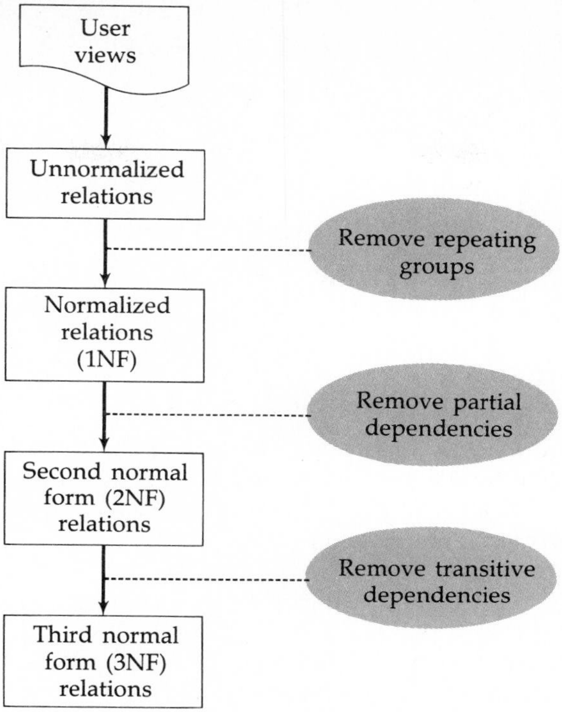

Figure 7-7
Steps in normalization

the unnormalized relation; the result is a set of relations in first normal form (1NF). Next, any partial dependencies are removed from these relations; the result is a set of relations in second normal form (2NF). Finally, any transitive dependencies are removed, creating a set of relations in third normal form (3NF).

Intuitively, normalization "untangles" the complex relationships among data items that exist in a typical user view (such as the one in Figure 7-3). Each user view is reduced to a set of simple relations (described in Chapter 6), each of which either describes an entity class (such as Student or Instructor) or describes an association between two or more entity classes. Normalization relies on the definition of functional dependency introduced in Chapter 6.

Unnormalized Relations

The analyst visualizes the data in each user view as if they were laid out in tabular form. Figure 7-8 shows a relational view of Grade-Report. We will refer to this view as the GRADE-REPORT relation. Notice that sufficient data have been recorded in GRADE-REPORT to clarify its structure.

GRADE-REPORT is an example of an unnormalized relation. An **unnormalized relation** is a relation that contains one or more repeating groups.

GRADE-REPORT

STUDENT#	STUDENT NAME	MAJOR	COURSE#	COURSE-TITLE	INSTRUCTOR NAME	INSTRUCTOR LOCATION	GRADE
38214	BRIGHT	IS	IS 350	DATA BASE	CODD	B104	A
"	"	"	IS 465	SYS ANAL	KEMP	B213	C
69173	SMITH	PM	IS 465	SYS ANAL	KEMP	B213	A
"	"	"	PM 300	PROD MGT	LEWIS	D317	B
"	"	"	QM 440	OP RES	KEMP	B213	C
...							

Figure 7-8
Example of an unnormalized relation

As a result, there are multiple values at the intersection of certain rows and columns. Since each student takes more than one course, the course data in GRADE-REPORT constitutes a repeating group within student data. For example, there are two entries in each column for STUDENT# 38214 starting with the attribute COURSE#.

In an unnormalized relation, a single attribute cannot serve as a candidate key. For example, in GRADE-REPORT suppose we examine STUDENT# as a candidate key. The relationships between STUDENT# and the remaining attributes are as follows:

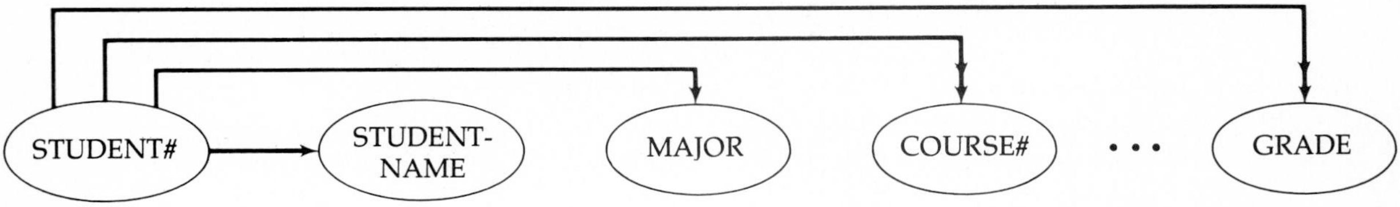

There is a one-to-one relationship from STUDENT# to STUDENT-NAME and MAJOR. However, the relationship is one-to-many from STUDENT# to COURSE# and the remaining attributes. Therefore, STUDENT# is not a candidate key, since it does not uniquely identify all the attributes in this relation.

A major disadvantage of unnormalized relations is that they contain redundant data. In GRADE-REPORT, for example, information pertaining to course IS 465 is contained in multiple locations (two tuples in the sample data shown in Figure 7-8). Suppose that we want to change the COURSE-TITLE for this course from SYS ANAL to SYS ANAL & DES. To make this change, we would have to search the entire GRADE-REPORT relation to locate all occurrences of COURSE# IS 465. If we failed to update all occurrences, the data would be inconsistent.

A shorthand notation for the unnormalized relation GRADE-REPORT is as follows:

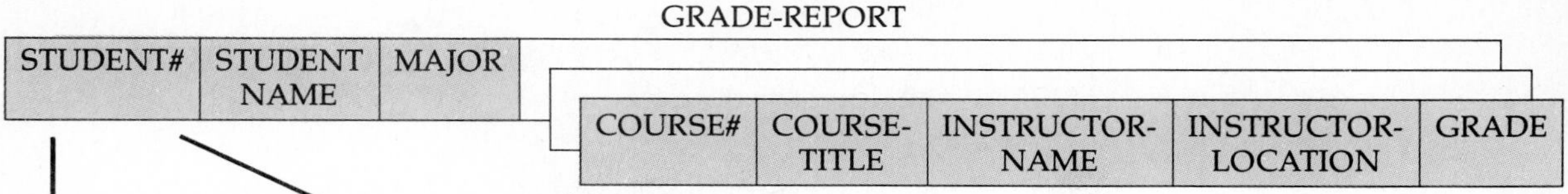

STUDENT

<u>STUDENT#</u>	STUDENT-NAME	MAJOR
38214	BRIGHT	IS
69173	SMITH	PM
...		

(3NF)

STUDENT-COURSE

<u>STUDENT#</u>	<u>COURSE#</u>	COURSE-TITLE	INSTRUCTOR-NAME	INSTRUCTOR-LOCATION	GRADE
38214	IS 350	DATA BASE	CODD	B104	A
38214	IS 465	SYS ANAL	KEMP	B213	C
69173	IS 465	SYS ANAL	KEMP	B213	A
69173	PM 300	PROD MGT	LEWIS	D317	B
69173	QM 440	OP RES	KEMP	B213	C
...					

(1NF)

Figure 7-9
Normalizing a relation by removing the repeating group

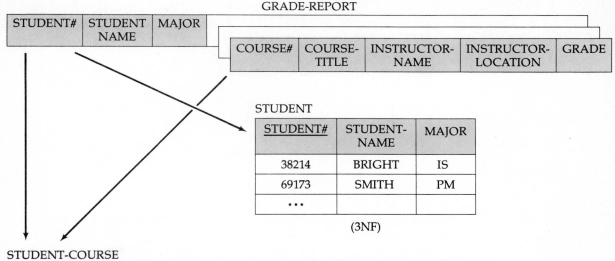

GRADE-REPORT (STUDENT#, STUDENT-NAME, MAJOR, {COURSE#, COURSE-TITLE, INSTRUCTOR-NAME, INSTRUCTOR-LOCATION, GRADE})

In this notation, the inner set of braces designates the repeating group.

Normalized Relations: First Normal Form

A normalized relation is a relation that contains only elementary (or single) values at the intersection of each row and column. Thus, a normalized relation contains no repeating groups.

To normalize a relation that contains a single repeating group, we remove the repeating group and form two new relations. This process is illustrated for GRADE-REPORT in Figure 7-9. The two new relations formed from GRADE-REPORT are the following:

1. The relation STUDENT, which contains those attributes that are not part of the repeating group: STUDENT#, STUDENT-NAME, and MAJOR. The primary key of this relation is STUDENT#. This relation is in third normal form, as we will see.
2. The relation STUDENT-COURSE, which contains those attributes from the repeating group. The primary key of this relation is a composite key: STUDENT# plus COURSE#. STUDENT# is the primary key in the first relation, while COURSE# is an attribute that identifies each course repeating group for a given student. Notice that it is necessary to use this composite key, since both STUDENT# and COURSE# are needed to uniquely identify a student's GRADE. Such composite or concatenated keys are typically (but not always) the result of a normalization step.

The STUDENT-COURSE relation in Figure 7-9 is in first normal form (1NF). A relation is in **first normal form** if it contains no repeating groups. Such a relation does not have to meet any other constraints, as we will soon see.

Although the STUDENT-COURSE relation is in first normal form, it is still not an ideal representation of these data. A glance at the sample data in this relation (Figure 7-9) reveals that there is considerable data redundancy. If we leave the data in this form, we will encounter anomalies (problems or inconsistencies) in inserting, deleting, and updating data.

Insertion Anomaly Suppose we want to insert data in this relation for a new COURSE# and COURSE-TITLE. For example, we may want to insert BA 200, INTRO DP. We cannot insert these data until at least one student has registered for this course, since STUDENT# is part of the composite key. Similar anomalies occur in attempting to insert new instructor data.

Deletion Anomaly Suppose that only one student is enrolled in a course (perhaps an independent study). If the student drops that course (or leaves school), we want to delete that tuple from the data base. Unfortunately, this will result in our losing information about the title and instructor of that course. If we attempt to leave the tuple in the data base to preserve information about the course, we are left with a null value for the STUDENT# part of the key.

Update Anomaly Suppose we want to change the course title for IS 465 from SYS ANAL to SYS ANAL & DES. Since the title of this course appears in STUDENT-COURSE a number of times, the user will have to search through all tuples in this relation and update the course title each time it occurs. This procedure will be inefficient and can result in inconsistencies if all occurrences are not correctly updated.

The reason for these anomalies in STUDENT-COURSE is that several of the nonkey attributes in this relation are dependent only on COURSE# and

STUDENT#	COURSE#	COURSE-TITLE	INSTRUCTOR-NAME	INSTRUCTOR-LOCATION	GRADE
38214	IS 350	DATA BASE	CODD	B104	A
38214	IS 465	SYS ANAL	KEMP	B213	C
69173	IS 465	SYS ANAL	KEMP	B213	A
69173	PM 300	PROD MGT	LEWIS	D317	B
69173	QM 440	OP RES	KEMP	B213	C
...					

(a)

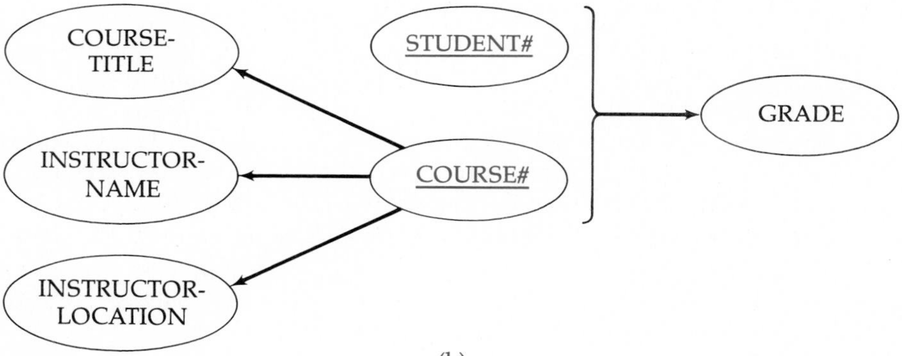

(b)

Figure 7-10
Dependencies of nonkey attributes on the composite primary key:
(a) Student-Course relation
(b) dependency diagram

not on the full primary key (STUDENT# plus COURSE#). This is shown in Figure 7-10. Figure 7-10a shows the dependencies of the nonkey attributes in tabular form, while Figure 7-10b shows a dependency diagram depicting the same information.

Notice that GRADE is the only attribute that is dependent on both STUDENT# and COURSE#. This is because we must know both the student and the course taken to determine a grade. An attribute that depends on the full composite key (rather than part of that key) is said to be **fully dependent** on that key.

The remaining nonkey attributes (COURSE-TITLE, INSTRUCTOR-NAME, and INSTRUCTOR-LOCATION) are dependent only on COURSE#, and not on the combination STUDENT# plus COURSE#. (We assume that only one instructor teaches a given course.) These attributes are said to be **partially dependent** on the primary key.

Second Normal Form

To eliminate the anomalies of the first normal form, we must remove partial functional dependencies. A relation is in **second normal form** if it is already in first normal form and any partial functional dependencies have been removed.

To convert a relation with partial dependencies to second normal form, we create two new relations, one with attributes that are fully dependent on the primary key and the other with attributes that are dependent on only part of that key. This process is illustrated in Figure 7-11 for the STUDENT-COURSE relation, where the following new relations are created:

1. A REGISTRATION relation, with composite key STUDENT# plus COURSE#. The nonkey attribute GRADE is fully dependent on the primary key. This relation is in third normal form.
2. A COURSE-INSTRUCTOR relation, with the primary key COURSE#. The nonkey attributes (COURSE-TITLE, INSTRUCTOR-NAME, and INSTRUCTOR-LOCATION) are those that are dependent only on COURSE# (as shown in Figure 7-11).

The anomalies described earlier for first normal form have been eliminated in these new relations. Notice that each course is described only once in the COURSE-INSTRUCTOR relation. As a result, any update to course data (such as a change in title) is confined to a single tuple. Also, since course data are separated from student data, new course data can be inserted or old course data deleted without reference to student data.

Although second normal form represents an improvement, additional

Figure 7-11 Conversion of a relation to second normal form by removing partial functional dependency

STUDENT-COURSE

STUDENT#	COURSE#	COURSE-TITLE	INSTRUCTOR-NAME	INSTRUCTOR-LOCATION	GRADE

REGISTRATION

STUDENT#	COURSE#	GRADE
38214	IS 350	A
38214	IS 465	C
69173	IS 465	A
69173	PM 300	B
69173	QM 440	C
...		

(3NF)

COURSE-INSTRUCTOR

COURSE#	COURSE-TITLE	INSTRUCTOR-NAME	INSTRUCTOR-LOCATION
IS 350	DATA BASE	CODD	B104
IS 465	SYS ANAL	KEMP	B213
PM 300	PROD MGT	LEWIS	D317
QM 440	OP RES	KEMP	B213
...			

(2NF)

refinement is required, since data concerning the entity Instructor are "hidden" within the COURSE-INSTRUCTOR relation. A diagram of the dependencies within this relation appears as follows:

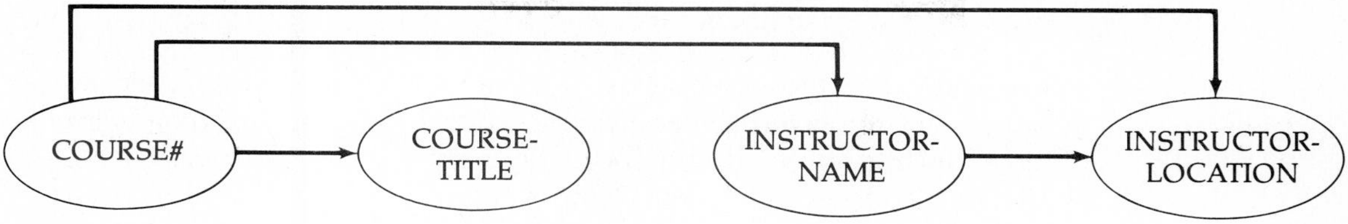

Notice that each of the nonkey attributes is dependent on COURSE#. However, INSTRUCTOR-LOCATION is also dependent on INSTRUCTOR-NAME. That is, there is a unique location (or office number) for each instructor. This is an example of a transitive dependency. A **transitive dependency** occurs when one nonkey attribute (such as INSTRUCTOR-LOCATION) is dependent on one or more nonkey attributes (such as INSTRUCTOR-NAME). A simple transitive dependency appears as follows:

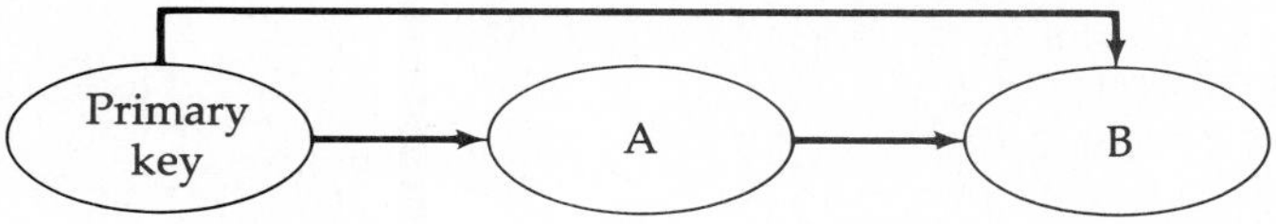

In this case, there is a transitive dependency between the primary key and attributes A and B. Transitive dependencies result in insertion, deletion, and update anomalies, similar to those for partial dependencies.

Insertion Anomaly Suppose we want to insert data for a new instructor in the COURSE-INSTRUCTOR relation (Figure 7-11). Since instructor data are dependent on COURSE#, we cannot insert instructor data until an instructor has been assigned to teach at least one course. For example, in Figure 7-11, we cannot insert data for the instructor Smith until one or more courses have been assigned to Smith.

Deletion Anomaly Deleting the data for a particular course may result in the loss of instructor data. For example, deleting the data for the course IS 350 will cause the loss of data concerning the instructor CODD.

Update Anomaly Instructor data occur multiple times in the COURSE-INSTRUCTOR relation (for example, instructor KEMP has two occurrences). As a result, any change to instructor data (such as a new instructor location) requires searching the entire relation to locate the desired occurrences and then updating each occurrence. The number of such occurrences in a relation will vary over time.

To eliminate these anomalies, a further normalization step is necessary. This step converts a relation to third normal form by removing transitive dependencies.

Third Normal Form

A relation is in **third normal form** (3NF) if it is in second normal form and contains no transitive dependencies. A relation in third normal form has the following simple dependency relationships:

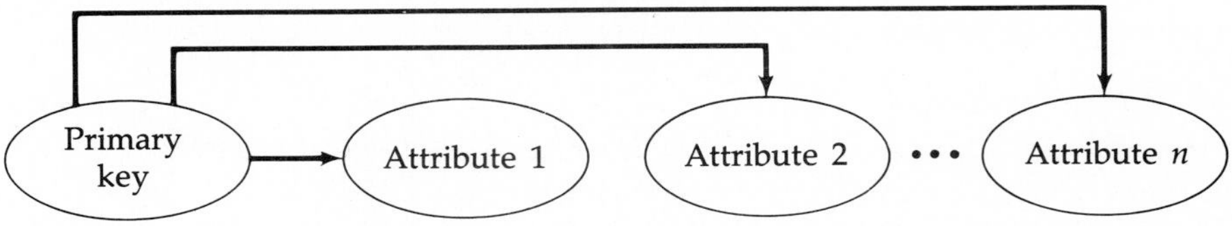

That is, each nonkey attribute is fully dependent on the primary key, and there are no transitive ("hidden") dependencies.

The process of removing a transitive dependency is illustrated for the COURSE-INSTRUCTOR relation in Figure 7-12. The nonkey attributes that participate in the transitive dependency (INSTRUCTOR-NAME and INSTRUCTOR-LOCATION) are removed to form a new INSTRUCTOR relation. The primary key of this relation is INSTRUCTOR-NAME, since we assume that this attribute uniquely identifies INSTRUCTOR-LOCATION. The data base analyst would have to investigate this assumption to ensure its validity, since names are often not unique. We assume that INSTRUC-

Figure 7-12
Conversion of a relation to third normal form by removing transitive dependency

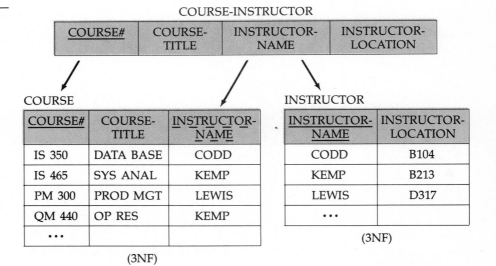

COURSE-INSTRUCTOR

<u>COURSE#</u>	COURSE-TITLE	INSTRUCTOR-NAME	INSTRUCTOR-LOCATION

COURSE

<u>COURSE#</u>	COURSE-TITLE	INSTRUCTOR-NAME
IS 350	DATA BASE	CODD
IS 465	SYS ANAL	KEMP
PM 300	PROD MGT	LEWIS
QM 440	OP RES	KEMP
• • •		

(3NF)

INSTRUCTOR

<u>INSTRUCTOR-NAME</u>	INSTRUCTOR-LOCATION
CODD	B104
KEMP	B213
LEWIS	D317
• • •	

(3NF)

TOR-LOCATION is not a candidate key in this relation since more than one instructor may be in a given location (or office).

Although the attribute INSTRUCTOR-NAME becomes the primary key in the new INSTRUCTOR relation, it is also a nonkey attribute in the new COURSE relation (see Figure 7-12). INSTRUCTOR-NAME is said to be a foreign key in the COURSE relation. A **foreign key** is a nonkey attribute in one relation (such as COURSE) that also appears, as a primary key in another relation (such as INSTRUCTOR). In this example, the foreign key allows us to associate a particular course with the instructor who teaches that course. We indicate a foreign key by underlining it with a dashed line, as in Figure 7-12.

The normalization process is now completed. The Grade-Report user view (Figure 7-3) has been transformed through a series of simple steps to a set of four relations in third normal form. The 3NF relations are summarized in Figure 7-13, both in tabular form and in shorthand notation.

These 3NF relations are free of the anomalies described earlier. Since each entity is described in a separate relation, data concerning that entity can easily be inserted or deleted without reference to other entities. Also, updates to the data for a particular entity are easily accomplished, since they are confined to a single tuple (row) within a relation.

STUDENT#	STUDENT-NAME	MAJOR
38214	BRIGHT	IS
69173	SMITH	PM
...		

STUDENT (STUDENT#, STUDENT-NAME, MAJOR)

INSTRUCTOR-NAME	INSTRUCTOR-LOCATION
CODD	B104
KEMP	B213
LEWIS	D317
...	

INSTRUCTOR (INSTRUCTOR-NAME, INSTRUCTOR-LOCATION)

COURSE#	COURSE-TITLE	INSTRUCTOR-NAME
IS 350	DATA BASE	CODD
IS 465	SYS ANAL	KEMP
PM 300	PROD MGT	LEWIS
QM 440	OP RES	KEMP
...		

COURSE (COURSE#, COURSE-TITLE, INSTRUCTOR-NAME)

STUDENT#	COURSE#	GRADE
38214	IS 350	A
38214	IS 465	C
69173	IS 465	A
69173	PM 300	B
69173	QM 440	C
...		

REGISTRATION (STUDENT#, COURSE#, GRADE)

Figure 7-13
Summary of 3NF relations for GRADE-REPORT

In the process of normalizing Grade-Report, no information is lost from the original user view. In fact, the Grade-Report in Figure 7-3 can be recreated by combining the data from the 3NF relations in Figure 7-13 using relational algebra (described in Chapter 6).

Normalization of Summary Data

Figure 3-2 indicated that data bases to support management control and strategic levels of an organization often contain subsets and summarizations of data from operational data bases. These "information bases" to support higher levels of management also need to be normalized to avoid all the same anomalies found in operational data bases.

Consider the GRADE-REPORT data base of Figure 7-13. Deans, degree program heads, and department chairs may be concerned only with grade summaries by department or major. For example, one report view for summarized data of grades by major would be represented by

MAJOR-GRADES (MAJOR, NO-STUDENTS, AVG-GPA)

Here NO-STUDENTS is the number of students in a given major and AVG-GPA is the average grade point for students in a given major. This primary relation is in 3NF; note that AVG-GPA, although *mathematically* related to NO-STUDENTS, is *functionally dependent* only on MAJOR.

The MAJOR-GRADES table is derivable from the STUDENT and REGISTRATION tables of Figure 7-13. Whether MAJOR-GRADES is a view on an operational data base or an independent table for an information base is a decision to be made later during physical design. This decision will be based on such factors as time to derive MAJOR-GRADES and response time required when MAJOR-GRADES is requested, cost of data storage for this table, and costs to keep MAJOR-GRADES contents consistent with operational data from which it is derived (for integrity).

At the requirements analysis and conceptual design stages, a data base designer should determine normalized relations for user views where possible, even of summarized data. Thus, MAJOR-GRADES would be added as another table to the GRADE-REPORT data base and the data base analyst should note how NO-STUDENTS and AVG-GPA are derived from data in other tables.

It is also possible that new data elements will be used in summary tables. For example, MAJOR-GRADES might also include data on the home department and its head or chairperson for each major, which would be represented by

MAJ-GRADES (MAJOR, DEPT, HEAD, NO-STUDENTS, AVG-GPA)

Since it is very likely that each department has only one head (HEAD functionally dependent on DEPT), MAJ-GRADES is not in 3NF (but is in 2NF). It can be put into 3NF as

MAJ-GRADES (<u>MAJOR</u>, DEPT, NO-STUDENTS, AVG-GPA)
DEPARTMENT (<u>DEPT</u>, HEAD)

Since information bases are frequently designed after operational data bases are implemented (especially if data bases are *not* planned as described in Chapter 3), a data base analyst must be careful to clearly identify derived data and recognize the associated operational data source. If this is not done, the result can be unplanned redundancy and inconsistency within the data base.

BEYOND THIRD NORMAL FORM

Relations in third normal form are sufficient for most practical data base design problems. However, 3NF does not guarantee that all anomalies have been removed. Recent research has identified additional normalization steps that can be performed to remove any remaining anomalies (Kent 1983). Although these refinements are not often required, you should be aware of them and the conditions under which they may be required.

Boyce-Codd Normal Form

When a relation has more than one candidate key, anomalies may result even though the relation is in 3NF. For example, consider the ST-MAJ-ADV relation shown in Figure 7-14a. The primary key of this relation is the composite key (STUDENT#, MAJOR). The semantic rules for the relation are as follows:

1. Each student may major in several subjects.
2. For each major, a given student has only one advisor (this condition must be true if STUDENT# + MAJOR is the primary key).
3. Each major has several advisors.
4. Each advisor advises only one major.

A dependency diagram summarizing these rules is shown in Figure 7-14b. The relation is clearly in 3NF, since there are no partial functional dependencies and no transitive dependencies. Nevertheless, there are still anomalies in the relation. For example, suppose that student #456 changes her major from BIOL to MATH. When the tuple for this student is updated, we lose the fact that DARWIN advises in BIOL (update anomaly). Also, suppose we want to insert a tuple with the information that WATSON advises in COMPSCI. This, of course, cannot be done until at least one student majoring in COMPSCI is assigned WATSON as an advisor (insertion anomaly).

Figure 7-14
Boyde-Codd normal form:
(a) relation in 3NF with anomalies
(b) dependency diagram
(c) relations in BCNF

ST-MAJ-ADV

STUDENT#	MAJOR	ADVISOR
123	PHYSICS	EINSTEIN
123	MUSIC	MOZART
456	BIOL	DARWIN
789	PHYSICS	BOHR
999	PHYSICS	EINSTEIN

(a)

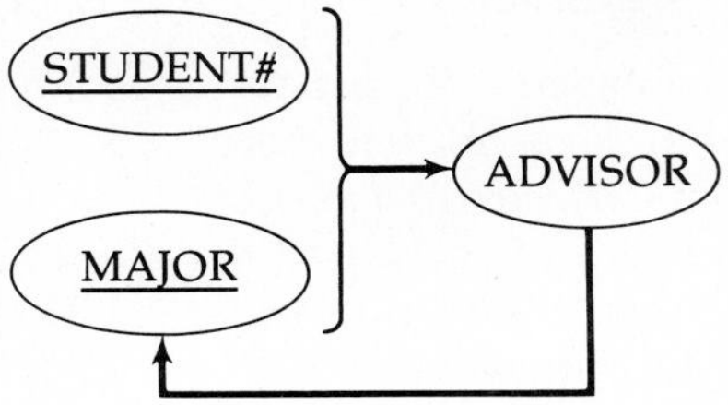

(b)

ST-ADV

STUDENT#	ADVISOR
123	EINSTEIN
123	MOZART
456	DARWIN
789	BOHR
999	EINSTEIN

ADV-MAJ

ADVISOR	MAJOR
EINSTEIN	PHYSICS
MOZART	MUSIC
DARWIN	BIOL
BOHR	PHYSICS

(c)

In the ST-MAJ-ADV relation, there are two candidate keys: (STUDENT#, MAJOR) and (STUDENT#, ADVISOR). Although the first of these candidate keys was chosen as the primary key, the second could equally well have been chosen. Notice that the two candidate keys overlap, since they have STUDENT# in common. The type of anomalies that exist in this relation can occur only when there are two or more overlapping candidate keys. Thus, the situation is relatively rare, but nevertheless can occur.

R. F. Boyce and E. F. Codd identified this deficiency and proposed a stronger definition of 3NF that remedies the problem. Their definition relies on the concept of a determinant. A **determinant** is any attribute (simple or composite) on which some other attribute is fully functionally dependent. For example, in the ST-MAJ-ADV relation, the attribute ADVISOR is a determinant, since the attribute MAJOR is fully functionally dependent on ADVISOR (see Figure 7-14b). We say that a relation is in Boyce-Codd normal form (BCNF) if and only if every determinant is a candidate key.

Applying the Boyce-Codd rule, we see that ST-ADV-MAJ is not in BCNF (even though it is in 3NF) because even though ADVISOR is a determinant, it is not a candidate key (one ADVISOR may advise many students). To overcome this problem, we project the original 3NF relation into two relations that are in BCNF. The result of one such projection for ST-MAJ-ADV is shown in Figure 7-14c. The first of these two relations (called ST-ADV) contains the attributes STUDENT# and ADVISOR, which form the primary

OFFERING

COURSE	INSTRUCTOR	TEXTBOOK
Management	White Green Black	Drucker Peters
Finance	Gray	Weston Gilford

(a) Unnormalized Relation

OFFERING

COURSE	INSTRUCTOR	TEXTBOOK
Management	White	Drucker
Management	Green	Drucker
Management	Black	Drucker
Management	White	Peters
Management	Green	Peters
Management	Black	Peters
Finance	Gray	Weston
Finance	Gray	Gilford

(b) Normalized Relation

Figure 7-15 Relation with multivalued dependency

key. The second relation (called ADV-MAJ) contains ADVISOR (the primary key) and MAJOR (a nonkey attribute). You should check that these relations are in BCNF by applying the basic definition.

Fourth Normal Form

Even when a relation is in BCNF it may still contain unwanted redundancies that result in update anomalies. For example, consider the unnormalized relation called OFFERING in Figure 7-15a. In this relation we make the following assumptions:

1. Each course has one or more instructors.
2. For each course, all of the textbooks indicated are used.
3. The text that is used for a given course is *independent* of the instructor—that is, the same set of textbooks are used regardless of the instructor.

In Figure 7-15b the OFFERING relation has been normalized. Thus, for each course, all possible combinations of instructor and text appear in the resulting table. Notice that the primary key of this relation consists of all three attributes (COURSE, INSTRUCTOR, and TEXT). Since there are no determinants (other than the primary key itself) the relation is in BCNF. However, it does contain many redundant data. These, in turn, can easily lead to update anomalies. For example, suppose that we want to add a third textbook (author: Middleton) to the Management course. This would require the addition of *three* new rows to the table in Figure 7-15b, one for each Instructor (otherwise that text would apply to only certain instructors!).

Despite the fact that the relation in Figure 7-15b is in BCNF, there is a form of dependence between the attributes. For each course, there is a well-defined set of instructors (a 1:*M* relationship), and a well-defined set of textbooks (a 1:*M* relationship). However, the instructors and textbooks are independent of each other, so that the relationships appear as follows:

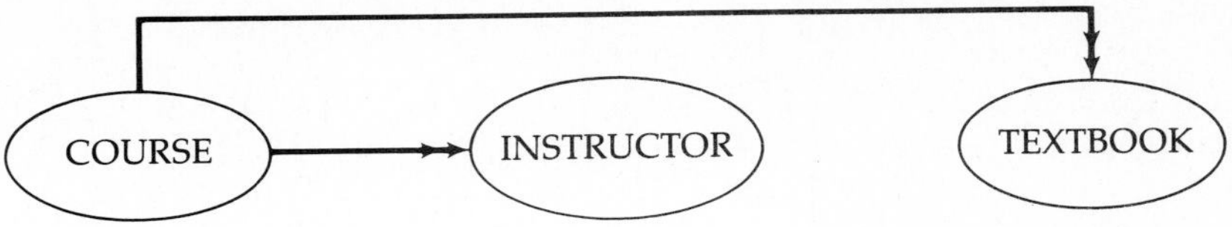

The type of dependency shown in this example is called a multivalued dependency. A *multivalued dependency* exists when there are three attributes (e.g., A, B, and C) in a relation, and for each value of A there is a well-defined set of values of B and a well-defined set of values of C. However, the set of values of B is independent of set C, and vice-versa.

To remove the multivalued dependency from a relation, we project the relation into two relations, each of which contains one of the two independent attributes. Figure 7-16 shows the result of this projection for the OFFERING relation of Figure 7-15b. Notice that the relation called TEACHER contains the INSTRUCTOR attribute, while TEXT contains the TEXTBOOK attribute (these two attributes are independent of each other in Figure 7-15b). A relation is in **fourth normal form** (4NF) if it is in BCNF and contains no multivalued dependencies. You can easily verify that the two relations in Figure 7-16 are 4NF. The original relation (OFFERING) can easily be reconstructed by joining these two relations.

Additional Normal Forms

Other normal forms (beyond 4NF) have been defined. We describe them only briefly here, since they appear to be mostly of research interest. For an extended discussion of these normal forms, see Date (1981).

Fifth Normal Form This normal form is designed to cope with a type of dependency called join dependency. A relation that has a join dependency cannot be decomposed by projection into other relations without spurious results. Fifth normal form (5NF) provides a definition for removing join dependencies if they exist and can be discovered. However, according to Date (p. 263), "it is tempting to think that such relations are pathological cases and likely to be rare in practice."

Domain-Key Normal Form Fagin (1981) has proposed a conceptually simple normal form called the domain-key normal form (DK/NF). According to this definition, a relation is in DK/NF if and only if every constraint on the relation is a logical consequence of key constraints and domain constraints. Fagin shows that if a relation is in DK/NF, it cannot have insertion or deletion anomalies.

Fagin's definition is an important contribution, since it provides a completely general definition of normal forms. Unfortunately, it does not provide a methodology for converting a given relation to DK/NF.

Limits of Normalization The objective of normalization is to reduce redundancy and produce a set of stable data structures. In most applica-

TEACHER

COURSE	INSTRUCTOR
Management	White
Management	Green
Management	Black
Finance	Gray

TEXT

COURSE	TEXTBOOK
Management	Drucker
Management	Peters
Finance	Weston
Finance	Gilford

Figure 7-16
Relations in fourth normal form

tions, the use of third normal form is adequate to achieve these objectives, but sometimes, further refinement to BCNF or 4NF is warranted.

It should be remembered that the normalization steps described in this chapter are only guidelines to be used by the data base designer. The designer's skill and experience also play a role, and sometimes the designer may choose not to normalize "all the way" to third normal form (or higher). For example, consider the following CUSTOMER relation:

CUSTOMER (NAME, STREET, CITY, STATE, ZIP)

The primary key of this relation is NAME. However, the relation is in 2NF because there is a "hidden," or transitive, dependence. A ZIP code uniquely identifies the CITY and STATE, so that within the CUSTOMER relation, we have the following functional dependence:

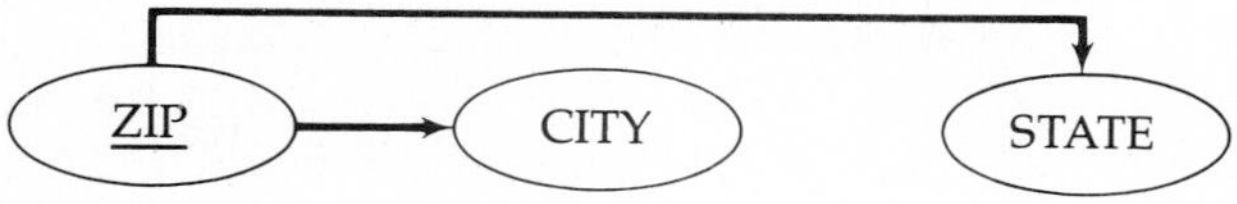

Normalization theory would suggest that we convert CUSTOMER to two relations in 3NF. These two relations are:

CUSTOMERDATA (NAME, STREET, ZIP)
LOCATION (ZIP, CITY, STATE)

However, in practice the designer would most likely choose *not* to decompose CUSTOMER into the two relations because the attributes STREET, CITY, STATE, and ZIP are almost always used together as a unit. Although conceptually correct, decomposing CUSTOMER into two relations would require the user to logically associate the CUSTOMERDATA and LOCATION data each time they are referenced. Thus, the designer should use judgment and common sense in applying normalization theory. In any event, any departures from 3NF should be justified and carefully documented. The use of normalization should be enforced for both network and relational implementations.

Normalization is also limited by the fact that it ignores operational considerations. Users may have to join several tables for retrieval, which requires additional computer time. Also, referential integrity is more difficult to enforce when a table is decomposed via normalization.

DATA VOLUME AND USAGE

The last step in requirements analysis is collecting information concerning data volume and usage patterns. This step is most easily accomplished after the conceptual schema is completed, as we will see. When the conceptual schema is completed, the data base designers should conduct a design review with users. Simultaneously, information can be gathered concerning data volume and usage.

We will illustrate the techniques of data volume and usage analysis with the conceptual schema for GRADE-REPORT. However, you should keep in mind that this schema was derived from a single user view. We illustrate the techniques for an extended example in the next chapter.

Conceptual Data Model

The four normalized relations for GRADE-REPORT shown in Figure 7-13 are a perfectly valid representation of a conceptual schema, and no additional transformation is necessary. However, it is often useful to map the relations onto a data structure diagram so that users can easily see the associations among entities. Also, the resulting data structure diagram (sometimes called a relational map) is useful to data base designers if the conceptual schema is to be implemented as a network or hierarchical model.

The conceptual data model for GRADE-REPORT, expressed as a data structure diagram, is shown in Figure 7-17. Each relation is represented by a rectangle containing the names of of its attributes (primary keys are underlined). The one-to-many association from STUDENT to REGISTRATION is the consequence of the composite key (STUDENT#, COURSE#) in REGISTRATION. This composite key implies that a given student registers in several courses. For the same reason, there is a one-to-many association from COURSE to REGISTRATION. Finally, the foreign key INSTRUCTOR-NAME in COURSE implies the association between INSTRUCTOR and COURSE. (This association is one-to-many, since each instructor teaches several courses.)

Data Volumes

Data volume figures are superimposed on the conceptual schema shown in Figure 7-17. These data volumes are necessary for physical data base design (described in Chapter 9). The figures shown in Figure 7-17 are based on the following assumptions:

1. There are 3000 students.
2. Each student registers for an average of 3 courses (thus, there are 9000 registration entries).
3. There are 100 instructors.

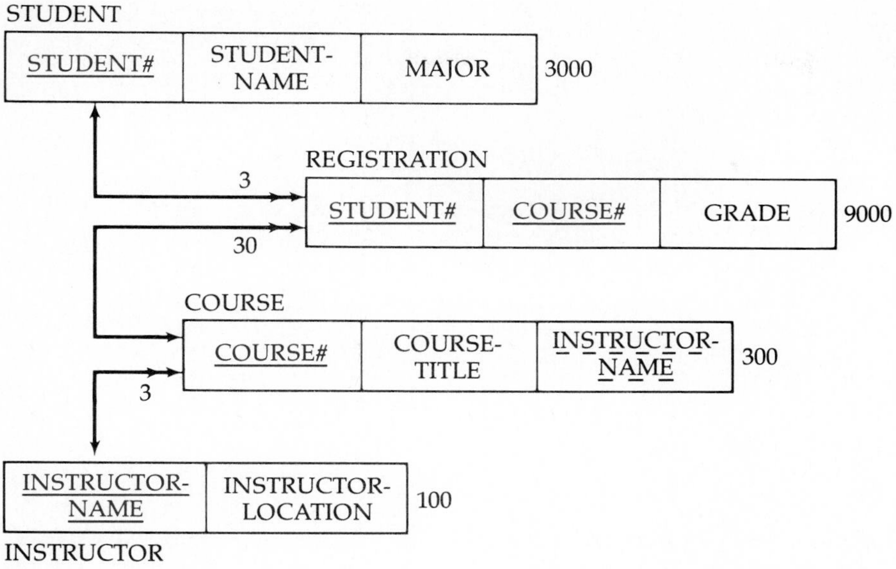

Figure 7-17 Conceptual data model (GRADE-REPORT)

4. Each instructor teaches an average of 3 courses (thus, there are 300 courses).
5. Each course has an average of 30 registrants (9000 ÷ 300 = 30).

In collecting such data volume figures, the analysts must allow for future growth. Often, two sets of figures are collected—one set representing current volumes, the other representing forecasted volumes for a future time frame (say, five years later). Also, whether the data base is to contain only current period data or, in addition, contain historical data (e.g., current semester, complete time period each student is in school, or even some longer time period), it is very important to calculate data volumes and to determine relationship types.

Data Usage Analysis

After data volumes have been estimated, the analyst must define how the data are to be used. This step requires that the following two tasks be performed:

1. Define data base transactions. A transaction is a record of an event, or a request for information, that causes certain actions to be taken against a data base.
2. Define the logical data base accesses required to process each transaction (expressed as a logical access map).

We will illustrate this process with another user view based on the GRADE-REPORT data base. Figure 7-18 shows a view called CLASS-LIST, which

Figure 7-18
Another user view (CLASS-LIST)

LAKEWOOD COLLEGE CLASS LIST FALL SEMESTER 198X			
COURSE#: IS 350 COURSE-TITLE: DATA BASE INSTRUCTOR-NAME: CODD INSTRUCTOR-LOCATION: B104			
STUDENT#	STUDENT-NAME	MAJOR	GRADE
38214	BRIGHT	IS	A
40875	CORTEZ	CS	B
51893	EDWARDS	IS	A
...			

provides a list of students registered in each class at Lakewood College. The list is produced three times each semester: after registration, at mid-semester, and when the semester is ended (GRADES are recorded in the final version only).

Now let us define the transaction CREATE-CLASS-LIST. This transaction is a request for information, namely, to produce one version of the CLASS-LIST view. This transaction will require the following logical steps:

1. Read the next COURSE record (or tuple).
2. Read the INSTRUCTOR record for that COURSE.
3. Print (or display) the report header.
4. Read the next REGISTRATION record for that COURSE.
5. Read the STUDENT record corresponding to that REGISTRATION.
6. Print a detail line for the report.
7. Repeat steps 4 through 7 for each REGISTRATION for the COURSE.

A **logical access map** (LAM) is a diagram showing the sequence of logical accesses to conceptual data base records (or relations). A LAM for the transaction CREATE-CLASS-LIST is shown in Figure 7-19. Figure 7-19a shows a preliminary LAM superimposed on the conceptual schema. Figure 7-19b shows the same map arranged in the logical sequence in which the records are accessed. This LAM also shows the total number of accesses that will be required for each conceptual record type in order to produce the entire set of 300 class lists. This information is also necessary for physical data base design—for example, in selecting file organizations and access methods.

The LAM in Figure 7-19b can be used directly to specify a procedure to create the class lists. We describe procedure design in Chapter 9.

Figures 7-3 and 7-18 illustrate how two different user views (or external schemas) may be derived from the same conceptual schema. Figure 7-17 is

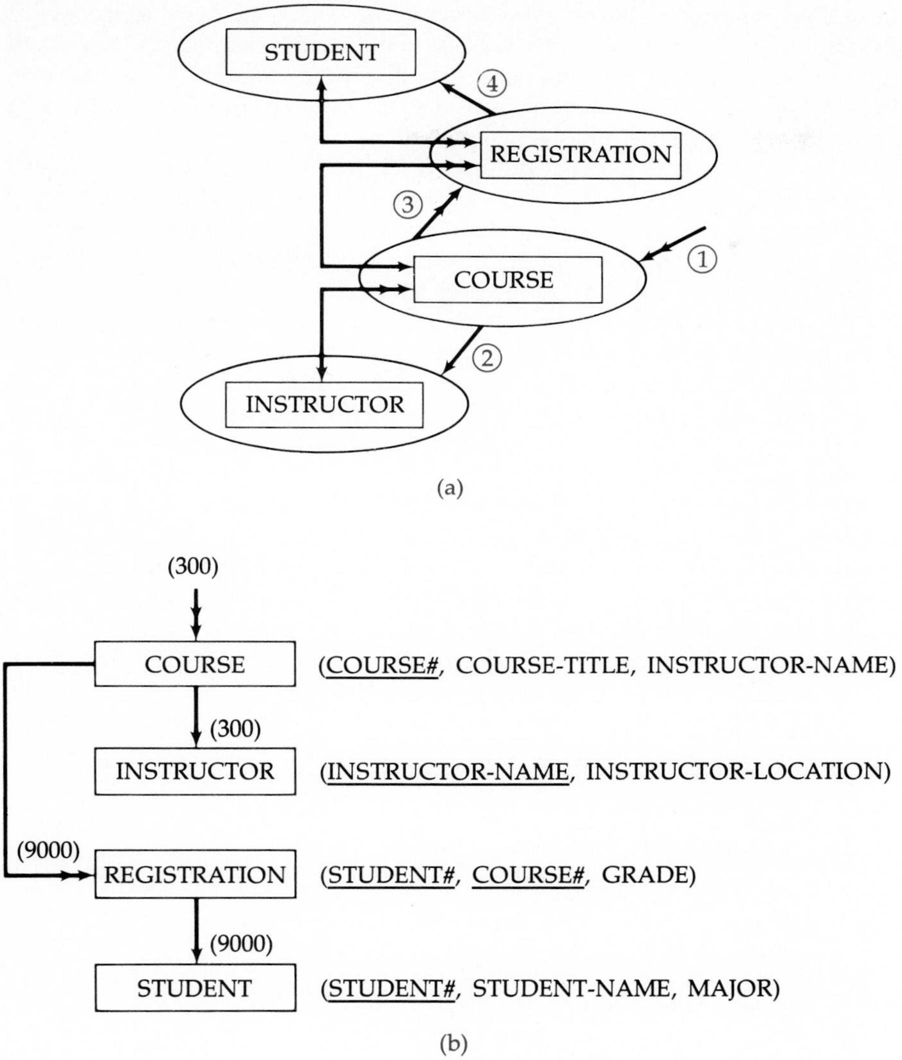

Figure 7-19
Logical access map (CREATE-CLASS-LIST):
(a) preliminary map
(b) final map

simply a different view of the same data. In fact, we could have created the conceptual schema by normalizing the data in Class-List (we ask you to do this in the chapter exercises).

SUMMARY

In this chapter, we have presented an introduction to data base design. First, we described the major steps: requirements formulation and analysis, conceptual design, implementation design, and physical design. Next, we described requirements formulation and analysis, which is the process of determining user requirements for data. Requirements analysis consists of defining the scope of the data base, establishing data collection standards, identifying user views, building the data dictionary, and identifying data volumes and usage patterns.

We also described normalization, which is the cornerstone of modern data base design. Normalization is the step-by-step process of removing unwanted dependencies from relations, thereby eliminating data redundancy and the anomalies that result when modifying data. Normalization should result in simple data structures that are easy to maintain.

We described a number of normal forms in this chapter. Third normal form is adequate for most practical data base design problems. However, 3NF relations should be checked to determine if there are any remaining unwanted dependencies. If such dependencies exist, there will be redundancy in the relations. These dependencies can be removed by applying the definitions of BCNF or 4NF.

When the conceptual schema is completed, it should be reviewed with users to ensure that all semantic rules have been followed and that no important data have been omitted from the model. At this time, additional information concerning data volumes and usage patterns should be collected and superimposed on the conceptual schema.

Chapter Review

REVIEW QUESTIONS

1. Define each of the following terms concisely:
   a. data base design
   b. user view
   c. semantic rules
   d. normalization
   e. determinant
   f. multivalued dependence
   g. interrelation constraint
   h. logical access map
   i. unnormalized relation

2. Contrast the following terms:
   a. unnormalized relation; normalized relation
   b. full dependence; partial dependence
   c. process-oriented approach; data-oriented approach
   d. transitive dependence; multivalued dependence
   e. insertion anomaly; deletion anomaly
   f. primary key; foreign key

3. Briefly define each of the following:
   a. first normal form
   b. second normal form
   c. third normal form
   d. Boyce-Codd normal form

e. fourth normal form
f. domain-key normal form

4. Describe the procedure required for each of the following:
   a. Convert an unnormalized relation to 1NF
   b. Convert a 1NF relation to 2NF
   c. Convert a 2NF relation to 3NF
   d. Convert a 3NF relation to BCNF
   e. Convert a BCNF relation to 4NF
5. Why are interrelation constraints significant?
6. Briefly describe the four major steps in data base design.
7. Briefly describe six steps of requirements analysis.
8. What is the significance of domain-key normal form (DK/NF)?
9. What are semantic rules? Why are they important?
10. Explain how procedure formation for data bases differs from that for conventional application programs.

PROBLEMS AND EXERCISES

1. Match the following terms to the appropriate definitions:

________ conceptual design
________ physical design
________ user view
________ 1NF
________ 2NF
________ 3NF
________ normalization
________ partial dependence
________ transitive dependency
________ foreign key
________ BCNF
________ 5NF

a. attribute does not depend on entire key
b. analysis of functional dependencies
c. attribute depends on a nonkey attribute
d. synthesizes user views
e. attribute appears as a primary key elsewhere
f. data required by a user for decision making
g. relies on the concept of a determinant
h. last stage of data base design
i. deals with join dependencies
j. contains no repeating groups
k. contains no transitive dependencies
l. partial dependencies have been removed

2. Draw a data flow diagram representing the registration procedure at your school.
3. Derive a set of 3NF relations for the Class-List user view (Figure 7-18). Use the assumptions stated in Figure 7-3. Compare your results with Figure 7-13.

4. The transaction CREATE-GRADE-REPORT is a request to produce the Grade Report shown in Figure 7-3.
   a. List the logical steps required to process this transaction.
   b. Draw a logical access map representing the logical data base accesses.
5. Write a sequence of relational algebra commands to create Grade-Report (Figure 7-3) from the 3NF relations in Figure 7-13. Refer to Chapter 6 for a discussion of relational algebra.
6. Classify each of the following relations as unnormalized, 1NF, 2NF, or 3NF (state any assumptions you make).
   a. EMPLOYEE (EMPLOYEE#,EMPNAME,JOBCODE)
   b. EMPLOYEE (EMPLOYEE#,EMPNAME {JOBCODE, #YEARS})
   c. EMPLOYEE (EMPLOYEE#,EMPNAME,JOBCODE,JOBDESCRIPTION)
   d. EMPLOYEE (EMPLOYEE#,EMPNAME,PROJECT#,HRS-WORKED)
7. For each of the following relations, do the following:
   a. State the normal form in its present state.
   b. Identify any unwanted dependencies.
   c. Give an example of an insertion and deletion anomaly.
   d. Further normalize the relation, stating what definition you are using.

EMPLOYEE

EMP#	COURSES	INTERESTS
123	COMM. I	BOWLING
123	COMM. II	BOWLING
456	Q.C.	SKIING
456	Q.C.	BOWLING

EMP# ←↠ COURSES
EMP# ←↠ INTERESTS

FOOTBALL

PLAYER	POSITION	COACH
EARL	FB	JOE
JOHN	G	ED
TONY	FB	PETE
CARL	T	JIM
MACK	FB	JOE

COACH ↞→ POSITION

8. A customer order form for Pine Valley Furniture Company is shown in Figure 7-20.
   a. Derive a set of 3NF relations.
   b. Create a data structure diagram.

Figure 7-20
CUSTOMER ORDER
(Pine Valley Furniture)

CUSTOMER ORDER

ORDER#: 61384 DATE: 11/4/8X
CUSTOMER#: 1273
CUSTOMER NAME: CONTEMPORARY DESIGNS
CUSTOMER ADDRESS: 123 OAK ST.
CITY-STATE-ZIP: AUSTIN, TX 28384

PRODUCT#	DESCRIPTION	QUANTITY ORDERED	UNIT PRICE
M-128	BOOKCASE	2	150
B-381	CABINET	1	725

ORDER# ↞→ CUSTOMER#
PRODUCT# ↞→ DESCRIPTION

9. Do the following for the conceptual data model derived for the user view in Figure 7-20:
   a. Add data volumes to the conceptual data model, using the following assumptions:
      (i) 200 customers
      (ii) 2 orders per customer (average)
      (iii) 3 products per order (average)
      (iv) 300 products
   b. Create a logical access map for the transaction CREATE-CUSTOMER-ORDER.
10. Refer to the conceptual data model for Grade-Report (Figure 7-17). Draw a logical access map for the transaction CREATE-GRADE-REPORT (Figure 7-3).
11. Obtain a user view such as a credit card statement of account, a phone bill, or some other common document. Perform the following:
    a. Fill out a user view form (Figure 7-4).
    b. Fill out a data element form (Figure 7-5) for a data item that identifies some entity.
    c. Derive a set of 3NF relations.
    d. Draw a data structure diagram.

REFERENCES

Date, C. J. 1981. *Introduction to Database Systems.* 3d ed. Reading, Mass.: Addison-Wesley.

Fagin, Ronald. 1981. "A Normal Form for Databases That Is Based on Domains and Keys." ACM *Transactions on Database Systems* 6 (September): 387–415.

Kent, William. 1983. "A Simple Guide to Five Normal Forms in Relational Database Theory." *Communications of the ACM* 26 (February): 120–125.

Martin, James. 1983. *Managing the Data-Base Environment.* Englewood Cliffs, N.J.: Prentice-Hall.

Teorey, T. J., and J. P. Fry. 1982. *Design of Database Structures.* Englewood Cliffs, N.J.: Prentice-Hall.

Weinberg, Victor. 1979. *Structured Analysis.* New York: Yourdon Press.

Chapter 8

Conceptual Design

INTRODUCTION

Before starting construction on a new house, a builder must consult a set of architectural plans. The architect who designs these plans determines the present and future needs of the prospective homeowner. Also taken into account are any constraints of the owner as well as the natural environment. In the same way, an organization must develop an "architectural plan" before creating a data base, to ensure that the data base will meet its present and future information needs.

Conceptual data base design is the process of developing a detailed "architectural plan" for the data base. We will refer to this plan as the conceptual data model (it is also called a conceptual schema). The conceptual data model represents the entities of the organization, the attributes of those entities, and the relationships among entities. It is defined by the data themselves and is entirely independent of application programs, computer hardware, the data base management system, or any other physical considerations.

Conceptual design is the second step in data base design, following requirements analysis. As shown in Figure 8-1, the major inputs to this activity are the requirements specifications representing user needs for data and the preliminary enterprise information model if a data base plan has been developed. Much of the metadata required for conceptual design should be organized in the data dictionary. The output of conceptual design is a conceptual data model that represents the information structure of the organization.

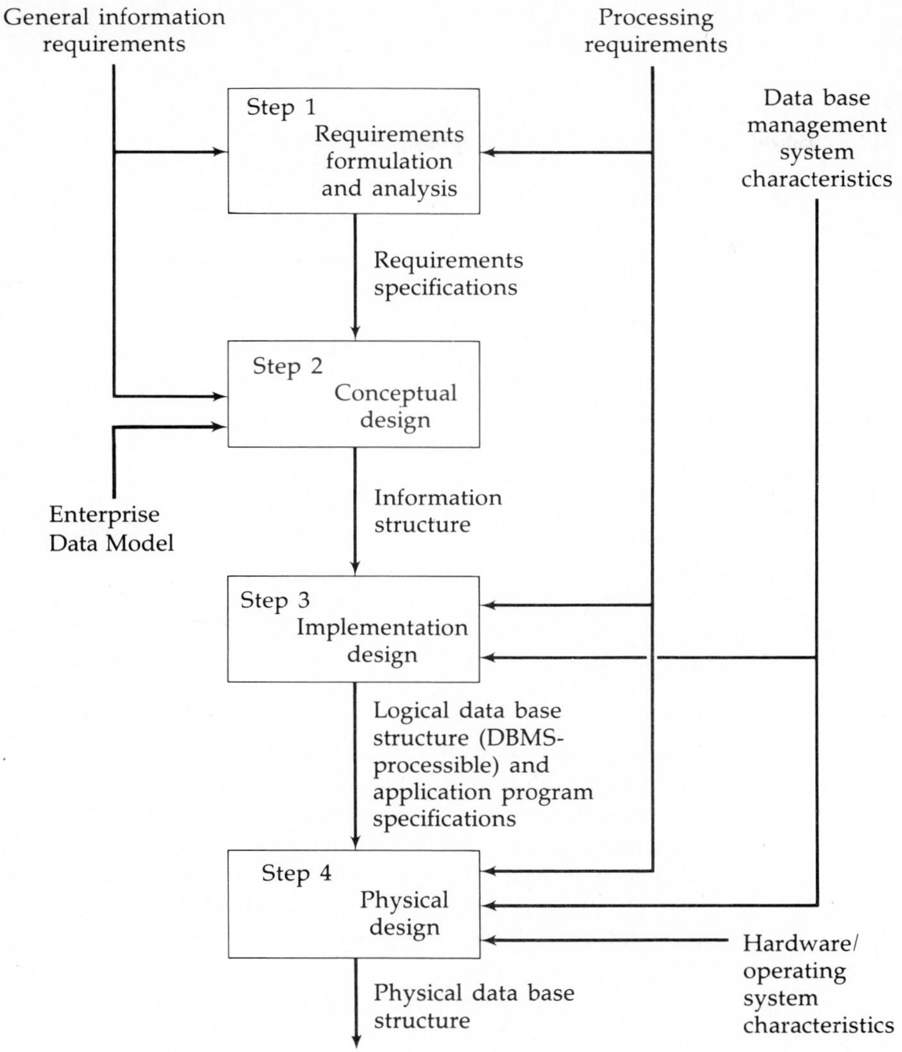

Figure 8-1
Position of conceptual design in the data base design process (Source: Teorey and Fry 1982)

TRADE-OFFS IN CONCEPTUAL DESIGN

The data base designer must perform a series of trade-offs during conceptual data base design. How these trade-offs are resolved will have an important bearing on the overall success of the data base project. Following is a brief description of several such trade-offs (Auerbach Publishers 1980).

Scope of the Design

Should an organization attempt to design a single large global data base to meet its information needs? Or should the organization design a separate data base for each of its applications? Perhaps an intermediate approach would be superior to either of these two extremes.

With the **global approach**, the designer attempts to design a single integrated data base to meet the organization's present and future information needs. This approach is basically the "total systems" approach that was widely advocated during the 1960s. However, the global approach has seldom proved successful. The design task is so complex and the time and resources required are normally so large that the global approach becomes quite risky. Any benefits from data base implementation are delayed for months or years, so that the project is in danger of losing organizational commitment and momentum.

With the **application approach**, the designer performs a requirements analysis and designs a separate data base for each new application. This reduces the design task to manageable size. However, there are two major disadvantages. First, there is no assurance that the various data bases will ever be integrated or shared. Second, the application data bases will probably be designed to resemble conventional application files, with extensive data redundancy and lack of data independence. Thus, the application approach is just as risky (perhaps riskier) as the global approach.

An intermediate design approach seems preferable to either the global or individual application approach. With this approach, the designers sketch a high-level enterprise model (see Chapter 3) based on an analysis of business processes and functions. This model shows the major entities that must be described in the data base and the relationships between those entities. The enterprise model is then used to partition the overall data base design into several smaller, more manageable data bases (or segments of a global data base). Each smaller data base should represent a natural grouping of data entities rather than a specific application or functional unit of the organization. The data base designers then develop a detailed logical design for each of these smaller data bases, using the strategic data model as an integrating framework. Davis (1974) refers to this approach as a federation of systems.

We do not rule out the global data base approach. That approach has been used successfully by a number of smaller organizations where the information structures are not unduly complex and where there was unquestioned organizational commitment. However, when these conditions are not present, we recommend the "partitioned" or "federated" approach.

Design Approach

The designer must choose between two possible design approaches: top-down and bottom-up. This choice is closely related to the design scope we have just described.

With the top-down approach (also called *entity analysis*), the designer

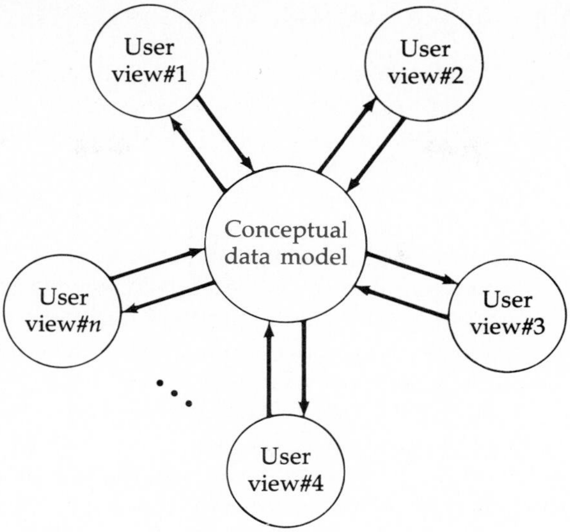

Figure 8-2
Bottom-up conceptual design process

starts with the enterprise model and adds detail to that model until a satisfactory conceptual design has been achieved. For example, the designer decides what attributes to associate with each entity, chooses primary keys, and so on. The main disadvantage of this approach is that there is no assurance that all user requirements will be represented in the model.

The other major approach to data base design employs a bottom-up analysis (also called *attribute synthesis*). With this approach, the analyst performs a detailed requirements analysis and models each user view separately. The relations for each user view are then merged to form a conceptual schema, as shown in Figure 8-2. Each user view in turn can be derived from this conceptual data model (shown by the outward-pointing arrows in Figure 8-2).

Actually, both the top-down and bottom-up approaches can be used, with each approach providing a check on the other.

When both approaches are used, we should anticipate that differences may arise between the two models. Some reasons for those differences are:

1. The two models are completed by different people at different times.
2. The enterprise information model is more global and future-oriented, while the bottom-up model is more detailed and incremental.
3. The enterprise information model is not necessarily normalized.

Despite the possible differences caused by these factors, the models, as noted, provide a valuable cross-check on each other.

In this chapter we stress the bottom-up approach since the top-down was emphasized in Chapter 3.

DBMS Dependency

Should the data base management system be selected and its features and constructs introduced early during the conceptual data base design process? Or should conceptual design proceed without reference to features of the DBMS that will be used?

We strongly recommend the latter approach. Although introducing the DBMS early may spread the overall implementation effort, it will greatly reduce flexibility. A data model expressed in the constructs of one DBMS cannot be mapped easily into the constructs of another DBMS. Therefore, we recommend that the conceptual design be completed before DBMS features are considered. In fact, the completed conceptual design is most useful in evaluating what DBMS features are required by the organization.

One major difficulty may arise in postponing the DBMS software decision until conceptual design is completed. In discussing requirements analysis (Chapter 7), we recommended that the organization use an automated data dictionary facility to record metadata. Yet a mainstream trend in data management systems is to integrate the data dictionary with the DBMS and other data management software (we describe these software products in Chapter 11). As a practical matter, then, an organization may be forced to choose its data management software before conceptual design begins if it is going to use the data dictionary to support requirements analysis. This compromise is acceptable (indeed, necessary), provided that conceptual design is performed without reference to the DBMS that is going to be used. The conceptual schema is mapped to a DBMS-dependent schema during implementation design.

STEPS IN CONCEPTUAL DESIGN

A number of different approaches and methodologies are used for conceptual data base design. The detailed steps, or tasks, naturally depend on the approach or methodology that is used. However, the steps shown in Figure 8-3 represent the major tasks that must be performed.

Data Modeling

Data modeling is the process of identifying and structuring the relationships among data elements. The analyst starts with the user views that are identified during requirements analysis and normalizes these data using the steps described in the previous chapter. The result of data modeling is a set of relations in third normal form for each user view.

View Integration

View integration is the process of merging the relations for each user view into a single set of relations in third normal form. The result of view integration is a conceptual data model for the organization's data base expressed in the form of normalized relations.

To illustrate how relations are merged, suppose that modeling a user view results in the following 3NF relation:

EMPLOYEE1 (EMPLOYEE#, NAME, ADDRESS, PHONE)

Modeling a second user view might result in the following relation:

EMPLOYEE2 (EMPLOYEE#, NAME, ADDRESS, JOBCODE, #YEARS)

Since these two relations have the same primary key (EMPLOYEE#), they describe the same entity and may be merged into one relation. The result of merging the relations is the following relation:

EMPLOYEE (EMPLOYEE#, NAME, ADDRESS, PHONE, JOBCODE, #YEARS)

Notice that an attribute that appears in both relations (such as NAME in this example) appears only once in the merged relation.

When merging two relations, the data base analyst should be aware that a transitive dependency may be introduced into the merged relation. For example, suppose that we have two relations with the following dependency diagrams:

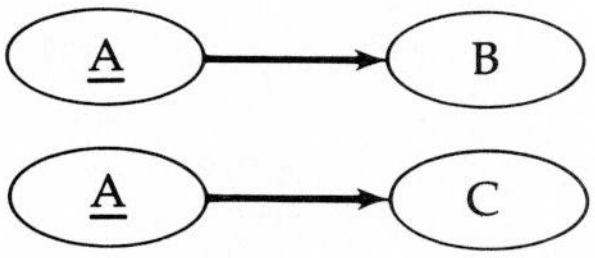

Since these two relations have the same primary key, they can be merged into a single relation. However, attribute C may be functionally dependent on attribute B. If so, we have introduced a transitive dependency into the merged relation, as shown in the following diagram:

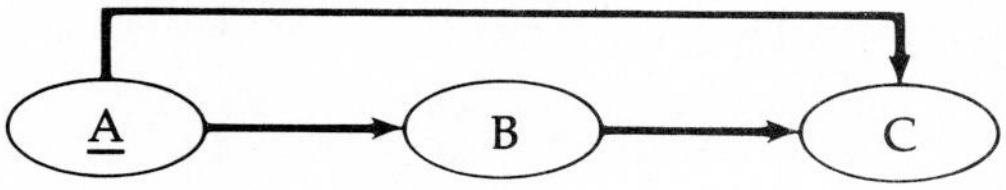

To resolve this dependency, the analyst can create the following two relations:

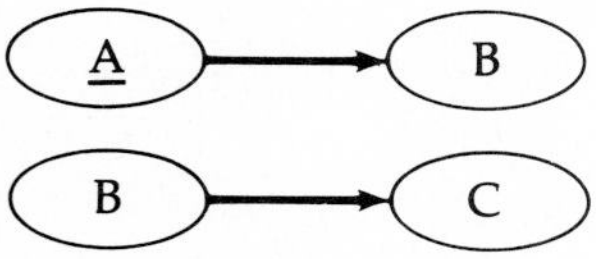

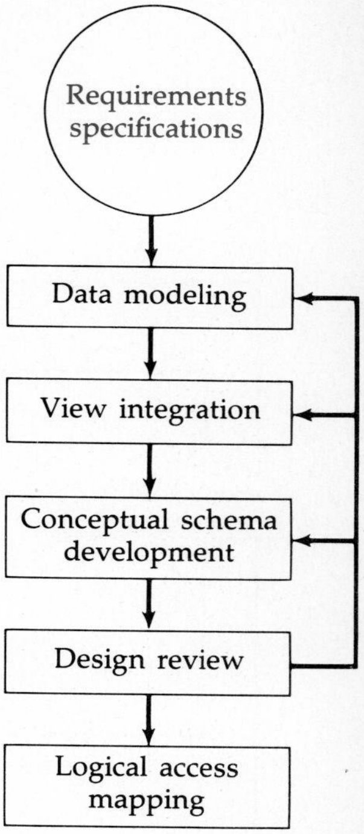

Figure 8-3
Steps in conceptual design

Conceptual Data Model Development

As we have indicated, when view integration is completed, the conceptual data model is expressed in the form of normalized relations. For better user understanding (and also for subsequent design steps), we may wish to

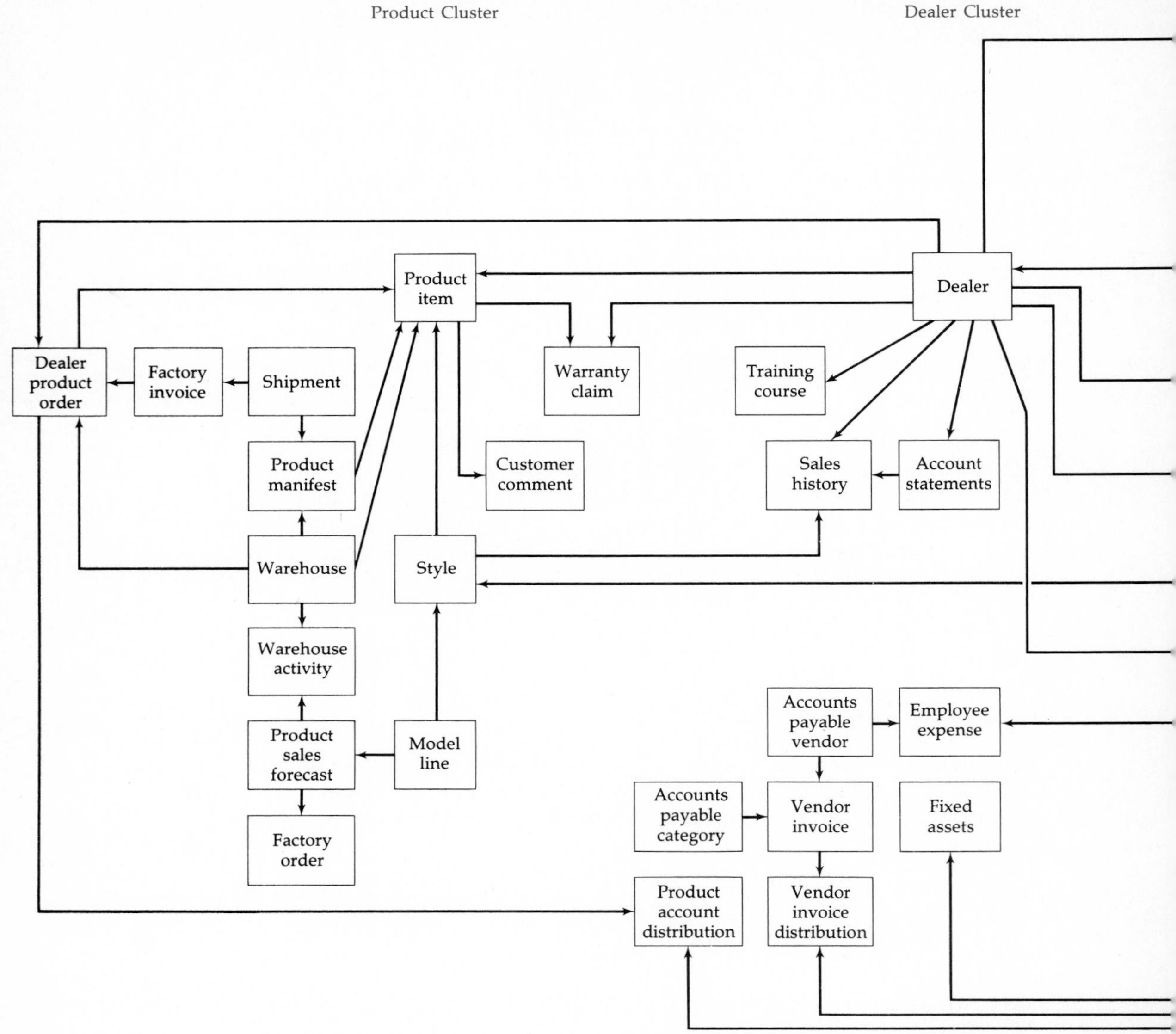

Figure 8-4
Sample conceptual data model (Courtesy Peat, Marwick, Mitchell & Co.)

transform these 3NF relations into a graphic model. We illustrated this process in Chapter 7, where the 3NF relations for Grade-Report (Figure 7-13) were transformed into a data structure diagram (Figure 7-17). The conceptual data model may be expressed in several different forms: a data structure diagram, an entity-relationship model, or a semantic data model. It may be drawn manually or by computer graphics.

A conceptual data model for a small to medium-sized company may

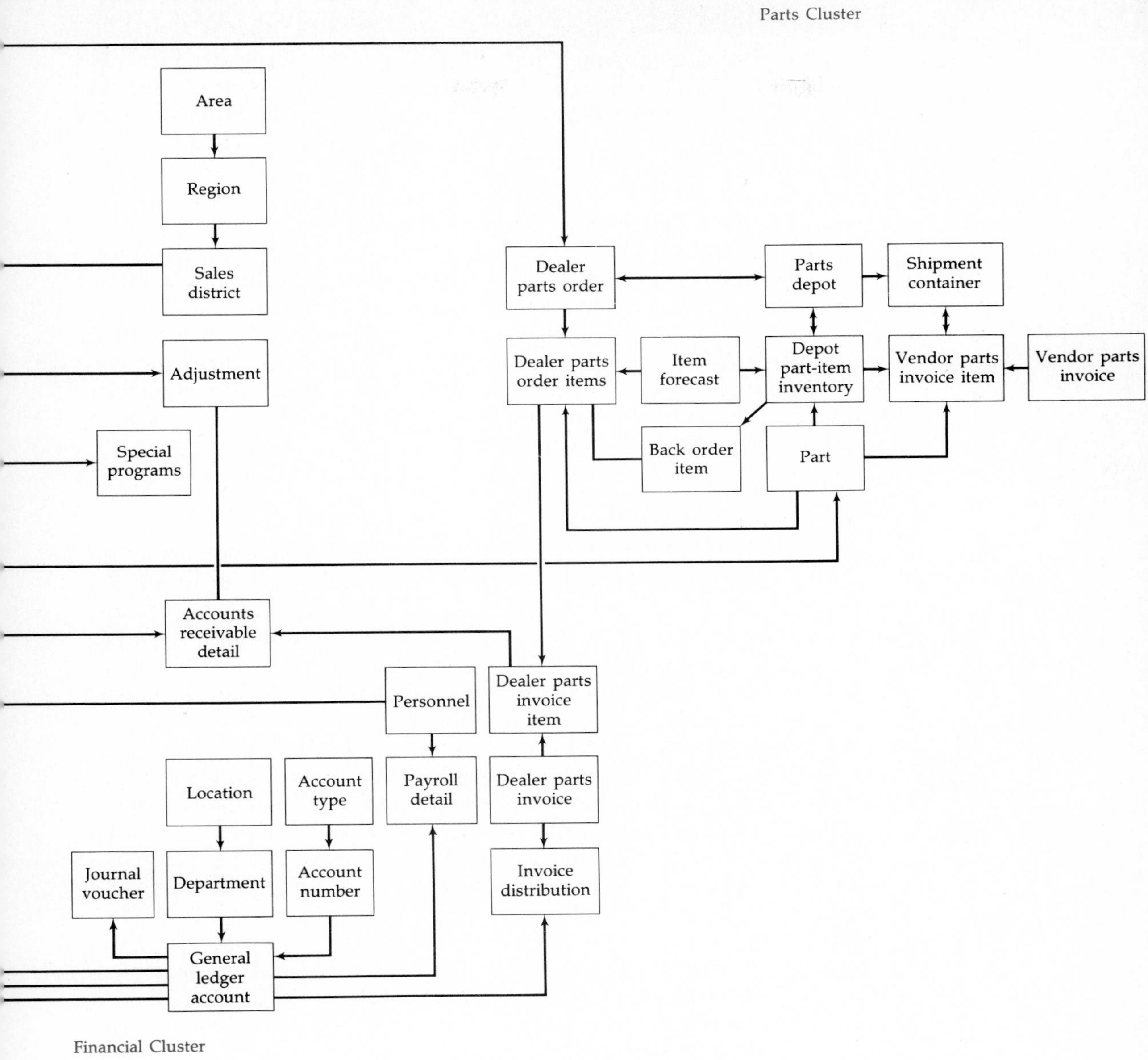

comprise some 50 to 100 entities. For example, Figure 8-4 shows a conceptual data model for a medium-sized distributor. There are some 50 entities in the diagram (a manufacturing company would typically define more entities). Notice that the entities fall into natural clusters or groups. Thus, there is a Product cluster, a Parts cluster, a Dealer cluster, and a Financial cluster. Each of these clusters might be physically implemented as a separate data base [Martin (1983) refers to these clusters as "subject" data bases].

Design Review

When the initial version of the conceptual data model is developed, it should be subjected to a formal design review. All managers and key users should evaluate the conceptual data model and suggest changes or improvements before the next step (implementation design) is attempted. The conceptual data model should be evaluated from two points of view: accuracy and completeness. Does the conceptual data model accurately reflect the organization's data and their relationships? For example, is the association between Suppliers and Materials one-to-many, or should it really be many-to-many? And is the data model complete, or are there important entities, attributes, or relationships that should be added?

A report or questionnaire posing specific questions about the conceptual data model should be prepared by the design team before the review is held. An example of such a questionnaire for a Customer Information data base is presented in Figure 8-5 [see Teorey and Fry (1982) for a discussion of alternative conceptual design techniques].

Logical Access Mapping

Logical access maps (introduced in Chapter 7) are diagrams showing the logical sequence for accessing the conceptual records required to process transactions. LAMs are used as a basis for developing data base procedures and are also used to estimate the frequency of logical accesses to records.

Logical access mapping may be considered part of conceptual design or a step in implementation design. We will regard logical access mapping as the last step in conceptual design, as shown in Figure 8-3.

We can illustrate the various steps of conceptual design by continuing the case of Mountain View Community Hospital, which was introduced in Chapter 3. We include requirements analysis in the following discussion.

Conceptual data base design at Mountain View Community Hospital was performed under the direction of Mr. Helms, the data base administrator. Mr. Helms was assisted in this effort by Mrs. Green, whose title was data analyst. Mrs. Green was previously a systems analyst with Mountain View Community Hospital and had attended a seminar on data base analysis and design. A data base consultant assisted in organizing the design effort and answered some technical questions. However, the analysis was performed almost entirely by the design team of Mr. Helms and Mrs. Green.

Conceptual data base design (together with requirements analysis) at Mountain View Community Hospital required approximately five months. This period was broken down as follows:

Requirements analysis: 2 months

Data modeling: 1 month

View integration: 1 month

Conceptual data model development: 2 weeks

Final review with users: 2 weeks

CUSTOMER INFORMATION

Statements About How Customer Information Is and Is Not Used in the Current Operating Environment

1. Each customer must be assigned to a salesperson before an account may be established.
   COMMENTS: ______________________
2. All orders must be from customers with established accounts.
   COMMENTS: ______________________
3. Each customer can be served by only one salesperson.
   COMMENTS: ______________________
4. Each customer may have an unlimited number of orders.
   COMMENTS: ______________________
5. If a salesperson is replaced, all customers must be immediately reassigned to a new salesperson and all sales agreements renegotiated.
   COMMENTS: ______________________
6. If a customer is deleted or inactivated, all of the customer's current orders will be removed and sales agreements nullified.
   COMMENTS: ______________________
7. Customers have no direct relationship to invoices, vendors, item numbers, or warehouses.
   COMMENTS: ______________________
8. More than one customer may be on a given order.
   AGREE ______________________
   DISAGREE ______________________
9. A customer buys from a warehouse and not a salesperson. Consequently, each customer may have a sales agreement with each warehouse.
   AGREE ______________________
   DISAGREE ______________________

Figure 8-5
Sample design review questionnaire (Source: Donna L.S. Rund in Teorey and Fry 1982)

Enterprise Information Model

An enterprise information model in the form of an entity-relationship diagram was developed for Mountain View Community Hospital in Chapter 3 (see Figure 3-12). This model is shown again in Figure 8-6 for ease of reference.

The entity-relationship diagram shown in Figure 8-6 was developed using a top-down process, proceeding from business functions, processes, and activities. It could be used to continue the design process. For example, the design team could attempt to identify the attributes or data items that should appear in the Patient entity. But what data items should in fact be included? It is safer to use a bottom-up process, which proceeds from actual detailed

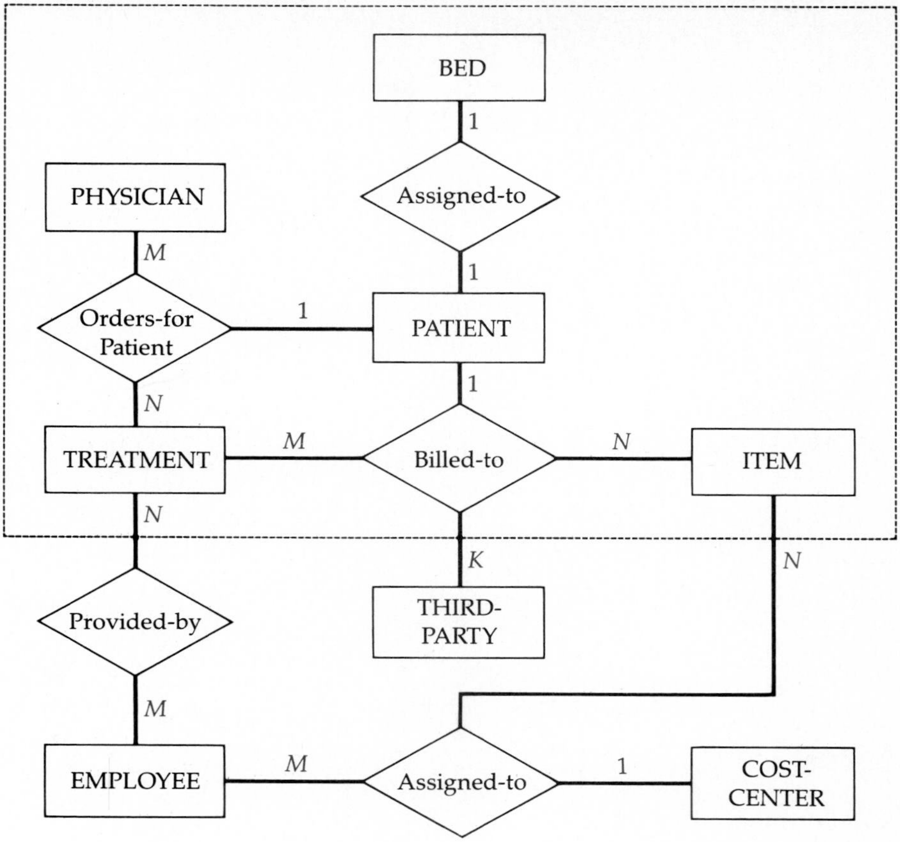

Figure 8-6
E/R diagram (Mountain View Community Hospital)

user views. However, the E/R diagram provides a valuable reference point to ensure that all entities have been included and that the relationships are correct.

In the analysis that follows, the design team considers four user views that we associated with the basic patient accounting system. They are: patient bill, patient display, room utilization report, and physician report. These views include or refer to the following entities: Physician, Patient, Treatment, Item, and Bed (or Location). Thus, the analysis pertains to the area enclosed within the dashed line in Figure 8-6. This example illustrates how the E/R diagram can be used to help partition a large data base design project into smaller, more manageable tasks.

The E/R diagram shown in Figure 8-6 reflects the state of the hospital (and its data base) at a given point in time. Thus the association between BED and PATIENT is 1:1 (actually, this is a conditional association; at a given instant a bed may or may not be assigned to a patient). Over a period of time, of course, a bed will be assigned to a number of patients.

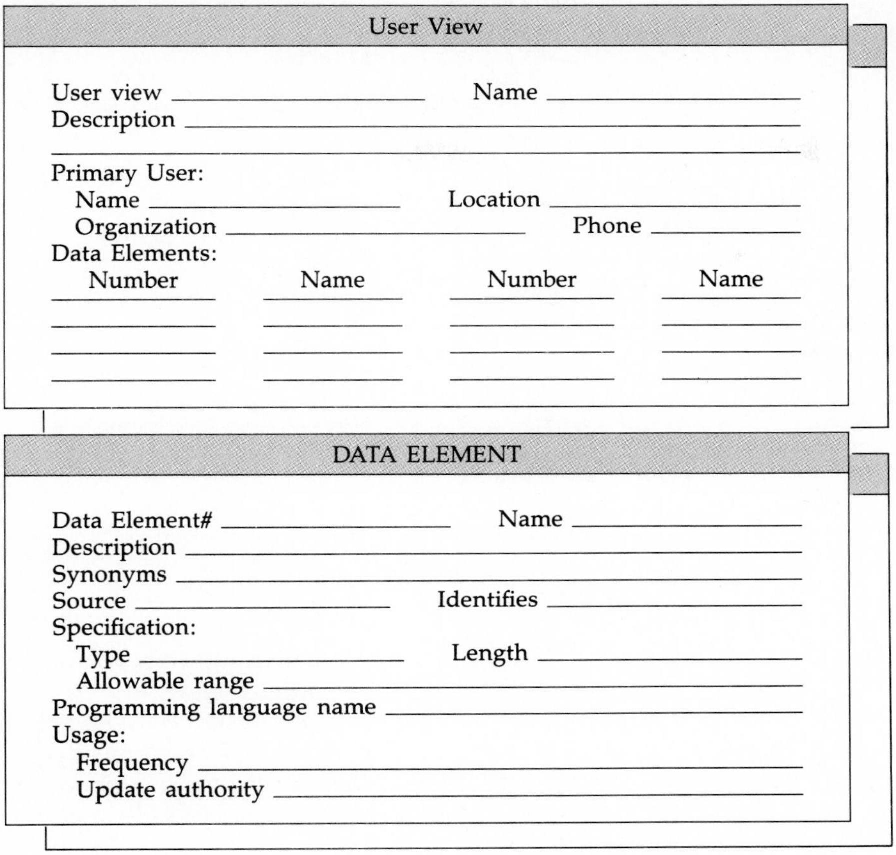
User View

User view ______ Name ______
Description ______

Primary User:
Name ______ Location ______
Organization ______ Phone ______
Data Elements:
Number | Name | Number | Name

DATA ELEMENT

Data Element# ______ Name ______
Description ______
Synonyms ______
Source ______ Identifies ______
Specification:
Type ______ Length ______
Allowable range ______
Programming language name ______
Usage:
Frequency ______
Update authority ______

Figure 8-7
Sample metadata (Mountain View Community Hospital)

Requirements Analysis

The design team interviewed users throughout Mountain View Community Hospital, including nurses, doctors, administrators, and clerks. Samples of existing reports and other operating documents were obtained.

As the design team accumulated these user views, they documented the data elements that were used throughout the organization. The meaning and usage of each data element were recorded, and any inconsistencies were resolved with the users. Information concerning each data element (metadata) was then recorded in the hospital's data dictionary system. Sample metadata collected during requirements analysis are shown in Figure 8-7.

When requirements analysis was nearly completed, the design team drew an overview diagram identifying the various user views to be used in designing a conceptual data model. Part of this overview diagram is shown in Figure 8-8. It identifies four significant user views of data for Mountain

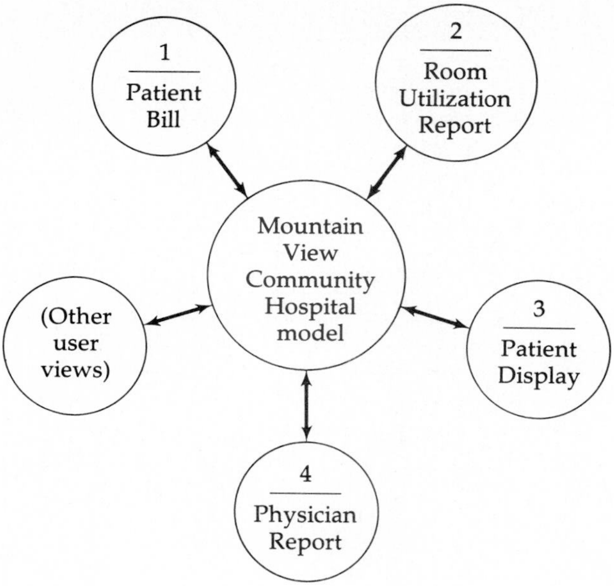

Figure 8-8
User views for Mountain View Community Hospital

View Community Hospital: Patient Bill, Room Utilization Report, Patient Display, and Physician Report.

When the overview diagram was completed, the design team reviewed it with users to ensure that all relevant user views had been considered. There were other user views in addition to the four we named. However, we will use these four views in the following discussion to illustrate the design of a conceptual data model for Mountain View Community Hospital.

User View 1: Patient Bill

The first user view is that of the Patient Bill (see Figure 8-9). Charges incurred by each patient are accumulated during that patient's stay at the hospital. After the patient is discharged, a statement is sent to the patient in the format shown in Figure 8-9.

The Patient Bill consists of header information for the patient, followed by an itemized list of patient charges, and ending with the Balance Due. To simplify the presentation we assume that a patient is only billed once for each item. If we view the Patient Bill as a relation, this itemized list constitutes a repeating group. To express the Patient Bill in shorthand notation, we list the attributes as follows:

BILL (PATIENT#, PATIENT-NAME, PATIENT-ADDRESS,
CITY-STATE-ZIP, DATE-ADMITTED, DATE-DISCHARGED,
{ITEM-CODE, DESCRIPTION, CHARGE}, BALANCE-DUE)

This is an unnormalized relation since it contains a repeating group (designated by the inner braces). To normalize this relation, we remove the repeating group, thus creating the following two new relations:

Mountain View Community Hospital
200 Forest Dr. Mountain View, Co.

Statement of account for:

Patient name: Baker, Mary
Patient address: 300 Oak St.
City-State-Zip:
Mountain View, Co. 80638

Patient#: 3249
Date admitted: 09-10-8X
Date discharged: 09-14-8X

Item Code	Description	Charge
200	Room semi-pr	150.00
205	Television	10.00
307	X-ray	25.00
413	Lab tests	35.00
	Balance Due	220.00

Figure 8-9
User view 1: Patient Bill

3NF: PATIENT (<u>PATIENT#</u>, PATIENT-NAME, PATIENT-ADDRESS, CITY-STATE-ZIP, DATE-ADMITTED, DATE-DISCHARGED, BALANCE-DUE)

1NF: DETAIL(<u>PATIENT#</u>, <u>ITEM-CODE</u>, DESCRIPTION, CHARGE)

In the PATIENT relation, PATIENT# is the primary key because it uniquely identifies a patient (PATIENT-NAME is assumed not to be a candidate key, since it may not be unique). In the DETAIL relation, the primary key is the composite of PATIENT# and ITEM-CODE.

PATIENT is in third normal form. However, DETAIL is in first normal form, since it contains a partial dependency, as shown in the following diagram:

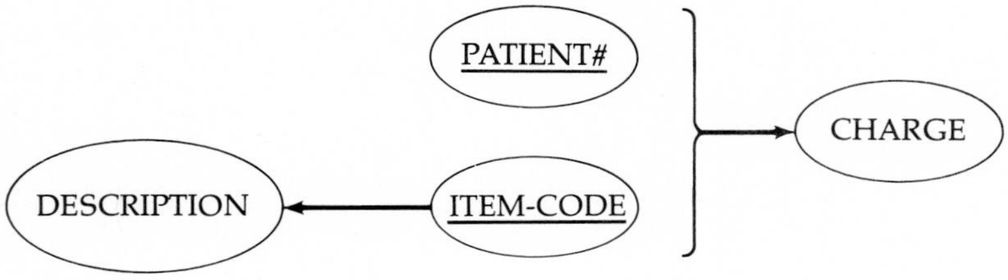

We assume that a particular CHARGE depends on both PATIENT# and ITEM-CODE. However, the ITEM-DESCRIPTION depends only on ITEM-CODE.

To convert DETAIL to 2NF, we remove the partial dependency, creating two new relations:

3NF: LIST (PATIENT#, ITEM-CODE, CHARGE)
3NF: ITEM (ITEM-CODE, DESCRIPTION)

Each of these relations is in 3NF, so the normalization steps are completed. The set of 3NF relations for the Patient Bill are:

1. (PATIENT#, PATIENT-NAME, PATIENT-ADDRESS, CITY-STATE-ZIP, DATE-ADMITTED, DATE-DISCHARGED)*
2. (ITEM-CODE, DESCRIPTION)
3. (PATIENT#,ITEM-CODE, CHARGE)

User View 2: Room Utilization Report

The Room Utilization Report (Figure 8-10) is a daily report that provides information about the current patient in each location. LOCATION specifies the room and bed numbers (e.g., 102-2 is room 102, bed 2). If a LOCATION is not assigned to a patient when the report is printed, then PATIENT#, PATIENT-NAME, and EXP-DISCHARGE-DATE are left blank (see the entry for 102-1 in Figure 8-10). This report is used by the hospital staff for room scheduling and utilization studies.

This user view is expressed as the following relation:

2NF: ROOM (LOCATION, ACCOM, PATIENT#, PATIENT-NAME, EXP-DISCH-DATE)

Notice that the attribute DATE (top of the Room Utilization Report) is omitted in the preceding relation. This is because DATE is assumed to be supplied by the system and need not be included in the conceptual view of the data base.

The ROOM relation does not contain any repeating groups and therefore is in 1NF. Also, since the primary key is a single attribute (LOCATION), there cannot be a partial dependency. Therefore, ROOM is already in 2NF.

Inspection of the ROOM relation reveals transitive ("hidden") dependencies involving patient information. Both PATIENT-NAME and EXP-DISCH-DATE depend on PATIENT#, not on LOCATION. A diagram of this dependency is:

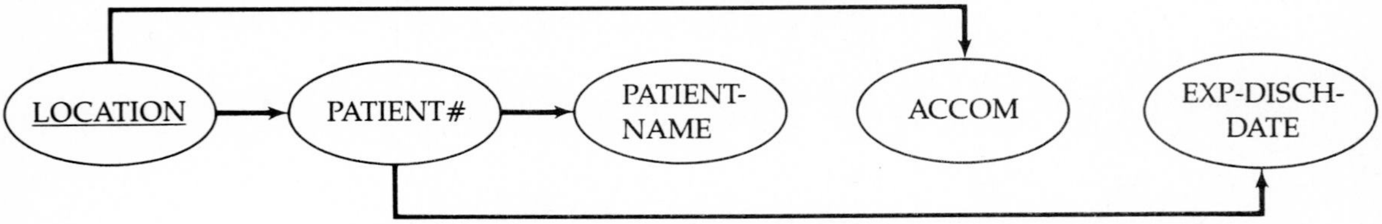

*In this relation we have chosen to omit the BALANCE-DUE attribute since that is a computed quantity.

Room Utilization Report
Date: 10-15-8X

Location	Accom	Patient#	Patient Name	Exp Discharge Date
100-1	PR	6213	Rose, David	10-17-8X
101-1	PR	1379	Cribbs, John	10-15-8X
102-1	SP			
102-2	SP	1239	Miller, Ruth	10-16-8X
103-1	PR	7040	Ortega, Juan	10-19-8X

Figure 8-10
User view 2: Room Utilization Report

Patient#: 3249
Patient Name: Baker, Mary
Patient Address: 300 Oak St.
City-State-Zip: Mountain View, Co. 80638
Date Admitted: 09-12-8X
Date Discharged: XX-XX-XX
Location: 437-2
Extension: 529
Third Party: Blue Cross

Figure 8-11
User view 3: Patient Display

To convert this relation to 3NF, we create two new relations, with PATIENT# the primary key of the relation containing patient data and a foreign key in the other relation.

4. (LOCATION, ACCOM, PATIENT#)
5. (PATIENT#, PATIENT-NAME, EXP-DISCH-DATE)

User View 3: Patient Display

The Patient Display (Figure 8-11) is presented on demand to any nurse or other qualified staff member who uses a visual display. We will assume that the user must enter the PATIENT# to display data for a particular patient (in practice, the system would probably support lookup based on patient name as well).

The Patient Display appears in relational form as follows:

2NF: PATIENT (PATIENT#, PATIENT-NAME, PATIENT-ADDRESS, CITY-STATE-ZIP, DATE-ADMITTED, DATE-DISCHARGED, LOCATION, EXTENSION, THIRD-PARTY)

This relation is in second normal form (you should verify this statement). There is a "hidden" dependency in this relation, since LOCATION determines EXTENSION (a particular bed location has a unique telephone extension). Removing this transitive dependency results in the following two 3NF relations:

6. (PATIENT#, PATIENT-NAME, PATIENT-ADDRESS, CITY-STATE-ZIP, DATE-ADMITTED, DATE-DISCHARGED, LOCATION, THIRD-PARTY)
7. (LOCATION, EXTENSION)

User View 4: Physician Report

The Physician Report is prepared daily for each physician treating patients at Mountain View Community Hospital (see Figure 8-12). It lists all patients currently in the hospital and the procedures that have been performed or prescribed by the physician. To simplify the presentation, we assume that a given patient's name does not appear more than once on the report for each physician (that is, a given procedure is performed only once by a given physician on the same patient and on a given day).

The relational view of this report in shorthand notation is as follows:

DOCTOR (PHYSICIAN-ID, PHYSICIAN-PHONE, {PATIENT#, PATIENT-NAME, LOCATION, PROCEDURE})

This is an unnormalized relation since there is a repeating group for patient information. Removing the repeating group results in the following relations:

3NF: DOCTOR (PHYSICIAN-ID, PHYSICIAN-PHONE)
1NF: PATIENT (PHYSICIAN-ID, PATIENT#, PATIENT-NAME, LOCATION, PROCEDURE)

The PATIENT relation is in 1NF, since the patient data in this relation depend

Figure 8-12
User view 4:
Physician Report

Mountain View Community Hospital
Physician Report

Date: 10-17-8X

Physician ID: Wilcox
Physician Phone: 329-1848

Patient#	Patient Name	Location	Procedure
6083	Brown, May	184-2	Tonsillectomy
3157	Miller, Ruth	216-1	Observation
4139	Majors, Carl	107-3	Chemotherapy

only on PATIENT# and not on PHYSICIAN-ID. Removing this partial dependency results in these two relations:

3NF: PATIENT (PATIENT#, PATIENT-NAME, LOCATION)
3NF: TREATMENT (PHYSICIAN-ID, PATIENT#, PROCEDURE)

These relations are now in 3NF. The set of relations for the Physician Report is therefore:

8. (PHYSICIAN-ID, PHYSICIAN-PHONE)
9. (PATIENT#, PATIENT-NAME, LOCATION)
10. (PHYSICIAN-ID, PATIENT#, PROCEDURE)

View Integration

At this point we have developed a set of ten 3NF relations from the four user views used to illustrate logical data base design at Mountain View Community Hospital. However, several of these relations have duplicate primary keys and therefore may be merged. Relations 1, 5, 6, and 9 all have PATIENT# as a primary key. All these relations are merged to form a single PATIENT relation with PATIENT# as the primary key. Similarly, relations 4 and 7 are merged, since they both have LOCATION as the primary key.

The final set of 3NF relations for Mountain View Community Hospital is shown in Figure 8-13. There is now a total of six relations representing the four user views. An analysis of each of these six relations indicates that no unwanted dependencies exist and that the relations are actually in 4NF.

Conceptual Data Model

After carefully checking the normalized relations, the design team developed a graphic version of the conceptual data model. A preliminary version

PATIENT (PATIENT#, PATIENT-NAME, PATIENT-ADDRESS, CITY-STATE-ZIP, DATE-ADMITTED, DATE-DISCHARGED, EXP-DISCH-DATE, LOCATION, THIRD-PARTY
ROOM (LOCATION, ACCOM, EXTENSION, PATIENT#)
PHYSICIAN (PHYSICIAN-ID, PHYSICIAN-PHONE)
ITEM (ITEM-CODE, DESCRIPTION)
TREATMENT (PHYSICIAN-ID, PATIENT#, PROCEDURE)
CHARGES (PATIENT#, ITEM-CODE, CHARGE)

Figure 8-13
3NF relations for Mountain View Community Hospital

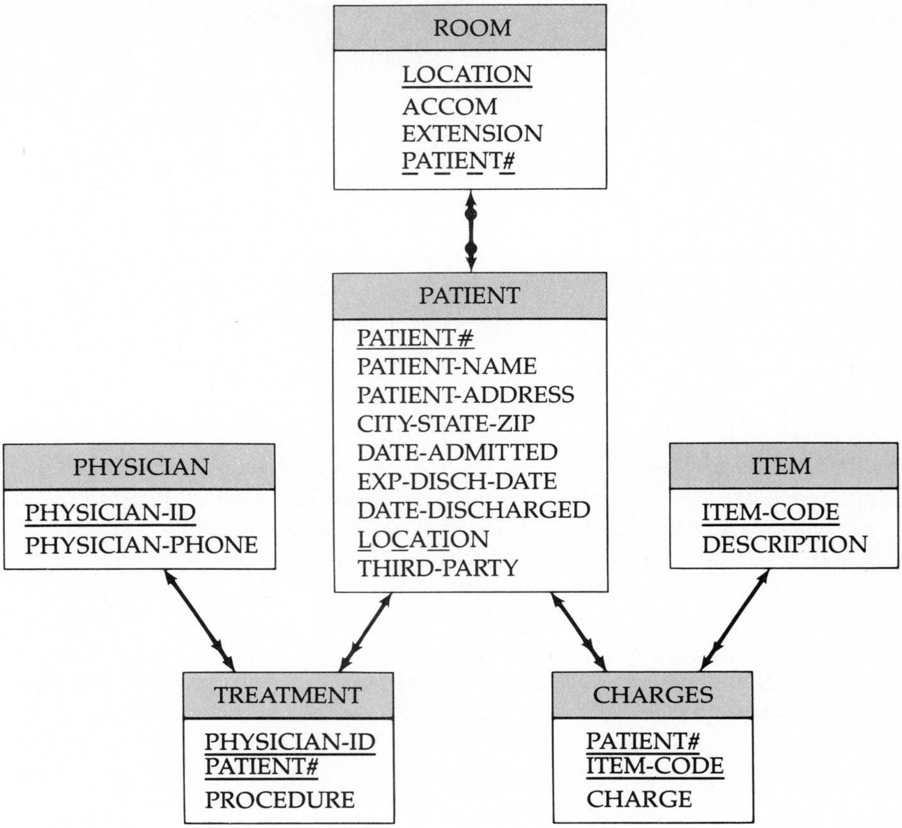

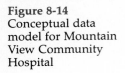

Figure 8-14 Conceptual data model for Mountain View Community Hospital

of the conceptual data model for the four user views considered in this analysis is shown in Figure 8-14.

Here are the rules for forming a graphic model from 3NF relations:

1. A relation that has a composite key represents an association between two or more entities. The graphic model shows the association between such a relation and the relations that contain the composite key.
2. A relation that has a foreign key has an association with another relation that uses this foreign key as its primary key.

The relation CHARGES has a composite key: (PATIENT#, ITEM-CODE). Therefore, there is an association between the PATIENT and CHARGES relations and between the ITEM and CHARGES relations. The association is one-to-many from PATIENT to CHARGES, since each patient will be charged for several items. Similarly, there is a one-to-many association from ITEM to CHARGES.

The relation TREATMENT represents the association between physicians and patients. There is a 1:*M* association between PHYSICIAN and TREATMENT and a 1:*M* association between PATIENT and TREATMENT.

The association between ROOM and PATIENT is a conditional association in both directions (the conditional association was introduced in Chapter 2). The association from ROOM to PATIENT is conditional because at a given time, a hospital bed may be assigned to a patient or it may be unassigned. Also, the association from PATIENT to ROOM is conditional since at a given time a patient may or may not be assigned to a hospital bed (for example, the person may be an outpatient or may have already been discharged from the hospital). These conditional associations are designated by an arrow with circles in Figure 8-14.

Notice the similarity between the conceptual model (Figure 8-14) and the corresponding E/R diagram (Figure 8-6). The conceptual model does contain a new entity (Charges) that is not shown in Figure 8-6. This entity replaces the Billed-to association shown in Figure 8-6. Recall from the discussion of Chapter 6 that entities and associations are often essentially interchangeable in an E/R diagram. Also, the entity Bed in Figure 8-6 has been renamed Room in Figure 8-14 because that term more accurately reflects the nature of the entity (the primary key of Room is LOCATION, which refers to the combination of room number and bed number). Despite these changes, the close correspondence between the two diagrams suggests that the analysis is complete for now (entities outside the scope of the present analysis such as Employee, Cost-Center, and Third-Party will be added at a later stage).

DATA VOLUME AND USAGE ANALYSIS

The conceptual data model completes the "architectural plan" (logical design) of the data base. However, once the design has been completed, the designer should return to the user and collect additional data concerning the prospective use of the model. In effect, data volume and usage analysis is an additional step in requirements analysis that is best postponed until after the conceptual model has been completed. In addition to providing useful data, this analysis may reveal inconsistencies in the conceptual model that need to be corrected.

Data volume analysis is concerned with estimating the number of each type of logical entity that must be represented in the data base, both now and in the future. For example, how many Patient data entities or records must be stored? **Data usage analysis** is concerned with estimating the frequencies with which each data entity will be accessed, given the various transactions that will be required to access and update the data base. The statistics collected during data volume and usage analysis are vital inputs to the physical data base design process.

Data Volume Analysis for Mountain View Community Hospital

A simplified picture of the conceptual data model for Mountain View Community Hospital is shown in Figure 8-15. Each entity is represented by a rectangle, but the attributes have been omitted. Inside each rectangle is a number representing the estimated average volume for that entity. For example, it is estimated that an average of 1000 Patient entities must be accommodated in the data base at any one time. The numbers adjacent to the arrowheads are estimates of the average number of a given entity type associated with a related entity type. For example, Figure 8-15 indicates that there is an average of ten Charges associated with each Patient at any given time.

The data base design team at Mountain View Community Hospital made the estimates in consultation with users. Since there are 100 beds at the hospital, the maximum number of admitted patients at any one time is limited to 100. However, the accounting staff indicated that the records for an average patient would probably be kept active for about 30 days. Since the average length of stay for a patient is 3 days, the total number of active patient records is expected to be 100 × 30/3, or 1000. After an average period of 30 days, a PATIENT record would be archived. The PATIENT-ROOM assignment is kept active only while the patient is in the hospital.

Further discussions with the hospital accounting staff revealed that each patient incurs an average of 10 Charges during a hospitalization. Thus, the number of Charge entities is expected to be 10 × 1000, or 10,000. Also, there are 500 separate Items (treatments, pharmacy items, and so forth) that may appear on a patient's bill. Thus, the average number of Charges outstanding for a given Item is 10,000/500, or 20, as shown in Figure 8-15.

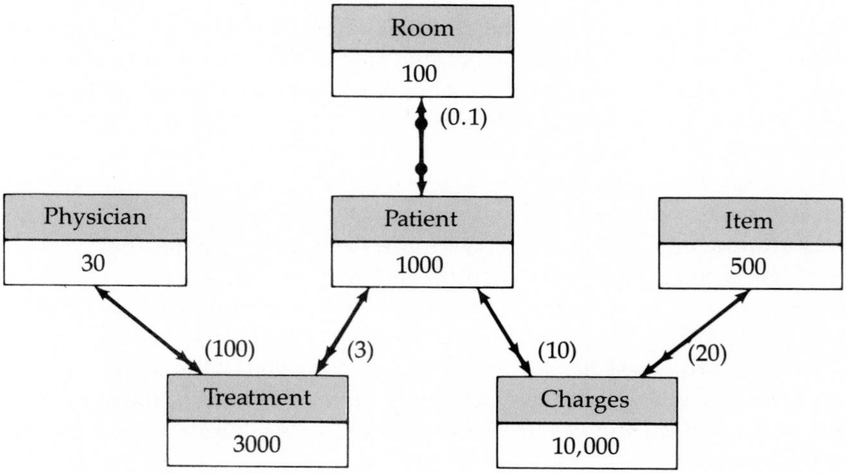

Figure 8-15
Conceptual data model with volumes and ratios

The design team also conferred with the medical staff and discovered that each patient receives an average of 3 treatments. Thus, the average number of Treatment entities in the data base is 3 × 1000, or 3000. Since Mountain View Community Hospital has a staff of 30 physicians who treat patients, the average number of Treatment entities for each Physician is 3000/30, or 100.

Data Usage Analysis for Mountain View Community Hospital

In data usage analysis, the analyst identifies the major transactions and reports required against the data base. Each is then analyzed to determine the access paths used and the estimated frequency of use. When all transactions have been analyzed, the composite load map is then prepared, showing the total usage of access paths on the conceptual model.

At Mountain View Community Hospital, a systems analyst (Mr. Thomas) was assigned to work with the design team in analyzing user transactions. The data administrator felt that there were three advantages in having an applications specialist assist the design team during this phase of the study. First, the systems analyst could assist the team in identifying access paths for each transaction. Second, the information developed during this phase would be a starting point for designing transaction processing programs. And finally, having a systems analyst work with the design team would foster cooperation between the data base group and the rest of the information systems organization.

The data base design team used a form for analyzing each transaction at the hospital. Figure 8-16 shows how this form is used to analyze the transaction Create Patient Bill. This transaction causes a PATIENT record to be read, along with the detail of patient charges, and also causes a bill to be produced in the format of Figure 8-9. After talking with persons in accounting, the analysts estimated an average transaction volume of 2 per hour and a peak volume of 10 per hour.

The number of logical references per transaction and per period are recorded on the form. Create Patient Bill requires only one PATIENT reference per transaction. At peak volume, this translates to 10 references per hour. Each PATIENT has an average of 10 CHARGES. Therefore, the average number of times the PATIENT-CHARGES path is used per transaction is 10; this translates to a peak volume of 10 × 10, or 100, per hour. Since the CHARGES-ITEM path is traversed once for each CHARGE, this also results in a peak usage of 100 per hour. The analysts chose to use peak volumes to estimate references per period, since this would measure the maximum load on the data base.

Logical Access Map A map for the transaction Create Patient Bill is shown in the middle of Figure 8-16. The dashed line that is superimposed on the

Figure 8-16
Analysis of the transaction Create Patient Bill

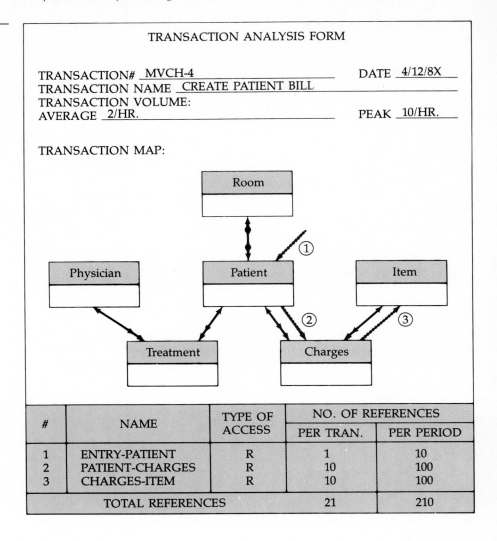

TRANSACTION ANALYSIS FORM

TRANSACTION# MVCH-4 DATE 4/12/8X
TRANSACTION NAME CREATE PATIENT BILL
TRANSACTION VOLUME:
AVERAGE 2/HR. PEAK 10/HR.

TRANSACTION MAP:

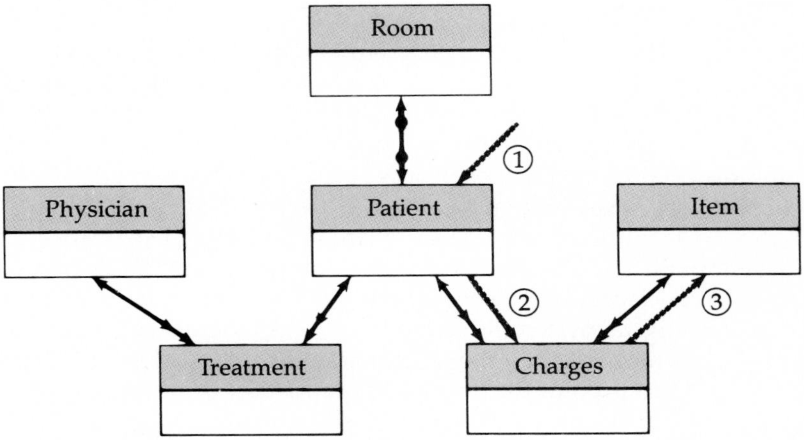

#	NAME	TYPE OF ACCESS	NO. OF REFERENCES	
			PER TRAN.	PER PERIOD
1	ENTRY-PATIENT	R	1	10
2	PATIENT-CHARGES	R	10	100
3	CHARGES-ITEM	R	10	100
TOTAL REFERENCES			21	210

conceptual model shows the access path for this transaction. The entry point is at the Patient entity, then to the entity Charges, then from each Charge to Item to pick up the description for that Charge.

A detailed analysis of each step in the access path is entered at the bottom of the form. The "type of access" to each entity is recorded using the following codes:

R designates to read an entity.

I designates to insert a new entity.

U designates to update an entity.

D designates to delete an entity.

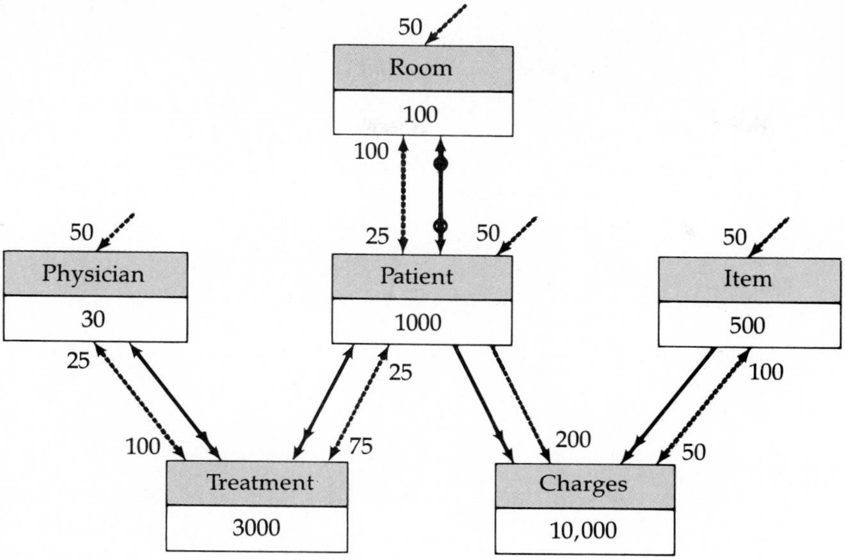

Figure 8-17
Composite usage map (Mountain View Community Hospital)

For the Create Patient Bill transaction, each access is coded with an R, since this transaction requires "read" only.

Composite Usage Map There are many other transactions for the data base in addition to Create Patient Bill—for example, Record New Treatment, Record New Patient Charge, and Display Patient Data. When all these transactions have been analyzed, the analysts can combine the data and display them in the form of a composite usage map. A sample composite usage map for Mountain View Community Hospital is shown in Figure 8-17. The number in each rectangle shows the estimated number of entities of that type (e.g., 1000 patients). The number at the head of each dashed arrow is an estimate of the total number of references on a given access path at a peak volume. For example, the number of references to the entity Treatment from the entity Patient is estimated at 75 per hour. Also, the number of references to Patient from outside the model is estimated at 50 per hour.

The composite usage map is a concise reference to the estimated volume and usage of data in the data base. It provides a basis for physical data base design, during which the analysts must design storage structures and access strategies to optimize performance.

SUMMARY

In this chapter, we introduced conceptual data base design, the second task in the overall data base design process. The steps in conceptual design include data modeling, view integration, conceptual schema development, design review, and logical access mapping. The major products (or deliverables) from this process are the conceptual data model, logical access maps for each transaction, and a composite usage map.

The information systems plan (described in Chapter 3) provides an overall framework for conceptual design. The enterprise model shows the major entities of the organization and their relationships. Also, the business charts delineate the functions, processes, and activities of the organization (see Figure 3-6), thereby helping to identify the transactions required to process the data base.

Chapter Review

REVIEW QUESTIONS

1. Give concise definitions for each of the following terms:
   a. conceptual data model
   b. entity analysis
   c. attribute synthesis
   d. data modeling
   e. view integration
2. Briefly describe five steps in conceptual design.
3. Describe four different forms in which the conceptual data model can be represented.
4. In the design review, the conceptual data model should be evaluated from two points of view. What are they?
5. Briefly summarize the rules for forming a graphic data model from a set of 3NF relations.
6. What conflict arises when an organization attempts to defer selecting a data base management system until after conceptual design is completed?
7. What is a composite usage map? What is its purpose?
8. What is the disadvantage of expressing the conceptual data model in the format of a particular DBMS?
9. Why is data volume and usage analysis performed after the conceptual data model is completed?
10. Why is a bottom-up approach favored over a top-down approach in conceptual design?
11. Contrast the following terms:
    a. global approach; application approach
    b. entity analysis; attribute synthesis
    c. data volume analysis; data usage analysis
    d. logical access map; composite usage map

PROBLEMS AND EXERCISES

1. Match the following terms to the appropriate definitions:

_____ global approach	a. "architectural plan"
_____ view integration	b. estimating frequency of data access
_____ logical access map	c. bottom-up data analysis
_____ conceptual data model	d. shows entities and relationships
_____ data usage analysis	e. single integrated data base
_____ attribute synthesis	f. identifies user views
_____ design review	g. improve productivity of design process
_____ enterprise model	h. merging relations
_____ requirements analysis	i. evaluation of conceptual model
_____ computer-assisted design	j. sequence of accessing records

2. Examine the sample conceptual data model for a distributing company (Figure 8-4).
   a. Draw a simplified version of this model by selecting between 10 and 15 of the most important entities. Use the convention of drawing arrows, which we have used throughout the text. This simplified model might correspond to a planning-level data model (or enterprise model).
   b. Suppose that the company represented in the model shown in Figure 8-4 decides to implement each cluster as a separate data base. Draw lines (or boxes) indicating the boundary of each data base.
   c. Discuss how an association between entities in different data bases might be implemented. For example, in Figure 8-4, there is an association between Style (Product cluster) and Part (Parts cluster).

3. Draw a logical access map for the Create Patient Bill transaction using the format shown in Figure 7-19.

4. Record sample metadata (such as those shown in Figure 8-7) for the Physician Report (Figure 8-12).

5. Expand the conceptual data model for Mountain View Community Hospital by including Third Party information. We want to include the following attributes: THIRD-PARTY-ID, ADDRESS, PHONE#. Assume that a given Patient may subscribe to only one third party.

6. Examine the Treatment entity for Mountain View Community Hospital (Figure 8-14). Suppose that the composite key (PHYSICIAN-ID, PATIENT#) does not uniquely identify a PROCEDURE (that is, a given physician performs more than one procedure on a given patient on a given day). Suggest how the Treatment entity could be modified to accommodate this situation. How would the Physician Report (Figure 8-12) have to be modified to reflect this change?

7. Devise a design review questionnaire (such as the one in Figure 8-5) for the Mountain View Community Hospital conceptual data model (Figure 8-14).

8. Draw logical access maps for each of the following transactions:
   a. Admit Patient.
   b. Transfer Patient (to a different room).
   c. Create Room Utilization Report (Figure 8-10).
   d. Create Physician Report (Figure 8-12).

9. The relations shown in Figure 8-13 are in 3NF. Examine each relation and state (and justify) whether it is (or is not) also in:
   a. BCNF
   b. 4NF

10. Examine the transaction Create Patient Bill (Figure 8-16). Suppose that during the design review, the transaction volume figures are revised as follows:

    Average: 5 per hour
    Peak: 15 per hour

    Revise the number of references in the diagram to reflect this change.

11. Following are several 3NF relations. Merge these relations to produce a new set of relations, also in 3NF. Then draw a graphic model of the merged relations.
    a. STUDENT (<u>ST#</u>, STNAME, PHONE#)
    b. COURSE (<u>CRS#</u>, NAME)
    c. MAJOR (<u>ST#</u>, MAJOR)
    d. ENROLL (<u>ST#</u>, <u>CRS#</u>, <u>SECTION#</u>)
    e. UNITS (<u>CRS#</u>, NAME, UNITS)
    f. TEXT (<u>CRS#</u>, <u>SECTION#</u>, TEXTNAME)
    g. LOCATION (<u>CRS#</u>, <u>SECTION#</u>, ROOM#)

Figure 8-18
Customer invoice (Pine Valley Furniture)

CUSTOMER NO: 1273 INVOICE NO: 06389

NAME CONTEMPORARY DESIGNS DATE: 11/5/8X

ADDRESS: 123 OAK ST. ORDER NO: 61384

CITY-STATE-ZIP: AUSTIN, TX. 28384

PRODUCT NO.	DESCRIPTION	QTY ORD.	QTY SHIP.	QTY BACK.	UNIT PRICE	TOTAL PRICE
B381	CABINET	2	2		150.00	300.00
M128	BOOKCASE	4	2	2	200.00	400.00
R210	TABLE	1	1		500.00	500.00

TOTAL AMOUNT 1200.00
5.0% DISCOUNT 60.00
AMOUNT DUE 1140.00

12. An invoice form used by Pine Valley Furniture Company is shown in Figure 8-18. One such invoice is submitted to a customer for each shipment. There may be one or more shipments for each customer order (multiple shipments result when items must be back-ordered).
    a. Derive a set of 3NF relations for this document (user view).
    b. Merge the 3NF relations for the invoice with the 3NF relations for the customer order (Figure 7-20).
    c. Develop a conceptual data model (graphic form) for the merged relations.

13. For the conceptual data model developed in Problem 12, develop logical access maps for the following transactions:
    a. Enter New Customer Order.
    b. Create Customer Invoice.

14. Express the conceptual data model for Mountain View Community Hospital as an entity-relationship diagram (similar to the one in Figure 6-24).

REFERENCES

Auerbach Publishers. 1980. *Practical Database Management*. Princeton, N.J.: Auerbach Publishers.

Couger, J. Daniel, Mel A. Colter, and R.W. Knapp. 1982. *Advanced System Development/Feasibility Techniques*. New York: Wiley.

Davis, Gordon B. 1974. *Management Information Systems: Conceptual Foundations, Structure, and Development*. New York: McGraw-Hill.

Hubbard, George V. 1981. *Computer-Assisted Data Base Design*. New York: Van Nostrand Reinhold.

Martin, James. 1983. *Managing the Data-Base Environment*. Englewood Cliffs, N.J.: Prentice-Hall.

Teorey, T. J., and J.P. Fry. 1982. *Design of Database Structures*. Englewood Cliffs, N.J.: Prentice-Hall.

Chapter 9

Implementation and Physical Design

INTRODUCTION

The conceptual data model described in Chapter 8 is a model of the organization and its data, completely independent of any data base management system or any other software or hardware considerations. That model must then be refined so that it can be implemented on the DBMS used by the organization.

As shown in Figure 9-1, the refinement of the conceptual data model occurs in two stages: implementation design and physical design. **Implementation design** is concerned with mapping the conceptual data model into a DBMS-processible logical model or schema. The logical model is usually in the form of a network, relational, or hierarchical data model (or some combination of these models). **Physical design** is concerned with selecting file organizations, access methods, and related factors.

Implementation design and physical design are the last steps in the data base design process and must be performed carefully, since they affect performance, integrity, security, and a number of other factors that have a direct impact on users.

IMPLEMENTATION DESIGN

Implementation design starts with the conceptual data model and maps (or transforms) that model into a logical model that conforms to a particular DBMS. Also, specifications for programs to access the data base can be formulated during implementation design.

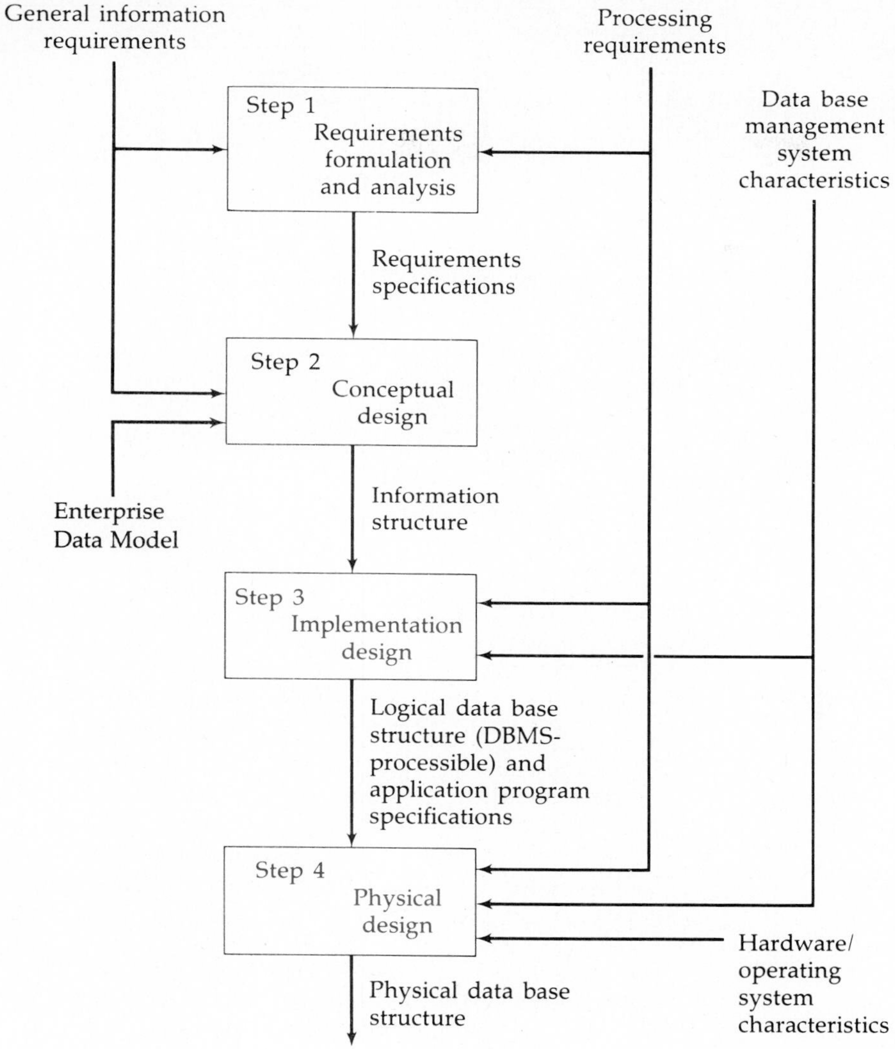

Figure 9-1
Implementation design and physical design (Source: Teorey and Fry 1982)

Components of Implementation Design

The major components (inputs and outputs) of implementation design are shown in Figure 9-2.

Inputs Following are the major inputs to implementation design (Teorey and Fry 1982):

1. *DBMS-independent schema:* the conceptual data model, described in Chapter 8.

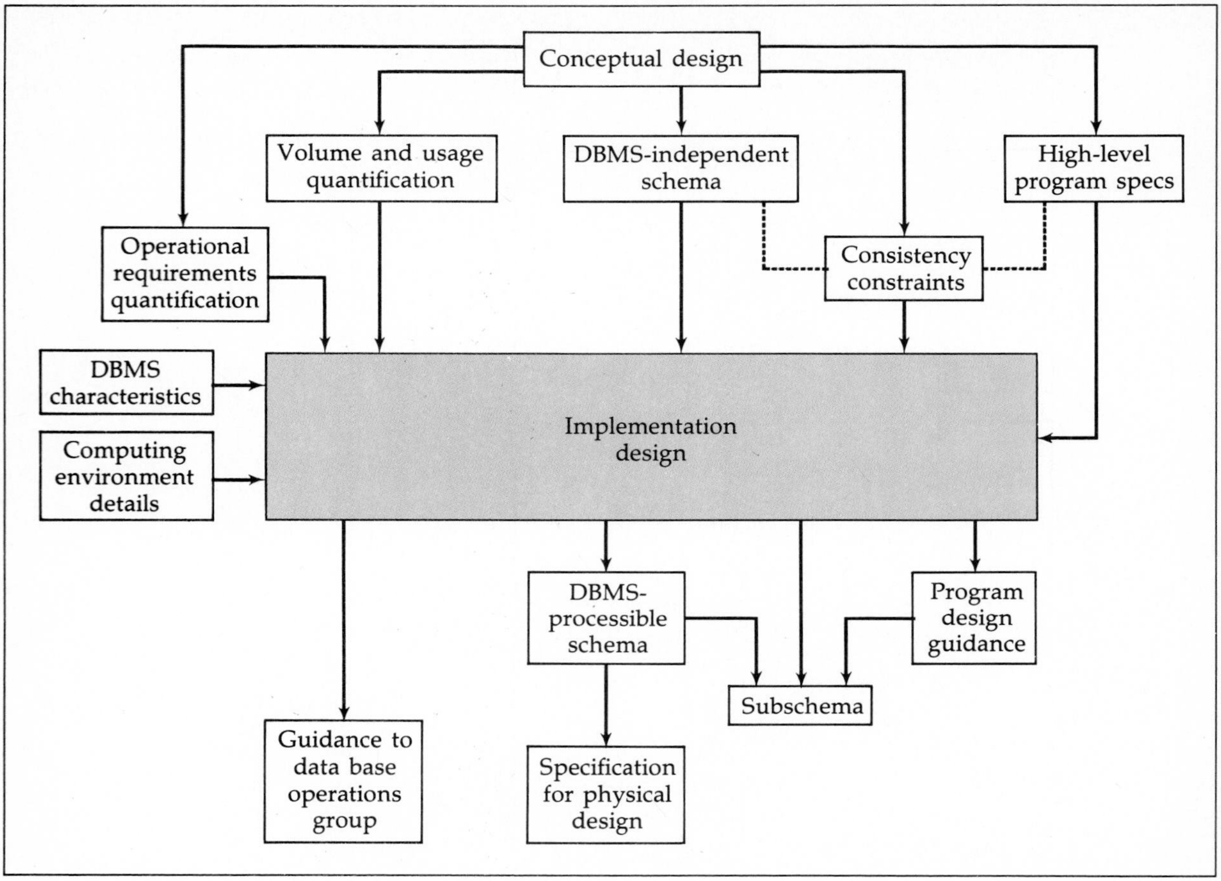

Figure 9-2
Implementation design process (Source: Teorey and Fry 1982)

2. *Operational requirements quantification:* specifications for response times, security, integrity, recovery, and archiving of data. These specifications are developed during requirements analysis (Chapter 7).
3. *Volume and usage quantification:* data volumes and usage figures, which are superimposed on the conceptual data model (described in Chapters 7 and 8).
4. *Consistency constraints:* rules for keeping data items mutually consistent, both within and between records.
5. *High-level program specifications:* definitions of access patterns for data base transactions. These definitions may be expressed in the form of logical access maps (described in Chapters 7 and 8).
6. *DBMS characteristics:* the logical constructs and data definition language of the DBMS to be used.

In contemporary relational DBMSs there is a clear distinction between logical and physical data bases. For these systems, some of the inputs shown in Figure 9-2 (computing environment details, operational requirements quantification, and volume and usage quantification) are inputs to physical design, rather than implementation design.

Outputs Following are the major outputs of implementation design (Teorey and Fry 1982):

1. *DBMS-processible schema:* a schema (or data model) that can be implemented directly on the chosen DBMS.
2. *Subschemas:* DBMS-processible external views and security constraints on these views.
3. *Specifications for physical design:* fully documented schemas, subschemas, and volume and usage information.
4. *Program design guidance:* skeleton program designs, which may be expressed in the form of data base action diagrams (described later).
5. *Guidance to data base operations:* summary of requirements and constraints for data administration and operations.

Steps in Implementation Design

The major steps in implementation design are shown in Figure 9-3. Although the steps are shown in the general sequence in which they are performed, the process is actually one of progressive refinement with feedback among the various steps.

Mapping to a Logical Model The most important step in implementation design is to map the conceptual data model into a DBMS-processible data model, which we will call a **logical model** (also referred to as a **schema**). The magnitude of this effort will depend on the form the expression of the conceptual data model takes and the logical model to which it is mapped.

The conceptual data model may be expressed in any one of several forms, the most typical being the entity-relationship model, the semantic data model, the data structure diagram (or relational map), and a set of relations in third normal form. On the other hand, most contemporary data base management systems support one or more of the following logical models: hierarchical, network, relational, and inverted file (a relational-like model). Thus, the mapping task may range from complex (such as mapping from an entity-relationship model to a hierarchical model) to trivial (such as when the conceptual and logical models are both relational).

We will illustrate mapping a conceptual data model to the hierarchical, network, and relational data models in the next section.

Designing Subschemas A **subschema** is a working subset of the schema (logical model). A large number of subschemas are normally defined on a given schema. Each subschema represents a user view and provides an

Figure 9-3
Major steps in implementation design

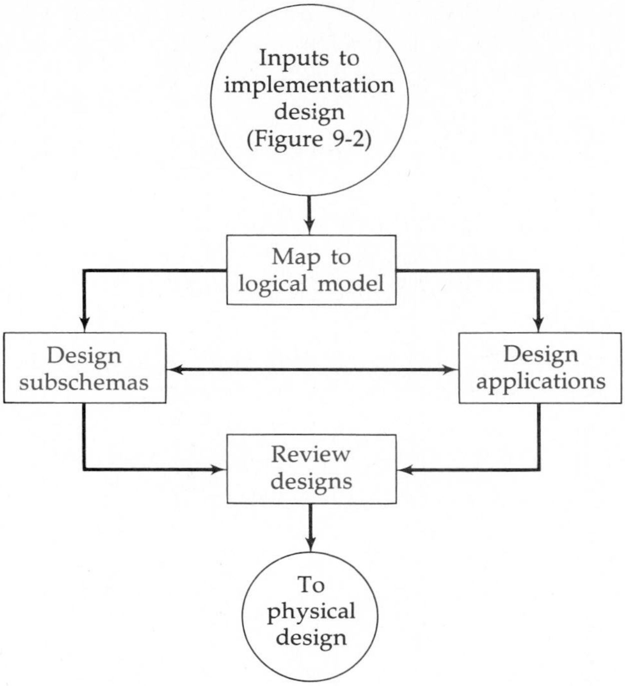

interface that allows a user application program to access the data base. To design subschemas, we start with the individual user views and map them into logical data submodels.

Designing Programs As each subschema is defined, the designers can develop outlines of program logic to process data represented in that subschema. The program designs can be most effectively expressed in structured forms referred to as data base action diagrams. We describe and illustrate data base action diagrams later in the chapter.

Conducting a Design Review When the preceding steps have been completed, a thorough review of the implementation design should be conducted. Any omissions or inconsistencies should be corrected before we proceed with the physical design.

MAPPING TO A LOGICAL DATA MODEL

The process of mapping to a logical data model depends on the form of the conceptual data model and the form of the target logical model. It may be performed manually, or it may employ computer-assisted design techniques.

We will use the case of Mountain View Community Hospital to illustrate

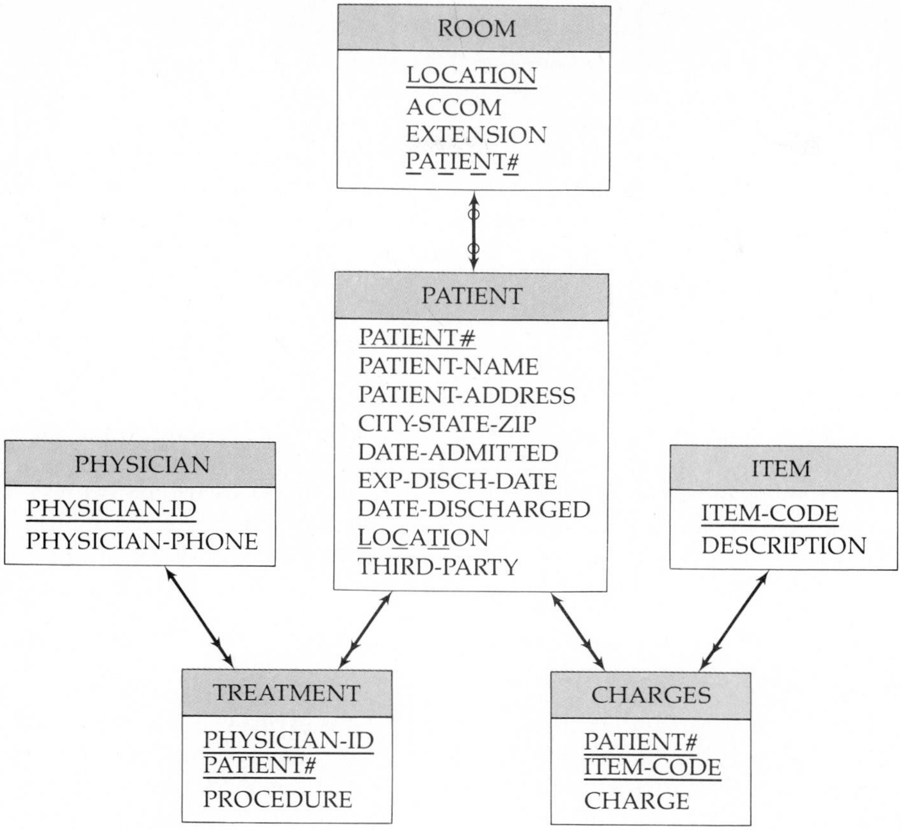

Figure 9-4
Conceptual data model (Mountain View Community Hospital)

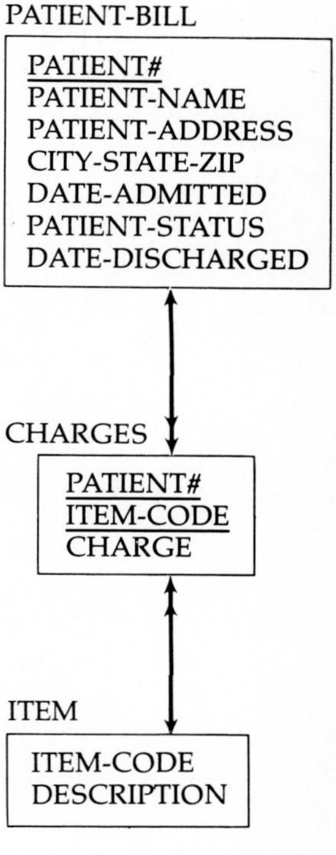

Figure 9-5
Conceptual user view: Patient Bill

mapping to a logical data model. A conceptual data model based on four user views was developed for this organization in Chapter 8. This model (expressed as a data structure diagram) is repeated in Figure 9-4.

One of the user views used to develop this conceptual data model was the Patient Bill (see Figure 8-9). Consider the set of 3NF relations that was derived from this user view in Chapter 8:

PATIENT-BILL (<u>PATIENT#</u>, PATIENT-NAME, PATIENT-ADDRESS, CITY-STATE-ZIP, DATE-ADMITTED, DATE-DISCHARGED)
ITEM (<u>ITEM-CODE</u>, DESCRIPTION)
CHARGES (<u>PATIENT#</u>, <u>ITEM-CODE</u>, CHARGE)

The conceptual model for these relations is shown in Figure 9-5. We refer to this model as the conceptual user view. It is a subset of the conceptual data model that provides the user with all the information required to create a patient bill. Like the conceptual model, each conceptual user view must be mapped to a logical model (or subschema) for the DBMS to be used.

Mapping to a Relational Model

The conceptual data models shown in Figures 9-4 and 9-5 are expressed in the form of relations connected by arrows. Therefore, mapping the conceptual models onto a relational model is a straightforward process. Each box in the conceptual model becomes a relation, and attributes in the boxes are attributes of the relations. Arrows in the conceptual data model are simply ignored, since they convey associations that are usually recorded as data within the relations. Thus, when the conceptual data model shown in Figure 9-4 is mapped to a relational model, there are six relations: ROOM, PATIENT, PHYSICIAN, ITEM, TREATMENT, and CHARGES. Also, when the external view in Figure 9-5 is mapped to a relational model, there are three relations: PATIENT-BILL, ITEM, and CHARGES. These two sets of relations are described to the relational DBMS using the schema and external view data definition languages, respectively. We give examples of these languages in Chapters 14 and 15.

For the relational model, *external views* (or user views) are usually expressed in the form of tables. External views for the Patient Bill are shown in Figure 9-6. Each table contains sample data to assist the user in understanding and using that view.

Mapping to a Network Model

Since the conceptual data model in Figure 9-4 is expressed in the form of a network data structure diagram, mapping to a network data model is also relatively straightforward. However, some additional steps are required. Assuming that the popular CODASYL data model (described in Chapter 13) is to be used, the following steps are usually required:

Figure 9-6
External views (Patient Bill):
(a) Patient Bill view
(b) Item view
(c) Charges view

PATIENT#	PATIENT-NAME	PATIENT-ADDRESS	CITY-STATE-ZIP	DATE-ADMITTED	DATE-DISCHARGED
3249	BAKER, MARY	300 OAK ST.	MT. VIEW, CO. 80638	09-10-8X	09-14-8X
1837	THOMAS, WM.	137 PINECREST	DENVER, CO. 80180	09-13-8X	09-21-8X
6251	MOORE, ANN	650 VADLE LN.	ASPEN, CO. 83149	10-01-8X	10-06-8X
...					

(a)

ITEM-CODE	DESCRIPTION
200	ROOM SEMI-PR
307	X-RAY
413	LAB TESTS
...	

(b)

PATIENT#	ITEM-CODE	CHARGE
3249	200	150.00
3249	307	25.00
1837	307	35.00
...		

(c)

1. Define record types and associations.
2. Define sets (owner-member relationships, including member sorting and membership rules).
3. Eliminate redundant keys (if unneeded).
4. Define record access strategies.

Figure 9-7 shows the result of transforming the conceptual data model (Figure 9-4) to a network data model. Notice that only relatively minor changes have been made in this mapping.

Defining Record Types Each box in the conceptual data model becomes a CODASYL record type. For example, there is a PATIENT record type in Figure 9-7. The primary keys are underlined, just as in the conceptual data model. Notice that the data item name PATIENT# in Figure 9-4 has been changed to PATIENT-NO in Figure 9-7 to conform to CODASYL specifications (we explain such details of the CODASYL model in Chapter 13).

In the CODASYL model, a one-to-many association between record types is usually represented by an arrow with a single head. We use this convention in Figure 9-7. For example, there is a 1:*M* association from PHYSICIAN to TREATMENT.

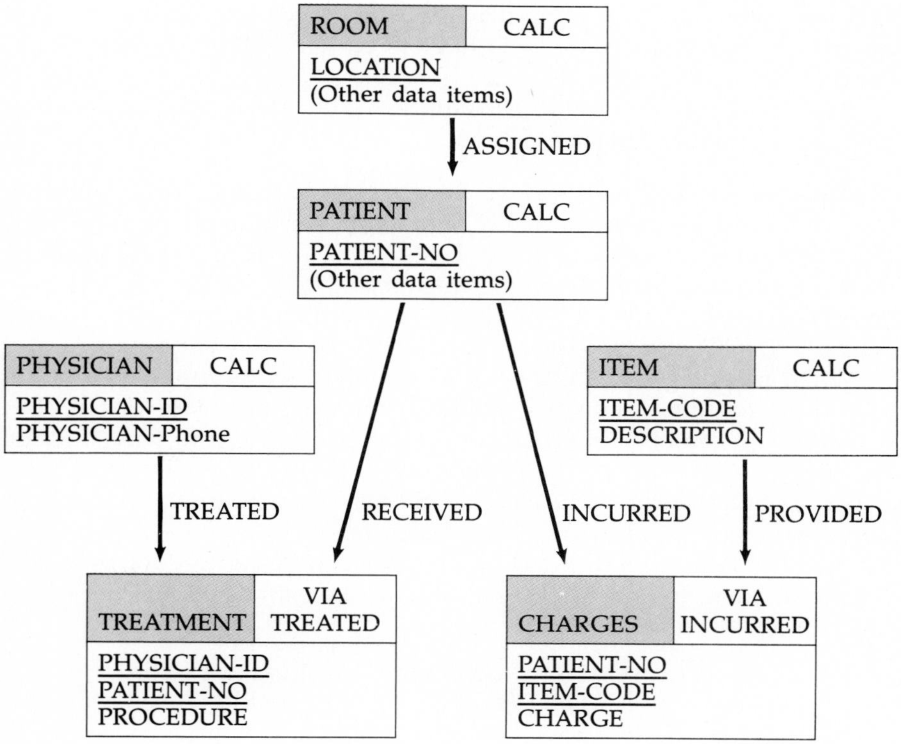

Figure 9-7
Network data model

The conditional associations between ROOM and PATIENT in the conceptual model (Figure 9-4) can easily be accommodated in mapping to a network model. The CODASYL model can be used to permit a PATIENT occurrence without an associated ROOM occurrence (e.g., for an outpatient). Further, the 1:*M* association from ROOM to PATIENT does permit zero, one, or more occurrences of PATIENT to be associated with each occurrence of ROOM. Therefore, in Figure 9-7 we show the association (or CODASYL set) from ROOM to PATIENT as a 1:*M* association.

Defining Sets The set is the basic building block in the CODASYL model. A **set** is a one-to-many association between two record types, where the first record type is called the **owner** and the second record type is called the **member.** Each set type is given a unique name.

In mapping to a network data model, we define a set for each 1:*M* association in the conceptual data model. For example, in Figure 9-7, the 1:*M* association between PHYSICIAN and TREATMENT is defined as a CODASYL set with the name TREATED. PHYSICIAN is the owner record type for this association, while TREATMENT is the member record type. For each occurrence of a PHYSICIAN record type, there may be zero, one, or many associated occurrences of the TREATMENT record type.

In the conceptual data model (Figure 9-4), the association between ROOM and PATIENT is conditional. This means that each patient is either assigned to a room location or else is not assigned (the converse is also true). In the CODASYL model, there is no provision for directly enforcing only one assignment per location; this will have to be handled by the application program for room assignment.

Additional properties and constraints of CODASYL sets (e.g., sorting members in a set and system-owned sets) are defined in Chapter 13.

Eliminating Redundant Keys In the conceptual data model, composite keys and foreign keys are normally redundant. For example, in Figure 9-4, the composite key for CHARGES is (<u>PATIENT#</u>, <u>ITEM-CODE</u>). Each of these data items is contained in the parent record type (in this case, PATIENT and ITEM). Also, the PATIENT relation (or record type) contains the foreign key LOCATION, which is the primary key of the ROOM relation.

When mapping to a CODASYL data model, these duplicate keys are candidates for elimination. For example, the composite key (<u>PATIENT#</u>, <u>ITEM-CODE</u>) can be eliminated from the CHARGES record type, and the LOCATION data item can be eliminated from the PATIENT record type. These duplicated keys can be eliminated because the associations they represent are represented by the CODASYL sets.

Whether keys should in fact be eliminated (to avoid redundancy) is a design decision. In general, keys should *not* be eliminated if either of the following two conditions holds:

1. The key in question is required for direct access to a record (e.g., the composite key (<u>PATIENT#</u>, <u>ITEM-CODE</u>) could be used for direct access to CHARGES records if this is a requirement).

2. The key in question is normally required for reference purposes and if removed will often necessitate referencing the owner record occurrence.

To illustrate the second situation, suppose that in examining an occurrence of a PATIENT record, we normally need to identify the patient's location. If LOCATION were removed from the PATIENT record type, we would have to reference a ROOM record occurrence (owner record) to determine this information. Or suppose that we eliminated (PATIENT#, ITEM-CODE) from the CHARGES record type. In examining a CHARGES record for a particular patient, the user could not determine the item code without referencing an ITEM record occurrence.

In summary, deciding whether or not to eliminate keys requires a tradeoff between redundancy and performance. The designers must consider the anticipated usage patterns (identified during requirements analysis) to evaluate each individual case. In Figure 9-7, we have retained the redundant data items so that they can be used for reference purposes.

Defining Record Access Strategies The last major step in mapping to a network model is to define the basic techniques to be used to access occurrences of each record type in the model. Although there are many variations, there are two basic record access strategies in the CODASYL model:

1. CALC: We access records directly by supplying a primary key value.
2. VIA: We access records through a set relationship; that is, we first access an owner record occurrence (often using CALC), and then we access each set member occurrence for that owner. VIA results in a *physical* clustering of records by the owner.

The access strategies to be used depend on the way data will be accessed by various users and their applications. These usage patterns are expressed in the form of a composite usage map (described in Chapter 8). A composite usage map for Mountain View Community Hospital was shown in Figure 8-17. Referring to this map, we see that four record types are normally accessed directly (that is, from outside the model). These record types are PATIENT, ROOM, PHYSICIAN, and ITEM. The remaining two record types (TREATMENT and CHARGES) are normally accessed by following set relationships. As shown in Figure 8-17, TREATMENT record occurrences are accessed from their owner PHYSICIAN records (100 references per period) and from their owner PATIENT records (75 references per period). Similarly, CHARGES records are accessed from PATIENT records (200 references per period) and from ITEM records (50 references per period).

Based on this information, the access strategies for the record types in the network data model are shown in Figure 9-7. The CALC (or random access) technique is used for PATIENT, PHYSICIAN, ITEM, and ROOM records. TREATMENT records are accessed VIA the TREATED set type since the frequency of access is greater than for the RECEIVED set type (100 references per period versus 75 references per period). For the same reason, CHARGES records are accessed VIA the INCURRED set.

The VIA clause defines the primary access path to records. Records can also be accessed through secondary access paths. For example, TREATMENT records can be accessed using the RECEIVED set relationship, as well as using the TREATED set relationship. However, secondary access paths are nearly always slower and less efficient. We describe the details of various CODASYL access strategies in much more detail in Chapter 13.

Ideally, record access strategies would not be defined during implementation design but during physical design. By defining these strategies during implementation design (and therefore in the schema), we lose some data independence. Thus, if we later decide to change the access strategy for a particular record type (say, from VIA to CALC), we will have to alter the schema. What is worse, changing the schema often requires that application programs be modified, since application logic often varies with the access strategies that are used.

In essence, the CODASYL approach to data base implementation provides efficient, rapid access, provided that predefined access paths are used. However, the CODASYL approach is somewhat less flexible and therefore more resistant to change than some other models (especially the relational model).

CODASYL Subschemas We obtain each CODASYL subschema by mapping the conceptual user view to a network model. Figure 9-8 shows the network user view that is obtained by mapping the conceptual user view for Patient Bill. Notice that the only difference in these two models is that the set names INCURRED and PROVIDED have been added in Figure 9-8. Record access strategies (CALC and VIA) are not specified in the subschema since they are the same as in the logical model (Figure 9-7).

Mapping to a Hierarchical Model

Since the hierarchical data model has several restrictions, mapping a conceptual model to a hierarchical model often presents some problems. Several arbitrary choices must be made, and there is no "correct" result. The mapping is usually performed in two stages: mapping the conceptual model to a DBMS-independent hierarchical model and then mapping the hierarchical model to conform to a particular hierarchical DBMS.

Hierarchical Data Model In mapping to a hierarchical model, each box in the conceptual model (Figure 9-4) becomes a "node type" in a hierarchy (or tree structure). Recall from Chapter 5 that each node type in a hierarchy can have only one parent node type. Therefore, it is necessary to refine the conceptual data model by identifying root node types and resolving multiple parentage.

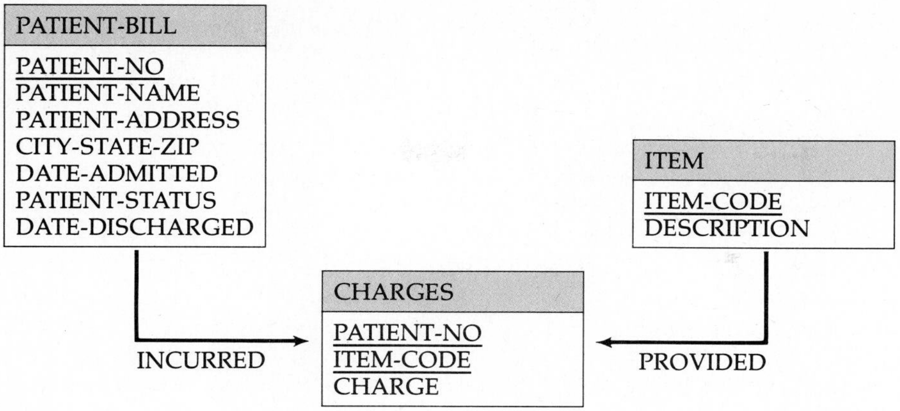

Figure 9-8 Network external view: Patient Bill

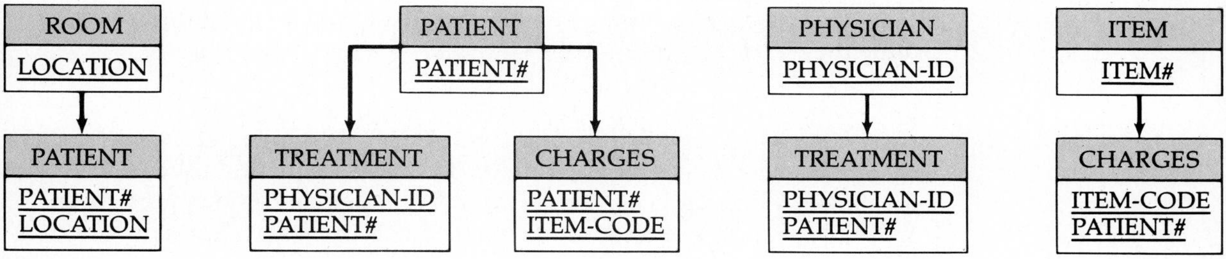

Figure 9-9 Hierarchical structures

Four hierarchical structures derived from the conceptual data model (Figure 9-4) are shown in Figure 9-9. In this diagram, only the keys are shown; other data items are omitted to simplify the diagram.

Identifying Root Node Types Each root node type in a hierarchical model defines a data base and provides an entry point to that data base. In Figure 9-9, we have selected four root node types—ROOM, PATIENT, PHYSICIAN, and ITEM—that define four distinct data bases. Thus, a user may access data by starting at any one of these four entry points.

Resolving Multiple Parentage Since each node type can have only one parent node type, it is necessary to resolve instances of multiple parentage. In Figure 9-4, TREATMENT and CHARGES each have two parents.

To resolve multiple parentage, we must introduce redundancy. One approach is to combine a child node with its parent node. For example, in Figure 9-4, we could combine the TREATMENT node with the PHYSICIAN node. An alternative approach is to repeat node types under two or more patients.

In Figure 9-9, we have resolved multiple parentage by repeating child node types under their parent node types. Thus, TREATMENT appears

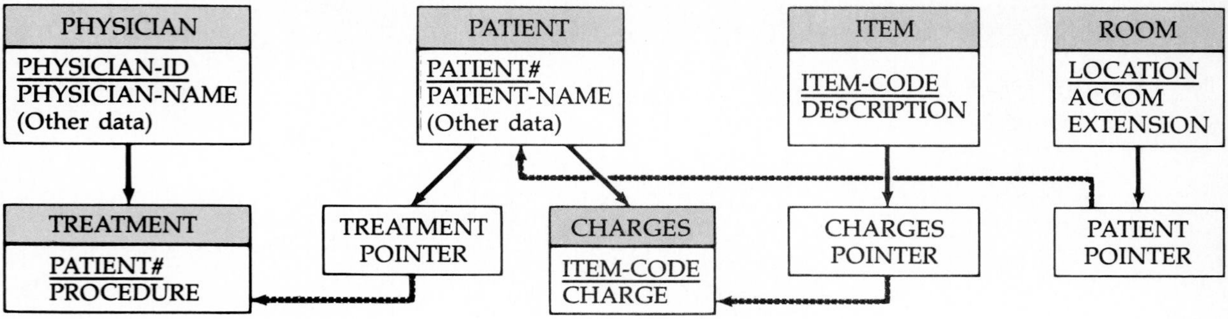

Figure 9-10
Structuring an IMS data base (incorrect version)

under both PATIENT and PHYSICIAN, and CHARGES appears under both PATIENT and ITEM. This solution is undesirable, since a great deal of redundancy has been introduced. However, we must remember that Figure 9-9 portrays a logical (not physical) model. Depending on the DBMS used, it may be possible to implement these data bases without excessive redundancy.

DBMS Implementation The hierarchical structures in Figure 9-9 must be mapped onto a data model for a particular DBMS. A number of hierarchical DBMS products are available. Of these, the most frequently used is IBM's Information Management System (IMS). We illustrate the mapping to an IMS data base in this section, and a detailed description of IMS is provided in Chapter 12.

In IMS, each node is called a **segment.** Although IMS supports a hierarchical data model, it does permit a limited networking capability. Each segment type in IMS can have two parents: a physical parent and a logical parent. The **physical parent** is the parent segment type in the hierarchy. The **logical parent** is a segment type in another hierarchy (or IMS data base) that has a parent/child relationship with the given segment. The logical parent relationship is implemented by means of a **logical pointer,** which is a segment that contains the addresses of logical child segments (but no actual data).

A first attempt at structuring IMS data bases from the hierarchical models is shown in Figure 9-10. Four IMS data bases are shown in the figure, with root segments PHYSICIAN, PATIENT, ITEM, and ROOM. Rather than duplicating the TREATMENT, PATIENT, and CHARGES data (as in Figure 9-9), the logical parent feature of IMS is used in Figure 9-10. For example, the TREATMENT segment type (which appears only once) has PHYSICIAN as its physical parent. PATIENT is the logical parent of TREATMENT, and this relationship is implemented by the logical pointer called TREATMENT POINTER. By using these relationships, a user can access TREATMENT segments using either PHYSICIAN or PATIENT segments as entry points.

Similarly, logical parent relationships are used to avoid duplicating PATIENT and CHARGES data. Unfortunately, the structure shown in Figure 9-10 is not feasible since it violates an important rule of IMS: A logical

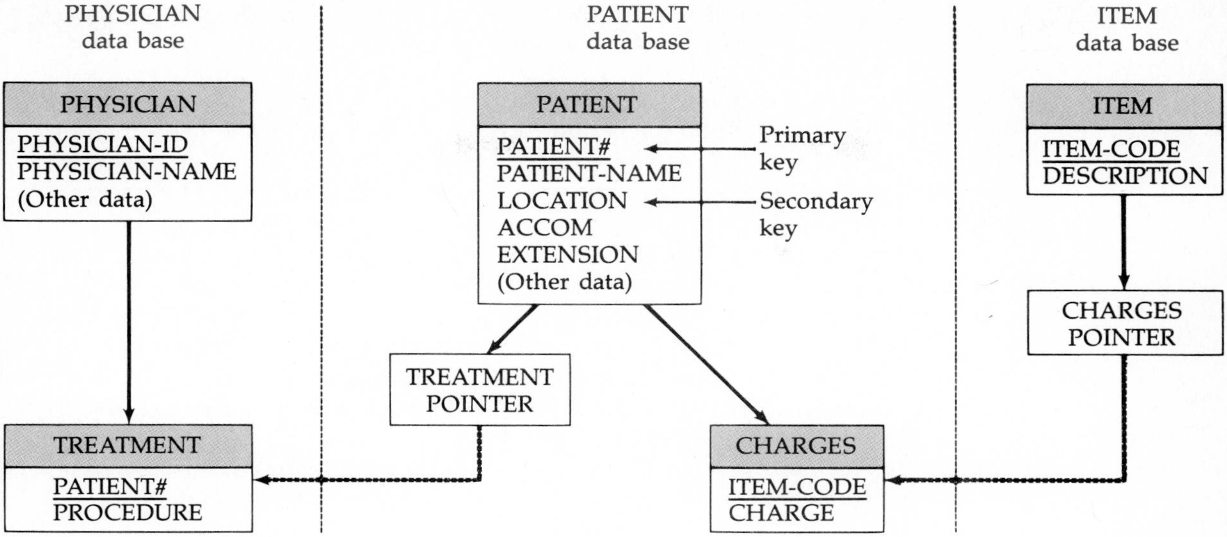

Figure 9-11
Structuring an IMS data base (revised version)

child cannot itself have a logical child. In Figure 9-10, PATIENT is a logical child of ROOM. But PATIENT, in turn, has a logical child of TREATMENT. Therefore, the structure must be modified. But how? We cannot eliminate the problem by rearranging the logical child relationships.

One solution to the problem is to combine the ROOM and PATIENT segment types into a single segment type. In Figure 9-11, data from the ROOM segment (LOCATION, ACCOM, EXTENSION) have been combined with PATIENT data. This introduces very little redundancy since the association between PATIENT and LOCATION is 1:1. However, it apparently introduces a new problem: To access room information, it is now necessary to provide a patient number (LOCATION is no longer an entry point).

Fortunately, IMS does provide a facility for secondary keys. As shown in Figure 9-11, PATIENT# is the primary key for the PATIENT segment type, while LOCATION is a secondary key. This allows the user to access a PATIENT segment by providing either a patient number or a location.

The IMS data base shown in Figure 9-11 is now feasible. It contains three data bases, called PHYSICIAN, PATIENT, and ITEM. There are two logical parent relationships: PATIENT is the logical parent of TREATMENT, and ITEM is the logical parent of CHARGES. For each data base, the root node type and its offspring are referred to as a **physical data base record.** For example, in Figure 9-11 the PATIENT, CHARGES, and TREATMENT POINTER segments constitute a physical data base record type.

In structuring an IMS data base, keys that appear in a parent segment (or any segment higher in the hierarchy) are not repeated in a child segment. For example, in Figure 9-11, the item PATIENT# does not appear in the CHARGES segment, since PATIENT# is the primary key of PATIENT, which is the physical parent of CHARGES. However, a key that appears in a logical parent (such as ITEM-CODE) *is* repeated in the logical child segment (in this case, CHARGES).

Alternative Designs The data bases shown in Figure 9-11 could have been structured differently. For example, CHARGES could have been made a physical child of ITEM and a logical child of PATIENT. How do designers make these choices? The answer is that in structuring an IMS data base, designers make some assumptions about how the data will be used. Access to a physical child segment is usually faster than access to a logical child segment (because of less overhead). Therefore, physical parent/child relationships are used for frequently used access paths, while logical parent/child relationships are used for secondary access paths. In Figure 9-11, the assumption is that CHARGES segments are most often accessed via PATIENT segments (as in preparing a patient bill). However, they may also be accessed from ITEM segments if necessary.

As we have seen, in designing an IMS (or other hierarchical) data base, the designer is forced into making some decisions about how the data will be used. This results in some loss in data independence; if the assumptions are wrong (or the usage patterns change), then the data base structure itself may have to be modified to improve performance. In Figure 9-11, for example, we may have to move the TREATMENT segment type so that it is a physical child of PATIENT and a logical child of PHYSICIAN. Such changes inevitably require changes to application programs.

IMS External Views An IMS external view is called a **logical data base record.** A logical data base record has the following properties:

1. It may represent a subset of a physical data base record.
2. It may span two or more physical data base records.

An external view (or logical data base record) for Patient Bill is shown in Figure 9-12. This view contains segments from two physical data base

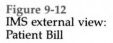

Figure 9-12
IMS external view: Patient Bill

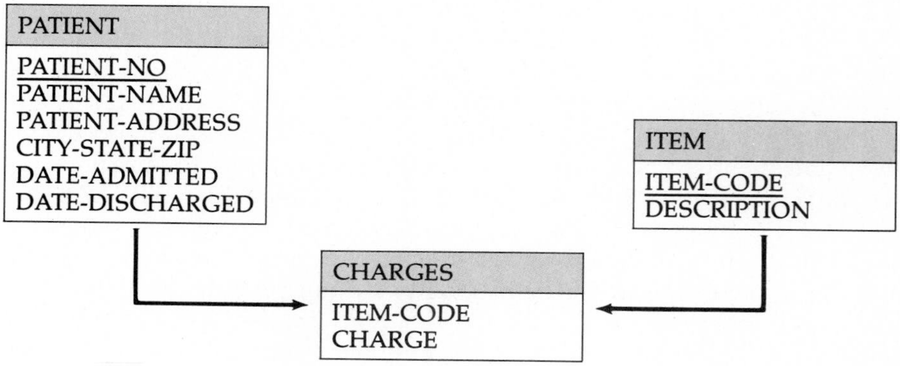

records: PATIENT and ITEM. It uses the logical parent relationship between ITEM and CHARGES shown in Figure 9-11. However, notice that the CHARGES POINTER segment is not shown in the external view. The user is unaware of the pointer segments used to implement logical parent relationships in IMS. The Patient Bill (Figure 8-9) can be created by manipulating the segments in the logical data base record in Figure 9-12, as we will show in Chapter 12.

DESIGNING APPLICATIONS

In this section, we describe a structured technique for designing data base applications. This technique, called data base action diagrams, is an extension of the logical access maps (LAMs) introduced in Chapters 7 and 8. Data base action diagrams are much easier to use than conventional structured program design techniques and in fact may be applied by end users with minimal training or experience.

Data Base Applications

The types of applications (or processes) required in a data base environment are shown in Figure 9-13. The data base is stored and maintained with data management software (described in Chapter 11). The processes on the left in Figure 9-13 are used to create and update the data base. These processes must include adequate controls to ensure the accuracy of input data. The applications on the right of Figure 9-13 generate routine documents (such as purchase orders and invoices), produce summary reports, and respond to management requests for information. The data base shown in the figure may be distributed, and users may interact with the data via remote terminals.

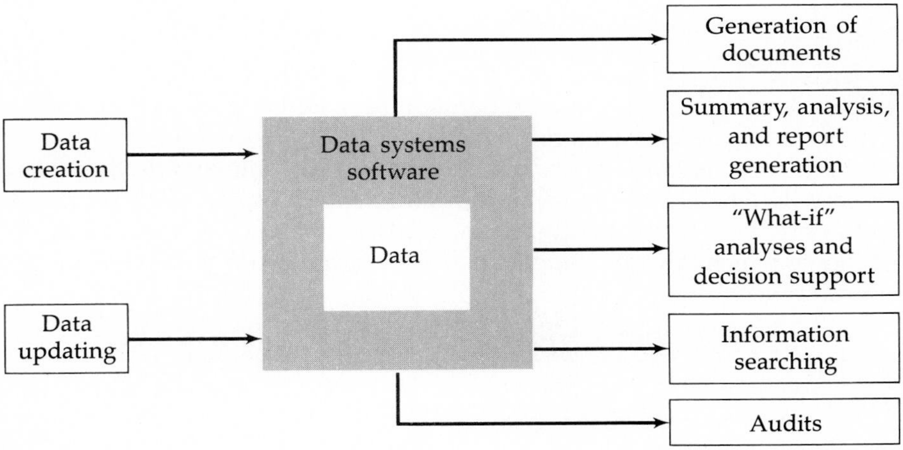

Figure 9-13
Types of data base applications (Source: Martin 1983, p. 380.)

One of the most significant developments in software today is the emergence of high-level languages for data base users. Many of these languages can be used by end users with little or no data processing experience to create, access, and update their own data bases. With such languages, users can perform many of the functions shown in Figure 9-13 without having to write conventional application programs. For example, report generators (such as Mark IV) can be used to generate routine reports; query languages (such as Query-by-Example and Easytrieve) can be used for information searching and retrieval; spreadsheet programs (such as Lotus 1-2-3 and Multiplan) can be used for analysis and decision support; and application generators (such as Mapper and Ramis II) can be used to develop complete application programs to perform specified functions.

With many of these high-level languages, data base action diagrams are not required. Instead, the user simply describes what information is required by "filling in the blanks" or writing simple English-language commands. However, some data base applications do require more complex procedures for processing data, and data base action diagrams are an effective tool for designing such applications.

Data Base Action Diagrams

A **data base action diagram** (or simply *action diagram*) is a map that shows a sequence of actions to be performed on a data base. The action diagram is normally drawn alongside a logical access map, extending the logical access map by defining the actions (including control structures) that are to be taken.

Actions An **action** is a step that is applied to one instance of one normalized record (Martin 1983). There are four basic types of action: Create, Read, Update, and Delete. In an action diagram, an action is drawn with an oblong symbol, as follows:

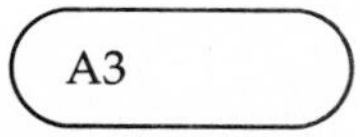

Actions may be numbered (as in the preceding example) for human reference purposes. However, action numbers are not necessary, since one action never references another.

Each action symbol contains a simple English-language declaration of the action to be taken. For a simple action, this declaration starts, as noted, with one of the verbs Create, Read, Update, or Delete. The name of the record to which the action applies is written *above* the symbol. Here are two examples:

Compound Actions Sometimes we wish to perform the same action against multiple instances of a given record type. For example, we may want to sort a file of records or select all records that satisfy a certain condition. Such actions are referred to as **compound actions.** A compound action is indicated by a double bar, as follows:

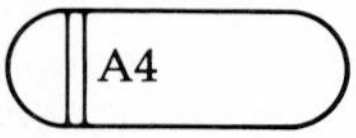
A4

Here are two examples of compound actions:

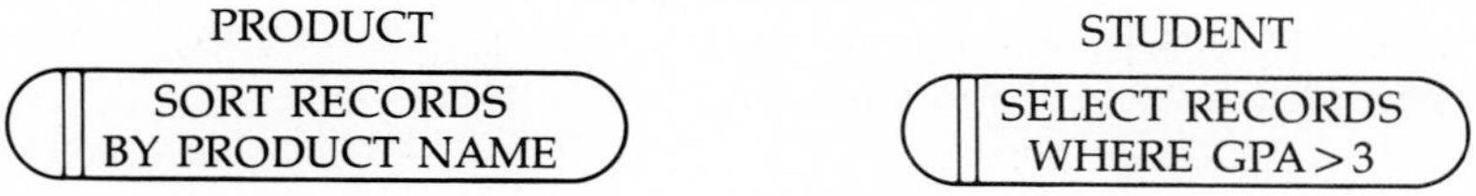
PRODUCT
SORT RECORDS BY PRODUCT NAME
STUDENT
SELECT RECORDS WHERE GPA > 3

Compound action symbols are used mostly with relational data bases, since each compound action can be implemented by a single relational command such as SELECT or JOIN.

Control Structures Three basic control structures are used in structured programming: sequence, selection, and iteration. These three structures are represented in data base action diagrams by a few additional symbols, as shown in Figure 9-14. This figure also shows notation for representing set relationships.

We indicate a **sequence** of actions by drawing the action symbols in top-to-bottom sequence in the order in which they are to be executed. **Selection** (or IF/THEN condition) is indicated by a partitioned bracket, as shown in

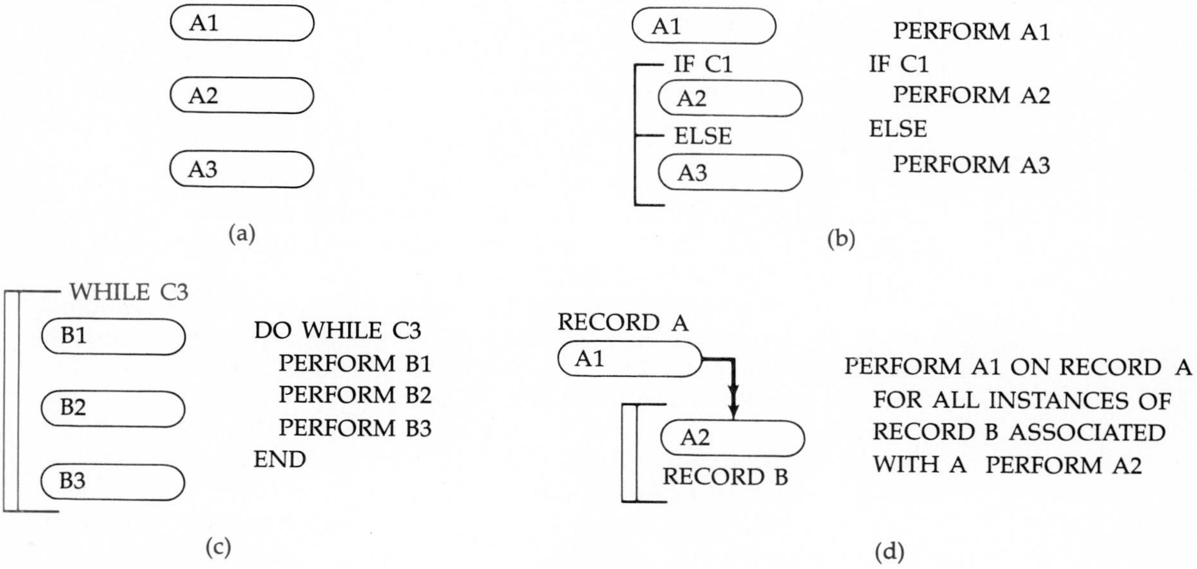
A1
A2
A3
(a)
A1
IF C1
A2
ELSE
A3
PERFORM A1
IF C1
PERFORM A2
ELSE
PERFORM A3
(b)
WHILE C3
B1
B2
B3
DO WHILE C3
PERFORM B1
PERFORM B2
PERFORM B3
END
(c)
RECORD A
A1
A2
RECORD B
PERFORM A1 ON RECORD A
FOR ALL INSTANCES OF
RECORD B ASSOCIATED
WITH A PERFORM A2
(d)

Figure 9-14
Basic control structures:
(a) sequence
(b) selection
(c) iteration
(d) set relationships

Figure 9-14b. The condition is shown at the top of the bracket. **Iteration** (or DO WHILE) is indicated by a bracket with a double line (Figure 9-14c). The actions contained within the bracket are executed repeatedly as long as the condition at the top of the bracket is true.

A **set relationship** is a one-to-many association between two record types. In a data base action diagram, we may wish to indicate that a particular action (or set of actions) is to be performed against all occurrences of records in this association. This is indicated by a double-headed arrow, as shown in Figure 9-14d.

The symbols in Figure 9-14 are nested, or combined, as necessary to express the actions in a data base action diagram. For a more complete discussion of data base action diagrams, see Martin (1983).

Correspondence of LAMs and Action Diagrams

Data base action diagrams are usually drawn alongside logical access maps. The LAM shows the sequence of accesses to data base records followed in processing a transaction or producing a desired result. The corresponding action diagram simply elaborates the LAM and shows the specific actions required.

An example showing this correspondence between the LAM and action diagram can be seen in Figure 9-15. The logical access map shows the sequence of accesses required to produce a class list. This logical access map was developed in Chapter 7 (see Figure 7-19). The corresponding action diagram shows the actions and control structures needed to perform this task. Notice that each access in the LAM has a corresponding action (in this case READ) in the action diagram. There is one set relationship in the diagram, representing the one-to-many association between COURSE and REGISTRATION.

Nested brackets are also illustrated in Figure 9-15. The outer bracket causes repetition of the entire sequence of actions for each course. The inner (or nested) bracket causes a repetition of the actions to read and print student data. Print statements are embedded in the action diagram at appropriate locations to produce the class list.

Data base action diagrams are normally related to external views. A logical map is drawn from the external view, and then an action diagram is prepared. That is why in Figure 9-3 we show the "design application" step interfaced with the "design subschema" (or external view) step.

We will now illustrate this procedure for Mountain View Community Hospital. A network data model for this organization (mapped from the conceptual data model) is shown in Figure 9-7 and one external view (representing the Patient Bill) is shown in Figure 9-8.

Suppose that we wish to develop an application called "Create Patient Bill." First, we draw a logical access map based on the external view (see Figure 9-16). The LAM is simply a rearrangement of the external view, showing in vertical arrangement the necessary sequence of accesses to the logical records.

The data base action diagram for this process is also shown in Figure

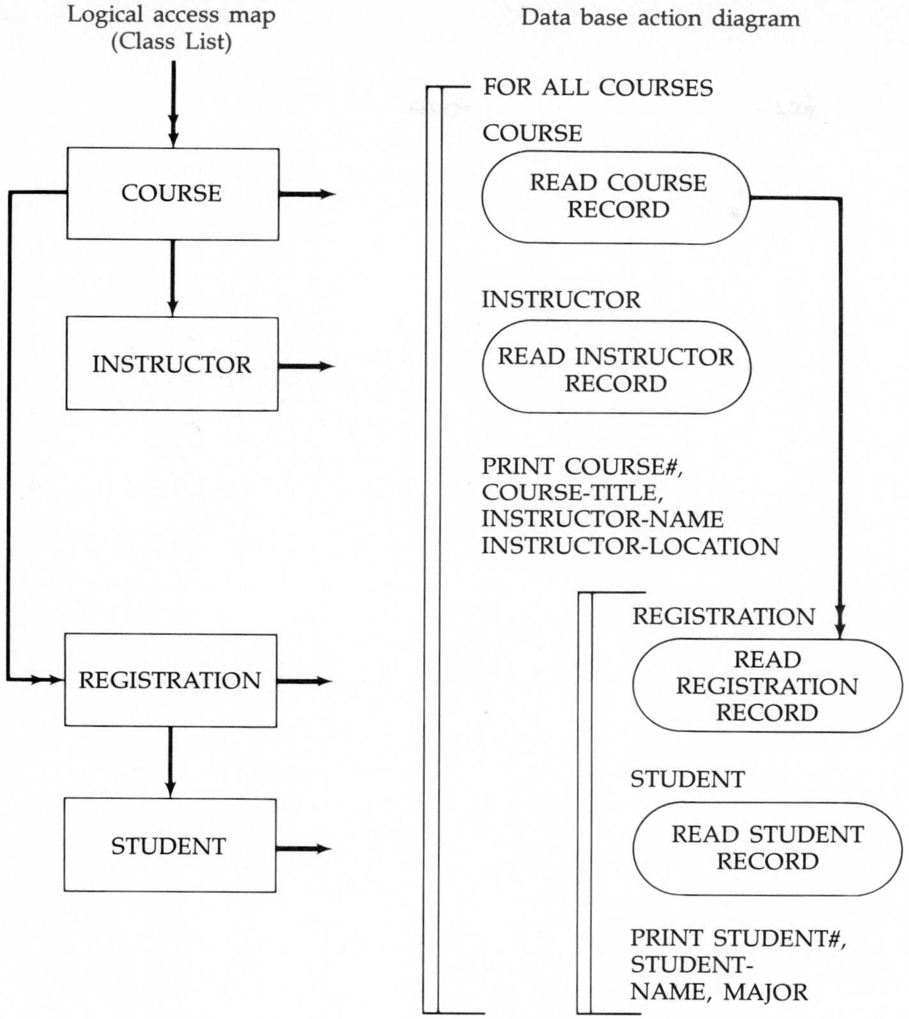

Figure 9-15 Correspondence between logical access map and data base action diagram

9-16. The outer bracket causes a record to be retrieved for each patient. If the patient has been discharged, the remaining steps are performed. If the patient is not discharged, a bill is not prepared (we assume that patients are not billed until after they are discharged). The inner bracket causes individual charges to be retrieved, printed, and accumulated for each patient. At the end, the total amount owed by the patient is printed.

Converting Action Diagrams to Program Code

A data base action diagram is an outline for an application program. It resembles structured English but is generally easier to understand because it is in graphic form. The action diagram is language-independent and may be converted to any third- or fourth-generation language.

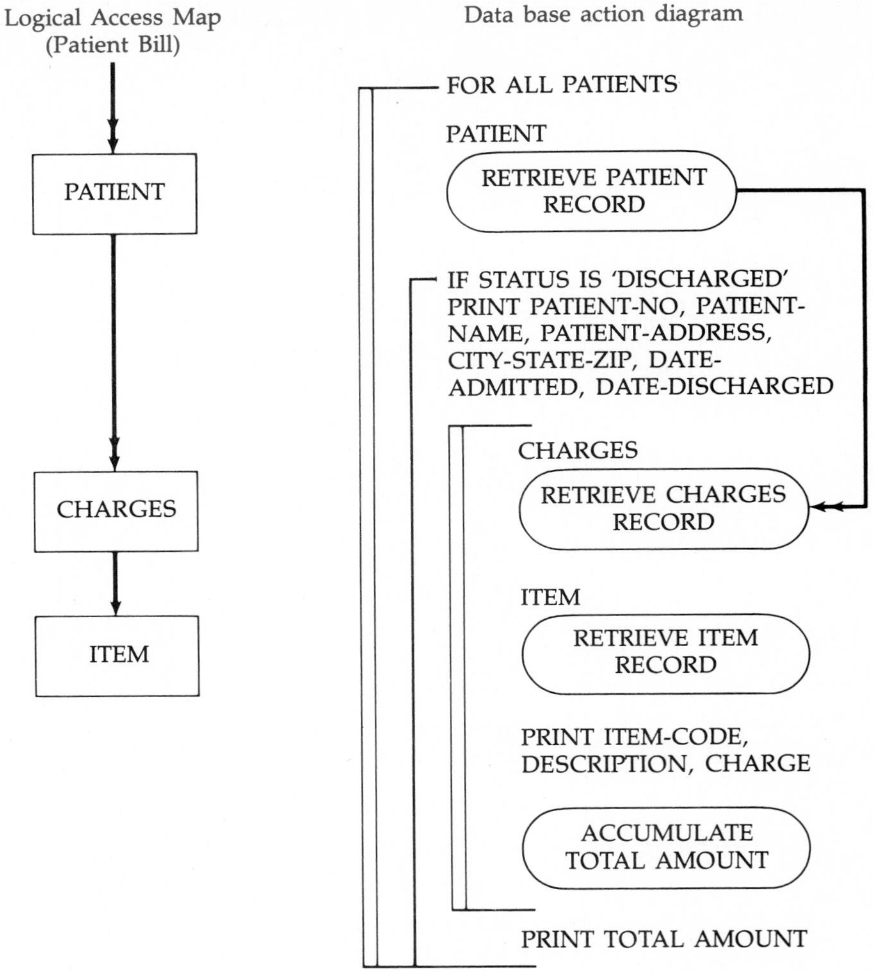

Logical Access Map
(Patient Bill)
PATIENT
CHARGES
ITEM
Data base action diagram
FOR ALL PATIENTS
PATIENT
RETRIEVE PATIENT RECORD
IF STATUS IS 'DISCHARGED' PRINT PATIENT-NO, PATIENT-NAME, PATIENT-ADDRESS, CITY-STATE-ZIP, DATE-ADMITTED, DATE-DISCHARGED
CHARGES
RETRIEVE CHARGES RECORD
ITEM
RETRIEVE ITEM RECORD
PRINT ITEM-CODE, DESCRIPTION, CHARGE
ACCUMULATE TOTAL AMOUNT
PRINT TOTAL AMOUNT

Figure 9-16
Data base action diagram for CREATE PATIENT BILL

Figure 9-17
Application code (MANTIS) for CREATE PATIENT BILL

```
WHILE PATIENTS>0
• DO PATIENT-INQUIRY
• IF PATIENT-STATUS='DISCHARGED'
•• PRINT PATIENT-NO, PATIENT-NAME,...
•• WHILE CHARGES>0
••• DO CHARGES-INQUIRY
••• DO ITEM-INQUIRY
••• PRINT ITEM-CODE, DESCRIPTION, CHARGE
••• TOTAL-AMOUNT=TOTAL-AMOUNT+CHARGE
•• END
•• PRINT TOTAL-AMOUNT
• END
END
```

An example showing the conversion of the action diagram in Figure 9-16 to a fourth-generation language (MANTIS) is given in Figure 9-17. Notice that with such a powerful fourth-generation language, there is approximately a one-for-one correspondence between actions and program language statements.

PHYSICAL DESIGN

Physical design is the process of developing an efficient, implementable physical data base structure. It is concerned with how the data are stored on physical devices rather than how they appear to the user. The major inputs to physical design are the logical structures (schemas and subschemas) from implementation design, characteristics of the DBMS and operating system to be used, and user operational requirements. Outputs of physical design are specifications for stored record formats, record placement, and access methods to be used.

As shown in Figure 9-1, physical design is the last stage in the data base design process. In terms of the three-level ANSI/SPARC model, physical design is concerned with the internal model (see the last column of Figure 2-17). The major objective of physical design is to provide an optimum balance between performance and operational costs.

There are three major steps in physical design: stored record design, record clustering, and access method selection. As with previous design stages, the steps are performed interactively rather than in linear sequence as shown in Figure 9-18.

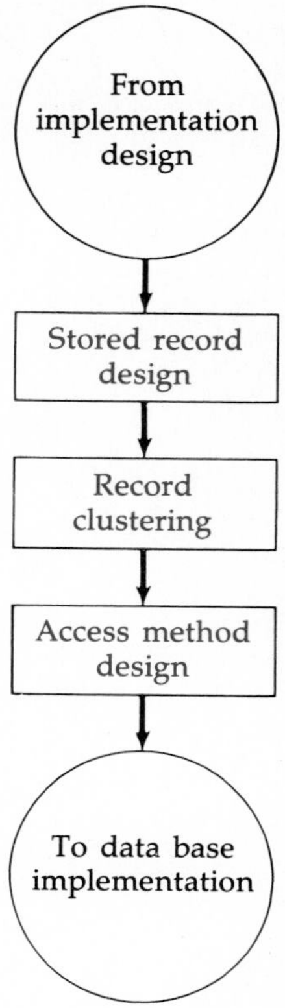

Figure 9-18
Steps in physical design

Stored Record Design

In the internal model, a data base is viewed as a collection of stored records. A **stored record** is a collection of related data items that corresponds to one or more logical records. In addition to data items, a stored record includes any necessary pointers and other overhead data, such as record length indicators. Thus, a stored record format represents data as they are actually stored on physical devices.

It is important to understand the difference between logical records and stored records. This difference is illustrated in Figure 9-19. As shown in Figure 9-19a, there are three levels, or views, of records: conceptual, external, and stored (or internal). A **conceptual record** is a collection of related data items (the conceptual record in Figure 9-19a has four data items: A, B, C, and D). An **external record** is a subset of the conceptual record and represents a local user view. Several external records may be derived from the same conceptual record. (Although not shown in the figure, an external record may also be derived from two or more conceptual records.) In addition to data items, a **stored record** contains pointers and other overhead data.

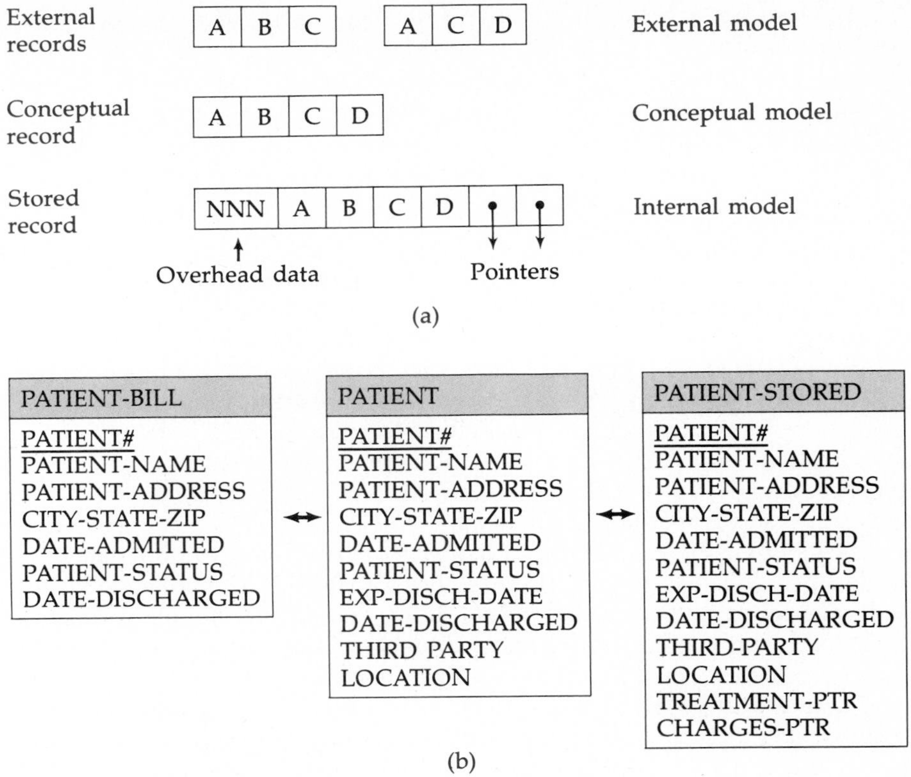

Figure 9-19
Contrast between logical and stored records:
(a) three levels (ANSI/SPARC model)
(b) examples of logical and stored records

Figure 9-19b shows an example of this three-level architecture. The PATIENT record is a conceptual record that appears in the conceptual data model (see Figure 8-14). PATIENT-BILL is an external record that is derived from PATIENT and appears in a user view (see Figure 9-5). And PATIENT-STORED is a stored record version of the PATIENT record type. It contains two pointer fields: CHARGES-POINTER and TREATMENT-POINTER. These fields contain addresses of occurrences of related records (CHARGES and TREATMENT, respectively). The pointer fields are unknown to users since they do not appear in the logical record descriptions (conceptual or external).

A **physical data base** is a collection of one or more types of stored records. For example, the collection of all stored records for Mountain View Community Hospital constitutes a physical data base.

Designing stored record formats essentially consists of deciding how to map the logical records to stored records. The stored records may closely resemble the corresponding conceptual records. For example, in Figure 9-19b, the PATIENT-STORED record format is the same as PATIENT, with two pointer fields added. On the other hand, several options exist for modifying stored records to improve performance, including data item storage

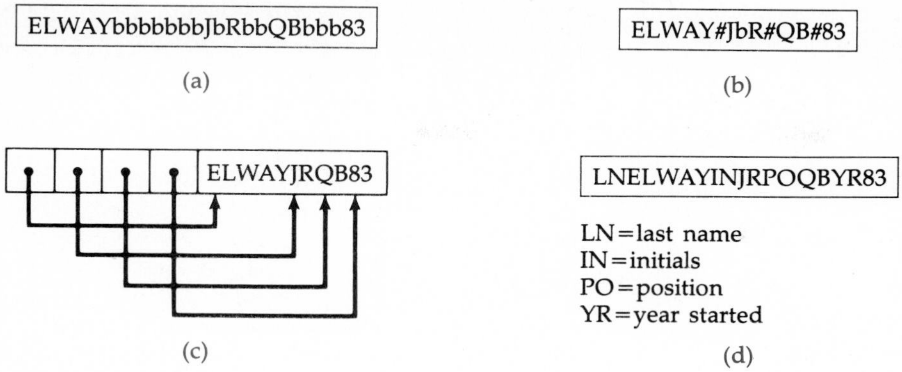

Figure 9-20 Data item representation techniques: (a) positional (b) relational (c) indexed (d) labeled

techniques, data compression, and record partitioning. The specific options available in a given application will depend on the DBMS being used.

Data Item Storage Techniques Four basic techniques are available for representing data in stored records: positional, relational, indexed, and labeled (see Figure 9-20). The positional technique is a fixed-length record representation; the remaining three techniques support variable-length records (these techniques were introduced in Chapter 5, and are summarized here for ease of reference).

With the **positional technique,** fixed-length fields are used for each data item. Thus, each field must be sufficiently large to accommodate the longest anticipated data item value. When data item values are stored, they are right- or left-justified, and blanks are used to pad unused space. (In Figure 9-20, the values are left-justified and the symbol b is used to represent blank space.) The positional technique is the most widely used technique for storing data items since it simplifies programming and data management tasks. However, it tends to waste storage space, which can be costly, especially for very large data bases.

With the **relational technique,** a special character (not valid in the stored data) is used to delimit data item values. In Figure 9-20b, the symbol # is used for this purpose. The special symbol eliminates strings of blanks and therefore conserves space.

The **indexed approach** (Figure 9-20c) uses pointers to specify the beginning of each data item value in the record. The pointers normally specify the relative displacement of each value within the record. As with the relational technique, the use of pointers supports variable-length records and eliminates wasted space.

With the **labeled technique** (Figure 9-20d), each data item value is preceded by a label indicating the data item type. This approach allows only certain data items to be included within each record; unwanted data items are simply omitted. The labeled approach is efficient for unstructured data or when a record has many defaulted data item values.

Original data: ATARIbbbbbbb120000
Compressed data: ATARI#712@4

(a)

Original data	Compressed data
TRS8093000X	@93#X
TRS8091000Y	@91#Y
TRS8094000Z	@94#Z

Pattern Table

TRS80	@
000	#

(b)

Original data

CUSTOMER#	CITY
0123	TUCSON
1467	MINNEAPOLIS
3247	DENVER
5914	MINNEAPOLIS
6789	DENVER

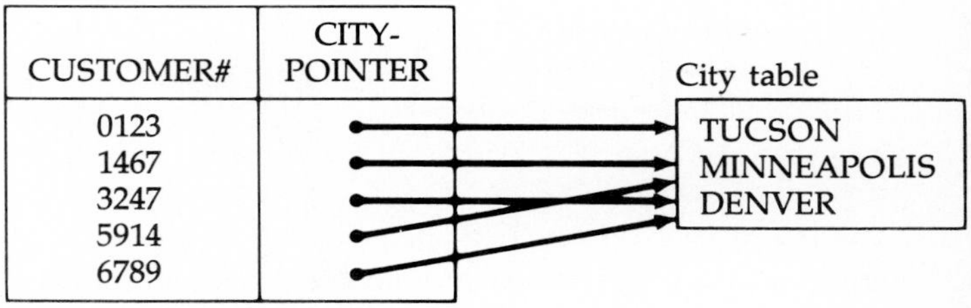

(c)

Figure 9-21
Data compression techniques:
(a) null suppression
(b) pattern substitution
(c) indexing

The physical designer may or may not be able to choose the data item storage technique, depending on the DBMS being used. When a choice exists, one of the variable-length record techniques (relational, indexed, or labeled) can be used to conserve storage space if this is an important consideration. However, variable-length records usually complicate the programming task and slow down input/output operations.

Data Compression Data compression is the process of reducing the length of data item values in stored records. Several techniques are used, the three most popular being null suppression, pattern substitution, and indexing (see Figure 9-21).

Null suppression techniques suppress blanks and zeros. One common technique that is used for zero suppression is a simple extension of the relational technique already described. A special character is used to indicate the beginning of a sequence of blanks or zeros (in Figure 9-21a, the symbol # represents the beginning of a sequence of blanks, the symbol @ the beginning of a sequence of zeros). The special character is followed by a digit that represents the length of the sequence. Thus, in Figure 9-21a, the symbol @4 is the compressed version for a sequence of four zeros. Null suppression is an effective technique for compressing "sparse" data that are dominated by zeros or blanks.

Pattern substitution is a technique in which sequences of characters that occur repeatedly in the data are recognized and then represented by shorter codes. An example of this technique is shown in Figure 9-21b.

In this example, two character strings (TRS80 and 000) were identified as patterns in the same data. These values were stored in a pattern table and coded with the characters @ and #, respectively. The compressed data then appear with these codes replacing the character strings. Notice that this type of data compression requires additional accesses to the pattern table to store and retrieve data. However, pattern substitution is an effective means of data compression when frequent patterns exist in the data.

Indexing is a variation of pattern substitution. Instead of using a code to replace patterns, a pointer is used for each data item value. For example, in Figure 9-21c there is considerable redundancy in the CITY data item values, since the names of two cities are repeated (if there were 10,000 records, each city name would appear many times). To compress the data, a separate CITY table is created. City names are then replaced by pointers that point to the appropriate names in the table (the pointer values must be shorter than the city names for compression to occur).

Some data base management systems automatically compress stored data. For example, ADABAS (DBMS from Software AG) has a compression algorithm that automatically suppresses trailing spaces on alphanumeric fields and leading zeros on numeric fields, packs numeric data, and compresses null value fields to a single character. The net result is that an ADABAS file typically requires only about 50% to 65% of the space required for the raw data (Software AG 1982).

Record Partitioning The last aspect of stored record design that we will consider is record partitioning. **Record partitioning** (or segmentation) is the process of splitting stored records into separate segments and then allocating those segments to separate physical devices or separate extents on the same device. The reason for partitioning records is that some data items are accessed far more frequently than others. In fact, the so-called 80-20 rule often applies: approximately 20% of the data items often account for about 80% of the input/output activity. We can improve performance by locating the active data items on fast devices (such as fixed-head disks) or in readily accessible locations (such as the middle cylinders on a disk pack).

The simplest form of record partitioning divides a stored record into two segments: the **primary segment** (with the most active data items) and the **secondary segment** (with the less active data items). An example of this segmentation for the PATIENT record at Mountain View Community Hospital is shown in Figure 9-22. The three most active data items (which account for about 80% of all requests) are located in the primary segment: PATIENT#, PATIENT-NAME, and LOCATION. The remaining PATIENT data items are located in the secondary segment. The primary segment might be stored for fast access, with the secondary segment stored on a slower device. In reality, the PATIENT records would probably not be segmented at all, since the data base for this hospital is relatively small. However, record partitioning may be an effective means of improving performance for large data bases.

Notice that the primary and secondary segments are connected by a pointer so that they can be retrieved together when necessary. All user requests for data first generate an access to the primary segment. If the data are not found, then another access to the secondary segment is made.

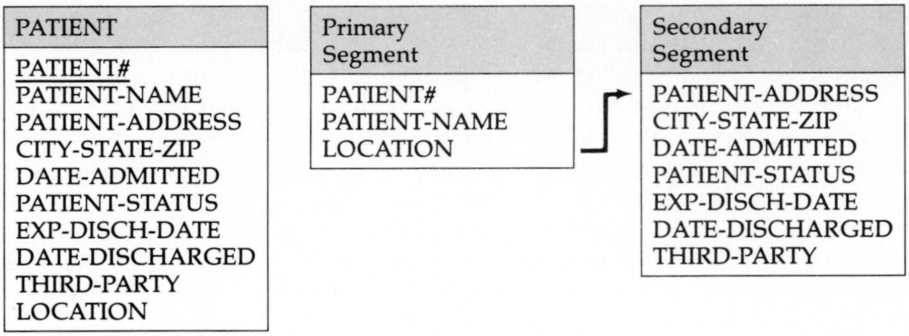

Figure 9-22
Example of record partitioning

Record partitioning occurs at the physical level and is not visible to data base users.

Record partitioning is part of the more general process of clustering data items into stored records. A cluster analysis technique called the **bond energy algorithm** has been developed to identify natural groupings that occur in large data arrays. Hoffer and Severance (1975) have applied the bond energy algorithm to the process of record partitioning. Their algorithm measures the "bond," or cohesiveness, among data items and groups data items that are used together into physical subfiles. As with all clustering techniques, the bond energy algorithm requires detailed analysis concerning the way that data are used.

Record Clustering

A physical data base consists of a collection of stored records of different types. **Record clustering** is the process of physically grouping these records according to the dominant access paths, thereby minimizing access times. For example, all stored records of a given type may be grouped together in a physical extent. However, it is often more efficient to group occurrences of different record types together when they are frequently accessed together. Optimum record clustering is a complex problem for large, integrated data bases.

Clustering in Hierarchical Data Bases In a hierarchical data base, record clustering is the process of grouping segment occurrences into physical blocks or extents. See Figure 9-23, for example. Figure 9-23a shows a physical data base record that consists of the four segment types A, B, C, and D (A is the root segment). Figure 9-23b shows one clustering option, where occurrences of each segment type are grouped together. This grouping is not likely to be efficient, since segments in a hierarchy are often retrieved in top-down, left-to-right sequence.

Another approach to grouping the segments is shown in Figure 9-23c. In this case, occurrences of segments A and B are grouped together (occur-

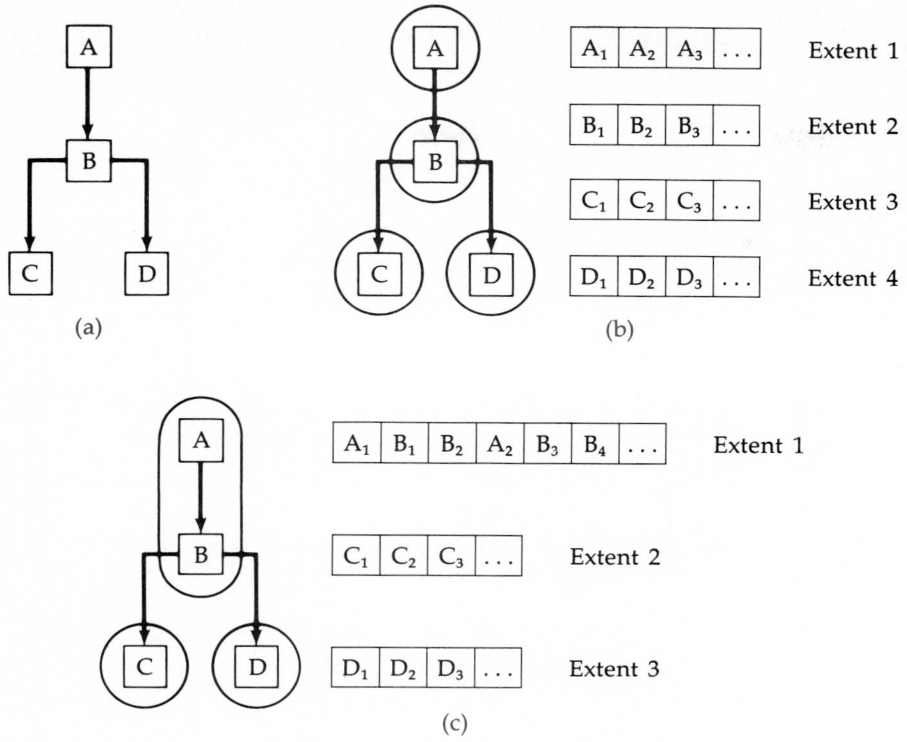

Figure 9-23
Record clustering in a hierarchical data base:
(a) sample physical data base record
(b) grouping individual segments
(c) alternative grouping

rences of segment B are grouped immediately following their parent segment occurrences). This grouping will probably be efficient if root segment (type A) occurrences are normally accessed sequentially with their child (type B) occurrences and if segments C and D are normally accessed sequentially. Certainly, many other groupings are possible even in this simple example.

Schkolnick (1977) has developed an algorithm for optimum clustering of segments in a hierarchical data base. This algorithm minimizes the expected number of I/O accesses for a given set of user applications by computing a distance function for each clustering option (nonoptimal clusterings are eliminated from further consideration). For details of this algorithm, see Teorey and Fry (1982) and Schkolnick (1977).

The IMS hierarchical data base for Mountain View Community Hospital is shown in Figure 9-11. The primary access path for TREATMENT segments is by means of PHYSICIAN segments, since PHYSICIAN is the root segment. Therefore, TREATMENT segment occurrences will be clustered with their PHYSICIAN parent segment occurrences in an IMS implementation of this data base. For the same reason, CHARGES segment occurrences will be clustered with their PATIENT parent segment occurrences.

Figure 9-24
Example of record clustering

PHYSICIAN RECORD# 1	TREATMENT RECORD A	TREATMENT RECORD B
TREATMENT RECORD C		
PHYSICIAN RECORD# 2	TREATMENT RECORD D	TREATMENT RECORD E
PHYSICIAN RECORD# 3	TREATMENT RECORD F	

If the usage patterns for this data base change over time, it may become necessary to revise this clustering scheme.

Clustering in Network Data Bases In a CODASYL (network) data base, the physical data base structure (or internal model) is specified in the Data Storage Description Language (DSDL). The DSDL is used to define the format of each stored record, the number and size of areas, and the placement of records in areas.

Record placement (or clustering) in a CODASYL data base is controlled by a PLACEMENT clause in the DSDL. For each CODASYL record type, one of three placement modes may be chosen:

1. CALC: A data item value (record key) is hashed to produce a storage address. This results in record occurrences being dispersed randomly throughout a storage area (or extent).
2. CLUSTERED VIA SET: Member record occurrences in a set are clustered together, usually with their owner record occurrence.
3. SEQUENTIAL: Occurrences of a given record type are stored in sequential order according to their primary key.

Referring to the network data model for Mountain View Community Hospital (Figure 9-7), there are two instances where the CLUSTERED VIA SET option will be used in the DSDL. CLUSTERED VIA SET TREATED will be specified for the TREATMENT record type. This clause will cause occurrences of TREATMENT records to be clustered with their PHYSICIAN owner record occurrences (see Figure 9-24). Also, a CLUSTERED VIA SET INCURRED will cause CHARGES record occurrences to be clustered with their PATIENT owner record occurrences.

Design Access Methods

We have described the first two steps in physical design: record design and record clustering. The last step is to select the access methods to be used for the stored records. An **access method** is a technique for storing and retrieving records. Access methods have two major components: a data structure and a search strategy. A **data structure** is a technique for physical data organization. Some important data structures (which are described in Chapter 5) are linear lists, multilists, inverted lists, and trees. A **search strategy** is a technique used to define an access path and locate a specific stored record. Examples include sequential search, binary search, and hashing (or random access).

The choice of access methods for stored records is a relatively complex process, requiring considerable knowledge of how the data will be used by various applications, as well as technical knowledge of the DBMS being used and the access methods that it supports. Some DBMS products support a wide variety of access methods, while other products constrain the user to a limited set of options. There are numerous formulas for predicting performance (such as average access times) for various access methods. For a detailed discussion of access methods and related performance measures, see Teorey and Fry (1982), Martin (1977), and Wiederhold (1977).

A detailed discussion comparing the performance of various access methods is beyond the scope of this text. However, a classification scheme proposed by Severance and Carlis (1977) can be used to simplify this process. They describe three classes of user applications and the type of access methods best suited to each class. The three classes are as follows:

1. GET ALL or MANY: This class of applications requires access to a significant proportion of the data base, usually between 10% and 100%. Examples of such applications are batch updating and report preparation. Sequential organizations are most efficient for this class of applications.

2. GET UNIQUE: Access is normally to a single target record. Organizations based on primary keys (such as hashing and B-trees) are most efficient for this class of applications.

3. GET SOME: This class of applications requires access to several records (but less than 10% of the data base) on each occasion. The most common example is ad hoc queries that traverse several records. Organizations based on secondary keys (such as inverted files and multilists) are most efficient.

A summary of the three application classes and the most efficient access methods for each class are shown in Table 9-1. The table also groups records from the network data model for Mountain View Community Hospital (Figure 9-7) into the classes, based on the anticipated dominant mode of usage for those records. Four of the record types in Figure 9-7 (ROOM, PATIENT, PHYSICIAN, and ITEM) have a CALC record placement mode. This indicates that the dominant access mode for these records is GET UNIQUE, as shown in Table 9-1. These records can be organized as a hashed file or, if

Table 9-1 Classification of Access Methods

Application class	Typical access methods	Hospital record type
GET ALL or MANY (10%–100%)	Sequential (physical or linked)	None
GET UNIQUE (one)	Random (hashed); Indexed sequential; B-tree	PATIENT; ROOM; PHYSICIAN; ITEM
GET SOME (0%–10%)	Inverted file; multilist	TREATMENT; CHARGES

sequential access is also required, as an indexed sequential file. The remaining two record types (TREATMENT and CHARGES) normally require a GET SOME discipline and may therefore be organized using inverted file or multilist techniques.

Handling Missing Data

It is not uncommon in data base management to encounter situations where data are missing, lost, or incomplete. When data are not normalized or when data are duplicated for high operational performance, different data values for the same data item may disagree, causing ambiguity or uncertainty as to the real data value (which may have to be handled as missing the real value).

As we will see in later chapters, many DBMSs now support a NULL VALUE that can be used to represent missing data. But, although missing data can be represented, reporting involving missing values may be cumbersome. For example, if the gender of some employees is missing, and the age of some other employees is missing, any comparison or relationship between age and gender is questionable since it would not be based on the same employees.

According to Babad and Hoffer (1984), there are six possible methods for dealing with missing data:

1. *Initialization of data fields.* Initialization ensures that all data elements have some value and that computations can always be performed. But the lack of data is masked and computations are biased.
2. *Automatic defaults.* Common default values are zero, smallest or largest possible value for numerical fields, or a blank space for nonnumeric fields. NULL VALUE also fits into this category. Although similar to initialization methods, defaults can be applied at any time data are found to be missing.
3. *Deducing values.* The DBMS can compensate for missing data by inferring values. The most common derived value would be to use the

mean of some set of values—either all values from all record instances, some appropriate or categorized subset, or simply of the range of possible values. More sophisticated methods could estimate the missing value from audit trails or from characteristics of similar records. It might even be possible to represent the missing value by a confidence interval or range (set in the case of discrete data) of likely values.

4. *TRACK missing data.* No matter how values may be stored in the place of missing data, it is equally important to tag or identify data as missing. Use of a NULL VALUE or some special code does this, but no value is actually stored. It may even be desirable to know for how long the value has been unknown or what attempts have been made to find the correct value. A tag with the "missing value" can indicate that the value stored was entered by some user, estimated in some way, reconstructed from an audit trail, or reviewed for reasonableness on same day, among many possible annotations.
5. *Determine impact of missing data.* How we handle missing data may depend on how the data will impact those who use it. If data are simply being listed in a report for descriptive purposes, then simply showing a null value may be sufficient. If the value would be crucial in putting a core summary statistic over an important threshold (e.g., cause a reorder of an expensive inventory item), then the missing value should cause a message to either find the missing value or interpret the results with caution. Vassiliov (1981) discusses this situation in detail.
6. *Prevent missing data.* Even if complete prevention of missing data is not possible, the incidence of missing data can be greatly reduced by certain procedures. In batch processing, preedit programs can scan for missing data and validate all data elements (a major source of missing data is an invalid field value that has been eliminated by an edit check at data load time). Reports of missing and invalid data elements can lead to an immediate search for actual values before the data have to be entered into the data base. Grouping transactions into logical sets and forcing the whole set to be valid before any single transaction takes effect is another procedure that can be used to prevent missing data (e.g., make sure that a patient discharge, which affects patient, bed, and charges data, can be processed as a whole). To avoid erroneous handling by application programs, programmers can write special utilities to scan for missing data, especially unrelated records.

No data model explicitly recognizes the possibility of missing data, yet it is an everyday fact of life for a living data base. If not dealt with during data base design, a data base can evolve into a low integrity state and cause interrupted or erroneous data processing. A data base designer must design the data base and data base utilities to deal with the inevitable situation of missing or ambiguous data.

SUMMARY

In this chapter, we described the final two steps of data base design—implementation design and physical design. Implementation design is concerned with mapping the conceptual model (described in Chapter 8) to a logical data base structure. This logical structure is usually expressed in the form of a hierarchical, network, or relational data model, or some combination of these models. The logical structure is expressed in the form of a DBMS-processible schema. Implementation design is also concerned with mapping conceptual user views into logical views. These logical views are then expressed in the form of DBMS-processible subschemas. Data base action diagrams that express program logic can also be developed during implementation design.

Physical design, which occurs at the level of the internal model, is concerned with developing an efficient, implementable physical data base structure. Several decisions that must be made during physical design concern stored record formats, record clustering, and selection of efficient access methods. Several trade-offs among access times, storage requirements, and data redundancy must typically be made during physical design.

When physical design is completed, the data base is ready to be implemented. In the following chapters, we describe and illustrate this implementation using several types of data base management systems.

Chapter Review

REVIEW QUESTIONS

1. Concisely define each of the following terms:
   a. logical model
   b. schema
   c. subschema
   d. set
   e. segment
   f. action
   g. stored record
   h. data compression
   i. physical data base
2. Contrast the following terms:
   a. physical design; implementation design
   b. conceptual model; logical model
   c. owner; member
   d. CALC; VIA
   e. physical parent; logical parent
   f. positional technique; relational technique
   g. null suppression; pattern substitution
   h. record clustering; record partitioning
   i. GET ALL; GET SOME

3. List the major steps for each of the following:
   a. implementation design
   b. physical design
4. List four steps in mapping a conceptual model to a CODASYL model.
5. Briefly describe four techniques for representing data in stored records.
6. Describe three techniques for data compression.
7. Describe three general classes of user applications in terms of their access patterns.
8. What is the difference in IMS between a physical data base record and a logical data base record?
9. Why should data access strategies be defined during physical design rather than during implementation design?
10. What is the relationship between LAMs and action diagrams?

PROBLEMS AND EXERCISES

1. Match the following terms to the appropriate definitions.

_____ physical design
_____ subschema
_____ set relationship
_____ segment
_____ physical parent
_____ logical parent
_____ action diagram
_____ action
_____ stored record
_____ external record
_____ physical data base
_____ pattern substitution
_____ record clustering
_____ access method

a. subset of a conceptual model
b. step applied to one record instance
c. collection of related data items
d. grouping records according to access paths
e. collection of stored records
f. technique for storing and retrieving record
g. representing a sequence of characters
h. selecting file organization and access methods
i. node in IMS
j. working subset of a schema
k. segment type in another hierarchy
l. 1:*M* association between two record types
m. parent segment type in a hierarchy
n. map showing a sequence of actions

Problems 2 to 6 are based on a conceptual data model (abbreviated version) for Pine Valley Furniture Company. This data model, shown in Figure 2-10, is repeated here:

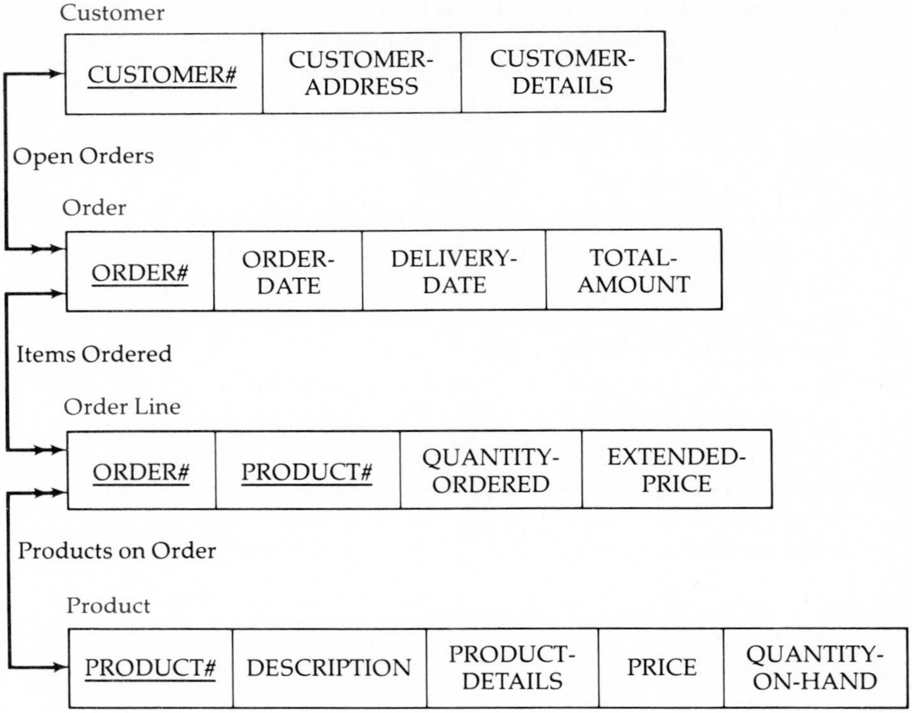

In answering the following questions, assume that the dominant access patterns for the record types are as follows:

(i) CUSTOMER: GET UNIQUE
(ii) ORDER; GET UNIQUE
(iii) ORDER-LINE: GET SOME (retrieve all ORDER-LINE occurrences for a given Order occurrence)
(iv) PRODUCT: GET UNIQUE (GET ALL sometimes required)

2. Map the model to a relational data model. Show sample data.
3. Map the model to a network (CODASYL) data model (similar to the one in Figure 9-7).
4. Map the model to a hierarchical (IMS) data model (similar to the one in Figure 9-11).
5. Suggest an efficient access method for each of the four record types in the data models.
6. Create a logical access map and data base action diagram for a procedure that will create a new customer order. The following steps are performed:
   (i) Create ORDER record occurrence.
   (ii) Retrieve CUSTOMER record.
   (iii) Check customer credit (contained in CUSTOMER record). If credit OK, proceed; otherwise, print message and stop.

(iv) Create ORDER-LINE record occurrence for each product on the order.
(v) Retrieve PRODUCT record occurrence for each ORDER-LINE occurrence.
(vi) Multiply PRICE (PRODUCT record) by QUANTITY (ORDER-LINE), giving EXTENDED-PRICE (ORDER-Line).

7. One of the user views for Mountain View Community Hospital is the Physician Report (see Figure 8-12).
   a. Referring to the hospital data model (Figure 8-14), draw a logical access map for the procedure CREATE-PHYSICIAN-REPORT.
   b. Draw a data base action diagram for the preceding LAM.

8. Consider the following data:

   APPLEbbbbbVISICALC60000
   APPLEbbbbVISICLONE70000

   a. Show these data with null suppression (use the same symbols as in Figure 9-21).
   b. Show these data with pattern substitution.

9. Refer to the conceptual data model (Figure 8-14) and Room Utilization Report (Figure 8-10) for Mountain View Community Hospital.
   a. Derive a conceptual user view (such as the one in Figure 9-5) by normalizing the relation in Figure 8-10.
   b. Using the views developed in part (a), draw a logical access map for the procedure CREATE-ROOM-UTILIZATION-REPORT.
   c. Draw a data base action diagram for the LAM in part (b).

10. Express each of the following data base action diagrams in structured English (or pseudocode):

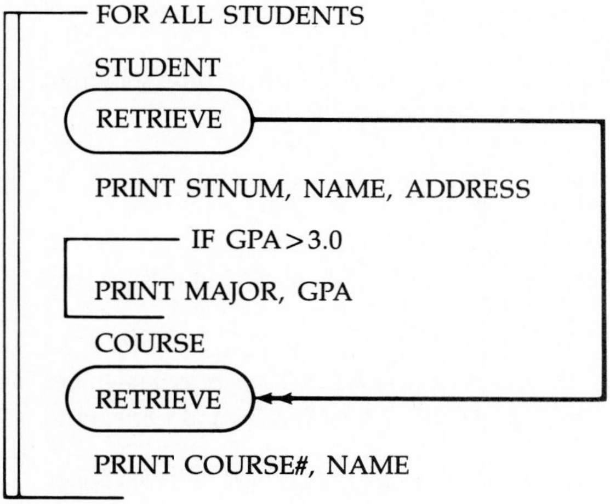

(a)

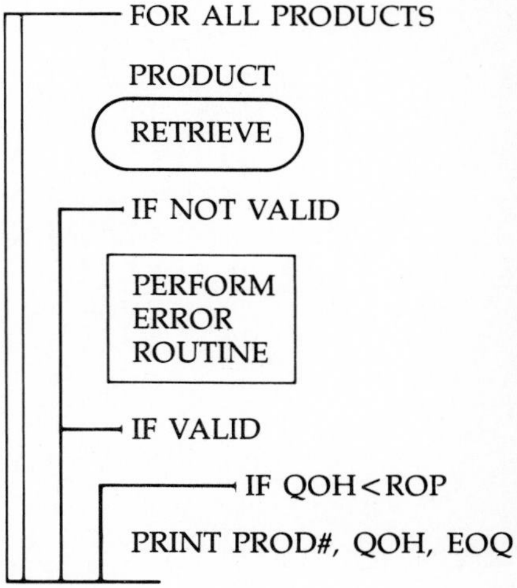

(b)

11. A simplified conceptual data model for a purchasing data base is shown in Figure 9-25. Map this conceptual model to a CODASYL logical model. Assume the following access patterns:

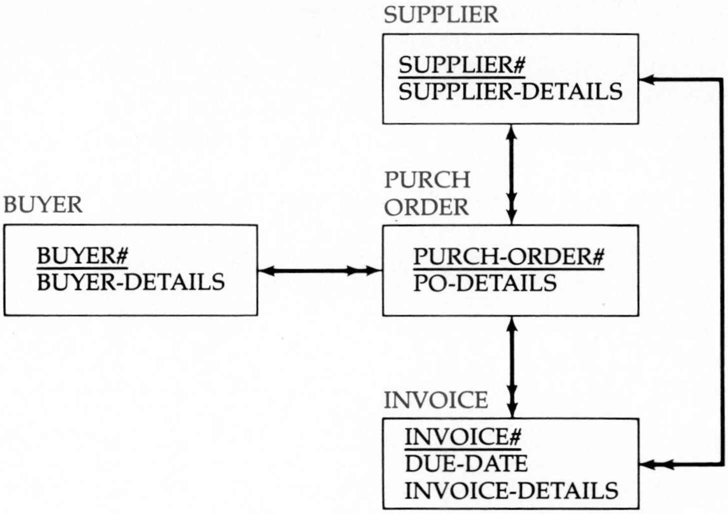

Figure 9-25
Purchasing data base

(i) SUPPLIER, BUYER, and PURCHORDER are normally GET UNIQUE.
(ii) INVOICE is normally GET SOME. There are two cases:
- Retrieve a PURCHORDER occurrence, then retrieve all associated INVOICE occurrences.
- Retrieve all INVOICE occurrences that have a particular DUE-DATE value.

12. Map the conceptual data model shown in Figure 9-25 to a hierarchical model (see assumptions in Problem 11).
13. Based on the assumptions stated in Problem 11, how are the records shown in Figure 9-25 likely to be clustered in a CODASYL data base?

REFERENCES

Babad, Yair M., and Jeffrey A. Hoffer. 1984. "Even No Data Has a Value." *Communications of the ACM* 27 (August): 748–756.

Hoffer, J. A., and D. G. Severance. 1975. "The Use of Cluster Analysis in Physical Data Base Design." *Proceedings of First Very Large Data Base Conference.* September.

Martin, James. 1977. *Computer Data Base Organization.* 2d ed. Englewood Cliffs, N.J.: Prentice-Hall.

———. 1983. *Managing the Data-Base Environment.* Englewood Cliffs, N.J.: Prentice-Hall.

Maxwell, W. L., and D. G. Severance. 1973. "Comparison of Alternatives for the Representation of Data Item Values in an Information System." *Proceedings Wharton Conference Res. Computer Organ. Oper. Res.* 20(5).

Schkolnick, M. 1977. "A Clustering Algorithm for Hierarchical Structures." *ACM Transactions on Database Systems* (March): 27–44.

Severance, D. G., and J. V. Carlis. 1977. "A Practical Approach to Selecting Record Access Paths." *ACM Computing Surveys* 9(4): 259–272.

Software AG. 1982. *ADABAS, Effective Data Base Management for the Growing Corporate Environment.*

Teorey, Toby J., and James P. Fry. 1982. *Design of Database Structures.* Englewood Cliffs, N.J.: Prentice-Hall.

Vassiliov, Y. 1981. "Functional Dependencies and Incomplete Information." *Proceedings of the 6th International Conference on Very Large Data Bases.* Montreal, Canada: 260–269.

Wiederhold, G. 1977. *Database Design.* New York: McGraw-Hill.

Chapter 10

Data Base Administration

INTRODUCTION

Increasingly, organizations are recognizing that data and information are resources that are too valuable to be managed casually. According to a study conducted by the Center for the Study of Data Processing of Washington University (Herbert and Hartog 1986), data utilization [that is, "assuring that data are made available to the right person in a timely manner" (79)] is the second most important issue in MIS management (the first was aligning MIS with business goals). Further, this issue moved from ninth place (1984) to fourth place (1985) and then to its current prominent position.

There are many causes of poor data utilization:

- Multiple definitions of the same data entity and inconsistent representations of the same data elements in separate data bases—which makes linking data across different data bases hazardous
- Missing key data elements—which makes existing data useless
- Low levels of data quality due to inappropriate sources of data or timing of data transfers from one system to another
- Not knowing what data exist, where to find them, and what they really mean

One organizational response to the data utilization issue is to create a new function called data base administration (DBA). The person who heads this function is called the manager of data base administration or, more popularly, the data base administrator (also abbreviated DBA). The term *DBA* is used in this chapter to mean both the person and the function.

Actual experience with computer data bases has established a fundamental principle: The data base administration function is *essential* to the success of managing the data resource. Establishing this function is an indication of top management's commitment to data resource management. When the DBA function is not established, or when it is weakly established, the chances of success of the data base approach are significantly diminished.

The data base is a shared resource, belonging to the entire enterprise. It is not the property of a single function or individual within the organization. The data base administrator is "custodian" of the organization's data, in much the same sense that the controller is custodian of the financial resources. Like the controller, the DBA must develop procedures to protect and control the resource. Also, the DBA must resolve disputes that may arise when data are centralized and shared among users, and must play a significant role in deciding where data will be stored and managed.

Data base administration is responsible for a wide range of functions, including data base planning, design, implementation, maintenance, and protection. Also, the DBA is responsible for improving data base performance and for providing education, training, and consulting support to users. The data base administrator must interact with top management, users, and computer applications specialists.

Selecting the data base administrator and organizing the DBA function are extremely important. The data base administrator must possess a high level of managerial skills and must be capable of resolving differences that normally arise when significant change is introduced into an organization. The DBA should be a respected, senior-level middle manager selected from within the organization, rather than a technical computer expert or a new individual hired for the DBA position.

Several concepts, methods, and tools are available to help a DBA manage the data resource to achieve high data utilization (as defined above). A data base (already covered) and a DBMS (to be addressed in detail in Chapter 11) are fundamental components of a DBA's portfolio. Fourth-generation languages (to be discussed in Chapter 14) and system prototyping (Boar 1984) can be used by a DBA and others to help users better understand their data processing requirements, but an almost complete and fully defined data base must be in place for 4GLs and prototyping to be of much assistance. Finally, but certainly very importantly, a data dictionary/directory is needed so that all data base users know exactly what data are available where, what "data" means, who controls access to the data, how data are stored, when they are maintained, and where they are used. The use of a data dictionary/directory is covered in considerable detail later in this chapter, and the structure of a data dictionary/directory is addressed in Chapter 11.

DATA BASE ADMINISTRATION VERSUS DATA ADMINISTRATION

The manager of the DBA function requires both managerial and technical skills. On the one hand, this person must be capable of enlisting cooperation from users, who may at first be hostile to the idea of "giving up" their "private" data to a shared data base. Also, these users must be convinced of the benefits of adhering to a set of standard procedures for accessing and protecting the data base. On the other hand, the DBA must be capable of managing a technical staff and dealing with technical issues in designing and managing the data base.

To resolve the managerial versus technical complexity of the DBA function, some organizations are distinguishing between data administration and data base administration. When this distinction is made, **data administration** is regarded as a high-level management function (perhaps a corporate vice-president) with responsibility for determining overall information needs from a management perspective. The data administration is "responsible for developing and administering the policies, procedures, practices, and plans for the definition, organization, protection, and efficient utilization of data within a corporate enterprise" (Guide International 1977). This function encompasses all corporate data, whether or not they are part of a stored data base. **Data base administration** is considered a "work group within an organization charged with managing the firm's data resource" (Canning 1972). Data base administration is normally responsible only for computer data bases. It usually reports within the data processing organization. In many organizations, data base administration is a technical group concerned mainly with system software and storage devices, operational efficiency of data base processing, selection of appropriate data base management systems, and the physical integrity of the data base through sound security and recovery from abnormal conditions.

Recently the concept of a data steward has emerged in the data resource management field. A **data steward** manages a specific logical data resource or entity (e.g., customer, product, or facility) for all business functions and data processing systems that originate or use data about the assigned entity. A data steward is the focal point for coordinating all data definitions, quality controls and improvement programs, access authorization, and planning for the data entity for which he or she is responsible. Data stewards may be coordinated by the data administrator or may collectively satisfy the responsibilities of data administration.

Usually a data steward is a user manager from a business management department that originates data about the entity or has primary interest in the entity. The intent of data stewardship is to distribute (not decentralize) data administration to those most knowledgeable of and dependent on high-quality data for key data entities.

An enterprise information model (see Figure 3-12) would be used to identify the key data entities to be assigned to data stewards. A data steward manages an enterprise data entity not just for the good of his or her own area of the organization but also to promote organizational data sharing and access. When the organization distinguishes local data from organizational data, a particular unit may appoint data stewards for entities local to that unit.

The process of describing and separating these various functions continues, and in all likelihood, standard definitions (and standard industry practice) will not be adopted for some time to come. In the meantime, the term *data base administration* is most widely used today (and is used in this text) to refer to the broad range of managerial and technical functions of data resource management. The question of organizational placement of the DBA function is addressed later in this chapter.

DATA BASE SYSTEM LIFE CYCLE

Data base administration is responsible for managing the data base system life cycle. Therefore, to understand the DBA functions, it is necessary to understand that life cycle. As shown in Figure 10-1, there are six stages in the life cycle of a typical data base system:

1. Planning
2. Requirements formulation and analysis
3. Design
4. Implementation
5. Operation and maintenance
6. Growth and change

Normally, these stages are performed in the order given here. However, iteration is often required between the various stages. For example, the design stage may reveal that some data have been inadequately defined, which would lead to further requirements analysis.

Chapter 3 addresses many aspects of stage 1, planning. Chapters 7–9 outline in detail stages 2 and 3, requirements formulation and design, respectively. Chapters 11–15 discuss implementation, stage 4, in a wide variety of data base management technologies. What follows is a brief overview of these six stages in the data base life cycle and their relationship to the role of the DBA. Keep in mind that parts of stages 2 through 6 will likely happen as part of the evolutionary development of systems that use a data base. Thus, these six stages do not comprehensively define all aspects of data base development. An organization will typically define a standard methodology for systems development that will include these data base life cycle stages as well as the stages of feasibility study, logical design, physical design, programming, testing, training, conversion, documentation and procedure writing, and so on, necessary to build a complete application system.

Figure 10-1
Stages in the data base system life cycle

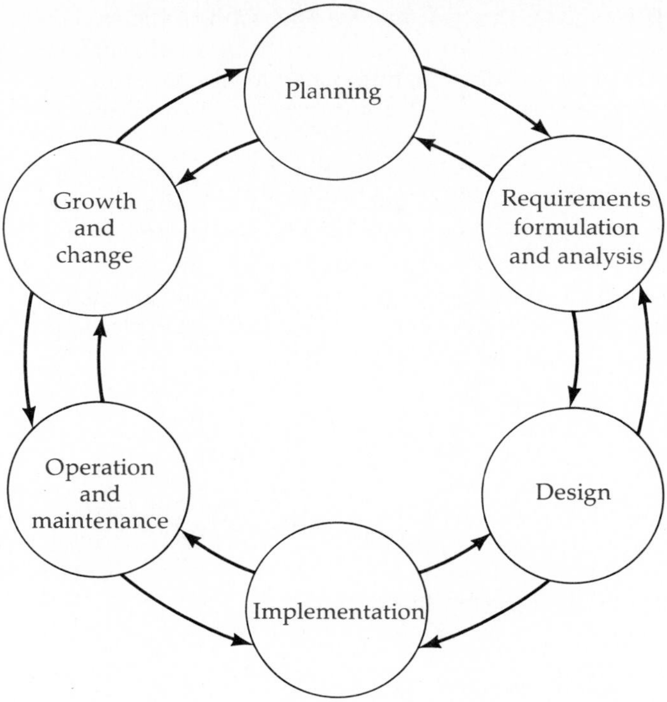

Planning The purpose of data base planning is to develop a strategic plan for data base development that supports the overall organizational business plan. Although the responsibility for developing this plan rests with top management, data base administration provides major inputs to the planning process.

Requirements Formulation and Analysis The process of requirements formulation and analysis is concerned with identifying data elements currently used by the organization, precisely defining these elements and their relationships, and documenting the results in a form that is convenient to the design effort that is to follow. In addition to identifying current data, requirements formulation and analysis attempts to identify new data elements (or changes to existing data elements) that will be required in the future.

Design The purpose of data base design is to develop a data base architecture that will meet the information needs of the organization, now and in the future. As we described in Chapter 7, there are three stages in data base design: conceptual design, implementation design, and physical design. Although data base administration is responsible for data base design, the

DBA group must work closely with users and systems specialists in performing these design activities.

Implementation Once the data base design is completed, the implementation process begins. The first step in implementation is the creation (or initial load) of the data base. The data base is simply an empty superstructure until it has been "populated" with actual data values. Data base administration manages the loading process and resolves any inconsistencies that arise during this process.

Operation and Maintenance Data base operation and maintenance is the ongoing process of updating the data base to keep it current. Examples of updating include adding a new employee record, changing a student address, and deleting an invoice.

Updating the data base is not the responsibility of data base administration. Rather, users are responsible for data base maintenance. However, DBA is responsible for developing procedures that ensure that the data base is kept current and that it is protected during update operations. Specifically, the DBA must perform the following functions:

1. Assign responsibility for data collection, editing, and verification.
2. Establish appropriate update schedules.
3. Establish an active and aggressive quality assurance program, including procedures for protecting, restoring, and auditing the data base.

Growth and Change The data base is a model of the organization itself. As a result, it is not static but reflects the dynamic changes in the organization and its environment. The DBA function must plan for change, monitor the performance of the data base (both efficiency as well as user satisfaction), and take whatever corrective actions are required to maintain a high level of system performance and success.

FUNCTIONS OF DATA BASE ADMINISTRATION

The major functions of data base administration are summarized in Figure 10-2 according to the data base system life cycle. Some of these functions have been described in previous chapters and are therefore discussed only briefly in this chapter. Functions that have not been covered in previous chapters are described in greater detail.

Planning Functions

Data base administration is responsible for developing a set of plans for data base implementation. Here are some of the major functions performed during this stage of the life cycle:

Figure 10-2
Major functions of data base administration

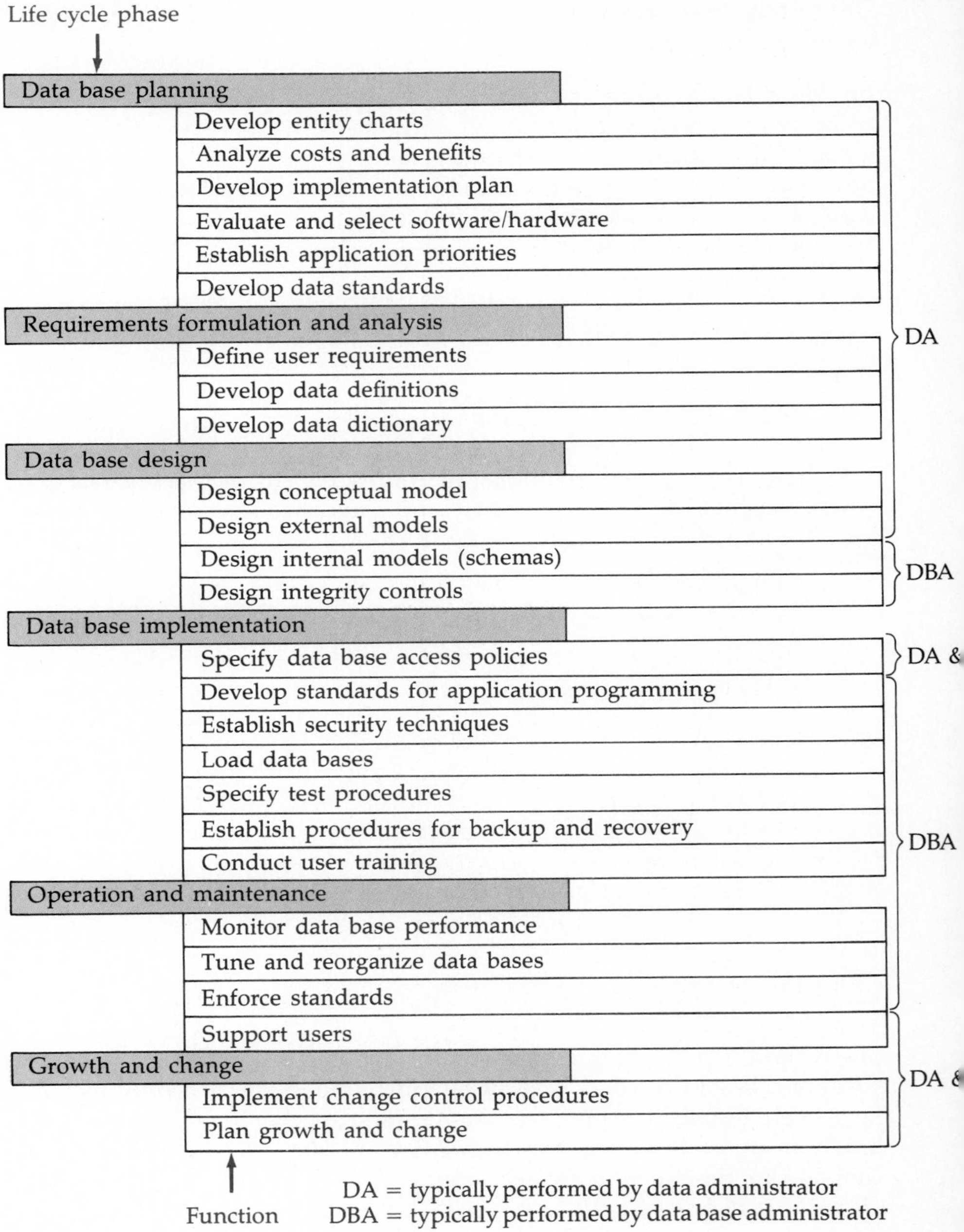
Life cycle phase
Data base planning
Develop entity charts
Analyze costs and benefits
Develop implementation plan
Evaluate and select software/hardware
Establish application priorities
Develop data standards
Requirements formulation and analysis
Define user requirements
Develop data definitions
Develop data dictionary
Data base design
Design conceptual model
Design external models
Design internal models (schemas)
Design integrity controls
Data base implementation
Specify data base access policies
Develop standards for application programming
Establish security techniques
Load data bases
Specify test procedures
Establish procedures for backup and recovery
Conduct user training
Operation and maintenance
Monitor data base performance
Tune and reorganize data bases
Enforce standards
Support users
Growth and change
Implement change control procedures
Plan growth and change
DA
DBA
DA &
DBA
DA &
Function
DA = typically performed by data administrator
DBA = typically performed by data base administrator

1. Develop entity charts.
2. Analyze costs and benefits.
3. Develop implementation plan.
4. Evaluate and select software and hardware.
5. Establish application priorities.
6. Develop data standards.

All of these activities were described in Chapter 3, except for analyzing costs and benefits and developing data standards. The DBA should help users analyze the prospective costs and benefits of a data base system. Although many of the benefits may seem intangible, they should be quantified as much as possible. These estimates provide a baseline for evaluating performance as data base implementation proceeds.

A DBA should also establish data standards, especially naming conventions and standard definitions for key data entities. Without such standards, users of the data base may not realize what data exist or the true meaning of data attributes and entities. For example, the entity Customer must be defined to clearly indicate if it includes prospective and/or prior and no longer active purchasers of products and services. Failure to produce such standards will mean that data base management technology is used simply as an advanced file access method, and the benefits of a shared data base will not be achieved.

A list of some of the important costs and benefits of data bases is presented in Table 10-1. The costs are divided into nonrecurring (one-time) and recurring costs and include hardware, software, and personnel additions. The benefits are divided into cost reduction (or avoidance) and value enhancement. The latter category is more difficult to quantify, since it includes improved resource utilization, more timely reports, and improved decision making.

Requirements Formulation and Analysis

We described the process of requirements formulation and analysis in Chapter 7. This is the period of greatest interaction between data base administration and user groups. As shown in Figure 10-2, here are the major functions performed by the DBA group during this stage:

1. Define user requirements.
2. Develop data definitions.
3. Develop data dictionary.

The result of requirements formulation and analysis is a complete set of data definitions that are recorded in the data dictionary.

Table 10-1 Major Costs and Benefits of Data Bases

Data base costs	
Nonrecurring:	Recurring:
Data base software	Personnel costs (DBA)
Hardware	Software lease, maintenance
Data communications equipment	Hardware lease, maintenance
Site and facility	Travel and training
Travel and training	Supplies and utilities
Data conversion	Support services
Studies (analysis, design)	Overhead
Data base benefits	
Cost reduction/avoidance:	Value enhancement:
Reduced program maintenance	Improved resource utilization
Reduced error rates	More timely reports
Reduced loss/fraud	Improved data accessibility
Reduced data storage and maintenance processing	Improved decision making
Reduced operating costs	Easier data definition change control
Reduced data documentation costs	

Data Base Design

As noted in Figure 10-2, data base design consists of four major phases: conceptual design, external design, internal design, and integrity control design. Data base administration is responsible for managing these four phases of the design cycle. Conceptual and external design are concerned with modeling the organization's data; therefore, during these phases, there is heavy interaction between the DBA group and users throughout the organization. Internal and integrity control design are DBMS-dependent, so that there is less interaction with users. However, during these phases DBA personnel may interact with other system specialists in the data processing organization.

Data Base Implementation

As shown in Figure 10-2, data base administration is responsible for implementing data bases and must perform a number of significant functions in supporting this phase of the life cycle.

Specifying Data Base Access Policies In implementing a data base, previously independent application files are consolidated into a corporate data base. Data base administration does not own these data, but instead acts as a custodian. The DBA must determine the rights and duties of the user community concerning use of the data base. For example, some users are responsible for updating certain data, while other users may only be allowed to access (but not update) the data. Still other users may not be permitted to access the same data. In general, the DBA should allocate to users only those rights that are necessary to satisfy their responsibilities.

Developing Standards for Application Programming A data base management system provides a number of new facilities, such as high-level languages, application development systems, and security mechanisms. If properly used, these facilities can greatly improve the productivity of application programmers. Data base administration must develop and enforce programming standards to ensure that these facilities are used consistently and correctly.

Establishing Security Techniques Since data are shared by many users, a data base tends to increase the vulnerability of data to improper use. Data base administration is responsible for developing adequate security measures, such as passwords, access tables, and encryption facilities. We describe such security techniques in Chapter 11.

Loading Data Bases Initial loading of a data base requires significant computer resources, including processor time, input/output channels, and disk storage units. Also, people are required to supervise, reconcile, and verify the process. Careful planning of these resources is required to minimize disruptions to normal operations. A schedule for data base loading must be worked out between DBA and computer operations. The data base load program must provide for checkpoints from which restarts can occur. Elapsed time is minimized by eliminating all unnecessary operator intervention such as disk mounts and dismounts. Finally, audits (random samples) of the newly created data base should be made to verify the loading process.

In most cases, creating a data base involves combining data from a number of existing master files. Frequently, special application programs must be written to extract data from relevant files and load the data into data base records. Since the same data often exist in multiple files maintained by different users, inconsistencies in the data element values are bound to exist. For example, an employee may be listed as having two different addresses in two separate files. Data base administration must anticipate and reconcile such inconsistencies.

Specifying Test Procedures New application programs must be carefully tested before they are allowed to go on-line with a data base. The DBA group is responsible for establishing policies concerning test procedures, coordinating with application programmers, end users, and operations personnel in carrying out these tests.

Establishing Procedures for Backup and Recovery As custodian of corporate data, data base administration is responsible for establishing procedures for data base backup and recovery. These procedures include transaction logs, backup copies of the data base, and recovery mechanisms. We describe backup and recovery in detail in Chapter 11.

Conducting User Training An important function of data base administration is to provide training in using the data base system to various user groups such as managers, other end users, and systems personnel. The DBA group should evaluate the training needs of these various user groups and should then schedule vendor-conducted training courses or conduct on-site training, as appropriate.

Operation and Maintenance

During the operation and maintenance phase, DBA functions center on monitoring, control, and user support. As shown in Figure 10-2, the DBA group monitors data base performance and responds to user complaints or suggestions. If necessary, the DBA "tunes" or reorganizes the data base for improved performance. Also, the DBA group performs a quality assurance function in checking that standards and procedures are being enforced. Finally, the DBA group actively seeks out ways to support users, for example, by suggesting new data base applications.

Growth and Change

Three major types of change may occur with data bases:

1. Change in size: addition of more data of the kind already contained in the data base (e.g., adding student records as the number of students increases).
2. Change in content or structure: adding new data types or data relationships through the implementation of new applications (e.g., implementing a new purchasing application might require adding a new VENDOR record type or association).
3. Change in usage pattern: changes in the relative frequency of accessing a particular record type or combinations of record types (e.g., a sudden increase in the frequency of access to ARREST records in a criminal justice data base).

These three major types of growth and change in a data base are managed by two DBA functions (see Figure 10-2) that implement procedures to recognize, plan, monitor, and control such dynamics. Methods available to a DBA for detecting change and determining the proper response to change are enumerated by Lyon (1976). In brief, these include the following.

Table 10-2 Responses to Data Base Change and Growth

Type of change	Method of detection	Possible response(s)
Size	Analysis of space utilization	Additional space allocation; space reallocation
Content/structure	New application requests	Altering logical and physical structure
Usage pattern	Performance monitoring	Reorganization; altering access methods; new hardware

Changes in Size Changes in size are detected by analyses of storage space utilization. Most data base management systems include a facility for measuring space utilization. Also, as space utilization increases, performance often tends to decrease. Two measures are available to the DBA to accommodate growth: allocation of additional space (e.g., more cylinders on a disk volume) and reallocation of existing space (requires an unload and reload of the data base).

Changes in Structures Changes in content and/or structure result from requests for new applications that cannot be met by the existing data base. The DBA must consult the data dictionary to verify that the required data are not available. Assuming that the request is to be satisfied, the response is to alter both the logical and physical data base structures. Hopefully, this type of change will be minimized by careful data base planning. However, the DBA must be open to change, since change reflects the normal dynamic growth of the organization. In any event, the impact of such changes will be minimized if the DBMS provides a strong measure of data independence.

Changes in Usage Patterns Changes in usage patterns are detected by a performance-monitoring system or (in its absence) by degraded performance. For example, average terminal response times may increase from 2 seconds to 2 minutes (or more!). Several responses are available.

Reorganization—that is, altering the physical characteristics of the data base—is one possible response. Examples include reassigning frequently accessed records to faster devices, changing the relative placement (or clustering) of records, and altering the content of records. Reorganization normally requires that the data base (or a portion of it) be unloaded and then reloaded.

Altering the access methods is another possible response—for example, changing from a sequential organization to a random organization. This process usually requires unloading and reloading the data base.

If the first two techniques do not improve performance, it may be necessary to resort to a third response, that of providing additional, higher-performance hardware devices (disk drives, controllers, and so on).

Performance in a data base environment is a joint responsibility. Data base administration must work with computer operations, systems programmers, and users to seek ways to improve performance.

INTERFACES OF DATA BASE ADMINISTRATION

Data base administration can be a highly political function that requires superb interpersonal skills in each data base administrator (DBA) in the group. A DBA lives between various groups that can, and frequently do, have conflicting views and expectations. A DBA must be able to retain credibility with each of these groups and be able to deal with a variety of issues from diverse interests. Additional insight into the functions of data base administration can be gained by studying the interfaces between DBA and other major groups in the enterprise. As shown in Figure 10-3, data base administration interfaces with four major groups: management, users, applications development, and operations.

Communications with Management

Data base administration has a number of important communications with top management. If the data resource management concept is in practice, the data base administrator may well be a top manager, or at least will report to a top manager.

Management communicates to the DBA function a continuing commitment to the data resource management concept. Hopefully, this includes the necessary budgetary support. Also, management communicates its business plans, goals, priorities, and constraints, which are the basis for data base planning. If there are any major contingencies, such as a reorganization or acquisition, these must also be communicated to the DBA.

The DBA, in turn, communicates to management its budget requirements and data base plans and schedules. The DBA should provide frequent status reports concerning data base projects. Often, the DBA is responsible for performing cost/benefit analyses of specific proposals.

One way for data base administration to sustain top management support is to show these managers how they can use the data base system to improve their own decision making. The DBA should make recommendations to management concerning the use of high-level query languages, graphic displays, simulation modeling, and other areas of decision support.

The DBA and management also jointly have responsibility for developing and maintaining the enterprise information model (see Chapter 3) and for developing plans for data base evolution and technology acquisition. The data base plan is typically part of a total MIS plan, so the DBA function works closely with both general and MIS senior management. Today, strategic systems planning methods include strategic data planning

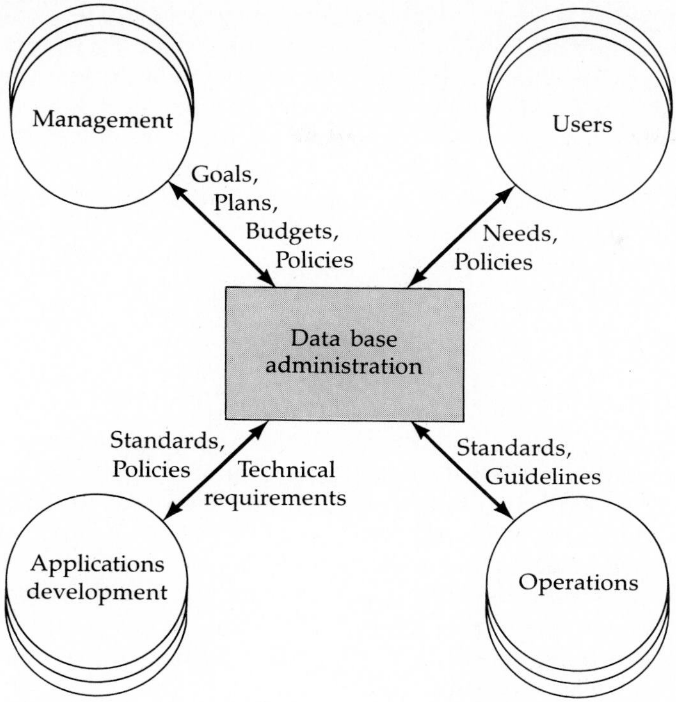

Figure 10-3
Major interfaces of data base administration

components. Many organizations establish the DBA function because long-range systems planning clearly indicates the need for a data management function to handle data and information in the same way other organizational resources are administered. Thus, the DBA has much to *learn* from general management, in order to acquire, plan, account for, secure, dispose, inventory, and so on the data resource as well as other resource managers undertake their responsibilities.

Communications with Users

The term *users* is a generic term, referring to any person in the organization who uses the data base. Thus, users may be managers (at any level), clerical personnel, shop workers, or computer personnel. The DBA provides users with the information they require to maintain and protect the data base and to develop new applications. This information includes data definitions, data relationships, and other information stored in the data dictionary. However, the DBA does not provide users with a "hard-copy" listing of the complete data dictionary—only that portion for which there is a "need to know."

One of the many advantages of the data dictionary is the ability to perform impact studies. This is the ability to show the impact that a data base change will have on programs and data processing (e.g., the change by the Postal Service from a five-digit to a nine-digit zip code). The DBA also consults with users regarding education and training needs, new applications, and methods for improving performance.

During the requirements analysis stage, users provide the DBA with their data requirements—data element descriptions, user views, priorities, access limitations, frequency of updating, and so on. Also, users must keep data base administration informed of possible future data base applications and changes in business practices and policies that necessitate changes in entity relationships.

Communications with Applications Development

The applications development group includes the analysts and programmers who are responsible for developing user application programs. Data base administration must develop and enforce standards for programs that interface with the data base. These standards include programming techniques, program documentation, and quality assurance. For example, a portion of the standards should address what data manipulation language commands must be used (or are recommended) to access and manipulate the data base. These standards are necessary both to protect the data base and for performance reasons.

For each new application program, the DBA provides the application designer with the controls required by the user. At the same time, the DBA keeps users informed about the data base itself, as well as providing documentation concerning the DBMS as needed.

Applications development provides the DBA with the required application view of data for each new program. Applications development also keeps the DBA informed of priorities and schedules, as well as the status of projects.

It is important that each new application program be carefully tested with test data before an attempt is made to interface it with the "live" data base. The application specialist must communicate the test plan to the DBA, and the two groups must work together to ensure that an adequate plan is developed.

Communications with Operations

Computer operations is concerned with the physical aspects of data processing—hardware operations, shift scheduling, security, tape and disk library, and so on. Operations is also concerned with the operating system and is often assigned technical support (systems programmers) to maintain this software.

Data base administration must provide operations with schedules and standard operating procedures for routine operations, such as updating, backup, and archiving. The DBA also provides operations with standard procedures for protecting the data base and for recovering from errors or abnormal conditions. It should be noted that these are not one-way communications between the DBA and operations; many of the issues must be worked on and resolved jointly. However, the DBA is responsible for the final results.

Operations provides the DBA with standard reports concerning data base usage, system performance, and any errors or problems encountered. Also, operations should provide periodic verification that the standard procedures are being implemented.

USING THE DATA DICTIONARY/DIRECTORY SYSTEM

The data dictionary/directory system (DD/DS) is an essential tool for data base administration and it is used by the data base administrator throughout the entire data base system life cycle. In this section, we describe how the DD/DS is used to support the various activities during this life cycle.

A **data dictionary** is an organized description or inventory of the data resource of an organization. A **DD/DS** is a software system that manages the data dictionary as a data base. Thus, a DD/DS is like a DBMS for metadata, or data about data. A DD/DS provides methods to enter data dictionary (DD) contents, update contents, and report and provide access to the DD in a variety of ways. A DD/DS is essential for proper data resource management. According to Wertz:

> If the people who will be using the system (data base) and the analysts and the programmers don't all share a common understanding of the data, the system (data base) may never work correctly. (1986, 52)

Since a DD/DS is a DBMS for data definitions, Chapter 11 provides extensive coverage of the contents and operation of a DD/DS. We will skip over many of the finer points of a DD/DS in this chapter and concentrate simply on its use in the DBA function.

The uses of the DD/DS during each stage of the life cycle are shown in Figure 10-4. There are four major types of usage:

1. Documentation support: recording, classifying, and reporting metadata
2. Design aid: documenting the relationships between data entities and performing impact analyses
3. Metadata generation: generating metadata in formats required by other software components of the data management system (such as DBMS and application programs)

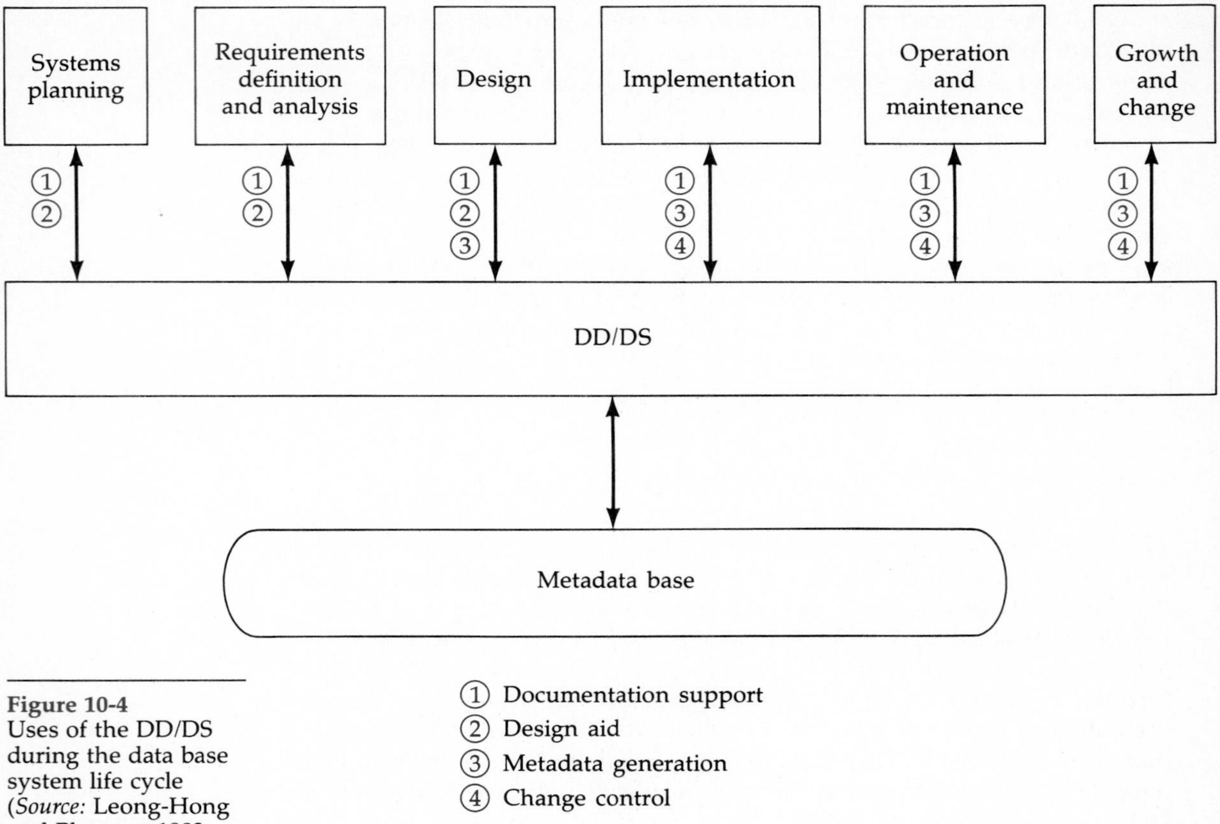

Figure 10-4
Uses of the DD/DS during the data base system life cycle (*Source:* Leong-Hong and Plagman 1982. Adapted with permission.)

4. Change control: enforcing standards, evaluating the impact of proposed changes, and implementing changes (such as adding new attributes or record types)

Use During System Planning

The DD/DS should be used to document the various "products" of data base planning, described in Chapter 3. These products include the business functions, processes, activities, entities, and transactions of the organization. As each of these objects is defined and described, it should be recorded in the DD/DS.

The DD/DS should also be used as a high-level design aid during data base planning. As described in Chapter 3, one of the major objectives of this phase is to develop a strategic data model or entity chart, such as the one for Mountain View Hospital shown in Figure 3-12. The DD/DS is used to document the associations among the entities and also may be used to map other associations, such as the relationships between transactions and business activities.

Use During Requirements Formulation and Analysis

During requirements formulation and analysis, analysts collect detailed information from users concerning existing and future uses of data. Data items are defined and described. Also described are existing documents, reports, displays, and other user views of data. All the data are associated with the business functions and activities that require their use. Thus, a vast amount of detailed metadata is collected and analyzed during requirements formulation and analysis. As shown in Figure 10-4, the DD/DS is used as a documentation tool and design aid during this phase.

Use During Design

Data base design consists of three phases: conceptual design, implementation design, and physical design. For each data base, the design effort results in a logical and physical design that can be implemented on a target data base management system. The DD/DS is used as a design aid and as a tool to document the logical and physical designs. The DD/DS is also used to generate metadata such as DBMS control blocks or COBOL file descriptions. Finally, the DD/DS can be used to generate user manuals and other forms of documentation.

Use During Implementation

During implementation, the data base is initially loaded and tested. New application programs for loading and updating the data base are also developed and tested. The DD/DS is used during this phase for documentation support, metadata generation, and change control.

The DD/DS is used to produce documentation for all users during implementation. For example, programmers require descriptions of data elements, record types, and other metadata in developing application programs. The DBA uses the DD/DS to resolve inconsistencies (such as synonyms and homonyms or conflicting data types) when loading the data base. Also, the DD/DS is used to enforce standards during implementation. For example, editing criteria and security locks or other mechanisms should be incorporated in the DD/DS. In addition, the DD/DS can be used to generate test data that are used to test various system components during implementation.

Use During Operation and Maintenance

The operation and maintenance phase represents the ongoing updating, operation, and maintenance of the data base. The DD/DS is the basic tool used by the DBA for documentation and control during this phase. For example, the DD/DS is used to enforce standards for security, data integrity, and backup and recovery. Also, the DD/DS is used to collect usage statistics and may be used as the basis for data base auditing and control.

Use During Growth and Change

During the last phase of the life cycle, the DBA monitors the usage and performance of the data base and plans for growth and change. Again, the DD/DS is the primary tool that supports these activities. For example, it can be used for **impact analysis,** determining the impact of a proposed change such as adding a new data item type, record type, or association. In addition, the DD/DS is used to analyze and record changes in business functions, processes, activities, and entities—thus completing the system life cycle.

ORGANIZING THE DBA FUNCTION

This section addresses three key management issues that arise in organizing the DBA function. The means by which top management resolves these issues is a good indication of their acceptance of data resource management. The three issues are initiating the DBA function, selecting the data base administrator, and placing the DBA function into the organization (including decentralized and other types of structures).

Initiating the DBA Function

The DBA function and its primary tool, the DD/DS, are often viewed as extraneous and unessential to data management, yet nothing could be further from the truth. DBA produces valuable results, but often, to those anxious to have access to data, its role seems to bottleneck or be an extra step in that process. A DBA function is developed over several years and usually evolves from a systems planning or project management function.

Wherever the DBA function obtains its start, several steps are essential to ensure its success from the beginning. These are:

1. Obtain management support for and commitment to the reason for the existence of the function and its role in data base development. This may require conducting a survey of other organizations to identify practical justification for the DBA function. Also essential here is

determining the relationship of the DBA function and any data systems planning group(s).

2. Determine the requirements for a DD/DS and acquire financial support to buy or develop a DD/DS appropriate for the data base environment.
3. Train the DBA staff in data base planning, DD/DS, data base trends, data security and recovery, and other areas in which the staff will be involved.
4. Develop standards of operation (for example, data naming conventions) and measures of performance for DBA staff (for example, meeting project deadlines) so they recognize that their job has professional practices and that their good performance can be identified and rewarded.

Many organizations acquire a DBMS before a DBA function is (formally) established, yet logic would indicate that this puts the cart before the horse (or the resource before the manager). In such an organization, the DBMS is used to implement a series of unrelated applications not using shared data. Thus, expectations for data base management may not be high, and user experience may not be conducive to change. The practical consequence of a situation like this is that the DBA function does not usually start with a clean slate. Data base design practices, data ownership, multiple data bases, multiple or no data dictionaries, and an essentially active but unorganized data management function are very likely to be in place already when the DBA function is started. The first chore then is to convince those with vested interests that methods must be changed. Thus, above all, a DBA is an agent of change that must be sensitive to organizational history, politics, existing technology and systems, and attitudes.

Because of this inertia based on past practices, the DBA function often begins with a new, major application of system planning, and then slowly integrates other data and systems under its management. A phased introduction is almost always the wisest way to start the DBA function.

Selecting the DBA

This chapter is essentially an extended job description for the position of data base administrator. A review of the functions of the DBA (see Figure 10-2) indicates that the DBA must possess an unusual collection of managerial, analytical, and technical skills. However, in reviewing the full range of responsibilities, it is apparent that the job is more managerial than technical. The DBA must perform the following typical managerial functions:

1. Planning: developing a comprehensive plan for the organization's data resource
2. Organizing: organizing and staffing the DBA function

3. Supervising: supervising the DBA staff
4. Communicating: communicating with managers, users, and computer specialists
5. Controlling: developing procedural controls for maintaining and protecting the data resource

Thus, the organization should define the data base administrator position as a management position. The ideal candidate is a person with at least middle management experience (line or staff), a broad knowledge and a "sense" of the enterprise (including its politics), and stature as a manager. Such a person requires some familiarity with computer-based information systems, but does not have to be a computer or data base expert.

Other candidates for the DBA position might include business analysts, user-oriented systems analysts, or a DBA with relevant experience in another, similar organization. However, a manager with experience in the enterprise is usually preferred.

Highly technical computer specialists such as system programmers are not usually good candidates for data base administrator. Selecting such persons normally results from an overly narrow, technical definition of the DBA position. Most of these individuals do not have the managerial experience, aptitude, or desire to be a data base administrator. However, computer specialists might be assigned to the DBA staff.

Placing the DBA Function

In most organizations today, the DBA function is placed within the information systems organization. Where the DBA function is placed within the MIS organization varies from one firm to another, depending on the role and tasks assigned to data base administration. Weldon (1981) has identified four common locations within MIS for the DBA function. These locations (shown in Figure 10-5) are described by their orientation (project or functional) and by the nature of the DBA role (advisory, support, or managerial).

Advisory DBA The advisory DBA is a small staff group (one or more persons) that reports directly to the MIS manager (Figure 10-5a). The functions of the advisory DBA are generally limited to planning, research, and policy formulation. The advisory DBA may be used during the early planning stages for a data base approach. Once a DBMS has been introduced, this organization is usually replaced by one of the other forms described here.

Functional-Support DBA The functional-support DBA reports to the manager of support services (Figure 10-5b). The DBA's services are available in a supporting role to all project groups, as needed. This organizational approach is generally not effective, since the DBA has no real input on application priorities or control over the data base.

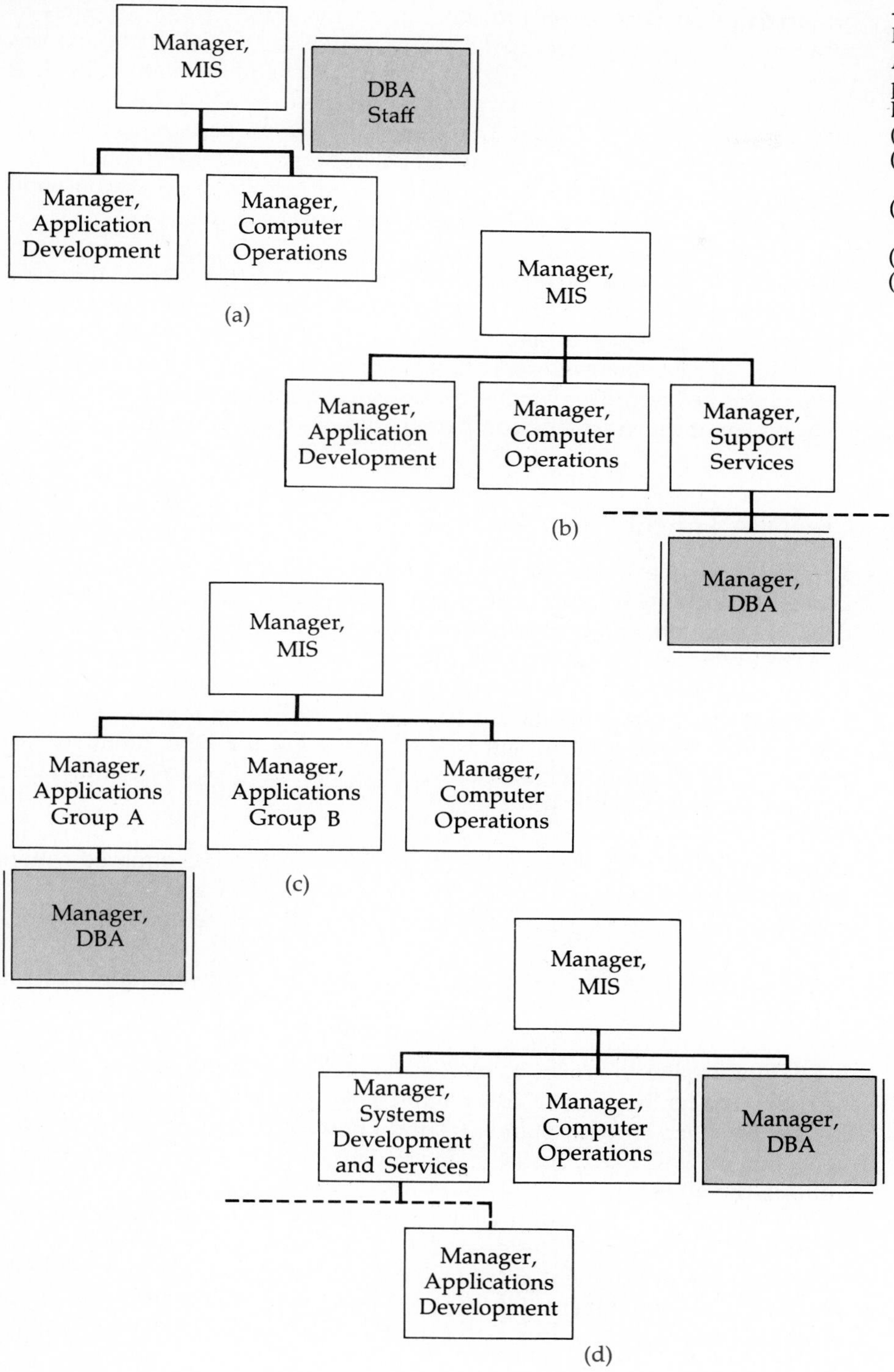

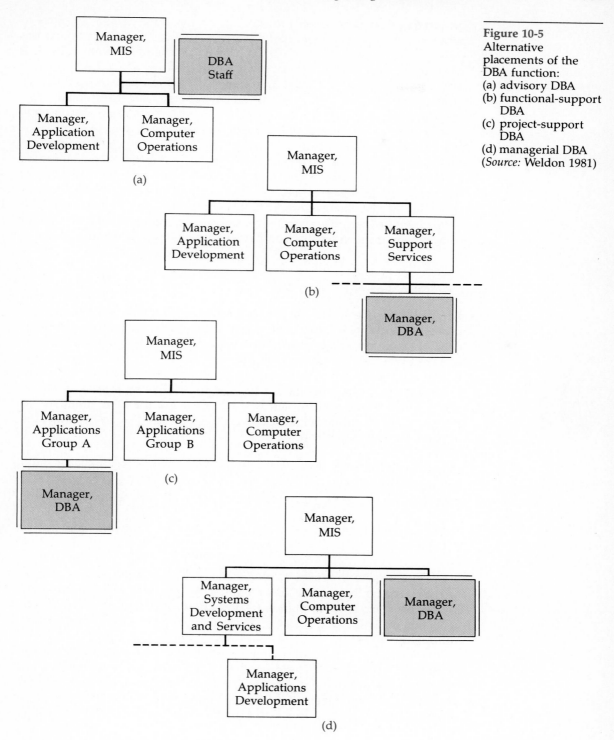

Figure 10-5 Alternative placements of the DBA function:
(a) advisory DBA
(b) functional-support DBA
(c) project-support DBA
(d) managerial DBA
(*Source:* Weldon 1981)

Figure 10-6
DBA organizations in a decentralized environment:
(a) centralized DBA
(b) decentralized DBA
(c) partially decentralized DBA
(*Source:* Weldon 1981)

Project-Support DBA The project-support DBA organization reports to an applications project manager (see Figure 10-5c). The DBA supports the project team by performing data base design tasks and by supporting data base operation and control. In large organizations that follow this approach, it is not unusual to find more than one DBA group, each reporting to a different project team. This organizational approach is generally not effective, since the DBA group should be concerned with an organization-wide view of data, rather than a single application area.

Managerial DBA The managerial DBA reports directly to the MIS manager and is located higher in the organization than project managers (see Figure 10-5d). In this position, the DBA is able to promulgate and enforce standards for system development and data control. The management DBA is the preferred approach among those described here, since it represents a strong commitment by the company to a data base approach.

The DBA Function in a Decentralized Organization

An advantage of establishing the DBA function is that numerous data management functions become centralized. Tasks such as data base planning, design, operation, and control (which were previously fragmented) are centralized under the DBA. However, this may lead to conflict in organizations where data processing is originally decentralized. Fortunately, several organizational arrangements can be used to resolve (or at least minimize) this conflict. Three typical methods of organizing the DBA function in a decentralized environment are shown in Figure 10-6 [for an extended discussion see Weldon (1981)].

Centralized DBA With this approach, the DBA function is centralized within corporate systems (Figure 10-6a). The centralized DBA acts in a support, advisory, or managerial role to decentralized system development groups.

Decentralized DBA In organizations where all hardware and system development activities are decentralized, decentralized DBA groups may be formed as needed within each organization (see Figure 10-6b). If there is a corporate system group, a DBA liaison may be established to coordinate activities among the several DBA groups. This approach promotes the move toward organizationwide standards and knowledge sharing. Lack of such coordination will likely result in incompatible systems and much "reinventing the wheel."

One technique for improving compatibility and avoiding excessive duplication of effort is to designate one of the sites as a "pilot project." As the data base development projects at the pilot site are completed, relevant portions may be transferred to the remaining sites. Also, DBA personnel at the pilot site may act as consultants to the other decentralized DBA groups.

(a)

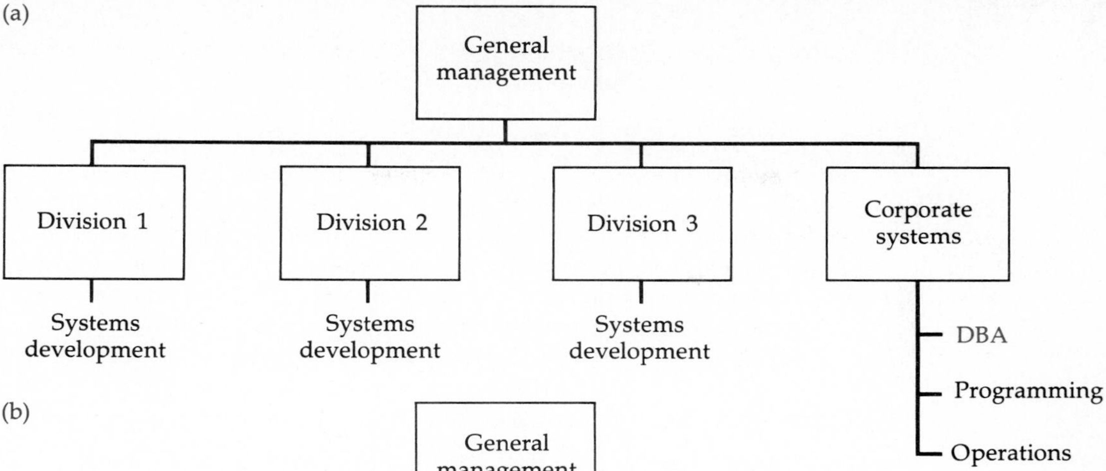
General management
Division 1
Division 2
Division 3
Corporate systems
Systems development
Systems development
Systems development
DBA
Programming
Operations

(b)

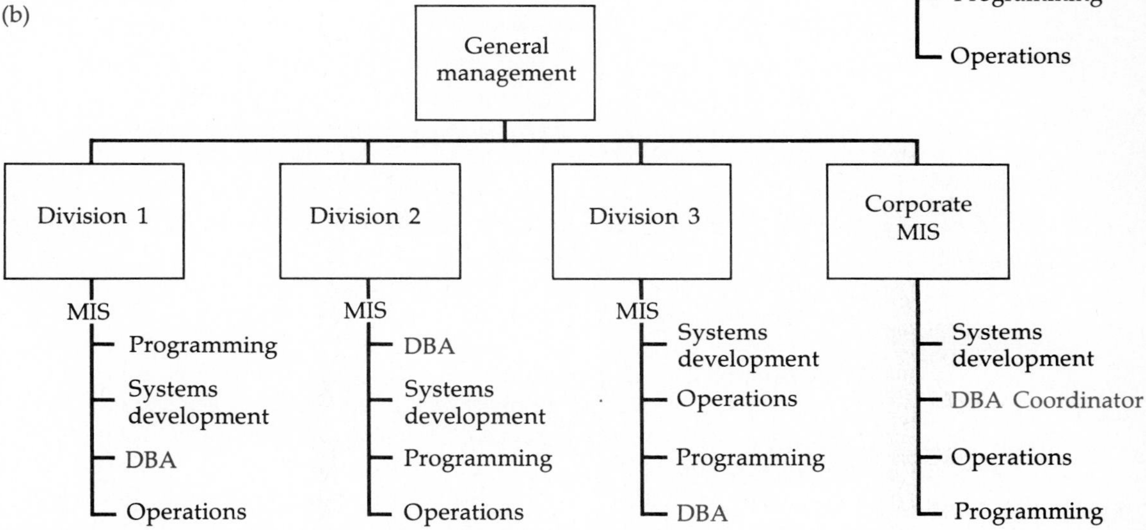
General management
Division 1
Division 2
Division 3
Corporate MIS
MIS
Programming
Systems development
DBA
Operations
MIS
DBA
Systems development
Programming
Operations
MIS
Systems development
Operations
Programming
DBA
Systems development
DBA Coordinator
Operations
Programming

(c)

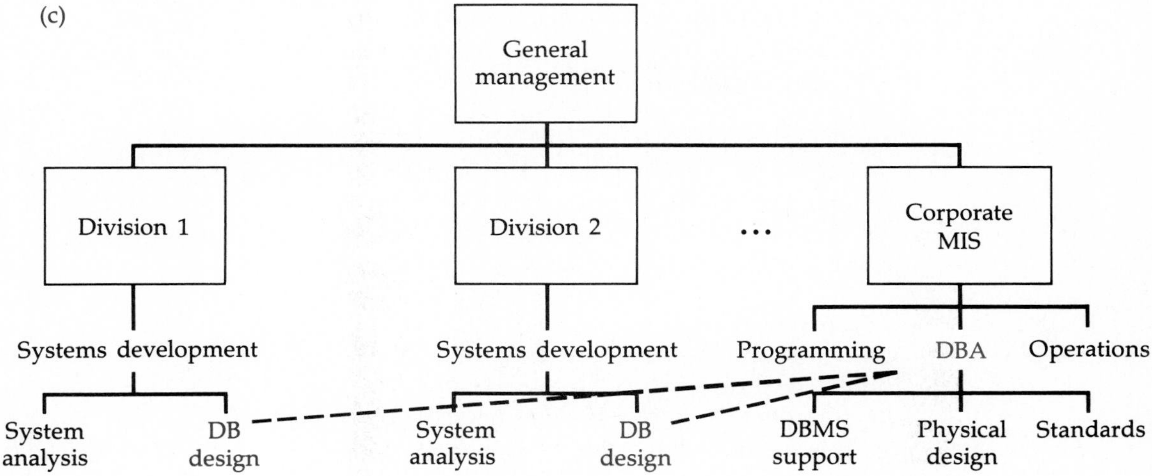
General management
Division 1
Division 2
...
Corporate MIS
Systems development
Systems development
Programming
DBA
Operations
System analysis
DB design
System analysis
DB design
DBMS support
Physical design
Standards

However, overall progress is likely to be slow, and there is no assurance that the resulting systems will be compatible.

Partially Decentralized DBA With this approach, the central DBA staff is partitioned and assigned, as needed, to local organizations. Typically, technical DBA staff (such as DBMS support) remain at the central location. Data base designers are separated and report to local operations managers, with a dotted-line responsibility to the DBA manager (see Figure 10-6c). This alternative is a compromise between the preceding approaches and provides a good balance between flexibility and control.

Types of DBA Organizations

The DBA group can be organized along functional or project lines. Weldon (1981) has described a number of alternative organizations for the DBA function. Four typical organizations are shown in Figure 10-7.

Flat DBA Organization The flat DBA organization (shown in Figure 10-7a) is typically used in the early stages of DBA development. The organization consists of a few individuals who report directly to the DBA manager. These individuals share the specialized tasks required, such as logical design, physical design, and data dictionary maintenance.

Functional DBA Organization As the DBA group becomes larger, it is necessary to organize along functional lines. A typical organization is shown in Figure 10-7b, where there are three functional groups: DB design, data dictionary, and DB operation and control. Each of these groups is headed by a manager who reports to the DBA manager. Data base planning tasks are either assumed by the DBA manager, or (as shown) a separate planning function may be established, as needed.

Project-Oriented DBA With a project-oriented DBA, the DB designers are assigned to individual applications or project areas (Figure 10-7c). Other support groups (such as DBMS and data dictionary) continue to report directly to the DBA manager. This approach allows data base designers to become thoroughly familiar with the requirements of a given area. However, it tends to discourage integration among the various areas and, as a result, is generally dysfunctional.

Matrix Organization In a matrix DBA organization, certain DBA tasks (such as design and support) are assigned to groups outside the DBA organization. These groups could be system development project groups, end user organizations, or even computer operations (see Figure 10-7d). The assigned groups maintain a dotted-line (indirect) reporting relationship to the DBA manager.

A matrix organization for the DBA function provides the advantage of

Figure 10-7
Typical internal DBA organizations:
(a) flat DBA
(b) functional DBA
(c) project-oriented DBA
(d) DBA with matrix
(*Source:* Weldon 1981)

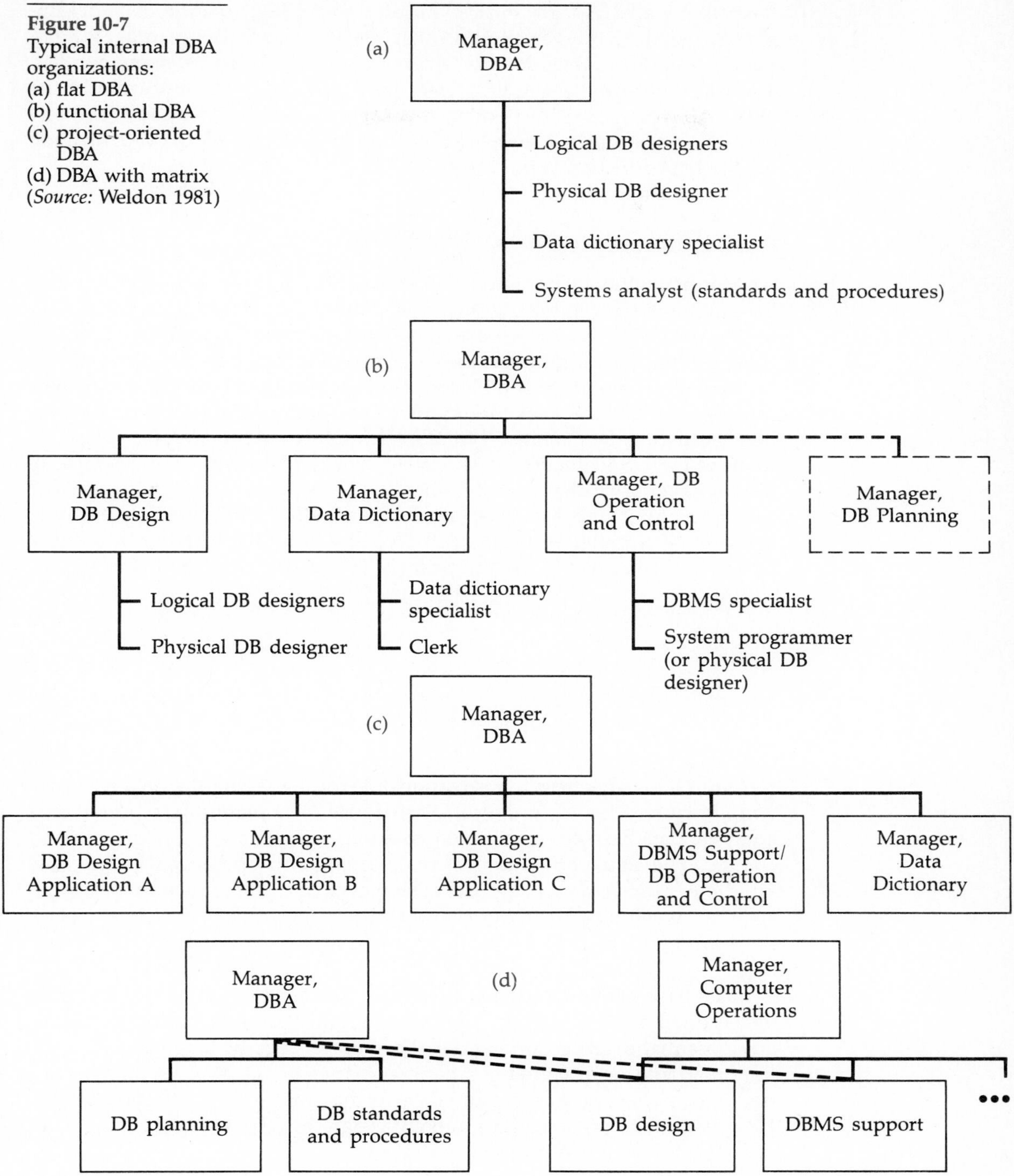

flexibility: Data base administration can easily adapt to immediate organizational needs. However, there are also two important disadvantages. First, the dual reporting relationship becomes a source of confusion and conflict. Second, the power of the DBA manager is eroded, since a portion of the DBA staff reports directly to other managers. Unless the company routinely (and effectively) uses a matrix form of organization, a matrix organization for the DBA function should be avoided.

Case Example

At Mountain View Community Hospital, Mr. Helms was appointed data base administrator following the initial planning study (described in Chapter 3). Mr. Helms is a systems analyst who is a new employee at Mountain View Community, but he has previous experience in data base design.

Mr. Helms reports to Mr. Heller, who is manager of information systems (an organization chart for Mountain View Community is shown in Figure 3-8). In turn, a data analyst (Mrs. Green) reports to Mr. Helms. The placement of the DBA function at Mountain View Community is an example of the managerial DBA approach, since the DBA reports directly to the MIS manager, along with two other project managers. As the data base becomes operational, another employee will probably be added to data base administration. However, a flat organization is likely to be used for the foreseeable future.

SUMMARY

Data base administration is essential to managing the organization's data resource. The DBA function is responsible for managing the data base system life cycle. This life cycle consists of data base planning, requirements analysis, data base design, implementation, maintenance, and growth and change. The actual operations of maintaining and updating the data base are the responsibility of the users. However, the DBA function is responsible for developing procedures and controls that ensure that these operations are performed so as to protect the integrity and security of the data base.

Data base administration is a resource management function. It should be assigned at a sufficiently high level within the organization to resolve any potential disputes among data base users. Ideally, data base administration should be assigned at a general management level, to an administrative or executive vice-president or to the chief executive officer's staff. However, many organizations initially assign the DBA to report to the manager of information systems.

The manager of data base administration (or data base administrator) should be defined as a management (rather than technical) position. The person selected for this position should have significant management experience within the enterprise. The DBA staff can then be filled out with the necessary technical skills appropriate to the maturity of the DBA function.

Chapter Review

REVIEW QUESTIONS

1. Contrast data administration, data base administration, and data stewardship.
2. List and briefly describe six stages in the data base system life cycle.
3. What are the four major interfaces of data base administration? Summarize the major types of communications with each of these groups.
4. Describe four ways the DBA could use the data dictionary/directory system.
5. Describe four typical placements (or locations) of the DBA function in actual organizations. Which placement is preferred?
6. Describe three basic types of changes that occur with data bases, and describe the responses available to DBA.
7. a. Where should data base administration be assigned when the function is first created?
   b. Where should it be assigned as the DBA function evolves?
8. Describe four alternative organizations for the DBA function.

PROBLEMS AND EXERCISES

1. Match the following terms with the most appropriate definitions:

_____ data naming convention	**a.** software for maintaining and reporting data definitions
_____ data steward	**b.** responsible for computer data bases
_____ data base administrator	**c.** determining the effect on data base of proposed data definition changes
_____ data administrator	**d.** standards for assigning names to entities, data elements, and other pieces of data
_____ data dictionary	**e.** responsibility for specific logical data entity
_____ DD/DS	**f.** evolutionary phases in life of a data base
_____ data base system life cycle	**g.** metadata
_____ impact analysis	**h.** overall data resource management responsibility

2. Customcraft, Inc., is a mail-order firm specializing in the manufacture of stationery and other paper products. Annual sales of Customcraft are $25 million and are growing at a rate of 15% per year. After several years' experience with conventional data processing systems, Customcraft has decided to organize a data base administration function. At present, they have four major candidates for the data base administrator position:

   - John Bach, a senior systems analyst with three years' experience at Customcraft who has attended recent seminars in structured systems design and data base.
   - Margaret Smith, who has been production control manager for the past two years after a year's experience as programmer/analyst at Customcraft.
   - William Rogers, a systems programmer with extensive experience with TOTAL and ADABAS, the two data base management systems under consideration at Customcraft.
   - Ellen Reddy, who is currently data base administrator with a medium-sized electronics firm in the same city as Customcraft.

   Based on this limited information, rank the four candidates for the DBA position, and state your reasons.
3. Evaluate the selection and organizational assignment of the data base administrator for Mountain View Community Hospital. Can you suggest a better candidate for the DBA position than the one selected?
4. Visit an organization that has implemented the data base approach. Evaluate each of the following:
   a. The functions performed by data base administration in the organization.
   b. The organizational placement of the DBA function.
   c. The background of the person chosen for data base administrator.
   d. The DBA staff and its functions.
5. List the major costs and benefits of a data base system at Mountain View Community Hospital.
6. List the major costs and benefits of a data base system at Pine Valley Furniture Company.
7. A major electronics firm has its corporate headquarters on the East Coast, and manufacturing plants located throughout the country. Each plant has its own computer and data processing organization. Describe three alternative ways for organizing the DBA function in this company.
8. Since a data dictionary is a data base of metadata, list the major costs and benefits of a DD/DS at Mountain View Community Hospital.

REFERENCES

Boar, Bernard H. 1984. *Application Prototyping*. New York: John Wiley & Sons.

Canning, R. G. 1972. "The 'Data Administrator' Function." *EDP Analyzer* 10 (November): 1–14.

Guide International. 1977. "Establishing the Data Administration Function." Chicago: Guide International.

Herbert, Martin, and Curt Hartog. 1986. "MIS Rates the Issues." *Datamation* (November 15): 79–86.

Leong-Hong, B. W., and Bernard K. Plagman. 1982. *Data Dictionary/Dictionary Systems: Administration, Implementation, and Usage.* New York: Wiley-Interscience.

Lyon, John K. 1976. *The Database Administrator.* New York: Wiley-Interscience.

McFadden, Fred R., and James D. Suver. 1978. "Costs and Benefits of a Data Base System." *Harvard Business Review* 56 (January-February): 131–139.

Perry, William E. 1982. *Evaluating the Cost/Benefits of Data Bases.* Wellesley, Mass.: Q.E.D. Information Sciences, Inc.

Weldon, J. L. 1979a. "The Changing Role of Data Base Administration." Center for Research on Information Systems, New York University.

———. 1979b. "Organizing for Data Base Administration." Center for Research on Information Systems, New York University.

———. 1981. *Data Base Administration.* New York: Plenum Press.

Wertz, Charles J. 1986. *The Data Dictionary: Concepts and Uses.* Wellesley, Mass.: Q.E.D. Information Sciences, Inc.

Part IV

Data Base Implementation

Part IV consists of five chapters that describe a number of implementations of data base management systems. These systems are illustrated and compared using common examples.

Chapter 11 introduces data management software. It describes the various components of a modern data management system, including data base management systems, data dictionary/directory systems, teleprocessing monitors, and query languages. Important functions of a data management system are described, including metadata management, security, backup and recovery, and concurrency control.

Chapter 12 describes implementations of the hierarchical data model. Most of the emphasis is placed on IBM's Information Management System, or IMS.

Chapter 13 examines network (or CODASYL) implementation. The various components of CODASYL are described in detail, including the data description language (DDL) and data manipulation language (DML).

Chapter 14 considers several implementations of the relational data model on mainframe computers. Some of the languages described in this chapter are SQL/DS, NOMAD, and QUERY-BY-EXAMPLE. Chapter 15 describes several relational implementations on microcomputers. Systems included in that chapter are dBASE III, R:base 5000, and Oracle.

Chapter 11

Data Management Systems

INTRODUCTION

Choosing the right software for data management is a key ingredient in managing the data resource successfully. In making this choice, the organization should place the highest priority on the productivity of its human resources. These resources take precedence over hardware, whose price and performance are expected to continue to improve dramatically over at least the next decade. Many progressive organizations today are selecting software products that allow end users to take greater responsibility in creating and managing their own data. The "information center" concept, whereby users do their own computing, portends the future.

We describe the major components of data management software in this chapter. Desirable features of these components are noted, and the interrelationships among the components are described. More detailed descriptions of individual products are presented in the following chapters.

DATA MANAGEMENT SOFTWARE COMPONENTS

Figure 11-1 shows the software components in Cullinet Software's integrated data management system. The architecture of this system is similar to that of other vendors of integrated systems. Cullinet Software's family of products is organized into several major categories:

Figure 11-1
Integrated Data Management System (*Source:* Cullinet Software)

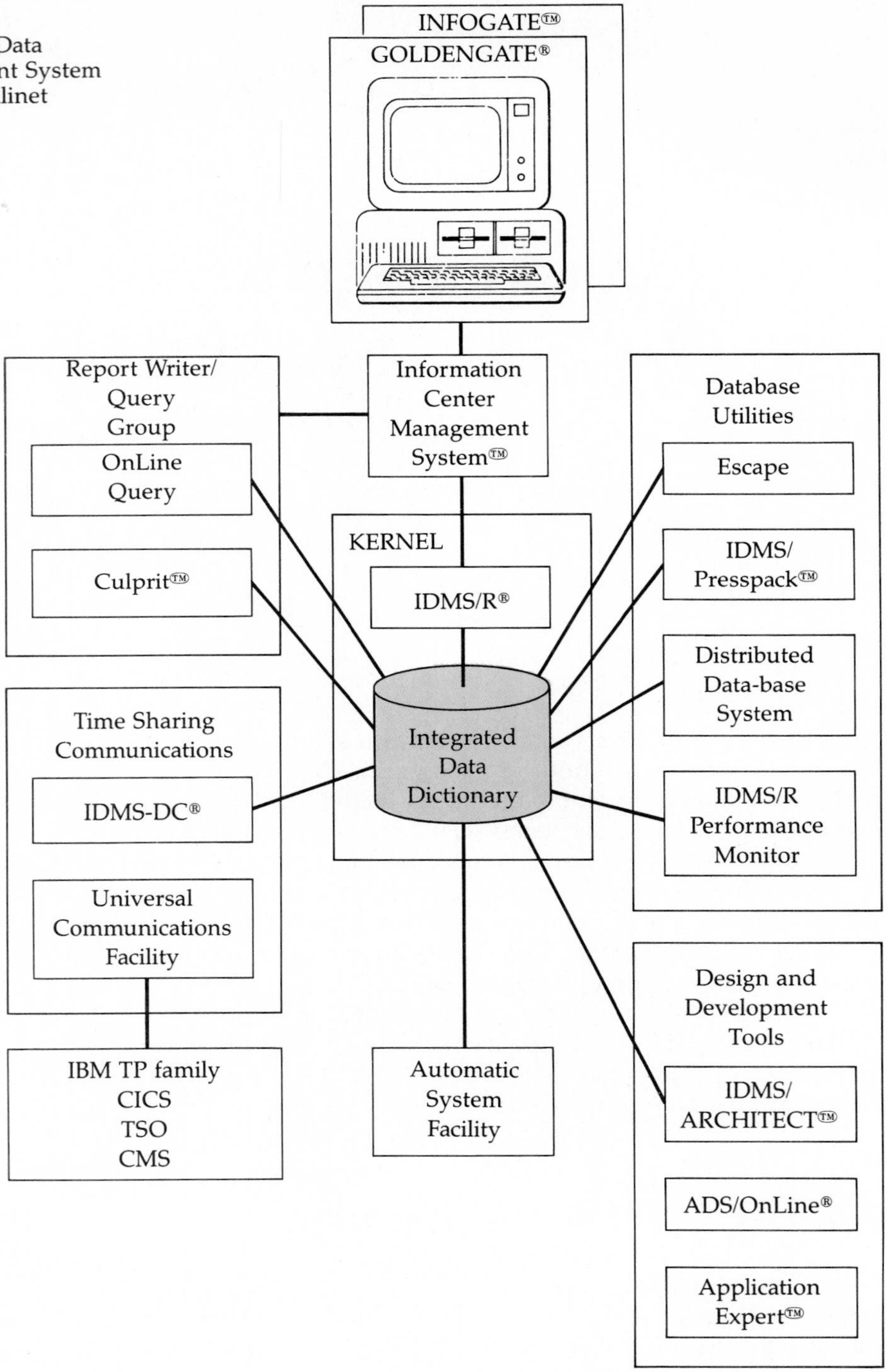

Kernel. The kernel (or heart) of the system consists of the IDMS/R data base management system and the Integrated Data Dictionary (IDD). These components manage the user data bases and the set of data definitions, respectively.

*Report Writer/Query Group.*This group consists of On-Line Query (an interactive query language) and Culprit (a report writer).

Time-Sharing Communications. These products provide interfaces to various teleprocessing monitors such as IBM's CICS and CMS. These monitors allow users at remote locations to access the data bases.

Data Base Utilities. This group consists of two utilities, Escape and Distributed Data Base System. Escape is used to convert older files or data bases for use with IDMS/R, while Distributed Data Base System provides the ability to access distributed data bases (we describe distributed data bases in Chapter 16).

Following is a brief description of several of the key components shown in Figure 11-1.

Integrated Data Dictionary (IDD) As shown in Figure 11-1, the Integrated Data Dictionary (IDD) is at the center of the Cullinet family of software products. The IDD provides a single, central repository for all data definitions in a company. All of the software products utilize the data definitions stored in the IDD. We describe the importance and functions of an integrated data dictionary in this chapter.

IDMS/R IDMS/R is the Cullinet data base management system (DBMS). IDMS/R combines the features of both CODASYL and relational data base management systems (the R stands for relational). IDMS/R is used to create and manage user data bases. We describe the functions of a DBMS throughout this chapter.

ADS/On-Line Application Development System/On-Line (or ADS/On-Line) is a fourth-generation application development system that allows users to generate new applications much more rapidly than with conventional languages such as COBOL. ADS/On-Line uses a nonprocedural language that prompts the user to enter problem specifications through the use of menus and forms. With such a language, prototypes can often be built in days or weeks, then refined and converted into production systems.

On-Line Query On-Line Query is an interactive retrieval language that allows managers and other end users to retrieve data by using simple commands and menus. No previous background in computer languages or systems is required.

On-Line English On-Line English is a natural language processor that allows users to retrieve data using English language statements. The dictionary of usable terms is expanded as the system grows.

Culprit Culprit is an end user–oriented report generator that allows users to specify and produce reports with a few simple commands.

Goldengate Goldengate is an integrated software package for personal computers. It provides support for data base management, word processing, spreadsheet, graphics, and data communications on a personal computer. Also, Goldengate provides a micro–mainframe link for downloading data from a mainframe to personal computers.

Information Data Base This component allows users to specify data that are to be extracted from production data bases and stored in a separate data base, called the Information Data Base. That data can then easily be downloaded to a PC and analyzed using the Goldengate product.

The trend in data management software today is toward such an integrated set of software products organized around a common data dictionary/directory. The data dictionary/directory provides all the metadata (or data definitions) used by the various software components. We describe many of these software products and their interaction with the data dictionary/directory in subsequent sections.

DBMS FUNCTIONS AND ARCHITECTURE

A **data base management system** (DBMS) is a generalized software system that manages the data base, providing facilities for organization, access, and control (Auerbach Publishers 1981). The term *generalized* means that the DBMS is independent of individual applications and therefore can be employed by any user requiring access to the data base.

DBMS Functions

According to Codd (1982), a comprehensive DBMS provides eight major functions.

Data Storage, Retrieval, and Update A data base may be shared by many users. Thus, the DBMS must provide multiple user views and allow users to store, retrieve, and update their data easily and efficiently.

Data Dictionary/Directory In Chapter 1, we defined the data dictionary/directory as the repository of all information about an organization's data.

The DBMS must maintain a user-accessible data dictionary/directory. (This service may be provided by a module of the DBMS itself or by an independent software package, as we will see shortly.)

Transaction Integrity A **transaction** is a sequence of steps that constitute some well-defined business activity. Examples of transactions are "Admit Patient" (in a hospital) and "Enter Customer Order" (in a manufacturing company).

Normally, a transaction requires several actions against the data base. For example, consider the transaction "Enter Customer Order." When a new customer order is entered, the following steps may be performed by an application program:

1. Input order data (keyed by user).
2. Read CUSTOMER record (or insert record if a new customer).
3. Accept or reject the order (if BALANCE-DUE plus ORDER-AMOUNT does not exceed CREDIT-LIMIT, accept the order; otherwise, reject it).
4. If the order is accepted:
   a. Increase BALANCE-DUE by ORDER-AMOUNT.
   b. Store the updated CUSTOMER record.
   c. Insert the accepted ORDER record in the data base.

In processing a transaction, we want the changes to the data base to be made only if the transaction is processed successfully, in its entirety. In this case, we say that the changes are **committed.** If the transaction fails at any point, we say that it has **aborted** and we do not want any of the changes to be made. For example, suppose that the program accepts a new customer order, increases BALANCE-DUE, and stores the updated CUSTOMER record. However, suppose that the new ORDER record is not inserted successfully (perhaps there is a duplicate ORDER# key, or perhaps there is insufficient file space). In this case, we want the transaction to abort and the changes not committed.

To maintain transaction integrity, the DBMS must provide facilities for the user or application programmer to define **transaction boundaries**—that is, the logical beginning and end of transactions. The DBMS should then commit changes for successful transactions and reject changes for aborted transactions.

Recovery Services The DBMS must be able to restore the data base (or return it to a known condition) in the event of some system failure. Sources of system failure include operator error, disk head crashes, and program errors. Measures for data base recovery are described later in this chapter.

Concurrency Control Since a data base is shared by multiple users, two or more users may attempt to access the same data simultaneously. If two users attempt to update the same data record concurrently, erroneous results may occur, since the transactions may interfere with each other. Safeguards must be built into the DBMS to prevent or overcome the effects of such interference. We will discuss this issue later.

Security Mechanisms Data must be protected against accidental or intentional misuse or destruction. The DBMS provides mechanisms for controlling access to data and for defining what actions (such as read-only or update) may be taken by each user.

Data Communications Interface Users often access a data base by means of remote terminals in a telecommunications network. A telecommunications monitor is used to process the flow of transactions to and from the remote terminals. The DBMS must provide an interface with one or more telecommunications monitors so that all the necessary functions are performed and the system will assist, rather than place a burden on, the end user.

Integrity Services The DBMS must provide facilities that assist users in maintaining the integrity of their data. A variety of edit checks and integrity constraints can be designed into the DBMS and its software interfaces. These checks are normally administered through the data dictionary/directory.

Most contemporary data base management systems provide all the functions named here, at least to some degree (although most do not yet provide a comprehensive set of integrity services). However, DBMS products differ in the manner in which the functions are performed. With some user-friendly products, the functions are performed more or less automatically by the DBMS, with little or no user involvement. With other products, the DBMS provides some facilities or interfaces, but the user must take major responsibility for defining the functions (either directly or through application programs). Thus, an organization must evaluate its needs and select its data management software carefully.

Data Base Definition

A DBMS must provide users with language facilities for describing their data bases. A **data definition language** (DDL) is a vocabulary, or set of commands, that is used to describe a data base to the DBMS. The data base specialist uses the DDL to describe metadata—schemas, subschemas, files (or relations), records, and data items (or attributes). In some systems, the DDL is also used to define integrity constraints and access controls.

Schemas A **schema** is a specification (or definition) of a data base using the DDL. In Chapter 2, we introduced the ANSI/SPARC three-level data base model (see Figure 2-17). This model allows us to view any data base at three levels of abstraction: the conceptual model, the external views, and the internal (storage) model. Thus, a DBMS that supports the ANSI/SPARC model must allow the user to express three types of schemas: a conceptual schema, one or more external schemas, and an internal schema. Separate data definition languages are often used to express each of these types of schemas.

DBMS Families The data definition languages that are used vary from one DBMS product to another. However, there are similarities among **families** of DBMS products. Following are the major DBMS families and the entities that are described in the DDL for each family:

1. Hierarchical family: schemas are used to describe fields, segments, data base records, and data bases; examples are provided in Chapter 12.
2. Network family: schemas are used to describe data items, records, sets, and user views (called subschemas); examples are provided in Chapter 13.
3. Relational family: schemas are used to describe attributes, domains, relations, and views; examples are provided in Chapter 14.

Conceptual Schema The conceptual schema defines a global model of the data base. The underlying data model may be hierarchical, network, or relational. Ideally, the data model should make no reference to how the data model is implemented (inverted list, multiple linked lists, and so on) or how the data are physically stored or accessed.

A simple model for a data base is shown in Figure 11-2 (this model was extracted from a more comprehensive model for Pine Valley Furniture Company). The conceptual model shown in Figure 11-2a (called ORDER-ACCOUNTING) has two record types, CUSTOMER and ORDER. There is a one-to-many association between these record types. Figure 11-2b shows sample data for this model, expressed in the form of the relations CUSTOMER and ORDER.

Figure 11-2c shows a sample relational schema for this data base. The relations are defined by means of CREATE TABLE commands. The attributes in each table are named in the command, and their types and lengths are specified. The schema is user-oriented and contains no information about physical implementation.

External Schemas External schemas are derived from the conceptual schema. They define subsets, or views, of the real data. Many external schemas are defined for a single conceptual schema.

The DDL used to define external views depends on the data model being used. Normally, the data model used to define external schemas is the same as the one used in the conceptual schema (e.g., both are network). However, some DBMS products allow the conceptual schema to be defined with

Figure 11-2
Conceptual model and schema:
(a) conceptual model (ORDER-ACCOUNTING)
(b) sample data
(c) sample schema (relational)

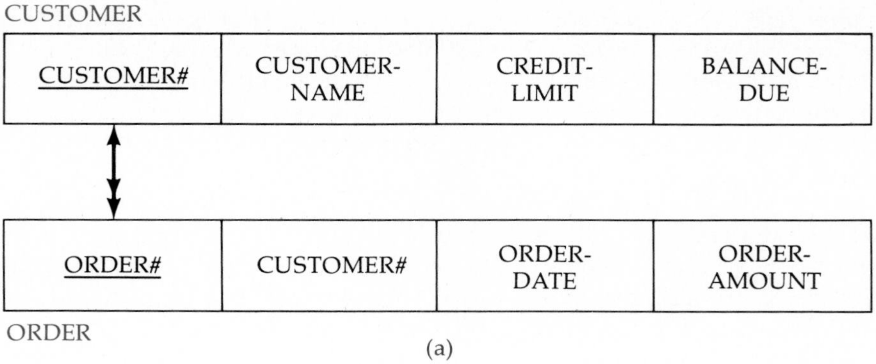

(a)

CUSTOMER#	CUSTOMER-NAME	CREDIT-LIMIT	BALANCE-DUE
S298	SUSAN'S PLACE	10,000	6,000
C039	CONTEMP DES	15,000	10,000
A123	CASUAL FURN	5,000	4,000

CUSTOMER

ORDER#	CUSTOMER#	ORDER-DATE	ORDER-AMOUNT
816	A123	12/20/8X	4,000
713	C039	12/8/8X	7,000
942	S298	1/12/8X	5,000
629	C039	12/2/8X	3,000
867	S298	12/28/8X	1,000

ORDER

(b)

```
CREATE TABLE CUSTOMER  (CUSTOMER#         (CHAR(4), NONULL),
                        CUSTOMER-NAME     (CHAR(20)),
                        CREDIT-LIMIT      (INTEGER),
                        BALANCE-DUE       (FLOAT))

CREATE TABLE ORDER     (ORDER#            (INTEGER, NONULL),
                        CUSTOMER#         (CHAR(4)),
                        ORDER-DATE        (CHAR(8)),
                        ORDER-AMOUNT      (FLOAT))
```

(c)

one data model and the external schemas defined with a different data model. In fact, IDMS (pictured in Figure 11-1) allows users to define their external views using either the CODASYL (network) model or the relational model.

Two external views for ORDER-ACCOUNTING and the associated external schemas are shown in Figure 11-3. These views are derived from the conceptual model by specifying relational commands that are applied

CUSTOMER#	CREDIT-LIMIT
S298	10,000
C039	15,000
A123	5,000

DEFINE VIEW USERVIEW1 (CUSTOMER#, CREDIT-LIMIT)
AS SELECT CUSTOMER#, CREDIT-LIMIT FROM CUSTOMER

(a)

CUSTOMER-NAME	ORDER#	ORDER-AMOUNT
CASUAL FURN	816	4,000
CONTEMP DES	713	7,000
SUSAN'S PLACE	942	5,000
CONTEMP FURN	629	3,000
SUSAN'S PLACE	867	1,000

DEFINE VIEW USERVIEW2 (CUSTOMER-NAME, ORDER#, ORDER-AMOUNT)
AS SELECT CUSTOMER-NAME, ORDER#, ORDER-AMOUNT FROM CUSTOMER, ORDER
WHERE CUSTOMER. CUSTOMER#=ORDER. CUSTOMER#

(b)

Figure 11-3
External schemas:
(a) user view 1
(b) user view 2

to the relations CUSTOMER and ORDER. Each view (or external schema) is defined by a DEFINE VIEW clause followed by a list of attributes that appear in that view. We define the first user view by selecting two attributes (CUSTOMER# and CREDIT-LIMIT) from the CUSTOMER relation. The second user view requires a join of the CUSTOMER and ORDER relations over the CUSTOMER# attribute. Three attributes (CUSTOMER-NAME, ORDER#, and ORDER-AMOUNT) are then selected to form the user view. The language used to form these user views simply names the necessary attributes and relations, but does not express their physical characteristics. Once these views are defined as in this example, users may produce reports or displays by simply invoking the views in a simple command.

Internal Schema The internal schema (or storage schema) for a data base defines the storage files that contain the actual data records for the data base. Normally, there is one storage file for each conceptual file or relation described in the conceptual schema. Also, the internal schema defines the details of the data structures that are used by the DBMS to locate records and to establish associations between records. For example, inverted lists that are used to implement secondary keys are defined in the internal schema, as are pointer fields used to link records.

For the ORDER-ACCOUNTING data base we have been describing, there are two stored files: a Customer file and an Order file. The characteristics of these files (including the names, types, and lengths of the

Figure 11-4
Index entries for internal schema

```
CREATE UNIQUE INDEX CUSTNO-INDEX ON CUSTOMER (CUSTOMER#)
CREATE INDEX CUSTNAME-INDEX ON CUSTOMER (CUSTOMER-NAME)
CREATE UNIQUE INDEX ORDERNO-INDEX ON ORDER (ORDER#)
CREATE INDEX CNBR-INDEX ON ORDER (CUSTOMER#)
```

data items or attributes) are specified in the conceptual schema (see Figure 11-2) and do not need to be repeated in the internal schema. However, the internal schema must specify the indexes used to locate records.

For each of the stored files, we have created two indexes: a primary key index (specified by CREATE UNIQUE INDEX) and a secondary key index (specified by CREATE INDEX). The index entries are shown in Figure 11-4. The first entry in this index is the following:

```
CREATE UNIQUE INDEX CUSTNO-INDEX ON CUSTOMER
(CUSTOMER#)
```

This statement instructs the DBMS to create an index (called CUSTNO-INDEX) for the primary key CUSTOMER# in the CUSTOMER file. This index will allow users direct access to customer records, given a value for CUSTOMER#.

The last entry in Figure 11-4 is the following:

```
CREATE INDEX CNBR-INDEX ON ORDER (CUSTOMER#)
```

This entry causes the DBMS to create a secondary key index (called CNBR-INDEX) for the ORDER records. With this index, a user can provide a customer number (such as C039) and obtain a list of all outstanding orders for that customer (for customer C039 there are two orders: 629 and 713).

Notice that the internal model does *not* specify any details of physical data organization. For example, the Customer file may be organized as a hash file, while the Order file may be organized as an indexed sequential file. These details (as well as the record blocking factors) are specified to the access method and are often unknown to the DBMS. On the other hand, the indexes and list organizations specified in the internal schema are created and maintained by the DBMS and are unknown to the access methods.

Data Independence

The main reason for using the three-level DBMS architecture that we have just described is that it provides a high level of data independence. In Chapter 2, we defined data independence as the ability to change the structure of data without having to modify application programs. There are two types of data independence—logical and physical—and we will now illustrate each type for the ORDER-ACCOUNTING data base.

Logical Data Independence Logical data independence is the property that allows us to change the conceptual schema (or overall logical structure of the data base) without changing external schemas or application programs. This property is vital because it allows the data base to grow and change without inflicting excessive maintenance costs.

Consider the following two changes to the conceptual schema for ORDER-ACCOUNTING (Figure 11-2):

1. Data item change: Suppose that it is necessary to change the length of the data item CUSTOMER-NAME from 20 to 30 characters. This is accomplished by changing the specification from CHAR(20) to CHAR(30) in the conceptual schema. Since data item characteristics are not specified in the external schemas (see Figure 11-3), no changes to these views or the programs that use them are required.
2. New data item: Suppose that we wish to add a data item called YTD-SALES to the Customer relation. Again, this change is introduced in the conceptual schema. Any existing views that are derived from the conceptual schema are unaffected by the change.

Each of these examples pertains to a relational data base, which uses a three-schema architecture (older DBMS systems may not provide the level of data independence implied here).

Physical Data Independence Physical data independence is the property that allows us to change physical data organization or access without changing the logical structure. This property is vital, since it permits us to improve performance without having to modify existing programs or user views.

Let us consider two examples of physical data independence for ORDER-ACCOUNTING:

1. Change in implementation procedure: Suppose we want to implement the secondary key CUSTOMER# in the ORDER records by linked list rather than by an index. This requires a simple change to the internal schema (Figure 11-4), in which the CREATE INDEX clause is replaced by a CREATE LINKED LIST clause. The conceptual schema (and therefore the external schemas) are unaffected by this change.
2. Change in access method: Suppose (for performance reasons) that we want to change the organization of the Customer file from hashed to indexed sequential. This change is specified in the access method specification (or job control language). No changes to the schemas are required and the DBMS is unaware of the change.

Schema Generation and Translation

In a system that does not use a data dictionary, the three schemas (Figures 11-2 through 11-4) are coded by a data base programmer. However, when a data dictionary/directory system is used, these schemas are generated by the DD/DS using data definitions stored in the data dictionary/directory (DD/D). We describe the data dictionary/directory in the next section.

The source versions of the three schemas (whether coded by hand or generated from the DD/D) are translated by a software module of the DBMS called the DDL translator.The translated versions of the schemas are stored in a library for use by run-time modules of the DBMS (see Figure 11-10).

DATA DICTIONARY/DIRECTORY SYSTEM

The data dictionary/directory system (DD/DS) is the cornerstone of a modern data management system. This system stores and manages all metadata (or "data about data") used by the organization. (We described metadata in Chapter 2; see Figure 2-1.) As we mentioned in Chapter 10, the data dictionary/directory is the principal tool used by data base administration in managing the information resource. Also, as shown in Figure 11-1, an integrated data dictionary/directory interfaces with all other software components of the data management environment.

Components of a DD/DS

A DD/DS has two major components: the data dictionary/directory and the data dictionary/directory manager.

The **data dictionary/directory** (DD/D) is the repository for all organizational metadata, such as data definitions, relationships, and authorities. In other words, the DD/D is a data base of metadata (in fact, it is sometimes referred to as a "metadata base").

The **data dictionary/directory manager** is a software module (or set of modules) used to manage the DD/D. Just as the data base management system is used to manage the user data base, the DD/D manager is used to manage the metadata base.

We can think of the DD/D as being divided into two sections: the data dictionary and the data directory. The **data dictionary** contains definitions of records, data items, relations, and other data objects that are of interest to users or required by data management software. These definitions are employed by users to answer the question: What data are contained in the organization's data bases, and what are their characteristics? The same definitions are used by the DD/D manager to generate conceptual and external schemas (such as those shown in Figures 11-2 and 11-3) that are required by the DBMS to access user data bases.

On the other hand, the **data directory** contains information about where data are stored (in a relational DBMS, the directory is instead called the *catalog*). For example, the internal schemas (such as the one shown in Figure 11-4) are contained in the data directory. Also, the indexes maintained by the DBMS (such as CUSTNO-INDEX and CNAME-INDEX) are stored in the data directory. If the data base is distributed over several geographical locations, the data directory contains information about what data are stored

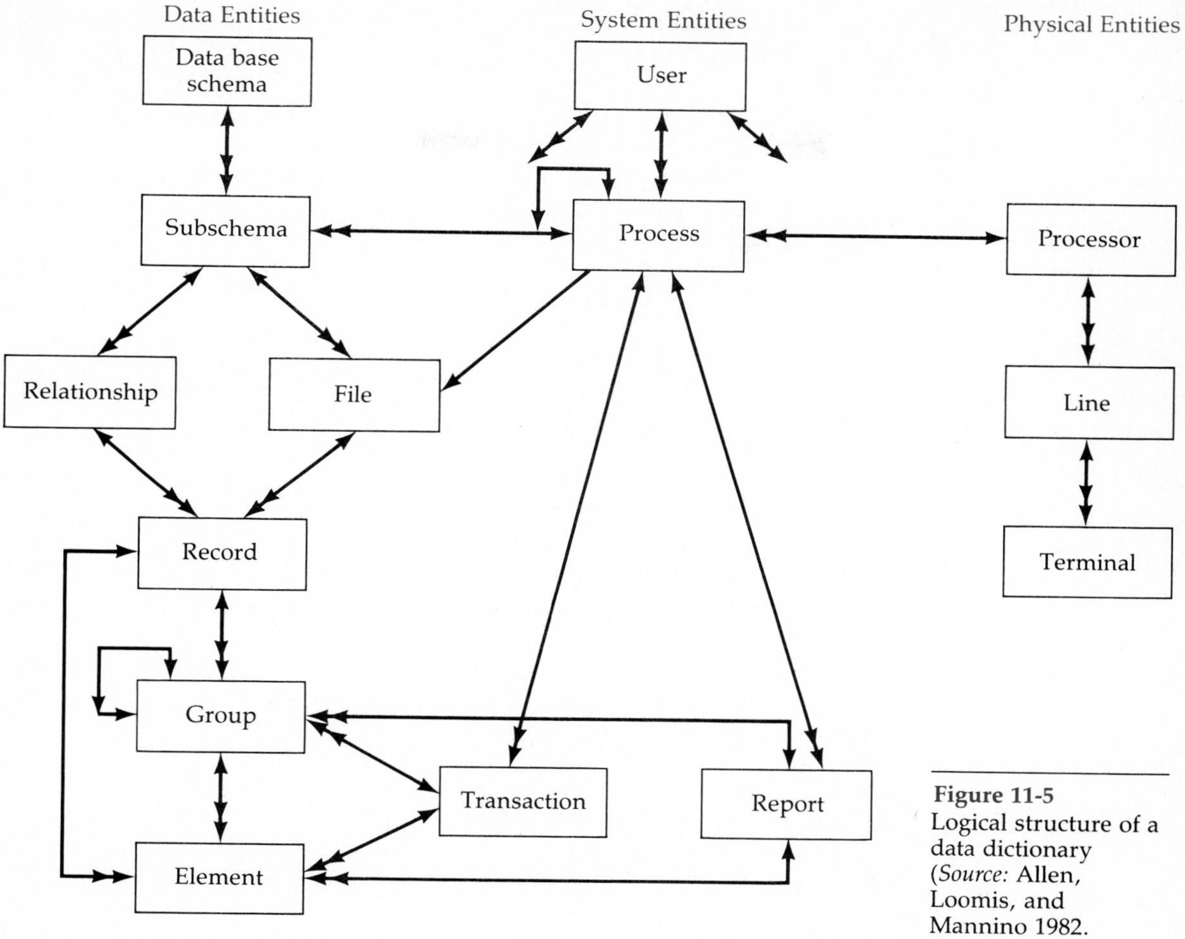

Figure 11-5
Logical structure of a data dictionary (*Source:* Allen, Loomis, and Mannino 1982. Copyright © 1982, Association for Computing Machinery, Inc.)

at each node (or location). Thus, the data directory (or catalog) contains information that is used exclusively by data management software rather than by users.

In the discussion that follows, we will emphasize the data dictionary section of the DD/D. However, both types of metadata are always included in the DD/DS.

Structure and Content of the DD/D

The data dictionary contains information about data entities and the relationships among those entities. Thus, the data dictionary is itself a complex data base. A diagram of the structure and contents of a typical data dictionary is shown in Figure 11-5. In this data structure diagram, the data dictionary is organized using a network data model. However, data dictionaries may also be organized using either the hierarchical or relational data models.

Some 14 types of entities are shown in the diagram in Figure 11-5 (additional entity types can often be created as needed). These entity types can be classified as data entities, system entities, and physical entities.

Data entities describe data objects in the user environment. The data entities included in Figure 11-5 are Element (or Data Item), Group, Record, File, Relationship, Subschema, and Data Base Schema. In a relational data base environment, the data objects would be relations, domains, attributes, and views.

System entities describe objects that process or are otherwise related to data entities. System entities included in Figure 11-5 are Transaction, Report, and Process (a process is a program or program module).

Physical entities are real-world objects that use or are otherwise associated with the data and system objects. The physical entities included in Figure 11-5 are User, Processor, Line, and Terminal.

The associations shown among entities in Figure 11-5 are all one-to-many (however, many-to-many associations can also be represented). The Process entity has a recursive association, since one process (or program) may "call" other processes. The Group (or data aggregate) entity has a nested association, since one group may contain other groups. The User entity may have an association with nearly any other entity type in the diagram.

A sample occurrence of the logical structure of this data dictionary is shown in Figure 11-6. This occurrence is for the ORDER-ACCOUNTING data base. Notice that there is one record occurrence in the data dictionary for each subschema, one record for each data element type, and so on. The associations between entities allow us to easily determine what data objects (such as elements) are used by other objects (such as records or transactions).

A typical DD/DS allows the user to define numerous attributes for each entity included in the DD/D. For example, typical attributes for an Element entity are shown in Table 11-1. The attributes are illustrated for the data item CREDIT-LIMIT. Notice that in addition to describing the data item, the attributes contain important editing criteria. Using these metadata, the DBMS can enforce the editing criteria when users input data. For example, the DBMS should reject any attempt to input a credit limit value that is not numeric, that exceeds 8 bytes, that is negative, or that exceeds the value 100,000.

A typical medium-sized company may have several thousand data items to describe. There will be one record in the data dictionary for each data item that is defined. Each record will contain the attributes shown in Table 11-1 (in reality, additional attributes may be used).

The entities shown in Figure 11-5 and the attributes given in Table 11-1 are typical of those provided in commercial data dictionary/directory systems. However, most vendors provide an **extensibility** feature that allows

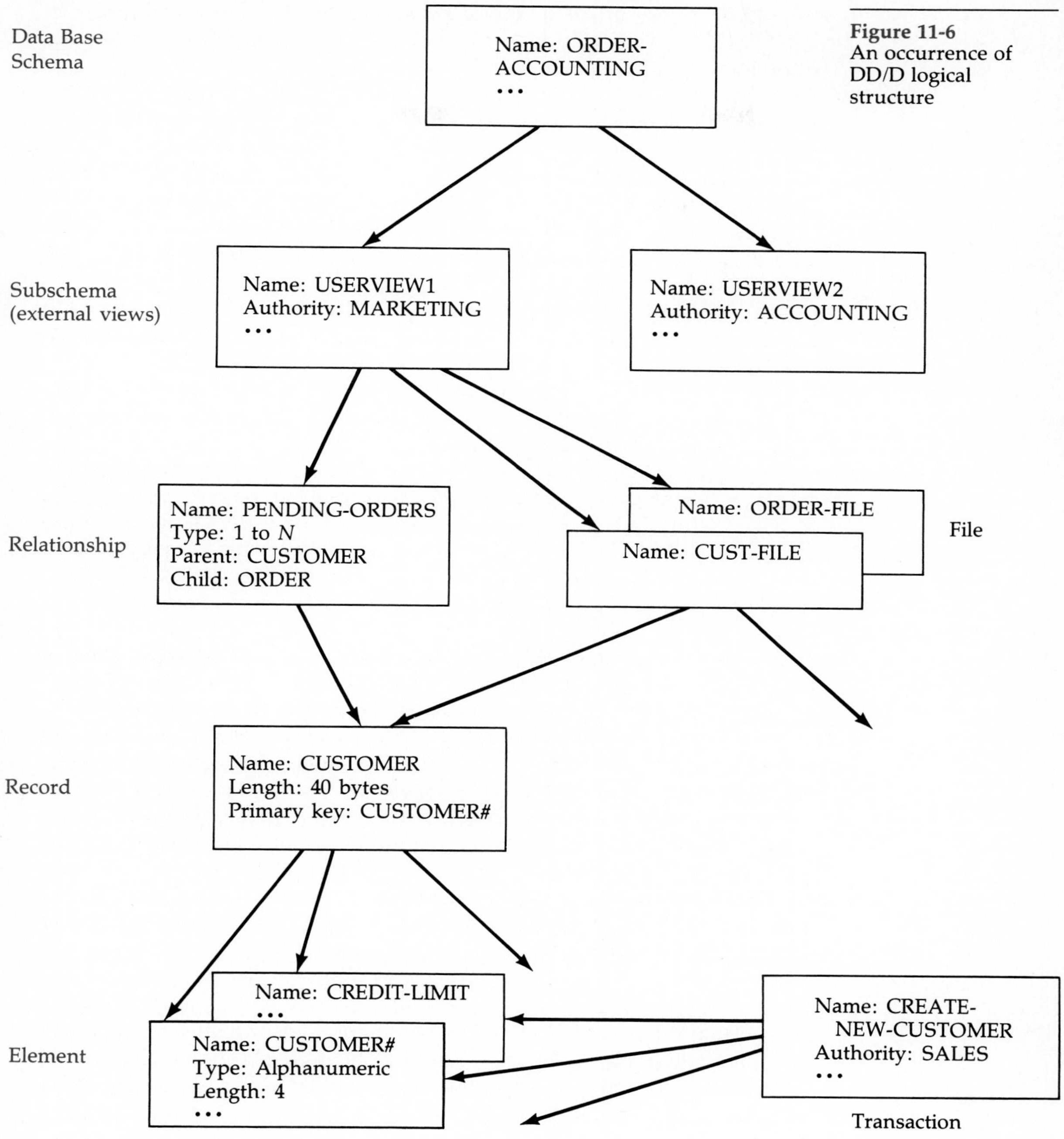

Figure 11-6
An occurrence of DD/D logical structure

Table 11-1 Typical Attributes for an Element Entity

Attribute	Example
User name	CREDIT-LIMIT
Type	Numeric
Length	8 bytes
Representation	Packed decimal
Lower limit	0
Upper limit	100,000
Default value	1000
Internal name	CRED-LIM
Display format	ZZZ,ZZ9.99
Description	Maximum unpaid balance for an approved credit customer

users to define additional entities, relationships, and attributes as needed. For example, with this feature, a user could define a new entity type called DEPARTMENT to be included in Figure 11-5. The user would define the attributes used to describe DEPARTMENT and the associations between this new entity and other entities in the figure.

Functions of the DD/D Manager

As we have seen, the data dictionary/directory is a complex data base that resembles any other data base in the organization in structure, but not in content (the DD/D contains metadata values rather than data values). Therefore, to manage the data dictionary/directory, the DD/D manager must provide many of the functions of a data base management system (these functions were given earlier in the chapter).

Six major functions normally provided by the DD/D manager are shown in Figure 11-7. Following are brief descriptions of these functions.

DD/D Definition The DD/D manager must provide a data definition language for describing entities, relationships, and attributes. We illustrated data definition languages in the previous section (see Figures 11-2 through 11-4).

DD/D Maintenance The DD/D manager must also provide language facilities for creating the DD/D and for adding, changing, and deleting its contents. This is normally an interactive language that allows the user to easily access the DD/D from a terminal.

DD/D Protection The DD/D manager must provide facilities for protecting the DD/D. Features that are required include security, concurrency control, and backup and recovery (all of these features are described later).

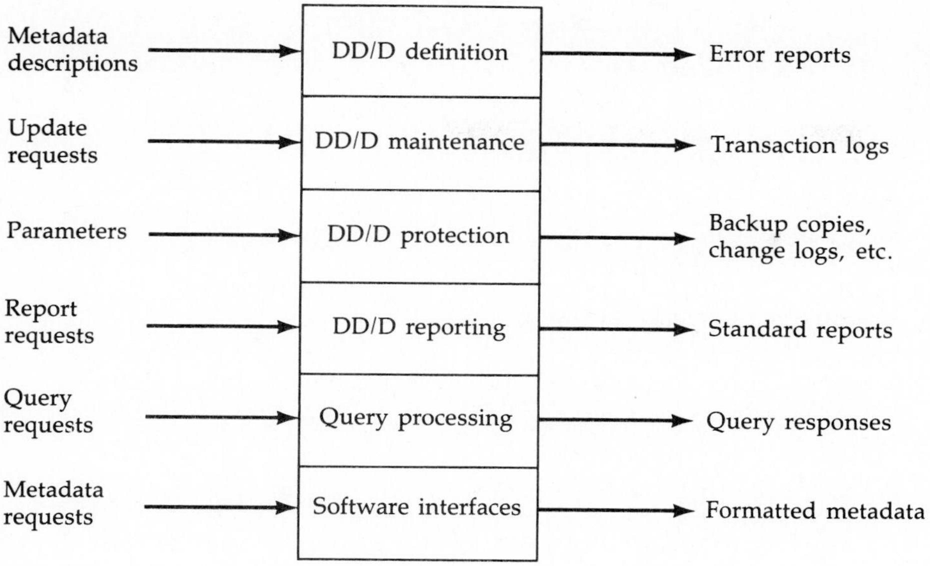

Figure 11-7
Major functions provided by DD/D manager

DD/D Reporting The DD/D manager must provide a facility for extracting metadata and producing reports describing the organization's data. The DD/D manager may include a report processor module or it may provide an interface to a standard report writer included in the data management system. For example, with Cullinet's data management system (Figure 11-1), the CULPRIT Report Generator is used to produce reports from the Integrated Data Dictionary.

An example of a standard user-oriented report produced from a DD/D (ADR's DATADICTIONARY) is shown in Figure 11-8. This report uses an indented format to show the entities (area, file, records, and fields) that make up a Human Resources data base. A comprehensive DD/DS is the source of much of the documentation required in a data base system.

Query Processing In addition to standard reports, the DD/D manager must provide a high-level query language interface so that users can easily formulate requests for dictionary data. A typical request for such data is shown in Figure 11-9. In this example, the user has requested a list of all programs that use the data item CUSTOMER-NUMBER. Using the associations between data dictionary entities, the query processor produces a list of five programs that use this element (you should examine the data structure diagram in Figure 11-5 and identify how this particular query is processed). The type of "where used" display shown in Figure 11-9 is very useful in **impact analysis**—analyzing the impact of a proposed change to one entity on other entities.

DATA

DATA BASE HUMAN RESOURCE

THE HUMAN RESOURCE DATA BASE CONTAINS THE INFORMATION RELATED TO PERSONNEL, PAYROLL, SKILLS, AND BENEFITS. IT IS MAINTAINED BY THE VARIOUS SUBSYSTEMS THAT MAKE UP THE HUMAN RESOURCES APPLICATION SYSTEM. IT IS USED FOR REPORTING BY THESE SAME SUBSYSTEMS AS WELL AS THE MANAGEMENT REPORTING SYSTEM AND ACCOUNTING REPORTING SYSTEM.

AREA PAYROLL

THE PAYROLL AREA CONSISTS OF THE PAYROLL MASTER FILE AND CONTAINS INFORMATION REGARDING ALL PAY UNITS. IT IS MANAGED BY THE PAYROLL DEPARTMENT.

FILE PAYROLL–MASTER

THE PAYROLL MASTER FILE CONTAINS A RECORD FOR EACH EMPLOYEE INCLUDING ACTIVE EMPLOYEES, TERMINATED EMPLOYEES, AND SUSPENSIONS.

RECORD PAYROLL

THE PAYROLL RECORD CONTAINS EMPLOYEE NUMBER, HIS/HER PAY CODE, AND RATE OF PAY, WHICH ALSO INCLUDES TAX INFORMATION

KEY PAYROLL NUMBER

THE EMPLOYEE NUMBER KEY IS USED TO RANDOMLY ACCESS PAYROLL RECORDS FOR IDENTIFICATION AND TAX REPORTING PURPOSES. ONCE ENTERED, AN EMPLOYEE NUMBER SHOULD NOT BE MODIFIED.

FIELD PAYROLL.ACTIVITY CODE

THE EMPLOYEE ACTIVITY CODE ELEMENT CONTAINS THE NUMBER AND EMPLOYEE PAY CODE AND STATUS CODE

FIELD PAYROLL.EMPLOYEE CODE

EMPLOYEE CODE IS ONE CHARACTER FIELD THAT CONTAINS EMPLOYEES' PAY TYPE. IT SHOULD CONTAIN "H" FOR HOURLY OR "S" FOR SALARY. THIS IS USED FOR PAY RATE AND YEAR INFORMATION.

Figure 11-8
Example of data dictionary report (Courtesy ADR)

```
WHICH PROGRAMS USE CUSTOMER-NUMBER?

THE FOLLOWING PROGRAMS USE THE ELEMENT CUSTOMER-NUMBER:
   CREATE-NEW-CUSTOMER
   ENTER-CUSTOMER-ORDER
   ACCOUNTS-RECEIVABLE
   SALES-ANALYSIS
   DELETE-OLD-CUSTOMER
```

Figure 11-9
Typical DD/D query

Software Interfaces Finally, the DD/D manager must accept requests for metadata from other software components (e.g., the DBMS or teleprocessing monitor). It must prepare the metadata in a format that can be accepted and used by the requesting program.

Implementing a DD/DS

Most data dictionary/directory systems used today are called active systems. An **active** DD/DS is one in which the DD/D is the sole source of metadata in the data management system (Allen, Loomis, and Mannino 1982). That is, all users and all software components obtain the metadata they require from a single source: the DD/D. This ensures a high degree of control over data definitions and standards. The Integrated Data Dictionary portrayed in Figure 11-1 is an active DD/DS.

An active DD/DS contrasts with earlier systems, which were passive. A **passive** DD/DS is one in which a dictionary of definitions is maintained for human users. However, these definitions are not used by the various software components. Each software product (such as the DBMS) generates and/or stores its own metadata. With a passive DD/DS, there is no assurance that the same definitions are used throughout the system.

Actually, the term *active* is a relative term in comparing DD/D systems. Vendors use different approaches in implementing their DD/DS, depending on their marketing strategy and other factors [for a comparison of these approaches, see Allen, Loomis, and Mannino (1982)]. The trend in data management systems today is to fully integrated, active data dictionary/directory systems that provide a single source of metadata for all users (human and software).

USING A DBMS

In this section, we describe the operations of a typical DBMS in managing a user data base. The major components of DBMS software are introduced, and their functions are described.

DBMS Software Components

The major software components in a DBMS operational environment are shown in Figure 11-10. This diagram shows how the DBMS interfaces with other software components such as user programs and access methods.

System Components A DBMS has two major operating components: a data base control system and a data base storage system. The **data base control system** (DBCS) is a module that interfaces with user programs. It accepts calls for data (such as READ and WRITE commands) and examines the external and conceptual schemas to determine what conceptual records are required to satisfy the request. The DBCS then places a call to the data base storage system to fill the request.

The **data base storage system** (DBSS) manipulates the underlying storage files. It establishes and maintains the lists and indexes that are defined in the internal schema. If hash files are used, the DBSS calls on a hashing routine to generate record addresses. However, the DBSS does *not* manage the physical input and output of data. It passes requests on to the appropriate access methods, which read data into and out of the system buffers.

The terms *data base control system* and *data base storage system* are generic and do not necessarily apply to a given DBMS. However, most DBMS products do have the equivalent of these operational modules.

Loading the DBMS In preparation for processing a data base, all the software components shown in Figure 11-10 are loaded into main memory. Precompiled versions of all the software modules—user programs, DBCS, DBSS, hashing routines, and access methods—are stored on a system disk. Also, compiled versions of the three schemas—conceptual, external, and internal—are stored in a disk library. When a program is to be run, all these components are loaded into main memory. They are linked together by an operating system module (sometimes called the linkage editor) so that they can communicate with one another. Also, system buffers are created by the operating system at this time. The resulting software system is represented in Figure 11-10.

Binding Times An important event that occurs in loading the DBMS is the linking of a user program to its external schema (normally each user program has one external schema). The process of linking an application program to its external schema (and therefore its data definitions) is referred to as **binding,** and the time when this occurs is called **binding time.** Binding

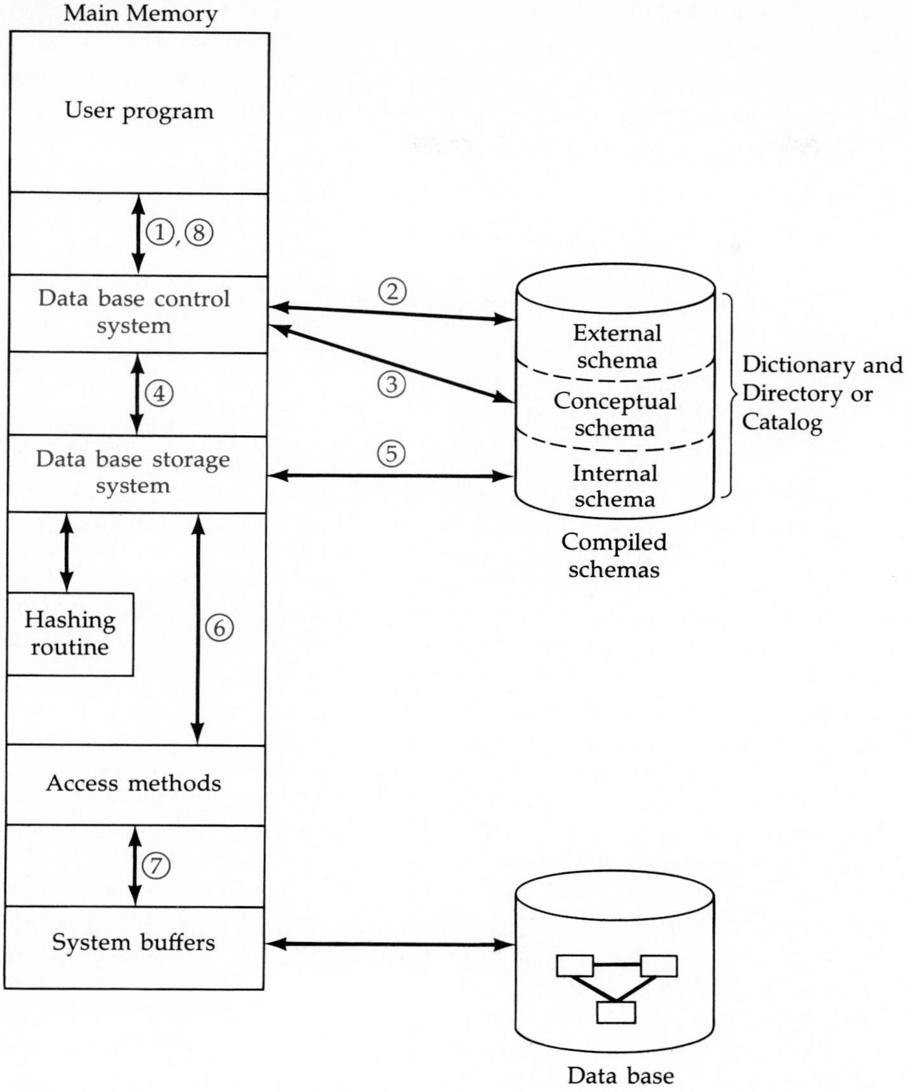

Figure 11-10
DBMS software environment

time is an important consideration for a DBMS because until the instant that binding occurs, changes can be made to data definitions without changing any process. For example, a data item length or type could be changed without the need to repeat the linking process. However, once binding occurs, any change to a data definition requires that the binding process be repeated.

In our description of the loading process, binding occurs during linkage editing (this is typical of contemporary data base management systems). However, binding may also occur at the following times:

1. When a program is written (such as when a constant is coded in the program logic)
2. When a program is compiled (such as a conventional application program that contains its own data descriptions)
3. When a program is linkage edited
4. When a data base is opened (readied for processing)
5. When a user program is executed (user supplies data definitions at run time)

These alternatives may be diagrammed as follows:

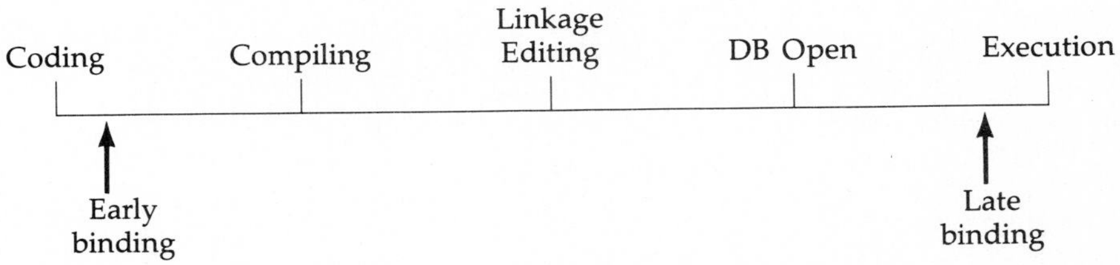

In general, late binding promotes data independence, since data definitions can be changed up until the time the program is executed. However, binding at execution time is normally too costly in terms of human and computer resources and is used only in exceptional situations.

Processing a Data Base

Let us now examine how the components in Figure 11-10 communicate with one another in processing a data base. We will illustrate each step by means of an example. Suppose that a user program called NEWORDERS is being used to update the ORDER-ACCOUNTING data base. This program uses the external schema USERVIEW1 (Figure 11-3). Assume that all the components shown in Figure 11-10, including the object (or compiled) versions of the three schemas, have been loaded into main memory and linked by the linkage editor. We assume that the name of the external schema (USERVIEW1) is specified in the NEWORDERS program, so that the system will know which external schema to select from the library.

Now let us suppose that the NEWORDERS program requests an occurrence of USERVIEW1 by means of a READ statement. In particular, the program requests the record for customer A123. Following are the essential steps that are performed (the steps are numbered also in Figure 11-10):

(1.) The program NEWORDERS issues a call to the data base control system to READ an occurrence of USERVIEW1. The key value (A123) is passed to the DBCS.

(2.) The DBCS examines the external schema and looks up the description of USERVIEW1. The DBCS notes that USERVIEW1 is derived from the CUSTOMER conceptual relation.

③ The DBCS examines the conceptual schema and looks up the description of the CUSTOMER relation.

④ The DBCS issues a request to the data base storage system to retrieve the CUSTOMER stored record with the primary key value A123.

⑤ The DBSS searches CUSTNO-INDEX and locates the relative address for customer A123.

⑥ The DBSS now issues a call to the access method to read the stored record at the relative address. The access method reads the stored record (including any pointer fields) and places it in the system buffer (if records are blocked, more than one record is placed in the buffer).

⑦ The DBCS extracts the required data items from the system buffer and moves them to the user work area (UWA) for the program NEWORDERS (pointer fields are not moved to the UWA). The user work area now contains the following data:

A123	5000

⑧ Required status information (such as error indications) is transferred from the DBCS to the user program, as required.

While the system is performing these steps, the computer operating system has transferred control to another program. When the I/O operation is completed, control may be transferred back to NEWORDERS.

Considering the preceding steps, you may well wonder about the performance of a data base management system. Eight steps to obtain two data items! True, individual input/output operations are often slower with a DBMS than with a conventional file processing system. Yet, overall productivity is often much higher. Remember that the overall goal is to improve the productivity of human resources, not to conserve machine cycles or byte positions.

Interactive Data Base Processing

In a typical data base environment, many users may be interacting with a data base from remote terminals. Some of the users want to interrogate the data base, while other users want to update the data base. More sophisticated data management software is required to supervise such interactive data base processing. We describe two such components in this section: query language processors and teleprocessing monitors.

Query Language Processors A query language processor (QLP) provides a high-level language that allows end users to easily access the data base. On-Line Query (pictured in Figure 11-1) is such a query language. We can illustrate the use of a query language by referring to

USERVIEW1 (see Figure 11-3a). Following is a typical query language statement:

SELECT CUSTOMER#
FROM USERVIEW1
WHERE CREDIT-LIMIT>10,000

This query requests a list of customer numbers whose credit limit exceeds 10,000. Referring to Figure 11-3a, we see that there is only one such customer, C039.

When this query is input from a terminal, the QLP analyzes the query and constructs a simple retrieval program. This program then interacts with the DBMS to retrieve the requested data, which are displayed by the program. If a particular query is used frequently, the retrieval program can be stored (thereby speeding up subsequent retrievals).

Teleprocessing Monitors When several on-line users are accessing a data base concurrently, a teleprocessing (TP) monitor is required to schedule and control the various activities. The TP monitor polls terminals for messages, places messages in an incoming message queue, and schedules the execution of programs that process the messages and produce output.

The position of a TP monitor in a data management system is illustrated in Figure 11-11. Clearly, the TP monitor is a vital component of the data management system, and it is important that the TP monitor be designed to interface with the DBMS and other system components.

Figure 11-11
Using a TP monitor

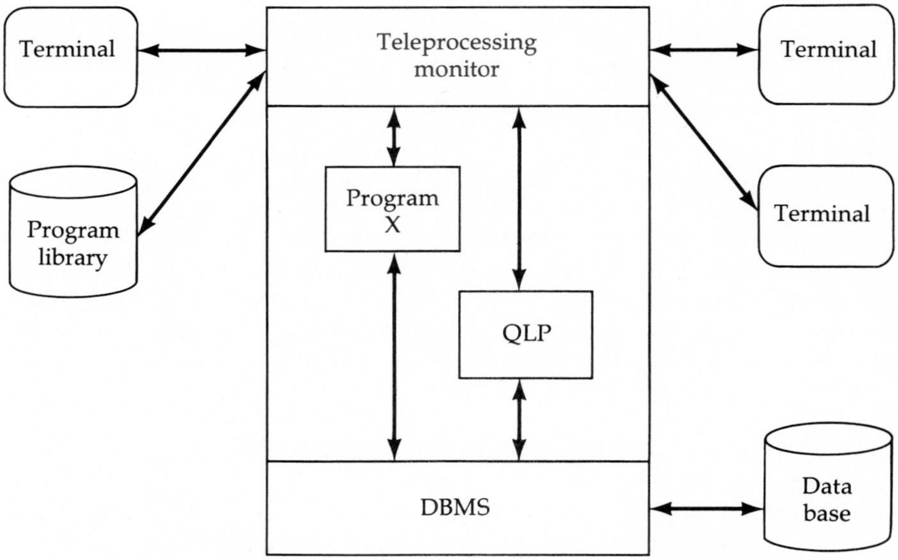

DATA BASE SECURITY

The problem of computer security is entertainingly illustrated in a popular movie called *War Games*. On a visit to his principal's office, a high school computer whiz easily obtains a password to the school's computer (it is scrawled on a piece of paper on the principal's desk). From his home computer, the student dials up the school computer and, using the password, logs on and alters his grades (favorably, of course). Using his newfound knowledge, he then penetrates other computer systems. Ultimately, he logs on to a national defense computer, where he nearly perpetrates a nuclear disaster. (The end of the movie is predictable; the student uses his computer knowledge to save the day.) Although fictional, the story does illustrate some important points concerning security. First, simple passwords are often ineffective security devices. Second, regardless of how rigorous the safeguards, no computer system is completely safe in the face of a determined adversary. And finally, the impact of a security violation may range from simple mischief to organizational disaster.

Computer Crime and Data Base Security

Computer crime—using (or misusing) computers and related technology for illegal purposes—is becoming increasingly common as computer technology becomes more accessible. As the use of computers spreads to a larger segment of the population, the opportunities for this type of "white collar" crime increase correspondingly. However, the rate of prosecution of computer criminals remains quite low. According to a census by the National Center for Computer Crime Data, there were only 75 prosecutions pursuant to computer crime laws in 38 states—fewer than two per state (Bloombecker 1986). The FBI has estimated that only 1 of 20,000 computer criminals goes to jail.

According to the National Center for Computer Crime Data census, the largest number of defendants in computer crime cases are employees of organizations. Such employees include programmers, bank tellers, students, and others with access to their companies' systems and data (see Figure 11-12a). The victims of these crimes are predominantly the organizations for whom these employees work (see Figure 11-12b).

Fortunately, a strengthened federal law (the Computer Fraud and Abuse Act of 1986) provides new weapons for prosecuting computer crime. Also, nearly all states now have computer crime laws. According to Bloombecker (1986), these crime laws attempt to combat the following types of crimes:

1. Money theft—ranging from complex bank or insurance company fraud to simple falsifications of records that allow money to be misappropriated
2. Service theft—use of computer services for one's own benefit (for example, using computer time or storage files)

3. Program and data theft—misappropriating programs and/or data for personal benefit (often involves trade secret theft)
4. Data alteration—including illegally altering credit information, motor vehicle records, and student grades
5. Data destruction—deliberate destruction of files or data bases as an act of mischief or revenge
6. Malicious access—gaining illegal access to a computer system, and reading files or data bases but not necessarily damaging the system
7. Violation of privacy—illegally gaining access to the private data of organizations or individuals

Figure 11-12
Survey results on computer crime (*Source:* Bloombecker 1986. © National Center for Computer Crime Data, Los Angeles.)

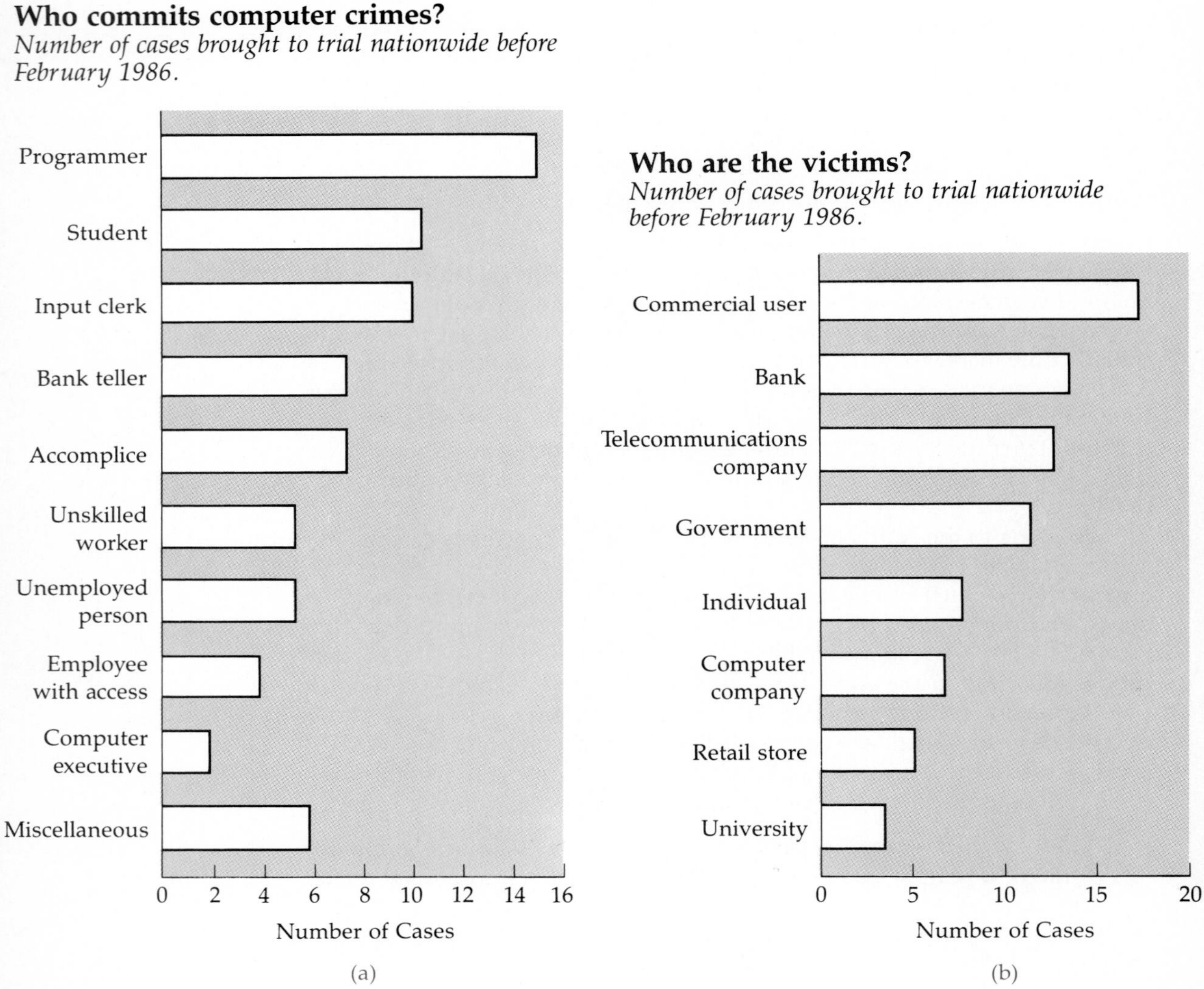

The best way to combat computer crime is to prevent it through the use of safeguards and security measures. Numerous organizational safeguards such as restricted access, careful employee selection and training, and division of responsibilities are included in a comprehensive security program. In this text we focus on one important aspect of computer security, data base security.

Data base security is defined as protecting the data base against accidental or intentional loss, destruction, or misuse. As noted in Chapter 10, data administration is responsible for developing overall policies and procedures to protect data bases. Data administration uses several facilities provided by data management software in carrying out these functions. The most important security features of data management software are the following:

1. External schemas, which restrict user views of the data base
2. Authorizations and controls, which identify users and restrict the actions they may take against the data base
3. User-defined procedures, which define additional constraints or limitations in using the data base
4. Encryption procedures, which encode data in an unrecognizable form
5. Authentication schemes, which positively identify a person attempting to gain access to a data base

External Schemas

External views and schemas promote security by restricting user views of the data base. Any data that are not included in a particular user view are presumably unknown to that user and cannot be accessed by a program that uses the external schema for that view. For example, USERVIEW1 shown in Figure 11-3 contains only the attributes CUSTOMER# and CREDIT-LIMIT. It contains no information about other attributes in the CUSTOMER relation and no information about the ORDER relation. Any user that uses USERVIEW1 cannot access these remaining attributes.

Although user views promote security, they are not adequate security measures. Unauthorized persons may gain knowledge of or access to a particular view. Also, several persons may share a particular view; all may have authority to read the data, but only a restricted few may be authorized to update the data. Finally, with high-level query languages, an unauthorized person may gain access to data through simple experimentation (as in *War Games*). As a result, more sophisticated security measures are normally required.

Authorization Rules

Authorization rules are controls incorporated in the data management system that restrict access to data and also restrict the actions that people may take when data are accessed. For example, a person who can supply the

Figure 11-13
Authorization matrix

Subject	Object	Action	Constraint
Sales Dept.	Customer Record	Insert	Credit limit LE $5000
Order trans.	Customer record	Read	None
Terminal 12	Customer record	Modify	Balance due only
Acctg Dept.	Order record	Delete	None
Luke Skywalker	Order record	Insert	Order amt LT $2000
Program AR4	Order record	Modify	None

password JEDI may be authorized to read any record in a data base but cannot necessarily modify any of those records.

Fernandez, Summers, and Wood (1981) have developed a conceptual model of data base security. Their model expresses authorization rules in the form of a table (or matrix) that includes subjects, objects, actions, and constraints. Each row of the table indicates that a particular subject is authorized to take a certain action on an object in the data base, perhaps subject to some constraint. An example of such an authorization matrix is shown in Figure 11-13. This table contains several entries pertaining to records in the ORDER-ACCOUNTING data base. For example, the first row in the table indicates that anyone in the Sales Department is authorized to insert a new CUSTOMER record in the data base, provided that the customer's credit limit does not exceed $5000. The last row indicates that the program AR4 is authorized to modify ORDER records without restriction. Data administration is responsible for determining authorization rules.

Subjects Subjects are organizational entities that can access the data base. Examples of subjects are individuals, departments (or groups of people), terminals, transactions, and applications (all of these are illustrated in Figure 11-13). Also, subjects may be combinations of entities—for example, a particular person entering a certain transaction at a particular terminal.

Positive identification of subjects is a continuing problem in computer security. In most systems today, individuals are identified by passwords (often in conjunction with names and account numbers). However, passwords are unreliable, as *War Games* clearly illustrates. More positive identification techniques, such as fingerprints and voiceprints, are being introduced to control access to sensitive data.

Objects Objects are data base entities to be protected by the security system. Examples of objects are records, relations, data items, programs, and data bases. In Figure 11-13, the objects are records.

In designing a security system, we must decide on the **granularity,** or size, of object to be protected by the system. A security system that permits (or denies) access to an entire data base is said to have large granularity, while a system that grants access to individual data items (or attributes) has small granularity. A system with large granularity exercises gross control over the data base. Individual users are either allowed access to the entire data base or else denied access. Systems with small granularity exercise close control: A user may be authorized to modify one data item in a record type but not authorized to modify another data item in the same record type. Such systems increase processing overhead since the system must exercise a security check every time a user attempts to access any data item. Most security systems compromise by providing security at the record level.

Actions The third attribute in the authorization table is the action that can be taken by the subject against the object. Typical actions that can be taken are shown in Figure 11-13: Read, Insert, Modify, and Delete. Additional actions that can be defined are Create (add a new record type, data item type, or other entity type to the data base) and Destroy (delete an entity type from the data base). These two actions require changes to the metadata, and authority is generally restricted to persons in data administration. Other data base actions may be defined by users and included in the authorization matrix.

Constraints Constraints on authorization rules are specified in the last column of the authorization matrix. As an example of a constraint, the fifth row of the table in Figure 11-13 indicates that a particular person (Luke Skywalker) can insert new ORDER records into the data base only if the amount of the order is less than $2000.

Implementing Authorization Rules Most contemporary data base management systems do not implement an authorization matrix such as the one shown in Figure 11-13. Instead, simplified versions are normally used. There are two principal types: authorization tables for subjects and authorization tables for objects. An example of each type is shown in Figure 11-14. In Figure 11-14a, for example, we see that salespersons (who are probably identified by passwords) are allowed to modify CUSTOMER records but not delete these records. In Figure 11-14b, we see that ORDER records can be modified by persons in Order Entry or Accounting but not by salespersons. A given DBMS product may provide either one or both of these types of facilities.

Authorization tables such as those shown in Figure 11-14 are attributes of an organization's data and their environment and therefore are properly viewed as metadata. Thus, the tables should be stored and maintained in the data dictionary/directory. Since authorization tables contain highly sensitive data, they themselves should be protected by stringent security rules. Normally, only selected persons in data administration have authority to access and modify these tables.

Figure 11-14
Implementing authorization rules:
(a) authorizations for subjects (salespersons)
(b) authorizations for objects (ORDER records)

	Customer records	Order records
Read	Y	Y
Insert	Y	N
Modify	Y	N
Delete	N	N

(a)

	Salespersons (password JABBA)	Order entry (password HUTT)	Accounting (password QUILL)
Read	Y	Y	Y
Insert	N	Y	N
Modify	N	Y	Y
Delete	N	N	Y

(b)

User Procedures

Some DBMS products provide user exits (or interfaces) that allow system designers or users to define their own security procedures in addition to the authorization rules we have just described. For example, a user procedure might be designed to provide positive user identification. In attempting to log on to the computer, the user might be required to supply a procedure name in addition to a simple password. If a valid password and procedure name are supplied, the system then calls the procedure, which asks the user a series of questions whose answers should be known only to that password holder (such as mother's maiden name). Other user procedures can be used to enforce constraints in authorization rules (such as those in Figure 11-14).

Encryption Procedures

For highly sensitive data (such as company financial data), data encryption can be used. **Encryption** is the coding (or scrambling) of data so that they cannot be read by humans. Some DBMS products include encryption routines that automatically encode sensitive data when it is stored or transmitted over communications channels. Other DBMS products provide exits that allow users to code their own encryption routines.

Any system that provides encryption facilities must also provide complementary routines for decoding the data. These decoding routines must of course be protected by adequate security, or else the advantages of encryption are lost. These routines also require significant computing resources.

Authentication Schemes

A long-standing problem in computer circles is how to positively identify persons who are trying to gain access to a computer or its resources. Passwords cannot, of themselves, ensure the security of a computer and its data bases because they give no indication of who is trying to gain access. To circumvent this problem, the industry is developing devices and techniques to positively identify any prospective user. The most promising of these appear to be *biometric devices,* which measure or detect personal characteristics such as fingerprints, voice prints, retina prints, or signature dynamics. To implement this approach, several companies have developed a *smart card*—a thin plastic card the size of a credit card, with an embedded microprocessor. An individual's unique biometric data (such as fingerprints) are stored permanently on the card. To access a computer, the user inserts the card into a reader device (a biometric device) that reads the person's fingerprint (or other characteristic). The actual biometric data are then compared with the stored data, and the two must match to gain computer access. A lost or stolen smart card would be useless to another person, since the biometric data would not match.

CONCURRENCY CONTROL

In most systems, several users can access a data base concurrently. The operating system switches execution from one user program to another to minimize waiting for input/output operations. With this approach, transactions are often interleaved; that is, several steps are performed on transaction A, then several steps on transaction B, followed by several more steps on transaction A, and so on. When transactions are interleaved, errors will occur in updating unless the DBMS has features to prevent interference between transactions.

Effects of Concurrent Updates

The effects of concurrent updates without concurrency control are illustrated in Figure 11-15. Two users are in the process of updating the same record, which represents a SAVINGS ACCOUNT record for customer A. At the present time, customer A has a balance of $100 in her savings account.

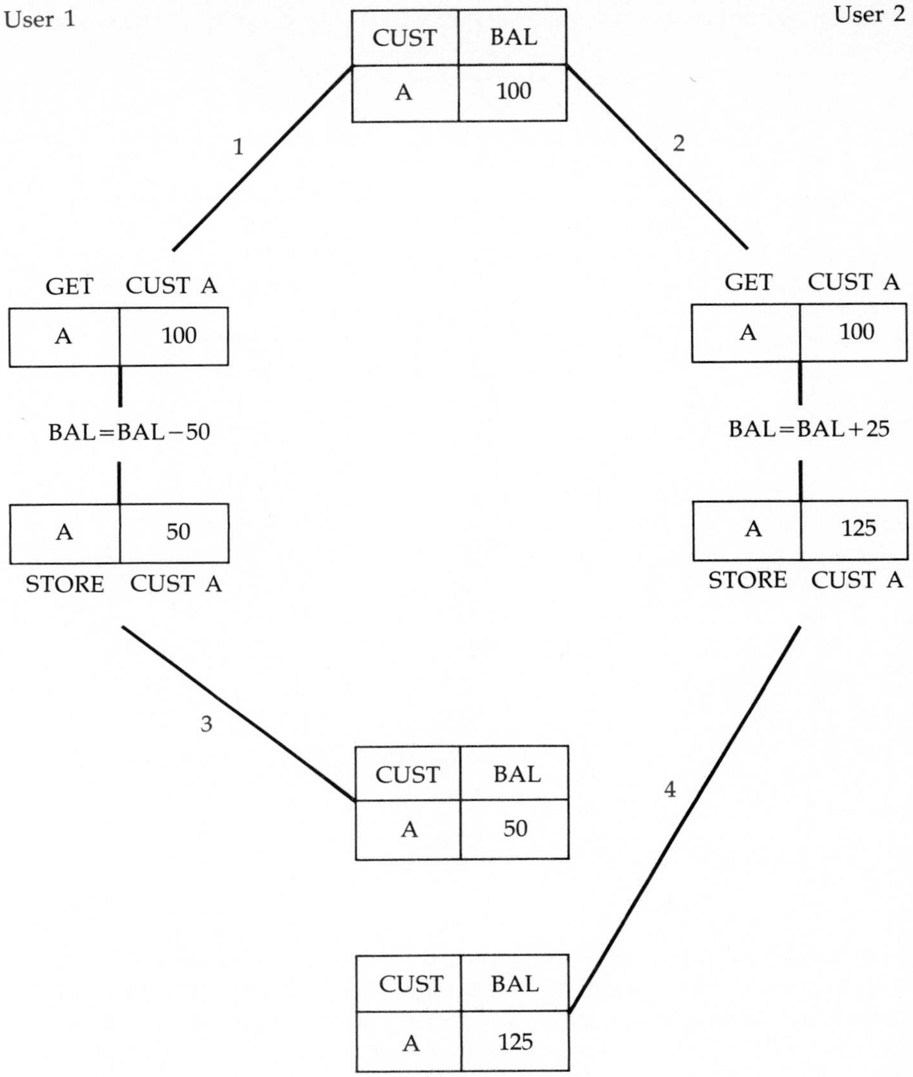

Figure 11-15
Effect of concurrent update

User 1 reads this record into the user work area, intending to post a customer withdrawal of $50. Next, user 2 reads the same record into that user work area, intending to post a customer deposit of $25. User 1 posts the withdrawal and stores the record, which now indicates a balance of $50. User 2 then posts the deposit (increasing the balance to $125) and stores this record on top of the one stored by user 1. The record now indicates a balance of $125 (customer A will be delighted by this turn of events!). In this case, the transaction for user 1 has been lost because of interference between the transactions.

Resource-Locking Mechanism

To prevent erroneous updates, the DBMS must incorporate a resource-locking mechanism. That is, any data that are retrieved by one user with the intent of updating must be "locked" or denied to other users until the update is completed.

Usually, data required by a program are locked when a transaction begins and released when the transaction is either completed (and committed) or aborted. Thus, to administer resource locking, the DBMS requires two pieces of information:

1. Intention to update—whether a particular program (or terminal session) will require updating the data base
2. Transaction boundaries—when a transaction begins and ends (discussed earlier)

An important consideration in evaluating the locking mechanism is the **lock level,** or granularity. The choices, which are the same as for security, are the data base, file (or relation), record (or tuple), or data item (or attribute).

At one extreme, the DBMS could lock the entire data base for each user update request. This is generally unacceptable, since most transactions would have to wait for the data base locks. At the other extreme, the DBMS could lock individual data items so that two data items in the same record occurrence could be updated concurrently by two different users. This approach would provide the fewest conflicts, but would increase processing overhead. Locking at the record level is the most common approach with contemporary systems.

Deadly Embrace

Resource locking (say, at the record level) solves the problem of erroneous updates, but it may lead to another problem: the deadly embrace. The **deadly embrace** (or "deadlock") is an impasse that results when two users each lock certain resources, then request resources locked by the other user. An example of this situation is shown in Figure 11-16. User A is waiting for record Y (locked by user B), and user B is waiting for record X (locked by user A). Unless the DBMS intervenes, both users will wait indefinitely.

There are two basic ways to resolve the deadly embrace: deadlock prevention and deadlock resolution.

Deadlock Prevention When deadlock prevention is employed, user programs must lock all records they will require at the beginning of a transaction (rather than one at a time). In Figure 11-16, user A would have to lock both records X and Y before processing the transaction (if either record is already locked, the program must wait until it is released).

Locking records in advance prevents deadlock. Unfortunately, it is often difficult to predict in advance what records will be required to process a

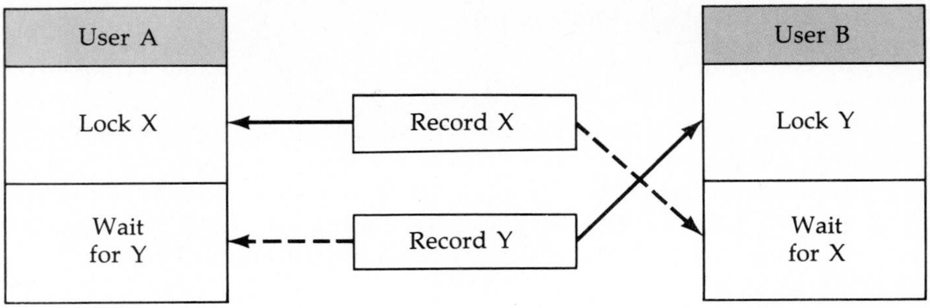

Figure 11-16 Example of the deadly embrace

transaction. A typical program has many processing paths and may call other programs. As a result, deadlock prevention is not often practical.

Deadlock Resolution The second (and more common) approach is to allow deadlocks to occur, but to build mechanisms into the DBMS for detecting and breaking the deadlocks. Essentially, this is how these mechanisms work: The DBMS maintains a matrix of resource usage, which, at a given instant, indicates what subjects (users) are using what objects (resources). By scanning this matrix, the computer can detect deadlocks as they occur. The DBMS then resolves the deadlocks by "backing out" one of the deadlocked transactions. Any changes made by that transaction up to the time of deadlock are removed, and the transaction is restarted when the required resources become available. We will describe the procedure for backing out shortly.

DATA BASE RECOVERY

Data base recovery is data administration's response to Murphy's law. Inevitably, data bases are damaged or lost because of some system failure. Such failures are caused by human error, hardware failure, incorrect or invalid data, program errors, and natural catastrophes. Since the organization depends so heavily on its data base, the data management system must provide mechanisms for restoring a data base quickly and accurately after loss or damage.

Basic Recovery Facilities

A data base management system should provide four basic facilities for backup and recovery of a data base:

1. Backup facilities, which provide periodic backup copies of the entire data base
2. Journalizing facilities, which maintain an audit trail of transactions and data base changes

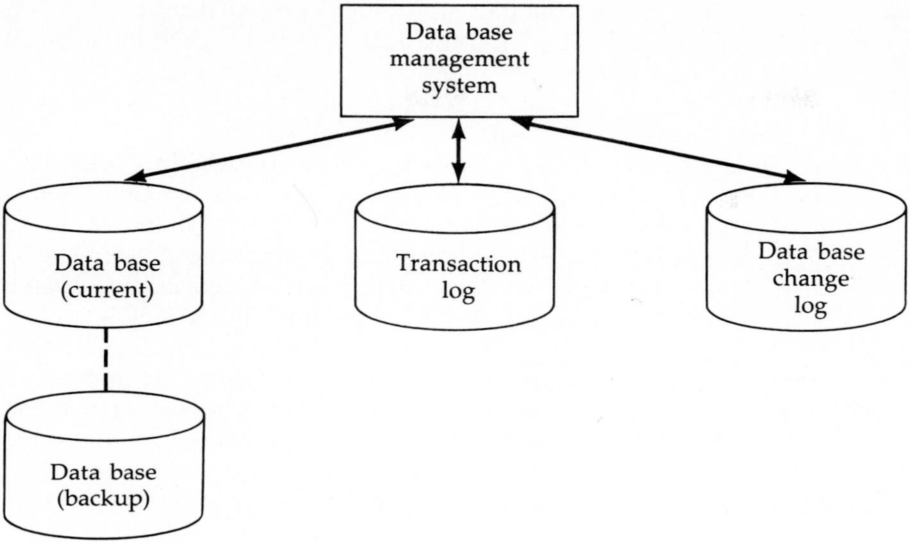

Figure 11-17
Data base journals and backup copy

3. A checkpoint facility, by which the DBMS periodically suspends all processing and synchronizes its files and journals
4. A recovery manager, which allows the DBMS to restore the data base to a correct condition and restart processing transactions

Backup Facilities The DBMS should provide an automatic dump facility that produces a backup copy (or "save") of the entire data base. Typically, a backup copy is produced at least once per day. The copy should be stored in a secured location where it is protected from loss or damage. The backup copy is used to restore the data base in the event of catastrophic loss or damage.

Journalizing Facilities A DBMS must provide an audit trail of transactions and data base changes. As shown in Figure 11-17, there are two basic journals or logs. First, there is the **transaction log,** which contains a record of the essential data for each transaction that is processed against the data base. Data that are typically recorded for each transaction include the transaction code or identification, time of the transaction, terminal number or user ID, data values input, records accessed, and records modified.

The second kind of log is the data base change log, which contains before and after images of records that have been modified by transactions. A **before image** is simply a copy of a record before it has been modified, while an **after image** is a copy of the same record after it has been modified.

Checkpoint Facility A *checkpoint* is a facility by which the DBMS periodically refuses to accept any new transactions. All transactions in progress are completed and the journal files are brought up to date. At this point, the system is in a "quiet state" and the data base and transaction logs are synchronized. The DBMS writes a special record (called a checkpoint record) to the log file. The checkpoint record contains information necessary to restart the system.

A DBMS may perform checkpoints automatically (which is preferred) or in response to commands in user application programs. Checkpoints should be taken frequently (say, several times an hour). When failures do occur, it is often possible to resume processing from the most recent checkpoint. Thus, only a few minutes of processing has to be repeated, compared with several hours for a complete restart of the day's processing.

Recovery Manager The recovery manager is a module of the DBMS that restores the data base to a correct condition when a failure occurs and resumes processing user requests. The type of restart used depends on the nature of the failure. The recovery manager uses the journal files shown in Figure 11-17 (as well as the backup copy, if necessary) to restore the data base.

Recovery and Restart Procedures

The type of recovery procedure that is used in a given situation depends on the nature of the failure, the sophistication of the DBMS recovery facilities, and operational policies and procedures. Following is a discussion of the techniques that are most frequently used.

Restore/Rerun Restore/rerun involves reprocessing the day's transactions (up to the point of failure) against the backup copy of the data base. The most recent copy of the data base (say, from the previous day) is mounted, and all transactions that have occurred since that copy (which are stored on the transaction log) are rerun.

The advantage of restore/rerun is its simplicity. The DBMS does not need to create a data base change journal, and no special restart procedures are required. However, there are two major disadvantages to restore/rerun. First, the time to reprocess transactions may be prohibitive. Depending on the frequency of making backup copies, several hours of reprocessing may be required. Processing new transactions will have to be deferred until recovery is completed, and if the system is heavily loaded, it may be impossible to catch up. The second disadvantage is that the sequencing of transactions will often be different from when they were originally processed. This may lead to quite different results. For example, in the original run, a customer deposit may be posted before a withdrawal. In the rerun, the withdrawal transaction may be attempted first and may lead to sending a "not sufficient funds" notice to the customer.

For these reasons, restore/rerun is not a sufficient recovery procedure and is generally used only as a last resort in data base processing.

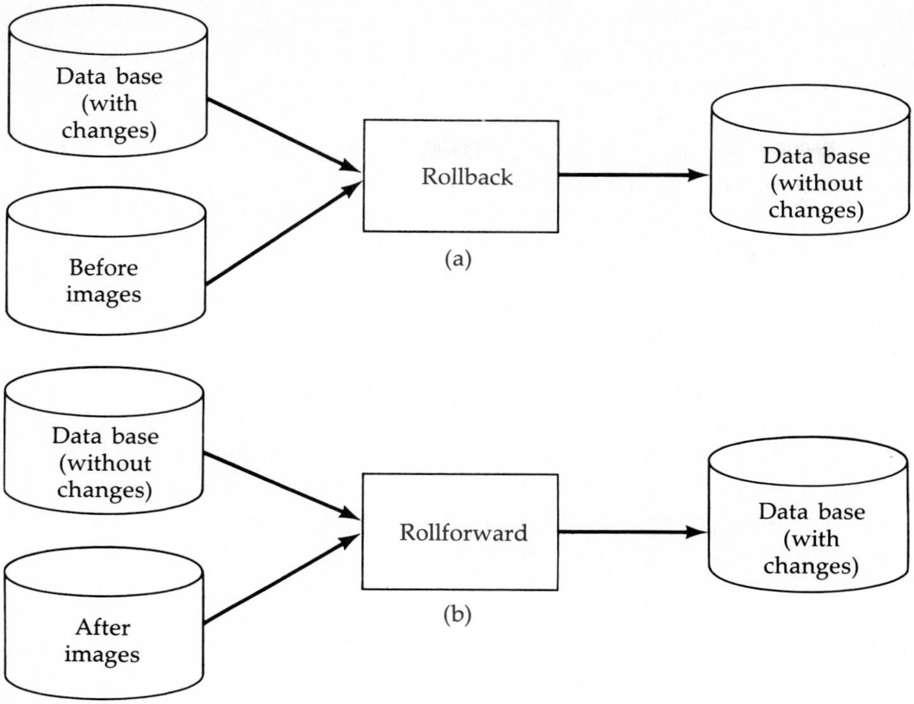

Figure 11-18
Basic recovery techniques

Backward Recovery Backward recovery (also called "rollback") is used to back out or undo unwanted changes to the data base. As shown in Figure 11-18a, before images of the records that have been changed are applied to the data base. As a result, the data base is returned to an earlier state (the unwanted changes are eliminated).

Backward recovery is used to reverse the changes made by transactions that have aborted, or terminated abnormally. To illustrate the need for backward recovery (or UNDO), suppose that a banking transaction will transfer $100 in funds from the account for customer A to the account for customer B. The following steps are performed:

1. The program reads the record for customer A and subtracts $100 from the account balance.
2. The program then reads the record for customer B and adds $100 to the account balance.

Now the program outputs the updated record for customer A to the data base. However, in attempting to output the record for customer B, the program encounters an error condition (such as a disk fault) and cannot write the record. Now the data base is inconsistent—record A has been updated but record B has not. Thus the transaction must be aborted. An

UNDO command will cause the recovery manager to apply the before image for record A to restore the account balance to its original value (the recovery manager may then restart the transaction and make another attempt).

Forward Recovery Forward recovery (also called "rollforward") starts with an earlier copy of the data base. By applying after images (the results of good transactions), the data base is quickly moved forward to a later state (see Figure 11-18b). Forward recovery is much faster and more accurate than restore/rerun, for the following reasons:

1. The time-consuming logic of reprocessing each transaction does not have to be repeated.
2. Only the most recent after images need to be applied. A data base record may have a series of after images (as a result of a sequence of updates). However, only the most recent "good" after image is required for rollforward.
3. The problem of different sequencing of transactions is avoided, since the results of applying the transactions (rather than the transactions themselves) are used.

Types of Data Base Failure

A wide variety of failures can occur in processing a data base, ranging from the input of an incorrect data value to complete loss or destruction of the data base. Four of the most common types of errors are aborted transactions, incorrect data, system failure, and data base loss or destruction. Each of these types of errors is described in the following sections, and the most common recovery procedure is indicated.

Aborted Transactions As we noted earlier, a transaction frequently requires a sequence of processing steps to be performed. Often, a transaction that is in progress will abort, or terminate abnormally. Some reasons for this type of failure are human error, input of invalid data, hardware failure, and deadlock. A common type of hardware failure is the loss of transmission in a communications link when a transaction is in progress.

When a transaction aborts, we want to "back out" the transaction and remove any changes that have been made (but not committed) to the data base. The recovery manager accomplishes this by backward recovery (applying before images for the transaction in question). This function should be accomplished automatically by the DBMS, which then notifies the user to correct and resubmit the transaction.

Incorrect Data A more complex situation arises when the data base has been updated with incorrect, but valid, data. For example, an incorrect grade may be recorded for a student, or an incorrect amount input for a customer payment.

Incorrect data are difficult to detect and often lead to complications. To begin with, some time may elapse before an error is detected and the data base record (or records) corrected. By this time, numerous other users may have used the erroneous data, and a chain reaction of errors may have occurred as various applications made use of the incorrect data. In addition, transaction outputs (such as documents and messages) based on the incorrect data may be transmitted to persons. For example, an incorrect grade report may be sent to a student, or an incorrect statement to a customer.

When incorrect data have been introduced, the data base may be recovered in one of the following ways:

1. If the error is discovered soon enough, backward recovery may be used. (However, care must be taken to ensure that all subsequent errors have been reversed.)
2. A series of compensating transactions may be introduced through human intervention to correct the errors if only a few errors have occurred.
3. If the first two measures are infeasible, it may be necessary to restart from the most recent checkpoint before the error occurred.

Any erroneous messages or documents that have been produced by the erroneous transaction will have to be corrected by appropriate human intervention (letters of explanation, telephone calls, and so on).

System Failure With a system failure, some component of the system fails, but the data base is not damaged. Some causes of system failure are power loss, operator error, loss of communications transmission, and system software failure.

When the system crashes, some transactions may be in progress. The first step in recovery is to back out those transactions using before images (backward recovery). However, it may not be possible to restart from this point after a system crash, since status information in main memory will likely be lost or damaged. The safest approach is to restart from the most recent checkpoint before the system failure. The data base is rolled forward by applying after images for all transactions that were processed after that checkpoint.

Data Base Destruction In the case of data base destruction, the data base itself is lost or destroyed or cannot be read. A typical cause of data base destruction is a disk drive failure (or head crash).

A backup copy of the data base is required for recovery in this situation. Forward recovery is used to restore the data base to its state immediately before the loss occurred. Any transactions that may have been in progress when the data base was lost are restarted.

SUMMARY

We conclude this chapter by summarizing some of the important considerations in evaluating and selecting data management software. For a more detailed discussion of selection criteria, see Martin (1983).

Integrated Data Dictionary/Directory System The foundation of a modern data management system is an integrated (or built-in) data dictionary/directory. Ideally, the DD/DS should be fully active—that is, it should provide a single source of metadata for all users and software components. Also, the DD/DS should be interactive and user-friendly.

Data Independence The system should afford a high level of data independence by providing clear boundaries between logical and physical data management. The three-level DBMS architecture described in this chapter provides this facility.

Data Base Recovery The DBMS must provide adequate mechanisms for recovery and restart following some system failure or data base loss. These mechanisms include transaction logs, data base change files, backward and forward recovery, and automatic system restarts.

Security Mechanisms The software should provide comprehensive controls to protect the data base. These controls include passwords, authorization tables, and audit trails.

Integrity Controls The software should provide at least the following controls over data integrity: concurrency controls, validity checks, and automatic range checks. More comprehensive integrity control mechanisms are under development but are not yet available in most systems today.

User-Oriented Languages The data management system *must* include high-level, user-oriented languages (query languages, report and graphics generators, spreadsheet programs, and so on). These languages must be easy to learn and use and should be supported by computer-assisted instruction in their use.

On-Line User Facilities The data management system should provide a number of facilities for on-line users: integrated teleprocessing monitor, on-line query language, and support for local area networks and distributed data bases (if appropriate).

Qualified Vendor The data management software vendor should be chosen very carefully. Some things to look for are financial stability, an excellent reputation for support, a full range of training courses, a sound commitment to an evolving product line, and satisfied customers.

The concepts described in this chapter provide a framework for the next four chapters, which describe implementations of specific data management systems.

Chapter Review

REVIEW QUESTIONS

1. Give a concise definition for each of the following terms:
   a. data base management system
   b. transaction
   c. schema
   d. data definition language
   e. logical data independence
   f. data dictionary/directory
   g. impact analysis
   h. active DD/DS
   i. data base control system
   j. binding time
   k. deadly embrace
2. Contrast the following terms:
   a. DBMS; DD/DS
   b. DBCS; DBSS
   c. data dictionary; data directory
   d. external schema; internal schema
   e. active data dictionary; passive data dictionary
   f. deadlock prevention; deadlock resolution
   g. backward recovery; forward recovery
3. List and briefly describe six software components of a typical data management system.
4. List and briefly describe eight functions of a DBMS.
5. What is meant by the term *transaction integrity*? How is it achieved?
6. Explain the purpose of each of the following:
   a. conceptual schema
   b. external schema
   c. internal schema
7. What is the "extensibility" feature of a DD/DS? Why is it important?
8. List and briefly describe six functions of a DD/D manager.
9. Why is the execution time for a query language processor likely to be slower than for a prewritten program?
10. Describe three important functions of a TP monitor.
11. Describe four basic DBMS facilities that are required for backup and recovery of a data base.
12. Why is forward recovery generally faster and more accurate than restore/rerun?
13. List and briefly describe four common types of data base failure.
14. List and briefly describe eight categories of computer crime.

PROBLEMS AND EXERCISES

1. For each of the following changes to the ORDER-ACCOUNTING data base, describe the changes that are required to the schemas (Figures 11-2, 11-3, and 11-4). Indicate whether each change provides an example of physical or logical data independence.
   a. Add a new relation (or record type) called ORDER LINE to the conceptual schema. This relation contains the following attributes: PRODUCT#, ORDER#, QTY-ORDERED.
   b. Expand USERVIEW1 to include the attribute CUSTOMER-NAME.
   c. Change the representation for the attribute BALANCE-DUE from "FLOAT" to "INTEGER."
   d. Change the index CUST-NAME from a secondary key index to a primary key index.
   e. Change the blocking factor for ORDER records from five to ten records per block.

2. Refer to the description of the movie *War Games* in the chapter. What type of security violation (or deficiency) is evidenced by each of the following incidents, and how could they be corrected?
   a. The student finds the computer password on the principal's desk.
   b. Using the principal's password, the student is able to modify student grade information.

3. Fill in the following authorization tables for Mountain View Community Hospital with Y (for yes) or N (for no), based on your own assumptions.

a.

	Patient records	Patient charges	Physician records	Employee records
Read				
Insert				
Modify				
Delete				

Authorizations for Nurses

b.

	Nurses	Physicians	Admissions	Administrator
Read				
Insert				
Modify				
Delete				

Authorizations for Patient Records

4. Fill in the following authorization tables for Pine Valley Furniture Company (Y or N), based on your own assumptions.

a.

	Customer records	Employee records	Product records
Read			
Insert			
Modify			
Delete			

Authorizations for Salespersons

b.

	Accountants	Quality inspectors	Personnel Department	President
Read				
Insert				
Modify				
Delete				

Authorizations for Employee Records

5. Write a conceptual schema (similar to the one in Figure 11-2c) for the following data model, which was extracted from the Mountain View Community Hospital conceptual model.

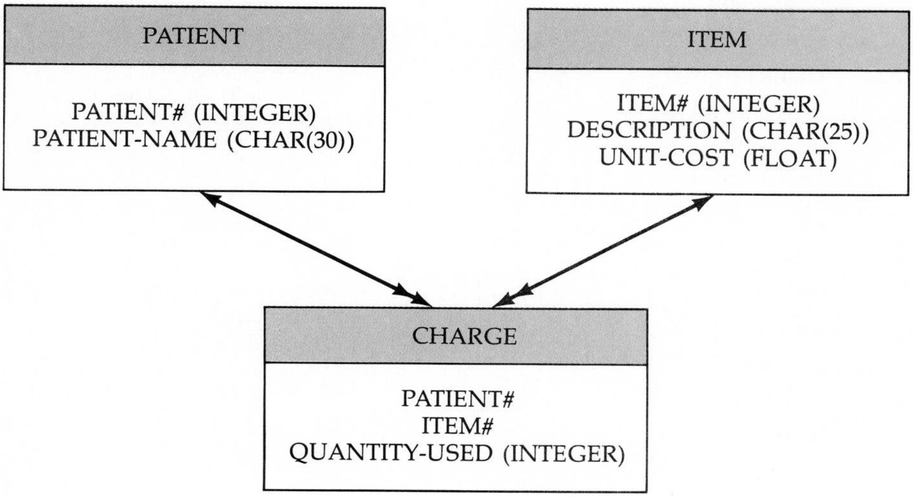

6. Develop two user views based on the conceptual model shown in Problem 5. For each user view, write an external schema similar to those shown in Figure 11-3.

7. Develop sample data dictionary entries (similar to those in Figure 11-6) for the conceptual model shown in Problem 5.

8. Explain what data base recovery technique is most appropriate for each of the following situations:
   a. A phone disconnection occurs while a user is entering a transaction.
   b. A disk pack is dropped and is damaged so that it cannot be used.
   c. A lightning storm causes a power failure.
   d. An incorrect amount is entered and posted for a student tuition payment. The error is not discovered for several days.
9. For the concurrent update situations shown in Figure 11-15, what balance would be shown if the transaction for user 2 was processed and the results stored before the transaction for user 1?
10. For the deadly embrace example pictured in Figure 11-16, what action should be taken by the DBMS?
11. Suppose that you are evaluating data management software for your own personal computer. Classify the factors named in the Summary as being of high (H) or low (L) importance.
12. Visit an organization that is using data management software.
   a. Which of the software components shown in Figure 11-1 are being used?
   b. Evaluate the procedures that are used for security and for data base recovery.
13. Match the following terms to the appropriate definitions:

_____ TP monitor
_____ transaction
_____ schema
_____ DDL
_____ data directory
_____ extensibility
_____ DBCS
_____ DBSS
_____ active DD/DS
_____ binding
_____ security
_____ granularity
_____ lock level
_____ deadly embrace
_____ encryption

a. definition of a data base using a DDL
b. contains information about where data are stored
c. allows users to define additional entities
d. module that interfaces with user programs
e. sequence of steps for a business activity
f. software that manages communications
g. sole source of metadata
h. commands used to describe a data base
i. application program linked to its schema
j. module that manipulates storage files
k. size of object protected by security system
l. two users have locked the same records
m. coding of data for protection
n. protecting a data base against loss
o. synonym for granularity

14. Find a recent example of computer crime in the press. Which type of computer crime (as discussed in the text) was involved? Was the person prosecuted?

REFERENCES

Allen, Frank W., Mary E. S. Loomis, and Michael V. Mannino. 1982. "The Integrated Dictionary/Directory System." *Computing Surveys* 14 (June): 245–286.

Auerbach Publishers. 1981. *Practical Data Base Management.* Princeton, N.J.: Auerbach Publishers.

Bloombecker, J. J. Buck. 1986. "New Federal Law Bolsters Computer Security Efforts." *Computerworld* 20, no. 43 (October 27): 53–62.

Codd, E. F. 1982. "Relational Database: A Practical Foundation for Productivity." *Communications of the ACM* 25 (February): 109–117.

Fernandez, Eduardo B., Rita C. Summers, and Christopher Wood. 1981. *Database Security and Integrity.* Reading, Mass.: Addison-Wesley.

Martin, James. 1986. *Fourth Generation Languages.* Vol. 2. *Representative 4GLs.* Englewood Cliffs, N.J.: Prentice-Hall, 37.

Martin, James. 1983. *Managing the Data-Base Environment.* Englewood Cliffs, N.J.: Prentice-Hall.

Chapter 12

Hierarchical Data Base Systems

INTRODUCTION

The earliest data base management systems were based on the hierarchical data model. As data base requirements have become better understood, these systems have had to evolve to handle a broader range of data structures. However, many organizations today continue to use hierarchical data base management systems because of the investment they have in these products and in the related application programs.

The leading hierarchical DBMS still in use today is IBM's Information Management System (IMS). IMS was developed during the mid-1960s in response to the data processing needs of the aerospace industry. This development was undertaken as a joint project of IBM and North American Aviation. Since its introduction in the late 1960s, IMS has evolved through several versions. The current version is IMS/VS (Information Management System/Virtual Storage). IMS is widely used among installations with IBM mainframe computers.

The IMS development team chose the hierarchical structure because they agreed with the philosopher who observed that all views of life are hierarchical in nature. They began by developing a physical hierarchical view, which unfortunately does not always mirror life. Finally, through logical relationships and other improvements, IMS was able to model life by becoming a logical hierarchical system.

IMS PHYSICAL DATA BASES

The physical data base record is a basic building block in IMS. A **physical data base record** (PDBR) consists of a hierarchical arrangement of segments. A **segment,** in turn, consists of a set of related fields. The top segment (or entry point) in a PDBR is called the **root** segment. A PDBR, then, consists of a root segment plus a hierarchical arrangement of subordinate segments called **child** segments.

A typical IMS physical data base record is shown in Figure 12-1. This PDBR contains information about departments, about equipment that is assigned to each department, and about employees assigned to each department. DEPARTMT is the name of the root segment type for this PDBR, and EQPMENT and EMPLOYEE are child segment types. The EMPLOYEE segment, in turn, has two child segments, DEPENDNT and SKILL. These segments contain information about each employee's dependents and skills, respectively.

PDBR Occurrences

The physical data base record shown in Figure 12-1 is a PDBR *type.* An occurrence of this PDBR type is shown in Figure 12-2. This occurrence represents data for one department (ACCTG) and contains two EQPMENT segments and two EMPLOYEE segments. The first employee (Evans) has three dependents and two skills. The second employee (Thomas) has one skill and no dependents.

Each occurrence of a root segment represents one PDBR occurrence.

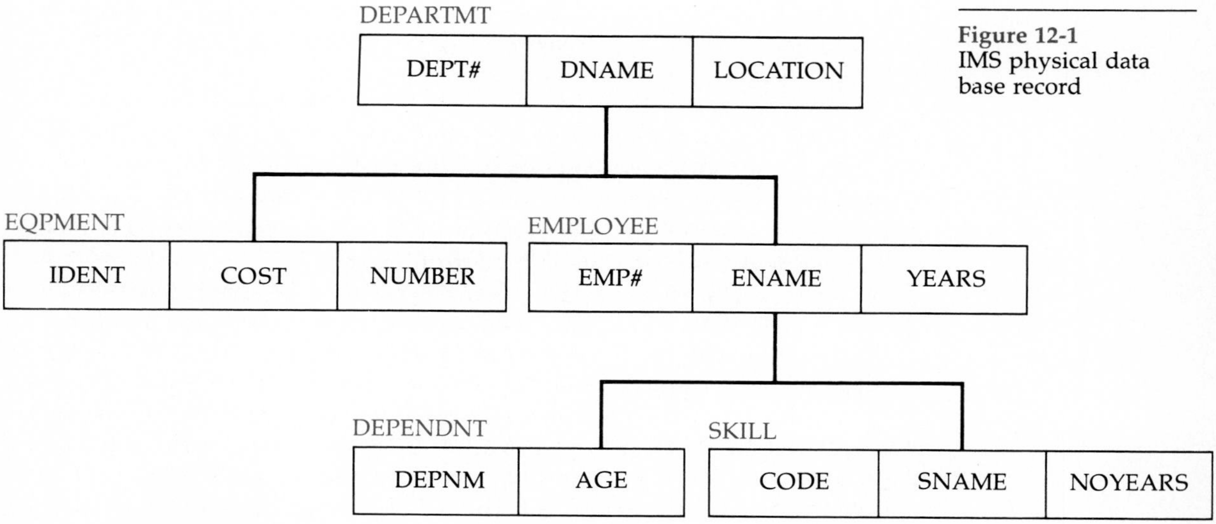

Figure 12-1
IMS physical data base record

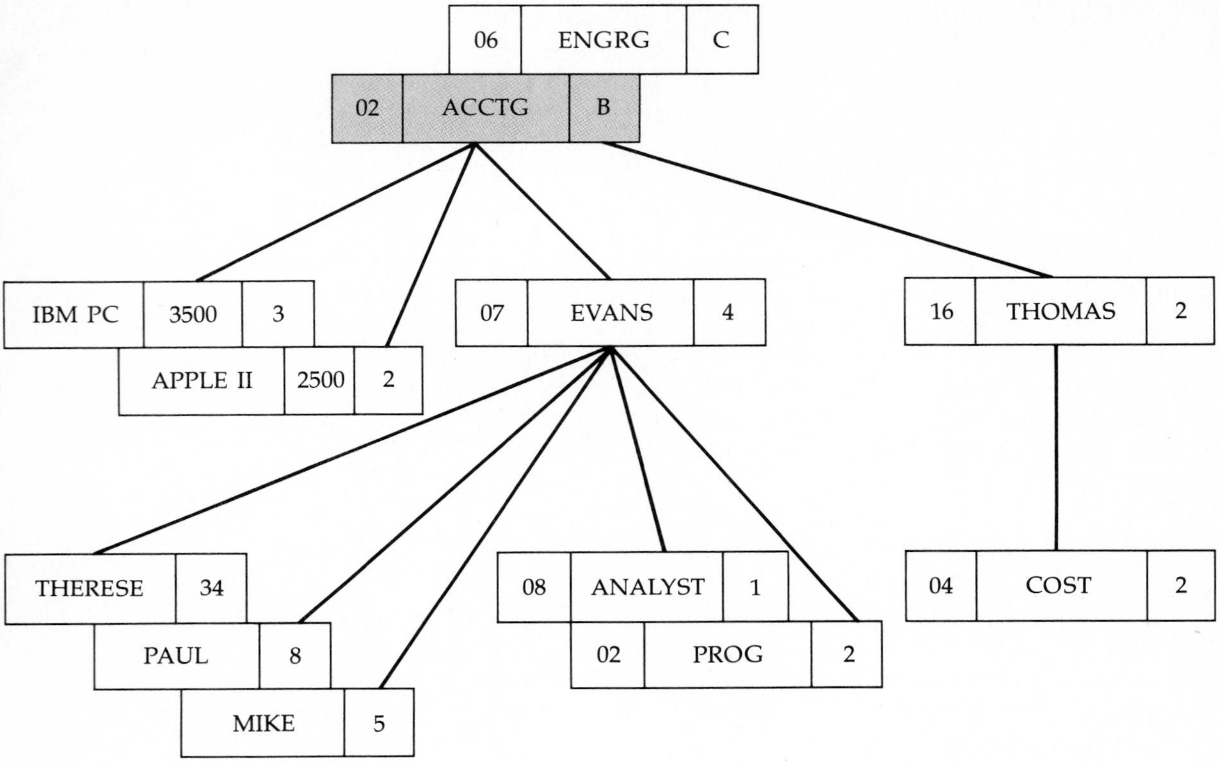

Figure 12-2
An occurrence of the PDBR

Thus, all the segments constitute one such PDBR occurrence (the ENGRG root segment shown would constitute a second occurrence of this record type).

Data Base Description

Each IMS physical data base record type is defined by a **data base description** (DBD). The DBD appears as a set of macro statements that define the segments and fields within a PDBR. These macro statements are coded by a programmer or data base analyst and then assembled into object form and stored in a library by the IMS control program.

A skeleton DBD for the department data base is shown in Figure 12-3. The statements have been numbered for reference in the following discussion; normally, these statement numbers are omitted.

Statement 1 assigns the name DEPTDB to the data base shown in Figure 12-1. Statement 2 then defines the root segment. This segment type is assigned the name DEPARTMT and is defined as 27 bytes in length. All names in IMS are limited to a maximum length of eight characters.

Statements 3 to 5 define the three field types that are included in DEPARTMT. Each FIELD definition statement defines the name, length,

```
 1  DBD    NAME=DEPTDB
 2  SEGM   NAME=DEPARTMT, BYTES=27, PARENT=0
 3  FIELD  NAME=(DEPT#, SEQ), BYTES=3, START=1
 4  FIELD  NAME=DNAME, BYTES=20, START=4
 5  FIELD  NAME=LOCATION, BYTES=4, START=24
 6  SEGM   NAME=EQPMENT, PARENT=DEPARTMT, BYTES=27
 7  FIELD  NAME=(IDENT, SEQ), BYTES=15, START=1
 8  FIELD  NAME=COST, BYTES=10, START=16
 9  FIELD  NAME=NUMBER, BYTES=4, START=26
10  SEGM   NAME=EMPLOYEE, PARENT=DEPARTMT, BYTES=42
11  FIELD  NAME=(EMP#, SEQ), BYTES=10, START=1
12  FIELD  NAME=ENAME,BYTES=30, START=11
13  FIELD  NAME=YEARS, BYTES=2, START=41
14  SEGM   NAME=DEPENDNT, PARENT=EMPLOYEE, BYTES=32
15  FIELD  NAME=(DEPNM, SEQ), BYTES=30, START=1
16  FIELD  NAME=AGE, BYTES=2, START=31
17  SEGM   NAME=SKILL, PARENT=EMPLOYEE, BYTES=28
18  FIELD  NAME=(CODE, SEQ), BYTES=6, START=1
19  FIELD  NAME=SNAME, BYTES=20, START=7
20  FIELD  NAME=NOYEARS, BYTES=2, START=27
```

Figure 12-3
Data base description (DEPTDB)

and starting position within the segment. Statement 3 contains the clause NAME=(DEPT#,SEQ). This clause defines DEPT# to be the sequence field for the DEPARTMT root segment type. As a result, physical data base record occurrences within the DEPTDB data base are sequenced in ascending department number sequence.

Statement 6 defines the EQPMENT segment type. The clause PARENT=DEPARTMT in this statement defines EQPMENT as a child segment of DEPARTMT. The segment is 29 bytes in length.

Statement 7 defines the IDENT field type within the EQPMENT segment type. The clause NAME=(IDENT,SEQ) means that for each occurrence of a parent DEPARTMT segment type, occurrences of the child EQPMENT segment type are stored in ascending sequence according to the IDENT field. Thus, for example, in Figure 12-2, the segment for APPLE II occurs before the segment for IBM PC. All occurrences of child segments of a particular parent occurrence are referred to as **twins.**

Statements 8 to 20 define the remaining segment types and field types in the department data base. Multiple physical data bases will often be needed to represent a given conceptual data base model effectively and efficiently.

IMS LOGICAL DATA BASES

External views of individual users in IMS are reflected in logical data base records (LDBRs). A **logical data base** (LDB) consists of all occurrences of a logical data base record (LDBR) type. Each LDBR type is a subset of a corresponding PDBR type (or more than one PDBR type). An LDBR may differ from the corresponding PDBR in the following ways:

1. Any segment type (except the root segment) of a PDBR may be omitted from an LDBR. If any segment type in the PDBR is omitted, then all of its dependents are also omitted.
2. Any field types that occur in a PDBR may be omitted in the corresponding LDBR. Also, the fields in a PDBR may be rearranged within the LDBR segment type.

Example LDBRs

Two examples of logical data base records derived from the department physical data base are shown in Figure 12-4. Figure 12-4a is an "equipment" LDBR that contains the DEPARTMT and EQPMENT segment types. Figure 12-4b is a "personnel" LDBR that contains the DEPARTMT, EMPLOYEE, and SKILL segment types. Each of these LDBR types represents the view of a different user. Notice that each LDBR type contains DEPARTMT as its root segment, as required.

Although not shown in Figure 12-4, any of the fields in a PDBR segment may be omitted in the corresponding LDBR segment. For example, the YEARS field in the EMPLOYEE segment could be omitted in the LDBR shown in Figure 12-4b. Also, the order of the fields EMP# and EMPNAME could be reversed if desired.

Program Communication Block

Each LDBR type is defined by a series of statements called a **program communication block** (PCB). The PCB for the personnel LDBR is shown in Figure 12-5.

Statement 1 defines the program communication block. The clause TYPE = DB is required for each PCB that defines a data base (as opposed to an on-line transaction). The clause DBNAME = DEPTDB specifies that the DBD for the underlying data base is DEPTDB (as defined in Figure 12-3).

The clause KEYLEN = 19 defines the maximum length of the concatenated key for the hierarchical path in this LDBR. In the LDBR shown in Figure 12-4b, the hierarchical path consists of the DEPARTMT, EMPLOYEE, and SKILL segment types. The fields on which these segments are sequenced, and the field lengths, are the following: DEPT#, 3 bytes; EMP#, 10 bytes; and CODE, 6 bytes. Thus, KEYLEN = 3 + 10 + 6, or 19 bytes. The KEYLEN clause is used by IMS to reserve space for concatenated keys in retrieving segments.

Statements 2 to 4 define the segments from the PDBR that are to be included in this LDBR. The term SENSEG means "sensitive segment." Segments from the PDBR that are included in an LDBR are said to be "sensitive"

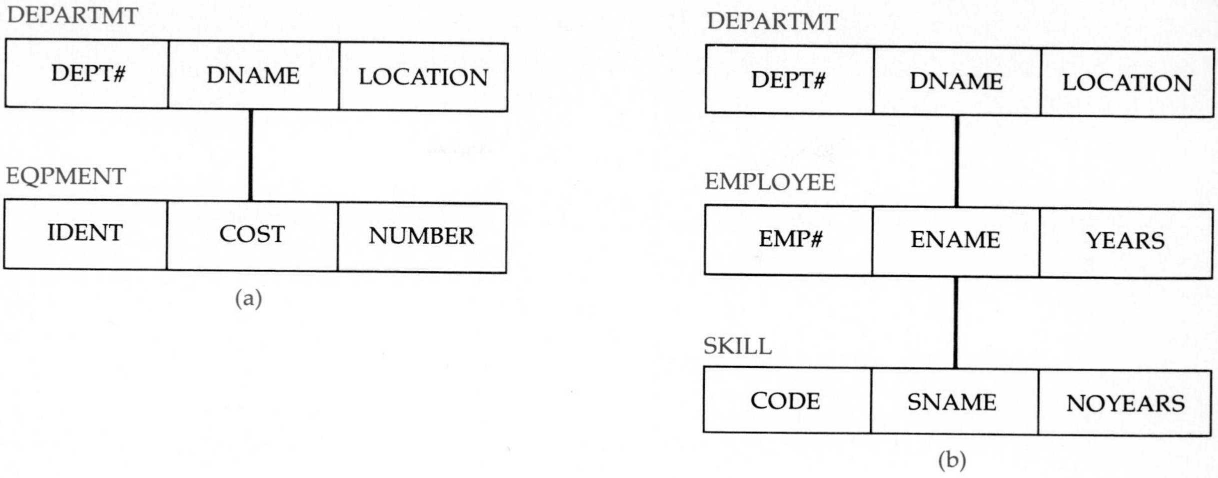

Figure 12-4
Examples of logical data base records:
(a) equipment LDBR
(b) personnel LDBR

(the term can also be applied to fields that are to be included). In this PCB, the sensitive segments are, of course, DEPARTMT, EMPLOYEE, and SKILL.

The term PROCOPT in Figure 12-5 stands for "processing options." The PROCOPT clause specifies the operations that a user of this LDBR can perform against each segment. In Figure 12-5, the clause PROCOPT=G specifies that a user can only "get" (G) or retrieve each segment occurrence. Other options that can be specified are I ("insert"), R ("replace"), and D ("delete"). Also, any combination of these options may be specified.

Caution must be used in specifying and using the delete (D) option in IMS. When an occurrence of a sensitive segment is deleted, all children of that segment are also deleted, whether they are sensitive or not. For example, the LDBR in Figure 12-4b is sensitive to the EMPLOYEE and SKILL segment types, but not to the DEPENDNT segment type. Suppose that a user deletes an EMPLOYEE segment occurrence. All DEPENDNT segment occurrences for that employee are also deleted, even though the user may not be aware of their existence.

The sensitive segment feature of IMS offers two significant advantages:

1. Data independence: a new type of segment can be added to the data base without affecting existing users. The LDBR for the existing user is not sensitive to this new segment type.
2. Data security: a user cannot access particular segment types if the user view (LDBR) is not sensitive to those segment types.

```
PCB     TYPE=DB, DBDNAME=DEPTDB, KEYLEN=19
SENSEG  NAME=DEPARTMT, PROCOPT=G
SENSEG  NAME=EMPLOYEE, PROCOPT=G
SENSEG  NAME=SKILL, PROCOPT=G
```

Figure 12-5
Program communication block for personnel LDBR

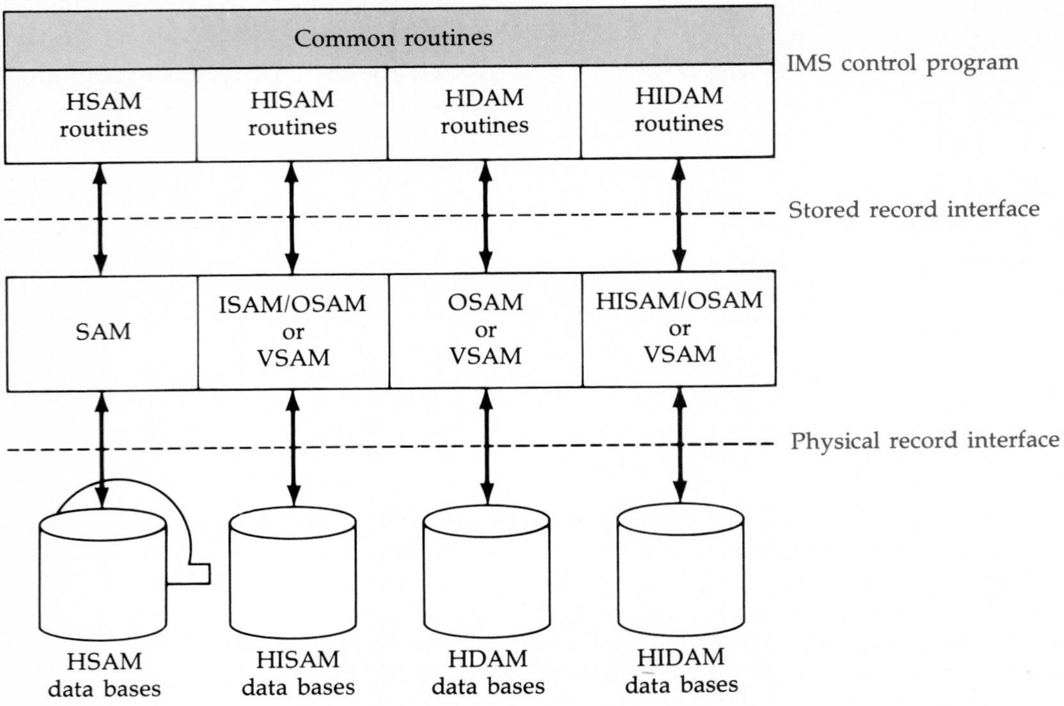

Figure 12-6
Overview of IMS internal models (*Source:* Date 1981, 312)

Program Specification Block

Each user may have one or more program communication blocks. The set of all PCBs for a given user is called a **program specification block** (PSB). The PSB for each user is assembled and stored in a system library by the IMS control program. The control program extracts the PSB from the library when a user program is executed.

IMS INTERNAL MODELS

IMS offers the user a wide variety of physical data organizations and access methods. Choosing the best internal model for each application requires a detailed knowledge of both IMS and the pattern of data usage defined during physical design. In this section, we provide only a brief overview of the IMS data structures.

Overview of IMS Internal Model

An overview of the IMS data structures and access methods that constitute the internal model is shown in Figure 12-6. As shown in this illustration, IMS supports four types of data bases:

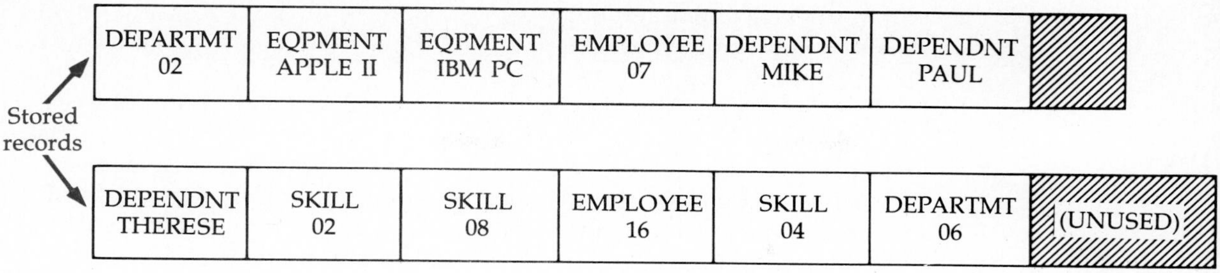

Figure 12-7
HSAM organization for DEPTDB

- Hierarchical sequential access method (HSAM)
- Hierarchical indexed sequential access method (HISAM)
- Hierarchical direct access method (HDAM)
- Hierarchical indexed direct access method (HIDAM)

The IMS control program contains routines to process each of these four data structures. Also, each of these routines "calls" (or uses) one of several standard access methods. The access methods used by IMS (and shown in Figure 12-6) are the following:

- Sequential access method (SAM)
- Indexed sequential access method (ISAM)
- Virtual storage access method (VSAM)
- Overflow sequential access method (OSAM)

The function of each of these access methods is to retrieve a physical record (possibly containing several stored records) and to present a stored record to the IMS control program.

HSAM

The simplest IMS data structure is the hierarchical sequential access method (HSAM). With this organization, the segments that make up a physical data base record are stored in physical sequence within one or more stored records. The root segment is stored first, followed by its dependent segments. The segments are stored in **hierarchical sequence,** which is a top-to-bottom, left-to-right ordering within the PDBR. Thus, the hierarchical sequence is represented by physical adjacency in HSAM.

An HSAM organization for the department data base (DEPTDB) is shown in Figure 12-7. The segment occurrences in this figure are taken from the PDBR occurrence shown in Figure 12-2. The segment occurrences are stored in two fixed-length stored records. First, the root segment (DEPARTMT 02) is stored, followed by the two EQPMENT segments in sequential order. The remaining segments are stored in hierarchical sequence as they appear within the PDBR. When the first stored record is filled, the remaining segments continue in the next stored record. Since fixed-length stored records are used, some unused space often results.

Although simple, HSAM has the same disadvantages as any physical sequential organization of records. Locating a particular segment requires an extensive sequential scan (each stored segment has a code that identifies the segment type for retrieval). Also, insertions and deletions are difficult to manage. As a result, HSAM has very limited use in most IMS installations. Normally, this method is used for historical or archival files.

HISAM

The hierarchical indexed sequential access method (HISAM) provides an indexed sequential organization for segments. As a result, the segments of a physical data base record can be retrieved either sequentially or by direct access. HISAM uses either ISAM or VSAM as its underlying access method (ISAM and VSAM are described in Chapter 4). ISAM is used with a special IMS access method called OSAM (overflow sequential access method).

A HISAM organization for the department data base is shown in Figure 12-8. In this example, two data sets (or physical storage files) are used, an ISAM data set and an OSAM data set. Each of these data sets is divided into fixed-length stored records. When an IMS data base is first loaded, each root segment that is stored causes a new ISAM stored record to be created. This root segment is stored at the front of the record (in Figure 12-8, DEPARTMT 02 is the first root segment). The remainder of that record is then filled with additional dependent segments in hierarchical sequence

Figure 12-8
HISAM organization for DEPTDB

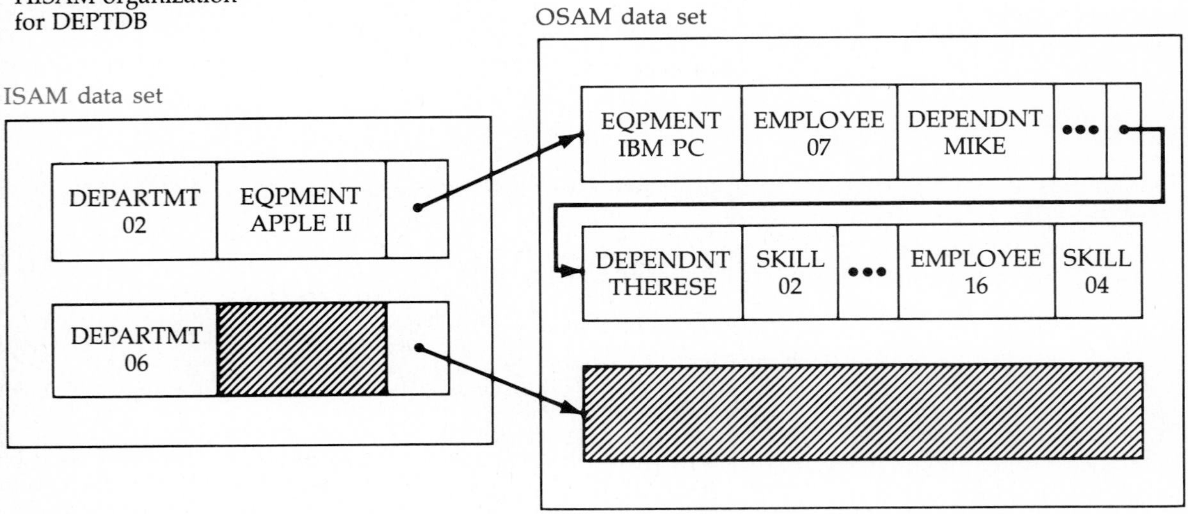

(in Figure 12-8, the first EQPMENT segment for department 02 is placed in the ISAM record).

If all dependent segments for a particular root segment fit into one ISAM record, then no OSAM record is required. However, if the dependent segments overflow this record (as in Figure 12-8), then they are stored in hierarchical sequence in an OSAM record. A pointer containing the relative address of that OSAM record is placed in the last ISAM segment. If the first OSAM record is filled, a second record is created, and so on. As shown in the figure, one ISAM record and two OSAM records were required for all the segments for department 02.

The segments in a physical data base record may be processed sequentially by following the pointers such as those shown in Figure 12-8. Also, each root segment can be located by direct access using the ISAM index. Thus, HISAM provides the advantages of both sequential and direct access.

When VSAM is used, the ISAM data set is replaced by a VSAM key-sequenced data set. Also, the OSAM data set is replaced by a VSAM entry-sequenced data set. Thus, the segments are stored within VSAM control intervals and managed by the VSAM indexes.

HISAM is not often used in most IMS installations. It should be used only when no logical relationships exist and adds and deletes are minimal (that is, the data base is not volatile).

HDAM and HIDAM

HDAM and HIDAM are both direct access methods. Both permit direct access to the root segment of a PDBR occurrence and therefore are frequently used. The dependent segments of that occurrence can then be accessed directly by following pointer chains. The main difference between HDAM and HIDAM is in the technique for addressing root segments, as we will now explain.

Pointer Structures HDAM and HIDAM both use pointers to represent the hierarchical sequence of segments within a PDBR occurrence. As shown in Figure 12-9, the hierarchical sequence may be represented either by hierarchical pointers or by child/twin pointers.

The use of hierarchical pointers is shown in Figure 12-9a. These pointers are simply "threaded" through the segments in hierarchical sequence. The last segment in the PDBR occurrence (in this case, 04 COST 2) does not contain a pointer to the next root segment. Hierarchical pointers are most efficient when the segments within a PDBR are normally processed in hierarchical sequence.

The use of child/twin pointers is shown in Figure 12-9b. Each parent segment contains a pointer to its first child segment occurrence. Each child segment occurrence then contains a pointer to the next twin segment (if

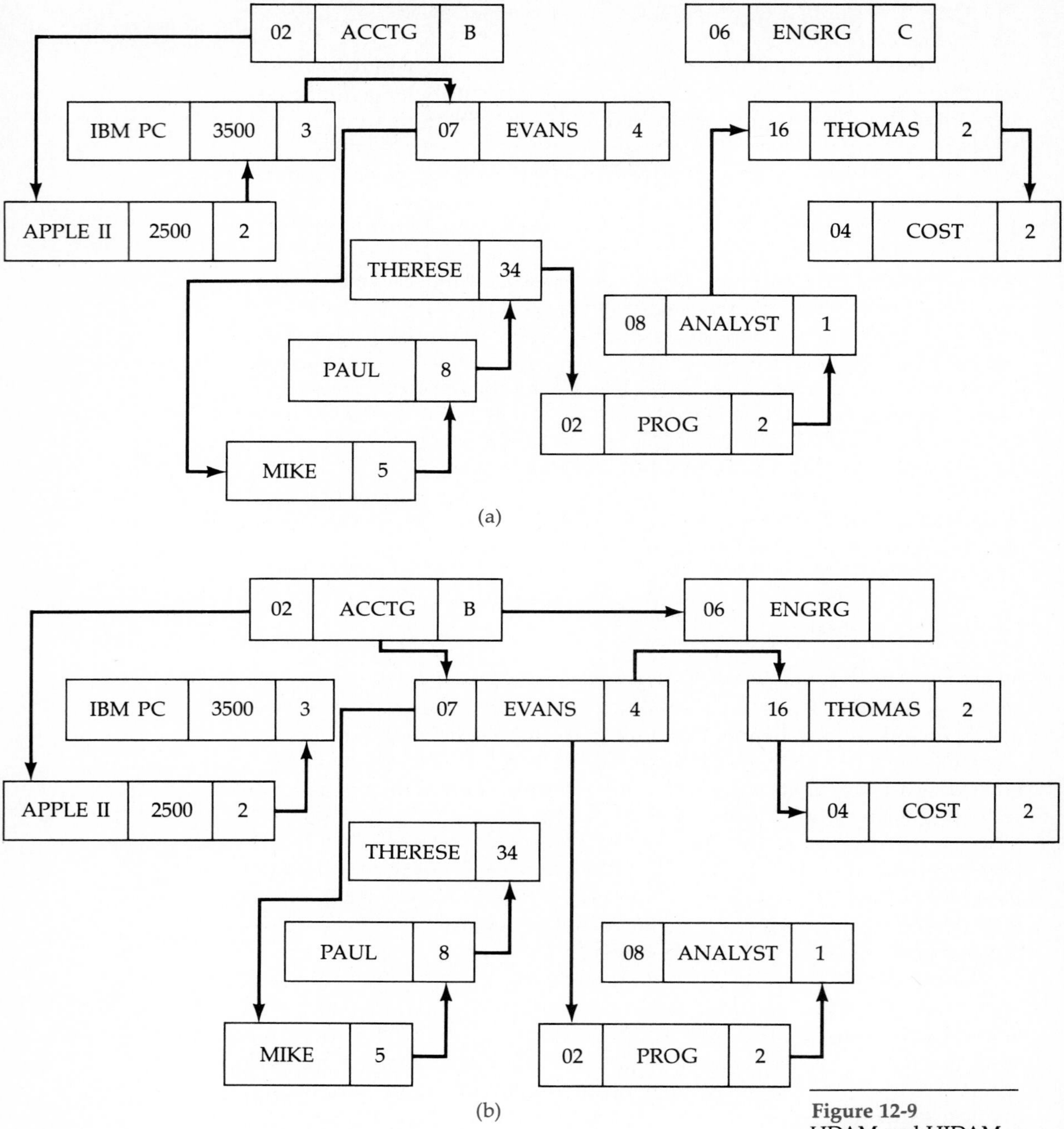

Figure 12-9
HDAM and HIDAM pointer structures:
(a) hierarchical
(b) child/twin

one exists). Also, each parent may optionally contain a pointer to the last (as well as first) child occurrence. Child/twin pointers are most efficient when only certain parent/child occurrences within a PDBR are normally processed each time (rather than the entire sequence).

Although not shown in Figure 12-9, both hierarchical and child/twin pointers may be bidirectional. That is, between any two segments, backward as well as forward pointers may be used.

HDAM Hierarchical direct access method (HDAM) provides direct access to root segments by means of a hashing algorithm. Segments are stored in fixed-length stored records. The hashing algorithm generates a relative record address that provides the location of a root segment occurrence. The dependent segments may then be accessed by following the segment pointers (hierarchical or child/twin).

When an HDAM data base is initially loaded, the root segments may be loaded in any order (key sequence is not necessary). However, all dependent segments for each root segment must be loaded in hierarchical sequence after the root segment. Dependent segments are stored as closely as possible to the root segment (recall our discussion of clustering in Chapter 9).

When two root segments collide (hash to the same relative address), the second root segment is placed in the next available stored record that contains sufficient space. A pointer to the second root segment is then placed in the first root segment (several colliding root segments may be linked by such a pointer chain).

HIDAM Hierarchical indexed direct access method (HIDAM) also provides direct access to root segments. However, instead of using a hashing algorithm, HIDAM uses a dense index to locate root segment occurrences. Root segments are linked to dependent segments by pointers, as with HDAM.

The main advantage of HDAM (compared with HIDAM) is the speed of access where direct access is required. HDAM should be used where random access is required almost exclusively. Sequential processing with HDAM is difficult or inefficient.

On the other hand, the main advantage of HIDAM is that both random and sequential access are handled effectively. Thus, HIDAM is probably the most frequently used of all access methods in IMS.

Specifying the Internal Model

In IMS, the mapping of a physical data base into storage is defined by adding additional statements to the data base description (such as the one in Figure 12-3). For example, if HISAM is to be used, the following statement would be added to DBD:

ACCESS = HISAM

Additional entries are required to define the access method (such as VSAM versus ISAM) and the type of pointers to be used (hierarchical versus child/twin). Full specification of the internal model is often quite complex and is beyond the scope of this text.

IMS DATA MANIPULATION

The IMS data manipulation language is called Data Language I (DL/I). DL/I consists of a set of commands that are used with a host language (COBOL, PL/I, or assembler language). The application program invokes (or uses) these commands by means of subroutine calls.

An overview of the DL/I commands is shown in Table 12-1. We describe and illustrate each of these commands below. The syntax is simplified in the following examples for ease of presentation. The examples are based on the department data base (Figure 12-2).

GET UNIQUE (GU)

The GET UNIQUE (GU) command is used to retrieve a specific segment occurrence. The segment may be a root segment or a dependent segment. The segment desired is specified in parentheses by a qualifying condition, called a segment search argument (SSA). For example, suppose that we want to retrieve the segment for department 06 (a root segment). The following command would be used:

```
GU DEPARTMT (DEPT#='06')
```

In this example, the SSA is DEPT#='06'. The GU command will retrieve the *first* segment that satisfies the SSA (presumably there is only one occurrence for each department).

Now suppose that we want to retrieve the segment for EVANS (EMP#=07) in ACCTG (DEPT#=02). The following commands would be used:

```
GU DEPARTMT (DEPT#='02')
   EMPLOYEE (EMP#='07')
```

In this example, a hierarchical path is specified. The GU command will retrieve only the segment at the *bottom* of this path. Thus, the employee segment for EVANS (but not the parent department segment) will be retrieved.

The SSA may be omitted from a DL/I command. For example, consider the following commands:

```
GU DEPARTMT
   EQPMENT (IDENT='APPLE II')
```

Table 12-1 Summary of DL/I Operations

Operation	Explanation
GET UNIQUE (GU)	Direct retrieval of a segment
GET NEXT (GN)	Sequential retrieval
GET NEXT WITHIN PARENT (GNP)	Sequential retrieval under current parent
GET HOLD (GHU, GHN, GHNP)	As above, but allow subsequent DLET/REPL
REPLACE (REPL)	Replace existing segment
DELETE (DLET)	Delete existing segment
INSERT (ISRT)	Add new segment

Source: Date 1981, 297

With this command, DL/I will retrieve the *first* occurrence of an EQPMENT segment that satisfies the indicated SSA. It will scan DEPARTMT segments sequentially until this first dependent segment is located.

GET NEXT (GN)

GET NEXT (GN) is used for sequential retrieval of occurrences of a particular segment type. For example, suppose that we use the following commands:

```
GU DEPARTMT (DEPT#='02')
    EQPMENT
GN EQPMENT
```

The GU command will cause the first EQPMENT segment (APPLE II) for DEPARTMT 02 to be retrieved. The GN command will then cause the next EQPMENT segment (IBM PC) to be retrieved.

The GN command cannot be executed until a "current position" has been established in the data base. In the preceding example, the GU command establishes the starting position by retrieving the first EQPMENT segment.

Now suppose that we add another GN command to the above example:

```
GU DEPARTMT (DEPT#='02')
    EQPMENT
GN EQPMENT
GN EQPMENT
```

These commands will attempt to retrieve a third EQPMENT segment. However, referring to Figure 12-2, we see that there are only two such segments under DEPARTMT 02. Will this result in an error condition? The answer is that it will not. Instead, DL/I will retrieve the next EQPMENT segment in the data base under a new root segment. In fact, we can retrieve *all* EQPMENT segments in the data base with the following commands:

```
          GU DEPARTMT
             EQPMENT
     MORE GN EQPMENT
             GO TO MORE
```

GET NEXT WITHIN PARENT (GNP)

Like GET NEXT, GET NEXT WITHIN PARENT (GNP) causes sequential retrieval of segment occurrences. However, unlike GN, only occurrences under the current parent segment are retrieved. For example, suppose that we wish to retrieve all DEPENDNT segments for EVANS in ACCTG. The following commands would be used:

```
          GU DEPARTMT (DEPT#='02')
             EMPLOYEE (EMP#='07')
             DEPENDNT
    NEXT GNP DEPENDNT
             GO TO NEXT
```

In this example, the GU command retrieves the first DEPENDNT segment for this employee. The GNP then sequentially retrieves the remaining segments for the same employee (EVANS has three dependents). When the last segment is retrieved, DL/I will return a status message indicating that there are no more subordinate DEPENDNT segments for this employee.

The GNP command can be used to retrieve *all* subordinate segment occurrences under a current parent. For example, suppose that we wish to retrieve all segment occurrences for DEPARTMT 02:

```
          GU DEPARTMT (DEPT#='02')
    NEXT GNP
             GO TO NEXT
```

Since no segment type is specified for GNP, the loop will cause all subordinate segments to be retrieved in hierarchical sequence. DEPARTMT 02 has ten subordinate segments (see Figure 12-2).

GET HOLD

There are three GET HOLD commands: GET HOLD UNIQUE (GHU), GET HOLD NEXT (GHN), and GET HOLD NEXT WITHIN PARENT (GHNP). These commands function in exactly the same manner as GU, GN, and GNP, respectively. However, the GET HOLD versions must be used to retrieve segments that are going to be replaced (REPL) or deleted (DLET).

Replacement (REPL)

The replace (REPL) command is used to replace a segment occurrence with an updated version of the same segment. First, the segment must be retrieved by using one of the GET HOLD commands. The segment is then modified, and the REPL command writes the updated segment.

Look again at Figure 12-2. Suppose that we wish to change the age of the DEPENDNT PAUL from 8 to 9. The following commands could be used:

```
GHU DEPARTMT (DEPT#='02')
    EMPLOYEE (EMP#='07')
    DEPENDNT (DEPNM='PAUL')
    MOVE '9' TO AGE
    REPL
```

Deletion (DLET)

A segment to be deleted must first be retrieved by using one of the GET HOLD commands. For example, suppose that we wish to delete the skill PROG for EVANS in ACCTG. The following commands would be used:

```
    GHU DEPARTMT (DEPT#='02')
        EMPLOYEE (EMP#='07')
        SKILL (CODE='02')
    DLET
```

A DLET command deletes not only a particular segment, but all of its subordinate children (there are some exceptions to this rule, but they are beyond the scope of this text). For example, the following command will delete the root segment for DEPARTMT 02 plus all ten of its subordinate segments:

```
GHU DEPARTMT (DEPT#='02')
DLET
```

As a result, caution must be exercised in using this command. In general, the processing options (PROCOPT) specification in the PCB should limit the delete operation to only a few qualified users.

Insertion (ISRT)

ISRT allows the user to insert a new segment into the data base. To insert a new subordinate segment, the parent segment must already exist in the data base. For example, suppose that we wish to insert a new DEPENDNT occurrence for EVANS in ACCTG. The following commands could be used:

```
MOVE 'CHRIS' TO DEPNM
MOVE '0' TO AGE
```

```
ISRT DEPARTMT (DEPT#='02')
     EMPLOYEE (EMP#='07')
     DEPENDNT
```

First, the new segment to be inserted is built in the application program output area (indicated by the first two statements above). Next, the ISRT statement defines the hierarchical path to the segment to be inserted. The new segment occurrence is inserted in sequence among the existing child occurrences for the specified parent.

ADVANCED IMS FEATURES

So far, we have described the basic features of IMS. All these features are based on a purely hierarchical data model. In this section, we describe two additional features that extend IMS beyond this hierarchical model. These two features are logical data bases and secondary indexing.

Logical Data Bases

Earlier in this chapter, we defined a logical data base record (LDBR) as a subset of an IMS physical data base record (PDBR). More generally, an LDBR may be defined as a subset of one or more PDBRs. In this section, we describe how an LDBR can be defined as a subset of two PDBRs.

Suppose that the department data base (DEPTDB) illustrated in Figure 12-1 already exists. Now suppose that the organization wants to create a project data base (PROJDB). The structure of this proposed data base is shown in Figure 12-10a. The root segment type is PROJECT, and the dependent segment is EMPLOYEE.

One possible approach is to create a new PDBR type with the structure shown in Figure 12-10a. However, the new EMPLOYEE segment occurrences will contain the same data that already exist in the EMPLOYEE segments within the department data base. A better approach (which avoids this redundancy) is to link the new PROJECT segment with the existing EMPLOYEE segment by means of a logical pointer segment (see Figure 12-10b). There are two PDBR types in this figure: DEPTDB and PROJDB. The logical pointer segment (called EMPLPROJ) links the two data bases. EMPLPROJ is the *physical* child of PROJECT and the *logical* child of EMPLOYEE.

As shown in Figure 12-10c, the new PROJECT data base may now be represented as a logical data base. The LDBR type in this figure is a subset of the two PDBR types shown in Figure 12-10b. The logical data base shown in Figure 12-10c does not actually exist. However, a user application program may process the data as if they existed in this form.

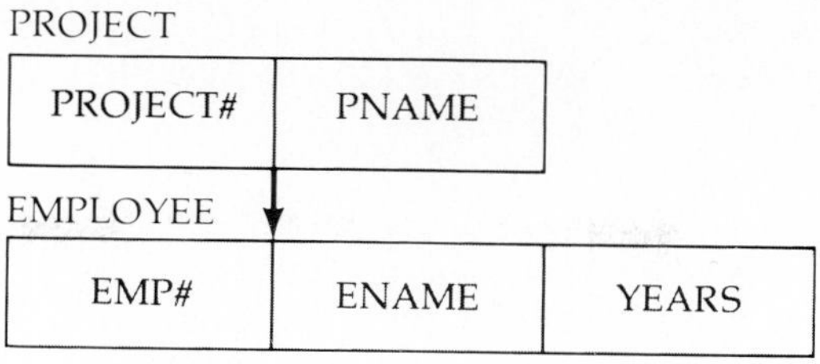

(a)

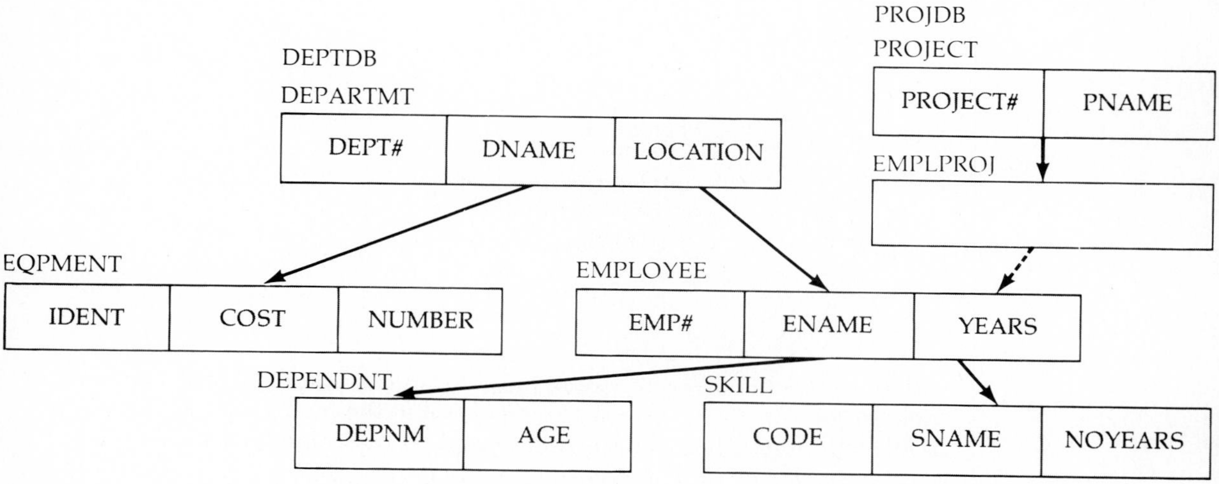

(b)

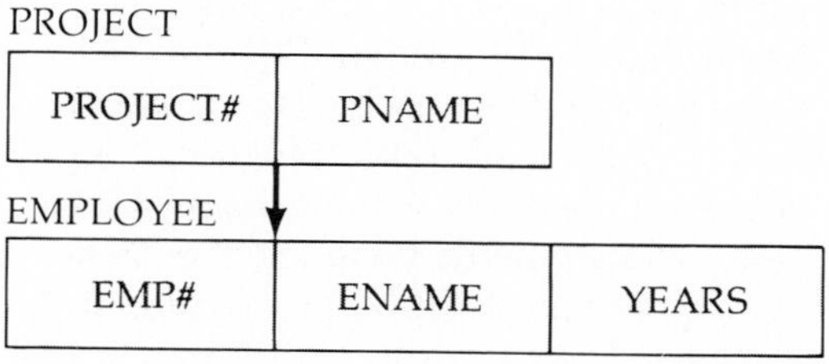

(c)

Figure 12-10
Logical data bases:
(a) proposed project data base
(b) two linked PDBRs
(c) one LDBR based on the first two PDBRs (PROJEMP)

Data Base Description Building a logical data base is a three-step process. The first step is defining a physical data base description of the project data base. In Figure 12-11a, statements 1 to 4 are similar to those in Figure 12-3 and the project segment is defined with two fields. Statement 5 is the description of the EMPLPROJ pointer segment. This statement identifies

```
1  DBD      NAME=PROJDB
2  SEGM     NAME=PROJECT, BYTES=27, PARENT=0
3  FIELD    NAME=(PROJECT#, SEQ), BYTES=7, START=1
4  FIELD    NAME=PNAME, BYTES=20, START=8
5  SEGM     NAME=EMPLPROJ, PARENT=((PROJECT), (EMPLOYEE, P, DEPTDB))
```

(a)

```
10 SEGM     NAME=EMPLOYEE, PARENT=DEPARTMT, BYTES=42
11 LCHILD   NAME=(EMPLPROJ, PROJDB)
```

(b)

```
1  DBD      NAME=PROJEMP, ACCESS=LOGICAL
2  DATASET LOGICAL
3  SEGM     NAME=PROJECT, SOURCE=(PROJECT, DATA, PROJDB)
4  SEGM     NAME=EMPLOYEE, PARENT=PROJECT,
            SOURCE=((EMPLPROJ, DATA, PROJDB), (EMPLOYEE, DATA, DEPTDB))
```

(c)

Figure 12-11
Building the logical data base:
(a) physical DBD
(b) change to EMPLOYEE segment of DEPTDB data base
(c) logical DBD for PROJEMP logical data base

PROJECT as the physical parent, and EMPLOYEE (in DEPTDB) as the logical parent. The "P" in this entry denotes that the pointer in EMPLPROJ is a logical pointer. If there are data related to the combination of a project and an employee (called intersection data), these data can be stored in the EMPLPROJ segment.

The second step is to amend the Department physical data base description (Figure 12-3) by adding an LCHILD (logical child) statement, as shown in Figure 12-11b. Statement number 11 in this figure indicates that EMPLOYEE has a logical child called EMPLPROJ in the PROJDB data base. This statement is then followed by the FIELD statements for EMPLOYEE.

The third step in building our logical data base is to define the logical data base itself. As seen in Figure 12-11c, this process is rather straightforward. In statements 1 and 2, the data base is named and is defined as logical. In statement 3, the PROJECT segment is defined and the source of the data to be used is shown to be the PROJDB. In statement 4, the EMPLOYEE is defined and the source of its data is the EMPLOYEE segment in the DEPTDB data base and the EMPLPROJ segment in the PROJDB data base.

There are two important restrictions in defining logical data bases:

1. The root of a logical data base must also be the root of a physical data base. In Figure 12-10, PROJECT is the root of the PROJEMP (logical data base) and PROJDB (physical data base).
2. A logical child segment must have one physical parent and one logical parent. In Figure 12-10, EMPLPROJ is the physical child of PROJECT and the logical child of EMPLOYEE.

In this section, we have presented a simplified description of IMS logical data bases. In reality, additional entries would be required. For a complete discussion of this topic, see IBM Corp. (1986).

Processing a Logical Data Base A logical data base is accessed in exactly the same way as a physical data base. The programmer does not have to know whether the data base is physical or logical.

Loading a logical data base is another matter. Again, it is a three-step process, assuming the logical data base has been correctly defined. First, the data must be loaded onto the first physical data base (DEPTDB in our example). Second, the data must be loaded onto the other physical data base (PROJDB). Finally, an IMS utility is run that causes the two data bases to be logically connected.

Once the logical data base has been loaded, a user can process it exactly as if it were a physical data base. That is, DL/I commands can be used to retrieve and manipulate the logical data base. For example, suppose that we wish to retrieve all EMPLOYEE segments for employees who are assigned to PROJECT ABCD. The following DL/I commands would be used:

```
          GU PROJECT (PROJECT#='ABCD')
             EMPLOYEE
    NEXT GNP EMPLOYEE
             GO TO NEXT
```

Notice that in filling this request, the program will retrieve segments from two physical data bases.

Secondary Indexing

One of the important features of IMS is the ability to access data bases using multiple keys. As an example, we normally access the DEPTDB by department number. If we now need to access the DEPTDB by location, we could use a logical data base, but a better approach would be to use a secondary index. Like HIDAM data bases, secondary indexes are implemented by means of a physical index data base. To implement a secondary index, the DBD of the data base to be indexed (DEPTDB in our example) needs to be changed.

The following two statements would need to be added to the DBD (Figure 12-3) immediately after the LOCATION field statement:

```
 LCHILD NAME=(LOCINDX, LOCDB), POINTER=INDX
XDFIELD NAME=XLOCN, SRCH=LOCATION
```

The first (or LCHILD) statement specifies that this data base (DEPTDB) is indexed by a segment called LOCINDX (location index). That index is defined in a data base called LOCDB. The POINTER=INDX entry specifies that LOCINDX is indeed an index (not a data record). The second (or XDFIELD) statement identifies the field that is indexed; in this example, it is LOCATION, as specified by the SRCH=LOCATION entry. The

Figure 12-12
DBD for secondary index

```
1  DBD      NAME=LOCDB, ACCESS=INDEX
2  SEGM     NAME=LOCINDEX, BYTES=4,
3  FIELD    NAME=LOCATION, BYTES=4, START=1
4  LCHILD   NAME=(DEPARTMT, DEPTDB), INDEX=XLOCN
```

NAME=XLOCN entry specifies that the variable name XLOCN will be used in referring to the indexed field.

Defining a Secondary Index The secondary index data base is described as shown in Figure 12-12. Statement 1 is a regular DBD statement and assigns the name LOCDB to this data base. Statement 2 assigns the name LOCINDEX to the segment in an index, and statement 3 defines the field (LOCATION) on which the secondary index is defined. This is the only field in the LOCINDEX segment. Statement 4 is the LCHILD that connects the index data base to the LOCATION field in the DEPTDB. A secondary index data base such as this one is loaded using IMS utilities.

Using a Secondary Index When an IMS data base is loaded, any secondary indexes that have been defined by the user are automatically constructed by IMS. Also, IMS automatically maintains the secondary indexes as the data base is modified.

To use a secondary index, the user specifies DL/I commands that invoke the variable names for the indexed field. To return to our original example, suppose that we wish to retrieve the segment for the department whose location is B100. The following statement will be used:

```
GU DEPARTMT (XLOCN='B100')
```

This statement causes IMS to retrieve the B100 index segment within LOCDB. That segment contains a pointer to the B100 data segment within DEPARTMT, which is the target segment.

In this example, we assume that values of the indexed field are unique (e.g., there is only one B100 segment). However, an IMS secondary index may also be defined for fields that do not have unique values. For example, there may be more than one department at a given location. Therefore, a secondary index for LOCATION must accommodate nonunique values. Minor modifications are required in the secondary index definition for this case [for details, see IBM Corp. (1986)].

Case Example

In this section, we illustrate the use of IMS to implement a data base for Mountain View Community Hospital. A structure of a data base for this hospital is shown in Figure 9-11 and again in Figure 12-13 for ease of reference.

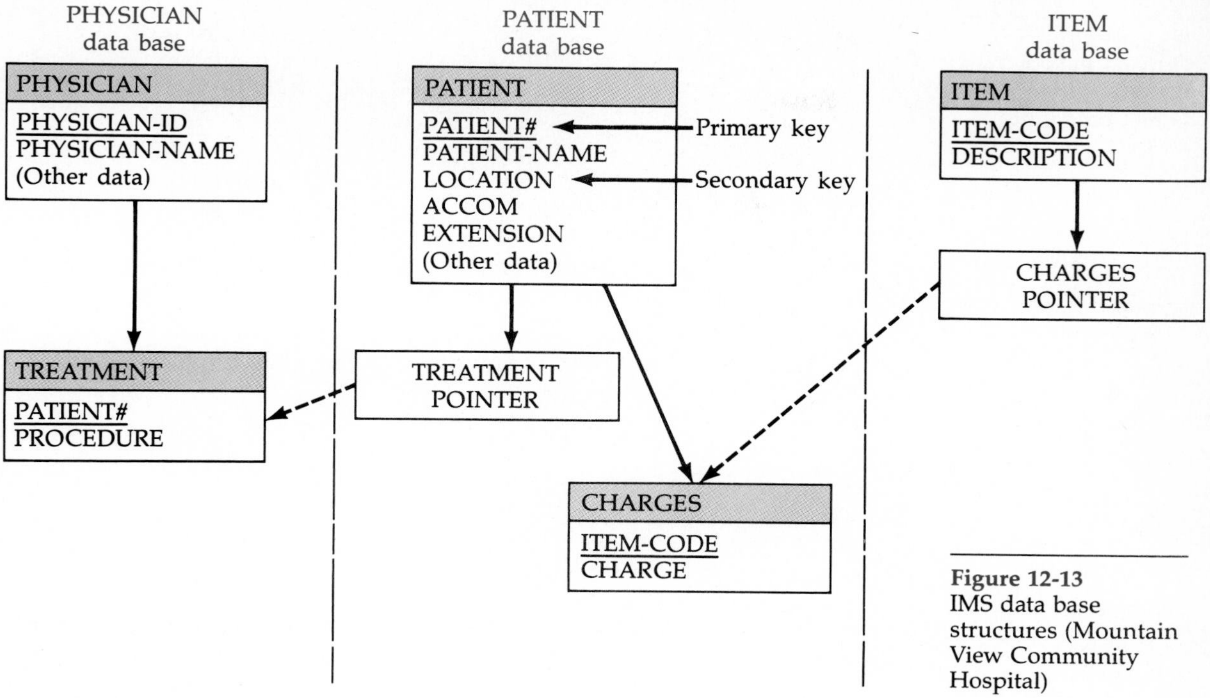

Figure 12-13
IMS data base structures (Mountain View Community Hospital)

Data Base Definition

Three distinct physical data bases are shown in Figure 12-13. These data bases are linked together by logical pointers for reasons already described. A DBD for the PHYSICIAN data base is shown in Figure 12-14 (we will ask you to develop DBDs for the remaining data bases in the chapter problems).

Two segment types are defined in the PHYSICIAN data base: PHYSICN (for physician) and TREATMT (for treatment). Notice that in statement 8, a logical child is defined for the TREATMT segment. This logical child is the treatment pointer (TREATPTR) in the PATIENT data base (PATNTDB). This pointer links the PATIENT and PHYSICIAN data bases.

Data Base Manipulation

To illustrate data base manipulation, we use DL/I statements to retrieve data from the hospital data bases. All the statements are based on the data base structures shown in Figure 12-13.

Simple Retrieval To retrieve patient data for patient number 1234, we use the following command:

```
GU PATIENT (PATIENT#='1234')
```

Figure 12-14
DBD for PHYSICIAN data base (Mountain View Community Hospital)

```
DBD     NAME=PHYSDB
SEGM    NAME=PHYSICN, BYTES=17, PARENT=0
FIELD   NAME=(PHYSID, SEQ), BYTES=10, START=1
FIELD   NAME=PHYPHONE, BYTES=7, START=11
SEGM    NAME=TREATMT, PARENT=PHYSICN, BYTES=19
FIELD   NAME=(PATIENT#, SEQ), BYTES=4, START=1
FIELD   NAME=PROCEDUR, BYTES=15, START=5
LCHILD  NAME=(TREATPTR, PATNTDB)
```

Indexed Retrieval To retrieve patient data for the patient in location 4321, we use the following command:

```
GU PATIENT (XLOCN='4321')
```

This command assumes that there is a secondary index for the LOCATION field. Also, we assume that XLOCN is the variable name for the indexed field LOCATION.

Retrieval of Child Segments To calculate total charges for patient number 1234, we use the following commands:

```
          MOVE 0 TO TOTAL
             GU PATIENT (PATIENT#='1234')
                CHARGES
                ADD CHARGE TO TOTAL
     MORE GNP CHARGES
                ADD CHARGE TO TOTAL
                GO TO MORE
```

The GET UNIQUE (GU) statement retrieves the first CHARGES segment for this patient (if one exists). The amount of the CHARGE is added to the running total (TOTAL). The GNP statement is then executed repeatedly to retrieve additional charges, and TOTAL is updated until there are no more charges for that patient.

Retrieval Using Logical Records To retrieve all TREATMT segments for patient number 1234, we use the following commands:

```
             GU PATIENT (PATIENT#=1234)
                TREATMT
     MORE GNP TREATMT
                GO TO MORE
```

In this retrieval, the PATIENT and TREATMT segments exist in separate data bases. However, use of the treatment pointer (TREATPTR) allows the user to manipulate the TREATMT segment as a child of PATIENT.

SUMMARY

In this chapter, we have presented an introduction to IMS, a data base management system based on the hierarchical data model. In IMS, data are viewed as hierarchical arrangements of segments. A data manipulation language called Data Language I (DL/I) allows the user to retrieve data by traversing the tree structure.

Although the design of IMS dates from the late 1960s, a stream of enhancements has been added to provide new features. Thus, through the use of logical data bases, the user can model limited networks. Also, secondary indexing permits access on fields other than primary keys. However, because these features are quite complex, IMS tends to be used only in relatively sophisticated data processing shops where considerable technical expertise is available.

Many other hierarchical DBMS products (not described in this chapter) are also available. Two of the more recent hierarchical products are FOCUS and DB Master. Although it represents older technology, the hierarchical model remains a viable alternative for some DBMS implementations. However, it should be evaluated against the more recent network and relational systems.

Chapter Review

REVIEW QUESTIONS

1. Give a concise definition for each of the following terms:
   a. segment
   b. root segment
   c. logical data base record
   d. physical data base record
   e. data base description
   f. program communication block
2. Contrast the following terms:
   a. physical data base record; logical data base record
   b. program communication block; program specification block
   c. root segment; child segment
   d. hierarchical pointers; child/twin pointers
3. Define each of the following acronyms:
   a. IMS
   b. PDBR
   c. LDBR
   d. PCB
   e. PSB
   f. GNP
   g. LCHILD
   h. SENSEG
4. Describe each of the following access methods briefly, and indicate the conditions favoring its use:
   a. HSAM
   b. HISAM
   c. HDAM
   d. HIDAM

5. Describe two ways in which an LDBR may differ from a PDBR.
6. Describe two advantages of the "sensitive segment" feature in IMS.
7. Why must caution be used in deleting a root segment with the DL/I DLET command?
8. Describe two restrictions in defining logical data bases.

PROBLEMS AND EXERCISES

Problems 1 to 4 are based on the following hierarchical data base structure for Pine Valley Furniture Company:

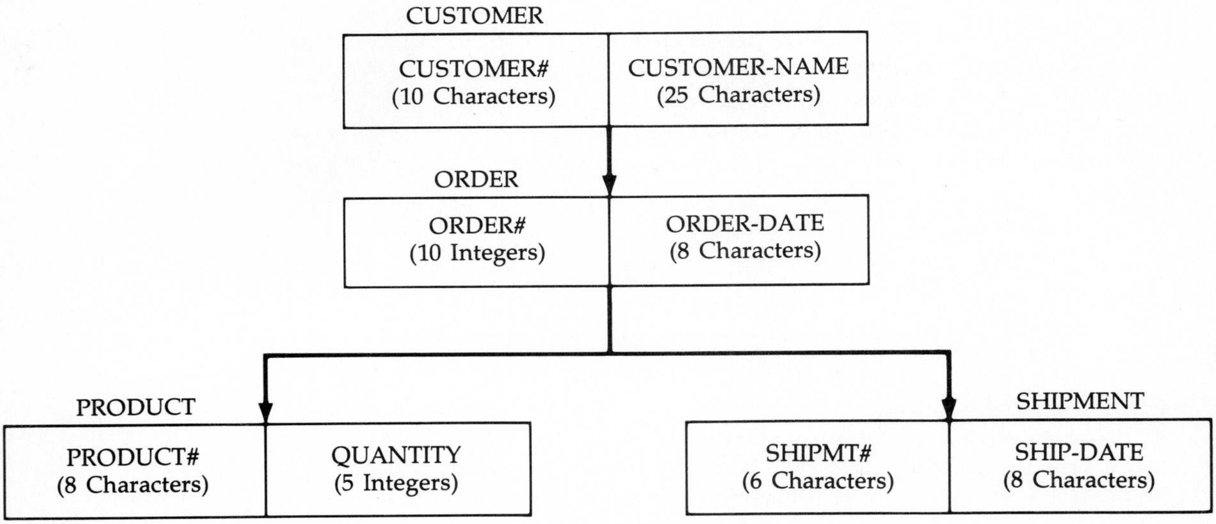

1. Write an IMS data base description (DBD) for the data base shown.
2. Based on the DBD in Problem 1, write a program communication block (PCB) for a logical data base record that contains the CUSTOMER, ORDER, and PRODUCT segments (but omits the SHIPMENT segment).
3. Write DL/I statements for each of the following retrievals:
   a. CUSTOMER segment for customer number ABCD
   b. ORDER segment for order number 1234, customer number ABCD
   c. All ORDER segments for customer number ABCD
   d. All PRODUCT segments for customer number ABCD, order number 1234
4. Write DL/I statements for the following updates:
   a. Change the QUANTITY for product number 10 in order number 1234 for customer number ABCD from 3 to 2.
   b. Delete shipment number WXYZ for order number 6789 from customer number ABCD.

c. Add shipment number CDEF to order number 6789 from customer number ABCD (shipment date is 6/18/8X).

5. Write an IMS data base description for the ITEM data base in Figure 12-13. Assume the following data item characteristics:

ITEM CODE	10 Characters
DESCRIPN	25 Characters

6. Write an IMS data base description for the PATIENT data base (Figure 12-13). Include the logical pointers. Assume the following data item characteristics:

PATIENT#	10 Characters
PATNAME	25 Characters
LOCATION	5 Characters
ACCOM	6 Characters
EXTENSN	4 Integers
ITEMCODE	10 Characters
CHARGE	Decimal XXXX.XX

7. In Figure 12-13, LOCATION is identified as a secondary key in the PATIENT segment. Write an IMS secondary index DBD for this field.
8. One logical data base record derived from the hospital data base (Figure 12-13) appears as follows:

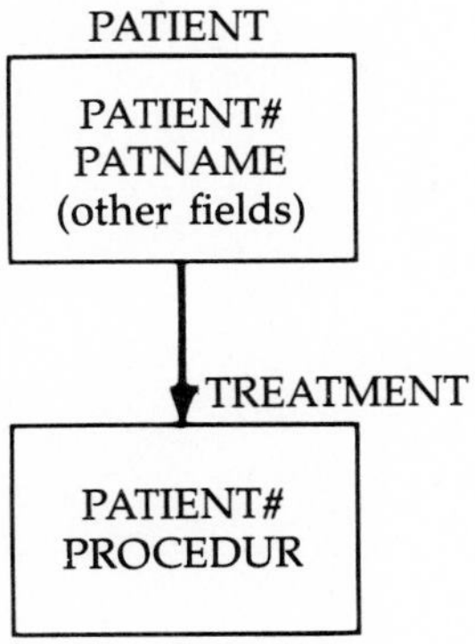

Write an IMS DBD for this logical record.

9. Write DL/I statements for the following retrievals in the hospital data base (Figure 12-13):
   a. CHARGE segment for item number 1234, patient number ABCD
   b. All CHARGE segments for patient number ABCD
   c. All TREATMENT segments for patient number ABCD performed by physician number P10

10. Referring to Figure 12-2, what segment(s) will be retrieved for each of the following statements?
    a. GU DEPARTMT (DEPT#='02')
            EQPMENT (IDENT='APPLE II')
    b. GU DEPARTMT (DEPT#='02')
            EMPLOYEE (EMP#='07')
            SKILL (CODE='02')

c.

```
          GU DEPARTMT (DEPT#='02')
             EMPLOYEE (EMP#='07')
             DEPENDNT (DEPNM='THERESE')
NEXT GNP DEPENDNT
             GO TO NEXT
```

REFERENCES

Atre, Shaku. 1983. *Data Base Management Systems for the Eighties.* Wellesley, Mass.: QED Information Sciences, Inc.

Date, C. J. 1981. *An Introduction to Data Base Systems.* 3d ed. Reading, Mass.: Addison-Wesley.

IBM Corp. 1986. *Information Management System/Virtual Storage General Information Manual.* IBM Form No. GH20-1260.

Tsichritzis, D. C., and F. H. Lochovsky. 1977. *Data Base Management Systems.* New York: Academic Press.

Chapter 13

Network and CODASYL Implementations

INTRODUCTION

The purpose of this chapter is to review the implementation of the network data model in industry standards and in commercial data base management systems. You may want to review "The Network Data Model" section in Chapter 6 before proceeding. Remember, the network data model can be used for modeling a conceptual data base (as presented in Chapter 6) or as the basis for a particular DBMS, as covered in this chapter.

The implementation of the network data model is an interesting example of the influence of industry standards in the computing field and of the influence of individual vendors. In preliminary form in 1969 and in an updated and better-outlined form in 1971 (CODASYL 1971), the COnference of DAta SYstem Languages (CODASYL), through its Data Base Task Group (DBTG), issued descriptions of languages for defining and processing data. These reports and updates in 1978 and 1981 define the general characteristics for all but a few network DBMSs (ANSI X3H2 1981; CODASYL COBOL Committee 1978; CODASYL Data Description Language Committee 1978).

Although represented on the original DBTG, IBM Corporation did not sign or endorse these standards and to this day has not implemented a network DBMS. But many other hardware vendors and numerous software firms have chosen to develop systems following the CODASYL guidelines (even for IBM computers). At the same time, IBM has installed IMS, its hierarchical DBMS, in many of its customers' data centers. Again, these events indicate that variety is the hallmark of data base.

The CODASYL Committee is a voluntary group of individuals who represent hardware and software vendors, universities, and major developers and users of data processing systems. Their original charge had been to discuss changes to the COBOL programming language and to write position papers in this area. Member organizations were in no way bound to implement these positions in their program products. It had become clear that COBOL needed radical extension to support multiple-file (data base) data processing, and the DBTG was formed.

In 1963, General Electric (later Honeywell Information Systems) began to market Integrated Data System (IDS), the forerunner of network DBMSs. The generally accepted leader of the development of IDS was Charles Bachman. Although Bachman was not on the DBTG itself, several individuals from Honeywell were represented, along with Richard Schubert of B.F. Goodrich Chemical Company, a primary user of IDS. Through these individuals and because IDS was the most fully developed DBMS by this time, the structure of IDS (and the ideas of Charles Bachman) greatly influenced the deliberations of the DBTG. Even today, many organizations draw "Bachman diagrams" to represent network data bases.

Although pleased with the capabilities of IDS, B.F. Goodrich worked on expanding these functions to meet more of the DBTG guidelines. Interest grew in the computing community in bringing a DBTG network DBMS to the marketplace. John Cullinane approached B.F. Goodrich and purchased the rights to further develop and market their initial DBTG implementation along with the existing CULPRIT reportwriter product. He named his new product Integrated Database Management System (IDMS), which is still, today, the leading DBTG DBMS on IBM (and other) computers. Charles Bachman has been, at various times, a consultant with Cullinane Database Systems (now Cullinet Software).

Many network DBMSs exist today. Most of these are DBTG implementations, but several significant exceptions have appeared. Table 13-1 lists many of these network DBMSs and pertinent information about them. Since DBTG network DBMSs dominate, most of this chapter reviews the definition and processing of data using these DBMSs; aspects of other network DBMSs are briefly covered. Also addressed are recent extensions to network DBMSs that provide nonnetwork views of a data base managed by a network DBMS. This topic is an important development that creates a great deal of confusion in distinguishing between DBMSs.

There are actually three official versions of the DBTG guidelines (1971, 1978, and 1981 reports); we have chosen to emphasize the 1978 report because most DBTG DBMSs today come closest to following these guidelines. Some exceptions will be noted when appropriate. Because of its prominence among IBM computer installations, we will draw heavily on IDMS as an example of a DBTG implementation. For greater depth on the DBTG model, Olle (1980) provides an excellent coverage of these guidelines through several minor modifications published in 1973.

Table 13-1 Summary of Some Network DBMSs

Package	Vendor	Equipment	Comments
CODASYL DBMSs			
IDMS	Cullinet Software	IBM 360/370, 30xx, 43xx, variety of operating systems, DEC VAX under VMS operating system, several minis and a few other mainframes	Various related packages, including: Integrated Data Dictionary, CULPRIT reportwriter, On-Line English natural language, distributed data base facility, and Application Development System (ADS/O)
PR1ME DBMS	PR1ME Computer	Various PR1ME mini and supermini computers under PR1MOS operating system	On-line query facility called QUERY/DBMS (DISCOVER)
DMS-170	CDC	Variety of hardware under NOS operating system	
DBMS 10	DEC	DEC 10 under TOPS operating system	PDP 11 version called DBMS 11
IDS II	Honeywell Information Systems	Variety of HIS computers	Extension of first network DBMS; works with many host languages
SEED	International Database Systems	PDP minis and CP/M operating system based micros	Has several associated reportwriters and query languages
DMS-1100	Univac (UNISYS)	Exec 8 and more recent operating systems for Univac 1100 computer family	Popular nonprocedural language MAPPER
Limited network DBMSs			
TOTAL	CINCOM Systems, Inc.	IBM 360/370, 30xx, 43xx, System/3, Harris, NCR, Honeywell, and CDC computers	ENVIRON/1 teleprocessing utility, SOCRATES report generator

(Continues)

Table 13-1 (Continued)

Package	Vendor	Equipment	Comments
IMAGE	Hewlett-Packard	HP3000 and other HP minicomputers	Basically same as TOTAL in design and function
Complex network/extended CODASYL DBMSs			
DMS II	Burroughs (UNISYS)	B1900 and higher, integrated with MCP operating system	Includes ALGOL host language interface
MDBS III	Micro Data Base Systems	CP/M and MS-DOS operating systems on micros and a few minis	Also hierarchical package HDMS; query language; BASIC, FORTRAN, and COBOL interfaces

INTRODUCTION TO CODASYL DBTG GUIDELINES

To begin to understand the DBTG guidelines and implementations of this data model, we must start by analyzing the concept of a DBMS that underlies the work of the DBTG. Figure 13-1 shows the conceptual data base management system envisioned by the DBTG. This diagram indicates that a DBMS is conceived as software that works in conjunction with an operating system to service multiple, concurrently executing, user programs.

DBMS Operation

To comprehend the nature of a DBTG DBMS, it is important to understand the operational sequence of events that occurs when such a DBMS is used. This sequence is depicted with numbered arrows in Figure 13-1 and can be summarized as follows:

1. A user program "calls" the DBMS with a request for service (retrieval, maintenance, and so on), which has been written using special data manipulation language (DML) statements. These statements are included in a host language (e.g., COBOL) user program.
2. The DBMS analyzes the request for service by matching the parameters of the request with a stored version of a definition of the data base (called a schema) and a definition of the part of the data base applicable to this program (called a subschema). These two data definitions have been predefined via data description languages (DDLs) and are maintained and stored separate from user programs in a library of data definitions.

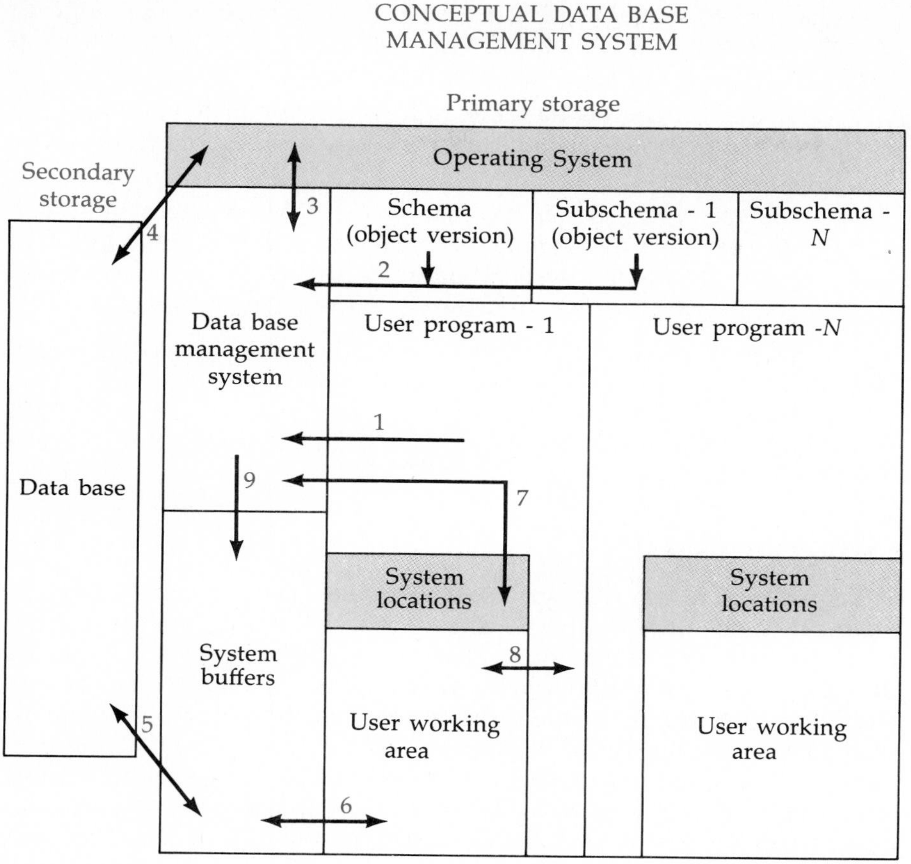

Figure 13-1 CODASYL conceptual data base management system (*Source:* CODASYL 1971)

3. As long as the request for service contains no inadmissible components (e.g., improper security passwords or references to data outside the invoked subschema), the DBMS composes a series of I/O commands for the access methods of the operating system.
4. The operating system interacts with secondary storage devices to initiate data base access.
5. The operating system performs the appropriate retrieval or modification of data base contents, using data buffers managed by the DBMS. These buffers contain blocks of data transferred between main and secondary memory in which data are formatted as defined by the schema.
6. In the case of data retrieval, data are then moved from the system buffers to a user work area or data section of the calling user's program (steps 5 and 6 are reversed for maintenance). This transfer also often includes the reformatting of data and the elimination of data in blocks not included in the subschema.

7. The DBMS then sets status-variable values in the user program with messages and error codes to indicate the nature of any problems, if any, that arose during data base interaction.
8. The user program is then free to further manipulate the data it has received from the data base or to compose new records for data base maintenance.
9. While each user program is executing, the DBMS manages the system buffers so that, for example, if a request for data is made that asks for data already in a system buffer, the DBMS can bypass steps 3 to 5 and provide the data immediately to the calling program.

Although the outline of this interaction could be interpreted in several ways, the resulting guidelines specified an implementation in which user calls occur at the record level; that is, the user program includes DML statements to retrieve or write *each* record required for processing, one at a time from each data base file.

DBTG Languages

The DBTG guidelines also specified or implied various new languages. Figure 13-2 illustrates the relationships between these languages and the roles of each in defining and using a network data base. First is a **schema data description language** (schema DDL), used to define the global data base. As previously mentioned, this is a combination of implementation-independent and -dependent statements. Since the schema DDL does not, however, cover all internal/physical declarations, a **device media control language** (DMCL) was proposed to specify assignment of data to particular devices, data block contents and format, data base update audit trail options, and so on.

Also proposed were standards for a **subschema data description language** (subschema DDL) for specifying data base structure to program compilers. Several user programs are allowed to share the same subschema. Originally, only a COBOL subschema DDL was proposed, but today a FORTRAN subschema DDL also exists. Each language requires its own subschema DDL since the idea was to define the external data base in a syntax that can be easily translated into the data definitions of a programming language.

Finally, standards for a **data manipulation language** (DML), also host-language-specific, were proposed. Initially, only a COBOL version was outlined, but today a FORTRAN version also exists. The DBTG assumed a host language environment in which there would be extensions to an already existing language (as opposed to defining a new self-contained language for data base manipulation). These extensions would be handled either by vendors creating new language compilers to translate the expanded vocabulary or by preprocessors (as illustrated in Figure 13-2) that would translate only the new language statements within a program into standard language sentences (usually CALL statements with parameters derived from the raw

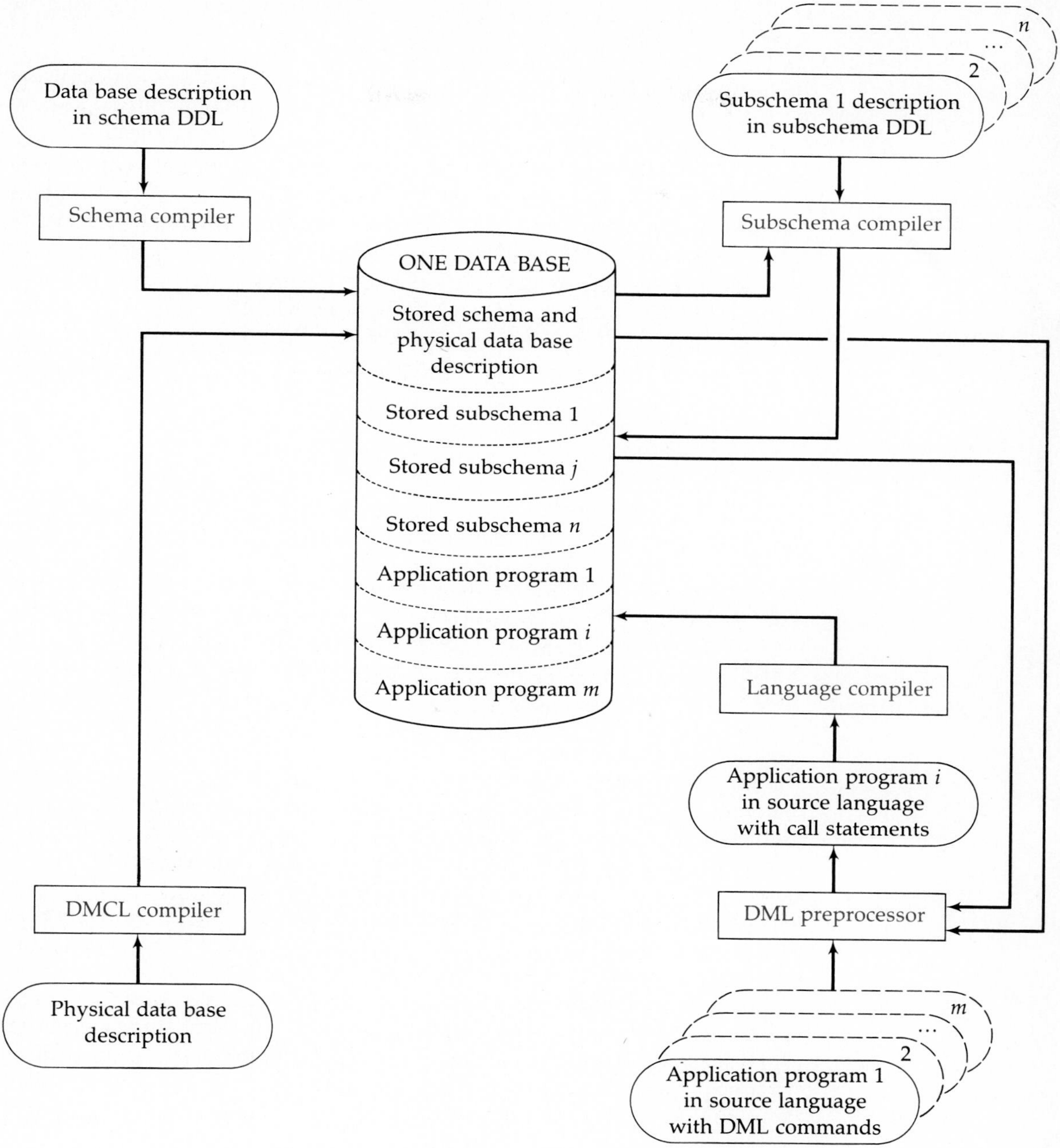

Figure 13-2
DBTG languages and compilation cycles

DML statement). The output from the DML preprocessor would then be given to a standard language compiler.

The DBTG proposals also called for extensive capabilities to define security controls in the schema DDL. Many initial implementations of the DBTG model chose not to include these capabilities since it was felt that given computing power in the early 1970s, data base processing performance would be seriously deterred by such overhead. Today, inclusion of security controls is a standard feature of DBTG implementations. Also standard today are nonprocedural (non-record-at-a-time) query languages for DBTG implementations that permit retrieval (but often *not* update) to be accomplished in fewer statements and less programming time than in conventional procedural languages like COBOL or FORTRAN.

This, then, is an overview of the DBTG DBMS environment. The following sections address the DBTG model and its languages in greater detail.

DBTG SCHEMA DDL: THE CONCEPTUAL/INTERNAL DATA BASE

The DBTG schema DDL uses some familiar terminology but has certainly done its part to create new terms. On occasion, this terminology has been disturbing enough to cause CODASYL to change terms to clarify usage of the data model. The schema DDL has many clauses and various options in most of the clause parameters. It is beyond our purpose here to cover all features of the schema DDL, so only the most salient and frequently used features and parameters will be shown. The general structure of a DBTG schema definition is shown in Figure 13-3a. The structure illustrated here generally obeys the 1978 DBTG guidelines; exceptions are indicated with footnotes. Figure 13-3b illustrates via a network diagram the parts of a network data model that correspond to the various sections of the schema DDL.

A **schema** (definition) is a named collection of record types and pairwise associations (sets) between owner and member record types, which are located in specified, named regions of secondary memory (areas or realms).

The structure shown in Figure 13-3a can be broken into three general segments. The first segment defines contiguous physical storage regions, called areas, into which all data values will be located. Because this deals with the physical or metaphysical data base, the 1981 guidelines have dropped this segment (and related clauses) to make the schema more independent of implementation.

The second segment describes all the record types or files and the data item contents that compose the data base. The third segment defines the data base representation, called sets, of all pairwise record type relationships designed in the conceptual data base. The data model is a simple network, and link and intersection record types (called junction records by IDMS) may exist, as well as sets between them (ORDER-LINE is an example of an intersection record in Figure 13-3b). Thus, the complete network of relationships is represented by several pairwise sets; in each set some (one) record type is owner (at the tail of the network arrow) and one or more record types are members (at the head of the relationship arrow). Usually, a set defines a 1:*M* relationship, although 1:1 is permitted.

Two types of clauses that can appear at various points in a schema will not be addressed in detail here; these are the ON ERROR and PRIVACY clauses. ON ERROR can be used to indicate that certain user-defined procedures are to be invoked in case of specified errors in data or commands. PRIVACY LOCKs specify passwords or procedures that are to be used to verify that certain data base manipulations are authorized for users of the data base.

Before we explain the schema DDL, it is worth mentioning that you may have the most trouble understanding three components of the DDL: LOCATION MODE, SET SELECTION, and set membership clauses. Carefully study examples and discussions that involve these most frequently misunderstood parts of a DBTG data base definition.

Areas or Realms

Consider the Pine Valley Furniture data base of Figure 2-10. If this data base were large enough to require many disk cylinders or disk packs, processing could become very expensive. If it were realized that a significant amount of data processing were related to customer geographical regions (e.g., sales reports produced by region or new orders batched by region), then it might be advantageous to cluster CUSTOMER and ORDER records (at least) from a common geographical region close together in the physical data base for more rapid access between these records. Similarly, suppose that marketing applications concentrate record usage to CUSTOMER and ORDER records and that production applications primarily use PRODUCT and ORDER-LINE record types. In this case, it is advantageous to cluster CUSTOMER and ORDER records close together, but separate from a cluster of PRODUCT and ORDER-LINE records, in order to provide rapid access between records that are used together in data processing.

An **area** (or **realm** in recent CODASYL terminology) is a named, contiguous portion of secondary memory. Operationally, this is equivalent to a range of adjacent pages of some physical disk file. The purpose of the area designation is to control physical proximity of records, as illustrated in the Pine Valley Furniture cases of geographical regions and segregated data processing. The data base of a schema will reside in one or more areas. Each area is named in the schema, and the definition of each record specifies which area or areas will hold records of that type (the WITHIN clause).

A skeleton of a schema for this Pine Valley Furniture situation would be:

```
SCHEMA NAME IS ____________
    [ON ERROR...]
    [PRIVACY LOCK...]
{AREA NAME IS ______________
    [ON ERROR...]
    [PRIVACY LOCK...]}*
{RECORD NAME IS ____________
     LOCATION MODE...
    [KEY IS...]**
    {WITHIN...}*
    [ON ERROR...]
    [PRIVACY LOCK...]
    [level-no data-base-data-name
     |((|PICTURE...| or |TYPE...|)
         |OCCURS...|) or
         (| SOURCE...|)|
         |RESULT...|
         |CHECK...|
         | FOR (ENCODING or DECODING)...|
         [ON ERROR...]
         [PRIVACY...]]}
[SET NAME IS ________________
     OWNER IS...
    |SET IS DYNAMIC or PRIOR|
     ORDER IS...
    [ON ERROR...]
    [PRIVACY LOCK...]
    {MEMBER IS ______________
     INSERTION IS ___________
     RETENTION IS ___________
    [KEY IS...]
    |SEARCH KEY IS...|
    |CHECK IS...|
    |SET SELECTION...|
    [ON ERROR...]
    [PRIVACY LOCK...]}]
 END SCHEMA

  *Deleted in 1981 CODASYL revision, but still a part of most DBMSs
 **Added in 1981 version, but not yet present in most DBMSs
   [...]-0, 1 or many occurrences of clause
   {...}-1 or many occurrences of clause
   |...|-0 or 1 occurrences of clause
```

(a)

Figure 13-3
General structure of DBTG schema definition:
(a) schema DDL
(b) schema diagram

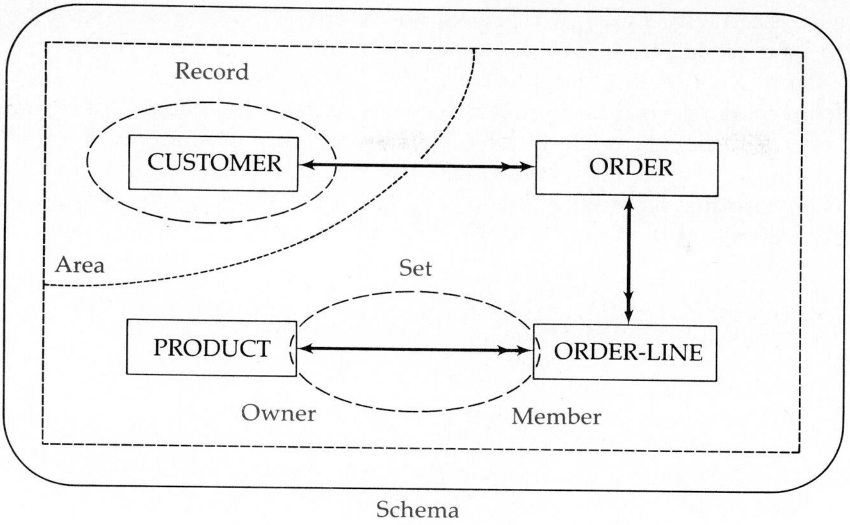

(b)

Figure 13-3 (continued)

```
AREA NAME IS SOUTH
. . .
RECORD NAME IS CUSTOMER
. . .
  WITHIN SOUTH, EAST, WEST AREA-ID IS CUST-REGION
. . .
  1 CUST-REGION ; TYPE IS CHARACTER 10
. . .
RECORD NAME IS ORDER
. . .
  LOCATION MODE IS VIA ORDERS-FOR-CUSTOMER SET
  WITHIN AREA OF OWNER
. . .
SET NAME IS ORDERS-FOR-CUSTOMER
  OWNER IS CUSTOMER
. . .
  MEMBER IS ORDER
. . .
```

In this example, it is assumed that three areas were desirable: SOUTH, EAST, and WEST (area definitions for EAST and WEST are similar to the one for SOUTH). CUSTOMER records are automatically placed in the proper area by the DBMS when a new record is stored. The customer's region (and area) name, loaded into the CUST-REGION field of a CUSTOMER record instance by a data entry program, is used to specify proper placement. ORDER records are placed in the same region as their associated CUSTOMER record (that is, their owner is the ORDERS-FOR-CUSTOMER set). Thus, if data processing requirements frequently require ORDER records associated with a given CUSTOMER record, then these records will be able to be accessed more rapidly than if placement is not controlled. For this reason, a set is said to define an access path to "walk" through a data base from owner record to members (or vice versa). This placement of ORDER records near their related CUSTOMER record is controlled by the WITHIN clause of the ORDER record (makes all ORDERs closer to all CUSTOMERs than to other records) and the LOCATION MODE clause of the ORDER record (places a specific ORDER close to its particular CUSTOMER record instance).

Records

The second major data construct in the DBTG model is that of a record. A **record** is a named entity, instances of which describe individual occurrences of the entity. We define a record by specifying how the physical location of a record instance is determined (LOCATION MODE clause) and by a list of data element (or data-base-data-name) definitions.

LOCATION MODE of a Record LOCATION MODE is a physical construct that has been removed in recent guidelines, but which is still present in most commercial implementations. **LOCATION MODE** specifies the method that will be employed to determine the precise disk address of an instance of a record when it is stored. Two methods are popular: CALC and VIA. Table 13-2 briefly summarizes the use of each of these methods.

Data processing frequently requires referring to records by logical key value. For example, a data entry operator may input a product number from a sales form and expect to see associated data in order to complete the entry of a customer order. The CALC LOCATION MODE would be appropriate to support this need.

The CALC LOCATION MODE can be illustrated with the following partial record definitions:

```
RECORD NAME IS PRODUCT
LOCATION MODE CALC USING PRODUCT# DUPLICATES NOT
  ALLOWED
. . .
  1 PRODUCT# ; PICTURE 9999.
. . .
RECORD NAME IS ORDER-LINE
LOCATION MODE CALC USING PRODUCT#, ORDER#
  DUPLICATES NOT ALLOWED
. . .
  1 PRODUCT# ; PICTURE 9999.
  1 ORDER# ; PICTURE 9999.
. . .
```

CALC was designed to specify that record instances will be stored and found by hashing on key values. For the preceding PRODUCT record,

Table 13-2 DBTG Record Placement Control Using LOCATION MODE

LOCATION MODE	Explanation	Examples
CALC	Indicates that a record instance will be placed and may be accessed in secondary memory based on a value for a primary or secondary key. Usually, this is implemented by key value hashing, but index methods are possible. That is, data base can be entered directly at a given record if a CALC key value is known.	RECORD NAME IS PRODUCT LOCATION MODE IS CALC USING PRODUCT# DUPLICATES NOT ALLOWED –defines a single, primary key ------------------------------ RECORD NAME IS CUSTOMER LOCATION MODE IS CALC USING CUST-ZIP DUPLICATES ARE FIRST –defines a single, secondary key
VIA	Indicates that a record instance will be placed in secondary memory close to its parent record instance for *one* specified set. This helps to improve performance when used with frequently referenced set. VIA and CALC may not both be used on same record; use of VIA prevents access to record on a key value.	RECORD NAME IS ORDER-LINE LOCATION MODE IS VIA ITEMS-ON-ORDER SET . . . SET NAME IS ITEMS-ON-ORDER OWNER IS ORDER . . . MEMBER IS ORDER-LINE –specifies that an ORDER-LINE instance should be stored close to its ORDER owner instance

PRODUCT# is a primary key (since DUPLICATES NOT ALLOWED); for the ORDER-LINE record given here, the concatenated key is PRODUCT# plus ORDER#, which is also unique. If duplicates are allowed, then the DBMS will permit two or more records to have the same hash key value. Otherwise, when not allowed, the DBMS will enforce, during storing and modification, the primary key property by returning error codes for data manipulation commands that would cause a violation of the duplicates clause. The CALC key must be defined as fields within the record being CALCed, even if part of the key can be found in a related record (in this case, PRODUCT# of ORDER-LINE is also in the related PRODUCT record).

Some DBTG systems permit only one LOCATION MODE clause; others permit several LOCATION MODE or the more recent KEY IS clauses. Some DBTG systems even permit a data base designer to use other than hashing methods for implementing CALC mode (e.g., indexes). In general, the CALC mode must be interpreted as any keyed access method (entry point into a data base) using primary or secondary keys, as allowed by the DBMS. Use of CALC does not preclude accessing a record by its association with other records; it simply says that records will be *physically placed* (and can be found) based on key values.

On other occasions, users of an information system do not know primary key values for desired records, but instead know the key for some associated record. For example, we might know a PRODUCT# but not know the CUSTOMER#s of customers who have open orders for this product.

The second LOCATION MODE alternative, designed to provide efficient record access by association, is VIA. VIA means that a record will be placed as close to its associated owner record instance as the DBMS can find *for the specified set*. Use of VIA in the DBTG model prevents a user from accessing a record directly by a key value. LOCATION VIA should be used for a given record when much data processing of this record involves first accessing an associated owner record before instances of this type are required (that is, access via relationships between records, since records to be retrieved are known only by their association with other records).

Consider again the ORDER-LINE record type. Although each of these record instances could be identified by a concatenated key of ORDER# plus PRODUCT#, careful review of data processing might indicate that ORDER-LINE records are retrieved or stored only after first retrieving associated PRODUCT or ORDER records. After additional review, it is determined that ORDER-LINE records are more often processed along with ORDER records than with PRODUCT records. The following LOCATION MODE clause could then be used in the definition of the ORDER-LINE record:

```
RECORD NAME IS ORDER-LINE
LOCATION MODE IS VIA ITEMS-ON-ORDER SET
. . .
SET NAME IS ITEMS-ON-ORDER
OWNER IS ORDER
. . .
MEMBER IS ORDER-LINE
. . .
```

Figure 13-4 illustrates the effect these schema commands might have on the data base of Figure 2-10 (Pine Valley Furniture).

A record can be located VIA only one set in the DBTG model, so ORDER-

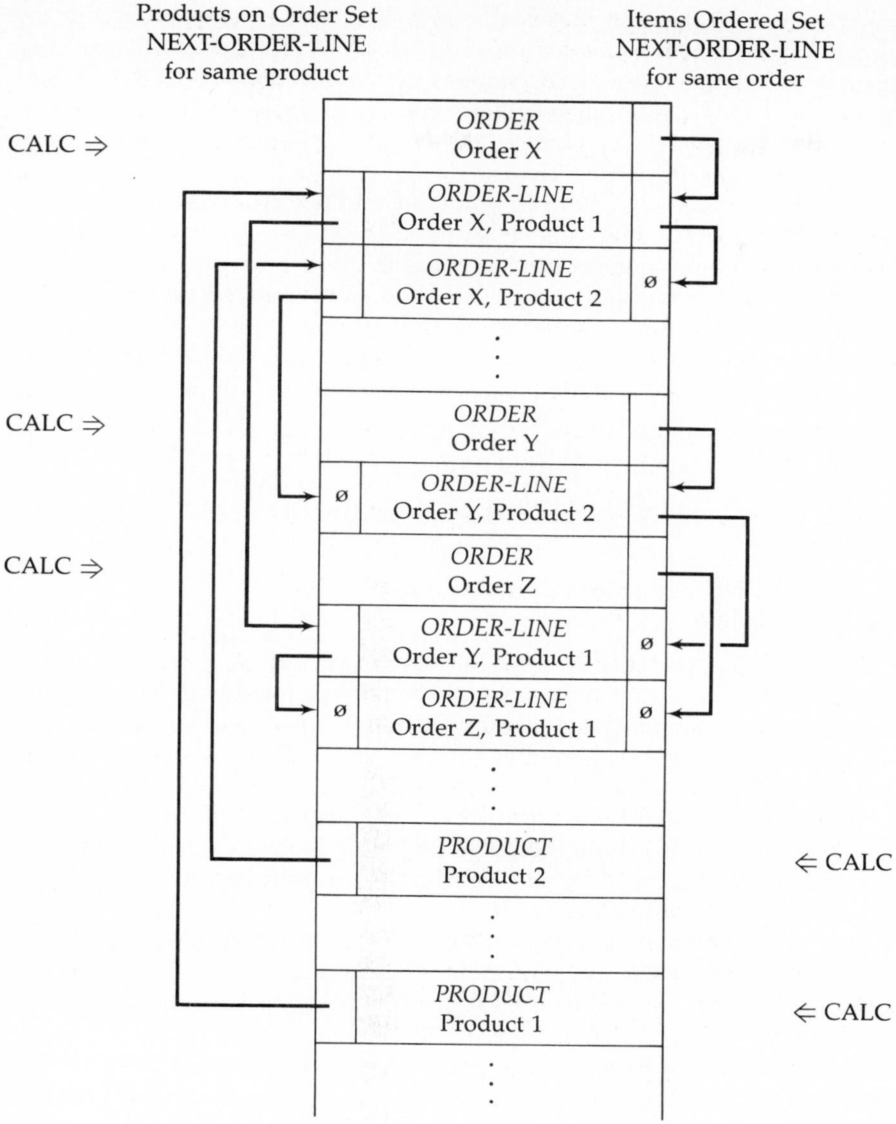

Figure 13-4
VIA placement control for Items Ordered set

LINEs cannot also be specified to be placed close to PRODUCT. It should be emphasized here that VIA does not establish which owner record instance is, in fact, the owner of a given member instance, but only that a member instance will be *placed* close to its owner instance. The SET SELECTION clause in the SET definition controls the method of determining ownership; we will discuss this clause later. As illustrated in Figure 13-4, a record type located VIA one set may participate as owner or members in other sets and may be accessed through these other sets; the most efficient access for the record will be through the set on which it is VIA. If a set member record instance located VIA its owner changes ownership (by a RECONNECT or similar command), its location will not change to be close to its new owner. Thus, after the ownership change, the member will not necessarily exhibit rapid access from its owner VIA the designated set.

In the most recent CODASYL guidelines, LOCATION MODE has been eliminated in favor of a more general and logical clause called KEY IS. Under the latest guideline, not yet implemented in all commercial systems, each record type may have one or more single or concatenated primary or secondary keys with either ascending or descending logical orderings maintained. For the primary key of CUSTOMER# in the CUSTOMER record of Figure 2-10, we could include (in place of the LOCATION MODE clause)

```
KEY CUSTOMER# IS ASCENDING CUSTOMER#
DUPLICATES ARE NOT ALLOWED
```

and for the secondary key of PRODUCT# in the ORDER-LINE record, we could include

```
KEY PRODUCT# IS ASCENDING PRODUCT#
DUPLICATES ARE FIRST
```

DUPLICATES ARE NOT ALLOWED specifies a primary key. The use of FIRST or LAST indicates how to sequence records for storage and retrieval with duplicate secondary key values. FIRST means that a new record with a duplicate value will be stored as the first record (first on a chain) among any with the same value for PRODUCT#; use of LAST would tell the DBMS to store the new record last (in this key sequence) after all existing records (on a chain) with this same PRODUCT# value. A KEY IS clause will cause some type of key access method, like hashing or indexing, to be employed, depending on the implementation.

Although not part of the most current CODASYL guidelines, LOCATION MODE has been presented here because most DBTG systems use some form of this clause, even if the KEY IS clause is also supported.

Data Elements in a Record Definition A record type may have no data elements, which is the case of a link record. Link records are possible because the DBTG data model can be classified as a simple network model. In most cases, a record type will have one or more data elements, or data-base-data-names, as part of its definition. A record type must contain data elements for each component of each key and for each data element used for sorting members of a set.

The schema not only defines what data elements are to be in each record, but also their format of representation in the data base (which may be different from that for corresponding fields in user working storage). Thus, each data element must have exactly one of the following as part of its definition:

- PICTURE clause
- TYPE clause
- SOURCE clause
- OCCURS clause (not allowed in some systems)
- OCCURS and PICTURE clauses
- OCCURS and TYPE clauses

and any of the other clauses shown in Figure 13-3a, with a few limitations.

The PICTURE format is similar to that used in COBOL. Both character and numeric formats are supported. A PICTURE is used to define a display format for data elements. Consequently, data are stored using the computer's typical coding scheme (e.g., EBCDIC or ASCII). TYPE is used to cause more efficient storage formats to be used. TYPE can specify base (BINARY or DECIMAL), scale (FIXED or FLOAT), and mode (REAL or COMPLEX); length specifications for arithmetic data, or BIT or CHARACTER strings; or DATA-BASE-KEY. For example, the PRODUCT file of Figure 2-2 (Pine Valley Furniture) could be defined as a DBTG record type as follows:

```
RECORD IS PRODUCT
LOCATION MODE CALC USING PRODUCT#
. . .
  1 PRODUCT# ; PIC 9999.
  1 DESCRIPTION ; PIC X(20).
  1 FINISH ; PIC X(8).
  1 ROOM ; PIC X(2).
  1 PRICE ; TYPE DECIMAL 6,2.
```

Here most data elements are to be used for display purposes. PRICE will be stored in the computer system's DECIMAL format, with four integer digits and two decimal places (some DBTG systems have a DOLLAR TYPE in which TYPE DOLLAR 4 would be identical to this specification).

An OCCURS clause may be used with PICTURE or TYPE to indicate a repeating group of elementary data items. In addition, an OCCURS clause may appear by itself to specify a repeating data aggregate. For example, we could expand the definition of PRODUCT in Figure 2-10 to include a set of PRICEs, depending on quantity purchased. Part of the record definition might then look like this:

```
RECORD IS PRODUCT
. . .
1 PRICE-SCHEDULE ; OCCURS 3 TIMES.
  2 QTY-UPPER ; PICTURE 99999.
  2 QTY-PRICE ; DECIMAL 6,2.
```

In this example, a three-tiered price schedule capability has been designed for each Product. If different Products have a different number of quantity-price breaks, then

```
RECORD IS PRODUCT
. . .
1 NO-BREAKS ; TYPE IS DECIMAL 2.
1 PRICE-SCHEDULE ; OCCURS NO-BREAKS TIMES.
  2 QTY-UPPER ; PICTURE 99999.
  2 QTY-PRICE ; DECIMAL 6,2.
```

would allow for 0 to 99 different quantity-price breaks for each PRODUCT.

Other Data Element Clauses Any data element can be further defined in a schema by CHECK and coding clauses. A CHECK clause specifies validation criteria to be checked each time the associated data element changes value or a new value is added. Implementations vary, but most permit specification of a list of legitimate values or ranges of values or the execution of a more general user procedure.

Coding clauses inform the DBMS what to do to ENCODE or DECODE a data element value. Again, implementations vary, but the effect of such clauses is to define code tables so that long, standard character strings that are input can be converted to more compact codes to save storage space (and vice-versa for reporting). For example, coding could be used for the DESCRIPTION of the PRODUCT record. Such coding could equate TABLE with a stored value of TA, WALL UNIT with a stored value of WU, and so on, to reduce space and eliminate wasted characters (if variable-length records are not supported). Entry of WALL UNIT for DESCRIPTION would result in only WU being stored; display of a TA stored value would result in TABLE actually being reported.

Relationship Definitions: Sets

A **set** is the definition of a directed relationship from an owner record type to one or more member record types. A set usually defines a 1:*M* relationship, say, an ORDERS-FOR-CUSTOMER set from CUSTOMER as owner to ORDER as member. A set may also define a 1:1 relationship, but this is unusual. A set may not define an *M*:*N* relationship, since the DBTG model prescribes a simple network data model. One can generally assume that a set is implemented as a ring data structure with the owner at the head of the chain and with the last member pointing to the owner. Other structures (bidirectional chains, pointer arrays, owner pointers, and so forth) can be defined in clauses not being considered here.

The Pine Valley Furniture data base of Figures 2-10 and 6-11 would result in three set definitions. The more extensive data base of Figure 6-12b would require five sets (and a link record definition). Figure 13-5 illustrates part of the data base of Figure 6-12b and a skeleton of the schema DDL necessary to define this part of the data base. This figure includes a complete record definition for the PRODUCT-VENDOR-LINK record. Assuming that this is only a link record, no data elements are defined, although some "data about

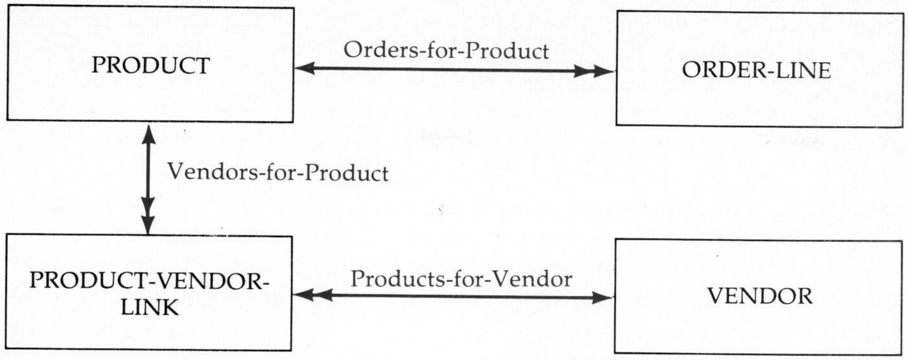

(a)

```
SCHEMA NAME IS PINE
•••
RECORD NAME IS PRODUCT
    LOCATION MODE IS CALC USING PRODUCT#
•••
1 PRODUCT# ; PIC 9999.
•••
RECORD NAME IS ORDER-LINE
    LOCATION MODE IS VIA ORDERS-FOR-PRODUCT SET
•••
RECORD NAME IS VENDOR
    LOCATION MODE IS CALC USING VENDOR#
•••
1 VENDOR# ; PIC 9999.
•••
RECORD NAME IS PRODUCT-VENDOR-LINK
    LOCATION MODE IS VIA VENDORS-FOR-PRODUCT SET
SET IS ORDERS-FOR-PRODUCT
    OWNER IS PRODUCT
    •••
    MEMBER IS ORDER-LINE
    •••
SET IS VENDORS-FOR-PRODUCT
    OWNER IS PRODUCT
    •••
    MEMBER IS PRODUCT-VENDOR-LINK
    •••
SET IS PRODUCTS-FOR-VENDOR
    OWNER IS VENDOR
    •••
    MEMBER IS PRODUCT-VENDOR-LINK
    •••
```

(b)

Figure 13-5
Skeleton of the schema for part of Pine Valley Furniture data base:
(a) network diagram
(b) schema definition

data" (e.g., pointers to maintain sets) may be allocated from the compilation of the schema DDL.

The inclusion of a set, say, from PRODUCT to ORDER-LINE, in a schema for Figure 6-12b informs the schema DDL compiler to establish some type of data structure to permit rapid access from an instance of a PRODUCT record to instances of associated set ORDER-LINE members (and possibly vice-versa). Whenever records are inserted, deleted, or modified in either of these files, the DBMS will perform much of the maintenance of the overhead data to continue correct record association. This schema in Figure 13-5 illustrates that a record type may be an owner of several sets and also a member of several sets; some DBTG systems even permit the same record type to be both owner and member of the same set!

However, a set is not the only means of relating records in the DBTG model. Consider the same PRODUCT to ORDER-LINE relationship just discussed. If both record types contain PRODUCT# and if this data element is used in a KEY IS clause in each record definition, then associated records may also be rapidly retrieved by accessing records by this logical key. Nevertheless, a set is the usual means employed in a DBTG data base to represent a relationship since this is the only way the DBMS will know about the relationship! If sets are not used to represent relationships, then the implementation is not any richer in structure and capabilities than multiple random access files.

Member Insertion Sequence When a member instance is inserted into a set, the DBMS must know what basis is to be used to determine where in the chain of existing members the new record should be placed. The typical choices available are:

- FIRST: at the beginning of the chain
- LAST: at the end of the chain (FIRST and LAST support chronological order of members by date/time of entry)
- SORTED: based on the value of some field in the member record
- NEXT: immediately after the most recently accessed member of the set
- PRIOR: immediately before the most recently accessed member of the set

We will discuss later in this chapter the difficult decision of choosing whether to sort members of a set. Very simply, the trade-off is between saving sorting time when data are reported versus storage space for the key field (this may be part of the record anyhow) and extra member insertion time to scan for the right place in the member chain. Long chains can, of course, be costly to scan, and frequent maintenance and infrequent reporting in sequence may negate the benefit of a sorted set.

Loop Relationship Several types of 1:*M* relationships need special illustration if we are to explain their representation in schema DDL. The first is a loop relationship. Figure 13-6 reproduces such a relationship from Figure 6-16 and indicates a skeleton of the schema parts required to represent this relationship between customers within the same parent organization under several different implementations in the DBTG model. This loop relationship would help to ascertain the total purchasing behavior of a client for which several purchasing agents or divisions are individual buyers.

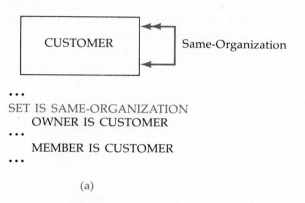

Figure 13-6
Alternative representations of a loop relationship in the CODASYL model:
(a) loop relationship with the same owner and member
(b) loop relationship using two record types
(c) loop relationship using secondary key

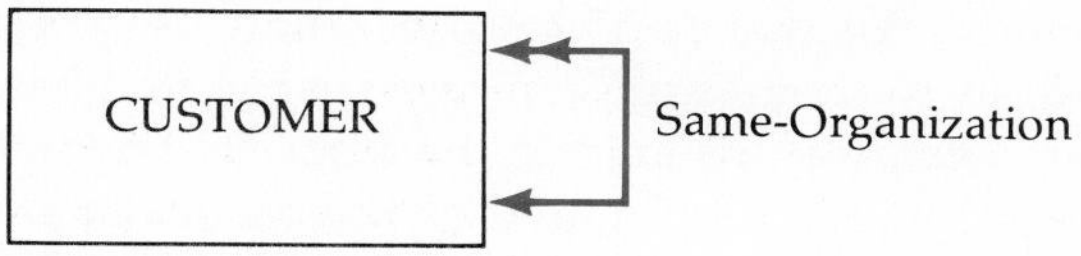


```
...
SET IS SAME-ORGANIZATION
    OWNER IS CUSTOMER
...
    MEMBER IS CUSTOMER
...
```

(a)

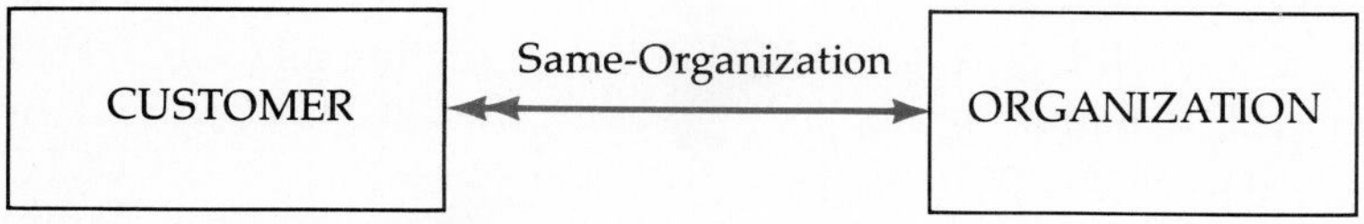


```
...
SET IS SAME-ORGANIZATION
    OWNER IS ORGANIZATION
...
    MEMBER IS CUSTOMER
...
```

(b)

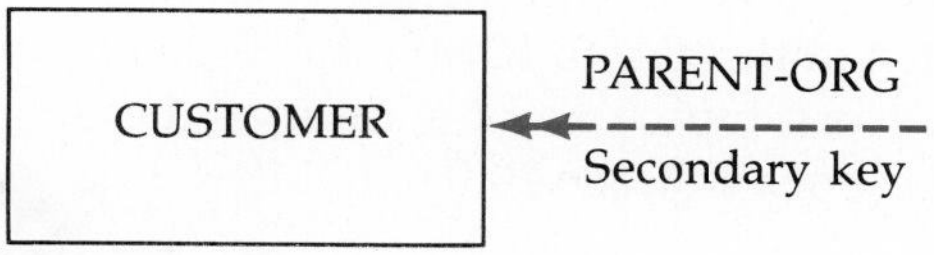

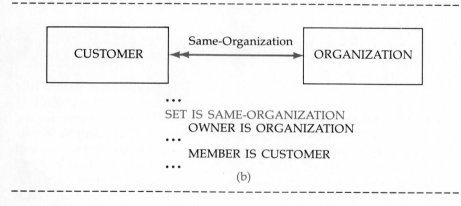

```
...
RECORD IS CUSTOMER
LOCATION MODE IS CALC USING CUSTOMER#
KEY IS PARENT-ORG DUPLICATES ARE FIRST
...
1 CUSTOMER# ; PIC 9999.
1 PARENT-ORG ; PIC 9999.
...
```

(c)

Figure 13-6a illustrates the basic loop relationship and the most direct way, if permitted, to represent this type of relationship. This representation requires that the DBMS support use of the same record type as both owner and member of the same set. In this case, both the parent organization as well as the individual buying groups are represented as CUSTOMERs (which, of course, they likely are).

The approach of Figure 13-6b is to define an additional ORGANIZATION record type, instances of which own a set of CUSTOMER member instances for that parent organization. Data manipulation statements can be used to move from one member to another in a given set instance or from a member instance to the associated owner instance. The approach of Figure 13-6c is, if permitted by the particular DBMS, to define a secondary key on the PARENT-ORG data element of the CUSTOMER record type; data manipulation statements can then be used to access all CUSTOMER records with a common value for this secondary key. In all of these cases, it is still possible to define a primary key of CUSTOMER# for the CUSTOMER record.

Singular Sets Singular or system relationships (called one-of-a-kind in IDMS) are easy to represent in a DBTG schema. The purpose of a singular relationship is to arrange all the instances of some record type into sorted sequence under a common owner, the "system."

Suppose we wanted to arrange all CUSTOMER records into ascending order by CUST-ZIPCODE to avoid the cost of sorting all CUSTOMER records for each mailing. Figure 13-7 illustrates the skeleton of the definition of a singular set that accomplishes this desired sequencing. CUSTOMER records can all be retrieved as members under one common parent (the singular system) in the zip code order because of the use of the ORDER IS SORTED clause and the KEY IS clause of the member specification for the set. Thus, now we would have two access points into CUSTOMER: (1) The primary key of CUSTOMER# is CALCed to provide direct addressing, and (2) the CUST-ZIPCODE set is used to access CUSTOMERs in zip code order.

Singular sets can also be used to logically group together records with a common characteristic (e.g., all customers who have exceeded their credit limit); that is, not all record instances from the set member record type *must* be included in the set. In IDMS, this type of set must be designed using an artificial record type (one-of-a-kind) as the owner, rather than the implicit "system" owner. Release 10.0 of IDMS (IDMS/R 10.0) allows system-owned sets.

It is very important to understand the distinct difference between singular sets and sets with an actual owner record. Singular sets create *one* set instance; other sets create one set instance *for each owner.* Thus, whereas sorted member records in a singular set provides a logical ordering for *all* the records of the member record type, sorted members in regular sets create logical orderings of a *subset* of member records, those with a common parent/owner.

```
...
RECORD IS CUSTOMER
    LOCATION MODE IS CALC USING CUSTOMER#
...
1 CUSTOMER# ; PIC 9999.
1 CUST-ZIPCODE ; PIC 99999.
...
SET IS CUST-SORT
    OWNER IS SYSTEM
    ORDER IS SORTED BY DEFINED KEYS
    ...
    MEMBER IS CUSTOMER
    ...
    KEY IS ASCENDING CUST-ZIPCODE
        DUPLICATES ARE LAST
    ...
```

Figure 13-7
Example of a schema DDL for a singular set

Sets with Multiple Member Types Any set definition contains reference to only one owner record type but may include several member record type clauses. This capability permits the representation of class relationships or any relationship in which a single owner record instance can be associated with many member instances, each of different types. Some DBTG systems permit all members to be sorted by such options as record name (all members of the same type sorted together under a common parent), data base key (that is, physical address sequence, which is convenient for efficiently traversing a member chain), or key values in each member record type.

Figure 13-8 illustrates a typical situation where CUSTOMER records are related to both OPEN- and CLOSED-ORDERs. The CUSTOMER-ORDERS set definition places into a common set instance all OPEN- and CLOSED-ORDERs, in ORDER# sequence, for each CUSTOMER owner. The sorting option is used here simply to facilitate reporting of order data. A hazard of such a set with multiple members is that long member chains can be created; if individual sets are not established from owner to each member type (e.g., CUSTOMER to only OPEN-ORDER), processing for only one of the member type records can be degraded by having to access unwanted set members.

Multiple Relationships Between Records Any number of sets may be defined between the same pair of record types. For example, if Pine Valley Furniture writes both blanket and special orders ("blanket" means an order for a series of deliveries over some extended time period, and "special" means a one-time, stand-alone order), then we might want to define two sets between CUSTOMER and ORDER: Blanket-for-Customer and Special-for-Customer. In this way, users interested in only one type of customer order could use the specialized set to find only orders of the desired type without wasted accesses to unwanted types. Multiple sets between the same pair of record types can also be used to handle different sorting sequences (e.g., orders by sale date, or orders by due date).

Figure 13-8
DBTG schema for a set with two member record types:
(a) example of a class relationship
(b) schema DDL for class relationship

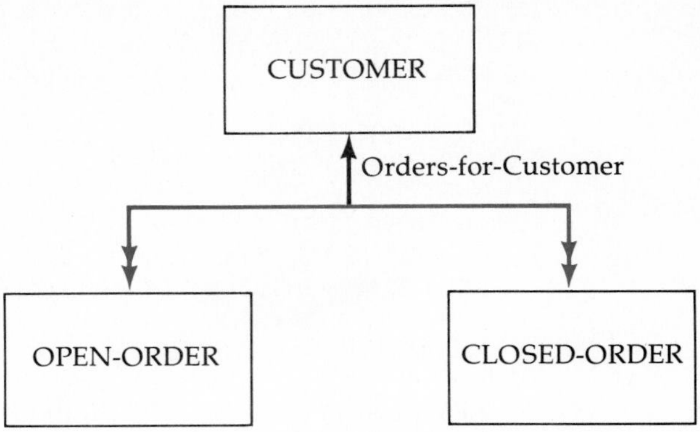

(a)

```
RECORD IS CUSTOMER
...
RECORD IS OPEN-ORDER
...
1 O-ORDER# ; PIC 9999.
...
RECORD IS CLOSED-ORDER
...
1 C-ORDER# ; PIC 9999.
...
SET IS ORDERS-FOR-CUSTOMER
OWNER IS CUSTOMER
ORDER IS SORTED BY DEFINED KEYS
    DUPLICATES NOT ALLOWED
...
MEMBER IS OPEN-ORDER
...
    KEY IS ASCENDING O-ORDER#
        DUPLICATES ARE NOT ALLOWED
...
MEMBER IS CLOSED-ORDER
...
    KEY IS ASCENDING C-ORDER#
        DUPLICATES ARE NOT ALLOWED
...
```

(b)

Many-to-Many Relationships Because the CODASYL network standard is a simple network architecture, many-to-many relationships have to be implemented using link records. Figure 13-9 illustrates, by way of an instance diagram, the result of representing an *M:N* relationship between PRODUCT and VENDOR. In this case, an intersection record containing the Vendor's

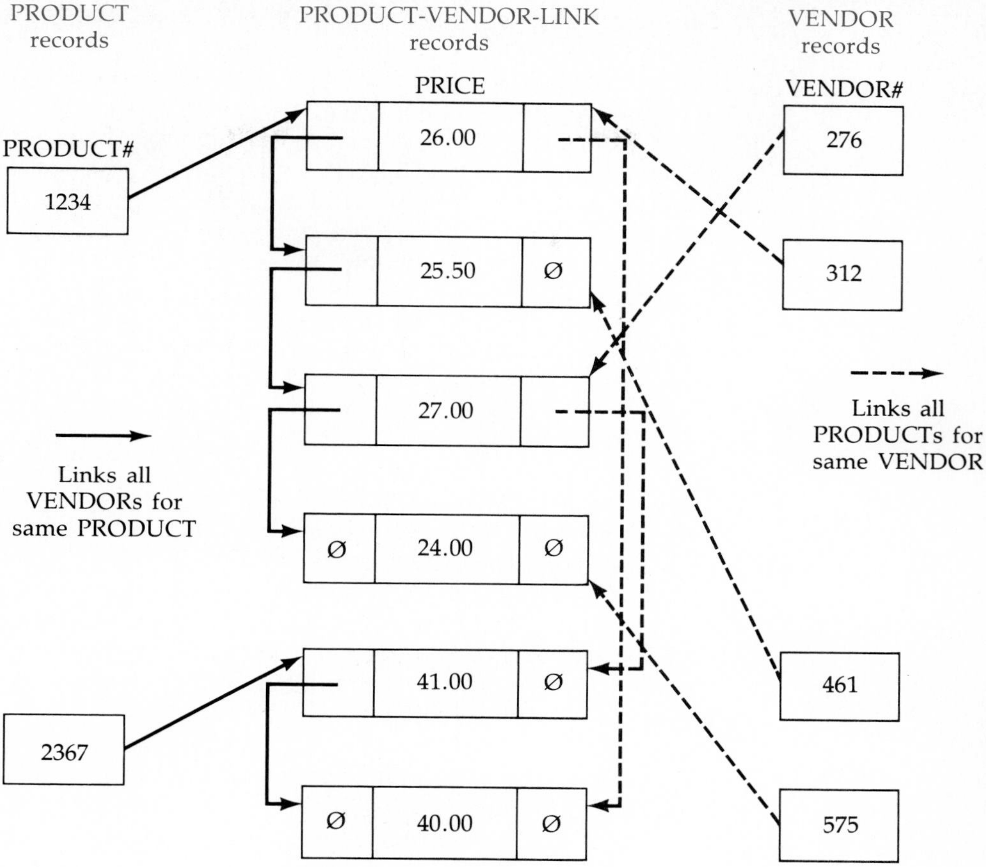

Figure 13-9
Example of records and sets implementations for a many-to-many relationship

PRICE for that Product is used to link a PRODUCT to a VENDOR when that Vendor supplies that Product. We assume here that meaningful data, PRICE, need to be retained on each PRODUCT-VENDOR relationship instance. If no such meaningful data exist, then the structure remains the same as in Figure 13-9, except there would be only pointers in the PRODUCT-VENDOR-LINK record. Since meaningful data exist most of the time there is a *M:N* relationship, the creation of the extra link record is almost always needed. In fact, it is recommended so that even if meaningful data are not recognized until after the data base is implemented, the structure of the data base will stay the same (thus minimizing reprogramming). Note that each VENDOR and PRODUCT record is stored only once, but a PRODUCT-VENDOR-LINK record instance appears each time a Vendor can supply some Product. As will be seen later, the three record types and two sets of this figure can be used to find both the Vendors of a given Product and the Products of a given Vendor. That is, sets may be processed from either owner to member or member to owner.

Set Qualifications A set may optionally be defined to be DYNAMIC or PRIOR. DYNAMIC means that this set has no specific member record type, but an instance of any record other than of the owner type may become associated in this set to a given owner instance. Use of DYNAMIC is rare. PRIOR, on the other hand, can be an important feature. Specification of SET IS PRIOR causes the DBMS to implement for the associated set a method that allows the set to be processed as efficiently in the backward (prior) direction as in the forward (next) direction. The effect is to create a bidirectional chain capability, although the guidelines do not specify that a bidirectional chain is *the* way PRIOR must be implemented.

Set Member Definition The set membership clauses are an important part of a schema. Not only do they provide a necessary companion to the OWNER IS clause, but they are instrumental in set integrity control and, hence, relationships in a data base. In addition, it is important to study this section of a schema carefully because three of its clauses—INSERTION, RETENTION, and SET SELECTION—typically are difficult to understand for people getting their first exposure to data base management. Further, you should be aware that INSERTION is called CONNECTION and RETENTION is called DISCONNECTION by some DBTG systems.

Any set may have one or more MEMBER IS and associated clauses, one each for each record type related to the set owner in the relationship represented by the set. In explaining these clauses, we will use sets with only *one* member record type.

For the purpose of explaining set membership clauses, consider the data base shown in Figure 13-10a and a possible schema definition for this data base shown in Figure 13-10b. The situation depicted here is an inventory accounting data base for unique, serial-numbered, limited-life products stored at various warehouses. For this situation, we will assume that the organization permits transshipment of products between warehouses. This example would be typical of certain chemical or pharmaceutical products. This situation is another example of an *M:N* relationship and illustrates how such a relationship would be defined in the DDL.

The STORAGE set relates a generic product to particular serial-numbered instances of that product stored in warehouses. An analysis of reporting requirements involving records of this set indicates that no special set ordering of INVENTORY members for the associated PRODUCT owner is necessary, so ORDER IS FIRST is chosen to speed member record creation (since a new record would be inserted in a chained set at the beginning of the chain, which we have seen is the easiest point to insert in a single-directional chain).

Controlling Member Insertion Since an INVENTORY record may not logically exist unless it is for an already existing PRODUCT, INSERTION IS AUTOMATIC is used. This means that the DBMS will automatically link a new INVENTORY record to its associated PRODUCT owner when we store a new INVENTORY record in the data base.

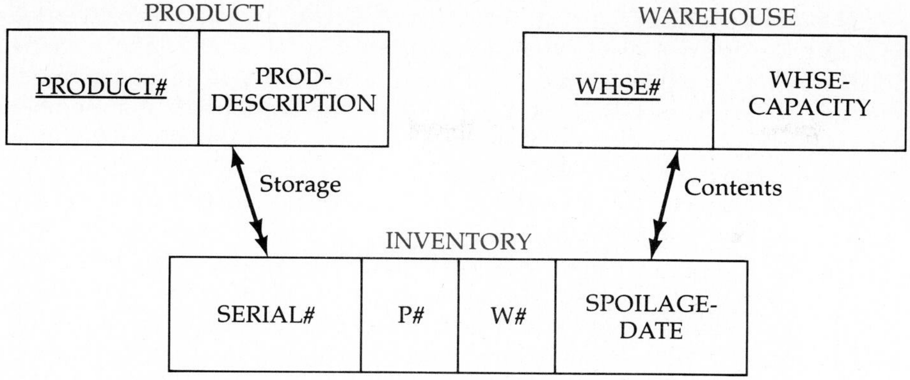

(a)

```
SCHEMA IS INVENTORY
AREA NAME IS STOCK
RECORD NAME IS PRODUCT
    LOCATION MODE IS CALC USING PRODUCT#
    1 PRODUCT# ; PIC 9999.
    1 PROD-DESCRIPTION ; PIC X(20).
RECORD NAME IS WAREHOUSE
    LOCATION MODE IS CALC USING WHSE#
    1 WHSE# ; PIC 99.
    1 WHSE-CAPACITY ; PIC 999999.
RECORD NAME IS INVENTORY
    LOCATION MODE IS VIA STORAGE SET
    1 SERIAL# ; PIC 99999.
    1 P# ; PIC 9999.
    1 W# ; PIC 99.
    1 SPOILAGE-DATE ; PIC 999999.
SET NAME IS STORAGE
    OWNER IS PRODUCT
    ORDER IS FIRST
    MEMBER IS INVENTORY
        INSERTION IS AUTOMATIC
        RETENTION IS FIXED
        CHECK IS PRODUCT# IN PRODUCT=P#
        SET SELECTION IS BY VALUE OF PRODUCT#
SET NAME IS CONTENTS
    OWNER IS WAREHOUSE
    ORDER IS SORTED BY DEFINED KEYS
    MEMBER IS INVENTORY
        INSERTION IS AUTOMATIC
        RETENTION IS MANDATORY
        KEY IS ASCENDING P# DUPLICATES ARE FIRST
        CHECK IS WHSE# IN WAREHOUSE=W#
        SET SELECTION IS STRUCTURAL WHSE#=W#
END SCHEMA
```

(b)

Figure 13-10 Illustration of set membership clauses: (a) sample inventory data base (b) schema DDL for inventory data base

The other choice for INSERTION IS is MANUAL, which means that we would have to explicitly and separately program when to connect a new INVENTORY record in a data entry program. AUTOMATIC saves a minimal amount of program coding. MANUAL would be appropriate if a member record might not have an owner record in a set when initially stored in a data base. For example, a set from department to employee might have INSERTION IS MANUAL, since many employees when hired are not immediately assigned to a department.

The CONTENTS set also uses INSERTION IS AUTOMATIC since it is assumed that a particular serial-numbered part must reside in some warehouse. The INSERTION IS clause is an effective mechanism for enforcing certain semantic data requirements (that is, existence dependencies upon original entry of a record). The appropriate value of AUTOMATIC or MANUAL for any given set can be established only after a careful analysis of the meaning of data and relationships involved in a set.

Controlling Member Retention Similar to the INSERTION IS clause is the RETENTION IS clause. In the STORAGE set, RETENTION IS FIXED is used. This means that once a serial number is associated to a generic PRODUCT record, it must be *permanently* associated with the same PRODUCT. The only way to change the association to another PRODUCT would be to delete the INVENTORY record and reenter it under a new owner PRODUCT.

On the other hand, since individual parts may be transshipped from one warehouse to another, RETENTION IS MANDATORY is used in the CONTENTS set. MANDATORY says that the member record, in order to exist, must always have some WAREHOUSE owner (the part has to be somewhere!), but that the particular owner may change. In terms of the data manipulation language to be introduced later, MANDATORY allows us to RECONNECT INVENTORY records as required to indicate current location of a part.

A third option for RETENTION IS, not illustrated here, is OPTIONAL. This choice means that we may actually DISCONNECT a member record from any owner and leave the member unowned for as long as is appropriate. For example, a part is not really in any warehouse during transshipment. To permit an INVENTORY record to have no WAREHOUSE owner during this period, we would use RETENTION IS OPTIONAL. OPTIONAL also permits the deletion of an owner record without having to delete members. For example, if a warehouse is closed, the associated part records will still exist until the parts are moved to a new location.

RECONNECTing records can have a subtle effect on data base performance. If, for example, INVENTORY records are located VIA the CONTENTS set instead of the STORAGE set, an INVENTORY record that changed its association to other than its original WAREHOUSE would *not* be physically moved to now be near its current WAREHOUSE owner record in the physical data base.

The RETENTION IS clause also provides a method to include semantic

Table 13-3 Summary of DBTG Semantic Controls in Set Membership Clauses

Retention	Insertion	
	AUTOMATIC	**MANUAL**
FIXED	Member record *must* have an owner when it is stored and will continue to have *same* owner until member is deleted. DBMS will automatically CONNECT member to owner, based on SET SELECTION clause, when member is stored.	Member record is permitted to *not* have an owner when it is stored, but once CONNECTed to an owner, it *must* keep same owner until member is deleted. DBMS will *not* CONNECT member to owner until told to do so by user program.
MANDATORY	Member record *must* have an owner when it is stored, but member can be RECONNECTed to other owners as required. DBMS will automatically CONNECT member to owner, based on SET SELECTION clause, when member is stored.	Member record is permitted to *not* have an owner when it is stored, and once CONNECTed may be RECONNECTed to other owners as required. DBMS will *not* CONNECT member to owner until told to do so by user program.
OPTIONAL	Member record *must* have an owner when it is stored, but member can be RECONNECTed to other owners or DISCONNECTed from any owner as required. DBMS will automatically CONNECT member to owner, based on SET SELECTION clause, when member is stored.	Member record is permitted to *not* have an owner when it is stored; once CONNECTed, if ever, it may be RECONNECTed or DISCONNECTed as required. DBMS will *not* CONNECT member to owner until told to do so by user program.

controls, after original loading of data, on proper data base record associations and data manipulation. Table 13-3 summarizes the impact of various combinations of INSERTION and RETENTION options. But be aware that the terms FIXED, MANDATORY, and OPTIONAL have not had the same meanings in all versions of the DBTG guidelines. Until 1978, FIXED did not exist and MANDATORY meant FIXED. If you are using a DBTG DBMS, read the reference manuals carefully to determine what is implemented by that vendor.

Cross-Reference Key Control The CHECK IS clauses provide yet another level of semantic control on record associations. Each of these clauses in the example of Figure 13-10 requires that key values in both member and owner of a set instance must be identical. These clauses provide an extra protection that the correct semantic connection occurs when records are originally inserted into the data base or CONNECTed to an owner. To fully appreciate the usefulness of the CHECK IS clause, the function of the SET SELECTION clause must be understood.

Determining a Member's Owner Instance Whereas the INSERTION and RETENTION clauses control *when* and *whether* a record type must have an owner, the SET SELECTION clause determines *which instance* of the owner record type of a set should become the "proud parent."

For the STORAGE set in Figure 13-10, SET SELECTION IS BY VALUE OF PRODUCT# means that when a new INVENTORY record is stored in the data base (if INSERTION IS AUTOMATIC) or CONNECTed to a PRODUCT owner, the DBMS will use the current value in PRODUCT# from user working storage as a key to find the appropriate owner. Thus, PRODUCT must have a keyed access (e.g., LOCATION MODE IS CALC or a KEY IS clause, whichever the DBMS uses) on the data element referenced (in this case, PRODUCT#). This type of SET SELECTION clause forces the DBMS to find the owner record automatically and forces the DBMS user to make sure that the correct PRODUCT# is in memory. As long as P# is correctly recorded, the CHECK IS clause on this set is a validity check that set selection was done properly. This form of the SET SELECTION clause is more often used when the member record type does *not* contain the key of the owner record.

The SET SELECTION clause of the CONTENTS set is the one that is more appropriate when a member record contains the key of the associated owner record instance. SET SELECTION IS STRUCTURAL means that the DBMS is to find the associated owner record for a new member when it is stored (if INSERTION IS AUTOMATIC) or CONNECTed by using the value of a data element in the member (e.g., W#) as the key value of the owner (e.g., WAREHOUSE#). In this case, the CHECK IS clause is of no operational value, since the SET SELECTION clause guarantees that the check will not be violated.

Proper use of INSERTION, RETENTION, CHECK, and SET SELECTION clauses requires practice. Although use of these clauses forces a data base designer to deal with many details, these clauses provide valuable tools for semantic controls of the data base maintenance and processing. A data base programmer also needs to be aware of these clauses in order to interpret error messages that indicate breaches of these integrity constraints.

Many DBTG DBMSs also permit a SET SELECTION THRU CURRENT OF SET option. This version is difficult to understand until one understands the DBTG data manipulation language and a construct used there called currency indicators. Basically, this form differs from the others in that the DBMS does not have to find the owner record, but rather uses the last owner record instance retrieved. This is, in fact, often the most efficient choice for SET SELECTION, especially in interactive programs. For example, if when entering a new INVENTORY record the program first finds the record for the WAREHOUSE indicated for the part, why make the DBMS find it again in order to store the INVENTORY record? The proper WAREHOUSE owner is "current"ly in working storage and does not need to be refound.

A SET SELECTION clause is not found in certain DBTG systems. In these (in particular, IDMS), the owner for a new member record being inserted into the data base is essentially the most recently retrieved record of each set, which must be an instance of the proper owner record type for each set.

Sorting Members Finally, the ORDER IS SORTED clause for the CONTENTS set needs to be explained. An analysis of reporting requirements from this data base indicated that warehouse contents frequently were desired in PRODUCT# (P#) sequence for easy reading. The ORDER IS SORTED and KEY IS clauses cause the data base to automatically maintain member INVENTORY records in this sequence (usually via a sorted list), thus avoiding sorting of records or report lines for each report.

Other Set Member Clauses Not illustrated in Figure 13-10 but appearing in Figure 13-3 is the SEARCH KEY IS clause of the member section of a set definition. The set itself establishes a method (usually a chain) to access all member instances, possibly in a sorted sequence, under a common owner record instance. The SEARCH KEY IS clause defines direct access from an owner instance to a member with a specific key value. That is, SEARCH KEY IS establishes functionally a key index in each owner record that points to each member record. For example, in the data base of Figure 13-10a, we might want to create a way to identify/access for each WAREHOUSE the INVENTORY that will spoil each day. To do so, we would include in the member clause of the CONTENTS set the clause

SEARCH KEY IS SPOILAGE-DATE DUPLICATES ALLOWED.

The design of efficient network data bases depends on careful study of data base usage maps, such as in Figure 8-17, and logical access maps, such as in Figure 7-19. These figures help a data base designer to

- identify frequent entry points into the data base (need for CALC keys)
- identify high activity access paths (possible use of VIA LOCATION MODE)

- identify entry into data base to a subset of records or a group of records of same type in sorted sequence (possible use of system or singular set)
- search through members of a set in a sorted sequence (possible use of ORDER IS SORTED to sort member records)

As a summary of this section on DBTG schema definition, Figure 13-11 contains the IDMS schema DDL for the Mountain View Community Hospital network data base of Figure 9-7. Numbered lines are explained in the footnotes to the figure.

DBTG SUBSCHEMA DDL: EXTERNAL DATA BASES

Each user of a data base usually wants to use only a portion of a global, conceptual data base. This portion may strictly be a subset but may also redefine, into more local terminology and different structures, selected components (records, data elements, sets) of the data base. Further, as a means to secure the data base against accidental damage by naive users or to ensure legislated, organizational, or personal privacy, a particular user may be limited in what components of the data base he or she may use and what data manipulations may be performed on the visible data.

The CODASYL Data Base Task Group provided for these capabilities by specifying subschemas. A **subschema** is a defined subset of an associated data base that gives a program invoking the subschema a customized view of the data base. The view of the data base as seen from a subschema may differ from the data base definition in that selected data elements, records, sets, and areas may be omitted; data elements, records, sets, and areas may be renamed using terms more understandable to a class of users; and data element formats (PICTURE, TYPE, length) may be changed to suit specialized data processing needs. Subschema capabilities in some DBTG systems even permit the subschema to define logical records that are combinations of data elements from several related schema records; this capability is similar to the "view" concept in relational data bases and can be considered the result of an implicit combination of record joins.

Subschemas provide a mechanism for data independence, since they yield a consistent view of the data base to a group of programs; if the schema changes but the local view is unaffected, then programs (which use a subschema, not the schema) are also unaffected.

Since subschemas are the definition of the view of a data base assumed by an application program, the subschema DDL is dependent on the programming language used in the application program. Over the years, subschema DDLs have been developed for COBOL, FORTRAN, PL/I, and assembler languages. A subschema is defined separately from any application program that uses it; a subschema is stored in a subschema library, managed by the DBMS, and can be invoked or included in an application

Figure 13-11 (pages 475–477) IDMS schema for Mountain View Community Hospital (see data base in Figure 9-7)

```
***********************************************************************
    SCHEMA DESCRIPTION.
***********************************************************************
    SCHEMA NAME IS MVCH.
(1) FILE DESCRIPTION.
    FILE NAME IS MVCHFILE                 ASSIGN TO MVCHDS
                                          DEVICE TYPE IS 3380.
    FILE NAME IS JOURNAL                  ASSIGN TO SYSJRNL.
***********************************************************************
    AREA DESCRIPTION.
***********************************************************************
(2) AREA NAME IS MVCH-CHG                 RANGE IS 770351 THRU 770420
                                          WITHIN FILE MVCHFILE
                                            FROM 1 THRU 70.
    AREA NAME IS MVCH-PHY                 RANGE IS 770421 THRU 770586
                                          WITHIN FILE MVCHFILE
                                            FROM 71 THRU 160.
***********************************************************************
    RECORD DESCRIPTION.
***********************************************************************
    RECORD NAME IS ROOM.
(3) RECORD ID IS 100.
    LOCATION MODE IS CALC                 USING LOCATION
                                          DUPLICATES NOT ALLOWED.
    WITHIN MVCH-PHY AREA.
        02 LOCATION                       PIC 9999.
        (other data items)
  *************
    RECORD NAME IS PATIENT.
    RECORD ID IS 101.
    LOCATION MODE IS CALC                 USING PATIENT-NO
                                          DUPLICATES NOT ALLOWED.
    WITHIN MVCH-CHG AREA.
        02 PATIENT-NO                     PIC 9999.
        (other data items)
  *************
    RECORD NAME IS PHYSICIAN.
    RECORD ID IS 102.
    LOCATION MODE IS CALC                 USING PHYSICIAN-ID
                                          DUPLICATES NOT ALLOWED.
    WITHIN MVCH-PHY AREA.
        02 PHYSICIAN-ID                   PIC X(10).
        02 PHYSICIAN-PHONE                PIC 9(7).
  *************
    RECORD NAME IS ITEM.
    RECORD ID IS 103.
    LOCATION MODE IS CALC                 USING ITEM-CODE
                                          DUPLICATES NOT ALLOWED.
    WITHIN MVCH-CHG AREA.
        02 ITEM-CODE                      PIC 999.
        02 DESCRIPTION                    PIC X(15).
  *************
```

(Continues)

```
    RECORD NAME IS TREATMENT.
    RECORD ID IS 104.
(4) LOCATION MODE IS VIA            TREATED SET.
    WITHIN MVCH-PHY AREA.
        02 PHYSICIAN-ID             PIC X(10).
        02 PATIENT-NO               PIC 9999.
        02 PROCEDURE                PIC X(15).
*********************************
    RECORD NAME IS CHARGES.
    RECORD ID IS 105.
(5) LOCATION MODE IS VIA            INCURRED SET.
    WITHIN MVCH-CHG AREA.
        02 PATIENT-NO               PIC 9999.
        02 ITEM-CODE                PIC 999.
        02 CHARGE                   PIC 9999V99 COMP-3.
*************************************************************
    SET DESCRIPTION.
*************************************************************
    SET IS ASSIGNED.
    ORDER IS FIRST.
(6) MODE IS CHAIN.
(7) OWNER IS ROOM                   NEXT DBKEY POSITION IS 1.
(8) MEMBER IS PATIENT               NEXT DBKEY POSITION IS 4
                                    LINKED TO OWNER
                                      OWNER DBKEY POSITION IS 5
(9)                                 OPTIONAL AUTOMATIC.
*********************************
    SET IS RECEIVED.
(10) ORDER IS LAST.
(11) MODE IS CHAIN                  LINKED TO PRIOR.
    OWNER IS PATIENT                NEXT DBKEY POSITION IS 1
                                    PRIOR DBKEY POSITION IS 2.
    MEMBER IS TREATMENT             NEXT DBKEY POSITION IS 1
                                    PRIOR DBKEY POSITION IS 2
                                    LINKED TO OWNER
                                      OWNER DBKEY POSITION IS 5
(12)                                FIXED MANUAL.
*********************************
    SET IS TREATED.
(13) ORDER IS SORTED.
    MODE IS CHAIN                   LINKED TO PRIOR.
    OWNER IS PHYSICIAN              NEXT DBKEY POSITION IS 1
                                    PRIOR DBKEY POSITION IS 2.
    MEMBER IS TREATMENT             NEXT DBKEY POSITION IS 3
                                    PRIOR DBKEY POSITION IS 4
                                    LINKED TO OWNER
                                      OWNER DBKEY POSITION IS 6
                                    FIXED AUTOMATIC
                                    ASCENDING KEY IS PATIENT-NO
                                      DUPLICATES ARE FIRST.
*********************************
```

Figure 13-11
(continued)

```
      SET IS INCURRED.
      ORDER IS SORTED.
      MODE IS CHAIN.
      OWNER IS PATIENT                 NEXT DBKEY POSITION IS 3.
      MEMBER IS CHARGES                NEXT DBKEY POSITION IS 1
                                       FIXED MANUAL
                                       ASCENDING KEY IS ITEM-CODE
                                         DUPLICATES ARE LAST.

*********************************
      SET IS PROVIDED.
      ORDER IS LAST.
      MODE IS CHAIN.
      OWNER IS ITEM                    NEXT DBKEY POSITION IS 1.
      MEMBER IS CHARGES                NEXT DBKEY POSITION IS 2
                                       LINKED TO OWNER
                                         OWNER DBKEY POSITION IS 3
                                       FIXED AUTOMATIC.
```

(1) Logical file names used in schema are matched with physical data set names and devices.
(2) Areas are assigned to page ranges in logical files. In this schema, we have chosen to have two areas: MVCH-CHG, which contains those record types related to a patient bill, and MVCH-PHY, which contains all other record types.
(3) RECORD ID simply assigns a number to identify each record type uniquely in the data dictionary.
(4) VIA is chosen here to group TREATMENT records close to PHYSICIAN records, since it is assumed that these related records are frequently used together in programs.
(5) Similar assumption as in (4), but this time for PATIENT and CHARGES records.
(6) This is a mandatory clause that simply says to create a chain from owner through members.
(7) The NEXT DBKEY POSITION clause specifies which relative pointer in the record associated with this clause (in this case, ROOM) is to be used for the next in chain pointer for this set.
(8) Again, the NEXT DBKEY POSITION clause specifies the pointer position (in this case in PATIENT); the LINKED TO OWNER indicates that each member record is to have a pointer (the pointer in the position specified) to its owner record to support rapid access to owner.
(9) OPTIONAL AUTOMATIC is used to allow PATIENTs to exist without being assigned a hospital location, but originally a PATIENT record can only be entered if the patient is admitted and placed in some location. The reader should note that IDMS does not have a SET SELECTION clause, as noted in the text.
(10) ORDER IS LAST is used to keep TREATMENT records in approximately ascending order by treatment date.
(11) LINKED TO PRIOR establishes backward chaining as well as forward chaining. The PRIOR clauses in the OWNER and MEMBER definitions indicate where in these records to find the PRIOR pointers.
(12) FIXED MANUAL is used here and in the INCURRED set to handle emergency treatment situations in which treatment is performed (and charges incurred) before the patient is admitted.
(13) ORDER IS SORTED is used to keep TREATMENT records grouped together by PATIENT (see ASCENDING KEY clause in member definition); DUPLICATES ARE FIRST is used in the member clause to keep TREATMENT records in reverse chronological order under each PATIENT.

Figure 13-11
(continued)

Figure 13-12
IDMS subschema for Patient Bill (Mountain View Community Hospital)

```
ADD SUBSCHEMA PATIENT-BILL
    OF SCHEMA MVCH.
ADD AREA . . .
ADD RECORD PATIENT
    ELEMENT PATIENT-NO.
ADD RECORD ITEM
    ELEMENTS ARE ALL.
ADD RECORD CHARGES
    ELEMENTS ARE ALL.
ADD SET INCURRED.
ADD SET PROVIDED.
```

program when that program is compiled, link edited, or loaded, depending on the DBMS.

Figure 13-12 illustrates the IDMS subschema DDL via the Patient Bill user view of Figure 9-8 for the Mountain View Community Hospital schema definition in Figure 13-11. Each subschema is named and is matched to a particular schema.

Areas, records, data elements, and sets to be included in the subschema are defined, along with restrictions on the use of data manipulation commands on these structural components. Also, depending on the features of the DBMS, this division may include privacy specifications and explanations of derivation of logical records as combinations of base records from the subschema. Some DBTG systems permit data names to be redefined into localized terms.

IDMS is one such DBTG DBMS that has a facility to define logical records and the process of deriving them (called a logical path). Figure 13-13 illustrates how the logical record concept could be used to define a DETAILED-BILL logical record for an identified patient.

In this case, the DBMS would automatically and transparently construct a DETAILED-BILL record for each CHARGES instance of each PATIENT record instance (that is, DETAILED-BILL represents the complete printed line item on the patient bill depicted in Figure 8-9). We derive a DETAILED-BILL logical record by first using the current value of PATIENT-NO to FIND (that is, locate but not load any PATIENT data in working storage) a uniquely identified PATIENT; the application programmer must make sure that the proper PATIENT-NO is in working storage before requesting a DETAILED-BILL record. Then the DBMS would OBTAIN (that is, transfer data element values into working storage) a CHARGES record for this PATIENT and conclude by OBTAINing the ITEM owner of this CHARGES in the PROVIDED set.

The operational benefit of a logical record, as will be seen later, is to reduce the application programmer's burden by creating virtual data that do not have to be constructed step by step in the application program. The result is less program coding (hence, faster development), less chance of

```
ADD LOGICAL RECORD IS DETAILED-BILL
      ELEMENTS ARE PATIENT, CHARGES, ITEM
ADD LOGICAL PATH OBTAIN DETAILED-BILL
      SELECT FOR FIELDNAME EQ PATIENT-NO
           FIND PATIENT WHERE CALCKEY IS
                PATIENT-NO OF REQUEST
           OBTAIN EACH CHARGES WITHIN INCURRED
           OBTAIN OWNER WITHIN PROVIDED
```

Figure 13-13
Example of IDMS logical record definition in a subschema

erroneous data processing (since common, complicated data accesses can be coded into the subschema by a senior data base programmer), and often a more understandable data model presented to the programmer (since excessive details have been masked from the programmer).

COBOL DML: RETRIEVING AND MAINTAINING DATA

We choose to illustrate here the data processing capabilities in the COBOL programming language for accessing and manipulating a DBTG data base. As mentioned before, this is not the only procedural language possible, but it is the one most likely encountered in business data processing. As will be seen in the next section, nonprocedural language access is also possible with many DBTG systems.

Procedural, step-by-step (record-by-record) processing of a data base requires frequent reference to some relative position in the data base from which to move. Recall the data structure processing procedures from Chapter 6. These procedures were based on knowing some current position in order to find the next record on a chain or in order to identify a position for record insertion or deletion. This same logic is an integral part of processing a DBTG data base.

Currency Indicators

The term used in the DBTG data manipulation language (DML) for relative position is *currency indicator.* In fact, the DBMS is constantly keeping track of numerous currency indicators. A **currency indicator** is a variable that holds the physical address (data base key) of the record instance most recently accessed or manipulated in a specified category of records. These categories result in the following currency indicators important in various DML statements:

Figure 13-14
LAM and AD for all customers by salesperson

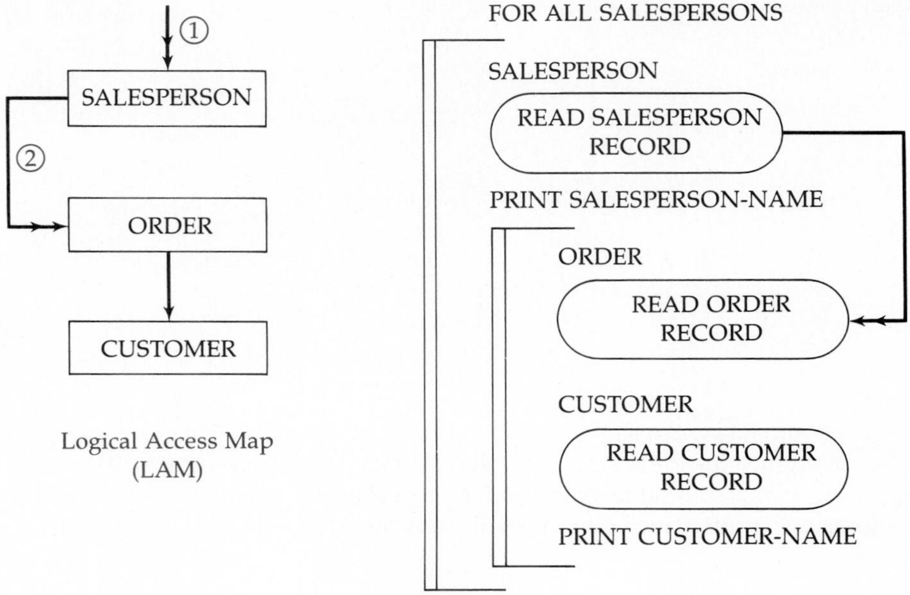

Logical Access Map (LAM)

Action Diagram (AD)

1. Current of run-unit: the most recent instance of any data base record referenced (that is, retrieved or maintained by some DML command, such as FIND, OBTAIN, CONNECT, or STORE)
2. Current of record type: for each record type in the subschema, the most recent record instance referenced
3. Current of set: for each set in the subschema, the most recent set record instance (owner or member) referenced
4. Current of area: for each area in the subschema, the most recent record occurrence referenced

Currency indicators are updated each time a record instance is accessed. Currency indicator updating may be suppressed, under application program control, to maintain a desired reference point. An application programmer must be well aware of the effect that each DML command has on currency indicator status.

Figure 13-14 shows the logical access map (LAM) and action diagram (AD) for a situation we will use to illustrate the maintenance of currency indicators. The situation illustrated here depicts part of the data processing necessary to produce a summary of the customers handled by each salesperson at Pine Valley Furniture. Figure 13-15 contains a network instance diagram and an accompanying table that illustrates the detailed maintenance of currency indicators. There is no need to sort the data in any way, so the process begins by accessing the first salesperson on file. To understand Figure 13-15, it is important to remember that user working storage contains only one instance of each record type at a time. Each time we OBTAIN (read) another ORDER record, for example, the prior ORDER record in main memory is overwritten.

In Figure 13-15b, a currency indicator is highlighted each time it is updated. A circle indicates that the currency indicator actually changes value; a box signifies that it was updated but no value change occurred. Logical values for currency indicators are used for clarity; currency indicators, in practice, are physical or relative disk addresses. Numbers on the arrows in the diagram (Figure 13-15a) correspond to the movement through the data base caused by execution of the DML statements in the table.

Several events shown in Figure 13-15 require explanation. The first step in the table can occur without any currency indicator values established since it accesses an absolute, not relative, record (the first SALESPERSON record found in the SALES-AREA). All the OBTAIN NEXT ORDER commands require that there be an established value for CURRENT OF SOLD-SET. Since there is no NEXT ORDER after orders X.2 and X.1, the DBMS

Figure 13-15
(pages 481-482)
Example of currency indicator maintenance in a DBTG DBMS:
(a) sample data base
(b) currency indicators

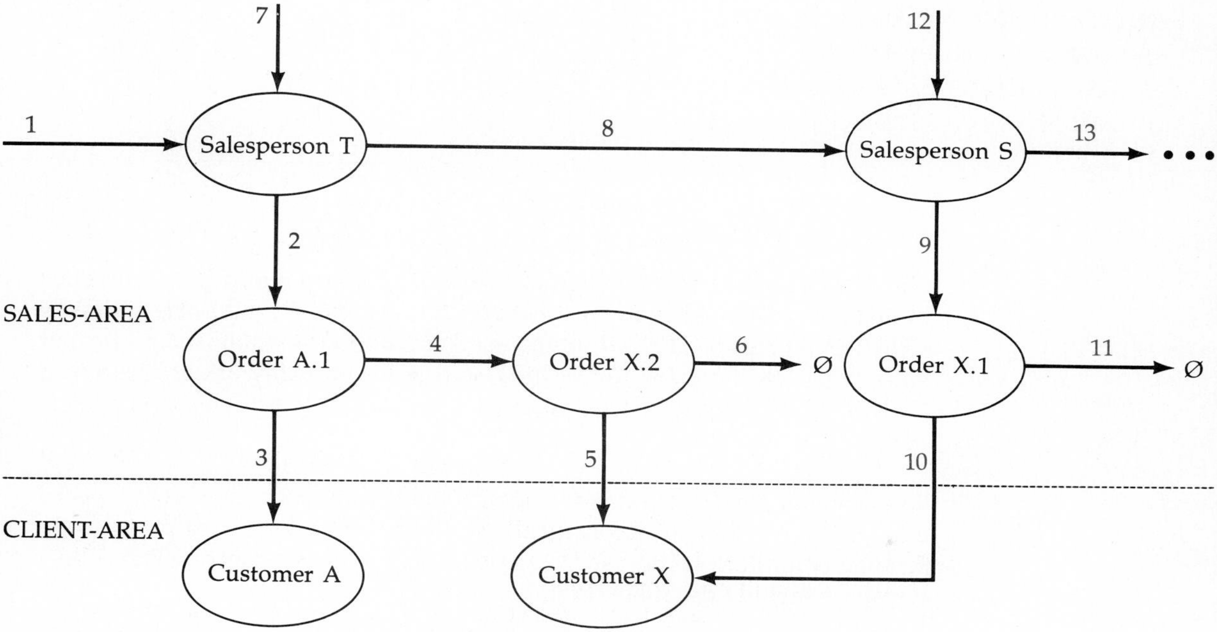

SALES-AREA: Salesperson and Order records
CLIENT-AREA: Customer records
SOLD-SET: Owner-Salesperson ; Member-Order
BOUGHT-SET: Owner-Customer ; Member-Order

(a)

		Records			Sets		Areas	
DML command	CURRENT OF RUN-UNIT	CURRENT OF SALESPERSON	CURRENT OF ORDER	CURRENT OF CUSTOMER	CURRENT OF SOLD-SET	CURRENT OF BOUGHT-SET	CURRENT OF SALES-AREA	CURRENT OF CLIENT-AREA
1 OBTAIN FIRST SALESPERSON WITHIN SALES-AREA	T	T			T		T	
2 OBTAIN NEXT ORDER WITHIN SOLD-SET	A.1	T	A.1		A.1	A.1	A.1	
3 OBTAIN OWNER WITHIN BOUGHT-SET	A	T	A.1	A	A.1	A	A.1	A
4 OBTAIN NEXT ORDER WITHIN SOLD-SET	X.2	T	X.2	A	X.2	X.2	X.2	A
5 OBTAIN OWNER WITHIN BOUGHT-SET	X	T	X.2	X	X.2	X	X.2	X
6 OBTAIN NEXT ORDER WITHIN SOLD-SET	X	T	X.2	X	X.2	X	X.2	X
7 OBTAIN CURRENT SALESPERSON	T	T	X.2	X	T	X	T	X
8 OBTAIN NEXT SALESPERSON WITHIN SALES-AREA	S	S	X.2	X	S	X	S	X
9 OBTAIN NEXT ORDER WITHIN SOLD-SET	X.1	S	X.1	X	X.1	X.1	X.1	X
10 OBTAIN OWNER WITHIN BOUGHT-SET	X	S	X.1	X	X.1	X	X.1	X
11 OBTAIN NEXT ORDER WITHIN SOLD-SET	X	S	X.1	X	X.1	X	X.1	X
12 OBTAIN CURRENT SALESPERSON	S	S	X.1	X	S	X	S	X
13 OBTAIN NEXT SALESPERSON WITHIN SALES-AREA	–	–	–	–	–	–	–	–

(b)

Figure 13-15
(continued)

would return an error message to the calling program and leave currency indicators unchanged after execution of these commands. The OBTAIN CURRENT SALESPERSON is necessary in step 7 to establish the proper value for CURRENT OF RUN-UNIT so that step 8 will work as desired (if CURRENT OF RUN-UNIT remained X.2, step 8 would actually access Salesperson T again).

Overview of DML Commands In addition to currency indicators, special data elements defined automatically in the user working area by the subschema compiler can be used for application program control. These data elements include the following:

- DB-STATUS: a code that is set after each DML command and that contains a value indicating the type of error, if any, that occurred; although implementation-dependent, this code is usually composed of an indicator for the type of command on which the error occurred (e.g., FIND) and several other characters symbolizing the specific error encountered (e.g., no next record found in set).

- DB-RECORD-NAME, DB-SET-NAME, DB-AREA-NAME, and DB-DATA-NAME: codes in which the DBMS places the subschema names for the record, set, area, and data element (where applicable) for the error that has just occurred (e.g., step 6 in Figure 13-15 would result in DB-RECORD-NAME equaling ORDER, DB-SET-NAME equaling SOLD-SET, DB-AREA-NAME equaling SALES-AREA); DB-DATA-NAME is applicable only on operations involving data elements (usually for violations of CHECK clauses on data values).

The DBTG COBOL DML commands can be divided into three categories: retrieval statements, modification statements, and control statements. Table 13-4 lists the various DML commands included in each of these categories.

Table 13-4 Typical COBOL DML Commands

Retrieval	
FIND	Locates record in data base
GET	Transfers record to working storage
OBTAIN	Combines FIND and GET
	With each command, we can retrieve • unique record • duplicate record • next or prior record in set or area • owner of a member record
Modification	
STORE	Puts a new record into data base and links it to all sets in which it is an automatic member
MODIFY	Changes data values in an existing record
CONNECT	Links an existing member record into a set occurrence
DISCONNECT	Removes (unlinks) an existing member record from its current set occurrence
RECONNECT	A combination of DISCONNECT and CONNECT to unlink a record from its current set and link it to a new set occurrence of the type
ERASE	Deletes record from data base, DISCONNECTs it from all set occurrences in which it participates, and deletes other records for which this is an owner in set
Control	
COMMIT	Makes permanent all data base updates made since last COMMIT command executed
ROLLBACK	Aborts all updates since last COMMIT and restores data base to status at time of last COMMIT
KEEP	Places concurrent access controls on data base records

Data Retrieval

In record-at-a-time processing, records can be retrieved on the basis of:

- Unique key or address value (entry into data base)
- Next with same or duplicate key value (secondary key)
- Next or prior in set or area possibly in a specified order (related records navigation)
- Owner of a member record in a set (usually used to change from processing along one set to processing along another)

Further, since retrieval is the basis for navigating/moving through a data base, we might want to (1) locate only the position of a record in order to verify its existence or as a reference point for subsequent movement (FIND); (2) once located (that is, current of run-unit), put the record's data into working storage for processing (GET); or (3) combine the first two steps into one for both data manipulation and subsequent movement (OBTAIN). In addition, we may want to retain exclusive access to data while retrieving in order to prohibit other programs from updating data. (The need to do this depends on the concurrency control of the DBMS; see Chapter 11.)

To understand some of these data retrieval capabilities, consider again the subschema in Figure 13-12 for the Mountain View Community Hospital Patient Bill user view; Figure 13-16a is a logical access map (LAM) for a variety of processing using this subschema. Recall that the DBTG COBOL DML contains statements that extend the standard COBOL examples; all the following examples represent parts of a COBOL program necessary to perform the data retrieval function specified (the IDMS COBOL DML is used as an example DML; IDMS uses the variable ERROR-STATUS instead of DB-STATUS).

Suppose we simply wanted to retrieve data for a specified patient (PATIENT-NO 1234). To do so, we need to store the desired key value (1234) in the PATIENT-NO field of the PATIENT record in working storage and then issue the proper DML OBTAIN command in order to enter the data base along the path labeled (1) in Figure 13-16a. This would be accomplished by

```
MOVE '1234' TO PATIENT-NO IN PATIENT.
OBTAIN CALC PATIENT.
IF ERROR-STATUS = 0 THEN NEXT SENTENCE
   ELSE . . . error routine . . .
```

The preceding OBTAIN command would make the PATIENT record for PATIENT-NO 1234 current of run-unit, current of PATIENT record type, and current of INCURRED set. If we then wished to calculate this patient's total charges, we would continue accessing along path (2) in Figure 13-16 with the following code (see Figure 13-16b for an AD of the procedure):

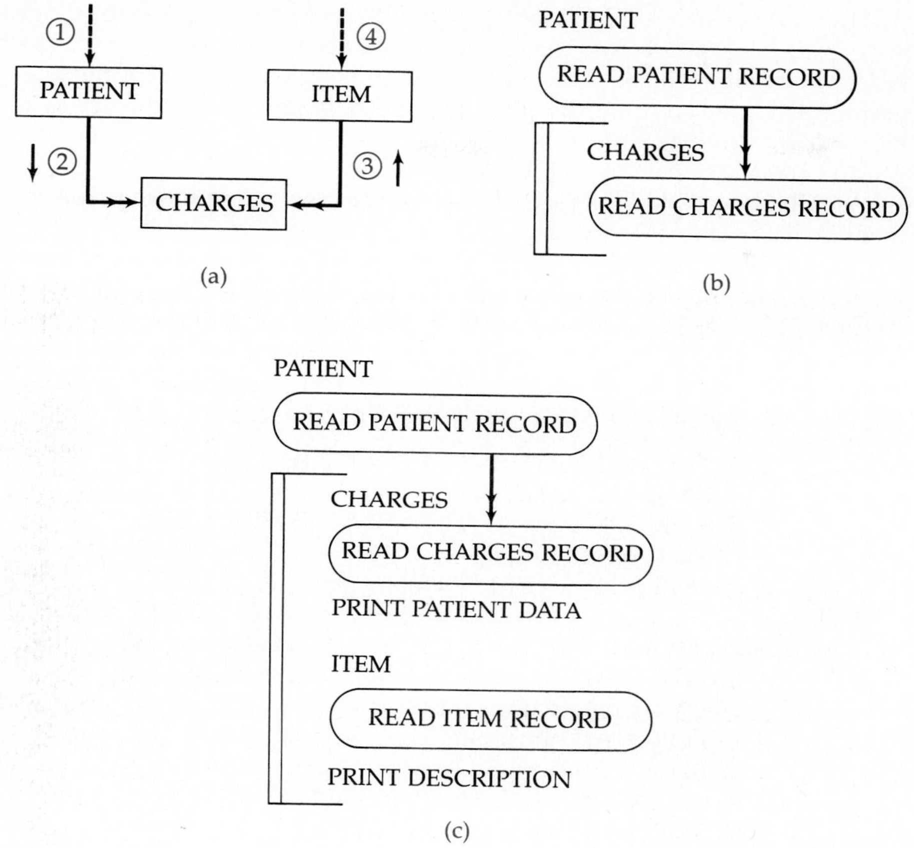

Figure 13-16 Mountain View Community Hospital subschema:
(a) logical access map (LAM)
(b) AD for a patient's total charges
(c) AD for description of all items for which a patient is charged

```
        MOVE 0 TO TOT-CHARGE.
    LOOP.
        OBTAIN NEXT CHARGES WITHIN INCURRED.
        IF ERROR-STATUS = error code for no next record
           THEN GO TO B.
        IF ERROR-STATUS = some other error code
           THEN GO TO error routine.
        ADD CHARGE IN CHARGES TO TOT-CHARGE.
        GO TO LOOP.
    B.
        . . .
```

In this example, CHARGES record instances related to the current of INCURRED set are (logically) sequentially retrieved and processed as required. At the first iteration, the set PATIENT owner (PATIENT-NO 1234) is current of set. The looping terminates when ERROR-STATUS indicates that there are no more CHARGES records within this set instance; any other error code in ERROR-STATUS indicates an unexpected error in the data base, which may require user intervention or even termination of the program. It is highly advisable to fully use the error-monitoring capabilities of the DBMS after every DML statement (some implementations have ON ERROR clauses as part of each DML command).

As a final example of retrieval statements, consider a reporting requirement to display the description of all the items charged to a specified patient (again, PATIENT-NO 1234). In this case, all three subschema records have to be accessed, but no data from the CHARGES record for this patient are desired. Figure 13-16c illustrates an AD for this retrieval, which is frequently referred to as a "V" retrieval since a path resembling a V is formed by accessing records in steps (1), (2), and then (3) in Figure 13-16a. The following DML statements could be used to retrieve the necessary data:

```
        MOVE '1234' TO PATIENT-NO IN PATIENT.
        OBTAIN CALC PATIENT.
        IF ERROR-STATUS = 0 THEN NEXT SENTENCE
           ELSE. . .error routine. . .
        Display or print desired PATIENT data.
    LOOP.
        FIND NEXT CHARGES WITHIN INCURRED.
        IF ERROR-STATUS = error code for no next record in set
           THEN terminate this procedure.
        IF ERROR-STATUS = some other error code
           THEN. . .error routine. . .
        OBTAIN OWNER WITHIN PROVIDED.
        IF ERROR-STATUS = any error code
           THEN. . .error routine. . .
        Display or print DESCRIPTION in ITEM.
        GO TO LOOP.
```

In this example, note that current of INCURRED set was not affected by accessing a CHARGES owner in the PROVIDED set. CHARGES records act in the same way as link records in this example; since link records have no meaningful contents, only FIND needs to be used to retrieve them.

Data Maintenance and Control

Data maintenance within the DBTG model, although limited to only six commands (see Table 13-4), requires careful development because of the various semantic controls that may be specified in a DBTG schema (refer to Table 13-3 for a summary of these controls). Further, to ensure the integrity of a data base against concurrent record update and abnormal program termination in the middle of a set of update statements, data maintenance routines require careful design.

When a data base (or data base area) is opened by a program, most DBTG DMLs require a specification of the mode of processing to be performed by the program (retrieval or update). If the mode is retrieval, then the DBMS will prohibit use of any data modification command in the program. If the mode is update, then two options are often permitted. The first, PROTECTED, means that concurrent update is prevented but that concurrent retrieval is allowed. The second, EXCLUSIVE, prevents any concurrent use of the data base (or area).

In addition, many DBTG DMLs permit record-level controls, called locks, to maintain a finer level of concurrent update management. In IDMS, for example, a program can place a SHARED lock on a record to prevent other run-units from updating a record temporarily while permitting retrieval. An EXCLUSIVE lock prohibits any other activity on a record until the lock is released. Exclusive locks are implicitly placed on a record that is altered by a STORE, MODIFY, or ERASE DML command.

Further control can be imposed to protect the integrity of a data base from abnormal termination of a program during the middle of a series of related maintenance statements. Consider the situation of entering a new customer order into the Pine Valley Furniture data base. Roughly, the procedure to enter this information into the data base is as follows:

1. Accept order header data and enter a new ORDER record.
2. Accept PRODUCT#, QUANTITY-ORDERED, and so on, for a LINE-ITEM and store the Line Item.
3. If there are more LINE-ITEMs, then repeat step 2.

Suppose that after accepting and storing the ORDER data and several LINE-ITEM records, an on-line order entry operator realizes that she has been reading data from several order forms. She then decides to abort this "logical transaction" and wants to delete all the previously entered data for this order. Using the ORDER# in working storage and the set between ORDER and LINE-ITEM, the program could ERASE these records. But a simpler approach in which the DBMS automatically performs these deletions is frequently available. The beginning of the logical transaction is indicated by some special DML control statement (a START TRANSACTION, COMMIT, or some other command). If during the logical transaction a user wishes to abort processing or if a fatal data base error occurs, the transaction can be aborted and the data base will be restored automatically to its state at the time the transaction began (the command ROLLBACK is used in IDMS).

Storing a New Record The data modification statements will be illustrated using the Mountain View Community Hospital subschema of Figures 13-12 and 13-16a and some variations. Consider the situation of storing the charge for an additional item charged to a patient. Since (from the schema in Figure 13-11) CHARGES is an AUTOMATIC member of the PROVIDED set and a MANUAL member of the INCURRED set, we will have to use a CONNECT command to insert the CHARGE into the proper INCURRED set instance. Further, since the SET SELECTION of the INCURRED set is implicitly THRU

CURRENT OF SET, we will have to first make the proper PATIENT record current. A CHARGES record instance is automatically linked to the correct ITEM owner in the PROVIDED set by common key values. The logical access path for this storage is step (1), then step (2) in Figure 13-16a. The DML for this update for PATIENT# 1234 would be as follows:

```
/* Verify patient record exists and make it current */
MOVE '1234' TO PATIENT-NO IN PATIENT.
FIND CALC PATIENT.
IF ERROR-STATUS = 0 THEN NEXT SENTENCE
   ELSE . . . error routine . . .
/* Build new CHARGES record in working storage */
MOVE 150 TO CHARGE IN CHARGES.
MOVE '1234' TO PATIENT-NO IN CHARGES.
MOVE 307 TO ITEM-CODE IN CHARGES.
STORE CHARGES.
IF ERROR-STATUS = 0 THEN NEXT SENTENCE
   ELSE . . . error routine . . .
/* Connect manual set member */
CONNECT CHARGES TO INCURRED.
IF ERROR-STATUS = 0 THEN NEXT SENTENCE
   ELSE . . . error routine . . .
. . .
```

Deleting an Existing Record The schema for this data base (see Figure 13-11) indicates that CHARGES is a FIXED member of both sets (INCURRED and PROVIDED). We may simply delete a CHARGES for PATIENT# 1234 and ITEM-CODE 307 in the case of misbilling by first FINDing the desired PATIENT (based on its CALC key), then searching for CHARGES for ITEM-CODE 307 among the members of the INCURRED set instance for PATIENT# 1234, and then ERASEing the proper CHARGES record. This is the same logical access path as in Figure 13-16b, but in this case searching can stop once the desired CHARGES record for deletion is found. Thus, we would

```
         /* Find desired PATIENT record */
         MOVE '1234' TO PATIENT-NO IN PATIENT.
         FIND CALC PATIENT.
         IF ERROR-STATUS = 0 THEN NEXT SENTENCE
            ELSE . . . error routine . . .
         /* Search for desired CHARGES record within INCURRED set */
LOOP.
         OBTAIN NEXT CHARGES WITHIN INCURRED.
         IF ERROR-STATUS = error code for no next record in set
            THEN indicate error and terminate.
         IF ERROR-STATUS = some other error code
            THEN . . . error routine . . .
```

```
IF ITEM-CODE IN CHARGES NOT = 307
  THEN GO TO LOOP.
ERASE CHARGES.
IF ERROR-STATUS = 0 THEN NEXT SENTENCE
  ELSE . . . error routine . . .
. . .
```

Changing a Member Record's Owner RETENTION IS FIXED prevents us from moving a CHARGES to a different owner record, which is a natural semantic for this data base. If, however, we had indicated RETENTION IS MANDATORY for CHARGES in the PROVIDED set, we could then RECONNECT (but not DISCONNECT) CHARGES records in this set. Suppose we want to change the CHARGES stored earlier to the 413 ITEM-CODE. To do so, we must first find the record for PATIENT# 1234 [access (1) in Figure 13-16a], then verify that the new ITEM record owner exists [access (4) in Figure 13-16a], then search through the CHARGES records under the desired patient looking for the CHARGES record to be reconnected [access (2) in Figure 13-16a]. Thus, assuming that we had used MANDATORY, not FIXED, for the PROVIDED set, we would

```
       /* Find the desired PATIENT record */
       MOVE '1234' TO PATIENT-NO IN PATIENT.
       FIND CALC PATIENT.
       IF ERROR-STATUS = 0 THEN NEXT SENTENCE
         ELSE . . . error routine . . .
       /* Find the ITEM to which CHARGES is to be connected */
       MOVE 413 TO ITEM-CODE IN ITEM.
       FIND CALC ITEM.
       IF ERROR-STATUS = 0 THEN NEXT SENTENCE
         ELSE . . . error routine . . .
       /* Search in INCURRED set for CHARGES to be reconnected */
LOOP.
       OBTAIN KEEP EXCLUSIVE NEXT CHARGES WITHIN
         INCURRED.
       IF ERROR-STATUS = error code for no next record in set
         THEN indicate error and terminate.
       IF ERROR-STATUS = some other error code
         THEN . . . error routine . . .
       IF ITEM-CODE IN CHARGES = 307 THEN NEXT SENTENCE
         ELSE GO TO LOOP.
       /* Change CHARGES record and reconnect to new owner */
       MOVE 413 TO ITEM-CODE IN CHARGES.
       RECONNECT CHARGES TO PROVIDED.
       IF ERROR-STATUS = 0 THEN NEXT SENTENCE
         ELSE . . . error routine . . .
       COMMIT.
```

The KEEP EXCLUSIVE clause on the OBTAIN command prevents any other run-unit from retrieving or modifying this CHARGES record while this run-unit is updating it. The COMMIT command releases this concurrency lock and makes the updates permanent (that is, the updates may not be aborted and undone after this point). KEEP EXCLUSIVE and COMMIT are vocabulary particular to IDMS but are representative of the data maintenance controls available in DBTG COBOL DMLs.

To illustrate DISCONNECT, suppose that miscellaneous charges (ITEM-CODE 999) do not have an ITEM record and that to support storage of such charges, we had made CHARGES an OPTIONAL member of the PROVIDED set. The logical access path for this situation is the same as in the previous example, except that the operation will be to DISCONNECT the record rather than to RECONNECT it. We could then change the charge for ITEM-CODE 413 to ITEM-CODE 999 for PATIENT# 1234 by

```
        /* Find the desired PATIENT record */

        MOVE '1234' TO PATIENT-NO IN PATIENT.
        FIND CALC PATIENT.
        IF ERROR-STATUS = 0 THEN NEXT SENTENCE
          ELSE . . . error routine . . .

        /* Find the ITEM from which CHARGES is to be disconnected */

        MOVE 413 TO ITEM-CODE IN ITEM.
        FIND CALC ITEM.
        IF ERROR-STATUS = 0 THEN NEXT SENTENCE
          ELSE . . . error routine . . .

        /* Search in INCURRED set for CHARGES to be disconnected */
LOOP.
        OBTAIN KEEP EXCLUSIVE NEXT CHARGES WITHIN
          INCURRED.
        IF ERROR-STATUS = error code for no next record in set
          THEN indicate error and terminate.
        IF ERROR-STATUS = some other error code
          THEN . . . error routine . . .
        IF ITEM-CODE IN CHARGES = 307 THEN NEXT SENTENCE
          ELSE GO TO LOOP.

        /* Disconnect CHARGES record and change contents */

        DISCONNECT CHARGES FROM PROVIDED.
        IF ERROR-STATUS = 0 THEN NEXT SENTENCE
          ELSE . . . error routine . . .
        MOVE 999 TO ITEM-CODE IN CHARGES.
        MODIFY CHARGES.
        IF ERROR-STATUS = 0 THEN NEXT SENTENCE
          ELSE . . . error routine . . .
        COMMIT.
```

Note that in this and the prior example, we had to OBTAIN, not just FIND, CHARGES in order to MODIFY its contents. It is also worth emphasizing again that it is wise not to execute the COMMIT until after all aspects of the logical transaction are complete. If we were to COMMIT after each DML modification command (e.g., after the DISCONNECT above), then, if for some reason the user program aborts before the MODIFY command, the data base would be left in a low integrity state, with only part of the total update done.

Special Maintenance Considerations In addition to deleting a record instance, the ERASE command can have a much broader effect on data base contents. Assuming the original schema and subschema from Figures 13-11 and 13-12, respectively, consider deletion of an ITEM record occurrence. Since CHARGES are FIXED members of the PROVIDED set (the same would be true of MANDATORY), they cannot exist without an ITEM owner. If we ERASE an ITEM record in this case, the CHARGES records associated with this ITEM would also automatically be erased by the DBMS.

If CHARGES were an OPTIONAL member of the PROVIDED set, then we would have a choice on what to do with CHARGES members (and members of any other set owned by ITEM) when deleting an ITEM owner. If we were to use

ERASE ITEM PERMANENT MEMBER.

then any MANDATORY or FIXED member for a set owned by ITEM would also be ERASEd, but OPTIONAL members (such as CHARGES under the preceding assumption) would only be automatically DISCONNECTed. If we

ERASE ITEM SELECTIVE MEMBER.

then all MANDATORY or FIXED members would be ERASEd, but OPTIONAL members would also be ERASEd *if* they do not currently have a member in any other set (e.g., INCURRED) occurrence. In the case of CHARGES records, since each must be a member of some INCURRED set, none would be ERASEd. This would apply only to members that are OPTIONAL members of other sets. All members can be ERASEd irrespective of other set membership by using ERASE ITEM ALL.

Logical Record Processing in IDMS

In Figure 13-13, we introduced the IDMS logical record construct that can be defined in a subschema. The purpose of a logical record is to define a simple view of the data base that consolidates several data base records into one virtual record. Logical records can be used to simplify OBTAIN, STORE, MODIFY, and ERASE processing by permitting *one* such DML statement to implicitly retrieve and appropriately process a group of related records.

Figure 13-13 contains a definition for a DETAILED-BILL logical record. We can use this logical record to produce a listing of all charges for a given PATIENT (say, PATIENT# 1234) by

```
PRINT-LIST.
   OBTAIN NEXT DETAILED-BILL WHERE PATIENT-NO = '1234'
      ON LR-NOT-FOUND GO TO AFTER-LIST.
   Display or print data from CHARGES and ITEM records
      (but not PATIENT, since logical record definition uses FIND for
      PATIENT record)
   . . .
   GO TO PRINT-LIST.
AFTER-LIST.
   . . .
```

The ON error clause also represents a logical/symbolic way to check data base error codes instead of using detailed IF statements involving ERROR-STATUS and other variables.

NETWORK DATA BASE DESIGN ISSUES AND ADVANCED TOPICS

The network data model presents a data base designer with many options to customize a data base for efficient processing. Many of the design decisions have been ignored or covered very briefly in the previous sections. This section elaborates on the topics of prior sections and introduces more subtle points and advanced options, as well as focuses on particular network implementation design decisions.

Because network systems frequently are used for high-volume, transaction processing applications, efficiency of data base design is important. Further, most of the topics addressed here deal with basic structural choices for a data base, which do not exhibit data independence. Thus, redesign to incorporate or change these design elements would typically require application program maintenance; for this reason, it is important to design the data base in the best way possible the first time.

Record Placement Control

Two internal network model constructs control the physical absolute and relative placement of records: areas and LOCATION MODE. Areas are physically contiguous disk tracks that are opened and closed together. In designing a data base, one would more likely choose to create an area and to place selected records in that area if:

- we wanted a single level of security control (that is, by area) on all the designated records
- data base navigation time would be noticeably improved by restricting placement of the related records to relatively nearby disk tracks (that is, to minimize disk head movement)

LOCATION MODE is determined by how records will be accessed. CALC is used when some application program will *know* (from user entry or other data base records) the key of a record (or records in the case of a secondary key) to be accessed. That is, the application needs direct entry into the data base on that record type. Such entry points would be apparent from a composite usage map like that in Figure 8-17. Choice of CALC requires the key to be a field (or fields, for a concatenated key) in the record being CALCed (so storage space is necessary to support CALC). The ability to CALC a record is unaffected by changes in set membership for that record. The existence of a primary key for a record type that is itself meaningful business data (e.g., ORDER# for an order, LADING# for a shipment) usually means that the record should be CALCed, whereas records with artificial primary keys or concatenated keys are less likely for CALC. One easy way to decide whether a record should be CALCed is to determine if it is a member of any set—if it is not a member of any set, it should be CALCed.

A data base designer will usually begin by CALCing the obvious entry points; other record types are then considered for VIA. Since many of the record types not CALCed may be members of several sets, the issue is really: VIA *which* set? A composite usage map (see, for example, Figure 8-17) is very useful. The set chosen for VIA would be the one associated with the path into the record that has the largest frequency of access. One caution with VIA: Since record placement is related to the owner of a member record when the member is first stored, MANDATORY and OPTIONAL sets (in which ownership may change) are not attractive as VIA sets.

Record Data Elements

Three particular data base design issues arise when determining the data elements of a record. First is the issue of whether to include the key of the associated owner record (and any of the other nonkey owner data) in the member record of a set. For example, consider the ORDER-LINE record in Figure 13-3b. Since pointers will be maintained by the DBMS for the two sets in which ORDER-LINE participates, PRODUCT# and ORDER# are not necessary in order to access the owner PRODUCT or ORDER for a particular ORDER-LINE. However, if we want to sort ORDER-LINE records in the ORDER to ORDER-LINE set by PRODUCT#, then we must include PRODUCT# in ORDER-LINE. In addition, we could include PRODUCT# in ORDER-LINE simply as insurance, to be able to relink an ORDER-LINE with the right PRODUCT if the physical pointers are damaged.

Owner nonkey data can be stored in a member to make accessing the owner in order to retrieve the data unnecessary, but this causes redundancy from unnormalizing the data. Thus, such storage would typically only be done when real-time processing requirements necessitate squeezing every extra record access out of a program.

The second design issue for data elements deals with the creation of repeating groups or definition of a separate record type. Use of a repeating group is not really feasible when repeating data are or could be related to multiple base records. That is, repeating data are very similar to the members of a set, and if the repeating data are members of only one set, then they can be embedded within the owner as a repeating group. For example, consider Figure 13-17, which depicts EMPLOYEE and DEPENDENT data, as well as other personnel data entities. Since the collection of DEPENDENT data for a particular EMPLOYEE is related only to the EMPLOYEE, this could easily be designated as repeating group data in the EMPLOYEE record type. On the other hand, ASSIGNMENT data are not a characteristic of just EMPLOYEE, but also JOB. Although we could make ASSIGNMENT a repeating group within EMPLOYEE (thus, unnormalizing the data base), we would then have to either duplicate it as a repeating group within JOB or create a *M:N* relationship between JOB and EMPLOYEE, which is not allowed in many network systems.

The third data element design issue is whether to store derived or calculated data for an entity in the associated record (and recalculate them as the parameters change) or to recalculate them in an application program as they are needed each time. For example, some users of a data base may want to manipulate the price and quantity ordered of products; other users, in accounting, perhaps, may only want to see the derived product amount due. But can we be sure that all accounting user programs will calculate amount due correctly?

The DBTG guidelines introduced the concept of virtual data, or data that appear to exist in a record but that do not physically reside in an instance of that record. Two clauses, the SOURCE and the RESULT clauses, deal with the distinction between ACTUAL and VIRTUAL data elements. These clauses and options together allow the data base to appear to contain data that, at least in the form or location perceived, do not actually exist.

If the SOURCE clause is associated with a given data element definition, it signifies that a value for that data element is to be the same as a specified data element from its owner in a designated set. For example, ORDER# in

Figure 13-17
Repeating group data in a network

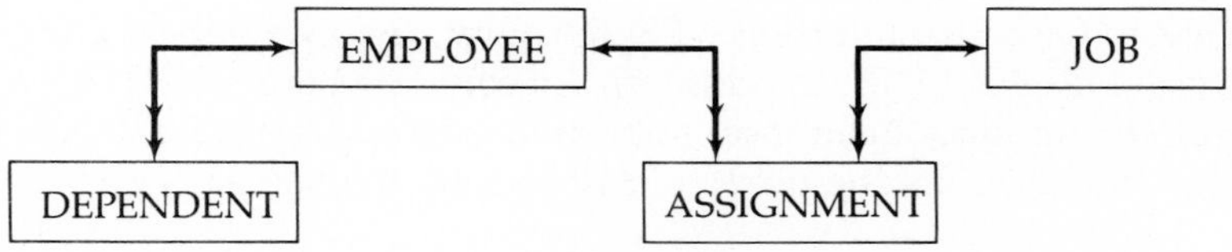

an instance of an ORDER-LINE record from Figure 2-10 (Pine Valley Furniture Company) must have the same value as the ORDER# in its associated ORDER record. SOURCE provides a form of integrity control of the data base. Use of SOURCE prohibits use of PICTURE or TYPE on the same data element since these are implied from the "source" data element. An appropriate SOURCE clause for this example would be

```
RECORD IS ORDER-LINE
. . .
1 ORD# ; ACTUAL SOURCE IS ORDER# OF OWNER
         ITEMS-ON-ORDER SET.
```

In this case, ACTUAL specifies that ORD# is to be redundantly stored again in the ORDER-LINE record. Use of VIRTUAL instead of ACTUAL would tell the DBMS to allow use of ORD# as if it were a data element of the ORDER-LINE record, but retrieve it from the associated ORDER record instead (and save the redundant space).

The RESULT clause also utilizes the ACTUAL and VIRTUAL designations. The RESULT clause says that the data element to which it applies is to be calculated or derived from a procedure involving other data elements from the same record; from all members for this record, in which the owner is some set (e.g., to calculate a total across all members, the equivalent of a class attribute in the semantic data model); or from some more general calculation. If ACTUAL RESULT is specified, then the derived value is constantly maintained by the DBMS and stored in the record. If VIRTUAL RESULT is specified, then the derived value is calculated by the DBMS each time a record instance is retrieved and appears to be included in the physical record but actually only exists in the user's working storage area (or subschema).

Sets

Since it is a set that provides navigation through a network data base, the choice as to which sets to include directly affects data base processing performance. A data base designer will certainly choose to build a set for each relationship between record types in the conceptual data model of the data base. The issue is whether to build extra, redundant sets. Such redundant sets serve two purposes:

1. **To maintain different member sorting sequences for the same relationship** (e.g., one set between CUSTOMER and ORDER for ORDERs in promised delivery date sequence and another set in salesperson sequence). Recall, each time we choose to sort the members of a set, the sorting variable must be included in the member records (e.g., salesperson id might have to be included in the ORDER record only if we were to sort ORDERs on this in some set). A data base designer, to be able to decide on this type of sorted set, needs to understand

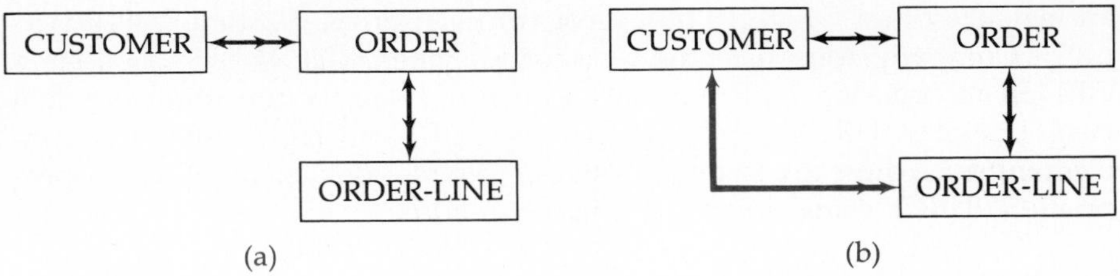

Figure 13-18 Redundant set for processing efficiency: (a) typical data base design (b) design with "shortcut" set

not only access paths in the composite usage map but also desirable member access sequence. A sorted set saves scanning members until the desired one or group is found in a random sequence and saves a post-data base access sort to rearrange the data.

2. **To "short cut" access along several component links.** For example, consider the network data base of Figure 13-18a. To determine the products ordered by a given customer, we must enter the data base on customer and navigate to ORDER, then to ORDER-LINE. In Figure 13-18b the redundant, transitive link from CUSTOMER to ORDER-LINE can be used to navigate directly to ORDER-LINE from CUSTOMER. Such shortcuts can only be made along a set of (nested) 1:1 or 1:*M* relationships. A shortcut 1:*M* link from CUSTOMER to PRODUCT, which is along a *M:N* transitive relationship, is infeasible since the same PRODUCT record can have only one owner for the set, yet it must be able to have several in the actual relationship.

The additional set design issues of choice of singular sets, and insertion and retention controls have been covered adequately in prior sections.

DEVICE MEDIA CONTROL LANGUAGE

Although the schema DDL specifies some internal data base characteristics, the schema still has a great deal of data independence from the internal data base. The device media control language (DMCL) is used to complete the data base definition.

Because the DMCL is used to prescribe physical data base characteristics, use of the DMCL should be limited to the data base administrator. PR1ME Computer, in fact, has made this implicit by calling their version of the DMCL for their DBTG DBMS the Data Base Administrator Control Program (DBACP) and by requiring that a user have special computer system privileges in order to perform most of the DBACP functions.

In IDMS, the DMCL is used to:

- Specify the number of secondary memory pages to keep in a main memory buffer area (this would specify the size of the system buffers block in Figure 13-1)

- Specify the characteristics of each area, such as the number of characters per page in the area, amount of space for expansion of variable-length records, and alias names for the area
- Define the physical characteristics of journal files used to store record and transaction images useful in data base recovery

Similar functions are performed by most DMCLs or equivalent utilities. In general, these functions allocate physical space for the data base, specify which options to use (if any) for representing sets, name all the various physical operating system files and/or data sets used to construct the data base, and indicate whether and how to create audit trails and data modification journals.

NONPROCEDURAL ACCESS: QUERY AND NATURAL LANGUAGES

Most vendors of DBTG systems provide nonprocedural query languages for ad hoc, interactive retrieval of data and/or report writer programs for nonprocedural production of customized reports. For example, PR1ME provides DBMS/Query (or DISCOVER) with its DBTG DBMS. Cullinet provides OnLine Query (OLQ) as a query language, IDMS/CULPRIT as a report writer, and OnLine English (OLE) as a natural language processor. (OnLine English is marketed by Cullinet, but is one version of Intellect, a product of Artificial Intelligence Corp.) Further, Cullinet now has a new version of IDMS, IDMS/R, which includes a relational-like query language. Their claim is that this marriage of network data storage with relational access provides both high performance and ease of access.

Query Languages

Query languages permit an interactive programmer, often a non–data processing professional, to write record retrievals using expressions that specify which records are desired, and not have to go through the process of record-by-record retrieval. Often such query languages resemble relational calculus; thus, it is possible to give an end user a relational-like view of a network data base.

As an example of a query language for a network data base, we will present a few sample queries using Cullinet's OnLine Query (OLQ). For this illustration, consider the inventory data base of Figure 13-10. We could retrieve the first sequential PRODUCT record in the data base by

(1) GET FIRST SEQUENTIAL PRODUCT RECORD

and OLQ would immediately display the contents of this record on the terminal. We could then retrieve the first INVENTORY for this PRODUCT by

(2) GET FIRST INVENTORY BELONGING TO THIS PRODUCT

and could continue to retrieve other INVENTORY records one by one using

(3) REPEAT WITH LAST

Otherwise, if we wanted to see all the INVENTORY records for this PRODUCT, we could issue the following command immediately after (1):

(4) GET ALL INVENTORY BELONGING TO THIS PRODUCT

Such query languages are helpful in that they can rapidly produce the result of a simple end user question, check on the contents of a data base after a series of COBOL data maintenance program executions, or provide a user with a prototype of the type of report that could be produced in a fancier format by a batch report writer or COBOL report program. These languages do, however, have a precise grammar and syntax that must be learned by anyone who wishes to write a query. Release 10.0 of OLQ from Cullinet has a menu-driven front end for end users.

Natural Languages

Natural language processors eliminate the need to learn a specific grammar, vocabulary, and syntax. Cullinet explains their package OnLine English (OLE) in this way:

> OnLine English (OLE) is an English-language query system that enables users to obtain computer-stored information by means of simple request. OLE accepts and interprets a freely worded request, retrieves the appropriate data, and performs all processing necessary to display the results in a meaningful format. The capacity to accept everyday English phrases is a powerful feature of OnLine English that distinguishes it from traditional query systems. (Cullinet 1982b)

Consider again the inventory data base of Figure 13-10. After signing on and being greeted by OLE, Figure 13-19 illustrates some possible dialogue between OLE and the user. In this figure, OLE prompts and responses are shown in capital letters and user questions in lowercase. Prior to processing each English question, OLE displays a structured query version of its interpretation of the original question. The user can abort the processing at this point in order to restate the query if OLE has misinterpreted the question. If the user uses key words such as *average, minimum,* or *bar graph,* OLE will generate the appropriate result.

Given that such nonprocedural languages exist for access to a network data base, why should we ever program in COBOL? First, most of these facilities are limited to only data retrieval and reporting; data update is usually not supported. Second, the computer time required to dynamically translate query or English statements into the record-level commands adds significant overhead to computer processing. A prewritten procedural language routine would execute the same type of retrieval much faster (but, of course, would take significantly more time to code). The trade-off, basi-

```
PLEASE ENTER YOUR FIRST REQUEST
What are the fields in the inventory file?
FIELDS IN THE INVENTORY FILE
S#      P#      W#
NEXT REQUEST
What is the S# and P# of all inventory in 04 warehouse?
PRINT THE S# AND P# OF ALL INVENTORY WITH W#=04
THE NUMBER OF RECORDS TO RETRIEVE IS 3
      S#        P#
    12345     1234
    72843     5436
    92371     3476
NEXT REQUEST
Where is part 1234 stored?
PRINT THE W# OF ALL INVENTORY WITH P#=1234
THE NUMBER OF RECORDS TO RETRIEVE IS 2
    W#
    04
    12
NEXT REQUEST
How many warehouses are there?
COUNT THE WAREHOUSE
ANSWER: 16
NEXT REQUEST
...
```

Figure 13-19
Example of IDMS OnLine English dialogue

cally, is between machine efficiency and programmer efficiency. When rapidly developed, ad hoc, frequently modified, or one-time reports are desired, nonprocedural languages are suitable; if high-volume transaction processing or repeated rapid response queries characterize the computing work load, then procedural languages will be more appropriate for processing the network data base.

SUMMARY

This chapter has reviewed the major network data model implementation, the CODASYL DBTG model (and IDMS, a leading commercial product). Although the discussion has been dominated by an examination of record-level access to data, we have also shown example query languages for access data in network data bases. Such query and natural languages can provide a relationlike front-end view of a network data base.

The network data model has been much maligned since the introduction of the relational model. Criticisms have primarily focused on issues of ease-of-use and processing complex queries, which generally favor the relational model. However, in practice, the network data model DBMSs have continued to be popular data management technologies, usually because of the better performance possible by the explicit record-level processing. Today, because of relational-like query language front ends, we can "have our performance and ease of use, too."

Chapter Review

REVIEW QUESTIONS

1. Define each of the following terms:
   a. CODASYL DBTG
   b. IDS
   c. DDL
   d. DML
   e. DMCL
   f. schema
   g. subschema
   h. area
   i. host language
   j. location mode
   k. manual insertion
   l. automatic insertion
   m. fixed retention
   n. mandatory retention
   o. optional retention
   p. CALC location mode
   q. virtual data
   r. currency indicator
   s. search key
   t. IDMS logical record
   u. natural language
2. Contrast the functions of the three DBTG retrieval commands FIND, GET, and OBTAIN.
3. Discuss the advantages of using a network DBMS with a relational-like query language.
4. Describe the use of the system buffers shown in Figure 13-1. When are data moved in and out of these buffers? What effect would paging in a virtual memory operating system have on buffer contents?
5. Describe the role of a computer operating system in data base access under the DBTG guidelines.
6. Explain why there are different subschema DDLs, one for each host programming language.
7. Explain why a record may not have a CALC key and also be located VIA some set.
8. Explain the factors to consider for selecting among FIRST, LAST, and SORTED for the ORDER IS clause of a set definition.
9. Explain the benefit of the IDMS logical record construct.
10. Explain the purpose of the IDMS COMMIT command and discuss where in a program this command can be usefully placed.
11. Under what circumstances (data base schema characteristics) is the DML command RECONNECT permitted?

PROBLEMS AND EXERCISES

1. Match each term with the appropriate definition:

_____ DBTG	**a.** language used to state data retrieval and modification operations
_____ schema	**b.** diagram indicating navigation path or steps through a data base
_____ subschema	**c.** task force that developed the CODASYL network standard
_____ status variable	**d.** most recent record accessed
_____ DDL	**e.** a natural language processor
_____ DML	**f.** contains error codes and other data about command execution
_____ VIA location mode	**g.** command that makes recent data base changes a part of the actual data base
_____ virtual data element	**h.** data that are not actually stored in the data base but appear as if they are
_____ singular set	**i.** a data base description for a DBMS
_____ RECONNECT	**j.** command that changes a set member's owner
_____ current of set	**k.** view of a data base used by an application program
_____ logical access map	**l.** placement of a member instance close to its owner instance
_____ COMMIT	**m.** language used to define a data base
_____ Intellect	**n.** used to sort all records of some type into sequence

2. Consider the entities of Agent, Policy, Client, Beneficiary, and Insurance Company in an independent insurance agency. Design a DBTG network diagram (similar to Figure 13-5a) for this situation.
3. For the data base designed in Problem 2, suggest several data processing requirements for which use of more than one area would be beneficial in the schema.
4. Specify the LOCATION MODE clause for each record type in Problem 2 and justify your choice of mode and duplicates specification.
5. For each of the sets in your answer to Problem 2, specify and justify INSERTION and RETENTION clauses. Write complete set definitions for this problem.
6. Consider the entities of Project, General Task, and Employee in a project management or job shop organization. Design a DBTG network diagram (similar to Figure 13-5a) for this situation.

7. For the situation in Problem 6, assume there is a need to report the employees working on a project in order by their job classification. Write the schema DDL necessary to support this requirement through the data base structure.
8. Consider the situation of an automobile dealership and entities Owner, Vehicle, Sale, and Salesperson. Assume all the usual relationships between these entities plus the association of a sale to vehicles traded in on that sale. Design a DBTG network diagram (similar to Figure 13-5a) for this situation and write the schema DDL, using data items of your choice.
9. In the situation in Problem 8, assume that the dealership's general manager frequently sends promotional mailings to owners of vehicles on file. To minimize mailing costs, she wishes this to be printed in customer zip code order. Add to your schema and network diagram for Problem 8 the constructs necessary to support this data processing.
10. Review the alternatives of representing a loop relationship presented in Figure 13-6. Evaluate each of these and suggest situations in which each would be a desirable approach.
11. For the data base schema of Problem 8, draw a logical access map and then write the COBOL and DML commands necessary to change ownership of a vehicle. Assume any data elements you believe are essential; include skeletons of data base error checks.
12. For the data base of Problem 2, write the COBOL and DML commands required to enter a new policy into the data base. Assume any data elements you believe are essential; include skeletons of data base error checks.
13. Consider again the data base of Problem 2. Draw a logical access map and action diagram and then write the COBOL and DML commands required (skeleton of the code is all that is necessary) to produce a report of the policy numbers and anniversary dates for each policy of each client. The policy numbers and dates are to be grouped by client; the clients are not to be printed in any particular logical order.
14. In the preceding data base design problems, you were not given much information about the data processing requirements of the situation, but instead were asked to design the data base in more general terms. Specifically, what clauses of a DBTG schema are affected by knowledge of particular data processing requirements? How is each affected?
15. Consider again the data processing required in Problem 13. Design some sample data for this problem and develop an illustration of currency indicator maintenance, as in Figure 13-15, for your sample data and the program fragment you wrote for Problem 13.

REFERENCES

ANSI X3H2. 1981. *Proposed American National Standard for a Data Definition Language for Network Structured Databases.* American National Standards Institute.

CINCOM Systems, Inc. 1982. *TOTAL Reference Manual.* Cincinnati: CINCOM.

CODASYL. 1971. *Data Base Task Group April 71 Report.* New York: Association for Computing Machinery.

CODASYL COBOL Committee. 1978. *COBOL Journal of Development*. Available from Federal Department of Supply and Services, Hull, Quebec, Canada.

CODASYL Data Description Language Committee. 1978. *DDL Journal of Development*. Available from Federal Department of Supply and Services, Hull, Quebec, Canada.

Cullinet. 1982a. *IDMS Database Design and Definition Guide*. Revision 0.0. Westwood, Mass.: Cullinet, September.

———. 1982b. *ONLINE ENGLISH User's Guide*. Revision 0.0. Westwood, Mass.: Cullinet, May.

———. 1983. *IDMS Programmer's Reference Guide—COBOL*. Revision 1.0. Westwood, Mass.: Cullinet, April.

Hewlett-Packard. 1983. *IMAGE Database Management System Reference Manual*. Cupertino, Calif.: Hewlett-Packard, March.

Olle, T. William. 1980. *The CODASYL Approach to Data Base Management*. Chichester, Eng.: Wiley.

Chapter 14

Relational Implementations on Mainframes: SQL, INGRES, and Others

INTRODUCTION

Data base management systems built for the relational data model (see Chapter 6) are abundant and rapidly increasing in number. As with the network data model implementations, more than one type of relational DBMS is available. Although the basics of the relational data model are present in all products, the style of relational data manipulation languages and the extent of vendor-introduced enhancements vary across products.

The purpose of this chapter is to review several of the most common styles (primarily SQL systems and INGRES), using example mainframe relational DBMS products to illustrate their features. We will emphasize the Structured Query Language (SQL) style since it has been widely adapted into many products and has been accepted as a standard by the American National Standards Institute. In Chapter 15 we will review the implementations of the relational data model in personal computer–based products.

A list of many of the most widely used mainframe relational DBMSs appears in Table 14-1. There has been considerable debate as to what constitutes a truly relational system, but the entries of this table have not been carefully screened for strict compliance with relational principles. The next section reviews the characteristics of a relational DBMS; these characteristics establish a set of factors consistent with the theory underlying the development of this type of DBMS.

Table 14-1 Summary of Some Mainframe Relational Systems

Relational algebra systems

Package	*Vendor*	*Equipment*	*Comments*
RIM	Boeing Commercial Airplane Company	PR1ME 750	Host language interfaces to FORTRAN, Pascal, and COBOL; logical views not supported; integrity assertions supported; typical algebra operators, including INTERSECT

Relational calculus systems

Package	*Vendor*	*Equipment*	*Comments*
SQL/DS	IBM	S/370, 3033, 43xx; VM/CMS operating system	Host language interfaces to COBOL, PL/I, and assembler; logical views supported; query language: SEQUEL
DB2	IBM	Same as SQL, except DOS/VSE operating system	Same as SQL/DS
DBC 1012	Teradata	DBC 1012 Data base machine	Uses SQL language
DG-SQL	Data General	DG MV	Adaptation of SQL; graphics, reporting, and query languages
HP-SQL	Hewlett-Packard	HP 3000; Spectrum	Uses SQL language
IDM 500	Britton-Lee	IDM 500 Data base machine	Uses SQL language
INGRES	Relational Technology	DEC VAX-11; VMS and UNIX operating systems; also IBM environments	Host language interfaces to C, Pascal, FORTRAN, BASIC, and COBOL; logical views supported; query language: QUEL; query-by-forms, report-by-forms, and graph-by-forms aids; SQL also supported
ORACLE	Oracle Corp.	DEC PDP-11, VAX (VMS, UNIX, RSX, RSTS) and IBM S/370, 3033, and 43xx (VM/CMS and MVS), and others	Host language interfaces to COBOL, PL/I, FORTRAN, C, BASIC, and assembler; logical views supported; query language: SEQUEL; very comprehensive implementation of SQL
Rdb-ELN	Digital Equipment Corp.	VAX VMS	Includes screen painter, Rally 4GL, and central dictionary

(Continues)

Graphical/Tabular systems

Package	*Vendor*	*Equipment*	*Comments*
Query-by-Example	IBM	S/370, 3033, and 43xx; VM/CMS and MVS	Unique graphical, fill-in-the-blanks query language

Relational-like systems

Package	*Vendor*	*Equipment*	*Comments*
ADABAS	Software AG	IBM S/370 and others; DOS/VSE, VM/CMS, MVS; DEC VAX/VMS	Inverted file organization with some network constructs; several query and report writer languages
DATACOM/DB	Applied Data Research	IBM S/370 and others; MVS, DOS/VSE operating systems	Inverted files; relational via high-level language, inverted via low-level DML; access to VSAM and IMS; generally considered a 4GL
FOCUS	Information Builders	IBM S/370 and others—VM/CMS and MVS; DEC-VAX—VMS; Wang	A leading 4GL; hierarchical and relational views of data; comprehensive systems-building tools
IDMS/R	Cullinet Software	IBM S/370 and others; MVS, VM/CMS, DOS/VSE operating systems	CODASYL system enhanced to support relational operators; application generator, natural language processor, integrated dictionary
Model 204	Computer Corp. of America	IBM S/370 and others; MVS, VM/CMS, DOS/VSE operating systems	Inverted file organization; no logical views; special query language; host language interfaces to COBOL, PL/I, FORTRAN, and assembler; generally considered a 4GL
NOMAD2	D&B Computing Services	IBM S/370 and others; VM/CMS and MVS	Hierarchical and relational models; limited logical views; special query language; generally considered a 4GL
RAMIS II	Martin Marietta Data Systems	IBM S/370 and others; VM/CMS and MVS	A leading 4GL; many system-building tools

A RELATIONAL DBMS—AN OVERVIEW

Many DBMSs are said to be relational. In fact, without even trying to generate an exhaustive list, we can safely say that more data management products claim to be relational than claim to be all other data models combined. Although for practical purposes it does not matter what it is called (what matters is that the DBMS has the features required for our data processing), an attempt to carefully distinguish relational from nonrelational systems will highlight the important features of relational implementations. Of course, a system that obeys the rules of a *truly* relational DBMS has certain desirable properties and capabilities that give it tremendous power and provide integrity of data base processing.

Most people agree that a relational data base is one perceived by its users as a collection of tables in which all data relationships are represented by common values, not links. A relational DBMS (or RDBMS), then, is a data management system that supports this view of data.

Kim (1979) has listed nine "requisite features for a hypothetical, comprehensive relational system" that are general features of any true DBMS (see Chapter 11), but several, which we emphasize here, have a unique form in relational systems. These nine features are as follows (Kim 1979, 185,186):

1. An interface for a high-level, nonprocedural data language that provides the following capabilities for both application programmers and nontechnical users: query, data manipulation, data definition, and data control facilities.
2. Efficient file structures in which to store the data base and efficient access paths to the stored data base.
3. An efficient optimizer to help meet the response-time requirements of terminal users.
4. User views and snapshots of the stored data base.
5. Integrity control—validation of semantic constraints on the data base during data manipulation and rejection of offending data manipulation statements.
6. Concurrency control—synchronization of simultaneous updates to a shared data base by multiple users.
7. Selective access control—authorization of access privileges to one user's data base to other users.
8. Recovery from both soft and hard crashes.
9. A report generator for a highly stylized display of the results of interactions against the data base and such application-oriented computational facilities as statistical analysis.

Since many of these features are, in fact, general characteristics of DBMSs, it is essential that a true relational DBMS be, first, a true DBMS (see Chapter

11). This may seem trivially obvious, but an evaluation of some "relational DBMS" products indicates deficiencies in these essential features. Several of these nine points require elaboration in order to be made specific to relational DBMSs.

High-Level Language Interface In his ACM Turing lecture, Codd (1982) states that relational data definition is via the construct of flat files or tables and that data can be manipulated, explicitly or implicitly, via at least three operators: SELECT, PROJECT, and JOIN. Further, to be truly relational, *any* table column must be capable of being manipulated with these operators, independent of the existence of data structures such as indexes, to make these manipulations efficient. The use of the word *join* in defining the minimal characteristics is somewhat unfortunate since it is not essential that such a verb actually be present in the DML. Rather, what is essential is that it be possible in one DML statement to refer to data in related records (*tuples* in relational terminology) from different tables. This was illustrated in Chapter 6 (see "Data Processing with the Relational Data Model"), where two relational DML styles were introduced: relational algebra (explicit join) and relational calculus (implicit join).

In this chapter, we explore relational calculus in detail since it is the primary style implemented in mainframe systems; relational algebra, common in personal computer implementations, will be discussed in Chapter 15. Also present in mainframe systems and illustrated here are other languages for manipulating relational data bases: tabular/graphic and host language interfaces. Although Kim (1979) states that both application programmers and nontechnical users are addressed by relational DBMSs, the primary emphasis has always been nontechnical users. Some relational DBMSs also have special procedural languages or interfaces to general-purpose programming languages that are used to develop data processing programs that require data manipulation not possible in the special-purpose languages of the relational DBMS.

Efficient File Structures Any DBMS attempts to provide efficient access paths to data. With relational DBMSs, this is typically achieved via B-tree key indexes (see Chapter 5) on data elements (*roles* or *columns* in relational terminology). Obviously, efficient access to data is a function of both the data structures used and the data processing workload. Relational DBMSs are designed for data processing environments in which data are to be retrieved based on a variety of complex multiple-key qualification statements (Boolean expressions). Often, such retrieval requests cannot be anticipated, but rather arise as new business problems or new insights to old problems occur. Multiple-key indexes are easy to combine in various Boolean patterns and are practical structures to use in such an environment. Thus, the combination of Boolean statements and multiple-key indexes makes it possible for relational systems to support more complex ad hoc inquiry into a data base than other types of DBMSs.

User Data Base Views The user view feature cited by Kim (1979) may have two dimensions for a truly relational DBMS. Minimally, it means that data jare viewed in tables (files), with possibly many rows/tuples (records) and columns/roles (attributes). Even the result of a DBMS manipulation must be a table. Values in the cells of these tables are restricted to certain domains (valid value sets).

For more richly developed relational DBMSs, there may also exist customized user views (external data bases). Such user views also conceptualize data into tables; these tables may be subsets of the complete data base (generated from SELECTions and PROJECTions from the complete data base) or a user view may be a table constructed from related (base) tables in the data base (generated from JOINing tables).

The more both base and view tables can be manipulated without knowledge of their physical implementation (e.g., whether an index exists or not, whether a table is a view or a base table), the more relational the DBMS is. However, as pointed out in Chapter 6, such logical manipulation often requires the user to know what data two or more tables have in common (that is, what roles relate to the same domain).

Integrity Control The last of Kim's (1979) relational DBMS features to require elaboration here is integrity control. We saw in Chapter 13 that network DBMSs include semantic and integrity controls in CHECK clauses and in various SET definition statements. In relational DBMSs, this is accomplished by means of integrity assertions. As explained by Kim:

> Integrity assertions may describe either valid states (state assertions) or valid state transitions (transition assertions). For example, the assertion "no employee should earn less than 10K" describes a valid state; while the assertion "no employee should be given a pay cut" constrains a state transition.
>
> Integrity assertions may be imposed on individual tuples (as above) or on groups of tuples of relations. For example, the state assertions "average salary of employees in any department should not exceed 20K" and "salary of employees in any department with 100 employees should not exceed 30K" are applied to groups of tuples. (1979, 203)

Not illustrated here is the typical network system set integrity capability, also present in many relational DBMSs, to restrict values across record types [e.g., a department number may not appear in an employee record unless there exists a department record (tuple) with that number]. This is known as referential integrity, and the ability to maintain this as the contents of a data base change is a difficult task. In many cases, more powerful integrity constraints have been implemented in relational DBMSs than in other types of systems.

Hardware Implementations

Not only have relational DBMSs been implemented in the classical fashion of DBMSs as software utilities, but also numerous special-purpose DBMS machines using the relational data model have been developed in laboratories (see Banerjee, Baum, and Hsiao 1978; Epstein 1983; McEnany 1985; Schuster et al. 1978; Su and Lipovski 1975) and for commercial sale (see *Computerworld,* January 28, 1985 and *Computerworld,* June 24, 1985). Data base computers will be discussed in detail in Chapter 16. Basically, such a special "back-end" computer is attached to a general-purpose computer. The data base computer receives a stream of requests for data base processing from the host computer's operating system (generated from application programs). These requests are queued, sequenced for efficient processing, and satisfied in parallel to the host CPU doing non–data base tasks. The data base computer is configured in ways to optimize data base processing (e.g., special architectures such as array or associative processors, table data distributed across different disk drives attached to the associative processors, fast channels for data transfer, and DBMS functions built into hardware or firmware). Relational DBMSs implemented in hardware are steadily emerging in commercial applications, and their progress requires attention.

What Then Is Truly Relational?

Since so-called RDBMSs appear in so many forms and with such fervent marketing, how can a system that truly follows the principles of relational data bases (with the associated functional capabilities) be easily distinguished from a system that does not? The founder of relational data base theory, E. F. (Ted) Codd, has outlined 12 rules to test whether a product that is claimed to be "fully relational" really is. These rules are summarized in Table 14-2.

Clearly a purist, Codd admits that "no existing DBMS product that I know of can honestly claim to be fully relational, at this time" when compared with these rules (Codd, October 14, 1985). Even the ANSI SQL standard comes under criticism by Codd as not complying, although he says it can be readily modified to comply.

The 12 rules and Codd's arguments are all based on a single foundation principle, which he calls Rule Zero:

> **Rule Zero.** For any system that is advertised as, or claimed to be, a relational data base management system, that system must be able to manage data bases entirely through its relational capabilities.

This is a tall order and one that, in practice, DBMSs following other data models have never had to meet in their own context in order to be considered network, hierarchical, or whatever. This and other rules are designed with users in mind; that is, they are designed to create an easy-to-use and consistent structure and user interface. Codd's orientation is that "any DBMS that advises users to revert to some nonrelational capabilities to achieve acceptable performance—for any reason other than compatibility with programs written in the past on nonrelational data base systems—should be interpreted as an apology by the vendor" (Codd, October 14, 1985, ID/4).

Table 14-2 Codd's Rules for a Truly Relational System

RULE 1: Information Representation.

> All information in a relational data base is represented explicitly at the logical level and in exactly one way—by values in tables.

Interpretation: Even metadata (that is, table names, columns names, etc.) are all stored in tables; coupled with Rule 4, data definitions are accessible via the relational manipulation sublanguage. Thus, data base administrators and developers of application and system software have access to up-to-date data definitions. "All information" can be widely interpreted. A reasonable definition of "all information" is any data or metadata defined or entered into the data base. This would include, for example, integrity rules and user names (since such names appear in security rules), but would reasonably exclude procedure/program documentation on references to data base data. The reference to "logical level" means that physical constructs such as pointers and indexes are not represented and need not be explicitly referenced in query writing, even if they exist.

RULE 2: Guaranteed Access.

> Each and every datum (atomic value) in a relational data base is guaranteed to be logically accessible by resorting to a combination of table name, primary key value, and column name.

Interpretation. This specifies a minimal accessibility in terms of content—the names of data and the one and only one primary key value. Thus, no data are to be accessible only by artificial paths, such as linked lists or physical sequential scanning. This rule is based on the fact that the relational data model deals only with data at a functional or logical level, devoid of physical constructs, and is a consequence of Rule 1.

RULE 3: Systematic Treatment of Null Values.

> Null values (distinct from the empty character string or a string of blank characters and distinct from zero or any other number) are supported for representing missing information and inapplicable information in a systematic way, independent of data type.

Interpretation: Given this rule, "nulls not allowed" can be specified to provide data integrity on primary keys or any other column for which nonexisting values are inappropriate. The systematic, uniform representation means that only one technique needs to be employed to deal with null values. Further, the treatment of null values must be persistent and be applied at any value change in order to maintain integrity.

(Adapted from Codd, October 14, 1985.) (Continues)

Table 14-2 (Continued)

RULE 4: Dynamic On-Line Catalog Based on Relational Model.

> The data base description is represented at the logical level in the same way as ordinary data, so that authorized users can apply the same relational language to its interrogation as they apply to the regular data.

Interpretation: Thus, only one data model is used for both data and metadata and only one manipulation sublanguage needs to be learned. In addition, it would be possible to then extend the catalog of definitions to become more like a data dictionary by including any "data about data" appropriate for an application. Data definitions are stored in only one place given this rule. A subtle consequence of this rule and Rule 1 is that the distinction between data and metadata is no longer clear since both can serve as the basis for information to and inquiry by a user.

RULE 5: Comprehensive Data Sublanguage.

> A relational system may support several languages and various modes of terminal use. However, there must be at least one language whose statements can express all of the following items: (1) data definitions, (2) view definitions, (3) data manipulation (interactive and by program), (4) integrity constraints, (5) authorization, and (6) transaction boundaries (begin, commit, and rollback).

Interpretation: The key word in this rule is *comprehensive.* The six specific items indicate that Codd does expect that most of the functions of a DBMS outlined in Chapter 11 are provided within the syntax of one language. The objective of this rule is to create a comprehensive environment that does not have to be left in order to accomplish another task. For example, if in the process of manipulating data the user decides to retain a result or record some new data, he or she does not have to exit one environment and enter another in order to define the new data, and then reenter the original to populate the new tables. Although the benefits of this rule are clear in concept, the motivation for this rule may not seem obvious from an analysis of relational theory. However, it is a consequence, in part, of Rule 4 since data definitions must be accessible from the manipulation sublanguage.

RULE 6: View Updating.

> All views that are theoretically updatable are also updatable by the system.

Interpretation: A view is "theoretically updatable" if there is an update (insert, delete, or modify) procedure that, when applied at any point in time to the base tables of a view, will have the same effect as the requested modification

Table 14-2 (Continued)

of the view. That is, the update of the base tables necessary to effect the change in the view must be unambiguously derivable by the system. For example, increasing an extended price column value in a view (where extended price is the multiple of price from a product base table and quantity from an order base table) does not have an unambiguous meaning in terms of base table data, so the relational DBMS would not have to be able to perform this update. But, updating a product description in a view that combines product and order base data could be interpreted unambiguously as an update of product description in the product base table, and must be supported according to this rule.

RULE 7: High-Level Insert, Update, and Delete.

> The capability of handling a base relation or a derived relation (that is, view) as a single operand applies not only to the retrieval of data but also to the insertion, update, and deletion of data.

Interpretation: This basically means that all operators are set operators, not record or tuple operators. Thus, a set of table rows can be deleted in one statement or a set of rows can all be modified in a common way in one command.

RULE 8: Physical Data Independence.

> Application programs and terminal activities remain logically unimpaired whenever any changes are made in either storage representations or access methods.

Interpretation: Again, "any changes" implies a very pure view of physical data independence. One typical example of the physical data independence advocated here would be that a query or program would be written the same no matter whether an index existed or not on a column qualified in the query; programs in a network system would likely change depending on the existence of an index, hashing function, or the like. This rule also implies that constructing an optimum retrieval sequence to compose the result of a query is the responsibility of the DBMS, not the user.

RULE 9: Logical Data Independence.

> Application programs and terminal activities remain logically unimpaired when information-preserving changes of any kind that theoretically permit unimpairment are made to the base tables.

Interpretation: This and Rule 8 permit a data base designer to make changes, to evolve, or to correct a data base definition at any point without having to completely redefine or reload the data base (and take it out of service to do so). As long as information is not lost from the restructuring, no application

(Continues)

Table 14-2 (Continued)

programs or inquiry activities should have to change. To comply with this rule, it must be possible to preserve prior definitions through views, and these views must be able to be updated (Rule 6) as long as the data base restructuring does not lose information. For example, the splitting of a table into two caused by recognition of new data requirements and the need to eliminate a transitive dependency (that is, a new entity is identified where only one domain of the entity was needed before the change) should not cause existing application procedures to change since the split table can be virtually reconstructed in a view.

RULE 10: Integrity Independence.

> Integrity constraints specific to a particular relational data base must be definable in the relational data sublanguage and storable in the catalog, not in the application programs.

Interpretation: This rule covers the ability to define as part of the data base definitions controls on the values columns may assume. Such rules may restrict values to be within a certain range, to be one of a set of permitted values, to be not null (if this column is part of a primary key, then this is called "entity integrity"), and to be a value from some other column of the data base (that is, a nonnull foreign key value must match some current value from a row of the table with that as primary key, so-called referential integrity). Even user-defined constraints (such as no more than five line items per order) should be possible. These integrity rules must be able to change over time; when changed, violations must be identified and existing programs or inquiries must still be able to work.

RULE 11: Distribution Independence.

> The data manipulation sublanguage of a relational DBMS must enable application programs and inquiries to remain logically the same whether and whenever data are physically centralized or distributed.

Interpretation: A distributed data base is one where data are physically dispersed across several remote computer sites and data processing requests at any one of those sites may require data stored at several of the sites. Each program treats the data base as if it were all local, so distribution and redistribution do not change the logic of programs. It is important to note that this rule does not say that to be fully relational the DBMS must support a distributed data base, but it does say that the data manipulation language would remain the same if and when this capability were introduced and when data are redistributed.

Table 14-2 (Continued)

RULE 12: Nonsubversion.

> If a relational system has a low-level (single-record-at-a-time) language, that low level cannot be used to subvert or bypass the integrity rules and constraints expressed in the higher-level relational language (multiple-records-at-a-time).

Interpretation: This basically means that all data manipulation languages supported by the relational DBMS must rely only on the stored data base definition (including integrity rules and security constraints) for control of processing. This and Rule 5 imply that it should not be possible nor is it necessary to access a relational data base using any language that bypasses the data definition catalog.

Rather than leaving these rules and the comparison of products against them as an academic debate, Codd argues that there are practical consequences for insisting on rule compliance (Codd, October 21, 1985), some of which are:

- Rules 1 and 4 allow a data base administrator to always know exactly what kinds of data are recorded, and hence they minimize the time needed to determine such while also reducing the data redundancy that would result if this information were unknowable.
- Rule 3 helps users of all types to avoid making foolish and costly mistakes (e.g., miscalculating summary data when null values are coded in some uninterpretable way).
- Rule 5 supports interactive program testing, which can mean improved programmer productivity.
- Rules 8–11 contribute to lowering program development and maintenance costs due to the inevitable system changes that occur in decision support and information retrieval applications systems.

People who firmly believe that RDBMSs are superior to other types of DBMSs argue that abusing the term *relational* reduces its meaning to the lowest common features of systems to which it is applied. Others—many of whom are proponents of commercial products that existed before the general popularity of relational systems—claim that user satisfaction with a tool and the ability of that tool to solve user problems should override definitions and categorization of products. Even with standards, vendors are motivated to enhance and otherwise distinguish their product from that of others. As long as this occurs, definitional debates are inevitable.

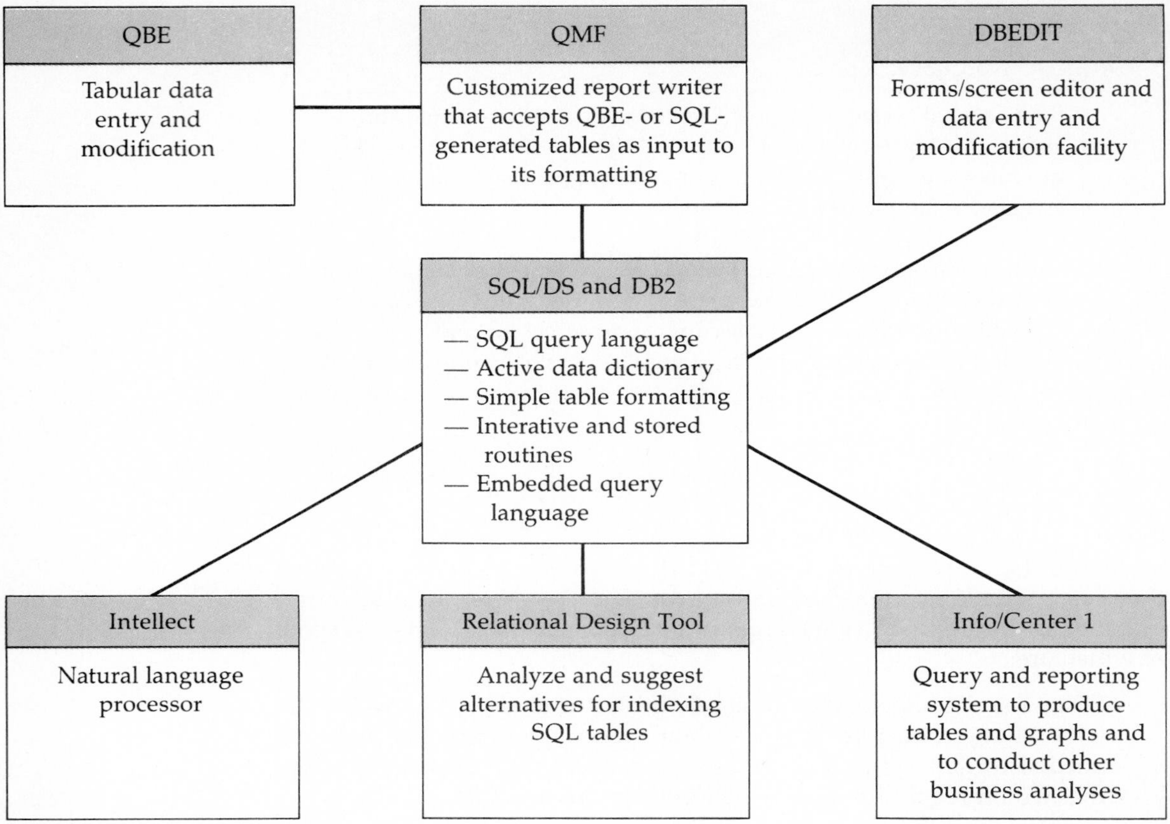

(a)

Figure 14-1 (pages 516–518) Relational DBMS environments: (a) SQL/DS and DB2 (b) INGRES (c) ORACLE

Structure and Components of Relational Systems

A modern RDBMS is typically a family of products or modules, each of which manipulates data in a particular way; for example, different modules may exist for line-by-line queries, screen or forms painting, stylized reports, and graphs. The ability to include RDBMS commands in procedural language programs is a rather standard feature, referred to as the embedded query language capability.

In addition, some RDBMSs have modules or associated products that support natural language processing against the data base, inclusion of data base data in an electronic spreadsheet (by using a data base query as a cell value), and merging data base contents with text documents in specific word processing packages. Because no one software package can provide

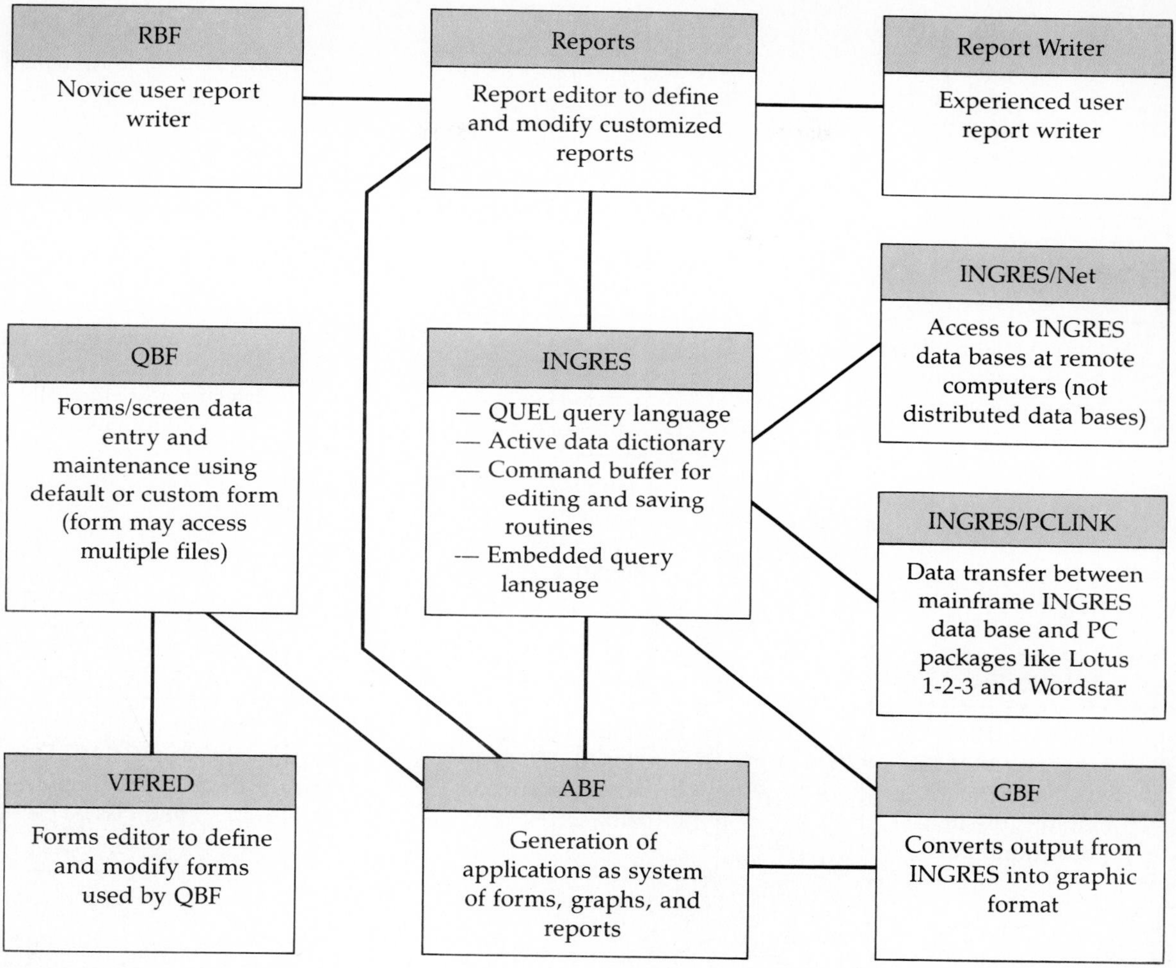

(b)

all the decision support or information processing capabilities a user may require, a RDBMS usually provides a file import/export facility for transfer of data (often in standard text file formats) between the RDBMS and other systems such as word processors, statistical packages, mathematical programming packages, and other DBMSs. Finally, a growing number of mainframe relational systems have associated personal computer products that provide all or nearly the same functionality as their mainframe counterpart, plus the ability to upload and download data between a package's mainframe data base and PC data base or other PC package (like electronic spreadsheet).

Figure 14-1 illustrates the environment of three popular and typical mainframe RDBMSs: SQL/DS and DB2, INGRES, and ORACLE (see IBM Corp. 1985, 1984; Relational Technology, Inc. 1984; and ORACLE Corp.

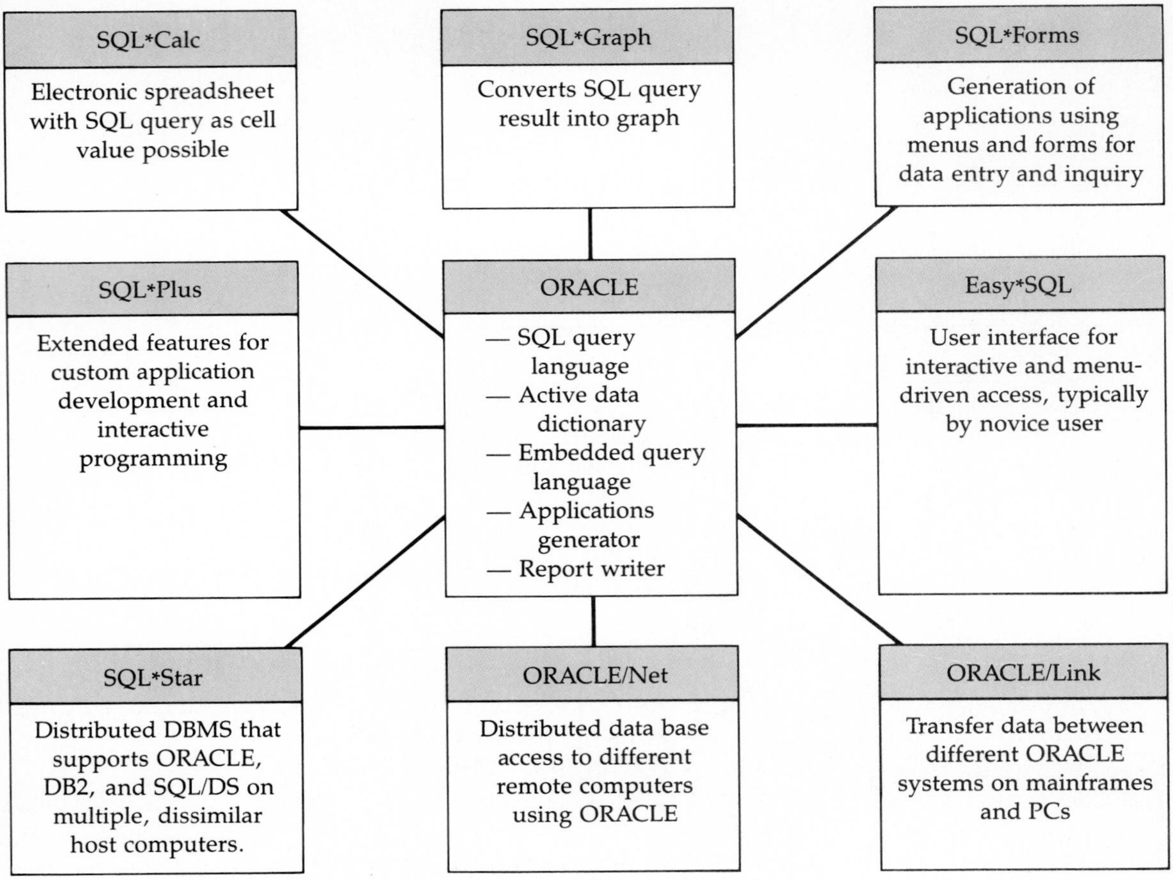

(c)

Figure 14-1
(continued)

1984). For each of these systems there is a kernel or core module and a variety of optional modules available at additional cost. A general trend is for new modules to be added periodically, each using similar command structures and syntax, and all sharing a common data definition and storage. In this way RDBMS products are being enhanced to be very similar to fourth-generation languages.

SQL: A Standard for Relational Systems

As was mentioned in Chapter 13, the development of network DBMSs has been guided by the work of the CODASYL Data Base Task Group and the published guidelines it has produced. These guidelines have had a major impact by strongly encouraging network DBMS vendors to provide a minimal set of capabilities and a general architecture for their products. The consequence is that different network implementations have very similar functional capabilities.

In order to provide some direction for the development of RDBMSs, the American National Standards Institute (ANSI) has approved a standard for the SQL relational query language (functions and syntax) proposed by the X3H2 Technical Committee on Database (Technical Committee X3H2—Database 1986). The ANSI X3 Committee is the same group that developed the three-level data architecture presented in Figure 4-1.

The purposes of this standard are

1. To specify the syntax and semantics of SQL data definition and manipulation languages
2. To define the data structures and basic operations for designing, accessing, maintaining, controlling, and protecting an SQL data base
3. To provide a vehicle for portability of data base definition and application modules between conforming DBMSs
4. To specify both minimal (Level 1) and complete (Level 2) standards, to permit different degrees of adoption in products
5. To provide an initial standard, although incomplete, that will be enhanced at later times to include specifications for handling such topics as referential integrity, transaction management, user-defined functions, join operators beyond the equi-join, and national character sets (among others)

An indirect effect, which may not have been intended, is that acceptance of *an* SQL standard has been interpreted by many as acceptance of SQL as *the* approved RDBMS query language. Even before the Technical Committee began its work, several SQL-based products were on the market (e.g., SQL/DS and DB2 from IBM and ORACLE from Oracle Corp.; see Table 14-1 for a list of other SQL-based RDBMSs). Since the adoption of the SQL standard, various mainframe and PC RDBMS vendors have announced that their packages will be enhanced to include an SQL language interface to their existing product. Thus, the market is accepting SQL as a necessary structured query language, although certainly not the only programming language, for relational data base access. In addition, the SQL standard is being reviewed by the International Standards Organization (ISO) and may become the international standard for relational query languages.

Because of this acceptance of the SQL standard, this chapter emphasizes the SQL language and its implementation in SQL/DS and ORACLE, although many examples of the QUEL language (used in INGRES), Query-By-Example, and other alternatives are also included. It should be noted, however, that SQL is not without its critics, who claim that the *initial* SQL standard, although a good start, has definite flaws. Date (1987) claims that important features (such as referential integrity rules and certain relational operators) are omitted and that the language is extremely redundant (that is, that there is more than one way to write the same query). These limitations will become clear in this chapter. It can be expected that, like the CODASYL DBTG network standard, the SQL standard will be modified, probably led by the capabilities of SQL-based DBMSs.

RELATIONAL DATA DEFINITION LANGUAGES

There is not much variety among relational data definition language (DDLs) since the relational data model is rather simple and standardized. Significant differences do occur, however, in embellishments such as the inclusion of integrity and security constraints, definition of user views (external data bases), and physical implementation clauses or commands to indicate, for example, creation of a key index. The process of designing a relational data base has been covered elsewhere in this text (see "Relational Data Model" in Chapter 6 and in Chapter 7); normalization is used to derive the relations to be defined. In this section we assume that this design has occurred, and we concentrate on the translation of these relations into DDL.

To illustrate the use of typical relational DDLs, we again refer to the Mountain View Community Hospital data base of Figures 8-13 and 9-7. Figure 14-2 contains a definition of this data base using the DDL of SQL/DS.

Various data definition commands are possible. In SQL/DS (see IBM Corp. 1985), seven are frequently used (these are typical of many relational DBMSs):

CREATE TABLE:	Defines a new table and its columns
DROP TABLE:	Destroys a table (definition and contents as well as any views and indexes associated with it)
ALTER TABLE:	Adds a new column to a table (in some RDBMSs this would also permit deleting columns)
CREATE INDEX:	Defines an index on one column (or a concatenation of columns) that enables rapid access of the rows of a table in a sequence or randomly by key value; a table may have many indexes and each may be specified to be UNIQUE (primary key) or not, and may be sequenced in ascending or descending order
DROP INDEX:	Destroys an index
CREATE VIEW:	Defines a logical table from one or more tables or views (views may not be indexed)
DROP VIEW:	Destroys a view definition (and any other views defined from the deleted view)

Table Definition

Tables, or more explicitly base tables, often correspond to the entities or normalized relations resulting from the conceptual design of the data base. Most relational systems allow dynamic or iterative table definition in order to support changes in the understanding of data base requirements. Dynamic definition is relatively easy to permit, since there are no physical links between tables; rather, indexes are used to support retrieving associated

```
CREATE TABLE ROOM
  (LOCATION          CHAR(4) NOT NULL UNIQUE,
   ACCOM             CHAR(2),
   EXTENSION         SMALLINT,
   PATIENT#          INTEGER)

CREATE TABLE PATIENT
  (PATIENT#          INTEGER NOT NULL UNIQUE,
   DATE-DISCHARGED   CHAR(8),
  . . . Other data elements . . .)

CREATE TABLE PHYSICIAN
  (PHYSICIAN-ID      CHAR(10) NOT NULL UNIQUE,
   PHYSICIAN-PHONE   CHAR(8))

CREATE TABLE ITEM
  (ITEM-CODE         SMALLINT NOT NULL UNIQUE,
   DESCRIPTION       CHAR(15))

CREATE TABLE TREATMENT
  (T-PHYSICIAN-ID    CHAR(10) NOT NULL,
   T-PATIENT#        INTEGER NOT NULL,
   PROCEDURE         CHAR(15))

CREATE TABLE CHARGES
  (C-PATIENT#        INTEGER NOT NULL,
   C-ITEM-CODE       SMALLINT NOT NULL,
   C-CHARGE          DECIMAL(6,2))
```

Figure 14-2
SQL/DS data definition for Mountain View Community Hospital

records (see "Implementation of the Relational Data Model" in Chapter 6).

Various data types are usually supported besides SMALLINT and CHARacter, which are used in the data base definition of Figure 14-2; these include a large integer size, decimal, floating point, and variable and very long character strings.

NOT NULL is a semantic control that informs the DBMS to not permit any tuple in the ITEM table to have a null value for ITEM-CODE; this is enforced on all data manipulation statements. NOT NULL is usually applied to key fields (the relational data model requires key columns to be not null in order to support unique rows), but may be applied to any column as appropriate.

UNIQUE is also a semantic control that specifies that the values of this column must be unique across all rows of the table. UNIQUE indicates a single primary key or candidate key column. As opposed to the DUPLICATES NOT ALLOWED in the network data definition language, UNIQUE is only applied to whole tables, not also to groups of rows related to a common row in another table. However, for example, by use of a concatenated key of ORDER# + PRODUCT#, one can specify in the SQL DDL that, although multiple rows of a table of order line item data may deal with the same product, there may not be multiple rows for the same product for the same order.

Table definitions may be changed in many mainframe RDBMSs by ALTERing column specifications. In SQL/DS, the ALTER TABLE command is provided to add new columns to an existing table; previously defined columns may not be dropped nor may the data type of an existing column be changed. To drop a column, one must define a view (see the following section, on view definition) on the base table that omits the column no longer desired. There are relational systems that do support column dropping and data type changes. The ALTER command is invaluable for adapting the data base to inevitable modifications due to changing requirements, prototyping, evolutionary development, and mistakes.

SQL/DS provides several commands to assist in documentation of table definitions and flexibility of using defined data. These commands are:

COMMENT:	Provides an explanatory remark for table columns (stored as part of the internal system definition tables and can be queried via SQL, thus extending the built-in data dictionary features of SQL/DS)
CREATE SYNONYM:	Specifies an alternative name for a table or view; often used to define an abbreviation or to avoid prefacing a table name with the owner name of the table
DROP SYNONYM:	Destroys a synonym declaration
LABEL:	Defines a column heading to be used in place of the column name in query results; an advantage is the uniform heading of columns across all applications

The following are examples of the use of these handy commands for the DESCRIPTION column of the ITEM table defined in Figure 14-2:

```
COMMENT ON ITEM COLUMN DESCRIPTION
  IS 'Selected from medical dictionary of terms'
CREATE SYNONYM IT FOR ITEM
DROP SYNONYM IT
LABEL ON TABLE ITEM COLUMN DESCRIPTION
  IS 'Standard Description'
```

View Definition

The major purpose of a view is to simplify query commands, as was the case with the logical record concept in IDMS (see Figure 13-13). Consider the Patient Bill of Figure 8-9. Construction of the lines of this bill requires access to three tables: PATIENT, CHARGES, and ITEM. A novice data base user may not be able to formulate properly or may be unproductive in formulating queries involving so many tables. A view allows this association to be predefined into a single virtual table as part of the data base, so that a user who wants only Patient Bill data does not have to reconstruct the joining of data in order to produce the report or any subset of it. In SQL/DS this view would be defined as:

```
CREATE VIEW DETAILED-BILL
  AS SELECT (PATIENT-NO,ITEM-CODE,DESCRIPTION,
    C-CHARGE,PATIENT-NAME and other columns as required)
    FROM PATIENT, CHARGES, ITEM
    WHERE PATIENT-NO = C-PATIENT-NO
    AND ITEM-CODE = C-ITEM-CODE
```

Not shown here is the ability to rename the columns included in the view. The SELECT clause (same as the DML SELECT command) indicates what data elements (columns) are to be included in the view table. The FROM clause lists the tables involved in the view development. The WHERE clause specifies the names of the common columns used to join CHARGES to ITEM and to PATIENT.

After this view definition is added to the data base, the DETAILED-BILL table may be used as any other (base) table. This view table is not maintained as real data; rather it is constructed automatically as needed by the DBMS. Therefore, a view is a virtual table. As the base data used to construct the view change values, so will the contents of the view table. A view always contains the most current derived values. Thus, a view is superior in terms of data currency to constructing a temporary real table from several base tables. Also in comparison to a temporary real table, it obviously consumes very little storage space. It is costly, however, since its contents must be calculated each time they are requested.

A view can be a SELECTion or a PROJECTion of a base table or may simply reorder the columns of a base table. As above, it may join multiple tables together and it may contain derived (or virtual) columns. A view may also be constructed from a combination of other views as well as base tables. For example, a user in Mountain View Community Hospital may simply want to know the total charges by patient for room and special items in the room (item codes between 200 and 300). A view for just this aggregate data can be created from the DETAILED-BILL view in SQL/DS as

```
CREATE VIEW ROOM-CHARGE (OCCUPANT,ROOM-CHARGES)
  AS SELECT (PATIENT-NAME,SUM(C-CHARGE))
    FROM DETAILED-BILL
    WHERE ITEM-CODE BETWEEN 200 AND 300
      GROUP BY PATIENT-NAME
```

Here, OCCUPANT is a renaming of PATIENT-NAME, local to only this view, and ROOM-CHARGES is the name given total charges by patient.

The power of such a view of can be illustrated by the following example of a query that asks for the names of all patients with total charges greater than $500. The ROOM-CHARGE based query is

```
SELECT OCCUPANT FROM ROOM-CHARGE
  WHERE ROOM-CHARGES > 500
```

which would be translated by the DBMS into a more complex, equivalent query on the DETAILED-BILL view:

```
SELECT PATIENT-NAME FROM DETAILED-BILL
  WHERE ITEM-CODE BETWEEN 200 AND 300
  GROUP BY PATIENT-NAME
  HAVING SUM(C-CHARGE) > 500
```

Access to a view may be restricted with GRANT and REVOKE statements (or their equivalents), so, for example, some users can be granted access rights to aggregated data (e.g., averages) in a view and denied access to base, detailed data.

Updating data directly from a view rather than from base tables is possible under certain limitations outlined in a later section on data modification in relational calculus. Both SQL-based RDBMSs and INGRES permit some update operations to data in a view, as long as the update is unambiguous in terms of base table data modification.

Internal Schema Definition in RDBMSs

The internal schema of a relational data base can be controlled for processing and storage efficiency. Typically a data base designer can tune the operational performance of the internal data model of a relational data base by

1. Choosing to index primary and/or secondary keys to increase the speed of row selection and table joining (and to drop indexes to increase speed of table updating)
2. Selecting file organizations for base tables that match the type of processing activity (e.g., keep table physically sorted by a frequently used reporting sort key) on those tables
3. Selecting file organizations for indexes (which are also tables!) suitable for how they are used
4. Clustering data so that frequently joined tables have related rows stored close in secondary storage to minimize retrieval time

Indexes may be created in most RDBMSs to provide rapid random and sequential access to tuples. Although not directly referenced by a user when writing any command, SQL/DS, for example, recognizes when existing indexes would improve query performance. The Relational Design Tool is provided with SQL/DS to help a data base designer decide on beneficial indexing. Indexes can usually be created for both primary and secondary keys and often on both single and concatenated keys. For example, to create an index on the TREATMENT relation for T-PHYSICIAN-ID (a secondary key) in SQL/DS, we would

```
CREATE INDEX T-PHYS
  ON TREATMENT
  (T-PHYSICIAN-ID)
```

and to create a concatenated key index on the CHARGES relation for C-PATIENT-NO and C-ITEM-CODE (a primary key), we would

```
CREATE UNIQUE INDEX C-PAT-ITEM
  ON CHARGES
  (C-PATIENT-NO,C-ITEM-CODE)
```

Indexes may be created at any time; if data already exist in the key column(s), index population will automatically occur for the existing data. Indexes will remain up to date with subsequent data maintenance. SQL/DS also permits specification of the percentage of space in each index page to reserve for later insertions; such free space reduces the time for subsequent key data maintenance.

When tables, views, or indexes are no longer needed, the associated DROP statements may be used. For example, to delete the T-PHYS index above, we would use

```
DROP INDEX T-PHYS
```

Several cautions should be applied when deciding on index creation. First, an index consumes extra storage space and requires maintenance time when indexed data change value. Together, these costs may noticeably retard retrieval response times and cause annoying delays for on-line users. Second, some RDBMSs do not use all indexes available for query keys or common columns for a JOIN. A system may use only one index even if several are available for keys in a complex qualification. The data base designer must know exactly how indexes are used by the particular RDBMS in order to make wise choices on indexing.

In INGRES, a user has control over the file organization of each file. A file can be organized as a heap (new tuples added to end of file), sorted/sequential, hashed, B-tree, or ISAM; a file may be dynamically reorganized, but each such reorganization requires indexes to be rebuilt (since the pointers to tuples need to be changed to refer to the new addresses). Each index, since it is a table, may also be organized using any of these file organizations.

Simply stated,

- **Heap** is useful when data sequencing in reporting is unimportant.
- **Sorted/sequential** is helpful for minimizing sorting costs or increasing the speed of tuple selection by continuous range key qualifications.
- **Hashing** is appropriate for tables and indexes where exact matches on unique values are used (e.g., find a row by primary key or join on equality of common columns).
- **B-tree** is suitable when volatile data will be accessed both randomly and sequentially.
- **ISAM** is useful to provide a balance of the benefits of sorted/sequential

and hashing (random access) when data insertion and deletion are infrequent.

A feature now becoming common in RDBMSs is the ability to cluster rows of different tables into adjacent physical storage in order to minimize access between related tables. Remember, the relational data model assumes that a table is a logical construct, so a table need not correspond to a physical file of contiguous records. For example, in ORACLE, we can specify that we want TREATMENT rows for a given PATIENT to be clustered with the associated PATIENT table row for that patient by using

```
CREATE CLUSTER PATIENT-DATA
  (PATIENT# INTEGER NOT NULL)
ALTER CLUSTER PATIENT-DATA
  ADD TABLE PATIENT
    WHERE PATIENT.PATIENT# = PATIENT-DATA.PATIENT#
ALTER CLUSTER PATIENT-DATA
  ADD TABLE TREATMENT
    WHERE TREATMENT.PATIENT# = PATIENT-DATA.PATIENT#
```

In this case, each distinct value of PATIENT# will be associated with a separate page of secondary storage and all PATIENT and TREATMENT data for a given PATIENT# will be stored together. Note that physical contiguity is used, not pointers, to tie together related rows. This is similar to the VIA SET file organization in the CODASYL guidelines for network DBMSs.

Data Integrity Control

Data integrity control tries to ensure that only valid data are entered and that data are consistent across all tables of a data base. A part of this is transaction integrity, or making sure that complete units of work are properly terminated and do not interfere with each other. Transaction integrity is covered in a later section.

The type of integrity discussed here is data validity. In relational systems, such validity is controlled by data type specification, valid ranges or lists of values (as in the CHECK clause in CODASYL systems), limitations on allowing null values (especially for primary key columns), and forcing values of foreign and cross-reference keys to exist in other tables.

Other than the data type specification and UNIQUE and NOT NULL qualifications on table columns, integrity assertions are not implemented in either the ANSI SQL standard or in SQL/DS. INGRES, however, does provide some data integrity control as part of its data definition facility (see Relational Technology, Inc. 1984). Suppose we wanted to limit the amount of a charge to a patient. If we wanted to restrict the C-CHARGE column in the CHARGE column in the CHARGES relation to be greater than $9.99 (charges less than this are recovered as overhead), but less than $1000.00 (requires special handling), we would include the following integrity definitions in the data base description:

```
DEFINE INTEGRITY ON CHARGES IS C-CHARGE > 9.99
DEFINE INTEGRITY ON CHARGES IS C-CHARGE < 1000.00
```

Cross-table integrity controls (e.g., to provide referential integrity) can also be specified using the Visual Forms Editor (VIFRED) or the PERMIT command of INGRES. For example, if we wanted to guarantee that a C-ITEM-CODE assumed an ITEM-CODE value of only existing ITEMs, then an appropriate PERMIT definition would be

```
DEFINE PERMIT ALL TO CHARGES TO ALL
   WHERE CHARGES.ITEM-CODE = ITEM.ITEM-CODE
```

Note that it would be necessary to first load a new item into the data base before any charges could be entered; this places certain constraints on the sequencing of data loading programs.

Such integrity constraints may become very complex. INGRES even supports the use of data aggregation functions such as sum or average in integrity statements. For example, suppose we wanted to limit the Mountain View Community Hospital data base to manage only patients with small to medium-sized bills and force high-expense patients to be handled by special procedures not included in the data base applications (when patient total charges exceed $100,000). INGRES could stop further data entry (either data REPLACEment or APPENDing new charges) once a patient exceeded this limit by monitoring the following integrity constraint:

```
DEFINE PERMIT REPLACE, APPEND TO CHARGES (C-CHARGE)
      TO ALL
   WHERE SUM(CHARGES.C-CHARGE BY CHARGES.PATIENT#) <
      100000
```

Such integrity constraints may be issued at any time; if issued after affected data have been entered into the data base, INGRES will not accept the integrity definition if any existing tuple violates the restriction. Subsequently, whenever new data are appended or existing data modified, INGRES will not process any update that would result in the violation of some integrity definition. Integrity constraints, if not carefully designed and specified, can cause operational problems. For example, if a data base owner accidentally revokes, say, retrieval access to a table to all users, access has also been revoked to the owner. Further, suppose that for some reason the hospital specified a minimum value for the sum of patient charges for each patient. Then, since the first charge entered is below the aggregate minimum, the data entry will be rejected. Fortunately, the dynamic definition of integrity constraints helps the data base designer deal with such problems.

Security Controls

Tables and views may also be given security restrictions. For example, in SQL/DS

```
GRANT INSERT ON ITEM TO INV-MANAGER
```

gives the user identified as INV-MANAGER privilege to insert tuples in the ITEM relation, and

REVOKE UPDATE ON ITEM FROM STOCKROOM

denies update capability to the ITEM table for the user identified as STOCKROOM. In most cases, data element- (column-) level restrictions are possible only by creating views with different column combinations and applying GRANTs and REVOKEs to views.

Control can be placed on commands SELECT (retrieval), INSERT (adding new rows), DELETE (deleting rows), UPDATE (data maintenance, as this may be applied to specified columns), INDEX (index creation), and ALTER (table redefinition). Privileges are granted on tables or views and each GRANT or REVOKE can be applied to all (PUBLIC) or selected users. Further, when a table owner grants a certain right (e.g., DELETE) to a user, the owner can specify whether the grantee may pass this right on to others. For example,

GRANT UPDATE (C-CHARGE), DELETE ON CHARGES TO NURSE
  WITH GRANT OPTION

gives the user identified as NURSE rights to update the C-CHARGE column, to delete rows from the CHARGES table, and to grant these same rights to others (WITH GRANT OPTION). Other, data base administrator privileges may also be granted to users and to stored data base routines. SQL/DS assumes that no one besides the table owner/creator can do anything with a table until granted the rights.

INGRES has an interactive command, PERMIT, that specifics who (by user name) can do what (by DML command) under certain conditions (e.g., time of day, day of week). A PERMIT is applied to a table and is checked each time that table is used. Suppose we wanted to allow only retrieval and adding new CHARGE data (APPEND command) by billing clerks in the Accounts Receivable office (terminal TTA4) only during normal business hours from Monday through Friday. The PERMIT command for this situation would be

DEFINE PERMIT RETRIEVE, APPEND ON CHARGE
  TO BILLING-CLERK AT TTA4 FROM 8:30 TO 17:50
  ON MON TO FRI

Other options can be used to restrict access to certain columns and to data in specified ranges of values (e.g., to permit an employee to be able to see only her own salary history).

Data Dictionary Facilities

Since RDBMSs typically store table, column, and view definitions, integrity rules, security constraints, and other data about data in tables, the RDBMS can itself be used to write queries and routines to produce data dictionary–type output. Further, understanding this definition structure, a user can build other or extend existing tables to enhance the built-in features (e.g., to include data on who is responsible for data integrity). A user is, however, often restricted from modifying the structure or contents of these definition tables directly since the DBMS depends on them for its interpretation and parsing of queries.

In SQL/DS a system catalog contains various tables of pertinent data definitions. For example, SYSTABLES contains such information on tables as the table name, owner/creator name, and number of columns. SYSCOLUMNS lists the names of all data base columns, the associated table (thus, if the same column name is used in more than one table, it will appear in several rows of SYSCOLUMNS), and data types. A user can query these tables to discover which tables contain an ITEM-CODE column by

```
SELECT TBNAME FROM SYSIBM.SYSCOLUMNS WHERE NAME =
  'ITEM-CODE'
```

In INGRES, three specific commands are available, and the user can build other queries to access the stored data definitions. These built-in commands are

CATALOGDB:	Lists the names of data bases created by the user
HELP:	Lists the names of relations in the data base currently being used
HELP relation:	Lists the column names and associated data formats for the specified relation as well as general relation statistics such as number of existing tuples and file organization

Summary of Data Definition

The preceding remarks describe the salient, typical data definition features of relational DBMSs. As can be seen, except for some syntactical differences, similar DDL features are provided in both SQL-based and INGRES systems. Differences are due more to style than to substance.

Similarities can be more pronounced in relational data manipulation languages than in the definition languages. Relational algebra and relational calculus represent two different forms of relational data manipulation. Since most mainframe systems use relational calculus and many personal computer products use relational algebra, in this chapter we address only the capabilities of and variations on calculus-based systems and associated products, and in Chapter 15 we address relational algebra.

DATA MANIPULATION—RELATIONAL CALCULUS

Some authors (e.g., see Date 1981, Kroenke 1983, and Ullman 1980) distinguish among three different but related forms of relational calculus: tuple calculus, domain calculus, and transform languages. INGRES (Relational

Technology, Inc. 1984) and the query language on which it is based, QUEL (Stonebraker et al. 1976), are representative of tuple calculus. A few rare implementations of domain calculus exist [see Date (1981) for a discussion]. Several popular products—SQL/DS and ORACLE, for example—are based on the transform language SEQUEL (Chamberlin et al. 1976). Since INGRES, SQL/DS, ORACLE, and their imitations are found most frequently, we will discuss aspects of both tuple calculus and transform languages. Because the differences are subtle, we will not dwell on these distinctions in any formal way. As pointed out by Date (1981, 224), the underlying concept of both of these forms is the same. Therefore, we will freely mix examples of both INGRES and SQL/DS to illustrate relational calculus.

General Structure of Relational Calculus

Commands in all relational calculus systems specify in some syntax which columns to manipulate, from what tables, and for what rows. For those already familiar with relational algebra–based products, there are two fundamental differences between relational algebra (see "Data Processing with the Relational Data Model" in Chapter 6 and see Chapter 15) and relational calculus: (1) calculus combines the SELECT and PROJECT commands and the binary operators (such as SUBTRACT) into one RETRIEVE (or similar) statement that lists the column names to appear in the result (PROJECT) and uses a WHERE clause to specify the selection criteria; and (2) calculus also uses the WHERE clause to specify the intertable associations used for implicitly JOINing relations in the RETRIEVE command. Thus, whereas the JOIN operator of the relational algebra is a binary operator (and a table that is the combination of n relations must be generated in $n-1$ JOINs), one RETRIEVE command can JOIN numerous tables (implicitly). Several examples of relational calculus were given in Chapter 6.

Basic Retrieval Command Structure

SQL structures data retrieval statements into three distinct clauses:

- SELECT: Lists the columns to be projected into the table that will be the result of the command
- FROM: Identifies the tables from which output columns will be projected and that possibly will be joined
- WHERE: Includes the conditions for tuple/row selection within a single table or between tables implicitly joined

For example, we can display the patient charges from the CHARGES relation of Figure 14-1 for C-PATIENT-NO = 1234 by

```
SELECT C-CHARGE
  FROM CHARGES
  WHERE C-PATIENT# = 1234
```

AND, OR, and NOT operators can be used to create complicated WHERE clauses, and parentheses can be used to properly group the logical operations. If the user does not wish to see duplicate tuples in the result, then SELECT DISTINCT may be used. All the columns of the referenced tables can be displayed by use of SELECT *, where * is shorthand for all columns.

INGRES combines the SELECT and FROM clauses into one RETRIEVE statement. Also, INGRES requires all data elements to be referred to with the syntax tablename.attributename. The equivalent INGRES query to the SQL/DS one above that retrieves the charges for patient# 1234 would be

```
RETRIEVE (CHARGES.C-CHARGE) WHERE
  CHARGES.C-PATIENT# = 1234
```

Functions such as COUNT, MAX, SUM, and AVG of specified columns can also be used to specify that the resulting table query answer is to contain aggregated data instead of row-level data. For example, in SQL

```
SELECT COUNT(PROCEDURE) FROM TREATMENT
  WHERE T-PATIENT# = 1234
```

would display the number of times a physician performed a procedure on patient with number 1234 (that is, would count the number of rows for patient 1234). This, however, is not the same as the number of distinct procedures performed on this patient when several physicians are involved in the same procedure (and, hence, there are multiple rows). To obtain the number of distinct procedures, the query would be slightly modified as

```
SELECT COUNT(DISTINCT PROCEDURE) FROM TREATMENT
  WHERE T-PATIENT# = 1234
```

Limitations on the use of data aggregate functions vary from system to system. In SQL/DS, data aggregates and individual row-level data may not be mixed in the same SELECT clause; that is, data aggregation is a function of groups of rows and row and group data cannot appear together. INGRES is more lenient. For example, it is possible in INGRES to request that C-CHARGE minus AVG(C-CHARGE) be displayed as a column in the query result, in which case the query is actually requesting a display of row-level data derived from both row and group data. SQL/DS cannot handle this type of derived data specification in the SELECT clause.

If the resulting tuples are desired in a sorted sequence, an ORDER BY clause may be added to the query to achieve ascending or descending sequence with major and several minor sort keys. A GROUP BY clause can be used to have functions performed on groups of rows with common values. INGRES has similar constructs.

The following illustrates the use of ORDER BY and GROUP BY clauses. We can produce a list of the total charges per patient for major medical items (item codes in the range 500–800) for those patients with large major medical expenses (total charges over $50,000) by

```
SELECT C-PATIENT#, SUM(C-CHARGE)
  FROM CHARGES
```

```
WHERE C-ITEM-CODE BETWEEN 500 AND 800
GROUP BY C-PATIENT#
ORDER BY C-PATIENT#
HAVING SUM(C-CHARGE) > 50000
```

Here the GROUP BY clause is used to specify subtotal control breaks. This query will display a subtotal of C-CHARGE for each patient. Since C-PATIENT# is the grouping variable, it may be used in the SELECT column list. The HAVING clause is necessary because of the qualification on group-level data. The ORDER BY phrase simply sorts the output into patient number sequence for easier scanning. Some relational languages require ORDER BY to accompany each GROUP BY phrase. This is used to sort tuples together with the same GROUP BY value to facilitate subtotal calculations.

In INGRES, functions may also be used in WHERE clauses. If we wish to display all the patient numbers for patients who have had charges above the average charge, we would

```
RETRIEVE (CHARGES.C-PATIENT-NO,CHARGES.C-CHARGE)
  WHERE CHARGES.C-CHARGE > AVG(CHARGES.C-CHARGE)
```

In addition to being able to use AND, OR, and NOT in qualifications, other options and keywords may be possible. For example, since SQL/DS recognizes a NULL value, qualifications can include NULL and NOT NULL. For example, WHERE DATE-DISCHARGED NOT NULL would limit a query to only discharged patients. Also, the OR operator can be replaced by IN, so that

```
SELECT T-PATIENT# FROM TREATMENT
  WHERE T-PHYSICIAN-ID IN ('BAKER,J.','FISCUS,A.')
```

would display the patient numbers of all patients treated by BAKER,J. or FISCUS,A. This use of IN is important when queries are nested inside other queries for joining tables, as illustrated in the next section.

Multiple Table Operations in Relational Calculus

Relational query languages are distinctive from network and most hierarchical languages in that explicit reference to access paths between related records is not necessary. Rather, data are related and related data are referenced simply by common values. How this is specified varies among different types of relational systems. One major difference between relational calculus and relational algebra (introduced in Chapter 6 in "Data Processing with the Relational Data Model" and to be discussed in greater detail in Chapter 15) is that all relational operators that deal with two (or more) related tables are combined into one command, SELECT or RETRIEVE. Further, SELECT or RETRIEVE can actually include references to more than two tables in the same command, whereas relational algebra commands are either unary or binary.

The most widely used relational operation that brings together data from several related tables into one resultant table is called JOIN. Relational calculus specifies a JOIN implicitly by referring in a WHERE clause to the matching of common columns over which tables are JOINed. Two tables may be JOINed when there is a column in each table that has the same domain of values, a condition that is frequently referred to as having common columns. The result of a JOIN is a table with columns possibly from all the tables being JOINed and with each row containing data from rows in the different input tables with matching values for the common columns.

Three types of JOINs are typically found in relational systems:

1. **natural JOIN**—in which common columns are redundantly kept in the resultant table
2. **equi-JOIN**—in which only one of the common columns is kept in the resultant table
3. **outer JOIN**—in which rows from each table that do not have matching common column values are also included in the resultant table, with null value for the columns from nonmatching tables.

Figure 14-3 illustrates the results of these three types of JOINs. The most commonly used of these is the equi-JOIN (Figure 14-3b). The SQL/DS command for this JOIN is:

```
SELECT PATIENT#, DATE-DISCHARGED, C-CHARGE
  FROM PATIENT, CHARGES
  WHERE PATIENT# = C-PATIENT#
```

The SELECT clause identifies all attributes to be displayed, the FROM clause identifies the tables from which attributes are selected, and the WHERE clause specifies the joining condition for common columns.

Although still not found in many relational systems, the outer JOIN (available in ORACLE) is appearing in newer versions of systems and is likely, in some form, to become a standard feature. The advantage of outer JOIN is that information is not lost; in Figure 14-3c, patients with no charges can be handled in the same table as patients with charges. Unless otherwise stated in this section, all JOINs will be equi-JOINs.

When columns from several different tables are referenced in one command, the DBMS must be able to identify unambiguously which columns are found in which table. This is especially difficult when the system permits the same column name to be used in several tables (which a designer may do if the columns have the same domain of values). When potentially each column name must be qualified by a reference to its associated table, commands can require many keystrokes. To minimize the length of commands, therefore, most relational systems support defining abbreviations for table names. For example, in INGRES we could define shorthand names for the tables of Figure 14-2 with the RANGE command as

```
RANGE OF R IS ROOM
RANGE OF P IS PATIENT
RANGE OF H IS PHYSICIAN
```

Figure 14-3
Example of different types of JOIN commands:
(a) natural JOIN
(b) equi-JOIN
(c) outer JOIN

PATIENT

PATIENT#	DATE-DISCH.
1234	05/20/83
0675	06/23/83
2345	02/28/83

CHARGES

C-PATIENT#	C-CHARGE
2345	23.00
2345	65.00
1234	80.50
1234	125.00

Result of natural JOIN

BILL-DATA

PATIENT#	DATE-DISCH.	C-PATIENT#	C-CHARGE
1234	05/20/83	1234	80.50
1234	05/20/83	1234	125.00
2345	02/28/83	2345	23.00
2345	02/28/83	2345	65.00

(a)

Result of Equi-JOIN

BILL-DATA

PATIENT#	DATE-DISCH.	C-CHARGE
1234	05/20/83	80.50
1234	05/20/83	125.00
2345	02/28/83	23.00
2345	02/28/83	65.00

(b)

Result of Outer JOIN

BILL-DATA

PATIENT#	DATE-DISCH.	C-CHARGE
1234	05/20/83	80.50
1234	05/20/83	125.00
2345	02/28/83	23.00
2345	02/28/83	65.00
0675	06/23/83	?

where ? indicates a NULL value.

(c)

```
RANGE OF T IS TREATMENT
RANGE OF I IS ITEM
RANGE OF C IS CHARGES
```

In SQL/DS when more than one table is being referenced, such abbreviations may be defined within the query as part of the FROM clause as, for example,

```
SELECT R.EXTENSION FROM ROOM R, TREATMENT T
  WHERE T.PROCEDURE = 'Tonsillectomy' AND
    T.T-PATIENT# = R.PATIENT#
```

which would tell us the telephone numbers of all patients who are in the hospital for a tonsillectomy. These abbreviations in SQL/DS are needed only when column names are not unique and when a table is joined with itself (a self-join), to be illustrated below.

This example also illustrates one of the two basic formats in SQL/DS for joining two tables: the joining technique. SQL/DS provides two different syntaxes for formulating such queries, which involve multiple related tables: (1) the subquery technique involves placing one query (SELECT, FROM, WHERE) within another query; (2) the joining technique uses one SELECT, FROM, WHERE and uses the WHERE clause in specifying the linking columns. This second approach is very similar to that found in INGRES.

The subquery approach to joining can be used when

- qualifications are nested (that is, one is within another) or when qualifications are easily understood in a nested way; nesting uses pairwise joining of *one* data element in an outer query with *one* in an inner query, much as in relational algebra (see Chapter 6 on data processing with the relational data model) and
- data from only the table(s) referenced in the outer query need to be displayed.

Suppose that as part of a hospital audit we wanted to know what patients had been charged more than twice the average rate for X-ray work (ITEM-CODE = 307). This would be specified in SQL/DS as

```
SELECT DISTINCT C-PATIENT#
  FROM CHARGES
    WHERE C-ITEM-CODE = 307
      AND C-CHARGE >
        (SELECT 2 * AVG(C-CHARGE)
          FROM CHARGES
            WHERE C-ITEM-CODE = 307)
```

This query also illustrates that a table (CHARGES) can be compared with itself, even using an inequality (>) operator. Such nesting of queries within queries may go several levels deep. The subquery approach is appropriate only when one column is being "passed up" to the next higher level (in the example above, only C-CHARGE is being passed up to match with itself), and only zero or one value will result from the inner query.

The preceding query is for X-ray work only; suppose we wanted to know which patients had been charged more than twice the average rate for any type of work performed on them. This question can be answered with correlated subqueries in which the preceding query is modified to have C-ITEM-CODE of the inner query refer to the C-ITEM-CODE in the outer query as each tuple is processed. This more general query is

```
SELECT DISTINCT C.C-PATIENT#, C.C-ITEM-CODE
  FROM CHARGES C
    WHERE C-CHARGE >
      (SELECT 2*AVG(C-CHARGE)
        FROM CHARGES
          WHERE C-ITEM-CODE = C.C-ITEM-CODE)
```

When an inner query returns a *set* of values and the matching is on equality to any of the values, then the keyword IN is used. Suppose we wanted to display the ITEM-CODE and DESCRIPTION for all work performed on PATIENT# 1234 in Mountain View Community Hospital. In SQL's subquery approach, we would

```
SELECT ITEM-CODE, DESCRIPTION
  FROM ITEM
  WHERE ITEM-CODE IN
    (SELECT C-ITEM-CODE FROM CHARGES
      WHERE C-PATIENT# = 1234)
```

Qualifiers NOT, ANY, and ALL may be used in front of IN or logical operators such as =, >, and < (see Figure 14-4 later in this section for examples).

SQL/DS has two special operators that can be useful for complex qualifications. In WHERE clauses, the logical operators EXISTS and NOT EXISTS restrict tuple display to situations in which subqueries have and have not, respectively, any qualified tuples. For example, suppose we wanted to know the patient numbers of any patient that had been charged for both treatments 307 and 807. We would write this query as follows in SQL/DS:

```
SELECT  DISTINCT C-PATIENT#
FROM    CHARGES A
WHERE   EXISTS
        (SELECT *
        FROM CHARGES B
        WHERE A.C-PATIENT# = B.C-PATIENT#
          AND A.C-ITEM-CODE = 307 AND B.C.-ITEM-CODE =
          807)
```

In this example both the outer query and the subquery refer to the same relation, CHARGES. To distinguish tuples from each, SQL permits assignment of unique names, A and B. Here, A and B are similar to range variables in INGRES. The subquery will be true if the same patient (qualified by the first WHERE clause of the subquery) has two CHARGES tuples, one for item 307 and another for item 807 (qualified by the second WHERE condition of the subquery).

Often a query is simpler to construct in the subquery approach than in the joining approach because the hierarchical decomposition is easier to understand. However, the subquery approach requires that the relationships over which tables are being joined be nested.

The joining technique for query construction, in contrast to the subquery approach, is useful when data from several relations are to be retrieved and displayed, and the relationships are not necessarily nested. The joining technique can be used to determine the items and associated descriptions charged to PATIENT# 1234, as

```
SELECT ITEM-CODE, DESCRIPTION
  FROM ITEM, CHARGES
    WHERE ITEM-CODE = C-ITEM-CODE AND
      C-PATIENT# = 1234
```

The equivalent subquery-style query would be

```
SELECT ITEM-CODE, DESCRIPTION
  FROM ITEM
  WHERE ITEM-CODE =
    (SELECT C-ITEM-CODE
      FROM CHARGES
      WHERE C-PATIENT# = 1234)
```

and could be used to display all the charges and names of all the patients discharged on 05/20/83 who were charged for television or X-rays as

```
SELECT PATIENT-NAME, C-CHARGE
  FROM PATIENT, CHARGE, ITEM
    WHERE PATIENT# = C-PATIENT# AND
              C-ITEM-CODE = ITEM-CODE AND
              DESCRIPTION IN ('X-Ray','Television') AND
              DATE-DISCHARGED = '05/20/83'
```

An equivalent to the outer JOIN operator can be constructed in SQL/DS by use of the UNION command. UNION is actually a way to combine the result of two queries into one table as long as the two tables being combined have compatible corresponding columns (that is, the same data types). A typical way in which UNION is used is to label or identify different types of similar rows. For example, the following would identify and label patients treated for tonsillectomy or charged for X-rays:

```
SELECT T-PATIENT#, 'Treated'
  FROM TREATMENT
    WHERE PROCEDURE = 'Tonsillectomy'
UNION
SELECT C-PATIENT#, 'Charged'
```

```
  FROM CHARGES, ITEM
    WHERE C-ITEM-CODE = ITEM-CODE AND
            DESCRIPTION = 'X-Ray'
```

We could produce a list of charges for all patients, even those for whom there were no charges so far (so that we could work with patients with zero charges) by using UNION in the following query:

```
SELECT C-PATIENT#, PATIENT-NAME, C-CHARGE
  FROM CHARGES, PATIENT
    WHERE C-PATIENT# = PATIENT#
UNION
SELECT PATIENT#, PATIENT-NAME, 0
  FROM PATIENT
    WHERE PATIENT# NOT IN
      (SELECT C-PATIENT#
        FROM CHARGES)
```

The second query in this union illustrates the equivalent of a SUBTRACT operator available in some systems, especially those using relational algebra (see Boeing Commercial Airplane Company 1982). The equivalent ORACLE outer JOIN command would simply be

```
SELECT PATIENT#, PATIENT-NAME, C-CHARGE
  FROM PATIENT, CHARGES
    WHERE PATIENT# = C-PATIENT# (+)
```

where the (+) indicates that the outer JOIN is to be performed.

As already mentioned, with only slight syntactical changes, this joining approach is identical to the transform language format in INGRES. One difference between INGRES and SQL/DS relates to what the DBMS does with the result of a SELECT (or RETRIEVE in the case of INGRES). With SQL/DS the result is simply displayed; in INGRES the user has the option to name a new table (automatically defined by INGRES) into which the results are to be temporarily stored. This resultant table can then be manipulated like any other table (it is essentially a dynamically created view), but unless explicitly SAVEd by the user, it will disappear after some period (usually seven days) when a PURGEDB command is executed.

Figure 14-4 illustrates some additional capabilities of relational calculus query languages and compares SQL/DS syntax with that of INGRES for the same queries.

Data Modification in Relational Calculus

The SQL/DS data maintenance operators, typical of relational systems, are:

INSERT: Places a new row in a table based on values supplied in the statement, or copies one or more rows computed from other data base data into a table

INPUT: Enters new rows into a table via an interactive command

UPDATE: Changes values in one or more qualified rows of a table by replacing current values with constants or the results of calculations

DELETE: Deletes one or more qualified rows of a table

INGRES has, in addition, a COPY command that permits tuples to be transferred between data base tables and external files. COPY is useful for batch loading of data, where the external file, containing new tuples, was created by a separate data entry or text editor program.

In SQL/DS, a new tuple could be added to the CHARGES relation by

```
INSERT INTO CHARGES
  VALUES (1234,300,220.00)
```

If values were to be supplied for only some of the columns, the table name can be qualified with the names of the columns to receive data. In addition, tuples may be copied from one table to another. Suppose there were also an OUT-PATIENT relation in the data base of Figure 14-2, for patients receiving treatment without occupying a hospital sleeping room. When such a patient is admitted for overnight, we could copy (without destroying) the demographic data by

```
INSERT INTO PATIENT
  SELECT PATIENT#, . . .
  FROM OUT-PATIENT
  WHERE PATIENT# = 1234
```

Whole groups of tuples can be copied when the WHERE clause involves secondary keys.

Similarly, tuples can be deleted individually or in groups. Deletion must be done with care when tuples from several relations are involved. For example, if we delete a PATIENT tuple before deleting associated CHARGES, we will have a referential integrity violation (integrity rules on CHARGES to ensure that C-PATIENT# must contain a value from the PATIENT# column of the PATIENT table are checked only when C-PATIENT# is entered or modified). Suppose we wish to delete all treatments performed by physicians in a given department (these physicians have the same phone extension, X3422). In this case, in order to preserve data base integrity, we must delete the TREATMENT tuples before we can delete the PHYSICIANs. Therefore, we would

```
DELETE TREATMENT
  WHERE T-PHYSICIAN-ID IN
        (SELECT PHYSICIAN-ID
        FROM PHYSICIAN
        WHERE PHYSICIAN-PHONE = 'X3422')
DELETE PHYSICIAN
  WHERE PHYSICIAN-PHONE = 'X3422'
```

Figure 14-4
SQL and INGRES (QUEL) command comparison

SQL	INGRES

What patients (displayed in PATIENT# order) have been charged more than $300 for item 307?

SQL:

```
SELECT     C-PATIENT#
FROM       CHARGES
WHERE      C-ITEM-CODE = 307
  AND      C-CHARGE > 300.00
ORDER BY   C-PATIENT#
```

INGRES:

```
RETRIEVE  (C.C.-PATIENT#)

WHERE     C.C-ITEM-CODE = 307
  AND     C.C-CHARGE > 300.00
SORT BY   C.C-PATIENT#
```

What physicians have not treated patient number 1234?

SQL:

```
SELECT     PHYSICIAN-ID
FROM       PHYSICIAN
WHERE      PHYSICIAN-ID NOT IN
           (SELECT T-PHYSICIAN-ID
            FROM TREATMENT
            WHERE T-PATIENT#=1234)
```

INGRES:

```
RETRIEVE  (PH.PHYSICIAN-ID)

WHERE     COUNT(T.T-PHYSICIAN-ID
          BY T.T-PHYSICIAN-ID
          WHERE T.T-PHYSICIAN-ID=
            PH.PHYSICIAN-ID) = 0
```

Create a new table containing data on the phone numbers of physicians and what procedures they have performed on what patients.

SQL:

```
CREATE TABLE WORK
    . . . Table definitions . . .
INSERT INTO WORK
SELECT     T-PHYSICIAN-ID,
           PHYSICIAN-PHONE,
           T-PATIENT#, PROCEDURE
FROM       PHYSICIAN,TREATMENT
WHERE      PHYSICIAN-ID =
             T-PHYSICIAN-ID
```

INGRES:

```
RETRIEVE INTO
   WORK(PH.PHYSICIAN-ID,
        PH.PHYSICIAN-PHONE,
        T.T-PATIENT#, T.PROCEDURE)

WHERE     PH.PHYSICIAN-ID =
            T.PHYSICIAN-ID
```

How many procedures have been performed on patient# 1234?

SQL:

```
SELECT     COUNT(*)
FROM       TREATMENT
WHERE      T-PATIENT# = 1234
```

INGRES:

```
RETRIEVE  (N = COUNT(T.PROCEDURE
               WHERE T.PATIENT#=1234))
```

Figure 14-4 (continued)

SQL	INGRES
How many (distinct) physicians have treated patient# 1234?	
SELECT COUNT(DISTINCT *) FROM TREATMENT WHERE T-PATIENT# = 1234	RETRIEVE (N = COUNTU(T.T-PHYSICIAN-ID WHERE T.T-PATIENT# = 1234))
What patients have total charges greater than $1000?	
SELECT C-PATIENT# FROM CHARGES GROUP BY C-PATIENT# HAVING SUM(C-CHARGE) > 1000	RETRIEVE (C.C-PATIENT#) WHERE SUM(C.C-CHARGE BY C.C-PATIENT#) > 1000
What is the total charge of items 307 and 415 to each patient who has had both items billed to their account?	
SELECT CA.C-PATIENT#, CA.C-CHARGE + CB.C – CHARGE FROM CHARGES CA, CHARGES CB WHERE CA.C-ITEM-CODE = 307 AND CB.C-ITEM-CODE = 415 AND CA.C-PATIENT# = CB.C-PATIENT#	RANGE OF CA IS CHARGES RANGE OF CB IS CHARGES RETRIEVE (CA.C-PATIENT#, TOT = (CA.C-CHARGE + CB.C-CHARGE WHERE CA.C-PATIENT# = CB.C-PATIENT# AND CA.C-ITEM-CODE = 307 AND CB.C-ITEM-CODE = 415)).

To update data in SQL/DS we must inform the DBMS what relation, columns, and tuples are involved. Suppose an incorrect charge were entered for patient# 1234 and item# 307. The following SQL/DS UPDATE statement would institute an appropriate correction:

```
UPDATE CHARGES
  SET C-CHARGE = 322.50
  WHERE C-PATIENT-NO = 1234
    AND C-ITEM-CODE = 307
```

Modifying Data Through a View Views are primarily intended for ease of data retrieval, but it is possible under limited circumstances to modify (INSERT, DELETE, and UPDATE) base table data by referring to a view. In SQL/DS, view data modification is limited by the following restrictions:

1. Only views that are simple row-and-column subsets of a single base table are updatable (that is, the view cannot include such operations as join, group by, distinct, or any data aggregation function).
2. A column in a view derived from mathematical expressions on base data may not be updated.
3. A view defined from another view is not updatable.
4. A new row may not be inserted into a view table when the base table affected would have a missing value for a column defined as NOT NULL.

Keller (1986) provides a discussion of interpreting and handling updates through a view.

Special Language Features

Relational DBMSs support both interactive entry and processing of commands as well as the ability to develop and save procedures or routines, possibly parameter-driven, for repeated execution. INGRES provides procedure processing through buffer management. As the user enters INGRES commands, they are placed in a workspace and held until a \GO is entered. This buffer may be edited at any time by entering \E, at which time INGRES is exited and the user is automatically put into his or her editor of choice, with the current buffer as the file being edited. When this editing is complete, the user terminates the editor in the normal way and is returned to INGRES right where he or she exited, but with the updated buffer. The user can then add more lines to the buffer and execute, or may at any time issue a \W and provide a file name to save the buffer. Later, whenever the user wishes to run this same procedure again, a \I with the file name will include this prewritten routine into the buffer for execution, editing, or enhancement.

SQL/DS provides procedures through a relational table called ROUTINE. The user may create the table and then store different routines or procedures for subsequent execution. Further, these routines may contain parameters, values for which are to be provided when executed. A user's routines are all stored in the same ROUTINE table and are identified by name in this table. Suppose we wanted to be able to display on demand the locations of a given physician's patients. The part of the ROUTINE table that would store this function would be

ROUTINE

NAME	SEQNO	COMMAND	REMARKS
PHREPORT	10	SELECT PATIENT#, LOCATION	
PHREPORT	20	FROM ROOM, TREATMENT	
PHREPORT	30	WHERE T-PHYSICIAN-ID IN &1	
PHREPORT	40	AND T-PATIENT# = PATIENT#	
PHREPORT	50	DISPLAY	

Remarks can be added to each line to document the routine for others who might use the routine. The – at the end of commands on lines 10 through 30 indicate a continuation of the command (we have left these off all SQL/DS commands in this section for simplicity). The &1 indicates that the user of the routine is to provide one value or a set of values for the parameter (T-PHYSICIAN-ID) of this procedure.

When using a RDBMS interactively it may be convenient for the user to create a transcript of the session in order to have a hard copy as a data entry audit trail or for other purposes. Many systems provide an automatic facility to accomplish this. In INGRES this is called the script function and can be activated by entering \SCRIPT and entering a file name into which the session log will be stored. Everything that appears to the user on the screen will be written to this file, which can then be printed or sent to other users. Session logging can be dynamically turned on and off by using \SCRIPT as a toggle switch. Note that this is a screen journal function, which is quite distinct from the data modification journalizing capability related to data base recovery (discussed later in this chapter).

Host Language Interface

Most relational DBMSs not only have a self-contained algebra or calculus language, but also permit access to the data base from a host procedural language. An interesting phenomenon has occurred: Network DBMSs, designed primarily to work with procedural languages like COBOL and FORTRAN, have been expanded to include relational calculuslike query languages; and relational systems, originally designed with stand-alone query languages, have been enhanced to include procedural language interfaces.

Both SQL/DS and INGRES have host language interfaces. We will demonstrate this capability with the INGRES FORTRAN interface. The capability is called EQUEL, for Embedded QUEL; QUEL is the calculus language that is the basis for INGRES's query language. EQUEL is available for BASIC, C, COBOL, and Pascal, as well as FORTRAN. EQUEL also supports use of forms defined by the Visual-Forms-Editor, so application programs can utilize these forms.

To use EQUEL, a programmer simply includes some query language–like statements in a FORTRAN program, indicating each with a special symbol, ##, at the beginning of each query line. A precompiler translates the FORTRAN program with query statements in it into standard FORTRAN code by replacing the query commands with correctly argumented FORTRAN CALL statements to the INGRES DBMS. The translated program is then given to the standard FORTRAN compiler, as would be any FORTRAN program. This process is very similar to the use of precompilers for network DMLs.

Suppose we wanted to write a FORTRAN subroutine to retrieve a PATIENT tuple and print the patient's name and address on the standard output device. In EQUEL, this could be done for PATIENT# 1234 in the following way:

```
        SUBROUTINE GETPATIENT
##      DECLARE
##      INTEGER          IPATNO
##      CHARACTER*30     PATNAM
##      CHARACTER*30     PATADD
        ID = 1234
##      RETRIEVE (PATNAM = PATIENT.PATIENT-NAME,
##                  PATADD = PATIENT.PATIENT-ADDR)
##        WHERE PATIENT.PATIENT# = ID
##      {
        WRITE(6,100)PATNAM,PATADD
100     FORMAT(' THE ADDRESS OF ', A, ' IS ' , A)
##      }
        END
```

This capability to access a relational data base by a procedural language can be important. Often, the relational query language (calculus or algebra) is not capable of summarizing or printing data in the format we desire. Use of a procedural language gives us this ability, and yet we are still able to use the high-level data retrieval facilities of a relational language.

TRANSACTION INTEGRITY FACILITIES

Relational DBMSs are no different from other types of data base managers in that one of their primary responsibilities is to ensure that data base maintenance is properly and completely handled. Data maintenance is defined in units of work called transactions, which, like the network systems of Chapter 13, involve one or more data manipulation commands. What is needed are commands to define the boundaries of a transaction, to commit the work of a transaction as a permanent change to the data base, and to purposely and properly abort a transaction. In addition, data recovery services are required to clean up after abnormal termination of data base processing in the middle of a transaction.

In SQL/DS, the relevant transaction integrity commands are

SET AUTOCOMMIT: Specifies whether changes to a table are made permanent after each command (ON) or only when work is explicitly made permanent (OFF) by the COMMIT WORK command

COMMIT WORK: Specifies that all changes made to a data base since the last COMMIT WORK command are to be made permanent (useful only when AUTOCOMMIT is OFF)

ROLLBACK WORK: Informs SQL/DS to undo all changes made to the data base since the last COMMIT WORK command

BACKOUT: Informs SQL/DS to nullify all changes made since the last SAVE (sub)command during the execution of an INPUT command (only relevant if AUTOCOMMIT is ON)

In SQL/DS, the effects of any data maintenance command do not occur immediately. If changes are *not* to be automatically made by the DBMS (AUTOCOMMIT OFF), then all changes are held in a workspace until the user explicitly issues the command that defines the end of one transaction and the beginning of the next (COMMIT WORK). If, before executing this command, the user enters ROLLBACK WORK, then the workspace is cleared and the data base retains the same contents present before the transaction began (and users have no idea any changes were attempted). (ROLLBACK WORK is equivalent to ABORT TRANSACTION in CODASYL network systems.)

If changes are to be automatically made (AUTOCOMMIT ON), then they still are not made until the next SQL command is given or an END command is issued; END indicates that the transaction is complete (in this case each transaction is composed of a single SQL command). Before the issue of END or the next command, a ROLLBACK WORK will undo the changes of the last modification command. Although the AUTOCOMMIT ON feature is convenient, it does force one to do work one command at a time, which may not correspond to the logical units of business transactions.

SET AUTOCOMMIT is an interactive command, so a given user session of SQL/DS can be dynamically controlled for appropriate integrity measures. Since each SQL INSERT, INPUT, UPDATE, and DELETE command typically works only on one table at a time and some data maintenance (such as deletion of all patient data for a given patient from the Mountain View Community Hospital data base) requires updating of multiple tables for the work to be complete, these transaction integrity commands are very important in clearly defining whole units of data base changes that must be completed in full for the data base to retain integrity.

Further, some RDBMSs have concurrency controls that handle the updating of a shared data base by concurrent users and journalizing data base changes so that a data base can be recovered after abnormal terminations in the middle of a transaction or to undo erroneous transactions. A relational data base designer, to ensure the integrity of a particular data base, must be sensitive to transaction integrity and recovery issues and must make sure that application programmers are appropriately informed of when these commands are to be used.

DATA MANIPULATION—TABULAR/GRAPHIC

Relational DBMSs have been designed for a variety of users, not all of whom want to use a structured query language, no matter how much more productive and easy it may be compared to conventional procedural programming languages. Several constructs or formats for viewing a data base have been devised in order to provide a simpler user interface to a relational data base. Since users are often accustomed to hard copy or screen-type forms, many relational systems provide a way to retrieve and possibly update data by filling in fields on a terminal screen. INGRES provides Query-By-Forms (QBF) and SQL/DS has DBEDIT for this purpose. INGRES also supports graphic output from table data produced by QUEL, the structured language, via the Graph-By-Forms (GBF) module. Stylized reports can be produced in INGRES with Report-By-Forms (RBF) and in SQL/DS with Query Management Facility (QMF). We will briefly review several of these visual table- or forms-oriented modules in order to illustrate the capabilities of such "friendly" user interfaces.

Query-By-Example

Zloof (1977) has developed a unique form of relational data manipulation language called QUERY-BY-EXAMPLE, or QBE (IBM Corp. 1980). Not only is it visually quite different, but several research studies (e.g., Greenblatt and Waxman 1978; Thomas and Gould 1975) have also shown that even with relatively little training, student subjects formulated QBE queries in less time and with greater accuracy than did subjects using SQL or a relational algebra–based language.

QBE is available under the Query Management Facility (QMF) as a data manipulation language (SQL may also be accessed through QMF). QMF takes the table that results from a query formulated in QBE or SQL and produces a stylized report to the users' specifications. QMF is, therefore, a shell under which QBE can be run. Since QBE (and SQL) produces only one kind of output, simple relational tables, QMF greatly enhances the output generation capabilities for relational data management, although business graphics output is not supported.

QBE is not really meant to provide any type of data definition facility, although table definition is possible. QBE is typically used to access an existing SQL data base, although under the IBM VM/CMS operating system it can also extract data from IMS data bases. QBE-like products are being introduced (e.g., PARADOX by Ansa Systems) and QBE-like interfaces will be typical with major RDBMSs.

A user interacts with QBE on a cathode ray tube (CRT) terminal by filling in values in different cells of a table template. QBE displays a skeleton table, and the user enters values:

Table name here	Column name here	Column name here
	Condition or examples in here	Condition or examples in here

The symbol P. may be entered in these cells to indicate what the user would like printed. For example, if we forget what columns there are in the PATIENT table, we can ask QBE to DRAW PATIENT or we can complete a blank table template:

PATIENT P.			

QBE would respond with

PATIENT	PATIENT#	PATIENT-NAME	PATIENT-ADDR

If a complete table is too wide to appear on one screen, only the left part of it is shown; function keys can then be used to scroll left and right to see other segments of the table. Other function keys can be used to scroll vertically, add a row or column, and widen columns.

If we do not know the names of any tables in the data base, we simply ask to use the TABLES table and enter P. under the TBNAME column. The TABLES table is part of the SQL data catalog.

Suppose we wanted to display in ascending order by patient number those patients who had been charged for item 307. With QBE we would formulate this query by indicating the condition directly in a table. This particular query would be formulated as

CHARGES	C-PATIENT#	C-ITEM-CODE	C-CHARGE
	P.AO.	307	

The equivalent SQL/DS query is

```
SELECT C-PATIENT# FROM CHARGES WHERE
  C-ITEM-CODE=307
    ORDER BY C-PATIENT#
```

The result would be a display of a similar table, with only the C-PATIENT# data column, listing all the patient numbers for people who have had a charge for item 307. If we wanted patients charged for item 307 or 807, we would complete a table template with two rows (and an implied OR logical operator between these rows), as follows:

CHARGES	C-PATIENT#	C-ITEM-CODE	C-CHARGE
	P.	307	
	P.	807	

The equivalent SQL/DS query is

```
SELECT DISTINCT C-PATIENT# FROM CHARGES
  WHERE C-ITEM-CODE IN (307, 807)
```

These examples clearly illustrate one of the main advantages of QBE—that is, a significant reduction in keystrokes compared to a structured query language such as SQL. This ease of use through minimal keystrokes, coupled with the input/commands and output being in the same format, makes QBE easy to learn. Also, the opportunity to use a data base is opened to more users—those who do not want to invest in learning a structured query language or who have a fear of such languages and keyboard usage.

We can also write queries that involve multiple conditions in QBE. To associate multiple conditions together we must use example column values (from which Query-By-Example gets its name). Consider the situation in which we want to know if anyone has been charged between $550 AND $600 for item 807. To answer this in QBE we would:

CHARGES	C-PATIENT#	C-ITEM-CODE	C-CHARGE
	P. _2222	807	> 550
	_2222	807	< 600

The equivalent SQL/DS query is

```
SELECT C-PATIENT# FROM CHARGES
  WHERE C-ITEM-CODE = 807 AND
          C-CHARGE BETWEEN 551 AND 599
```

The second condition line in the QBE example specifies finding all CHARGES tuples with item code 807 and with a charge less than $600; the example 2222 in the second line stands for whatever patient number is stored in a qualified tuple (the _ in front of the 2222 signifies that 2222 is an *example* value, not a constant qualifier, as 807 is in the following column). The first condition line says print this patient number if the charge is also greater than $550. The example patient number is used to link these two joint conditions together.

Frequently used queries can be stored by name and recalled. Stored commands can be simply recalled (printed in their table form) and possibly modified/customized, or can be directly executed.

Data maintenance is performed in a similar fashion. For example, we indicate update with a U., instead of P., under the table name. The symbols D. and I. are used, respectively, to indicate delete and insert. To illustrate, if we wanted to increase the charge 10% for all people who have been charged for item 807, we would complete the template as follows:

CHARGES	C-PATIENT#	C-ITEM-CODE	C-CHARGE
U.		807	_500 * 1.1

The equivalent SQL/DS update command is:

```
UPDATE CHARGES SET C-CHARGE = CHARGE * 1.1
  WHERE C-ITEM-CODE = 807
```

In this case, __500 is an "example" of an existing value for C-CHARGE. QBE will take whatever value actually exists and multiply it by 1.1. It is from the use of such "example" data that QBE gets its name.

Other more complex queries are possible in QBE. Suppose we know that patient with number 1234 had been charged for item 450 and we wanted to know if anyone else had been charged more for this item than had patient 1234. This would be written in QBE as

CHARGES	C-PATIENT#	C-ITEM-CODE	C-CHARGE
	1234	450	__500
	P.	450	> __500

In this situation we do not even need to know exactly what patient 1234 was charged for item 450; we simply use an example to relate the two tuples. The equivalent SQL/DS query is

```
SELECT C-PATIENT# FROM CHARGES CA
  WHERE CA.C-ITEM-CODE = 450 AND CB.C-CHARGE >
    (SELECT C-CHARGE FROM CHARGES CB
      WHERE CB.C-ITEM-CODE = 450 AND
              CB.C-PATIENT# = 1234)
```

When these conditions are too difficult to state by linking different condition rows or too long to enter in a column cell, QBE supports a Condition Box, separate from the table template, for entry of such conditional statements. Suppose we wanted to know what patients had been charged more than $500 combined for item codes 307 (X rays) and 413 (lab tests). Since the condition involves arithmetic across two rows of the CHARGES table, the condition box is required. This query would be represented in QBE as

CHARGES	C-PATIENT#	C-ITEM-CODE	C-CHARGE
	P.__1234	307	__Q
	__1234	413	__P

CONDITIONS
__Q + __P > 500

Refer to Zloof (1977) for additional examples of this powerful capability.

Data aggregation functions are also permitted in QBE. For example, the total charges for patient no. 1234 would be specified as

CHARGES	C-PATIENT#	C-ITEM-CODE	C-CHARGE
	P. 1234		P.SUM.ALL.__Q

for which the equivalent SQL query would be

SELECT SUM(C-CHARGE) FROM CHARGES GROUPED BY
C-PATIENT# HAVING C-PATIENT# = 1234

Other aggregation functions for counting number of rows, averaging, and finding minimum and maximum values are available.

As a final example of the capabilities of QBE we will illustrate how two tables can be linked and queries written that place conditions on the related tables. Suppose we want to know the descriptions of the items for which patient 1234 has been charged. This query involves both the CHARGES and the ITEM tables. There is a way to get QBE to display two table templates. We would then fill these templates in as follows:

CHARGES	C-PATIENT#	C-ITEM-CODE	C-CHARGE	
	1234	__333		P.__D

ITEM	ITEM-CODE	DESCRIPTION
	__333	__D

Here again, the example item code of 333 is used to link tuples. Since the result of any query must be a single table, the __D is used to "pull" the description into the one table.

QBE is especially interesting when we use a color CRT. QBE is designed to highlight column names in different colors, depending on their usage (condition, example, printing, and so on).

Query-By-Forms

Query-By-Forms (or QBF) is one of the several customization modules available to assist an application developer in building INGRES-based operational systems (see Relational Technology, 1983). Like most forms or screen painters, QBF assumes that a data base already has been defined by some data management system, in this case INGRES. QBF (like DBEDIT, its SQL/DS counterpart) is designed to support a visual fill-in-the-blank forms orientation for simple data retrieval and maintenance (insert new rows, update rows, and retrieve rows).

Each INGRES table has a default form format that can be changed by using VIFRED, the VIsual FoRms EDitor module provided with INGRES. Thus, QBF and VIFRED work together; VIFRED is used to edit forms and QBF is used to edit data via forms. A form is composed of both fields and trim—that is, characters that make the form readable (e.g., borders and headers, help messages). Each field can be given a title to be displayed, a window in which data for a field are to be displayed or modified, and attributes for fields to, for example, edit values entered. A field is the physical positioning on the screen of a column from an INGRES table.

The use of QBF is then simply a matter of entering a command such as

QBF – A MVCH CHARGES ADD__FORM

which invokes QBF in APPEND mode, opens the MVCH data base and the CHARGES table, and uses the ADD__FORM created by VIFRED. A customized screen is then displayed to the user who may fill in values in specified screen locations to add new rows to the CHARGES table. Tables referenced may be either base or view tables. APPENDing and UPDATEing of a view table via QBF is limited, just as in INGRES. The user moves the cursor around the screen, positioning for data entry or changes. When the form is completely filled in to the user's satisfaction, a special key commits the changes to the data base. When multiple rows are being entered or updated, the value from the previous form can be automatically repeated on a field-by-field basis by typing another special key when the cursor is positioned at the appropriate field.

Special keys may be used to move between fields, move between characters and words within fields, move to the beginning or end of a field, and find specific characters within a field. An UNDO command can be used to cancel the editing and the user can UNDO an UNDO! Typical text editor commands for inserting, deleting, and replacing characters are available. Thus, QBF acts as a full screen table row editor.

QBF is typical of forms-based data manipulation modules available with relational DBMSs. These and associated tools for customized reports (Report-By-Forms or RBF with INGRES and QMF with SQL/DS) and building applications involving many related screens or forms (Applications-By-Forms or ABF with INGRES) are very helpful in rapidly building applications systems, or prototyping. Features of such modules may be limited by the types of devices (such as a terminal) used, but color, blinking characters, changes of intensity, highlighted error messages, sounds, and other convenience features may often be utilized. As demonstrated by QBE, a visual or forms-oriented view of data is a very powerful and easy-to-use construct, and, to be commercially viable, such modules are now typically part of a modern RDBMS.

RELATIONAL-LIKE DBMSs AND FOURTH-GENERATION LANGUAGES

There are numerous data base management systems that, although they are not usually considered relational, have many relational characteristics (see Table 14-1 for a list of some of these systems). The purpose of this section is to introduce briefly a few of these relational-like DBMSs as examples of this class of DBMS.

NOMAD2 [see National CSS (1982); National CSS is now part of Dun & Bradstreet Computing Services] is a combination of relational and hierarchical data structures, so it cannot be classified as a pure relational system. With relational tables, joining is done dynamically as required to satisfy queries. When data will be frequently accessed in different tables (tables are called masters and columns are called items in NOMAD) that have nested 1:*M* relationships, the data base designer can define these files to have explicit pointers linking masters (owners) to segments (members). This capability allows the data base designer to structure the data base efficiently. The same data base may contain both relational tables and hierarchical structures. Further, NOMAD supports the definition of virtual data, where items in a master can be items from direct parent masters in the hierarchy. This simplifies references to data and makes the joining (called extracting in NOMAD) automatic over the common columns/items in parent and child masters.

NOMAD supports a variety of relational operators. The basic NOMAD DML command is LIST, similar to the RETRIEVE command in INGRES. With LIST, the user may project a table on specified columns and qualify which tuples to display in a WHERE clause. The LIST command is combined with the NOMAD relational operators to perform more complex manipulations. For example, if we wanted to list the items and their descriptions for which patient 1234 had been charged in Mountain View Community Hospital, we could say, in NOMAD,

```
FROM CHARGES
  LIST BY C-ITEM-CODE NOPRINT C-ITEM CODE
       WHERE C-PATIENT-NO = 1234
       FROM ITEM
       EXTRACT MATCHING ITEM-CODE
         ITEM-CODE
         DESCRIPTION HEADING 'EXPLANATION'
```

The EXTRACT MATCHING phrase identifies the equivalent of a JOIN and the BY clause on the original table (CHARGES), and the columns listed in the EXTRACT MATCHING clause are the columns to be matched for joining. EXTRACT MATCHING is equivalent to the outer join operation. The HEADING clause illustrates one of the many built-in report writer features of NOMAD, which also includes page titles and footers, totaling and subtotaling, and many other features, all part of one language.

Other multiple table operators in NOMAD are

EXTRACT ALL: Used for joining in the 1:*M* direction (EXTRACT is for the *M*:1 direction)

SUBSET: Same as EXTRACT but is equivalent to the equi-join

SUBSET ALL: Same as EXTRACT ALL but is equivalent to the equi-join

REJECT: Used in the same way as a SUBTRACT command or a NOT EXISTS qualifier to select the rows of the table referenced in the BY clause that have no match in the MATCHING table

MERGE: An extension of the EXTRACT command that includes rows from both the tables referenced in the BY clause and in the MATCHING clause in the resultant table for both matching and nonmataching original table rows (kind of a double outer join)

NOMAD also has graphics capabilities to plot data; it can work with arrays; and it is able to produce textual reports with data base contents embedded in the text. NOMAD can even be used to answer "what if" questions from the data base. By entering SAVE OFF, any changes to the data base are not permanent and will be undone at the end of the user's session. NOMAD can also calculate simple descriptive statistics (mean, median, etc.) and perform multiple regression, *t*-tests, chi-square tests, and others. Because such a variety of data management, analysis, and display functions are integrated into one high-level language, NOMAD can best be classified as a fourth-generation language, 4GL; like many other fourth-generation languages, a relational-like view of data is a feature.

FOCUS is a full-function, fourth-generation language combining data management, financial modeling, statistics, reportwriting, screen management, and a procedural applications development language (see Information Builders 1980). Both mainframe and personal computer versions contain these capabilities; in addition, the PC version is able to upload and download data with a mainframe FOCUS data base. Also unique with FOCUS is TableTalk, a menu-driven module that assists the user in completing a query; while responding to prompts and selecting menu choices, the actual FOCUS structured query is displayed to the user. This facility not only simplifies the user interface but is also an excellent learning tool. Like many 4GLs, FOCUS also provides interfaces to other products. In the case of FOCUS these include Intellect for natural language processing, IFPS for financial modeling and decision support system generation, and other DBMSs (including SQL/DS, IDMS/R, TOTAL, and ADABAS).

FOCUS is not a truly relational system since its data base structure is a multiple root hierarchy. Each hierarchy is called a master file. FOCUS hierarchies are very similar to those in IMS. Structured queries in FOCUS require that tables be traversed from root to leaf, but a dynamic file inversion feature (possible because of extensive use of pointers) permits a user to temporarily redefine a hierarchy to have any child segment become the root. Thus, a user often has to be aware of the physical positioning of segments.

A data base supports cross-references between segments in different hierarchies. Relational tables can also be defined and different tables and segments can be joined to create virtual relational tables (even foreign files from VSAM and other DBMSs can be involved in joining). The ability to join tables greatly reduces a user's need to understand the physical hierarchy of the data base. Since both pointer-based hierarchies as well as relational tables are supported, FOCUS purports to have both record/segment data processing for high-performance applications and the ease of use of a relational system.

Other systems, such as Model 204 and ADABAS (see Computer Corporation of America 1982; Software AG of North America 1981), are also relational-like. These two products in particular view a data base as a set of inverted files or lists (see Chapter 5). Although many relational DBMSs also use inverted lists (key indexes) to support rapid access to data based on content (the tuple selection clause), many inverted file–type systems restrict certain language commands to be used only when a data item is indexed. Most relational systems would use whatever indexes were helpful and then resolve the rest of the qualifications after retrieving only the records found from the index searches.

Another difference between ADABAS and Model 204 and a relational DBMS is that ADABAS and Model 204 permit repeating groups to be defined in a record. This, of course, violates one of the basic rules of the relational data model, that of each column being a simple, single-valued data element.

ADABAS also differs from a relational system in that explicit linking of relations must be defined. In the relational model, when two relations have a domain in common, these relations may be joined without the DBMS being told about this commonality when the data base is defined. In ADABAS, however, data elements that are to be used to associate two files must both be indexed. For example, both ITEM-CODE and C-ITEM-CODE would have to be indexed in order to find associated records in the CHARGES and ITEM files. Further, C-ITEM-CODE would not only have to be defined to be a search key (the designation for indexed) but would also have to be declared as "coupled," since it is used to "couple" the CHARGES file to the ITEM file. That is, the record type that is the "many" member of a 1:*M* relationship requires a special indexing designation.

ADABAS organizes indexed data in an ingenious fashion, as depicted in Figure 14-5. Indexes themselves do not point directly to data records. Rather, indexes refer to an internal sequence number, ISN. This ISN is a cell number in a table that matches each ISN to a pointer to the associated data record. Thus, if a record changes physical position (e.g., because of file reorganization or because of file rewriting stemming from variable-length record changes), only the ISN table, called the associator, must be changed. No index needs to be updated except when records are added or deleted or key values changed.

Other systems, such as RAMIS II and DATACOM/DB (see Mathematica, Inc. 1980; Applied Data Research 1976), can be classified as relational-like. The features of these systems will not be reviewed here. What is important is that we can achieve some of the benefits of data independence found in the relational data model or some of the ease of data retrieval found in relational query languages even in data base management systems that are not purely relational.

Note, from this discussion, that claims or labels are not as precise in practice as they may be depicted in textbooks. What is important for a prospective DBMS user is to know what his or her data processing requirements are and to determine what data modeling and manipulation will meet those needs. Whether a DBMS is hierarchical, network, relational, relational-like, or whatever is not the real problem.

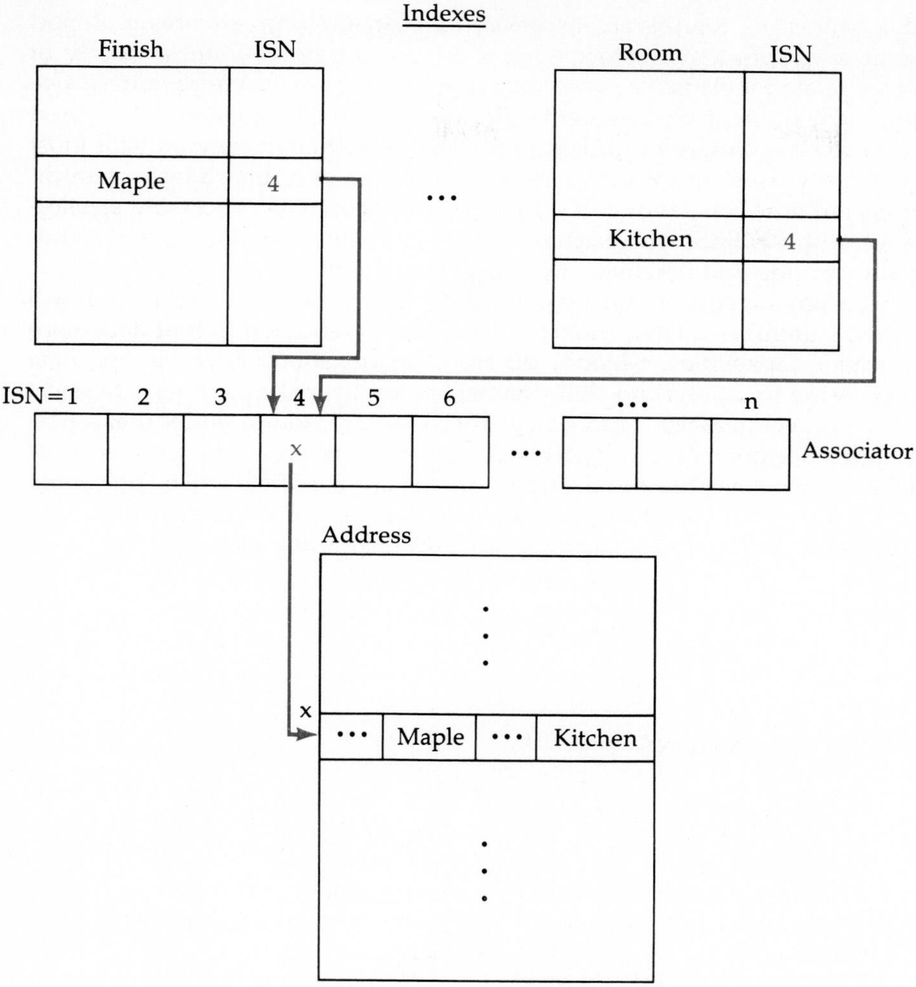

Figure 14-5
ADABAS general data base organization

SUMMARY

Relational DBMSs have been characterized in this chapter as viewing data in flat files or tables; manipulating data using commands that are, or are equivalent to, the relational algebra operators of PROJECT, SELECT, and JOIN; and providing an implementation-independent access to data (e.g., independent of the existence or nonexistence of key indexes).

Relational systems were criticized for many years because of their relative inefficiency compared with network systems. However, with recent performance improvements, with judicious use of key indexes, or with the implementation on a data base machine, a data base designer is now able to construct relational data bases that can be efficiently processed. Host language interfaces to relational systems can be used to provide the detailed data processing controls still necessary for customized programming. Report writers, graphics generators, screen and form painters, and a variety of other related tools make many relational DBMSs very comprehensive system development environments. Relational query languages can be used to develop a variety of information systems; although they are still most frequently used for information-retrieval-intensive applications, organizations are now considering developing production data processing applications with RDBMSs. Increasingly, relational systems are being used to initially develop and iteratively evolve all types of information systems.

It is our suggestion that no one DBMS architecture, even relational, will become dominant. First, different applications require different data management capabilities. Second, different organizations have various data processing traditions and skills that will naturally make them tend to select different technologies. And finally, there is no reason to doubt that a new Charles Bachman or Ted Codd is already at work on a new generation of DBMS. Some insights into the trends in the data base field will be presented in Chapter 16. One of these trends, the increasing use of personal computers for data management, will be addressed in the next chapter.

Chapter Review

REVIEW QUESTIONS

1. Define each of the following terms:
   a. view
   b. relational algebra
   c. relational calculus
   d. embedded query language
   e. index
   f. integrity assertion
   g. equi-join
   h. natural join
   i. outer join
   j. SQL/DS subquery
   k. SQL/DS joining
   l. relational-like
   m. internal sequence number (ISN)
   n. null value
   o. Boolean operator
   p. on-line catalog
   q. commit
   r. rollback
2. Explain the following statement regarding SQL/DS: Any query that can be written using the subquery approach can also be written using the joining approach, but not vice-versa.
3. Explain the difference between features like HELP in INGRES and the ability to query the data definition catalog in SQL with the capabilities of a data dictionary/directory.
4. Explain why JOIN is called a binary operator. How is JOIN accomplished, in general, in relational calculus?
5. Drawing on material covered in prior chapters, explain the factors to be considered in deciding whether to create a key index for a table.
6. Explain why it is sometimes necessary to prefix a column name with a table name in query language statements.

7. Explain the purpose of the RANGE statement in INGRES.
8. The section "Data Manipulation: Tabular/Graphic" illustrates two queries: one for an implied OR logical operator between the two rows of the query template and one for an implied AND logical operator between the two rows of the query template. What construct was used to distinguish between ORing and ANDing the conditions in two rows?
9. What is the benefit of the ISN in ADABAS?
10. Explain why it is necessary to limit the kinds of updates performed on data when referencing data through a view.
11. What kinds of modules are typically found in a RDBMS or in related products for the total management and presentation of data?
12. What makes a RDBMS truly relational?

PROBLEMS AND EXERCISES

1. Match the following terms to the appropriate definitions.

_____ equi-join
_____ natural join
_____ outer join
_____ relational algebra
_____ relational calculus
_____ SQL
_____ view
_____ index
_____ commit
_____ rollback
_____ data base machine
_____ null value
_____ host language interface

a. a standard relational query and definition language
b. provides rapid access to tuples
c. accomplishes JOIN within WHERE clause
d. also called a virtual table
e. all rows are kept in result table
f. changes to a table are made permanent
g. redundant columns are kept
h. uses SELECT, PROJECT, and JOIN commands
i. changes to a table are undone
j. redundant columns are not kept
k. allows access to a relational data base from procedural language programs
l. hardware that performs DBMS functions
m. missing or nonexisting value

Problems 2–10 are based on the Mountain View College data base from Chapter 7 (Figure 7–13). The 3NF relations for that application are repeated at the top of the next page.

2. Write a full data base description using the SQL data definition language. Assume the following attribute data types:

   STUDENT# (integer, primary key)
   STUDENT-NAME (25 characters)

STUDENT#	STUDENT-NAME	MAJOR
38214	BRIGHT	IS
69173	SMITH	PM
...		

STUDENT (STUDENT#, STUDENT-NAME, MAJOR)

INSTRUCTOR-NAME	INSTRUCTOR-LOCATION
CODD	B104
KEMP	B213
LEWIS	D317
...	

INSTRUCTOR (INSTRUCTOR-NAME, INSTRUCTOR-LOCATION)

COURSE#	COURSE-TITLE	INSTRUCTOR-NAME
IS 350	DATA BASE	CODD
IS 465	SYS ANAL	KEMP
PM 300	PROD MGT	LEWIS
QM 440	OP RES	KEMP
...		

COURSE (COURSE#, COURSE-TITLE, INSTRUCTOR-NAME)

STUDENT#	COURSE#	GRADE
38214	IS 350	A
38214	IS 465	C
69173	IS 465	A
69173	PM 300	B
69173	QM 440	C
...		

REGISTRATION (STUDENT#, COURSE#, GRADE)

MAJOR (5 characters)
INSTRUCTOR-NAME (25 characters, primary key)
INSTRUCTOR-LOCATION (5 characters)
COURSE# (6 characters, primary key)
COURSE-TITLE (10 characters)
GRADE (1 character)

3. Write commands to document your table definitions as follows:
   a. Include the following comment for the COURSE-TITLE column of the COURSE relation: "Title must be approved by the curriculum committee."
   b. Permit the name COURSE-GRADE to be used as an alternative name for the REGISTRATION table.
   c. Permit the name OFFICE to be used instead of the column heading INSTRUCTOR-LOCATION in queries.

4. Define the following view using a SQL view definition.

STUDENT#	**STUDENT-NAME**	**MAJOR**	**COURSE#**	**GRADE**
38214	Bright	IS	IS 350	A
38214	Bright	IS	IS 465	C
69173	Smith	PM	IS 465	A
69173	Smith	PM	PM 300	B
69173	Smith	PM	QM 440	C

5. Write a SQL command to create an index called FIND-GRADE for the concatenated primary key (STUDENT# and COURSE#) in the REGISTRATION relation.
6. Write ORACLE commands that will cause rows from the REGISTRATION table to be clustered with the associated row from the STUDENT table (call the cluster STUDENT-DATA).
7. Before any row can be entered in the REGISTRATION table, it is important that the COURSE# to be entered already exist in the COURSE table (referential integrity). Write a PERMIT definition (INGRES) that will enforce this constraint.
8. Write SQL retrieval commands for each of the following queries:
   a. Display the instructor location for the instructor Lewis.
   b. Display the student number and student name for all information system (IS) majors.
   c. Display the total number of students who are IS majors.
9. Write a SQL retrieval command to produce the table shown in Problem 4 above. Note the similarity between the view definition (Problem 4) and the retrieval command (Problem 8). Under what conditions would each of these commands be used?
10. Write SQL commands to perform the following operations:
    a. Add a row to the REGISTRATION table for student number 12345 who received a B in IS 200.
    b. Delete all rows for student number 56789 in the REGISTRATION table.
    c. Change the grade for student number 38214 in IS 465 from C to B.
11. Formulate the following using Query-By-Example:
    a. Queries in Problem 8
    b. Query to produce the table in Problem 4
    c. Listing of all students numbers for students who received an A or a B in IS 350
    d. Listing of all student names for students who received a B in QM 440.
12. Suggest several alternative ways for a relational DBMS, such as SQL/DS, to handle the ALTER TABLE command. Consider the possibility of both adding and deleting columns.
13. Write a relational calculus–like query (use SQL or INGRES) to answer the following question from the Mountain View Community Hospital data base of Figure 14-2: What physicians have performed a tonsillectomy?
14. Write relational calculus commands to answer the following question from the data base of Figure 14-2: What patients (display PATIENT-NAME) have been charged for the item TELEVISION?
15. Show how you would complete QBE skeleton templates to answer the question of Problem 13.
16. Write an SQL/DS query to answer the following question about Mountain View Community Hospital: What patients (display PATIENT#) are being treated by both Dr. Wilcox and Dr. Franklin?
17. Write an SQL/DS or INGRES query to answer the following question about Mountain View Community Hospital: What patients (display PATIENT#) have not been treated by Dr. Jefferson?

18. Write integrity assertions for INGRES to restrict DATE-DISCHARGED in Figure 14-2 to values greater than DATE-ADMITTED for each patient in the data base.
19. Write SQL/DS or INGRES commands to find those physicians that have not yet treated any patients at Mountain View Community Hospital.
20. Assume that the ITEM relation of Figure 14-2 is altered to also include STD-CHG, the standard charge for an item. Write the SQL/DS or INGRES commands to display the patient numbers for those patients that have been charged above standard.
21. Suppose you are designing the application program that deletes all patient-related information at the predetermined purging date (six months after discharge). The update of what tables would have to be included in the logical transaction for this data base maintenance?
22. Compare the data integrity capabilities of the CODASYL data model with the SQL data definition facilities. What types of data integrity problems (if any) can be avoided in the one and not in the other?
23. Discuss the advantages and disadvantages of creating a standard for a relational system as ANSI has done for SQL.
24. Sketch a QBE query template to answer the query in Problem 16 above.

REFERENCES

Applied Data Research. 1976. *Datacom/DB: User's Guide.* Dallas, Tex.: Applied Data Research.

Ashton-Tate. 1981. *dBASE II Users' Manual.* Culver City, Calif.: Ashton-Tate.

Banerjee, J., Richard I. Baum, and David K. Hsiao. 1978. "Concepts and Capabilities of a Database Computer." *ACM-TODS* 3 (December): 347–383.

Boeing Commercial Airplane Company. 1982. *User Guide: RIM 5.0.* Seattle, Wash.: Boeing Commercial Airplane Company.

Britton-Lee Corporation. 1982. *IDM 500.* Los Angeles, Calif.: Britton-Lee Corporation.

Chamberlin, D. D., M. M. Astrahan, K. P. Eswaran, P. P. Griffiths, R. A. Lorie, J. W. Mehl, P. Reisner, and B. W. Wade. 1976. "SEQUEL: A Unified Approach to Data Definition, Manipulation and Control." *IBM Journal of Research and Development* 20 (November): 560–574.

Codd, E. F. 1985. "Does Your DBMS Run by the Rules?" *Computerworld* (October 21): 49–64.

Codd, E. F. 1985. "Is Your DBMS Really Relational?" *Computerworld* (October 14): ID/1-ID/9.

Codd, E. F. 1982. "Relational Database: A Practical Foundation for Productivity." *Communications of the ACM* 25 (February): 109–117.

Codd, E. F. 1970. "A Relational Model of Data for Large Shared Data Banks." *Communications of the ACM* 13 (June): 377–387.

Computer Corporation of America. 1982. *Model 204: User Language Manual.* Cambridge, Mass.: Computer Corporation of America.

Computerworld. 1985. "Britton Lee Unwraps Trio of Data Base Machines." (January 28): 5.

Computerworld. 1985. "DBC/1012 Tool Upgraded." (June 24): 42.

Date, C. J. 1981. *An Introduction to Database Systems*, 3d ed. Reading, Mass.: Addison-Wesley.

Date, C. J. 1987. "Where SQL Falls Short." *Datamation* (May 1): 83, 84, 86.

Epstein, Robert. 1983. "Why Database Machines?" *Datamation* (July): 139, 140, 144.

Greenblatt, D., and J. Waxman. 1978. "A Study of Three Database Query Languages." In *Database: Improving Usability and Responsiveness*, ed. B. Shneiderman. New York: Academic Press.

IBM Corp. 1984. *IBM DATABASE 2 (DB2) General Information*. Form GC26-4073. Endicott, N.Y.: IBM Corp.

IBM Corp. 1980. *Query-by-Example: Terminal User's Guide*. Form SH20-2078-1. Irving, Tex.: IBM Corp.

IBM Corp. 1985. *SQL/Data System: Concepts and Facilities for VM/System Product*. November. Form GH24-5065-1. Endicott, N.Y.: IBM Corp.

Information Builders. 1980. *FOCUS: Query Language Primer.* New York: Information Builders.

Keller, Arthur M. 1986. "The Role of Semantics in Translating View Updates." *IEEE Computer* (January): 63–73.

Kim, Won. 1979. "Relational Database Systems." *ACM Computing Surveys* 11 (September): 185–211.

Kroenke, D. 1983. *Database Processing*. 2d ed. Chicago: Science Research Associates.

Mathematica, Inc. 1980. *RAMIS II*. Princeton, N.J.: Mathematica, Inc.

McEnany, Maura. 1985. "Data Base Machine's Appeal Rising." *Computerworld* (May 20): 63, 70.

National CSS. 1982. *NOMAD 2 Reference Manual*. Norwalk, Conn.: National CSS.

ORACLE Corp. 1984. *ORACLE SQL/UFI Reference Guide*. Menlo Park, Calif.: ORACLE Corp.

Relational Technology, Inc. 1983. *INGRES QBF (Query By Forms) User's Guide*. (Version 2.1, VAX/VMS). September. Berkeley, Calif.: Relational Technology.

Relational Technology, Inc. 1984. *INGRES Reference Manual*. (Version 3.0, VAX/VMS). January. Berkeley, Calif.: Relational Technology.

Schuster, S. A., N. B. Nguyen, E. A. Ozkarahan, and K. C. Smith. 1978. "RAP.2—An Associative Processor for Data Bases." *Proceedings of the Fifth Annual IEEE Symposium on Computer Architecture*. April.

Software AG of North America. 1981. *ADABAS Reference Manual*. Reston, Va.: Software AG of North America.

Stonebraker, M. R., Eugene Wong, Peter Kreps, and Gerald Held. 1976. "The Design and Implementation of INGRES," *ACM-TODS* 1 (September): 189–222.

Su, S., and G. Lipovski. 1975. "CASSM: A Cellular System for Very Large Data Base." *Proceedings of the First Very Large Data Base Conference*. September: 456–472.

Technical Committee X3H2—Database. 1986. *Database Language SQL*. (January). American National Standards Institute.

Thomas, J. C., and J. D. Gould. 1975. "A Psychological Study of Query by Example." *Proceedings of National Computer Conference*. New York: AFIPS Press.

Ullman, J. D. 1980. *Principles of Database Systems*. Potomac, Md.: Computer Science Press.

Zloof, M. M. 1977. "Query-by-Example: A Data Base Language." *IBM Systems Journal* 16 (4): 324–343.

Chapter 15

Relational Implementations on Personal Computers

INTRODUCTION

The purpose of this chapter is to introduce the features of personal computer relational DBMSs (or PC-RDBMSs) that are found in some of the most widely used products. As in Chapter 14, this chapter does not present a complete, in-depth description of any particular PC-DBMS. Instead, the goal is to prepare you to rapidly understand any package you might use by knowing the salient features of that type of product and the comparative features of several typical products.

It is difficult to put boundaries around the topic of DBMSs on personal computers. The power of personal computers (PCs) today, the migration of mainframe DBMS software to PCs, and the increasing sophistication of personal computer DBMSs all contribute to the difficulty in clearly distinguishing the unique characteristics of PC-DBMSs from products on mainframes. Further, it is difficult to clearly delineate relational from nonrelational DBMSs on personal computers because the PC marketplace is even looser than the mainframe marketplace in using the term *relational*. To refresh yourself on this topic, you may want to refer to the discussion in Chapter 14 about what is "truly relational."

To a great extent, a PC-DBMS mimics the capabilities of its mainframe ancestors. For example, we find hierarchical data models (HDMS), network (e.g., MDBS III), and relational (e.g., dBASE III Plus, R:base 5000, KnowledgeMan, and ORACLE) PC-DBMSs (see Micro Data Base Systems

1981a, 1981b, 1983; Ashton-Tate 1985; Microrim, Inc. 1985; and Oracle Corp. 1984). Further, we find that these products may also have screen formatters, report writers, query languages, multiple host language interfaces, and special procedural or command languages for data base processing.

Since so many of the features are similar to the features of mainframe RDBMSs, we will concentrate on differences from the mainframe environment. We will cover the structure of relational algebra, the typical language form in current PC-RDBMSs; user interfaces, menu-driven front-end processors, and capabilities to exchange data between different PC and mainframe file and data base systems; and some advanced features and trends of products in this field. dBASE III Plus and R:base 5000, primarily, and ORACLE, to some small degree, will be used to illustrate PC-DBMSs; these products will be used because they are among the most popular products and because they are characteristic of many other products. A few other products for both MS/PC-DOS and Macintosh environments will be briefly reviewed. A list of many of the most widely used PC-RDBMSs appears in Table 15-1.

Unique Features of PC-DBMSs

What makes a PC-DBMS unique from its mainframe counterparts? First, some DBMS functions are often missing from PC-RDBMS products. Such functions have frequently been eliminated because (at least in the past) PC data bases have been used by only one user and applications have been too simple to require the full capabilities of a mainframe product (which is why a PC implementation was chosen in the first place). For example, there is frequently no restart and recovery support, and often there are no data security procedures. In dBASE III Plus, for instance, copies of data base files are not automatically made by the DBMS, nor are transactions COMMITed or logged, or an audit trail maintained. If a user accidentally defines a new relational table to have the same name as an existing table, the existing table is destroyed and written over by the new data if the user responds Yes to a single prompt. Unless the user has explicitly made a backup copy of that file or diskette, the previous data base file is permanently lost. However, the trend today is clearly to include more and more features from the mainframe environment (e.g., R:base 5000 and ORACLE have some functions to assist in data base backup and recovery).

The second difference between a mainframe system and a PC-RDBMS is in the operating environment of data base processing. With mainframe systems, it is assumed that data base processing occurs in a multiprogramming, multiuser environment. Concurrent access to the data base must be controlled, and security protection is essential because of the shared data. In the PC arena, there are, in contrast, varying environments.

Single-User, Stand-Alone Approach The single-user stand-alone approach remains the most common PC-DBMS environment. Here, a single user at a time uses a PC dedicated to that user's processing. The data base is private

Table 15-1 Summary of Some Personal Computer Relational Systems

Relational algebra systems

Package	*Vendor*	*Equipment*	*Restrictions*	*Comments*
dBASE III Plus Version 1.0	Ashton-Tate	IBM PC or compatible, PC-DOS 2.0 or later; 256K minimum, but usually 384K RAM, and 1 disk	128 data elements per table; 4000 bytes per row, 2 billion bytes per table; 1 billion rows per table; 254 bytes per data element; no integer, money or time data types; maximum number of open tables is 10	Assistant pull-down menu-driven user interface; views supported and catalogs of related tables (logical data base) can be defined; file importing supported; runtime and local area network versions available
R:base 5000 Version 1.01	Microrim, Inc.	IBM PC or compatible, PC-DOS 2.0 or later; 256K RAM, 2 disks	400 data elements per table; 1532 bytes per row and per data element; no logical data type; no long text data type; maximum number of open tables is 40	Semantic rules can be entered that define validity checks for data entry and data modification operations; File Gateway supports importing files; Express menu-driven application generator; Clout natural language front-end
R:base System V	Microrim, Inc.	IBM PC or compatible, PC-DOS 2.0 or later; 512K RAM	400 data elements per table; 4096 bytes per row; 4092 bytes per data element; no logical data type; maximum number of open files is 80	Includes menu generator; Runtime and FileGateway; virtual column capability; extended forms and report capabilities over R:base 5000

Relational calculus systems

Package	*Vendor*	*Equipment*	*Restrictions*	*Comments*
KnowledgeMan Version 2.0	Micro Data Base Systems	IBM PC or compatible, PC-DOS 2.0 or later; 328K RAM, two disk drives	255 data elements per table; 64K bytes per row; 64K bytes per data element; no time data type; maximum number of open tables is 13	Compatible package available on several minis; integrated spreadsheet and word processor capabilities; forms painter, reportwriter, LAN version, mouse driver available

Table 15-1 (continued)

Relational calculus systems (continued)

Package	*Vendor*	*Equipment*	*Restrictions*	*Comments*
ORACLE Version 4.1.4	Oracle Corp.	IBM PC or compatible, PC-DOS 2.0 or later; 512K RAM, one floppy and one hard disk with at least 5MB	254 data elements per table; 90K bytes per row, 190K bytes per table (default, can be increased by user); 240 bytes per data element; no logical data type; no programming language per se, but can access data base from the C language	Compatible with mainframe version; uses SQL standard query language with a few extensions; data stored in variable-length format to conserve space; user-friendly interface shell assists users in composing, modifying, and debugging

Graphic/Tabular systems

Package	*Vendor*	*Equipment*	*Restrictions*	*Comments*
DataEase Version 2.5	Software Solutions, Inc.	IBM PC or compatible, PC-DOS 2.0 or later; 384K RAM, two disk drives	255 data elements per table; 4000 bytes per row, 64K rows per table, 168 rows per data base; 255 bytes per data element; no long text data type; maximum number of open tables is 28	Includes data types for social security numbers, phone numbers, and multiple-choice fields; backup and restore subsystem also checks data integrity
Paradox Version 1.1	Ansa Software	IBM PC or compatible, PC-DOS 2.0 or later; 512K RAM, two disk drives	255 data elements per table; 4000 bytes per row, 65,000 rows per table, 260 M bytes per table; 255 bytes per data element; no logical, time, or long text data types	Application generator, APGEN, and PAL programming language support dBASE type custom programming; QBE-type user interface; run-time version, but no multiuser or network version

(continued)

Table 15-1 (continued)

Relational-like systems

Package	*Vendor*	*Equipment*	*Restrictions*	*Comments*
PC/FOCUS Version 1.5	Information Builders, Inc.	IBM PC or compatible, PC-DOS 2.0 or later; 640K RAM, hard disk drive	256 data elements per table; 4096 bytes per row; 250 bytes per data element; no logical or long text data type; maximum number of files open is 16	PC version of mainframe product, designed, in part, to relieve processing from mainframe; TableTalk user interface prompts user to enter command components and displays actual statements for review and learning
Q&A Version 2.0	Symantec	IBM PC or compatible, PC-DOS 2.0 or later	2400 data elements per table; 16,780 bytes per row, 16 million rows per table; 1678 bytes per data element; only 1 file open at a time	Natural language interface file manager

Relational systems for the Macintosh

Package	*Vendor*	*Equipment*	*Restrictions*	*Comments*
Reflex for the MAC	Borland International	Macintosh 512K, Macintosh Plus, or Mac XL; second disk drive recommended	254 data elements per table; 1002 bytes per data element; 1008 bytes per row; rows per table limited by disk space; maximum number of open tables is 15	Visual layout of table design, data entry form and reports; graphics may be easily placed in data entry forms or reports; fully supports user interface of Macintosh including pull-down menus, dialogue boxes, and multiple windows open at once

in the sense that the user can take the diskettes away after use to prohibit other users from accessing the data. The data base, too, is personal, and frequently private. Further, the data base on the PC is separate from any other data base, including those on the mainframe from which the PC data base may have been extracted. Thus, data may be duplicated, and synchronization of updating is a problem that must be dealt with.

Multiuser, Stand-Alone Approach The multiuser stand-alone approach is different from the single-user stand-alone approach in that usually a hard-disk-based data base is shared among a number of concurrent users. These different users may all be using the same microprocessor with a multiprogramming-type operating system, or they may be sharing a hard-disk file server from several PCs in a local area network (LAN). In either case, concurrency control and security are limited or handled at a very coarse level (e.g., file-level lockout for update control, rather than record- or element-level lockout). Here, as in the prior situation, the PC data base is maintained separately from any mainframe data base.

Mainframe Link Approach The mainframe link is a relatively new but rapidly expanding class of PC-DBMSs, in which the same or very similar DBMS products are provided at both the PC and mainframe computers. A communications link (hardware and software) is provided as part of the PC package. From the PC, a user can access a mainframe data base as he or she would from a terminal (in so-called terminal emulation mode, in which the PC is made to act as a special terminal, such as an IBM 327x). The user can also have selected data from the mainframe transferred to the PC (often using the same type of retrieval command as in any data access statement, but with an extra clause to indicate that the destination of the result is a file, data base, or table on the PC). And finally, the user can manipulate data at the PC using the same language and range of commands as on the mainframe. Thus, users familiar with the mainframe product require minimal training time to learn the PC version. The benefit is that the PC can be used to relieve a mainframe doing production data base processing from also having to perform ad hoc inquiry processing, which can be expensive to support and can degrade the performance of the production data base. Besides ORACLE, products such as PC/FOCUS, PC/204, and Cullinet Personal Computer Software are examples of this category of product (see Information Builders, Inc. 1983; *Computerworld* 1983; Cullinet Software, Inc. 1983).

Multifunction Package Approach Multifunction packages include packages that have integrated DBMS functions along with other management support tools. For example, several spreadsheet packages combine some simple DBMS functions with spreadsheet and graphics capabilities. KnowledgeMan provides more relational DBMS functions with limited spreadsheet facilities (see Micro Data Base Systems 1983). This category of PC-DBMS should continue to expand as more general decision support system generators are created for personal computers.

Besides these environmental differences, a PC-DBMS differs from its mainframe predecessors in the size of the data base that they can manage. See Table 15-1 for examples of such restrictions. Newer versions of PC-DBMS products relax such size constraints considerably. For example, R:base 5000 from Microrim, Inc. (1985) permits as many records as the storage medium can handle and 400 data elements per record type. As word sizes and operating system capabilities on PCs expand, larger data bases will become possible via PC-DBMSs. A PC-DBMS is also limited by the processing speed of a personal computer, especially the time required to access disk or diskette storage.

Role of PC-DBMS in Data Management

A PC-DBMS has several distinct features that make it attractive as part of a general data management strategy:

1. It provides *mainframelike DBMS functions* for organizations or organizational units that do not require the power of a mini- or mainframe computer.
2. A PC-DBMS allows computer users in organizations that have an existing mainframe DBMS to develop data base *end user applications that are truly independent from production, high-transaction volume data bases* so that the costly unstructured end user access does not degrade production data base processing and does not interfere with the performance of these production data bases.
3. Newer PC-DBMS technologies essentially permit an organization to create *a type of distributed data base* that both achieves greater host performance as well as reduces communication traffic in the computer network (see Chapter 16 for a discussion of distributed data bases).
4. For those already using personal computers for management support, a PC-DBMS provides an additional *powerful tool to manage and present relevant data and information.*
5. A PC-DBMS is *portable,* since for many of these products the DBMS and data bases can be easily transported by moving diskettes. This not only benefits mobile managers, but also means that the same DBMS and data base can be used on mixed, yet compatible, machines (e.g., several PCs running the MS-DOS operating system). This portability also impacts education, since students learning a DBMS can do so at home or in a classroom or laboratory, and they can learn without disrupting other students (when their errors crash the DBMS or destroy a file of input transactions).

The principles of data base management hold whether we deal with mainframe or PC data bases. The major issues are shareability, integrity, consistency, security, and accessibility. PC and mainframe products alike should be measured on the same features and data processing requirements. As with many mainframe products, the label DBMS is often ascribed to a PC product that may only manage a single file of data or may only assist in producing stylized reports from single flat files. Thus, care should be taken to apply the same stringent requirements for PC data management products as have been introduced elsewhere in this text for DBMS products in general. PC-DBMSs exist on a different type of computer but should provide the same functionality.

PC-DBMSs and End User Computing

End user computing involves the development and use of computer-based applications by managers, executives, and occupational professionals, with little or no involvement by trained information system professionals. The proliferation of personal computers and the ease of use of spreadsheet, file management, word processing, business graphics, and desktop publishing software have opened new opportunities for the explosive, and potentially uncontrolled, deployment of systems in organizations.

Personal computer data base applications can range from very simple data systems to data bases with as complex a structure as any mainframe system. Today, personal computer DBMSs should not be treated as toy systems. They are sophisticated software packages that can be used to effectively solve significant data management problems, or that can be abused. Users of a PC-DBMS should be thoroughly trained in:

- The use of the package
- Principles of good data base design
- The need for proper backup and recovery practices
- The application of appropriate date security measures

In addition, the experience with end user computing to date indicates that the introduction of PC-DBMSs should be managed within organizationwide support systems and policies. Most organizations will standardize on one or just a few PC-DBMSs in order to more effectively provide training and consulting support. This control also means that the organization can enter into agreements with DBMS vendors that can result in significant savings from large-quantity purchases.

Equally important is the need to manage data as a corporate resource, which requires that data bases on personal computers be defined and designed to be consistent with corporate methods. For example, data element naming conventions should still be applied. The need for a data base on a PC should be reviewed by a data administrator or end user consulting specialist in order to help the user determine if a PC-DBMS is the appropriate technology and, if so, what is the best source of data for the PC data base (e.g., a mainframe data base, local data entry, or possibly an external public data source). The end user consultant can also help the user establish a local area network or PC–mainframe connection if the data base is to be used by multiple employees.

Experience with PC data bases and DBMSs should be shared throughout an organization. An information center or computer club is an excellent forum. A newsletter or users' group can also be effective in helping users better utilize the DBMS and in keeping issues of organizationwide data management before those using the PC-DBMS.

Structure and Components of PC Relational Systems

A PC-RDBMS is a multiple component product that frequently includes

- The **core DBMS,** which provides data definition, a relational query language, and data definition retrieval functions
- An optional **run-time version** of the DBMS (basically the data base control program; see Chapter 11) that allows only prewritten (and precompiled) programs to execute (that is, the user cannot enter ad hoc, interactive queries); this facility is provided to reduce the main memory requirements for more efficient processing and to allow software developers to bundle the DBMS with application software without requiring the purchaser to buy the complete DBMS
- A **programming language** that provides IF-THEN-ELSE logic, forms input and output, and presentation of menus and prompts to interactive users; programs can then be stored in command files to be used by nonprogrammers or to provide frequently used routines for inclusion in interactive sessions
- A **menu-driven front-end** that uses "pop-up" or "pull-down" menus to prompt the user in completing each clause of each DBMS data definition, retrieval, modification, or other command; frequently this user-friendly aid will display the actual structured query on the screen as menu selections are made—this then allows the user to verify visually the correctness of the query as interpreted, to be able to use the DBMS quickly without extensive training, and to learn the structured language by actually doing some data base processing
- A **report writer** that supports extensive reporting features beyond those provided by the query or programming languages; such features include subtotals and totals, custom report layouts, control breaks, data value formatting, statistical analysis, page numbering and dating, and column labeling; often the reportwriter accepts only one data base file as input, so a query or program must first merge data from related tables into a single file, if necessary
- A **natural language or tabular language processor** that allows a user to state a query in near English or indicate desired data by filling in a form or template on the screen

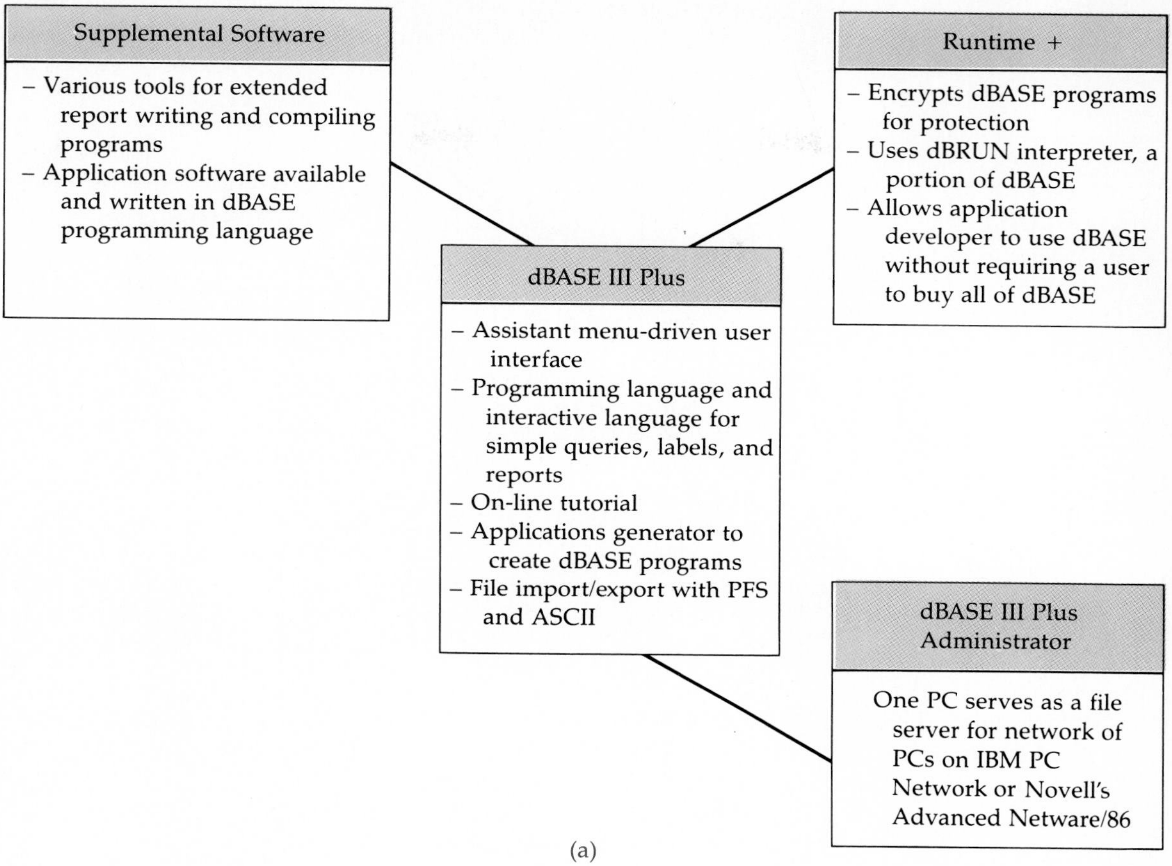
Supplemental Software
– Various tools for extended report writing and compiling programs
– Application software available and written in dBASE programming language
Runtime +
– Encrypts dBASE programs for protection
– Uses dBRUN interpreter, a portion of dBASE
– Allows application developer to use dBASE without requiring a user to buy all of dBASE
dBASE III Plus
– Assistant menu-driven user interface
– Programming language and interactive language for simple queries, labels, and reports
– On-line tutorial
– Applications generator to create dBASE programs
– File import/export with PFS and ASCII
dBASE III Plus Administrator
One PC serves as a file server for network of PCs on IBM PC Network or Novell's Advanced Netware/86

(a)

Figure 15-1 (pages 571–573) PC relational DBMS environments: (a) dBASE III Plus (b) R:base 5000 (c) ORACLE

Usually the standard version of the PC-RDBMS is designed for single-user data base access. Special versions of the DBMS are required for local area network environments or when interacting with both mainframe and PC data bases.

Figure 15-1 illustrates the environment of three popular and typical PC-RDBMSs: dBASE III Plus, R:base 5000, and ORACLE (see Ashton-Tate 1985; Microrim, Inc. 1985; Oracle Corp. 1984).

The main structural difference between mainframe and PC relational systems is the style of query language. As indicated in Chapter 6, relational calculus (typical of almost all mainframe products) and relational algebra (typical of many PC products) are the two major general styles. Chapter 14 deals extensively with relational calculus. A relational algebra language essentially has unary and binary table operators, whereas a relational calculus allows more than two tables to be referenced in one command. Thus, relational algebra decomposes complicated retrieval statements into many statements, each of which deals with operations on one or two tables. A

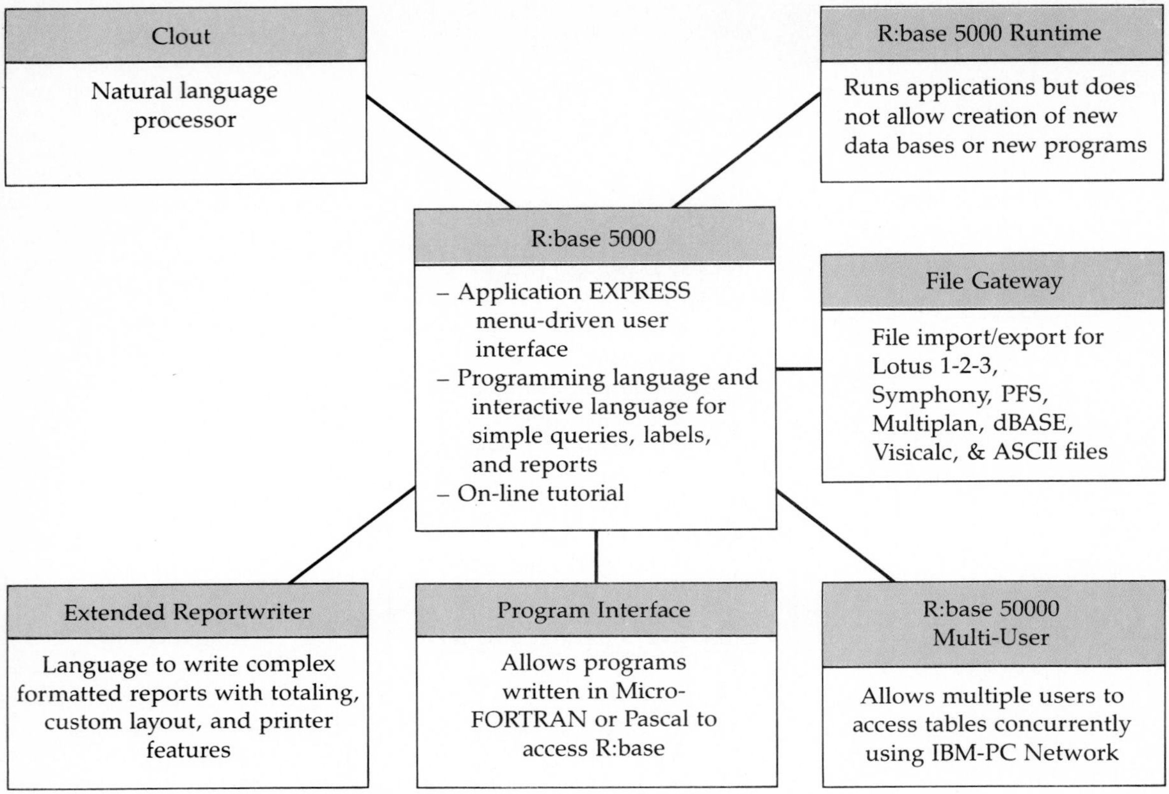

(b)

Figure 15-1 (continued)

single relational algebra statement can be simpler to construct than a calculus statement, but the full effect of data base processing cannot be seen in algebra unless one analyzes potentially many statements.

One trend in PC-RDBMSs is to provide an SQL language processor either as the query language or as an additional component. Although, as we will describe in the next section, many PC-RDBMSs have a query language that is different from SQL and often is relational algebra–based, the movement to standardize on SQL (a relational calculus language discussed in Chapter 14 for mainframe RDBMSs) is also occurring for PC products.

DATA DEFINITION, REDEFINITION, AND INTEGRITY CONTROLS

Since the data model is still relational and differences between relational calculus and algebra appear in data manipulation, not definition, the data definition capabilities of PC-RDBMSs are very similar to those of mainframe relational systems. The major difference is not in capability but rather in

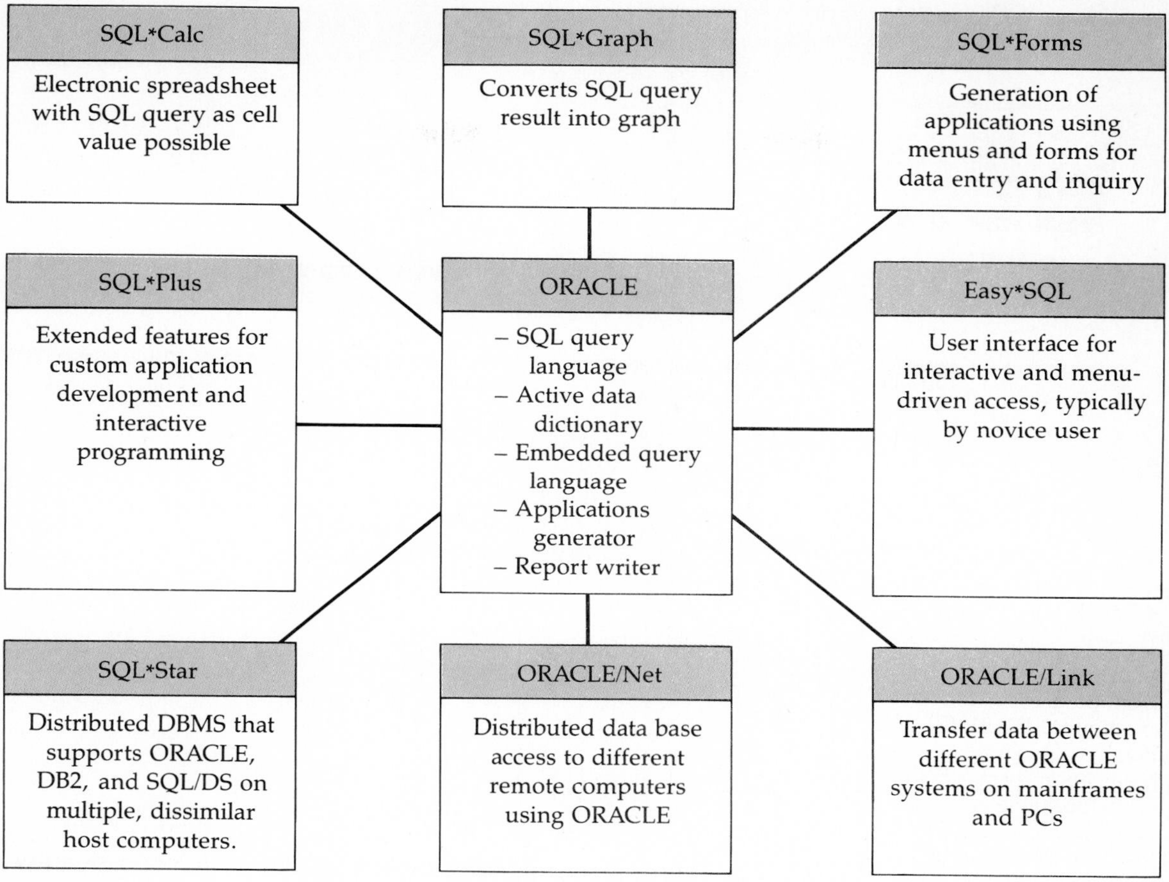

(c)

Figure 15-1
(continued)

the user interface. Data definition is usually done by filling in blanks and choosing options on a data definition screen, which is displayed upon entry of the table definition command, typically called CREATE.

For example, Figure 15-2 illustrates what would be entered on the screen generated by dBASE III Plus upon entry of the command

```
. CREATE ROOM
```

for the Room table of the Mountain View Community Hospital data base of Figures 8-13 and 9-7. In this and other examples involving dBASE commands, the period (.) at the beginning of a line is the prompt from dBASE that indicates that the user is to enter a command. dBASE limits table/file names to eight characters.

A table is defined by specifying for each "field" (PC-RDBMSs commonly refer to attributes by the traditional file processing term of *field*): its name,

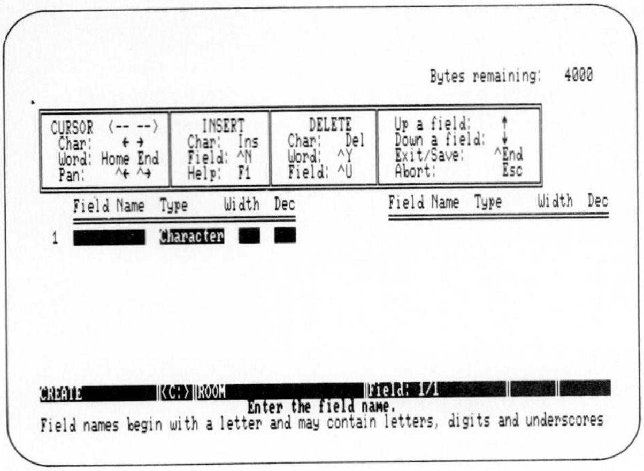

(a)

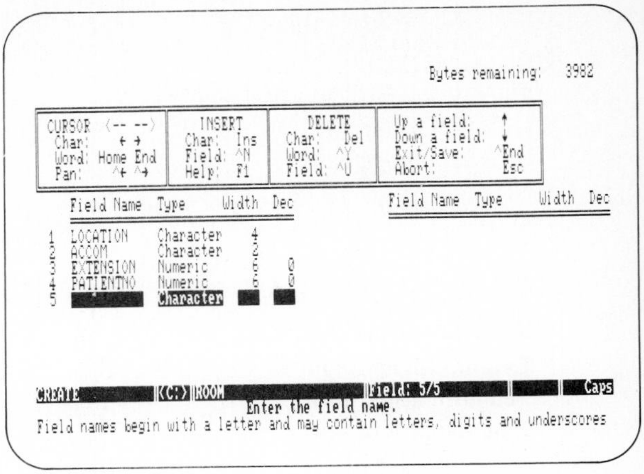

(b)

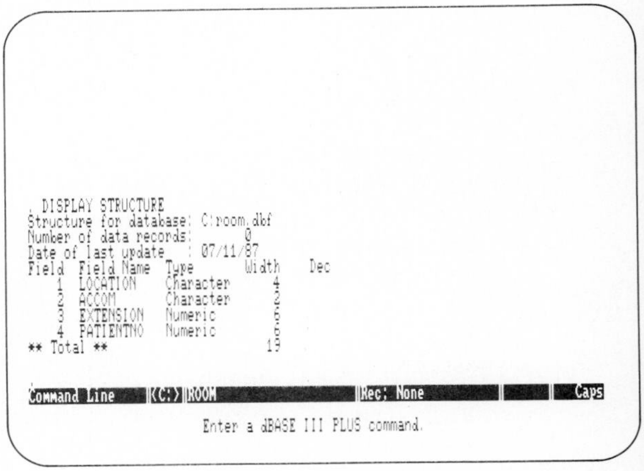

(c)

Figure 15-2
Example table creation in dBASE III Plus:
(a) creation form before table is defined
(b) creation form after table is defined
(c) table definition from dictionary

data type (choices are character; numeric; logical—Y/N or T/F Boolean value; date; or memo—memo is a long, variable-length character string), width (for character and numeric types), and number of decimal places (for numeric type). The person defining a table can use the cursor control keys to move around this data definition form, making changes until the definition is complete (as in Figure 15-2b). Pressing Ctrl-End or pressing the RETURN key when prompted to define a new field indicates that the definition is to be saved. The user is then asked if data are to be input at this point. We will illustrate the process of entering and modifying data later in this chapter. In Figure 15-2c we also illustrate the command DISPLAY STRUCTURE, which is the dBASE command used to display the definition of the table currently in use. Note that dBASE defines the ROOM table to be stored in the PC-DOS file called ROOM.DBF; DBF stands for data base file, and clearly indicates this as a dBASE data file. dBASE limits field names to ten characters.

Tables do not have to be defined interactively in dBASE III Plus, but rather the definition can be stored in a table and the data table created from the definition table. This is especially useful when two tables are to have very similar structures. For example, the dBASE commands

```
. USE ROOM
. COPY TO LOCATION STRUCTURE EXTENDED
```

creates a table LOCATION that contains four fields: field name, field type, field length, and number of decimal places. Each row is the definition of a field from the ROOM table. Data modification statements (to be covered later) could then be used to change the contents of the LOCATION table (that is, change field names or lengths, add new fields, delete fields, etc.). Then, the command

```
. CREATE HOUSING FROM LOCATION
```

would define a new table, HOUSING, for which field definitions would come from the contents of the LOCATION table. This CREATE (table) FROM (structure) command is especially useful as part of a prewritten program to perform all the necessary data definition building functions for a novice user.

The data base definition philosophy is slightly different in R:base 5000. Here, when a data base is defined, the columns to be used in all the tables are defined separately from the definition of the tables; in this way, the complete column definitions are incorporated as the columns of a table are indicated. When the same column (domain) is used in multiple tables (usually primary, foreign, and cross-reference keys), the DBMS can then ensure that exactly the same data types, lengths, and so on are used each time the column is referenced. This type of dictionary-driven data base definition is very helpful in achieving data base integrity.

The process of creating a data base in R:base 5000 is begun by issuing the DEFINE command. For example,

```
R> DEFINE c:\MVCH\MVCHDB
D>
```

would open a data base called MVCHDB in the MVCH subdirectory on the c: disk drive (usually a hard disk). The R> prompt is from R:base and then the D> prompt indicates that the user has been placed in definition mode.

R:base 5000 supports date, dollar, integer, real, text, and time data types for columns. Columns are defined interactively when the COLUMNS command is issued; the following indicates the definition of just those columns for the ROOM table, although all data base columns could be defined:

```
D> COLUMNS
D> LOCATION TEXT 4 KEY
D> ACCOM TEXT 2
D> EXTNSION INTEGER
D> PATIENTN INTEGER
```

KEY is used to qualify a column that is frequently used for data base access or sorting. A column name cannot be longer than eight characters in length in R:base 5000.

The ROOM table is then defined by

```
D> TABLES
D> ROOM WITH LOCATION ACCOM EXTNSION PATIENTN
```

Changing a Data Base Definition

Because PC-RDBMSs are frequently used to prototype an application and because data base needs change, it is very convenient to be able to redefine a data base from time to time. To illustrate the redefinition capabilities, we will consider various R:base facilities. In R:base, we can completely redefine a column of a table; the column name, data type, and length can all be modified. The following command would be used to change the patient number column in the ROOM definition above to permit alphanumeric values:

```
R> CHANGE COLUMN PATIENTN IN ROOM TO PATNUM TEXT 8
```

If the PATIENTN column were used in multiple tables, its format would have to be changed *separately* in each table.

In addition, R:base supports adding columns to a table (the EXPAND command), creating and deleting column keys (the BUILD/DELETE KEY commands), removing columns from a table (the REMOVE COLUMN command), removing tables from a data base (the REMOVE TABLE command), and renaming columns and tables (the RENAME command).

Integrity and Security Controls

Handling null values and specifying columns that must have unique values across all rows of a table are not common semantic controls available in PC-RDBMSs. R:base 5000, however, provides a facility, called Rules, that enables specification of integrity conditions to which data must comply. A rule, which is applied to a column of a table, is checked during all data entry and modification statements. Rules can be used to check referential integrity, prevent duplicate values, or limit data to a certain range of values.

To illustrate the R:base Rules feature, consider again the Mountain View Community Hospital data base of Figures 8-13 and 9-7. Figure 15-3a contains an R:base definition for this data base, and several rules to assist in data integrity are defined in Figure 15-3b. A rule begins with a message that is displayed whenever a data modification statement causes the condition specified to be violated. Rules can

- Compare the value of a column with a specified constant [e.g., CHARGE greater than or equal to (GE) 10]

- Check that a value exists for a specified column (equivalent of NOT NULL clause in some languages; e.g., PATIENTN EXISTS)
- Compare values in two columns of the same row
- Compare values in two columns from different tables [this can be used to check referential integrity; e.g., to store a PHYSID in TREATMNT, the value must equal a (EQA) PHYSID in PHYSCIAN]
- Compare the value of a column with values for that column in other rows of the table [e.g., LOCATION not equal a (NEA) value of an existing value of LOCATION; this implements a primary key restriction]

Rules are applied to the data base. A LIST RULES command can be entered at any R> prompt in order to display the rules for the currently open data base (see Figure 15-3c). It is common practice in relational systems to store all data base definitions in the data base as tables. This allows any part of the data base description to be retrieved using commands similar to those used to retrieve real data. Rules, therefore, are stored as part of the data base in a table called RULES; specific rules may be deleted from the RULES table by use of the DELETE ROWS command with a specification of exactly which rules (rows) are to be eliminated. One restriction to the RULES capability is that rules cannot be used to check concatenated key duplication (e.g., to verify that an ITEMCODE + PATIENTN pair is unique for each CHARGES tuple).

R:base also has the capability to assign passwords to a data base in order to provide security against unauthorized use of data. Passwords can be applied to the whole data base or to individual tables. A data base password is called an "owner password" and restricts use of commands to define, dump, and restore a data base. A table password restricts access to tables by limiting use of modification and/or retrieval commands. For example, to specify a modification password of "move" on the ROOM table of Figure 15-3a, a data base developer would specify in define mode

```
D> PASSWORDS
D> MPW FOR ROOM IS move
```

Passwords can be changed or removed by the creator of the data base. As can be seen from this example, security controls are very limited in PC-RDBMS products compared to mainframe systems. This limitation has not been much of a problem for single-user data bases in which physical access to the storage medium of the data base can be restricted. As multiple-user data bases become more prevalent, however, expanded security features will be necessary.

Internal Schema Definition

As with mainframe RDBMSs, PC products allow the data base designer some control over the physical storage of data base tables. These controls are implemented through the creation of key indexes and, in some systems,

Figure 15-3
Definition of a data base in R:base 5000:
(a) columns and tables definitions
(b) data integrity rules definitions
(c) listing rules from dictionary

```
R>DEFINE C:\MVCH\MVCHDB
 Begin R:base Database Definition
D>COLUMNS
D>LOCATION TEXT 4 KEY
D>ACCOM TEXT 2
D>EXTNSION INTEGER
D>PATIENTN INTEGER
D>DATEDISH TEXT 8
D>PHYSID TEXT 10 KEY
D>PHYSPHNE TEXT 8
D>ITEMCODE INTEGER KEY
D>DESCRIPT TEXT 15
D>PROCDURE TEXT 15
D>CHARGE DOLLAR
D>TABLES
D>ROOM WITH LOCATION ACCOM EXTNSION PATIENTN
D>PATIENT WITH PATIENTN DATEDISH
D>PHYSCIAN WITH PHYSID PHYSPHNE
D>ITEM WITH ITEMCODE DESCRIPT
D>TREATMNT WITH PHYSID PATIENTN PROCDURE
D>CHARGES WITH PATIENTN ITEMCODE CHARGE
```

(a)

```
D>RULES
D>"Duplicate Location" LOCATION IN ROOM NEA LOCATION IN ROOM
D>"Duplicate Patient" PATIENTN IN PATIENT NEA PATIENTN IN PATIENT
D>"Duplicate Physician" PHYSID IN PHYSCIAN NEA PHYSID IN PHYSCIAN
D>"Duplicate Item" ITEMCODE IN ITEM NEA ITEMCODE IN ITEM
D>"Charge Too Large" CHARGE IN CHARGES LT 10000
D>"Charge Too Small" CHARGE IN CHARGES GE 10
D>"Invalid Item-code" ITEMCODE IN ITEM GE 300 AND +
D>                    ITEMCODE IN ITEM LT 8000
D>"Physician Does Not Exist" PHYSID IN TREATMNT EQA PHYSID IN PHYSCIAN
D>"Patient Does Not Exist" PATIENTN IN TREATMNT EQA PATIENTN IN PATIENT
D>"Patient Does Not Exist" PATIENTN IN CHARGES EQA PATIENTN IN PATIENT
D>"Item Does Not Exist" ITEMCODE IN CHARGES EQA ITEMCODE IN ITEM
D>"Patient# Must Exist" PATIENTN IN PATIENT EXISTS
D>"Location Must Exist" LOCATION IN ROOM EXISTS
D>"Physician ID Must Exist" PHYSID IN PHYSCIAN EXISTS
D>"Item-Code Must Exist" ITEMCODE IN ITEM EXISTS
```

(b)

```
R>
R>LIST RULES
  RULE checking = ON
RULE    1  LOCATION IN ROOM NEA LOCATION IN ROOM
  Message: Duplicate Location
RULE    2  PATIENTN IN PATIENT NEA PATIENTN IN PATIENT
  Message: Duplicate Patient
RULE    3  PHYSID IN PHYSCIAN NEA PHYSID IN PHYSCIAN
  Message: Duplicate Physician
RULE    4  ITEMCODE IN ITEM NEA ITEMCODE IN ITEM
  Message: Duplicate Item
RULE    5  CHARGE IN CHARGES LT 10000
  Message: Charge Too Large
RULE    6  CHARGE IN CHARGES GE 10
  Message: Charge Too Small
RULE    7  ITEMCODE IN ITEM GE 300
      AND  ITEMCODE IN ITEM LT 8000
  Message: Invalid Item-code
RULE    8  PHYSID IN TREATMNT EQA PHYSID IN PHYSCIAN
  Message: Physician Does Not Exist
RULE    9  PATIENTN IN TREATMNT EQA PATIENTN IN PATIENT
  Message: Patient Does Not Exist
RULE   10  PATIENTN IN CHARGES EQA PATIENTN IN PATIENT
  Message: Patient Does Not Exist
RULE   11  ITEMCODE IN CHARGES EQA ITEMCODE IN ITEM
  Message: Item Does Not Exist
RULE   12  PATIENTN IN PATIENT EXIS
  Message: Patient# Must Exist
RULE   13  LOCATION IN ROOM EXIS
  Message: Location Must Exist
RULE   14  PHYSID IN PHYSCIAN EXIS
  Message: Physician ID Must Exist
RULE   15  ITEMCODE IN ITEM EXIS
  Message: Item-Code Must Exist
R>
```

(c)

Figure 15-3 (continued)

the ability to cluster close together in secondary memory related rows from different tables. Another physical control, use of a variety of file organizations tuned to the type of data base processing to be encountered, is usually not available on PCs, since PC operating systems typically have only sequential and relative record random accessing.

Typical of the indexing capability is the dBASE III Plus INDEX command, which creates an index file (that is, a file for the index table) on a specified field of some table. Index entries are maintained in alphabetical, chronological, or numerical order (depending on the data type). The placement of actual data records is unaffected by indexing. Logical and long text (memo) data type fields may not be indexed. Primary keys can be specified by requiring index entries to be unique. For example, an index on the LOCATION field of the ROOM table of the Mountain View Community Hospital data base would be specified by

```
. INDEX ON LOCATION TO LOCINDEX UNIQUE
```

Concatenated key indexes may be created by forming one key expression involving string operators to append the different fields together. For example, to form a concatenated (primary) key index on PATIENTNO and ITEM_CODE in the CHARGES table, the dBASE command would be

```
. INDEX ON STR(PATIENTNO) + STR(ITEM_CODE) TO CHGINDEX
  UNIQUE
```

The STR() function converts the numeric PATIENTNO and ITEM_CODE into character strings to form the index value. The INDEX command causes the current contents of the table to be indexed. As long as an index is open, it will be updated whenever the associated base table is changed. If one forgets to open an associated index for a table and the table is updated, a REINDEX command will update the index contents without creating a new index. Updating a file with all indexes open can significantly delay update times, so a user may elect not to open all indexes during file updating; updates to the index are then in a sense batch processed via the REINDEX command.

Indexes are opened when the associated table is put into use by dBASE. To use a particular table in dBASE, one must enter a USE command. For example, to use the CHARGES table and open with it the CHGINDEX index table, one would enter the following command:

```
. SELECT 1
. USE CHARGES INDEX CHGINDEX
```

Each table is put to use in a particular buffer area (in this case buffer 1). Until the CHARGES table is closed, the CHGINDEX can be used to provide rapid access to rows of the CHARGES table by qualifications on values for the concatenated key index.

View Definition

As defined in Chapter 14, a view is a virtual table composed of columns from one or more related tables. It is a way to give the user the impression of manipulating data from just one table and, hence, making data manipulation easier. Views are fairly recent constructs in most PC-RDBMSs. ORACLE has had a view capability since the product's inception, dBASE III Plus includes such a facility, and a view feature has been introduced into R:base in Version V.

dBASE III Plus allows up to nine tables to be used to build a view. Any indexes on a base table of a view are automatically included in the view (recall from Chapter 14 that data are still stored in the base tables, and the view table data are virtually built into single table form whenever the view table is referenced). dBASE requires that the different base tables of a view be defined along a linear chain or single path through all the base tables of the view.

For example, if the ITEM, CHARGES, and PATIENT tables of the Mountain View Community Hospital data base are to be used to form a view, then the view could be defined as a chain of relations from ITEM to CHARGES (linking on the common value of ITEM_CODE), and then from CHARGES to PATIENT (linking on the common value of PATIENTNO). Further, dBASE requires that the domain in the table to which the view is chaining (e.g., ITEM_CODE for the link from ITEM to CHARGES) must be indexed. This chain can be specified from the CREATE VIEW menus or by the use of a series of SET RELATION commands in the dBASE command language. The CREATE VIEW options menu or the SET FIELDS TO command in the command language can be used to include only selected fields (columns) in the view.

One can specify that only selected records (rows) from a base table are to be included in the view; this is accomplished in the CREATE VIEW options menu or by using the SET FILTER TO command. Once all the view specifications have been entered, the user exits the CREATE VIEW menu and saves the current view definition; in the command language, the CREATE VIEW FROM ENVIRONMENT can be used to save the view. Figure 15-4 illustrates a definition of a view; Figure 15-4a is an example of the view table (with columns from three base tables) and Figure 15-4b shows the dBASE III Plus command language commands that could be used to specify this view (here the CREATE viewname VIEW FROM ENVIRONMENT option is used rather than the CREATE VIEW menus).

Figure 15-4b begins with three SELECT workarea and USE tablename commands to establish which tables are involved in the view. Since a table being related to must be indexed on the domain used for linking tables, two index commands are needed to establish an ITEM_CODE index on the CHARGES table (to link from ITEM to CHARGES) and a PATIENTNO index on the PATIENT table (to link from CHARGES to PATIENT). After building each index, the table must be put into USE again, this time indicating that an index file should be opened along with the table file, before the SET RELATION command to link the tables is issued. SET FIELDS commands are then used to limit the view to only selected columns from each table and, to illustrate, a SET FILTER command limits the view to only items with codes greater than or equal to 200 and under 400. The DISPLAY STATUS is shown only as a convenience to verify that the view definition components have been accepted by dBASE. Finally, the CREATE VIEW command is issued to establish the view definition.

Figure 15-4
Example of a view in dBASE III Plus:
(a) example view table
(b) dBASE view definition

PATIENTNO	DATE_DISH	ITEM_CODE	DESCRIPTION	CHARGE

(a)

```
. SELECT 1
. USE ITEM
. SELECT 2
. USE CHARGES
. SELECT 3
. USE PATIENT
.
. SELECT 1
. DISPLAY STRUCTURE
Structure for database  :  C:ITEM.dbf
Number of data records:        0
Date of last update      :  11/29/86
Field  Field Name    Type        Width   Dec
    1  ITEM_CODE     Numeric         6
    2  DESCRIPT      Character      15
** Total **                         22
```

(a)

```
. SELECT 2
. DISPLAY STRUCTURE
Structure for database  :  C:CHARGES.dbf
Number of data records:           0
Date of last update      :  11/29/86
Field  Field Name    Type        Width   Dec
    1  PATIENTNO     Numeric         6
    2  ITEM_CODE     Numeric         6
    3  CHARGE        Numeric         7     2
** Total **                         20


. INDEX ON ITEM_CODE TO ITEMNDX
 100% indexed                  0 Records indexed
. SELECT 2
. USE CHARGES INDEX ITEMNDX
. SELECT 1
. SET RELATION TO ITEM_CODE INTO CHARGES

. SELECT 3
. DISPLAY STRUCTURE
Structure for database  :  C:PATIENT.dbf
Number of data records:        0
Date of last update      :  11/29/86
Field  Field Name    Type        Width   Dec
    1  PATIENTNO     Numeric         6
    2  DATE_DISH     Character       8
** Total **                         15
```

(b)

Figure 15-4
(continued)

```
. INDEX ON PATIENTNO TO PATNDX
  100% indexed                0 Records indexed
. SELECT 3
. USE PATIENT INDEX PATNDX
. SELECT 2
. SET RELATION TO PATIENTNO INTO PATIENT

. SELECT 1
. SET FIELDS TO ITEM_CODE,DESCRIPT
. SELECT 2
. SET FIELDS TO CHARGE,PATIENTNO,ITEM_CODE
. SELECT 3
. SET FIELDS TO PATIENTNO,DATE_DISH
. SET FIELDS ON
. SELECT 2
. SET FILTER TO ITEM_CODE >=200 .AND. ITEM_CODE <400

. DISPLAY STATUS

Select area:   1, Database in Use:   C:ITEM.dbf    Alias:  ITEM
    Related into: CHARGES
    Relation: ITEM_CODE

Currently Selected Database:
Select area:   2, Database in Use:   C:CHARGES.dbf    Alias:  CHARGES
    Master index file:  C:ITEMNDX.ndx    Key:  ITEM_CODE
Filter:  ITEM_CODE >=200 .AND. ITEM_CODE <400
   Related into:  PATIENT
   Relation:  PATIENTNO

Select area:   3, Database in Use:   C:PATIENT.dbf    Alias:  PATIENT
    Master index file:  C:PATNDX.ndx    Key:  PATIENTNO

File search path:
Default disk drive:  C:
Print destination:  PRN:
Margin =   0
Current work area =      2


. CREATE VIEW BILL FROM ENVIRONMENT
```

(b) (continued)

With relational calculus, the view shown in Figure 15-4 can be created with a single command, such as:

```
CREATE VIEW DETAILED-BILL
  AS SELECT (PATIENTNO,DATE_DISH,ITEM_CODE,
             DESCRIPTION, CHARGE)
  FROM ITEM,CHARGES,PATIENT
  WHERE PATIENT.PATIENTNO = CHARGES.PATIENTNO
    AND ITEM-ITEM_CODE     = CHARGES.ITEM_CODE
```

This example illustrates the power of relational calculus (typical of mainframe RDBMSs and of ORACLE) compared to relational algebra (typical of PC-RDBMSs).

Data Dictionary Access

Most PC-RDBMSs store data definitions in specially defined tables that are allocated to a data base when it is created (thus, an R:base user may not, for example, have a real data table called RULES since a table with this name is automatically created to store rule definitions). dBASE also has a feature called a catalog that allows tables and associated screen forms, labels, reports, and other definitions to be logically grouped, usually because of their common use in applications. This helps to isolate not only data manipulation but also definition access to only relevant portions of all the data maintained.

Table 15-2 lists and defines the various data definition access and manipulation commands built into dBASE III Plus, R:base 5000, and ORACLE. This table also indicates the predefined data definition tables created by each package, which, because these are tables to the DBMS, can be accessed, displayed, and changed just like any other data base table.

DATA MANIPULATION IN RELATIONAL ALGEBRA

Relational algebra–based data manipulation languages were, historically, the first type of "programming language" developed for the relational data model (see Codd 1970). Relational algebra uses certain primitive operators (select, project, join, union, product, and others) that take tables as input and produce tables as output. Each operator performs its data manipulation on one or two tables at a time (that is, all operators are unary or binary). Thus, queries that involve more than two tables have to be broken into a series of binary (or unary) algebra commands.

Relational algebra languages are special-purpose languages. That is, they are basically self-contained languages that are by themselves sufficient for a wide variety of data retrieval and maintenance operations. These languages are relation-at-a-time (or set) languages in which all tuples, possibly

Table 15-2 PC-DBMS Data Definition Access Commands

Explanation	dBASE III Plus	R:base 5000	ORACLE**
Show complete definition of a table	DISPLAY STRUCTURE	LIST tablname	SELECT * FROM COL WHERE TNAME = 'tablename'
Show complete definition of all tables	N/A	LIST ALL	**
Show names of all tables in data base	N/A	LIST TABLES	SELECT * FROM TAB WHERE TABTYPE = 'TABLE'
Show names of all columns in data base	N/A	LIST COLUMNS	SELECT * FROM COL
Show names of all data bases	N/A	LIST DATABASES	**
Show information about active/open data base	DISPLAY STATUS	N/A	N/A
Show all rules applied to current data base	N/A	LIST RULES	N/A
Change table definition	MODIFY STRUCTURE		
—rename a column		RENAME COLUMN oldname TO newname IN tablename	N/A
—change column definition		CHANGE COLUMN colname IN tablename TO newspec	ALTER TABLE tablename MODIFY newcolspec
—add new column		EXPAND tablename WITH colname newspec	ALTER TABLE tablename ADD colspec
Change table name	RENAME oldname newname	RENAME TABLE oldname newname	N/A
Delete table from data base	ERASE tablename	REMOVE tablename	DROP TABLE tablename
Duplicate structure of a table	COPY STRUCTURE TO newtablename	N/A	N/A
Store table definition in another table	COPY TO tabledefname STRUCTURE EXTENDED	N/A	N/A
Define new table from stored table definition	CREATE newtablename FROM tabledefname	N/A	N/A

**Since all definitions are stored in tables, the proper SELECT command can retrieve any data definition, even those qualified by who created, who may access, and so on.

Table 15-3 Summary of Relational Retrieval Operators in dBASE III Plus and R:base 5000

Explanation	dBASE III	R:base 5000
Single-Table Operators		
Compute the mean of a domain or an expression of domains for specified rows	AVERAGE	COMPUTE . . . AVE
Display the number of rows in a table (with specified qualification)	COUNT	COMPUTE . . . COUNT (qualified) COMPUTE . . . ROWS (unqualified)
Display the row with the minimum (maximum) column value	N/A	COMPUTE . . . MIN (COMPUTE . . . MAX)
Display sum of a column or an expression of domains for specified rows	SUM	COMPUTE . . . SUM
Display distribution of values for a specified column	N/A	TALLY
Display selected columns of a table for qualified rows	DISPLAY or LIST	SELECT PROJECT (to store result in a table) —both commands can involve sorting)
Position row pointer of table to first row with specified value	FIND (indexed col.) LOCATE (unindexed)	N/A
Position row pointer of table on specific relative row in table	GO TO	N/A
Cause current row pointer to advance or back up a specified number of rows	SKIP	NEXT
Create a row-ordered copy of a table	SORT TO	(sorting part of SELECT command)
Create a summary table with subtotals by key value	TOTAL TO	(requires report definition)
Copy a table into another table	COPY TO	COPY
Two-Table Operators		
Join of two tables into a third table	JOIN (only = comparison)	JOIN (permits noncomparison)
Intersection of two tables into a third table	N/A	INTERSECT
Difference of two tables into a third table	N/A	SUBTRACT
Union of two tables into a third table	N/A	UNION

from several relations, are manipulated in one language statement without explicit looping.

The basic relational algebra commands were introduced in the first major paper published by Codd (1970) on the relational model and are common, in some form, to all relational algebra systems. SELECT (originally called restriction), PROJECT, and JOIN were described in Codd's paper and have been discussed in Chapter 6. Other relational algebra operators are union, difference, intersection, and product. Table 15-3 lists the most frequently used relational operators found in dBASE III Plus and R:base 5000 (remember, ORACLE is an SQL calculus language).

Single-Table Algebra Commands

Single-table operators are used to display in table form all or some row or column subsets of a specified data base table. As an option, some systems allow the result to be stored as a new data base table. The ability to store the result as a table means that one result can be used in another operation without the need to manipulate the original, larger table. This can mean significant operational time savings. However, storing the result of an operation in a table creates redundant data and this "intermediate" table should be treated as transient and destroyed as soon as possible after it is no longer useful (since there is no guarantee that the intermediate table will remain consistent with the table(s) from which it was created).

Figure 15-5 contains several examples of single-table algebra commands for dBASE III Plus and R:base 5000. The Mountain View Community Hospital data base defined in Figure 15-3 for R:base 5000 is used in these examples (some of the definitions for this data base in dBASE III are shown in Figure 15-4). The major difference between dBASE and R:base syntax is that some results that can be produced in one R:base command must be produced by more than one dBASE command. This is primarily, but not exclusively, due to the fact that there is a separate dBASE USE command—the table name is not embedded within a command, as is done in R:base.

Figure 15-5
dBASE III Plus and R:base 5000 single-table command examples

dBASE III Plus	R:base 5000
Display the identifiers of physicians who have treated patient with patient number 1234.	
.USE TREATMEN .LIST ALL PHYSID FOR PATIENTNO = 1234	R>SELECT PHYSID FROM TREATMNT WHERE PATIENTN = 1234

(continued)

Figure 15-5
(continued)

Display the number of procedures that have been performed on patient with patient number 1234.
(See Figure 14-4 for calculus versions of this query)

dBASE III Plus	R:base 5000
.USE TREATMEN .COUNT ALL FOR PATIENTNO = 1234	R>COMPUTE COUNT PATIENTN FROM TREATMNT WHERE PATIENTN = 1234

Display the total charges for patient with patient number 1234.

dBASE III Plus	R:base 5000
.USE CHARGES .SUM CHARGE FOR PATIENTNO= 1234	R>COMPUTE SUM CHARGE FROM CHARGES WHERE PATIENTN= 1234

Display by procedure the patient number (in numerical order) for those patients given that procedure.

dBASE III Plus	R:base 5000
.USE TREATMEN .SORT TO TSORT ON PROCEDURE, PATIENTNO .USE TSORT .LIST ALL PROCEDURE, PATIENTNO	R>SELECT PROCDURE,PATIENTN FROM TREATMNT SORTED BY PROCDURE, PATIENTN

Display the patient numbers in order for those patients that have been charged more than $300 for item 307.
(See Figure 14-4 for calculus versions of this query)

dBASE III Plus	R:base 5000
.USE CHARGES .SORT TO SCHG ON PATIENTNO .USE SCHG .LIST ALL PATIENTNO FOR ITEM_CODE = 307 .AND. CHARGE > 300.00	R>SELECT PATIENTN FROM CHARGES SORTED BY PATIENTN WHERE ITEMCODE = 307 AND CHARGE > 300.00

JOIN—THE HEART OF RELATIONAL ALGEBRA

The **JOIN** operator requires special attention for two reasons. First, it is the most powerful of the algebra operators frequently implemented in relational DBMSs. Second, although only two types of JOINs, the equi-JOIN and the natural JOIN, appear in most relational algebra implementations (and are implied in many relational calculus implementations), other more general JOIN operators have been defined (see Chapter 14 for a discussion of these different types of JOINs).

With the equi- and natural JOINs, tuples from the two relations being joined (that is, JOIN is a binary operator) are concatenated only if they have common values in matching columns (matching columns must have the same domains and, in some systems, must also have the same column name). With the natural JOIN (e.g., dBASE III Plus without the use of the FIELDS clause to change the result), these common columns are redundantly kept in the resulting relation; with the equi-JOIN (e.g., R:base 5000) only one of the redundant, matching columns is kept. PROJECTion can be combined into this concatenation by restricting the resultant table to only certain columns. Some systems will, in this case, automatically eliminate duplicate tuples; others, such as R:base, leave to the discretion of the user the decision whether to use the DELETE DUPLICATES command.

Figure 15-6 contains some examples of JOINs in both dBASE and R:base. Both dBASE and R:base permit the columns over which joining is to occur to have different names in the two tables. The "B – > column name" notation in the dBASE examples is a prefix that indicates that the column name is from the table in buffer 2, or the B buffer. R:base allows joining over other than just equality of common domains, whereas dBASE supports only equality. dBASE allows the user to specify that only selected columns are to be included in the resultant table, whereas R:base automatically includes all columns from both tables (the common column appears only once); a subsequent PROJECT command is necessary in R:base to accomplish the same effect. dBASE, but not R:base, supports row qualifications in either table, which allows only qualified rows to be joined (e.g., to only join CHARGES and ITEM tables for selected patients). dBASE supports joining on multiple columns (that is, joining on a concatenated key), but R:base does not. Finally, the last example in Figure 15-6 indicates what has to be done in relational algebra to join data from more than two tables.

Although the need for joining on other than equality is rare, the requirement may arise. Consider the following two relations:

CURRENT-SALES	
PRODUCT#	SALES-YTD
1234	10000
3256	8000
5426	12000
6788	9500
7392	6600

PAST-SALES	
YEAR	AVG-TOTAL-SALES
1980	9000
1981	11000
1982	10500

Figure 15-6
Examples of relational algebra JOINs in dBASE III Plus and R:base 5000

dBASE III Plus	R:base 5000

Create a new table containing data on the phone numbers of physicians and what procedures they have performed on what patients. (See Figure 14-4 for calculus versions of this query)

dBASE III Plus:

```
.SELECT 2
.USE PHYSCIAN
.SELECT 1
.USE TREATMEN
.JOIN WITH PHYSCIAN TO
 PHONETBL
 FOR PHYSID = B->PHYSID
 FIELDS PHYSID, B->PHYSPHNE
      PATIENTNO, PROCEDURE
```

R:base 5000:

```
R>JOIN PHYSCIAN USING PHYSID
     WITH TREATMNT USING PHYSID
     FORMING PHTBL
R>PROJECT PHONETBL FROM PHTBL
     USING PHYSID, PHYSPHNE,
               PATIENTN, PROCDURE
```

Create a new table containing location and patient number for each patient that has been charged for item 307.

dBASE III Plus:

```
.SELECT 2
.USE CHARGES
.SELECT 1
.USE ROOM
.JOIN WITH CHARGES TO PLACE
 FOR PATIENTNO = B->PATIENTNO
 .AND. B->ITEM_CODE = 307
 FIELDS PATIENTNO, LOCATION
```

R:base 5000:

```
R>JOIN CHARGES USING PATIENTN
     WITH ROOM USING PATIENTN
     FORMING PL
R>PROJECT PLACE FROM PL
     USING PATIENTN, LOCATION
     WHERE ITEMCODE = 307
```

Create a new table containing physician identification, physician phone, patient identification, and date discharged for all treatments on all patients.

dBASE III Plus:

```
.SELECT 2
.USE PATIENT
.SELECT 1
.USE TREATMEN
.JOIN WITH PATIENT TO PT
 FOR PATIENTNO = B->PATIENTNO
 FIELDS PATIENTNO, PHYSID,
   B->DATE_DISH
.SELECT 2
.USE PHYSCIAN
.SELECT 1
.USE PT
.JOIN WITH PHYSCIAN TO RESULT
 FOR PHYSID = B->PHYSID
 FIELDS PATIENTNO, DATE_DISH,
   PHYSID, B->PHYSPHNE
```

R:base 5000:

```
R>JOIN PATIENT USING PATIENTN
     WITH TREATMNT USING
     PATIENTN  FORMING PL

R>JOIN PHYSCIAN USING PHYSID
     WITH PL USING PHYSID
     FORMING PL2
R>PROJECT RESULT FROM PL2
     USING PATIENTN, DATEDISH,
       PHYSID, PHYSPHNE
```

If we wanted to know what products, to date, have exceeded prior average total product sales, in R:base 5000 we could

```
JOIN CURRENT-SALES USING SALES-YTD
   WITH PAST-SALES USING AVG-TOTAL-SALES
   FORMING WINNERS WHERE GT
```

and the resulting table would be

WINNERS

PRODUCT#	SALES-YTD	YEAR	AVG-TOTAL-SALES
1234	10000	1980	9000
5426	12000	1980	9000
5426	12000	1981	11000
5426	12000	1982	10500
6788	9500	1980	9000

There are other types of JOINs, but these are not commonly implemented in commercial packages. Refer to Codd (1970), Date (1981), and Ullman (1980) for a discussion of these other types. In addition, these references define other relational algebra operators that are also not typically implemented.

OTHER MULTIPLE-TABLE OPERATIONS

Although not present in many relational algebra systems, there are several other multiple-table (two-table) operators present in some PC-RDBMSs [these operators were introduced by Codd (1970)]. R:base 5000 has several of these operators, as previously indicated in Table 15-3. We will illustrate these operators using R:base 5000.

Union

In general, with **union,** two tables that have corresponding columns with identical domains can be merged into one table with duplicate tuples eliminated. Two tables that have the same number of columns and corresponding columns with identical domains are called **union compatible.**

R:base redefines these general restrictions. In R:base, the two tables need only have one column in common, although more than one is permitted. Thus, the resultant table contains a union of the columns from the two original tables. Also, when the two rows, one from each table, have the same values for the common columns, the two rows are simply attached to one another. Null values are filled in for missing column values for rows from each table that do not have a matching row in the other table. Thus, UNION is similar to JOIN in R:base, except that UNION includes the nonmatching rows as well in the resultant table.

Consider the following example of the PATIENT and ROOM tables from the Mountain View Community Hospital data base:

Room				**Patient**	
LOCATION	ACCOM	EXTNSION	PATIENTN	PATIENTN	DATEDISH
C204	PR	1053	1234	1234	12/07/86
C303	DB	1645	3334	2222	—
B105	PR	7652	2222	3334	12/08/86
				4433	12/02/86

These two tables can be UNIONed over the common PATIENTN column. In R:base this command and the result would be

```
R>UNION PATIENT WITH ROOM FORMING RESULT
```

Result

PATIENTN	DATEDISH	LOCATION	ACCOM	EXTNSION
1234	12/07/86	C204	PR	1053
2222	—	B105	PR	7652
3334	12/08/86	C303	DB	1645
4433	12/02/86	—	—	—

Difference

The **difference** of two tables, A − B, is a third table, C, which contains the tuples that are in A but not in B. We can only perform difference if the two tables are union compatible. Obviously, A − B does not equal B − A. R:base 5000 has such an operator, called SUBTRACT. With R:base, the difference can be restricted to selected columns, in which case only the relations defined by projection on these selected columns need to be union compatible.

Difference (SUBTRACT) is often useful to compare two tables that are the result of other data manipulation statements. For example, in the Mountain View Community Hospital data base, we might first derive table A, which is a list of those patients treated by physician WILCOX, and then derive a similar table, B, for physician HENRY. The difference A − B would be those patients treated by WILCOX but not treated by HENRY. The particular R:base commands to derive tables A and B and to perform the difference would be

```
R>PROJECT A FROM TREATMNT USING PATIENTN WHERE
      PHYSID='WILCOX'
R>PROJECT B FROM TREATMNT USING PATIENTN WHERE
      PHYSID='HENRY'
R>SUBTRACT B FROM A FORMING C USING PHYSID
R>SELECT ALL FROM C
```

Intersection

The **intersection** of two tables is a third table that contains those tuples that are common to both original tables. Again, the tables must be union compatible. R:base 5000 provides a rather general form of INTERSECT, in which possibly selected columns may be used to define common tuples. For example, assume the following two instances of relations:

EMPLOYEE

NAME	DEPT	JOB
Smith	A	Writer
Jones	C	Prgmr
Smith	B	Writer
Franks	C	Writer

SALARY

DEPT	JOB	PAY
A	Writer	1000
B	Writer	700
C	Writer	600

Then

```
R>INTERSECT EMPLOYEE WITH SALARY FORMING CLASSIFIED
        USING DEPT NAME JOB
```

would produce the following table:

CLASSIFIED

DEPT	NAME	JOB
A	Smith	Writer
B	Smith	Writer
C	Franks	Writer

The CLASSIFIED table contains three columns, those named in the USING clause. Matches are made on the common columns, DEPT and JOB, to determine which rows to include in CLASSIFIED. When not all the columns of the intersected tables are used, duplicate rows can result; in this case, R:base provides the DELETE DUPLICATES command for the user, if desired, in order to eliminate duplicate tuples.

ALGEBRA MODIFICATION STATEMENTS

Data base modification commands in relational algebra vary in name among DBMSs. In R:base 5000, the modification commands include the following (equivalent dBASE III Plus commands are listed in parentheses):

LOAD:	Enters additional tuples onto end of a table (APPEND; INSERT to insert new tuple into specified row position)
APPEND:	Copies selected rows from one table into another table (APPEND FROM)
ENTER:	Adds rows to a table using a predefined form

	for data entry (a form can be used for APPEND, CHANGE, and so on by simply opening the form)
CHANGE:	Replaces existing values in tuples with specified new values for tuples that satisfy a selection clause (REPLACE; CHANGE or EDIT used to interactively change values and UPDATE for batch modifications)
EDIT:	Browses through the rows and columns of a table to change values or delete rows (BROWSE)
DELETE ROWS:	Deletes selected rows from a table (DELETE to mark rows for deletion, then PACK to actually delete the marked rows)
DELETE DUPLICATES:	Removes duplicate rows from a relation

An important observation that can be made after reviewing these commands is that they are all *single*-table commands. That is, rows cannot be directly changed or deleted based on relationships with data in other tables. Except in the case where the contents of one table can be loaded into another table, a user must determine pertinent data relationships from one set of commands, record these manually, and then provide the necessary commands to complete the data modification.

For example, suppose we wanted to delete the CHARGES records from the Mountain View Community Hospital data base (see Figure 15-3 for an R:base definition of the data base) for all discharged patients. This could be done in one command in relational calculus by performing an implied JOIN in the WHERE clause of the deletion command. But in R:base, several multiple-step approaches would be possible:

1. Discharged patients could be determined from inquiry on the PATIENT table, and then the list could be used to compose individual DELETE ROWS commands on the CHARGES table for the PATIENTNs identified.
2. A table, say DISCHG, of discharged patients could be generated from a PROJECT command, and a SUBTRACT command could be used to construct a new table, NCHARGES, which would be CHARGES − DISCHG and would have only the desired rows remaining in it.

Although most of these modification commands perform with very natural results, several require elaboration. As indicated, the dBASE III DELETE command for removing rows from a data base file simply marks the rows and the rows are actually removed in a second step upon execution of the PACK command. The RECALL command or special keystrokes in the BROWSE and EDIT commands can unmark rows. The greatest benefit of this two-step process is that it is a safety feature that prevents accidental deletion. Marked records appear in displays of the file contents, but their status as marked for deletion is indicated. Data in marked records are used in numerical and alphabetic operations, just as if they were still active.

One goal of the modification languages is to give the user several options for entering or modifying data; this, the language designers believe, contributes to greater user friendliness (since ease of use is relative to the skills and experience of each user). For this reason, the command list shows several commands for the same basic operation, and also for this reason a given command often has several forms. For example, consider the R:base LOAD command for adding rows to a table. The full syntax of this command is

```
                 ┌ WITH PROMPTS             ┐
LOAD tablename   │ FROM filename            │   [USING columnlist]
                 └ FROM filename AS ASCII   ┘
```

where none or one of the items in each set of brackets may be used. As an option via the USING clause, a user can choose to load values for selected columns or to rearrange the order of column data entry into any convenient sequence—not just the order used in the table definition. In the basic LOAD tablename form, the user has to enter both the column names and values in the desired entry order (useful when each row has variable missing columns). The WITH PROMPTS option causes R:base to display the column names to remind the user of what data are to be entered. The two FROM options allow batch data entry from external data files. The ENTER and APPEND commands provide additional options for data entry.

Also common in most data modification languages is the ability to conduct a full-screen browsing of a data base table and to replace in-place selected values. The R:base EDIT command (for display of existing data in typical table row and column format) and EDIT USING command (for browsing via a predefined custom table format) support such full-screen operations. For example, with the EDIT command R:base displays a tabular window on the table for the specified rows and columns to be browsed. The user may scroll up, down, left, or right. When more rows or columns than can fit on the screen are to be browsed, scrolling will rewrite the screen to move a new row or column onto the screen and move another off. Page up and down keys move through the file in complete window segments. Values can be written over or eliminated, new characters in current values can be inserted, or selected current characters deleted. Whole rows can be deleted in one keystroke. Full-screen editing of a file is convenient for reviewing the contents of a file and selectively making changes as errors are found. It is not practical for large files, and it is not efficient if the desired changes can be easily and explicitly specified in CHANGE or DELETE commands.

Transaction and Recovery Control

Most PC-RDBMSs have few if any constructs to assist in recovering corrupt data bases or in rollback of partial transactions. Users of a PC-DBMS should periodically back up or copy critical data base components; a convenient way to do this is to code such backup directly into stored routines so that users do not have to remember to do this.

R:base has three commands that help provide backup protection:

COPY: Works like an operating system copy command to duplicate the contents of one (or several if wild card characters are used) file(s) into another (set of) files

UNLOAD: Converts data and/or data definitions for a complete data base or selected parts for later recovery or transfer to another system

RELOAD: Copies the contents of the active data base into another data base (this is *not* the opposite of UNLOAD)

Both R:base and dBASE III Plus have the ability to log terminal activity into a text file in order to produce an audit trail of data base transactions; however, this audit trail cannot be automatically reapplied in the event it becomes necessary to restore a data base. This feature is, nonetheless, handy for producing documentation or class assignments. In R:base, the command is

OUTPUT filename WITH TERMINAL

This command can be entered at any time during a session. Once executed, R:base will begin to log all command line operations into this file, overwriting any prior contents. Only line-oriented commands and output are logged; interactive or screen-oriented functions cannot be recorded. The equivalent dBASE command is SET ALTERNATE TO filename; logging can be dynamically turned on and off with the SET ALTERNATE ON/OFF command.

Regrettably, the preceding discussion covers all the transaction and recovery controls available in dBASE and R:base, which are typical of PC-RDBMSs. This is clearly an area in which personal computer products have not met the standards of their mainframe counterparts.

USER INTERFACES

One way in which the personal computer industry has led the information systems field is in providing computer system interfaces for the casual and non–data processing professional user. Besides some of the features mentioned previously in this chapter, menu-driven subsystems are now a standard component of PC-RDBMSs.

A menu-driven system displays current options available to the user and prompts the user to enter required parameters or to indicate suboptions. Often the menus are so-called pull-down in form so that new menus appear on the screen to expand a selected alternative. A very important fact to remember about such menu systems is that they do not usually provide all the functionality of the full PC-DBMS command language. For

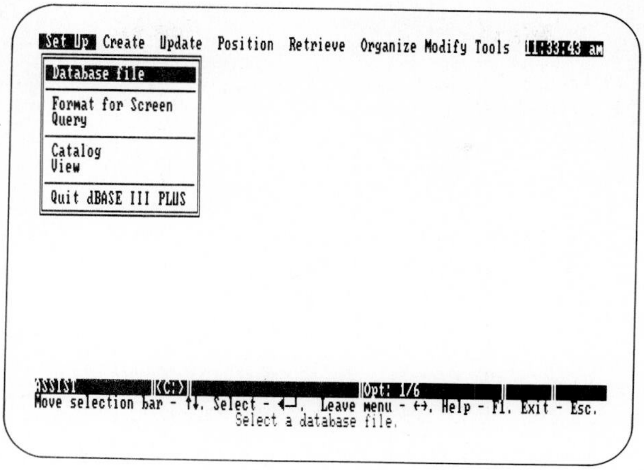

Figure 15-7
dBASE III Plus ASSIST main menu screen

example, the dBASE menu system does not support the JOIN command (yet, the casual user might need the most help in walking through the components of this "advanced" command).

The dBASE III Plus menu system is called The Assistant Menu (or simply ASSIST) and the R:base version is named The Application EXPRESS (or simply EXPRESS). In order to describe the type of features available in such systems, we will use ASSIST to illustrate the style of such user interfaces.

Figure 15-7 shows the initial screen displayed by ASSIST. Submenu names are displayed on the top line and the highlighted item (in this case the Set Up menu) has a pull-down submenu written below it. Cursor control keys can be used to move left and right to select different menus or up and down to select different options in the highlighted menu. Pressing the RETURN key will cause an option to be taken, and most often to display another menu or set of choices. The bottom status lines describe the current defaults and provides very brief prompts on what the user is to do.

The current submenu highlighted is the Set Up menu, which is where a user starts a session. This menu provides options for defining the environment for subsequent processing. The other menus are:

- **Create** menu—supports interactive definition of data base files, reports, mailing labels, and other format type items
- **Update** menu—provides the various data modification functions
- **Position** menu—provides options for positioning the current file row pointer on specific rows, which is necessary for the proper operation of some retrieval and update commands
- **Retrieve** menu—lists the range of single-table data retrieval and manipulation commands
- **Organize** menu—highlights commands for indexing, sorting, and copying tables

Figure 15-8
dBASE III Plus
ASSIST menus

Set Up	Create	Update	Position
Database file	Database file	Append	Seek
Format for Screen	Format	Edit	Locate
Query	View	Display	Continue
Catalog	Query	Browse	Skip
View	Report	Replace	Goto Record
Quit dBASE III	Label	Delete	
		Recall	
		Pack	

Retrieve	Organize	Modify	Tools
List	Index	Database file	Set drive
Display	Sort	Format	Copy file
Report	Copy	View	Directory
Label		Query	Rename
Sum		Report	Erase
Average		Label	List structure
Count			Import
			Export

- **Modify** menu—lists the range of commands that support modification of previously created reports, files, views, and so on
- **Tools** menu—provides a variety of commands dealing with use of the PC and movement of data between the data base and external file systems

Figure 15-8 shows the complete range of options in each of these submenus.

The Set Up menu provides options for indicating which data base table to open, what screen format to use for data entry and modification, what filter or query to use to limit access to records, what catalog of definitions and data base files to use, what view of the data base to use, and when to quit or leave dBASE. Since frequently the first step is to indicate what data base file is to be used, we illustrate in Figure 15-9 the sequence of menus that would be chosen to activate use of the Mountain View Community Hospital TREATMENt data base file.

When the RETURN key is pressed with the highlight bar over the Database file option in Figure 15-7, the screen in Figure 15-9a is displayed to indicate on which diskette or hard-disk drive the data base is to be found. The highlight bar is moved, so that Figure 15-9a indicates that the C: drive option is to be chosen. Then Figure 15-9b shows that the next screen displays the list of files on this drive (if the Catalog option had been chosen beforehand, then only the file names from the chosen catalog would be displayed). The desired file (TREATMEN) is highlighted for subsequent use. Again, note that ASSIST can work with only one file (base or view

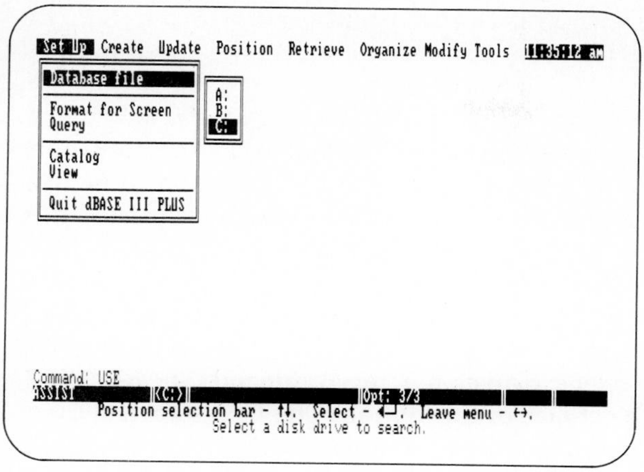

(a)

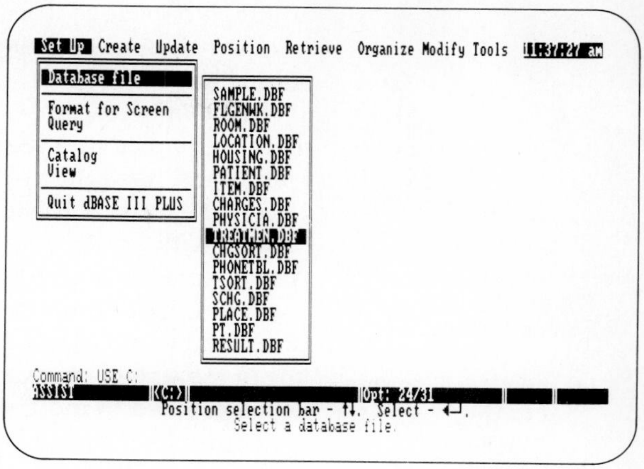

(b)

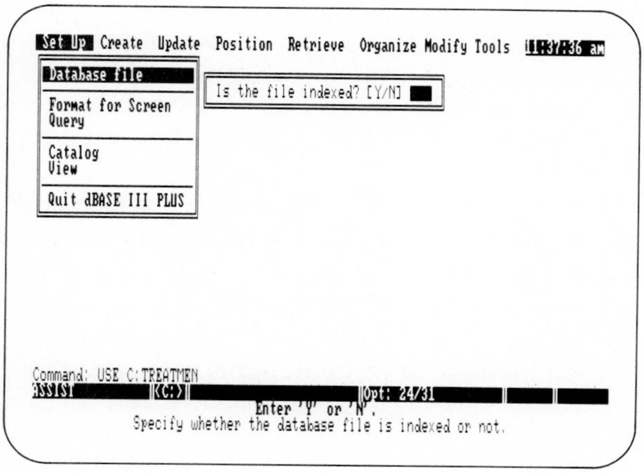

(c)

Figure 15-9
Activating a data base file in dBASE III Plus:
(a) indicating disk drive storage
(b) indicating file
(c) indicating if file is indexed

table) at a time. Finally, in Figure 15-9c the user indicates whether the file is indexed, and if so, the user would be prompted for what indexes to open along with the file.

As we worked through these menus in Figure 15-9 you may have noticed that the actual dBASE command (in this case USE) is being automatically written from the menu options chosen; the constructed command appears on the line labeled Command. This dynamic construction of the structured command helps the user to learn the command language, which is a much more direct way to accomplish the same result. Over time a user will learn dBASE and be able to bypass the somewhat verbose system of menus. However, people who use a variety of software, who are very infrequent users of dBASE, or who use several different PC-DBMSs and cannot remember what commands work in which languages, may only infrequently do anything outside of the menu system. This same pattern of working through a sequence of menus to provide more parameters to dBASE is used in each submenu.

Many options can be demonstrated, but we will illustrate just one Retrieve menu sequence in order to suggest the general style for data manipulation operations. We will use the menu system to develop the query in Figure 15-5 that asks that the identifiers of those physicians who have treated the patient with patient number 1234 be displayed. Figure 15-10 contains the proper screens to produce this query via ASSIST.

Figure 15-10a shows the first Retrieve menu, where the type of retrieval commands are listed. The List command is highlighted, and the bottom line of the screen provides a brief explanation of this command. The RETURN key is pressed to indicate the choice of this option. The next screen shown in Figure 15-10b lists the possible clauses that can be included in a List command, with the scope clause option (which indicates to which physical rows of the table the command should be applied) highlighted as our choice (notice that LIST has been filled in on the Command line). Pressing RETURN to this scope option generates the screen in Figure 15-10c. We will use the default scope, ALL (meaning every record in the file), and continue processing. ASSIST would return to the screen in Figure 15-10b, where we choose the next option in order to construct a list of field names (an implicit projection).

Since we only need to display the physician identifier, we will construct a field list to limit the output to the single desired column; Figure 15-10d shows the screen after choosing the field list option. The highlight bar is placed over the PHYSID field in the box listing all the columns in the TREATMEN table, and the center box provides this column's definition from the built-in data dictionary (this helps the user to verify that this is the desired

Figure 15-10
Query example in dBASE III Plus:
(a) indicating which retrieval command
(b) indicating a new scope is to be developed
(c) indicating choice of default scope (ALL)
(d) indicating which fields to include in result
(e) indicating field to include in row qualification
(f) indicating row qualification on PATIENTNO
(g) indicating value for qualification
(h) indicating end of search condition

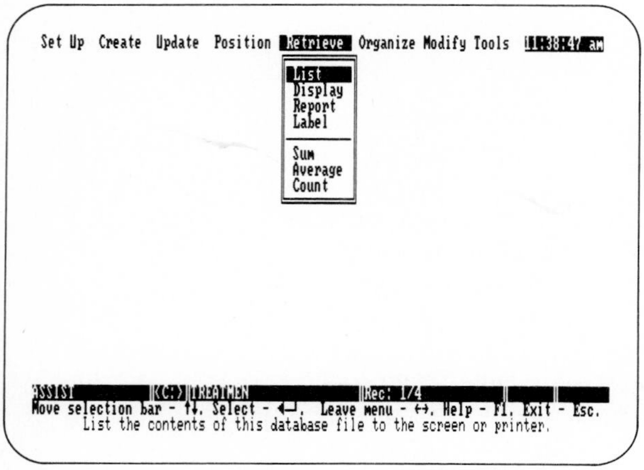

(a)

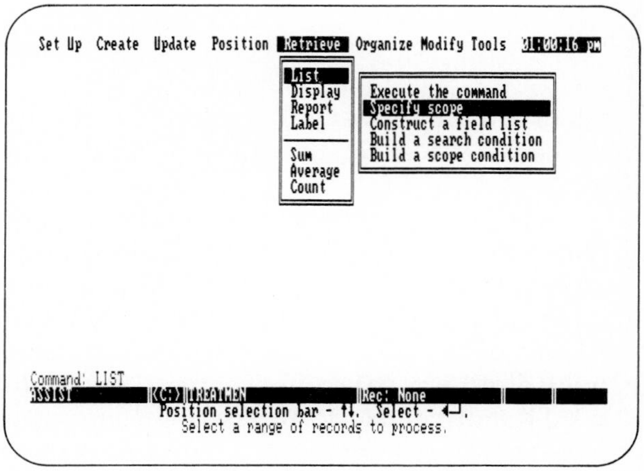

(b)

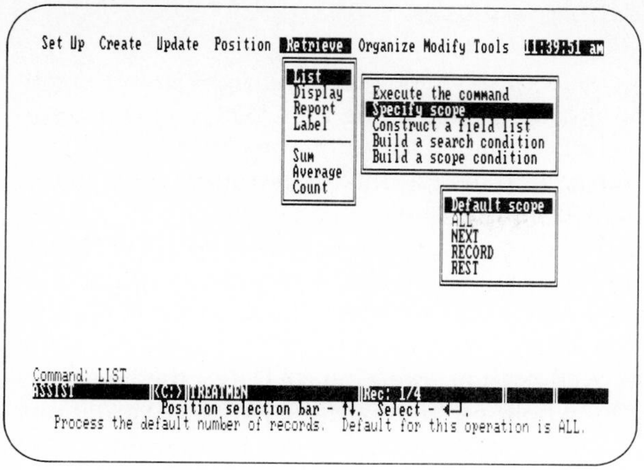
Set Up Create Update Position Retrieve Organize Modify Tools 11:39:51 am
List
Display
Report
Label
Sum
Average
Count
Execute the command
Specify scope
Construct a field list
Build a search condition
Build a scope condition
Default scope
ALL
NEXT
RECORD
REST
Command: LIST
ASSIST <C:> TREATMEN Rec: 1/4
Position selection bar - ↑↓. Select - ↵.
Process the default number of records. Default for this operation is ALL.

(c)

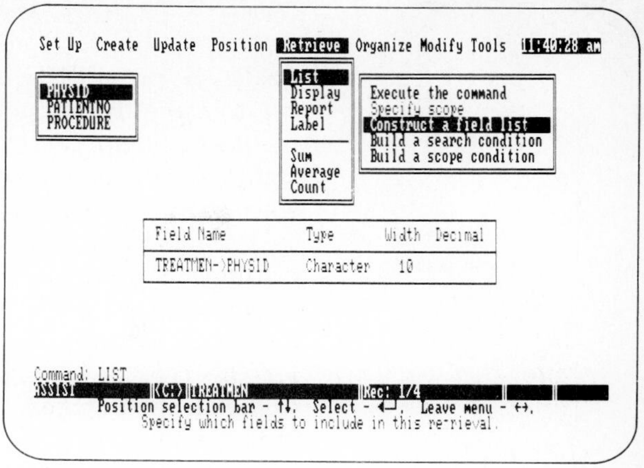
Set Up Create Update Position Retrieve Organize Modify Tools 11:40:28 am
PHYSID
PATIENTNO
PROCEDURE
List
Display
Report
Label
Sum
Average
Count
Execute the command
Specify scope
Construct a field list
Build a search condition
Build a scope condition
Field Name Type Width Decimal
TREATMEN->PHYSID Character 10
Command: LIST
ASSIST <C:> TREATMEN Rec: 1/4
Position selection bar - ↑↓. Select - ↵. Leave menu - ↔.
Specify which fields to include in this retrieval.

(d)

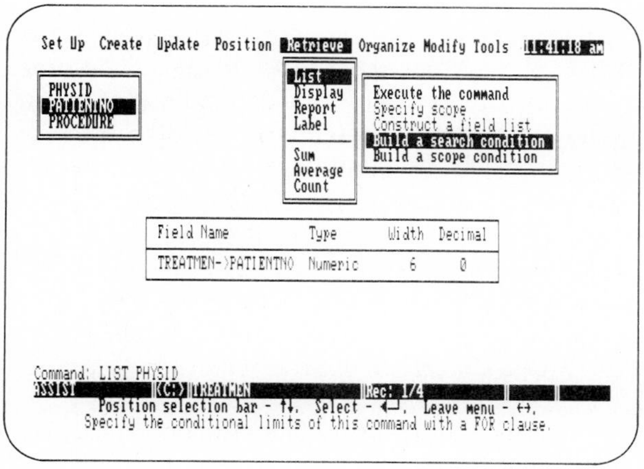
Set Up Create Update Position Retrieve Organize Modify Tools 11:41:18 am
PHYSID
PATIENTNO
PROCEDURE
List
Display
Report
Label
Sum
Average
Count
Execute the command
Specify scope
Construct a field list
Build a search condition
Build a scope condition
Field Name Type Width Decimal
TREATMEN->PATIENTNO Numeric 6 0
Command: LIST PHYSID
ASSIST <C:> TREATMEN Rec: 1/4
Position selection bar - ↑↓. Select - ↵. Leave menu - ↔.
Specify the conditional limits of this command with a FOR clause.

(e)

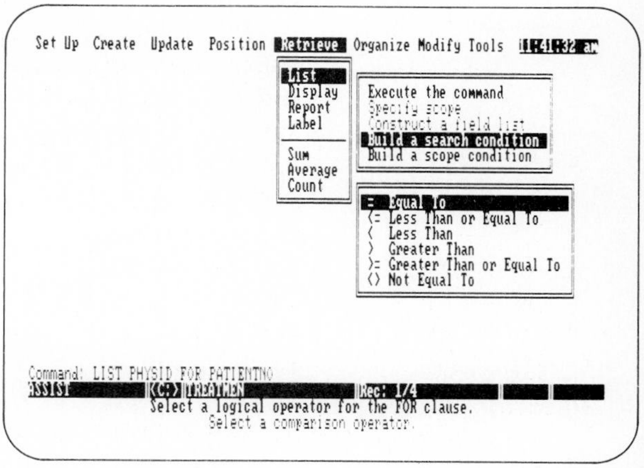
Set Up Create Update Position Retrieve Organize Modify Tools 11:41:32 am
List
Display
Report
Label
Sum
Average
Count
Execute the command
Specify scope
Construct a field list
Build a search condition
Build a scope condition
= Equal To
<= Less Than or Equal To
< Less Than
> Greater Than
>= Greater Than or Equal To
<> Not Equal To
Command: LIST PHYSID FOR PATIENTNO
ASSIST <C:> TREATMEN Rec: 1/4
Select a logical operator for the FOR clause.
Select a comparison operator.

(f)

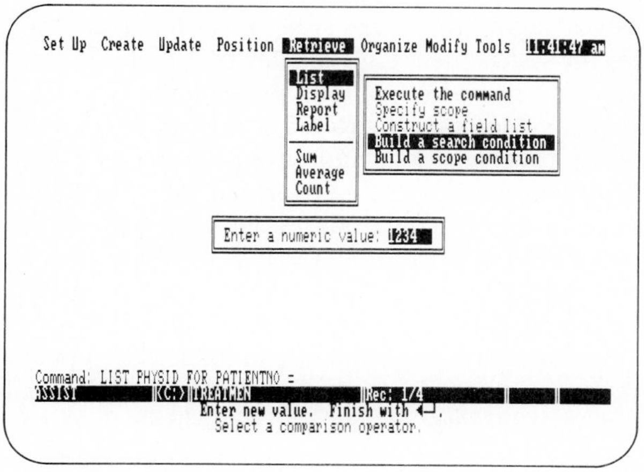
Set Up Create Update Position Retrieve Organize Modify Tools 11:41:47 am
List
Display
Report
Label
Sum
Average
Count
Execute the command
Specify scope
Construct a field list
Build a search condition
Build a scope condition
Enter a numeric value: 1234
Command: LIST PHYSID FOR PATIENTNO =
ASSIST <C:> TREATMEN Rec: 1/4
Enter new value. Finish with ↵.
Select a comparison operator.

(g)

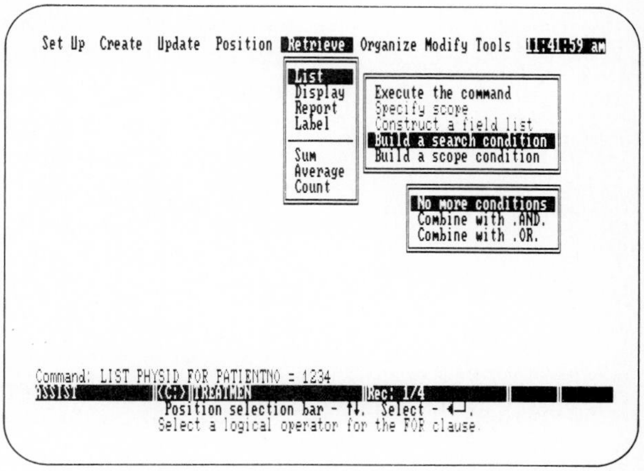
Set Up Create Update Position Retrieve Organize Modify Tools 11:41:59 am
List
Display
Report
Label
Sum
Average
Count
Execute the command
Specify scope
Construct a field list
Build a search condition
Build a scope condition
No more conditions
Combine with .AND.
Combine with .OR.
Command: LIST PHYSID FOR PATIENTNO = 1234
ASSIST <C:> TREATMEN Rec: 1/4
Position selection bar - ↑↓. Select - ↵.
Select a logical operator for the FOR clause.

(h)

field). We press RETURN to select this field, press the right or left arrow key to leave this submenu, and then choose the next clause to complete: the search condition (row selection qualification). Figure 15-10e shows the status of the screen at this point, with the PATIENTNO column highlighted since the query qualification is on this column.

When RETURN is pressed while the highlight bar is on the PATIENTNO column name, the screen in Figure 15-10f appears, to provide options on what comparison operator to apply to the selected column. In this case we choose =, and the screen in Figure 15-10g appears, on which we fill in the PATIENTNO of 1234 for the qualification. Pressing RETURN then leads us to the screen in Figure 15-10h, where we highlight the No more conditions option and press RETURN. Note that the Command line now shows the complete dBASE structured command to be executed. We would then indicate that the command is to be executed, and a table of relevant physician identifiers would appear.

This example emphasizes the verbosity of menu systems as well as the step-by-step approach that can allow an inexperienced user to quickly become functional. The industry trend is clearly to expand the capabilities of menu systems to support more commands and clauses of the underlying command language. The goal is to open DBMS technology to a wider market of users.

FORMS FOR INPUT AND OUTPUT

A **form** is simply a stylized format used to prompt data entry or to display data base contents on a screen. One form can be shown on a screen at a time, and data from usually only one record can be accepted or displayed in a form. A computer form, like a printed invoice or tax form, can contain instructions, can include boxes for highlighting areas to enter data, can have shaded or colored areas for special use (e.g., display only), and might show derived values not actually entered (e.g., total price as the result of multiplying price times quantity). More sophisticated forms management systems might support blinking, reverse video, colored, underline, or high-intensity field displays, as well as multiple screen forms. Some systems even provide data entry validation and can be programmed to display error messages or other prompts depending on the data values entered or displayed. Several different forms might be used to display the contents of the same data base file, where each format is appropriate for a different user or users or when the record has so many fields that not all fields can appear on the screen at the same time.

Most form subsystems permit the user to move from field to field on the screen at will in order to enter or modify data. Special keys can be used to move to the next or prior field, to move between the next or prior character within a field, to insert or delete characters within a field, or to inform the system when to move to the next or prior record in the file for display or entry.

A form is defined in a special language that basically indicates on what row and starting at what column of the screen certain text or field values should be placed. However, the form designer or painter may be able to use a menu-driven system that will allow the designer to develop or paint the form on the screen and then the system will generate the actual form definition code from the visual layout.

Figure 15-11 illustrates the process of describing a form (stored in file TREATED) for entry of data into the TREATMENt file using the dBASE III Plus Assistant Menu system. Only single screen forms can be built this way; the dBASE III programming language can be used to code routines that display multiple screens for the entry or display of data. ASSIST allows the user to design the screen interactively, and it automatically builds the form definition, the code for which is displayed in the last panel of Figure 15-11 for this example.

A screen or form is defined under the Create menu by defining a display Format; the submenu where the format file is named is shown in Figure 15-11a. The data base file to be associated with this form is selected from the Set Up submenu (see Figure 15-11b), and the fields to be used on the form are identified on the Load Fields submenu. In this case, we wish to use all the fields of the TREATMENt file, so each one is marked for inclusion (see Figure 15-11c). We leave this submenu by pressing Function Key 10, and dBASE places us into the default form layout as displayed on its "blackboard" (see Figure 15-11d).

In the initial blackboard layout of the form each field is simply listed on separate lines with the fieldnames as labels. Format symbols of X for alphanumeric and 9 for numeric indicate minimal validation rules for data entry. Although this form would be sufficient for data entry, it is not very aesthetic or informative. It would be easier for a user if the form were titled, more descriptive field labels were used, and the data were placed in a more readable format.

Figure 15-11e shows the result of some simple rearranging of the default format. In this version of the form a title has been added and the lines for the various fields have been separated for readability. This rearrangement was accomplished by inserting blank lines and typing in the title text. Figure 15-11f shows even more formatting—the physician id and patient number fields have been moved to the same line with labels above, a prompt indicating that both values need to be entered (since they form a concatenated key) has been added, and the procedure value has been centered and relabeled.

Figure 15-11f is a rather workable form. Some additional data entry control can be added by restricting the procedure field to a certain style; this is accomplished on the Modify submenu. While the cursor is located over the procedure field, the Modify menu can be accessed by pressing Function Key 10 (to invoke the menu), and moving the highlight bar to the Modify choice. Then pressing RETURN causes the screen in Figure 15-11g

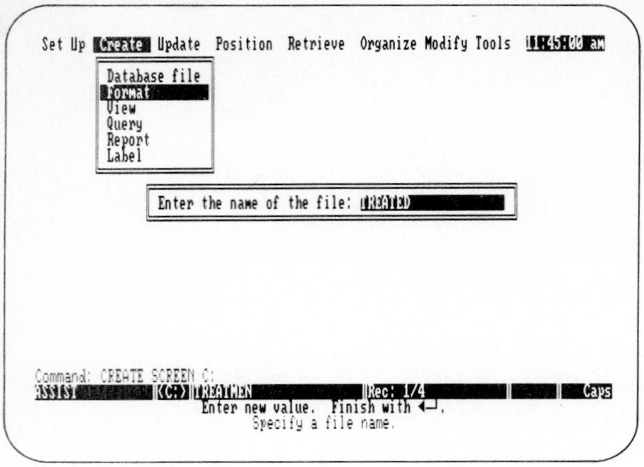
Set Up Create Update Position Retrieve Organize Modify Tools 11:45:00 am
Database file
Format
View
Query
Report
Label
Enter the name of the file: TREATED
Command: CREATE SCREEN C:
ASSIST <C:> TREATMEN Rec: 1/4 Caps
Enter new value. Finish with ←┘.
Specify a file name.

(a)

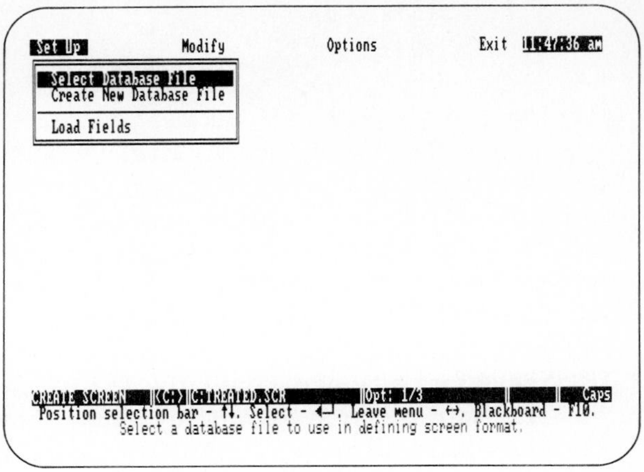
Set Up Modify Options Exit 11:47:36 am
Select Database File
Create New Database File
Load Fields
CREATE SCREEN <C:> C:TREATED.SCR Opt: 1/3 Caps
Position selection bar - ↑↓. Select - ←┘. Leave menu - ↔. Blackboard - F10.
Select a database file to use in defining screen format.

(b)

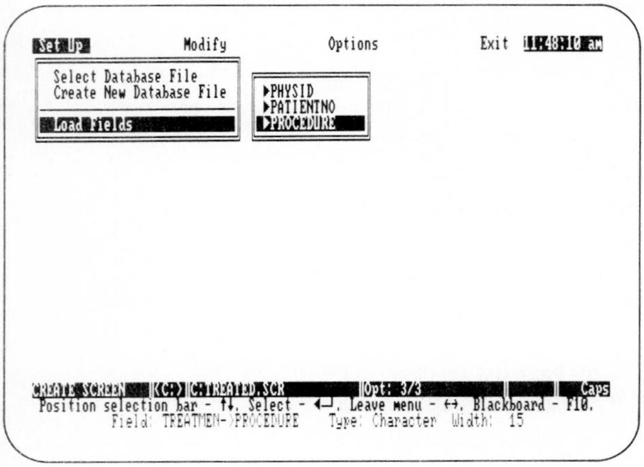
Set Up Modify Options Exit 11:48:10 am
Select Database File
Create New Database File
Load Fields
▸PHYSID
▸PATIENTNO
▸PROCEDURE
CREATE SCREEN <C:> C:TREATED.SCR Opt: 3/3 Caps
Position selection bar - ↑↓. Select - ←┘. Leave menu - ↔. Blackboard - F10.
Field: TREATMEN->PROCEDURE Type: Character Width: 15

(c)

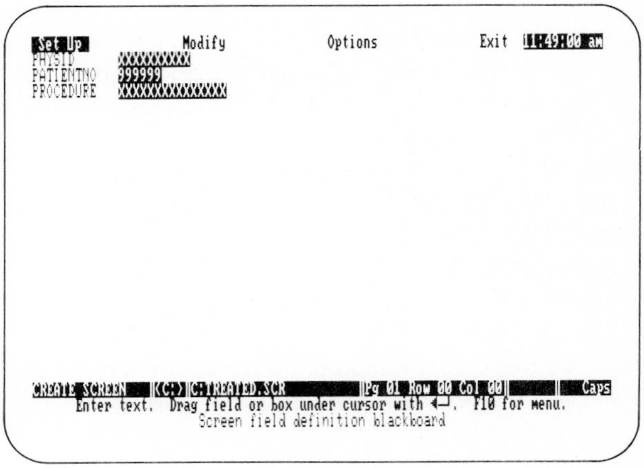
Set Up Modify Options Exit 11:49:00 am
PHYSID XXXXXXXXXX
PATIENTNO 999999
PROCEDURE XXXXXXXXXXXXXXX
CREATE SCREEN <C:> C:TREATED.SCR Pg 01 Row 00 Col 00 Caps
Enter text. Drag field or box under cursor with ←┘. F10 for menu.
Screen field definition blackboard

(d)

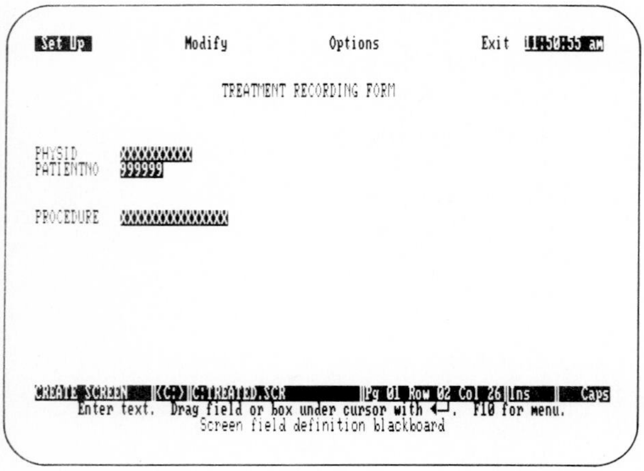
Set Up Modify Options Exit 11:50:55 am
TREATMENT RECORDING FORM
PHYSID XXXXXXXXXX
PATIENTNO 999999
PROCEDURE XXXXXXXXXXXXXXX
CREATE SCREEN <C:> C:TREATED.SCR Pg 01 Row 02 Col 26 Ins Caps
Enter text. Drag field or box under cursor with ←┘. F10 for menu.
Screen field definition blackboard

(e)

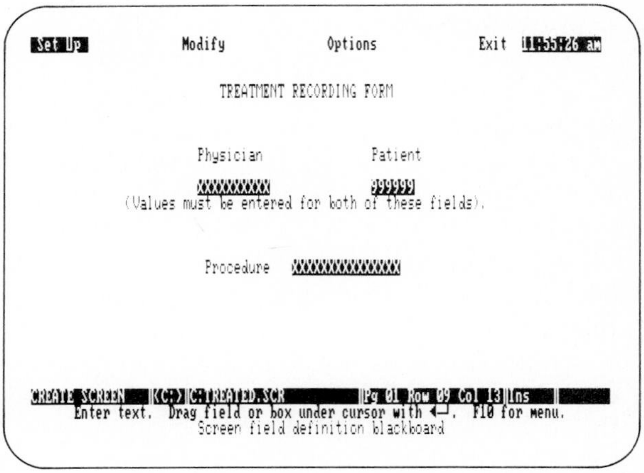
Set Up Modify Options Exit 11:55:26 am
TREATMENT RECORDING FORM
Physician Patient
XXXXXXXXXX 999999
(Values must be entered for both of these fields).
Procedure XXXXXXXXXXXXXXX
CREATE SCREEN <C:> C:TREATED.SCR Pg 01 Row 09 Col 13 Ins
Enter text. Drag field or box under cursor with ←┘. F10 for menu.
Screen field definition blackboard

(f)

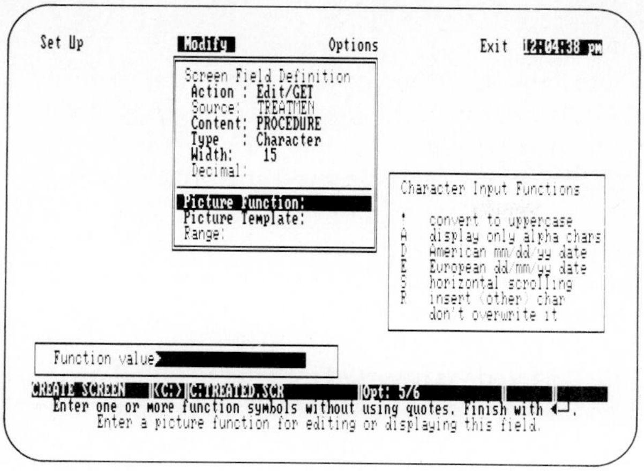

(g)

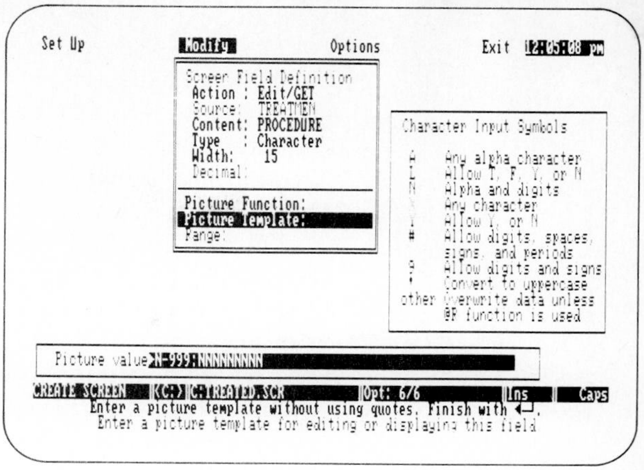

(h)

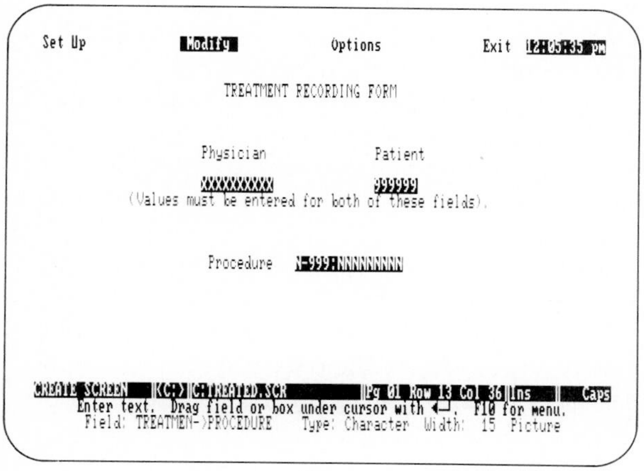

(i)

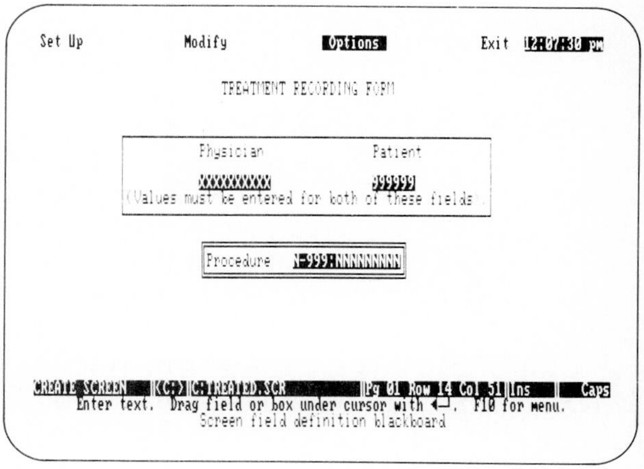

(j)

(k)

```
@  2, 26  SAY "TREATMENT RECORDING FORM"
@  6, 23  SAY "Physician                      Patient"
@  8, 23  GET TREATMEN->PHYSID
@  8, 47  GET TREATMEN->PATIENTNO
@  9, 13  SAY "(Values must be entered for both of these fields)."
@ 13, 24  SAY "Procedure"
@ 13, 36  GET  TREATMEN->PROCEDURE    PICTURE "N-999:NNNNNNNNN"
@  5, 12  TO 10, 63
@ 12, 23  TO 14, 51        DOUBLE
```

Figure 15-11
Form definition example using dBASE III Plus ASSIST:
(a) naming format file
(b) selecting data base file for form
(c) selecting fields for display in form
(d) default form on blackboard
(e) simple rearrangement of default form
(f) use of meaningful labels
(g) field picture specification
(h) field template specification
(i) form with pictures and templates
(j) final form with boxes for highlighting data entry areas
(k) form definition code

to appear. This screen prompts, among other options, the type, width, picture, and template of a field to be changed. As displayed here, the Picture Function has been highlighted, so the character codes for a picture specification are shown. Here a single code can be entered into the Function value box to set a picture for the whole field.

We will use the Picture Template option to establish a character-by-character template for entry of the PROCEDURE field. This is shown in Figure 15-11h, where the Picture Template option is highlighted and the Picture value has been set. The template says that any PROCEDURE value must begin with an alphanumeric, then a fixed - is inserted into the field, followed by three digits. A fixed : is then inserted, and the user can enter up to nine alphanumerics to complete the PROCEDURE value. The - and : will be displayed for the user on the screen and passed over during data entry. After entering this template, pressing Function Key 10 returns the designer to the Blackboard, where the new template for the PROCEDURE field is shown in Figure 5-11i.

One final screen display formatting step is indicated in Figure 15-11j. This figure shows the result of adding single and double line boxes to more clearly indicate different data entry areas on the screen. The boxes were drawn in the Options submenu by indicating whether single or double lines were desired and by placing the cursor at the northwest and southeast corners for the boxes.

The form is now ready for use in data entry or retrieval. We will illustrate the use in data entry. In Figure 15-12a we choose the Append command from the Update menu. Append adds new records/rows to the end of the selected table, TREATMEN. Figure 15-12b shows the data entry screen using the form just developed. Areas for entry of physician id and patient number are highlighted. Since the picture behind the patient number is all numeric,

Figure 15-12
Example of form usage:
(a) selection of command in which form is used
(b) form as displayed to user

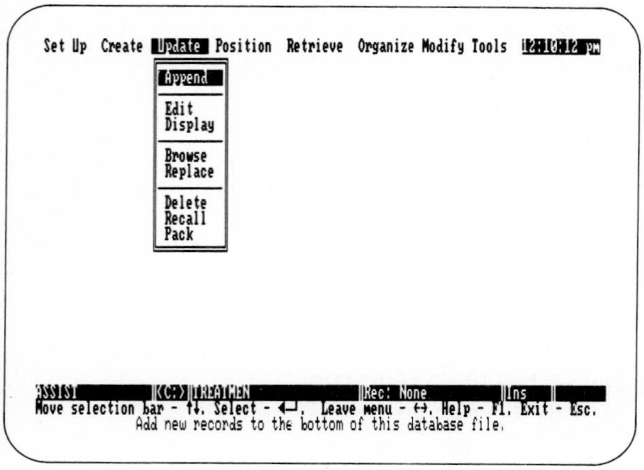

(a)

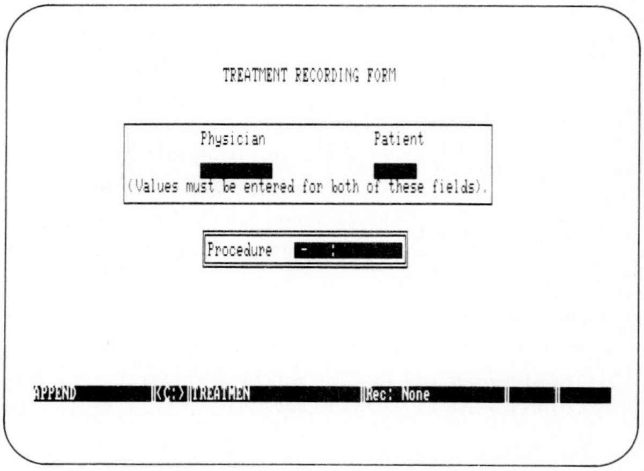

(b)

if the user enters an alphabetic, dBASE will indicate an error. dBASE has also displayed the template for the procedure, and as the user enters characters, the - and : will be skipped, keeping these special characters in their proper place. Further, they cannot be deleted by the user.

Figure 15-11k shows the dBASE form definition code that has been generated by these menu choices. A user, once familiar with this language, can enter a screen definition directly by using such commands. SAY writes a value to the screen at the row and column indicated, and GET accepts a value into a specified field from the data entered at a particular location on the screen. The TO commands draw the boxes, and the PICTURE clause results from the template specification for the PROCEDURE field.

One final note about forms. A dBASE command,

SET CARRY ON/OFF

can be used to control whether data entered onto one screen are carried forward as default values for the next screen. If this flag is ON, then the user will see the values from the last record entered displayed on a new screen. This is very convenient if data are entered in a sorted sequence where only a few values change from record to record.

Most systems analysis textbooks provide guidelines for screen and form displays. Fields should be clearly labeled in a similar fashion within and across screens. To minimize misentry, the sequence of fields should resemble the source documents. Forms should not be cluttered or contain too many fields. For ease of human search, titles, prompts, and help messages should appear in approximately the same location on each form for the same system. Finally, it is advisable that each screen be uniquely identified with some code and that each be marked to indicate whether it is one of several used for the total data entry task (e.g., 3 of 5). When these guidelines are followed and easily readable forms are created, forms data entry and display can contribute to building a user-friendly data base application system.

REPORT GENERATORS

Many PC-RDBMSs also include a subsystem for specifying customized printed reports. Whereas a form generator builds a screen format (a screen contains data from one record), a report generator (or report writer) builds printed report formats (a report contains data from usually multiple records, each record displayed in one or several printed rows and in the same format). Most report generators are limited to the use of one data base file, but some permit data from multiple, related files to be included in a report line.

As we have seen, the standard command languages of PC-RDBMSs contain commands that can display or even print tables of data, but these appear in a plain columnar style with few options. A report generator will support: including header and footer titles, page numbers, and date and time of printing the report; substitution of field names with more meaningful column headings; calculation of column totals, control break subtotals, and averages and counts; and possibly production of multiple-line-per-record layouts. As an alternative, a report generator or similar subsystem will produce mailing labels instead of reports. Even more complex and data-dependent formats can be built using a procedural programming language, but this requires special programming skills.

The mechanics of defining a report are similar to those of defining a screen form, so we will illustrate the *results* of using a report generator or writer rather than the details of building the report definition. We will use the REPORT FORM capability of dBASE III Plus, which is typical of report definition capabilities in PC-RDBMS products.

Figure 15-13 shows a report generated from dBASE that we will use for

Figure 15-13
Example report from dBASE III Plus (Mountain View Community Hospital)

```
Page No.     1
01/18/87
                         PATIENT CHARGE SUMMARY
                     Mountain View Community Hospital

  Patient    Charged   Amount
  Number        Item   Charged
===========  ===========  ===========

** Patient   1234
      1234        200    150.00
      1234        200    165.00
      1234        413     35.00
** Subtotal **
                         350.00

** Patient   2222
      2222        200    150.00
      2222        307     25.00
      2222        307     35.00
      2222        413     45.00
** Subtotal **
                         255.00

** Patient   3249
      3249        307     35.00
      3249        307     35.00
** Subtotal **
                          70.00
*** Total ***
                         675.00
```

illustration. The report contains a summary of charges from Mountain View Community Hospital. The report contains data on three patients and is produced from the CHARGES file. In order to perform subtotalling of data, the CHARGES file was sorted on the control break field, the patient number, after data were entered but before the report was printed.

The page number and printing date were automatically included by dBASE. We requested dBASE to display subtotals for total charges by patient as well as produce a grand total across all patients. Each control break at a patient number is clearly indicated by an identifying comment line supplied by dBASE. Descriptive, multiple line column headings were specified by the designer, as was a two-line header title. dBASE would also have allowed us to:

- Change the width of columns from the length used in the field definitions in the CHARGES file
- Change the number of decimal places shown for the amount charged
- Specify left and right margins, number of lines per page, single or double spacing, or omission of page numbers and date
- Specify a second level of subtotalling (e.g., on item code)

A limitation of the dBASE report generation capability is that data from only one file can be included in a report. When data from multiple, related files must appear in the same report line, then the user must perform a JOIN or other multiple-table operation first in order to merge all desired data into one file.

The R:base 5000 REPORTS function has several features in addition to the ones described for dBASE. These are:

- Subtotalling up to ten levels
- Retrieval of data from multiple, related records on the same report

One of the most popular add-on products for PC-RDBMSs is extended report writers that allow users to produce even more complex reports than that in Figure 15-13 without having to use a procedural programming language. Specialized reporting systems for maintaining and reporting personal telephone directories or customer/personal address lists are available for many PC-RDBMSs.

FILE IMPORT AND EXPORT

Since most personal computer users do not just use a PC-DBMS, it can be very convenient to be able to transfer data between different personal computer file formats. A typical personal computer user will use, in addition to one or more PC-DBMSs, word processors, electronic spreadsheets, simple filing systems, and operating system files. The ability to convert files

Table 15-4 Summary of File Import and Export Formats in dBASE III Plus and R:base 5000

dBASE III	**R:base 5000**
IMPORT and APPEND FROM	*FileGateWay and LOAD*
PFS:FILE	PFS:FILE
—Data file	—Data file
—Screen format	
ASCII	ASCII
—Delimited with any character	—Delimited with any character
—SDF	—SDF
DIF (Visicalc)	DIF
SYLK (Multiplan)	SYLK
WKS (Lotus 1-2-3)	WKS
*dBASE II	dBASE II
Export	*Export*
PFS:FILE	PFS:FILE
—Data file	—Data file
—Screen format	
ASCII	ASCII
—Delimited with any character	—Delimited with any character
—SDF	—SDF
DIF	DIF
SYLK	SYLK
WKS	WKS

*Available via separate file conversion utility.

among these various file formats eliminates the need to reenter data and keeps data more consistent across multiple application systems.

Table 15-4 summarizes the file import and export capabilities of dBASE III Plus and R:base 5000. File conversion is not necessarily a straightforward process. Different data types between the systems for conversion mean that the data after conversion may not be in the most desirable and understandable format (e.g., if one system does not have a date data type, then a date will be stored as a character string after conversion).

Conversion between a spreadsheet and a data base presents special considerations. A spreadsheet must not have any summary rows or else each row of the data base table will not be about the same type of entity. Further, data base field names and spreadsheet column labels are not equivalent, but the fields are named upon conversion by applying the column labels. For these and other reasons, R:base provides an exception reporting and handling scheme to deal with those data that cannot be directly converted.

Of growing importance is the ability to upload and download data between personal computer files and mainframe computer files. This is even more difficult than between different PC systems since PCs and mainframes

- Often have different word sizes and very different data types
- Use different character and number coding or representation schemes
- Require data communication software to support file transfer between technologies that use vastly different transmission speeds

As indicated in Chapter 14, mainframe vendors are developing personal computer versions of their DBMS products, and these will usually include the software to transfer data between mainframe and PC data bases of that type, but likely not the whole range of file types. Special upload/download software products are necessary to expand PC–mainframe file transfer capabilities to a more complete set of file types. Personal computer vendors, recognizing that many organizations that acquire their PC-RDBMSs also have considerable mainframe data, are increasingly announcing special arrangements with mainframe software vendors to provide specific file upload/download facilities.

PROGRAMMING LANGUAGES

Rather than allowing the use of DBMS data manipulation commands to be placed in programs written in traditional procedural programming languages, which is the practice for mainframe RDBMSs, most personal computer systems provide a separate programming language customized for the particular PC-RDBMS. This language typically supports looping, conditional IF-THEN-ELSE and other control logic, subroutine calls (with parameter passing), and input and output in interactive or batch mode with a variety of devices.

The purpose of a programming language with a PC-RDBMS is, as with any programming language, to execute a sequence of stored instructions so that these commands do not have to be reentered each time they are to be run. Specifically, a PC-RDBMS provides the ability to:

- Display predefined and tailored menus to guide a user through the steps of some application function
- Support customized input and output formats not possible with screen or report generators
- Provide a way to build and use frequently used procedures
- Give a novice user turn-key functions on whole application systems
- Provide a data base processing language that is easier to learn and use than traditional procedural programming languages such as COBOL, FORTRAN, C, or Pascal

Table 15-5 lists and describes the various programming language commands, in addition to those commands listed earlier, that are available in dBASE III Plus and R:base 5000. They are typical of other PC-RDBMSs. All

Table 15-5 Summary of Programming Language Commands in dBASE III Plus and R:base 5000

Explanation	dBASE III	R:base 5000
Get user-supplied data from keyboard and display input on screen at specified row and column	@ GET*	FILLIN*
Display data on screen or printer at specified row and column	@ SAY*	WRITE*
Abandon program execution	CANCEL	QUIT
Abandon program for another program	N/A	QUIT TO
Erase contents of memory variable(s)	CLEAR MEMORY*	CLEAR*
Assign a value to a memory variable	var = expression*	SET VAR*
Display/print contents of memory variable(s)	DISPLAY MEMORY*	SHOW VAR*
Execute a stored program rows	DO programname WITH parameters	RUN
Conditionally execute one of several sections of program based on value of some data item	DO CASE*	DO CASE*
Execute a section of a program while a condition is satisfied	DO WHILE*	WHILE . . . THEN*
Send a formfeed signal to the printer	EJECT	NEWPAGE

the commands illustrated previously in this chapter to define, retrieve, update, sort, index, and so on data all are valid in a stored program. Not listed are commands that set values for status or environment variables (e.g., that set the default number of decimal places for display of numeric data, the default input device) that can be used interactively or in a program.

Since only one record of each type can be stored in memory at a time and since a user might be using a programming language to calculate certain summary or statistical values for which there is no built-in function, a PC-RDBMS programming language supports a memory variable capability. A **memory variable** is a temporary location in computer main memory that can contain numbers, characters, dates, true/false indicators, or any other types of data the DBMS supports. Commands that are relevant to memory variables are indicated with an * in Table 15-5.

Table 15-5 (continued)

Explanation	dBASE III	R:base 5000
Transfer program flow out of a DO WHILE section to next command after this section	EXIT	BREAK
Transfer program flow from within a DO WHILE section to the beginning of the section	LOOP	N/A directly
Conditionally execute a section of a program	IF . . . [ELSE]*	IF . . . THEN [ELSE]*
Branch to a specified point in program	N/A	GOTO
Insert a comment in a program	NOTE or &&	*( )
Execute the specified command when an error occurs	ON ERROR	N/A
Store screen input into a field or memory variable	READ*	N/A directly
Execute a non-DBMS program	RUN	N/A
Temporarily stop execution of a program	SUSPEND	PAUSE
Resume execution of a temporarily halted program	RESUME	any keystroke after PAUSE
End a program and return to calling routine	RETURN	RETURN
Display a menu of choices	N/A	CHOOSE

(Note: Commands indicated with * can be used with memory variables)

Data can be entered into a memory variable from the keyboard, memory variable values can be saved to disk and restored (for example, to pass temporary variables between different program sessions), built-in functions and commands that store a value into memory can place the result of a calculation into a memory variable, and data stored in memory variables can be displayed on the PC screen and on reports. In addition, a variable may be declared to be relevant only to a single program (Local or Private) or to be operative in all program modules.

Figure 15-14 is an illustration of a simple program written in the dBASE III programming language. A program is stored in a program file and can be created and changed from a text editor or the dBASE MODIFY COMMAND statement (MODIFY COMMAND operates similarly to a word processor, and dBASE can be told to use whatever word processor the user

Figure 15-14
Sample dBASE III Plus program:
(a) program statements
(b) sample screen from program

```
USE CHARGES              && Open the CHARGES file
CLEAR                    && Clear the PC screen
SET HEADING OFF          && Suspend display of field names
SET TALK OFF             && Do not allow display to screen
STORE 0 TO execute       && Dummy variable for do while loop
SET TALK ON              && Allow display to screen
DO WHILE execute=0       && Program will continue to ask for patients
NOTE Next three commands display a title at top of screen
   @ 1,0 SAY ' '
   @ 2,0 SAY 'Calculate Patient Charge Deviations from Average'
   @ 3,0 SAY '                    By Item Code'
   SET TALK OFF            && Do not allow display to screen
   STORE 0 TO patid        && Variable for desired patient id
   STORE 0 TO patcount     && Variable for # of charges for patient
   STORE 0 TO item         && Variable for item code of patient
   STORE 0 TO place        && Variable for record number of charge
   STORE 0 TO avgchg       && Variable for avg charge for item
   SET TALK ON             && Allow display to screen
   @ 5,0 CLEAR             && Clear screen rows 5-end
NOTE Prompt and accept patient number
   @ 5,0 SAY 'Enter Patient Number: ' GET patid
   READ             && Read patient number from screen
   SET TALK OFF     && Do not allow display of anything on screen
NOTE Determine if there are no charges for this patient
   COUNT FOR PATIENTNO=patid TO patcount
   IF patcount=0    && If no charges, then ask for different patient
     STORE ' ' TO rest
     @ 7,0 SAY "NO CHARGES EXIST FOR THIS PATIENT; PRESS RETURN" GET rest
     READ           && Pause for user to see message
     LOOP           && Transfer control to beginning of loop
   ENDIF
   GO TOP           && Reposition record pointer at top of file
   LOCATE FOR PATIENTNO=patid      && Find first charge for patient
@ 7,0 SAY 'Patient    Item   Charge   Charge-Average'
   DO WHILE .NOT. EOF()            && Repeat until end of file
      SET TALK OFF                 && Do not allow display of anything on screen
      STORE ITEM_CODE TO item      && Note item for finding avg. charge
      STORE RECNO() TO place       && Remember which charge is being processed
NOTE Calculate the average of all charges for current item
      AVERAGE ALL CHARGE FOR ITEM_CODE=item TO avgchg
      GOTO place    && Return file pointer to charge record for printing
      diff=CHARGE-avgchg     && Calculate deviation from average
      SET TALK ON            && Allow display to screen
NOTE Print data starting on next print line/row
      @ ROW()+1,0 SAY PATIENTNO     && Display patient number
      @ ROW(),8 SAY ITEM_CODE       && Display item code
      @ ROW(),15 SAY CHARGE         && Display charge
      @ ROW(),21 SAY diff           && Display deviation from average
```

(a)

(continues)

```
        SET TALK OFF                      && Suppress display to screen
        CONTINUE                          && Find next charge for same patient
      ENDDO
      SET TALK ON                         && Allow display to screen
      STORE ' ' TO rest
NOTE Pause for user to see data before continue to next patient
      @ ROW()+2,0 SAY 'Press Y to continue to next patient' GET rest
      READ
      IF rest = 'Y' .OR. rest = 'y' LOOP ENDIF
      CLEAR                               && Clear screen before terminating
      RETURN TO MASTER                    && Terminate program
ENDDO
CLEAR
RETURN TO MASTER
```

(a) (continued)

Figure 15-14 (continued)

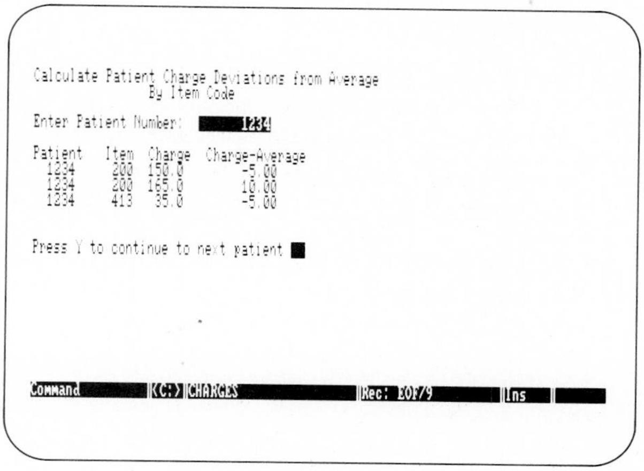

(b)

requests for such modifications). This program would be initiated by executing a

. DO programname

command either interactively from the keyboard or by placing this command in another routine. dBASE can also be made to start a program automatically when dBASE itself is activated.

The program in Figure 15-14a receives the patient number for a user-selected patient, then calculates and displays, for each item charged to that patient, the difference between the amount charged and the average charge for all patients. This query cannot be produced in the command language alone since dBASE does not permit the computation of the generic expression

fieldname − AVG(fieldname)

The comments in the program explain what each command does. Figure 15-14b shows the screen transcript from a sample session using this program.

Programming languages add tremendous power to PC-RDBMSs. Complex, structured programs can be written using commands that provide record-by-record (row-by-row) file processing control, as well as support intricate user–machine dialogues. Because these languages have been built along with the DBMS, they are especially tuned to data base processing (as opposed to COBOL, FORTRAN, and the like, which were designed for file processing). Frequently, users do not write programs but rather contract with the data processing department to build such routines for them since procedural programming training (e.g., experience in detecting and handling user data entry error) is important for writing effective programs. Programs should be designed to mask the inner workings of the DBMS from the user by:

- Handling errors within the program logic where possible, and passing only user-understandable error messages for user response when necessary
- Anticipating user data entry errors and providing easy mechanisms for the user to use to backtrack to a previous step, correct data entry mistakes, and fill in data with minimal keystrokes
- Responding to the user in meaningful terms when special circumstances (such as when no records satisfy a qualification) arise

Structured programming principles should be followed, and internal and external program documentation is still essential.

LOCAL AREA NETWORKS FOR SHARING A DATA BASE

Since many organizations have discovered that if data are valuable to one employee, those data are probably also valuable to many other employees, PC-DBMS vendors have introduced local area network (LAN) modules for many of the most popular packages. A **LAN** is cabling and data communications software that supports a network of personal computers, each with its own storage, that are also able to share common devices (such as a hard disk) and software (such as a DBMS) attached to the LAN. Each PC and workstation on a LAN is typically within one hundred feet of the others, with a total network cable length of under one mile. At least one PC is designated as a file server, where the shared data base is stored and accessed and where a shared copy of the PC-DBMS is located. The LAN modules of a DBMS add concurrent access controls, possibly extra security features, and query or transaction queuing management to support concurrent access from multiple users of a shared data base.

The dBASE III Plus LAN version is called dBASE ADMINISTRATOR, which is what we will use to discuss the special features and new commands needed for a LAN environment. In addition to dBASE ADMINISTRATOR, each PC workstation on a LAN requires dBASE ACCESS (a shell program that must interact with dBASE ADMINISTRATOR). Also necessary is PROTECT, a separate security module. PROTECT provides network data base log-in security, file- and field-level access protection, and data encryption. File protection includes adding rows to a table, deleting rows from a table, displaying rows from a table, and changing row contents. Field-level protection covers displaying and writing new field values, display only, and no privilege for any kind of access. PROTECT creates a user profile and arranges users into groups (thus, the same person may be a different user in different groups, with different privileges in each group).

dBASE ADMINISTRATOR controls concurrent access through the use of special commands in application programs. These commands essentially allow a user to specify exclusive or shared use of files, temporary lock-out from use of specified files or records by other users while critical functions (such as value changing) are occurring, and support for retrying commands when a data base access command is blocked by temporary locking or exclusive use of files and records by other users.

Certain commands require exclusive use of a file and will not work unless the user has opened the file for exclusive use; these are INSERT (inserts a new row at a specified position), MODIFY STRUCTURE, PACK (deleted marked records), REINDEX, and ZAP (deletes all the records in a file). Explicit exclusive use of a file is indicated by

```
. SET EXCLUSIVE ON
. USE filename
```

After the SET EXCLUSIVE ON command, all subsequent files put into use will be used without allowing sharing among users. SET EXCLUSIVE OFF then allows shared use, but any files previously opened in EXCLUSIVE mode remain exclusive. If a user wants to open only one or selected files for exclusive use, the USE EXCLUSIVE filename command can be issued.

In addition to explicit file locking commands that a user can place in a program, certain other commands imply automatic file locking while the command is being executed; these commands include all data modification commands plus COPY, COUNT, INDEX, JOIN, SORT, SUM, and TOTAL. A file is automatically unlocked after any of these commands completes execution.

As discussed in Chapter 11, file deadlock can occur when several users are trying to access for exclusive use the same set of files. Refer to Chapter 11 for methods to deal with deadlock.

Explicit locking is done via two commands: FLOCK(), for locking the file currently in use, and RLOCK(), for locking the current record in the current file in use. These functions not only lock an unlocked file or record but also test for a lock and return a T or F to indicate the result. If the file or record being tested is already locked, the locking function cannot be performed, and the program must execute a loop to try the locking request later. For example, DO WHILE .NOT. RLOCK() would start a loop that would cause a program to pause until the current record of the file in use were unlocked (that is, available to be locked) by another program. As an alternative, an ON ERROR command can be used to perform a subroutine that puts the program into a temporary wait and then RETRYs the blocked command—in the case of a locked record error, ERROR() = 158. An explicitly locked file (record) remains locked until the lock is released by the UNLOCK command, until another file (record in same file) is locked, or until the relevant file is closed. The form commands GET and READ require the user to issue record-level locks.

dBASE ADMINISTRATOR also includes some commands that can help a user or network manager control data base access. The DISPLAY STATUS command in a LAN environment not only includes the information we saw earlier in Figure 15-4, but now also indicates current settings for file exclusive usage and encryption. DISPLAY USERS lists the names of the workstations currently logged on to dBASE.

The features that we have described for dBASE ADMINISTRATOR—log-in security, concurrency control, deadlock resolution, and access control—are necessary features of any multiuser DBMS software that is to be used in a LAN environment.

DATA BASE MANAGEMENT ON THE MACINTOSH

The IBM PC and compatibles no longer are the only personal computers to support business data processing and give decision support. Several powerful data base management systems exist for use on the Macintosh. Omnis 3 Plus from Blyth Software and Odesta Corporation's Double Helix lead the pack as the two most powerful (Mace 1987). Both provide full relational capabilities, and each may be purchased in either single-user or multiuser versions. REFLEX for the Macintosh (Borland International 1986), while lacking some of the power of the DBMSs just mentioned, is an example of an extremely flexible PC-RDBMS that combines the ease of use of the Macintosh and its windowing user interface with the power of a relational DBMS. REFLEX will be a good illustration of a relational DBMS in use on the Macintosh.

Like most other data base packages available for the Macintosh, REFLEX fully supports the Macintosh user interface of pull-down menus and dialogue boxes in all aspects of operations from data base design through report generation. Some of REFLEX's most noteworthy features include the ability to create visual links between data base files and, through its report writing capabilities, to support the ease of reporting from more than one data base file at a time.

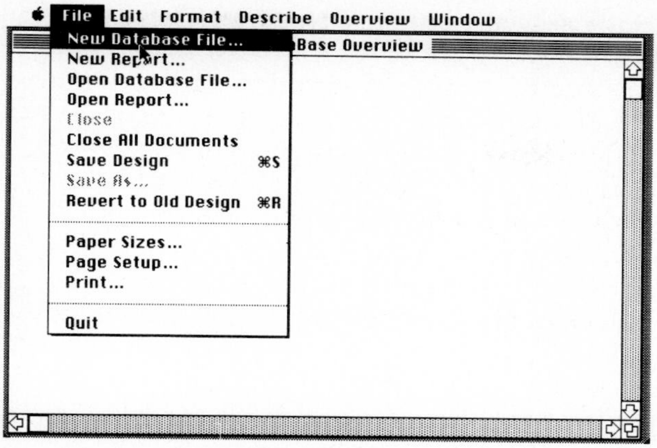

Figure 15-15
REFLEX file menu

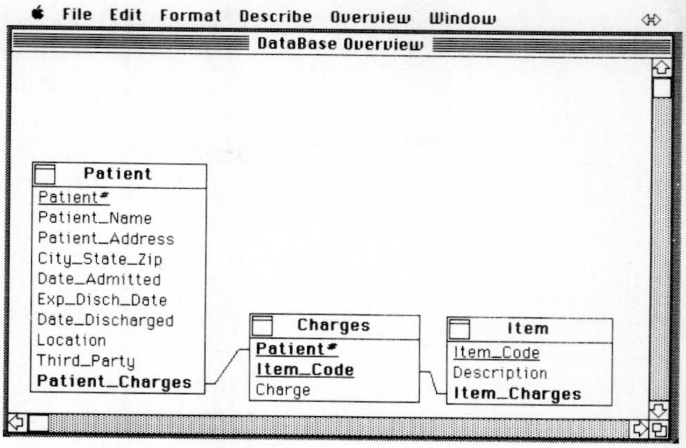

Figure 15-16
REFLEX Database
Overview Window

Data Base Definition

The first screen one encounters when entering REFLEX is a blank Database Overview window. All data base tables are created, linked, and modified from within this window. To create a new table you just select the **New Database File** . . . entry from the File menu at the top of the window, as shown in Figure 15-15.

REFLEX requests the name of the new table, and the user may then begin entering the names and types of the columns (called fields in REFLEX) to be stored in the table. Data base fields may be text, number (real), integer, date, time, logical, or sequence number data types. Fields defined as a type of sequence number are integer fields that will automatically be incremented by REFLEX for each new data base record. The starting point for a sequence number field may be specified by the user when the first record is input to the file. Field types are entered by selecting the field and choosing the data type from the **Describe** menu. In addition to choosing data types for each field, REFLEX requires that every file have at least one key field identified. REFLEX will automatically maintain all records in ascending order of their key fields. Any key fields that are identified are shown with their field names underlined in the Overview window.

In order to give a concrete example of designing and reporting from a REFLEX data base, we will implement a portion of the Mountain View Community Hospital data base of Figures 8-13 and 9-7. Only three of the tables from the full design will be implemented: Patient, Charges, and Item tables. Figure 15-16 illustrates the Database Overview Window that shows the design of the file as well as the linkages between the files.

As explained earlier, the underlined fields Patient# and Item_Code are the key fields that have been identified to REFLEX, just as they were key

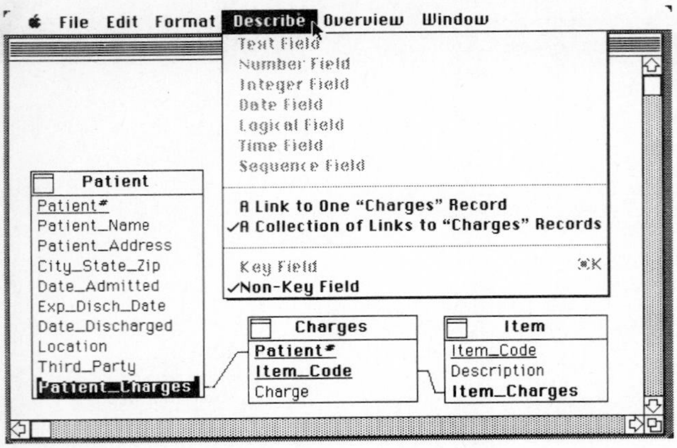

Figure 15-17
Display of link fields in REFLEX

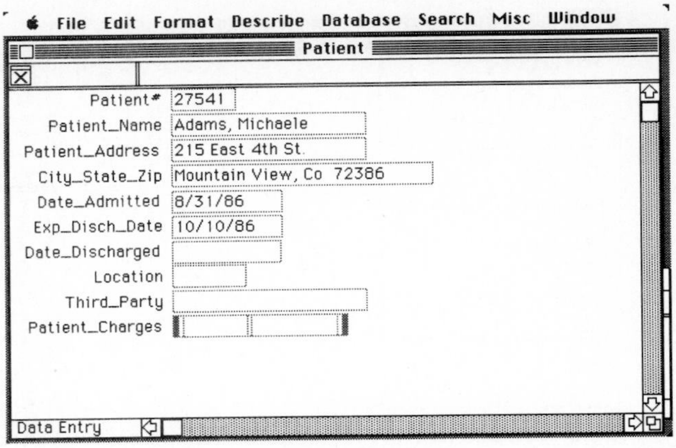

Figure 15-18
Example of default data entry form in REFLEX

fields from the data base design effort in Chapter 8. The fields that appear in **bold** type are the link fields between the tables in the data base. REFLEX supports 1:1, 1:*M*, and *M*:*N* links between tables. The link **Patient_Charges** is a 1:*M* link from the Patient file to the Charges file, just as **Item_Charges** is a 1:*M* link between the Item file and the Charges file.

These links are established graphically by selecting the fields to be linked and drawing a line between the two fields with a mouse. This operation is very similar to the Set Relation command in dBASE III. REFLEX automatically portrays the names of the linked fields in **bold** text to easily identify them from nonlink fields. The type of link must then be chosen from the Describe menu. This is accomplished by selecting with the mouse the link to describe, and choosing the link type from the menu. The operation for the link **Patient_Charges** is shown in Figure 15-17.

The field Patient_Charges is highlighted, showing it as the link that has been described, and the check mark in the Describe window identifies it as **A Collection of Links to "Charges" Records,** or a 1:*M* relationship. The same operation would be performed to classify the link between the Charges and the Item file. Once a link between files is established, REFLEX automatically maintains the referential integrity of the link. For example, if a Patient# that did not exist in the Patient file were entered into the Charges file, REFLEX would notify the user of the error and query if a record with the key specified should be added to the Patient file. The user would not be able to enter the CHARGES record without a corresponding PATIENT record. REFLEX would generate the same type of error if an attempt were made to add a record to the Charges file that contained a value for the Item_Code field that did not exist in the Item file. While this maintains the consistency of the data between linked files, it does make it difficult to

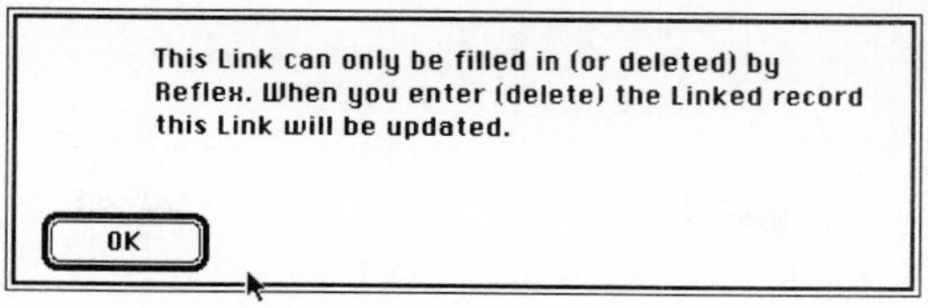

Figure 15-19
Error message in REFLEX when trying to store data in a link field

design optional relationships into data base files. REFLEX also maintains referential integrity when deleting records from the data base. For example, any attempt to delete a record from the Item file that is linked to a patient through the Charges file will generate an error stating that the record cannot be deleted. First, any associated charges for the item must be deleted. Once this is accomplished, then the item may be deleted.

Storing Data in a Data Base

When entering data into a file, REFLEX creates a default data entry screen utilizing the field names from the file design as labels for each of the data entry fields. This screen may be customized by the user by changing the labels on the fields or by dynamically moving and resizing fields on the screen by using the mouse. REFLEX automatically type checks each data value entered for consistency with the file design, but the user may easily specify more complex data entry checks on each field. Figure 15-18 shows a record being entered into the default data entry screen created for the Patient file.

In this Patient data entry window the user would enter data down through the Third_Party field. The field Patient_Charges is the link field to the Charges file, so no data are entered here by the user. REFLEX populates this field whenever a CHARGES record is entered identifying a charge for an individual patient. Any attempt by users to populate this field causes a message to appear (see Figure 15-19) reminding them that REFLEX maintains any creation and/or deletion of links in the data base files automatically.

Since REFLEX permits up to 15 files to be opened concurrently, there will usually be more than one window available to be operated in by the user. The individual windows might be data entry windows, report windows, or the Database Overview window. Each window is labeled at the top with its appropriate name, and the user may move from window to window through the use of the Window menu. In addition, each window may be sized so that more than one window could be shown on-screen at once; in this case, the user may switch to a particular window simply by clicking the mouse somewhere within the desired window. This feature is particularly useful since REFLEX allows for automatic retrieval of linked records through its data entry screens. Figure 15-20 shows a record retrieved for Mary Baker as well as the Window menu illustrating that three other windows are available to us at this time as well.

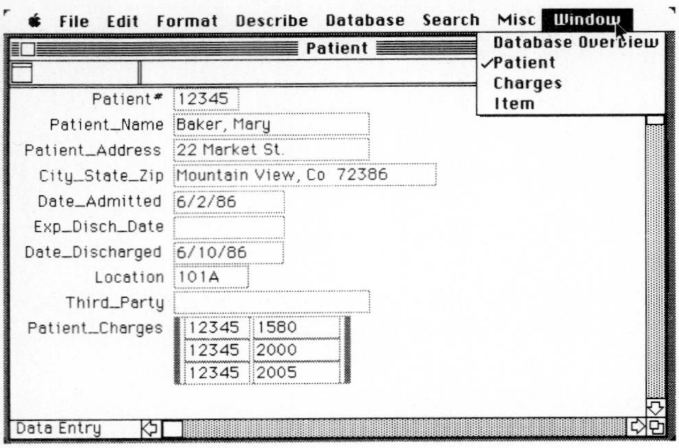

Figure 15-20
Example data display in REFLEX

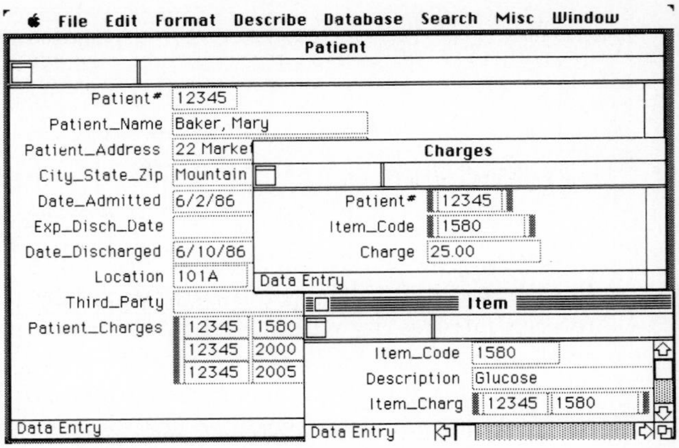

Figure 15-21
Example of multiple-window data display in REFLEX

Through the Patient_Charges link we can see that Mary Baker will be billed for items 1580, 2000, and 2005. By selecting one of the links in the retrieved record and choosing the **Show Linked Record** command from the Database menu, REFLEX will automatically retrieve the associated record from the Charges file. Through the careful sizing and placement of windows on the screen, we can see the relevant information from all three open files at the same time (Figure 15-21). Each of the three windows shown is a data entry window for the individual files. We can now clearly see that item 1580 being billed to Mary Baker is glucose, and the associated charge for that item is $25.00. We can obtain the information for any of the other items charged to Baker by simply selecting another link and requesting that REFLEX retrieve the necessary record.

Data Retrieval

Once data are entered into the data base, individual records may be retrieved by providing record qualifications to REFLEX through its Querybuild facility or by producing reports through its powerful reporting features. The Querybuild facility allows the user to simply point and select the fields to be included in the query and any operations to be performed on those fields. Through the use of the Search menu, REFLEX then retrieves all records matching the given qualifications. Figures 15-22 and 15-23 show a sample query being built to answer the question: Which patients that live in Colorado were discharged after May 1, 1986?

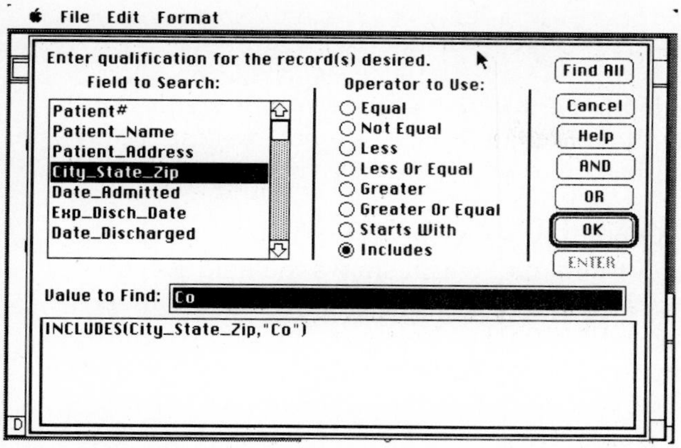

Figure 15-22
Building a query in REFLEX

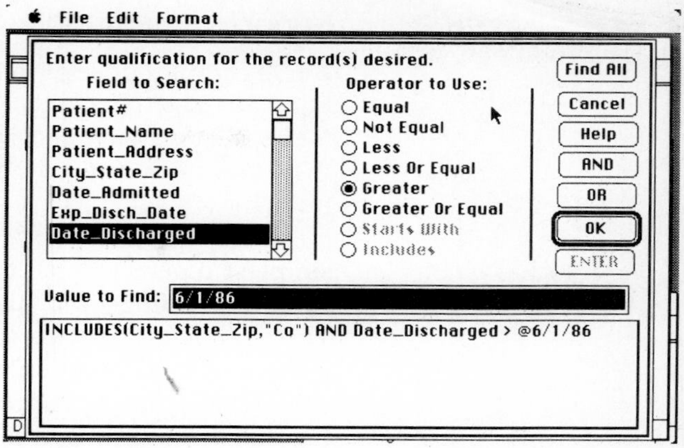

Figure 15-23
Completion of example query in REFLEX

Figure 15-22 shows the beginning of the query. The first step is to select the field we wish to include in this portion of the query. In this case the field **City_State_Zip** is chosen so that it can be searched for the string "Co", the two-character abbreviation for the state of Colorado. Next the user must select an operator to use in the query. This is done by simply pointing and clicking the mouse in the circle to the left of the desired operator. The INCLUDES operator, which has been selected, searches the entire length of the field chosen looking for the characters that have been entered in the **Value to find:** field of the Querybuild screen.

Note that as the user is selecting items with the mouse, REFLEX is displaying in the bottom box on the screen the actual query it is building. Once a user is familiar with the syntax and functions of the query language, it is unnecessary to go through this Querybuild function. All queries can also be typed directly into REFLEX from a data entry screen. By allowing two separate methods for searching data base files, REFLEX supports the needs of both the new and experienced users of the product.

To complete the request for information, the query must be expanded to also perform a search based on a patient's discharge date. To link the two queries into one, the user would select the **AND** option from the dialogue box shown in Figure 15-22. He or she would then be faced with the screen shown in Figure 15-23. The user would select the search field and operator just as before, and also enter the search value 5/1/86. The query is now complete and the selection of **OK** from the Querybuild dialogue will cause REFLEX to retrieve the desired records and place them in the format of a data entry form for viewing.

Report Generation

While complex queries may be created through the use of REFLEX's Query-build feature, the user is limited to performing search requests on only one file in the data base at a time. It is through REFLEX's report writing facility that data from multiple data base files may be easily combined into one report.

REFLEX allows for two different types of reports to be produced. The simplest type is a default report for a file, which shows the field names as column headings and displays individual records as rows on the report. The user is allowed to select which fields to view in the report, and to provide record qualifications to limit the records included in the report. While this is simple to produce, the report designer is still limited to including data from only one file in a report.

The second type of report allowed is a custom report that the user designs. It is this type of report that gives the user complete control over which data elements from what files are included in the report. This report is designed visually by placing elements and labels on the screen, sizing them to the width desired, and defining what data are to be retrieved and what calculations are to take place. As an example, a sample revenue report will be built combining data from all three files in the data base. The report should show the patient's number, location, and name, as well as all items charged to the patient and their costs. In addition, total charges should be calculated for each individual patient.

Shown in Figure 15-24 is the design of the sample report. In order to understand the design, it is first important to understand the term **repeating collection,** and what its purpose is within REFLEX. A repeating collection is the method by which REFLEX allows the user to specify various views of the data stored in data bases. The default for a repeating collection is that all records in a chosen data base file be included in a report. Record qualifications may be specified for repeating collections so that only records containing specific criteria are included in the report. Record qualifications in repeating collections limit the records to be included in the report and the user specifies in the report design what fields for each included record are to be displayed.

Figure 15-24 illustrates two separate parts in the report design. The first part consists of the labels that are placed at the top of each column. These labels are typed by the user and placed in the desired spot on the report through use of the mouse. The second part contains the specifications of the repeating collections and the identification of the individual fields and calculations that are to be included in the report.

Looking beneath the labels for the columns you will notice the outline of a rectangle with thick vertical bars around it surrounding many smaller rectangles. The outermost rectangle (or box) is the first repeating collection (or view). It appears darker than the other boxes because it has been selected with the mouse so that you can see how this view has been defined. Directly beneath the name of the report (Revenue_Report) is the definition for this

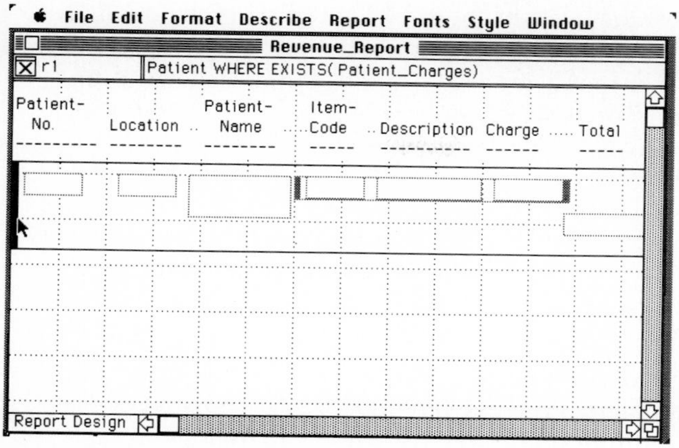

Figure 15-24
Report design in REFLEX

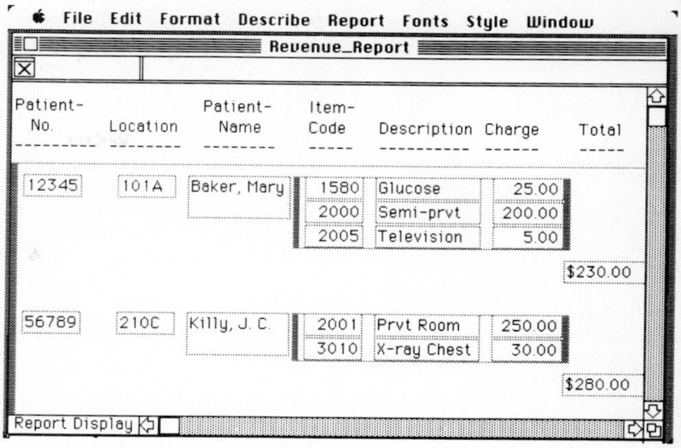

Figure 15-25
Example report output in REFLEX

repeating collection—**Patient WHERE EXISTS (Patient_Charges).** This tells REFLEX that we are going to include in this report only records from the Patient file that have an existing link to the Charges file (that is, charges have been entered for the particular patient). REFLEX will then filter out of the report any patients that have no charges associated with them yet. The boxes under the labels Patient-No., Location, and Patient-Name are simply defined as the field names from the Patient file.

Note that there is a second repeating collection following the Patient-Name field. This repeating collection provides a view into the other two files of Charges and Items. REFLEX is told in this collection to follow the link fields of Patient_Charges and Item_Code in order to obtain the necessary fields of Item_Code, Description, and Charge. The last box shown in the report design under the Total column is defined as a function in order to sum up all the charges for individual patients. This is done by defining the field as the function **SUM(Charge FROM r2).** The function tells REFLEX to sum any values in the Charge field from what we have defined as the second repeating collection. Once this report is run, it will dynamically join the necessary data from our three defined files to produce the report. It is not necessary, as in many other PC-RDBMSs, for the user to perform any intermediate file operations in order to join the data for the report. REFLEX, through the links defined in the initial design of the data base, has made that an unnecessary step. Shown in Figure 15-25 is the screen output of the sample report. While the grid boxes in the report are shown on the screen, they would not appear if the user requested the report be printed.

We hope that this brief section has provided a good introduction to the use of a sample relational data base package on the Macintosh, as well as showing some of the unique features to be found within the Macintosh user interface itself. The Macintosh has slowly gained acceptance in the personal computer area as another "standard," and its contribution to and effect on the MS-DOS world are clear through the importance of graphic user interfaces such as Microsoft Windows as well as the wide use and acceptance of memory-resident utilities such as Borland International's Sidekick (Grayson 1987; Petzold 1985).

SUMMARY

This chapter has summarized the salient features of personal computer relational data base management systems (PC-RDBMSs). These systems support many of the data definition and manipulation capabilities of their mainframe counterparts, but typically are weakest in functions most useful in multiuser environments. On balance, this chapter demonstrates that PC-RDBMSs are viable for meeting many data management needs in organizations.

For a small business, a PC-RDBMS may be quite sufficient as a tool to assist in managing and processing organizational data. In a large organization, one would typically find both mainframe and personal computer DBMSs in use. A major organizational issue is how to manage data as a corporate resource when data are distributed among many different processors, some of which may be stand-alone with their own separate sources of input. This chapter, as well as Chapter 10, suggests that decentralized data bases can have the same shortcomings as the departmental-based file systems outlined in Chapter 1. All data must be catalogued and definitions managed for consistency; data must be purposely placed on distributed machines with recognized redundancy. A well-organized and powerful data administration function is also needed when both mainframe and PC data bases exist.

Data have been categorized in many organizations into three tiers: corporate, departmental, and individual. Data cannot by default be placed in the individual category just for the expediency of the individual worker. The power of data is not linear, but grows exponentially as it is shared. A PC-RDBMS is a valuable tool that, when used within an overall organizational scheme for providing rapid access to relevant data, can serve both the needs of individual end users as well as the corporate desire for well-managed data and information.

Data base management on personal computers has become rather commonplace, but only a few years ago such technology was immature and innovative. The data base field ever changes, and now new areas have emerged as the leading edge of data base management. The next chapter reviews some of the most important of these emerging topics. A data base manager must become familiar with them in order to leverage the most out of the data base resource.

Chapter Review

REVIEW QUESTIONS

1. Define each of the following terms:
   a. relational algebra
   b. single-user DBMS
   c. mainframe link
   d. end user computing
   e. run-time version
   f. report writer
   g. join
   h. intersect
   i. union
   j. difference
   k. view
   l. mark and pack
   m. form
   n. memory variable
2. In what ways are PC-RDBMSs different from their mainframe counterparts?
3. What are the additional data management issues that arise in a multiuser data base environment that are not present in a single-user, stand-alone environment?
4. What are the advantages of a run-time version of a PC-RDBMS?
5. Contrast the data definition philosophy in dBASE to that in R:base 5000. What are the limitations or disadvantages of each approach?
6. What can the R:base rules capability accomplish?
7. Why is a DELETE DUPLICATES command found in some PC-RDBMSs?
8. What capabilities seem to be present in PC-RDBMSs for the Macintosh that do not appear in those for PC-DOS?
9. What is the purpose of a template in a dBASE form definition?
10. Why are file import and export capabilities important for a PC-RDBMS?

PROBLEMS AND EXERCISES

1. Match the following terms to the appropriate definitions.

_____ mainframe link
_____ referential integrity
_____ form
_____ session log
_____ lock
_____ catalog
_____ product

a. communication between DBMS on PC and mainframe
b. every pairwise combination
c. mandatory matching of keys in two tables
d. grouping of tables, forms, and so on that are typically used together
e. transcript of PC data base activity
f. stylized screen format
g. mechanism to prohibit use of a piece of data

Problems 2–8 are based on the Mountain View Community College data base from Chapter 7 (the 3NF relations for that application are repeated here):

STUDENT#	STUDENT NAME	MAJOR
38214	BRIGHT	IS
69173	SMITH	PM
...		

STUDENT (STUDENT#, STUDENT-NAME, MAJOR)

INSTRUCTOR-NAME	INSTRUCTOR-LOCATION
CODD	B104
KEMP	B213
LEWIS	D317
...	

INSTRUCTOR (INSTRUCTOR-NAME, INSTRUCTOR-LOCATION)

COURSE#	COURSE-TITLE	INSTRUCTOR-NAME
IS 350	DATA BASE	CODD
IS 465	SYS ANAL	KEMP
PM 300	PROD MGT	LEWIS
QM 440	OP RES	KEMP
...		

COURSE (COURSE#, COURSE-TITLE, INSTRUCTOR-NAME)

STUDENT#	COURSE#	GRADE
38214	IS 350	A
38214	IS 465	C
69173	IS 465	A
69173	PM 300	B
69173	QM 440	C
...		

REGISTRATION (STUDENT#, COURSE#, GRADE)

2. Write dBASE III and R:base 5000 commands for each of the following queries (refer to Figure 15-5 for sample commands):
   a. Display the instructor location for the instructor Lewis.
   b. Display the student number and student name for all information systems (IS) majors.
   c. Display the total number of students who are IS majors.
3. Write dBASE III and R:base 5000 commands to produce a table with columns STUDENT#, STUDENT-NAME, MAJOR, COURSE#, and GRADE (*Hint:* Data are contained in multiple base tables).
4. What dBASE III command would be used to:
   a. Add a new row to the end of the REGISTRATION table.
   b. Delete all rows for student number 56789 in the REGISTRATION table.
   c. Change the grade for student 38214 in IS 465 from C to B.
5. Write the R:base 5000 command(s) necessary to display those students who have taken IS 465 but who have not taken IS 350.
6. Write the dBASE III and R:base 5000 command(s) to display the names and locations of all instructors for courses taken by student with STUDENT# 69173.
7. Write the dBASE III command to create a primary key index on the REGISTRATION table.

8. Write the dBASE III and R:base 5000 commands to display the STUDENT# and STUDENT-NAME of those students who have taken a course from both instructor CODD and instructor KEMP.
9. Write a relational algebra query using either dBASE III or R:base to answer the following question from the Mountain View Community Hospital data base of this chapter: What physicians have performed a tonsillectomy?
10. Use the SUBTRACT operator of R:base to find those physicians that have not yet treated any patients at Mountain View Community Hospital.
11. Assume that the ITEM relation in the Mountain View Community Hospital data base is altered to also include STD-CHG, the standard charge for an item. Write the R:base 5000 commands to display the patient numbers for those patients that have been charged above standard.

REFERENCES

Ashton-Tate. 1985. *Learning dBASE III Plus.* Torrance, Calif.: Ashton-Tate.

Borland International. 1986. *REFLEX for the MAC.* Scotts Valley, Calif.: Borland.

Computerworld. 1983. "CCA's PC/204 Links Its DBMS to IBM Micro." November 7, pp. 53, 62.

Codd, E. F. 1970. "A Relational Model of Data for Large Shared Data Banks." *Communications of the ACM* 13 (June): 377–387.

Cullinet Software, Inc. 1983. *Cullinet Personal Computer Software: Summary Description.* October. Westwood, Mass.: Cullinet Software, Inc.

Date, C. J. 1981. *An Introduction to Database Systems.* 3d ed. Reading, Mass.: Addison-Wesley.

Grayson, Paul. 1987. "Windows of Opportunity." *PC Tech Journal* 5 (February): 70.

Information Builders, Inc. 1983. *PC/FOCUS Product Description.* March. New York: Information Builders, Inc.

Mace, Scott. 1987. "High End Mac Database Market Heats Up." *Infoworld* 9 (January 26): 25.

Micro Data Base Systems. 1981a. *Application Program Reference Manual: MDBS-DMS.* Lafayette, Ind.: Micro Data Base Systems.

Micro Data Base Systems. 1981b. *HDMS Users' Guide.* Lafayette, Ind.: Micro Data Base Systems.

Micro Data Base Systems. 1983. *KnowledgeMan Users' Guide.* July. Layfayette, Ind.: Micro Data Base Systems.

Microrim, Inc. 1985. *R:base 5000 User's Manual.* Bellevue, Wash.: Microrim.

Oracle Corp. 1984. *ORACLE Programmer's Guide.* Menlo Park, Calif.: Oracle.

Petzold, Charles. 1985. "Organize Your Desk and Your PC." *PC Magazine* 4 (January 22): 205.

Ullman, J. D. 1980. *Principles of Database Systems.* Potomac, Md.: Computer Science Press.

Part V

Future Directions

This concluding part consists of a single chapter, "Advanced Opportunities in Data Base Management." In this chapter we discuss emerging technologies and the opportunities and issues that these technologies bring to the data base management arena. Many of these technologies are already being used in pioneering companies but are still not well understood or in widespread use. Topics that are discussed in this chapter include distributed data bases, data base computers, and intelligent data base systems. We believe that these technologies are having a major impact on the future of data management.

Chapter 16

Advanced Opportunities in Data Base Management

INTRODUCTION TO THE FUTURE

The previous chapters of this book have concentrated on developing the principles of data management required for information systems analysis, design, and programming. We have tried in these chapters to illustrate these principles through the major data base management system technologies now in common practice. Although the principles of data modelling and administration outlined here should prevail well into the future, the data management technologies now in use are inevitably being replaced or enhanced by advanced equipment and software and ingenious combinations of DBMSs with other technologies. The purpose of this chapter is to introduce some of these advanced data management opportunities and to outline their future role in effective data management.

The technologies to be discussed in this chapter are distributed data bases, data base computers, and intelligent data base systems. Our goal is not to give a comprehensive review of these data management technologies (because each is a major topic by itself), but rather to present the salient features of these technologies and the opportunities and issues that they bring to the data base management arena.

The technologies that we will review here are not speculative but already exist in limited practice or are used but not well understood. Each, we believe, has a definite role to play in the near future of data management in organizations.

All these technologies are constantly evolving; they are on the leading edge, and standards and definitive principles do not exist. For this reason, it would be useful to seek out additional information on these topics, since the actual implementation of these technologies is likely to change rapidly. However, the salient features, opportunities, and issues should be the same.

DISTRIBUTED DATA BASES

When an organization is geographically dispersed, it may choose to store its data bases on a central computer or to distribute them to local computers (or a combination of both). A **distributed data base** is a single logical data base that is spread across computers in multiple locations that are connected by a data communications network. The network must allow the users to share the data; thus a user (or program) at location A must be able to access (and perhaps update) data at location B. The sites of a distributed system may be distributed over a large area (such as the United States or the world), or over a small area (such as a building or campus). The computers may range from micros to large-scale computers or even supercomputers.

It is important to distinguish between distributed and decentralized data bases. A **decentralized data base** is also stored on computers at multiple locations. However, the computers are not interconnected by a network, so that data cannot be shared by users at the various sites. Thus a decentralized data base is best regarded as a collection of independent data bases, rather than the geographical distribution of a single data base.

Objectives and Trade-offs

A major objective of distributed data bases is to provide ease of access to data for users at many different locations. To meet this objective, the distributed data base system must provide what is called location transparency. **Location transparency** means that a user (or user program) requesting data need not know at which site these data are located. Any request to retrieve or update data at a nonlocal site is automatically forwarded by the system to that site. Thus, ideally the user is unaware of the distribution of data, and all data in the network appears as a single logical data base.

Compared to centralized data bases, there are numerous advantages to distributed data bases. The most important of these are discussed in the following sections.

Increased Reliability and Availability When a centralized system fails, the data base is unavailable to all users. However, a distributed system will continue to function (at some reduced level) even when a component fails. The reliability and availability will depend (among other things) on how the data are distributed (discussed in the following sections).

Local Control Distributing the data encourages local groups to exercise greater control over "their" data. This promotes improved data integrity and administration. At the same time, users can access nonlocal data when necessary. Hardware can be chosen for the local site to match the local, not global, data processing work.

Modular Growth Suppose that an organization expands to a new location or adds a new work group. It is often easier and more economical to add a local computer and its associated data to the distributed network, than to expand a large central computer. Also, there is less chance of disruption to existing users than is the case when a central computer system is modified or expanded.

Lower Communication Costs With a distributed system, data can be located closer to its point of use. This can reduce communication costs, compared to a central system.

Faster Response Depending on how data are distributed, most requests for data by users at a particular site can be satisfied by data stored at that site. This speeds up query processing since communication and central computer delays are minimized. It may also be possible to split complex queries into subqueries that can be processed in parallel at several sites, thus providing even faster response.

A distributed data base system also faces certain costs and disadvantages.

Software Cost and Complexity More complex software (especially DBMS) is required for a distributed data base environment. We discuss this software briefly later in the chapter.

Processing Overhead The various sites must exchange messages and perform additional calculations to ensure proper coordination among the sites.

Data Integrity A by-product of the additional complexity and need for coordination is the additional exposure to improper updating and other problems of data integrity.

Slow Response If the data are not distributed properly according to their usage, or if queries are not formulated correctly, response to requests for data can be extremely slow. These issues are discussed later in the chapter.

Options for a Distributed Network

We have defined a distributed data base as one that is spread across computers in multiple locations that are connected by a data communications

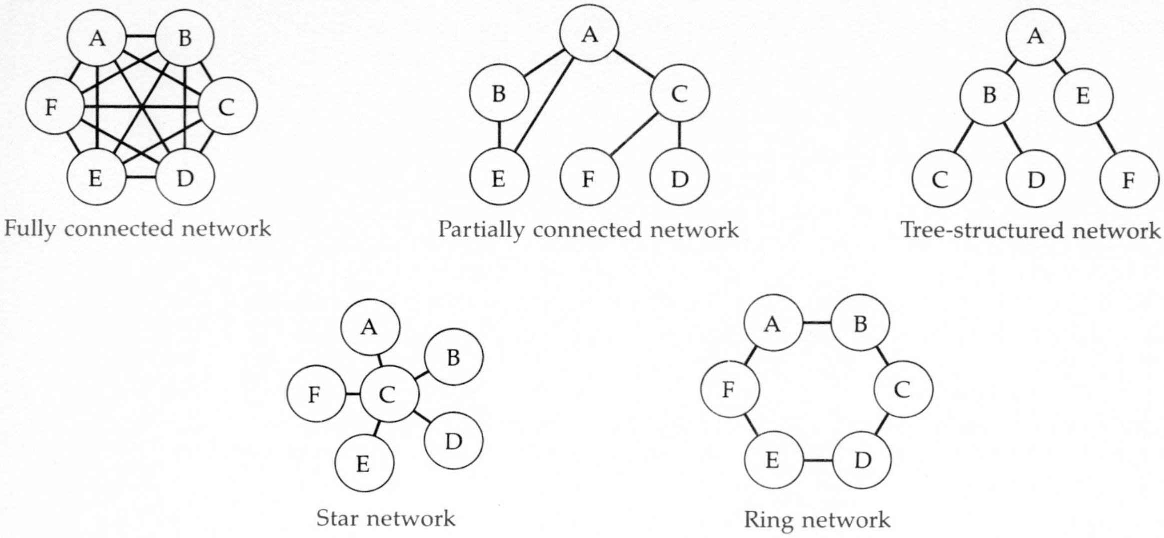

Figure 16-1
Alternative network configurations (*Source:* Korth and Silberschatz 1986)

network. As shown in Figure 16-1, there are a variety of ways to configure such a network.

A **fully connected** network is one in which each site (or computer) is physically linked to every other site. This approach provides the greatest reliability and flexibility. However, it is also the most costly to install.

A **partially connected** network has links between some (but not all) of the sites. Links are generally installed between sites where the traffic density is greatest.

A **tree-structured** network is a hierarchical arrangement of nodes. It is often used in organizations that have a hierarchical organization structure that corresponds to the network.

A **star** network connects numerous satellite computers with a central computer (in Figure 16-1, computer C is the central computer). This approach is often used in companies that have branch locations that must communicate with a central corporate computer.

A **ring** network interconnects sites in a closed loop. This approach is often used to link personal computers in a local area network.

In practice, combinations of these options are often used. For example, Figure 16-2 shows a common distributed processing approach in a manufacturing company that combines the tree-structured and ring approaches. The network contains three types of computers: a corporate mainframe, departmental computers (for engineering and manufacturing), and microcomputers or workstations. The corporate data base (including personnel, marketing, and financial data) is maintained on the corporate computer. The engineering and manufacturing departmental computers each manage data bases relative to their respective areas. The engineering computer is

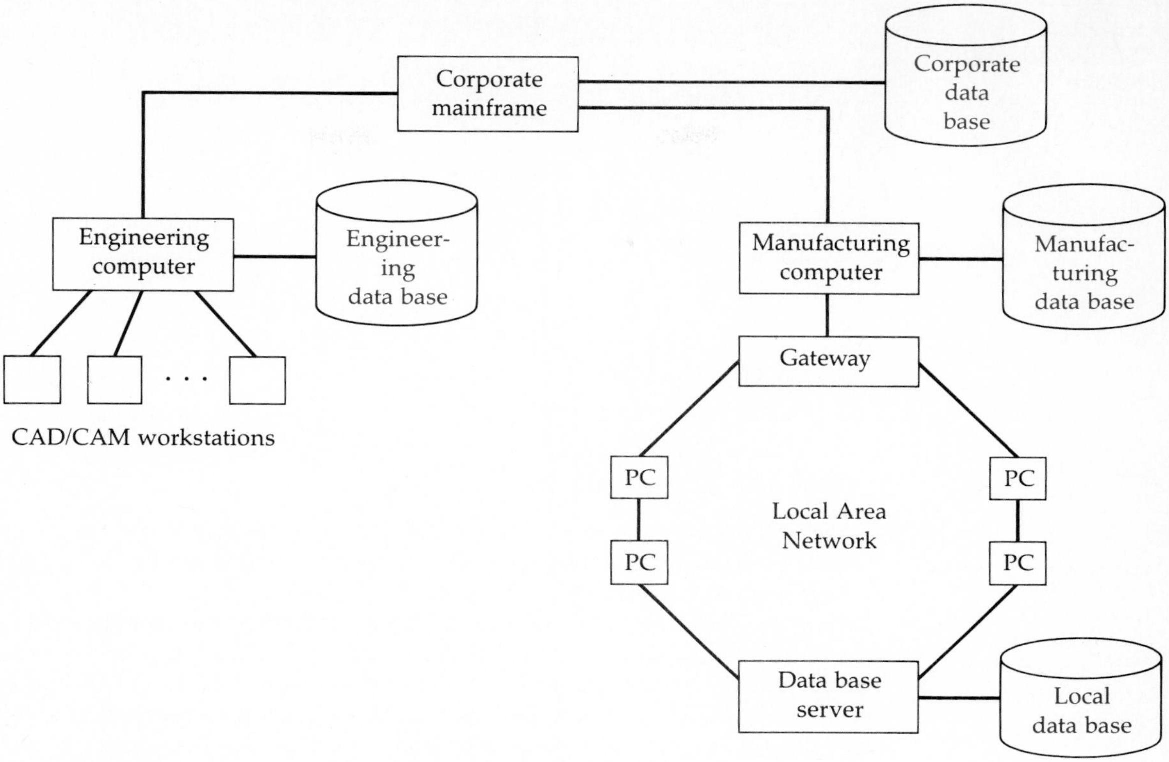

Figure 16-2 Distributed processing system for a manufacturing company

networked to several workstations (powerful microcomputers) for computer-aided design and computer-aided manufacturing (CAD/CAM).

In manufacturing, numerous personal computers are linked in a local area network (ring). These PCs are used for a variety of functions such as controlling machines and robots, controlling materials handling equipment, and reading manufacturing data. The local area network (LAN) has a dedicated microcomputer, called a **data base server,** that manages a local data base (this data base might contain work assignments, movements of materials, and so on). Notice that this data base is centralized with respect to the local area network, but in the overall scheme is just one component of the distributed data base. The LAN communicates with the manufacturing computer by means of a **gateway**—a microcomputer with special software to coordinate such communications.

Options for Distributing a Data Base

How should a data base be distributed among the sites (or nodes) of a network? This is an important issue in physical data base design (other issues in physical design were discussed in Chapter 9). There are four basic strategies for distributing data bases:

Figure 16-3
CUSTOMER relation for bank

ACCT-NO	CUSTOMER-NAME	BRANCH-NAME	BALANCE
200	Jones	Lakeview	1000
324	Smith	Valley	250
153	Gray	Valley	38
426	Dorman	Lakeview	796
500	Green	Valley	168
683	McIntyre	Lakeview	1500
252	Elmore	Lakeview	330

1. Data replication
2. Horizontal partitioning
3. Vertical partitioning
4. Combinations of the above

We will explain and illustrate each of these approaches using relational data bases. The same concepts apply (with some variations) for other data models such as hierarchical and network.

Suppose that a bank has numerous branches located throughout a state. One of the base relations in the bank's data base is the CUSTOMER relation. The format for an abbreviated version of this relation is shown in Figure 16-3. For simplicity, the sample data in the relation apply to only two of the branches (Lakeview and Valley). The primary key in this relation is account number (ACCT-NO). BRANCH-NAME is the name of the branch where customers have opened their accounts (and therefore presumably perform most of their transactions).

Data Replication One option for data distribution is to store a separate copy of the data base at each of two or more sites. Thus, the CUSTOMER relation could be stored at two or more sites (such as Lakeview or Valley). If a copy is stored at every site, we have the case of **full replication.**

There are two advantages to data replication:

1. Reliability—if one of the sites containing the relation (or data base) fails, a copy can always be found at another site.
2. Fast response—each site that has a full copy can process queries locally, so queries can be processed rapidly.

There are also two primary disadvantages to data replication:

1. Storage requirements—each site that has a full copy must have the same storage capacity that would be required if the data were stored centrally.
2. Complexity and cost of updating—whenever a relation is updated, it must be updated at each of the sites that holds a copy. This requires careful coordination, as we will see later.

ACCT-NO	CUSTOMER-NAME	BRANCH-NAME	BALANCE
200	Jones	Lakeview	1000
426	Dorman	Lakeview	796
683	McIntyre	Lakeview	1500
252	Elmore	Lakeview	330

(a) Lakeview Branch

ACCT-NO	CUSTOMER-NAME	BRANCH-NAME	BALANCE
324	Smith	Valley	250
153	Gray	Valley	38
500	Green	Valley	168

(b) Valley Branch

Figure 16-4
Horizontal partitions of the CUSTOMER relation

For these reasons, data replication is favored for data where most transactions are read-only, and where updates are relatively infrequent. Such data include catalogs, telephone directories, train schedules, and so on. CD-ROM storage technology has promise as an economical medium for replicated data bases.

Horizontal Partitioning With horizontal partitioning, some of the rows of a table (or relation) are put into a base relation at one site, and other rows are put into a base relation at another site. More generally, the rows of a relation are distributed to many sites.

Figure 16-4 shows the result of taking horizontal partitions of the CUSTOMER relation. Each row is now located at its "home" branch. If a customer, in fact, conducts most of his or her transactions at the home branch, then such transactions are processed locally and response times are minimized. When a customer initiates a transaction at another branch, then the transaction must be transmitted to the home branch for processing, and the response transmitted back to the initiating branch (notice that this is the normal pattern for persons using automated teller machines, or ATMs). If a customer's usage pattern changes (perhaps because of a move), the system may be able to detect this change and dynamically move the record to another location where most transactions are being initiated.

The horizontal partitions shown in Figure 16-4 (such as for the Valley branch) may be formed by manipulating the data in the original CUSTOMER relation using relational algebra or calculus (as an exercise, the reader should write the relevant commands). The original relation can be reconstructed by taking the union of all the partitions (the operation of forming unions was discussed in Chapters 14 and 15).

In summary, horizontal partitions for a distributed data base have three major advantages:

Figure 16-5
PART relation for manufacturing company

PART #	NAME	COST	DRAWING #	QTY-ON-HAND
P2	Widgit	100	123-7	20
P7	Gizmo	550	621-0	100
P3	Thing	48	174-3	0
P1	Whatsit	220	416-2	16
P8	Thumzer	16	321-0	50
P9	Bobbit	75	400-1	0
P6	Nailit	125	129-4	200

1. Efficiency—data are stored close to where they are used and separate from other data used by other users or applications.
2. Local optimization—data can be stored to optimize performance for local access.
3. Security—data not relevant to usage at a particular site are not made available.

Thus, horizontal partitions are usually used when an organizational function is distributed, but each site is concerned with only a subset of the entity instances (frequently based on geography).

Horizontal partitions also have two primary disadvantages:

1. Inconsistent access speed—when data from several partitions are required, the access time can be significantly different from local-only data access.
2. Backup vulnerability—since data are not replicated, when data at one site become inaccessible or damaged, usage cannot switch to another site where a copy exists; data may be lost if proper backup is not performed at each site.

Vertical Partitioning With the vertical partitioning approach, some of the columns of a relation are projected into a base relation at one of the sites, and other columns are projected into a base relation at another site (more generally, columns may be projected to several sites). The relations at each of the sites must share a common domain, so that the original table can be reconstructed.

To illustrate vertical partitioning, we use an application for the manufacturing company shown in Figure 16-2. A PART relation with PART# as the primary key is shown in Figure 16-5. Some of these data are used primarily by manufacturing, while other data are used mostly by engineering. The data are distributed to the respective departmental computers using vertical partitioning, as shown in Figure 16-6.

Each of the partitions shown in Figure 16-6 is obtained by taking projections of the original relation. The original relation in turn can be obtained

PART #	DRAWING #
P2	123-7
P7	621-0
P3	174-3
P1	416-2
P8	321-0
P9	400-1
P6	129-4

(a) Engineering

PART #	NAME	COST	QTY-ON-HAND
P2	Widgit	100	20
P7	Gizmo	550	100
P3	Thing	48	0
P1	Whatsit	220	16
P8	Thumzer	16	50
P9	Bobbit	75	0
P6	Nailit	125	200

(b) Manufacturing

Figure 16-6
Vertical partitions of the PART relation

by taking natural joins of the resulting partitions (as an exercise, the reader should illustrate each of these operations using relational algebra and/or calculus).

In summary, the advantages and disadvantages of vertical partitions are identical to those for horizontal partitions. However, whereas horizontal partitions support an organizational design in which functions are replicated, often on a regional basis, vertical partitions are typically applied across organizational functions with reasonably separate data requirements.

Combinations of Operations To complicate matters further, there are almost unlimited combinations of the preceding strategies. Some data may be stored centrally, while other data are replicated at the various sites. Also, for a given relation, both horizontal and vertical partitions may be desirable for data distribution. The overriding principle in distributed data base design is that data should be stored at the sites where they will be accessed most frequently (although other considerations such as security, data integrity, and cost are also likely to be important). The DBA plays a critical and central role in organizing a distributed data base in order to make it distributed, not decentralized.

Structure of a Distributed DBMS Environment

To have a distributed data base, there must be a distributed data base management system that coordinates the access to data at the various nodes. Although each site may have a DBMS managing the local data base at that site, a distributed DBMS is also required to perform the following functions:

1. Determine the location from which to retrieve requested data.
2. If necessary, translate the request at one node using a local DBMS into the proper request to another node using a different DBMS and data model.
3. Provide data management functions such as security, concurrency and deadlock control, query optimization, and failure recovery.

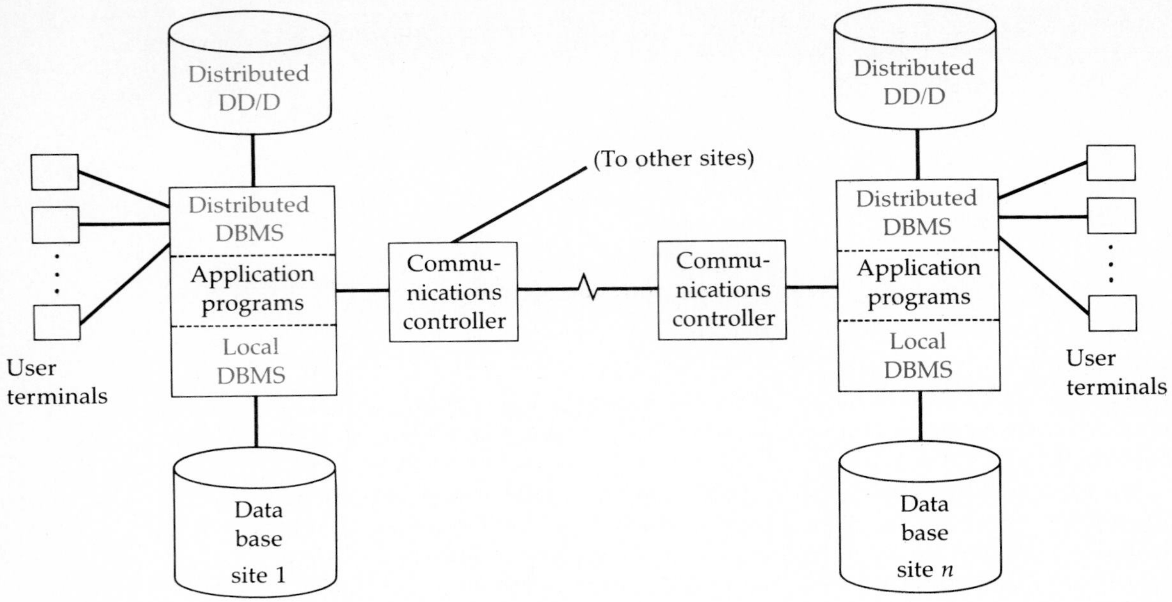

Figure 16-7
Architecture for distributed DBMS

One popular architecture of a computer system with a distributed DBMS capability is shown in Figure 16-7. Each site has a local DBMS that manages the data base stored at that site. Also, each site has a copy of the distributed DBMS and the associated distributed data dictionary/directory (DD/D). The distributed DD/D contains the location of all data in the network, as well as data definitions. Requests for data by users or application programs are first processed by the distributed DBMS, which determines whether the transaction is a local or global transaction. A **local** transaction is one in which the required data are stored entirely at the local site. A **global** transaction is one that requires reference to data at one or more nonlocal sites to satisfy the request. For local transactions, the distributed DBMS passes the request to the local DBMS to be satisfied. For global transactions, the distributed DBMS routes the request to other sites as necessary. The distributed DBMSs at the participating sites exchange messages as necessary to coordinate the processing of the transaction until it is completed (or aborted if necessary). This process may be quite complex, as we will see.

It may be that the DBMS (and its data model) at one site may be different from that at another site. For example, site A may have a relational DBMS while site B has a network DBMS. In this case, the distributed DBMS must translate the request so that it can be processed by the local DBMS. The capability for handling mixed DBMSs and data models is a state-of-the-art development that is beginning to appear in some commercial DBMS products.

In our discussion of an architecture for a distributed system (Figure 16-7) we assumed that a copy of the distributed DBMS and DD/D exist at each site (thus the DD/D is itself an example of data replication). An alternative is to locate the distributed DBMS and DD/D at a central site (other strategies are also possible). However, the centralized solution is vulnerable to failure and therefore is less desirable.

In the following sections we briefly describe some of the functions of the distributed DBMS.

System Recovery

Each site (or node) in a distributed system is subject to the same types of failure as a centralized system (erroneous data, disk head crash, and so on). However, there is the additional risk of failure of a communications link (or loss of messages). For a system to be robust, it must be able to *detect* a failure, *reconfigure* the system so that computation may continue, and *recover* when a processor or link is repaired (Korth and Silberschatz 1986).

Error detection and system reconfiguration are probably the function of the communications controller or processor, rather than the DBMS. However, the distributed DBMS is responsible for data base recovery when a failure has occurred. The distributed DBMS at each site has a component called the **transaction manager** that performs the following functions:

1. Maintains a log of transactions and before and after data base images
2. Maintains an appropriate concurrency control scheme to ensure data integrity during parallel execution of transactions at that site

For global transactions, the transaction managers at each participating site cooperate to ensure that all update operations are synchronized. This is necessary since without such cooperation, data integrity could be lost when a failure occurs. To illustrate how this might happen, suppose the bank we used in the earlier example stores a copy of its CUSTOMER relation (Figure 16-3) at each branch (data replication). Now suppose that the customer Smith, whose account is located at the Valley branch, moves and her account should now be moved to the Lakeview branch. This transaction, which is initiated (say) at the Lakeview branch, is global since every copy of the data base must be updated. However, without proper coordination, if the communications link between the Valley and Lakeview branches fails while the transaction is being processed, then the change would not be reflected in Smith's record at the Valley branch.

To ensure data integrity for update operations, the cooperating transaction managers execute a commit protocol. A **commit protocol** is a well-defined procedure (involving an exchange of messages) to ensure that a global transaction is successfully completed at each site, or else it is aborted. The most widely used protocol is called a **two-phase commit.** First, the site originating the global transaction sends a request to each of the sites that will process some portion of the transaction. Each site processes the subtransaction (if possible), but does not immediately commit (or store) the result to the local data base. Each notifies the originating site when it has completed its subtransaction. When all sites have responded, the originating site now initiates the two-phase commit protocol:

1. A message is broadcast to every participating site, asking whether that site is willing to commit its portion of the transaction at that site. Each site returns an "OK" or "not OK" message.
2. The originating site collects the messages from all sites. If all are "OK," it broadcasts a message to all sites to commit the transaction. If one or more responses are "not OK," it broadcasts a message to all sites to abort the transaction.

This description of a two-phase commit protocol is highly simplified. For a more detailed discussion of this and other protocols, see Date (1983) and Korth and Silberschatz (1986).

Concurrency Control

We introduced the topic of concurrency control in Chapter 11. Briefly, the DBMS must provide a mechanism for protecting the data base when transactions can be executed in parallel against the data base. The problem of concurrency control is more complex with distributed data bases, since programs at different sites may concurrently attempt to update records at a particular site.

The transaction managers (introduced above) at each site must cooperate to provide concurrency control. Two basic approaches may be used: locking (introduced in Chapter 11), and timestamping.

Locking There are two locking modes: shared and exclusive. If a transaction locks a record in shared mode, then it can read that record but cannot write the record (other transactions can also access the record). If a transaction locks a record in exclusive mode, then it can both read and write the record (but no other transaction can access the record while it is locked).

Before executing an update operation, a transaction must acquire an exclusive lock on every copy of the record to be accessed. For example, in the bank application, a transaction to modify a customer record would have to put an exclusive lock on each copy of the customer record at the various branches. The distributed DBMS at each site has a component called a **lock manager** that performs this function.

Recall from Chapter 11 that a problem with using locks is the occurrence of deadlocks (or deadly embrace). This problem is magnified in a distributed environment since there may be a **global deadlock**—a deadlock involving two or more sites. A simple example of this is illustrated in Figure 16-8, involving two sites (A and B). In processing a transaction, program A at site A has locked record X (we assume all locks are exclusive). The program then requests a lock on record Y at site B. Concurrently, program B at site B has locked record Y and has requested a lock on record X. The system is deadlocked; no further processing can occur without intervention.

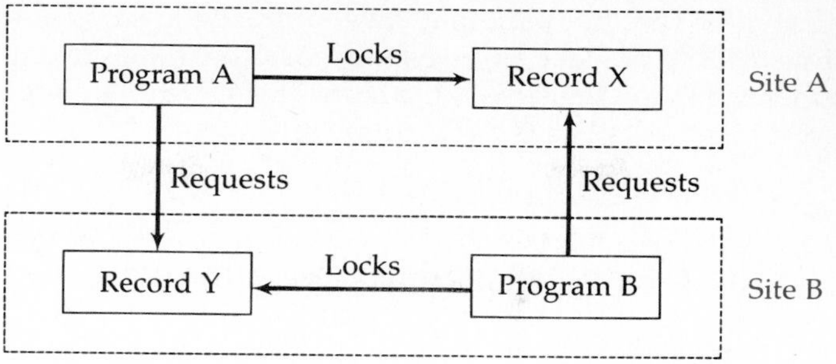

Figure 16-8
Example of global deadlock

The situation shown in Figure 16-8 is the simplest example; global deadlock may also involve multiple sites. Notice that the lock manager at each site cannot detect the deadlock using only the information available at that site. To detect and then resolve the deadlock, there must be a global deadlock detection manager that assembles the information from the sites that are involved. This function may be performed either in a centralized or distributed manner [see Date (1983) for an extended discussion]. Global deadlock detection and correction incurs additional communications overhead, and remains an active area of research in distributed data base management.

Timestamping With this approach, every transaction is given a globally unique timestamp. This timestamp generally consists of the clock time when the transaction occurred, plus the site ID. Timestamping ensures that even if two events occur simultaneously at different sites, each will have a unique timestamp.

The purpose of timestamping is to ensure that transactions are processed in serial order, thereby avoiding the use of locks (and the possibility of deadlocks). Every record in the data base carries the timestamp of the transaction that last updated it. If a new transaction attempts to update that record, and if its timestamp is *earlier* than that carried in the record, then the transaction is assigned a new timestamp and it is restarted. Thus, a transaction cannot process a record until its timestamp is *later* than that carried in the record, and therefore it cannot interfere with another transaction.

The obvious advantage of timestamping is that locking and deadlock detection (and the associated overhead) are avoided. The disadvantage is that transactions that are in conflict must be rolled back and restarted, which increases processing and response times.

Query Optimization

With distributed data bases, the response to a query may require that data be assembled from several different sites (although with location transparency, the user is unaware of this need). The way in which the query is formulated by the user may have a drastic impact on the response time. Date (1983) provides an excellent yet simple example of this problem. Consider the following situation adapted from Date. A simplified procurement (relational) data base has the three relations:

SUPPLIER(SUPPLIER#,CITY)	10,000 records, stored in Detroit
PART(PART#,COLOR)	100,000 records, stored in Chicago
SHIPMENT(SUPPLIER#,PART#)	1,000,000 records, stored in Detroit

and a query is made (in SQL/DS) to list the supplier numbers for Cleveland suppliers of red parts:

```
SELECT  SUPPLIER.SUPPLIER#
FROM    SUPPLIER, SHIPMENT, PART
WHERE   SUPPLIER.CITY       ='Cleveland'
AND     SUPPLIER.SUPPLIER#  =SHIPMENT.SUPPLIER#
AND     SHIPMENT.PART#      =PART.PART#
AND     PART.COLOR          ='Red'
```

Further, suppose that each record in each relation is 100 characters long, there are 10 red parts, a history of 100,000 shipments from Cleveland, and a negligible query computation time compared with communication time. Also, assume a communication system with a data transmission rate of 10,000 characters per second and a 1-second access delay to send a message from one node to another.

Date identifies six plausible query-processing strategies for this situation and develops the associated communication times; these strategies and times are summarized in Table 16-1. Depending on the choice of strategy, the time required to satisfy the query ranges from 1 second to 2.3 days! Although the last strategy is best, the fourth strategy may also be acceptable.

In general, this example would indicate that it is often advisable to break a query in a distributed data base environment into components that are isolated at different sites, then determine which site has the potential to yield the fewest number of qualified tuples/records, and then move this result to another site where additional work is performed. Obviously, more than two sites require even more complex analyses and more complicated heuristics to guide query processing. The Bernstein et al. (1981) text contains an excellent discussion of optimization of query processing in probably the most sophisticated distributed DBMS now available, SDD-1 from Computer Corporation of America. As we will see in the next section, expert systems may be employed in conjunction with a distributed DBMS for query optimization.

Summary of Distributed Data Bases

Distributed data base management in some form is a necessity in the data communications–oriented world of the future. Recent introductions of DBMSs on personal computers that link a PC data base to an associated mainframe

Table 16-1 Query-Processing Strategies in a Distributed Data Base Environment (Adapted from Date 1983)

Method	Time
Move PART relation to Detroit and process whole query at Detroit computer.	16.7 minutes
Move SUPPLIER and SHIPMENT to Chicago and process whole query at Chicago computer.	28 hours
JOIN SUPPLIER and SHIPMENT at the Detroit computer, PROJECT these down to only tuples for Cleveland suppliers, and then for each of these, check at the Chicago computer to determine if associated PART is red.	2.3 days
PROJECT PART at the Chicago computer down to just the red items and for each, check at the Detroit computer to see if there is some SHIPMENT involving that PART and a Cleveland SUPPLIER.	20 seconds
JOIN SUPPLIER and SHIPMENT at the Detroit computer and PROJECT just SUPPLIER# and PART# for only Cleveland SUPPLIERs and move this qualified projection to Chicago for matching with red PARTs.	16.7 minutes
Select just red PARTs at the Chicago computer and move the result to Detroit for matching with Cleveland SUPPLIERs.	1 second

data base provide a new dimension to distributed data bases. Whatever the form, distributed data bases will be necessary in many environments that are not efficient enough or reliable enough with only centralized data processing. Several commercial DBMS products—including ORACLE, INGRES, and IDMS/R—now have distributed versions that provide many of the facilities discussed in this section. With current technology, the same brand of DBMS must be running at each node in the network, but this is changing to allow a heterogeneous set of products. Crucial to the success of a distributed data base is a distributed DD/DS to inventory what data are stored where, how they are stored and formatted, and how they synchronize updates across distributed sites.

DATA BASE COMPUTERS

It is common practice to use specialized front-end communication processors to off-load computer network communication functions from a general-purpose host computer. Not only have these functions been separated into distinct machines, but these separate machines have been uniquely designed to handle the specific type of data processing in telecommunications. Simply from the viewpoint of symmetry, a back-end data base computer would seem possible to be able to handle the specialized and high-volume activity of data base processing.

It is not uncommon in large data centers today to find separate general-purpose computers performing the bulk of the data base processing, especially data inquiry. Periodically, files are transferred to such separate, independent computers from others that perform transaction processing and data base maintenance. Such copies of production data bases frequently support information center or end user computing tasks; some people refer to these data base extracts or copies as "shadow data bases." The growth in data base size and processing activity creates an expensive data processing burden that one centralized computer cannot safely handle by itself.

A major problem with this use of a general-purpose computer for data base processing is cost. Epstein (1983) has reported that typical mainframe computer technology costs from $100,000 to $400,000 per million of instructions per second (MIPS). However, with the use of special-purpose data base computers connected to a general-purpose host, data base processing cost can be reduced to as little as $10,000 per MIPS on a data base computer. Because of their special architecture to handle data base searching and query processing, data base computers can search as many as 30,000 records per second. Curtice and Casey (1985) predict that this price/performance advantage means that specialized data base processors will play a significant role in data base processing within the next five or so years. By 1987, there were approximately 1000 data base computers installed in organizations worldwide (including financial, manufacturing, government, telecommunications, and many other industries). Experience has shown that the use of data base computers is, in general, justified when an organization exhibits a steady, high-volume stream of data base transactions.

Data Base Computer Environment

Figure 16-9 depicts the difference between a conventional DBMS environment and a DBMS in a data base computer environment. We will discuss several alternative implementations of this general picture shortly, but basically the data base computer contains a customized operating system and the run-time components of the DBMS. Data dictionary, data definition, and other DBMS functions may or may not be moved to the data base computer (DBC).

Operationally, with the DBC present, data manipulation commands or DBMS calls are transferred via a high-speed data channel to the DBC as encountered in an application program in the host. These commands are interpreted and queued for processing in the DBC. The data base is searched for the required data and the requested data and/or DBMS messages are passed back to the host into the working storage area of the calling program. This whole process is transparent to the application program, since the DBMS call and the result apparently occur to the user as they would in the conventional environment.

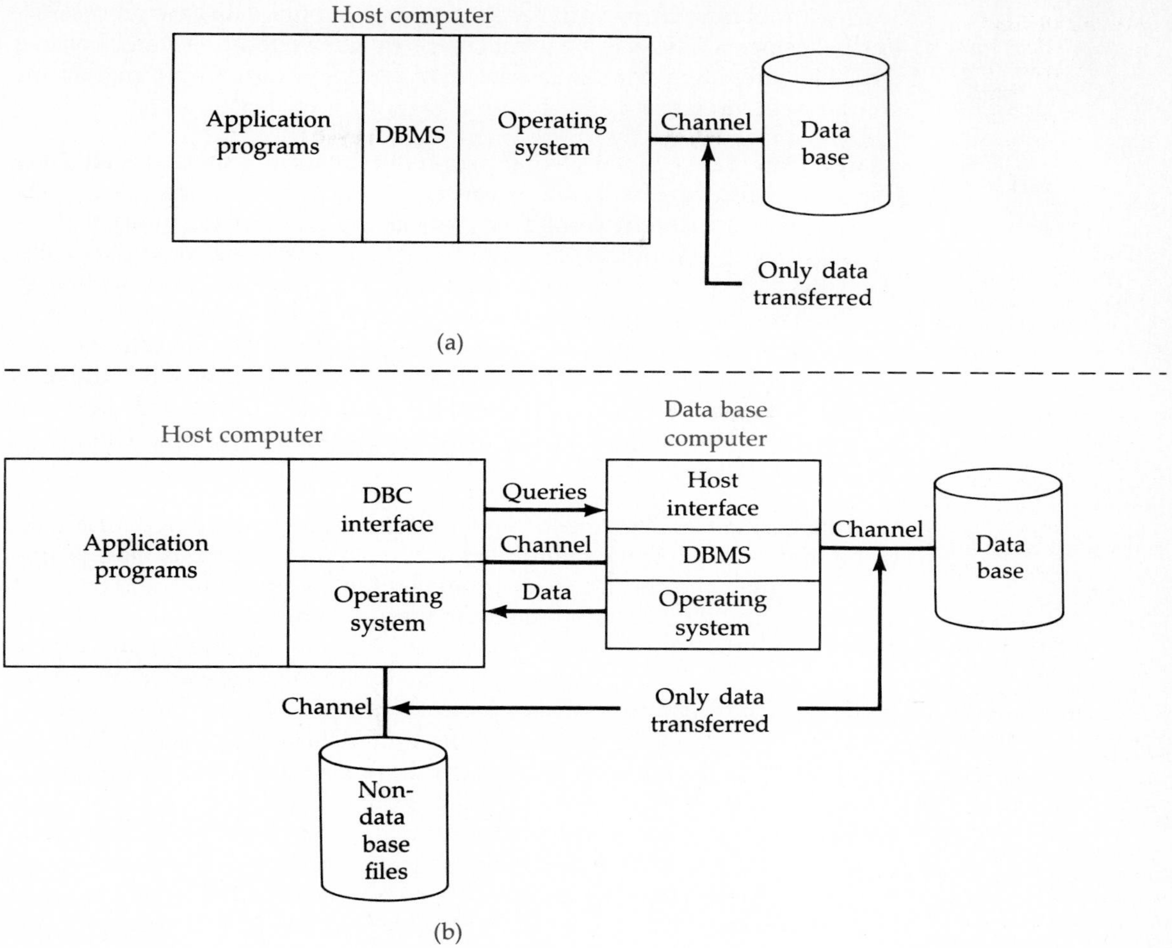

Figure 16-9 Comparison of conventional and data base computer configurations:
(a) conventional DBMS configuration
(b) data base computer configuration

Objectives and Hazards of Data Base Computers

Data base computers provide a number of benefits.

Portability The DBMS, residing in its own hardware, can be connected to a wide variety of general-purpose computers. This allows an application user to use a desired DBMS (on the separate DBC) even though that DBMS was not designed to run on the host computer being used. This not only gives users greater flexibility, but also opens up new markets for DBMS vendors.

Security Data security protection can be a costly overhead expense in a data base environment, since security enforcement consumes CPU cycles while other programs wait. A DBC allows extensive security controls to be used without interfering with the productivity of non–data base processing. Further, since a DBC can be simultaneously connected to several hosts, a DBC can provide a centralized security service in a multiple mainframe computer environment.

Shared Data Base Since several mainframe host computers can all share the same DBC, an organization can achieve greater sharing of its data. Specialized department computers, laboratory computers, internal time-sharing service computers, and the like can all share the same data base. The DBC handles concurrency control for all hosts, as well as providing an efficient data base processing service. It is even possible for each host to be running a different DBMS, as long as there is software to translate the local host query into the language (usually SQL) of the DBC. One DBC, the IDM 500 from Britton Lee Corp., can support up to 4096 hosts, and these can be from different vendors (including IBM mainframes and PCs, DEC VAX, and Univac (UNISYS)).

Cost Performance The most frequently mentioned advantage for a DBC is the more cost-effective manipulation of data that results. A DBC is specially designed and configured to provide rapid data searching and retrieval at an economical price. A special operating system can be utilized to concentrate on efficient secondary storage management. Some highly repetitive and stable DBMS functions can be built into the hardware or firmware of the DBC. Off-loading data base processing to a DBC also makes available more time on the host(s) for doing other non–data base processing. Various estimates of performance improvement have been reported, but a conservative figure is that a user can expect at least a 25% reduction in data base processing time compared to conventional DBMS software (although as much as a 90% reduction has been reported). Higher performance gains can be achieved when single data base commands require significant data base processing. This is why the relational data model (set processing) is the standard for DBCs, not the network model (record processing).

These benefits of DBCs are balanced by some potential hazards.

Vulnerability All the data in the data base attached to a DBC are accessible only through the DBC. If the DBC suffers a severe failure, all data base processing can cease, unless appropriate backup has been performed that will allow the hosts to take over data base retrieval and maintenance duties. On the other hand, most DBC technology has the capability for planned data redundancy, so that if selected disk storage devices or channels cannot operate, alternate paths to redundant data can be utilized; this means less vulnerability than with conventional data base technology.

Applicability A DBC is not cost-effective in all data base environments. In order for a DBC to provide significant cost/performance improvements, Champine (1977) has estimated that at least 40% of the host workload should be data base accessing.

Complexity A DBC does add complexity to the data base environment. Additional hardware vendors may be necessary in the data center, one for the host computer and another for the DBC (as of 1987, IBM still does not have a DBC product; some industry experts suggest that a DBC will never be a major product until IBM offers one). Problems can go unresolved as different vendors try to blame each other. The DBC, because of its possibly different architecture, is not a widely understood technology. Special training, reliance on vendor personnel, and a small user base all contribute to unexpected DBMS support costs.

Conversion Most organizations that have developed the need for a DBC have been using DBMS technology for many years and usually have many data bases under hierarchical or network architectures. All the major DBC products work with the relational data model and the SQL processing language (see Chapter 14). Conversion can be a very time-consuming and costly effort with a large installed base of applications. Thus, typically a DBC is applied first to a new application, and existing data base applications are converted only when major enhancements or redesigns are needed, or when severe processing schedule bottlenecks have developed.

Data Base Computer Architectures

Various technologies are being used for data base computers (see Banerjee, Baum, and Hsiao 1978; Champine 1977; Epstein 1983; Hawthorn 1981; and Maryanski 1980). Some of the alternatives are depicted in Figure 16-10. These alternatives include the back-end general-purpose processor, the intelligent peripheral control unit, and the special-purpose processor.

Back-End General-Purpose Processor With the back-end general-purpose processor, a master host uses a dedicated slave general-purpose computer to perform the data base processing. The host may be a large mainframe and the slave may be a minicomputer, although other combinations are possible. This alternative achieves the advantages of simultaneous data base and other processing, but does not utilize a more cost-effective data base processing technology in the dedicated slave. When several hosts share the same dedicated slave data base computer, this DBC can be viewed as one node in a computer network.

Intelligent Peripheral Control Unit With the intelligent peripheral control unit, highly repetitive and detailed functions of the DBMS are moved out of the host and placed in the logic of a mass storage unit controller device. This relieves the host from such processing steps. Such functions can include data content searching, sorting, data validation and error correction, data access scheduling, and even data recovery. Data may also be read in parallel across several surfaces of a multiple-surface secondary storage medium like magnetic disk. This type of associative storage and parallel processing means

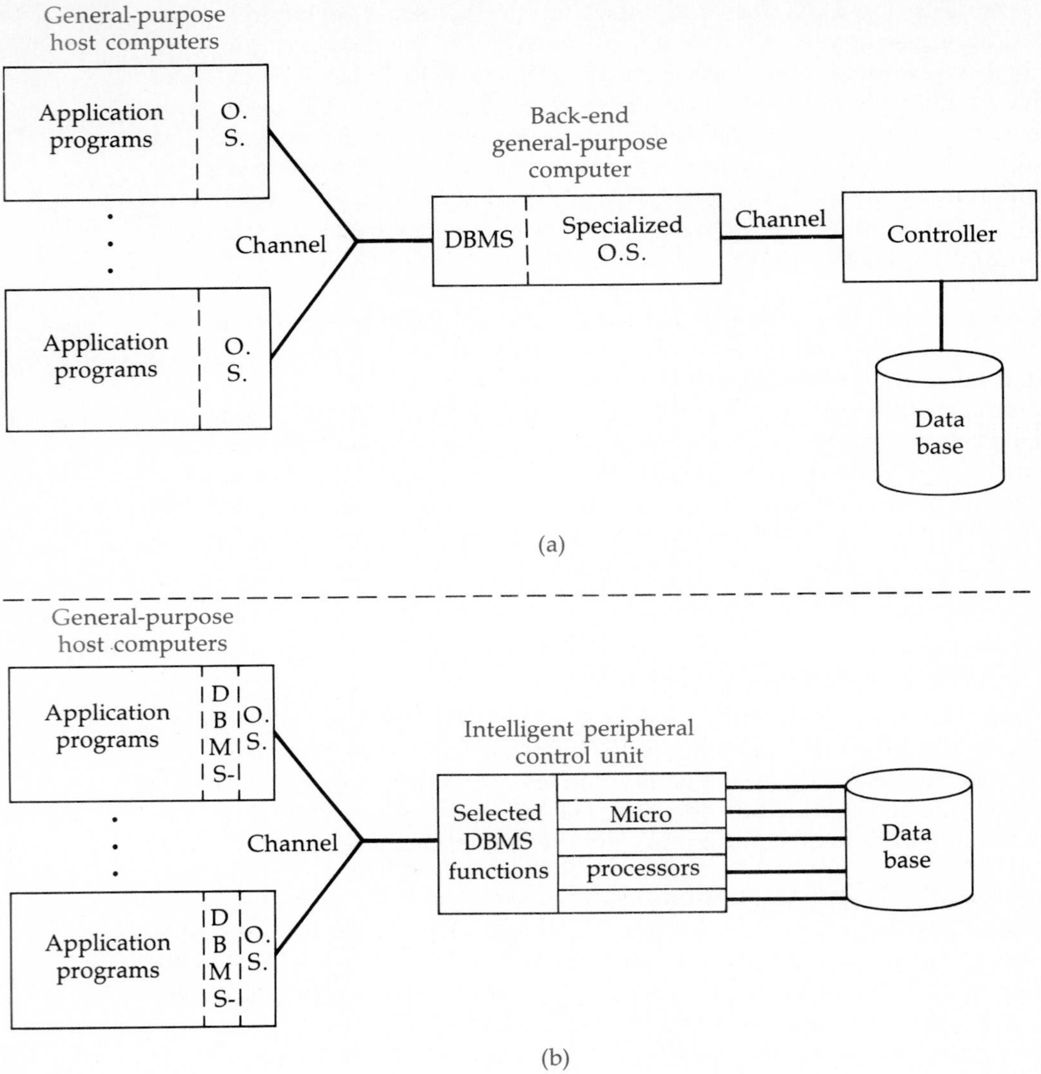

Figure 16-10
Alternative data base computer (DBC) configurations:
(a) back-end general-purpose processor DBC
(b) intelligent peripheral control unit DBC
(c) special-purpose processor DBC

that a whole disk cylinder can be searched for qualified data in approximately the time of one disk revolution. One version of this approach moves these data base processing functions literally to the read/write heads of the secondary storage devices. Some authors refer to this approach as *logic-per-track*.

Special-Purpose Processors The approach of the special-purpose processor is similar to the logic-per-track disk drives, except that such associative processing is done in the main memory of the special processor. Data are

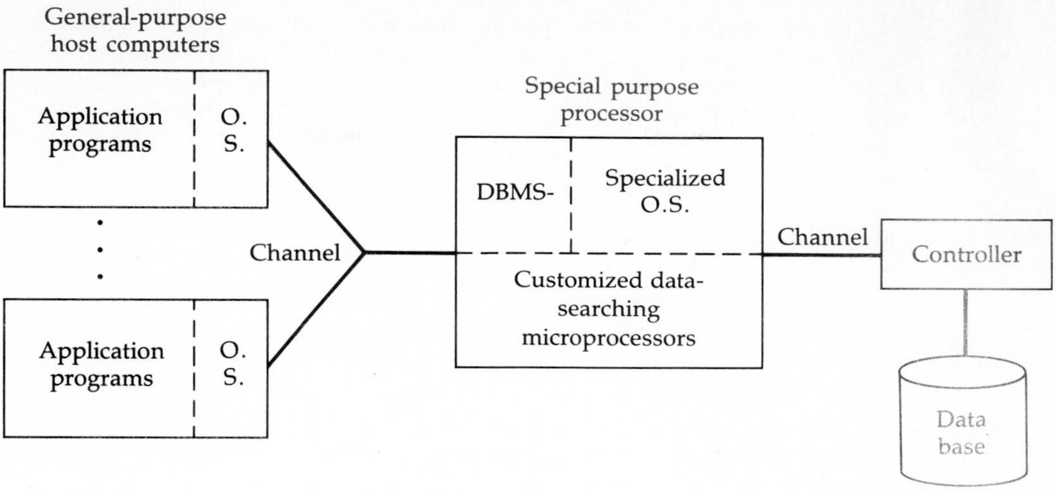

(c)

Figure 16-10
(continued)

staged into the DBC main memory, where they can be searched rapidly in predetermined patterns; these patterns often correspond to certain relational operations such as SELECT or JOIN. Although specifically designed hardware can be most cost-effective in this case, existing array processor technology, such as the Goodyear Aerospace STARAN computer, has been used as a DBMS staging device (Maryanski 1980). Most of the DBC products today are special-purpose processors. Frequently, a DBC is an array of microprocessors, each responsible for performing the same data base operation in parallel for a segment of the data base. For example, the DBC/1012 from Teradata Corp. can be configured with as many as 1024 microprocessors. A more typical 60-processor configuration offers 24MIPS of processing power and 19 gigabytes of on-line disk storage capacity. Each data base logical file is physically spread across multiple disk drives and channels so that multiple access arms and channels can work simultaneously to retrieve the desired data. Thus, a major limiting factor in DBC speed is the transfer rate (and associated recording density) between secondary and main memory.

Summary of Data Base Computers

Because of the continued rapid advances in microcomputer and disk technologies, there is no clear trend in data base computers. Some of the developments in personal computer DBMSs in which inquiry (especially ad hoc access) processing is being downloaded to desktop computers naturally reduces the data base workload on mainframes (see Chapter 15 for more details). This plus increased capabilities for networking personal computer data bases may reduce the need for data base computers as now defined. Some authorities have argued that the DBCs of the future will be file servers on computer networks. DBCs, however, still have a number of advantages, and high data base activity data centers should consider their application.

INTELLIGENT DATA BASE SYSTEMS

Artificial intelligence is the use of computers to carry out tasks that, if performed by humans, would be considered intelligent. Artificial intelligence techniques are being applied to data base systems on a variety of fronts, and promise to have a dramatic impact in the near future. Two branches of artificial intelligence that are already being used to enhance data base systems are natural language systems and expert systems. We discuss each of these developments briefly in this section.

Natural Language Systems

Natural language systems allow users to carry on a dialogue with the computer in everyday language, rather than having to use a structured command language. For example, a user can type a query such as "WHICH SALESPEOPLE SOLD MORE THAN $100,000 IN THE LAST 6 MONTHS" rather than a structured query such as:

```
RETRIEVE SALESID FROM SALESTABLE WHERE TOTALSALES >
  100,000
```

The most common use of natural language today is for data base query. Natural language systems facilitate data base access for novice and occasional users, and also often provide experienced users with a faster, more natural way to accomplish a particular task.

The components of a natural language system are shown in Figure 16-11. A program called the **parser** examines the syntax of each sentence and breaks the sentence into components (nouns, verbs, adjectives, and so on). The result of this step is a "parse tree" that resembles a sentence diagram in a high school English class. The next step is a semantic analysis of the sentence, performed by a program called the semantic analyzer. This program refers to a dictionary that contains a list of synonyms for key English words. For example, the verb "get" may be translated as "retrieve" by the analyzer. Once the whole sentence has been analyzed, the **code generator** translates the request to an application language (such as SQL), which contains the necessary instructions to respond to the user's request.

At the present time relatively few natural language systems are being marketed. A system called Intellect (Artificial Intelligence Corporation) has been available for some time as a natural language interface for mainframe data base management systems such as DB2 and IDMS/R (see in Chapter

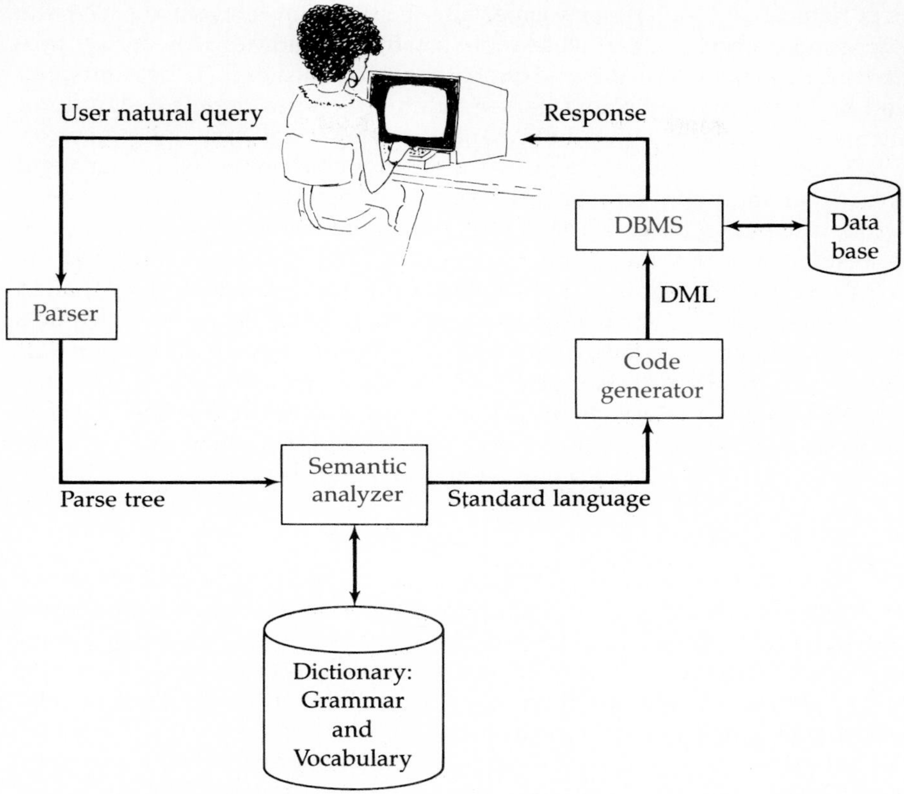

Figure 16-11
Components of a natural language system

13 the section "Natural Languages"). One of the first natural languages for personal computers was Clout (Microrim), a natural language interface for R:base 5000. Also, the Intelligent Assistant (Symantec) is a natural language interface for the Q&A data base system.

At the present time, natural language interfaces have two disadvantages:

1. Response time may be slower than for structured languages due to the need for sentence analysis and operational query composition.
2. Current systems are limited in their ability to understand natural languages such as English. For example, at the present time, the Intelligent Assistant has a vocabulary of about 400 words. It is necessary for a system administrator to maintain a "lexicon" of terminology to match natural language phrases to structured language command elements. The construction of this lexicon can be time-consuming and costly.

A consequence of this limited and application-specific vocabulary is that user queries can be frequently rejected as nonunderstandable or, even worse, misinterpreted, thus resulting in an erroneous response. Frequent rejection of a natural language query, especially if little help is given on why the parser has rejected it, can cause more frustration and even lower user productivity than with a structured query language, such as SQL. The difficulty can be overcome with more parser training, but this means a significant increase in human overhead for managing the natural language processor.

Despite these disadvantages, natural languages are easier to learn and to use than more conventional interfaces, and they save time for most users. It may also be that natural language queries promote better human retention of results since the query and response are both in a form similar to the user's conceptualization or motivation for the query. It seems likely that, in the future, most PC software (including data base packages) will include a natural language interface, thus expanding the set of potential users of data bases. One threat to this evolution toward natural language is icon and mouse human interfaces (see Chapter 15 on Macintosh DBMSs) that may be as easy to use as natural language but without the ambiguity.

Expert Systems

An **expert system** is a system that captures the knowledge and experience of an expert, in the form of facts and rules, in order to aid others make decisions in a subject domain (see Sprague and McNurlin 1986). Expert systems have been built in medicine, engineering, geology, and other fields to encode the knowledge of experts and to allow others to improve their decision making by using these systems. Expert systems are especially useful in business applications, where a combination of knowledge and judgment is required. For example, Campbell Soup Company built an expert system to help troubleshoot and maintain the large cookers used to sterilize soup.

The major components of an expert system are shown in Figure 16-12. At the center of the expert system is the knowledge base, which contains the facts, rules, and other information relative to a problem domain. Facts represent knowledge that is generally available to, and accepted by, experts in a certain field, such as accounting principles, tax regulations, labor costs, engineering standards, and so on. An example of a fact is the following: "The lead-time for Supplier A is two weeks."

Rules are the set of heuristics (or guidelines for searching for a solution) that experts typically use to reach a decision. Rules are often expressed as IF-THEN statements such as the following:

IF INVENTORY < REORDER POINT
THEN PLACE NEW ORDER

Most existing rule-based systems contain hundreds or thousands of rules such as this. The rules are captured by interviewing one or more experts for weeks or months. As shown in Figure 16-12, a special analyst called a **knowledge engineer** may be involved in interviewing or observing the experts and encoding their knowledge (in the form of rules) into the knowl-

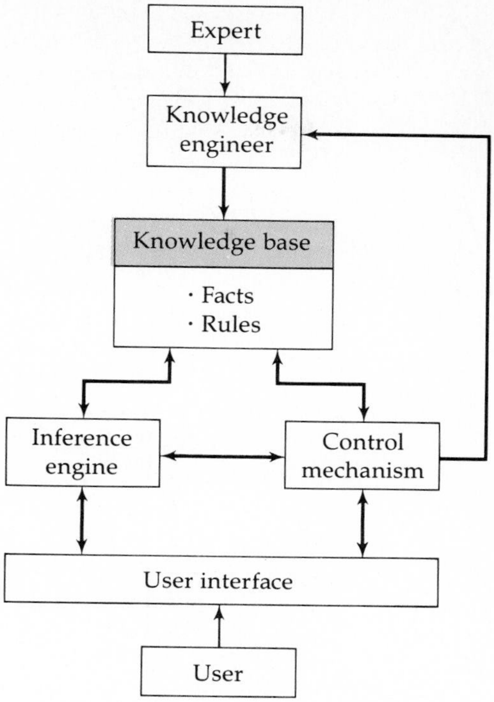

Figure 16-12 Components of an expert system (*Source:* Adapted from Moser 1986)

edge base. The many rules in a knowledge base are connected together to form a network that can be traversed in solving a given problem.

Rules in the knowledge base are processed or interpreted by a program called the **inference engine.** The user engages in a dialogue through an interface, which prompts the user to answer a series of questions concerning the problem. The inference engine may also call outside programs to query a data base for information or perform mathematical calculations. The inference engine may employ one of two principal strategies: backward chaining, or forward chaining. With forward chaining, the program starts with the appropriate IF clauses and works forward until a desired goal-state (or solution) is found. With backward chaining, the program starts with a desired goal or result and scans the rules to find those whose consequent actions can achieve the goal. In practice, an expert system may employ both strategies.

The control mechanism in Figure 16-12 serves as a system manager. It administers all of the resources of the system, decides when to start the inference engine, when to query the user for additional information, when to stop the process, and so on.

The use of expert systems is growing rapidly. The following are considered prerequisites for the success of an expert system [see Andriole (1985) for an elaboration]:

Figure 16-13
Expert data base system (*Source:* Kerschberg 1986)

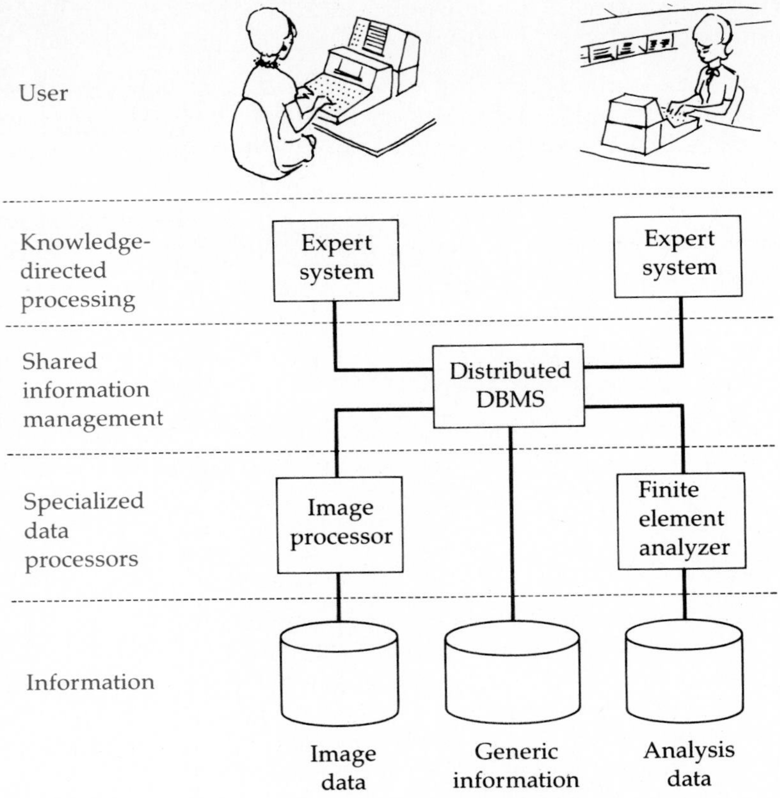

1. There must be at least one human expert acknowledged to perform the task well.
2. The primary source of the expert's exceptional performance must be special knowledge, judgment, and experience.
3. The expert must be able to explain the special knowledge and experience and the methods used to apply them to particular problems.
4. The task must have a well-bounded domain of application.

Expert Data Base Systems

Work is moving ahead rapidly on the knowledge-based approach to data base management. An evolving architecture is shown in Figure 16-13. In this model, there are three kinds of system components between the users and the data or information: expert systems for guiding the users in accessing and using the data base, a DBMS for shared information management, and (if appropriate) specialized processors for handling data in special formats (such as images). The DBMS and expert systems may be distributed across multiple processors.

Expert systems can provide numerous functions for data base users. Some of the more important of these are:

1. Provide assistance to users in composing data base queries. An expert system may provide instructive help messages, compose queries on the user's behalf, and/or reformulate queries to minimize response times.
2. Consult with users or data base designers on performance evaluation and suggest ways to "tune" the data base for improved performance.
3. Assist users and data analysts in constructing new external schemas to meet new data base requirements.
4. Assist data base administrators in developing improved schemes for data base security and integrity.

It seems likely that in the future, knowledge-based systems will have a major impact on data base management, and that most DBMS products will have natural language and/or expert system "front ends."

Knowledge-Based Decision Support Systems

We introduced decision support systems in Chapter 1. A decision support system (DSS) consists of a data base, a model base, and a user-friendly interface. It is used by managers and others to assist the decision-making process. A simple DSS may consist of a personal computer with decision support tools that is linked to a mainframe computer and its data bases (see Figure 1-9).

A natural extension of the DSS concept is to add an expert system that helps the user use the DSS in the decision-making process. We call such a system a knowledge-based decision support system, or KBDSS.* A model of such a system (called EXSYS) is shown in Figure 16-14.

EXSYS is an expert system development tool or shell, which allows users to develop knowledge-based decision support systems. As shown in Figure 16-14, it contains a user knowledge base, a system knowledge base, and a model library. The user knowledge base contains the facts and rules described earlier that are associated with an expert system. The model library consists of a set of simulation models that are used to model a corporation over time. The results of the business simulation are stored in the system knowledge base in a form called T-Matrices (T represents time). The system knowledge base also includes system functions such as net present value, internal rate of return, and others.

As noted, the system shown in Figure 16-14 is a KBDSS. It allows the user to build a corporate model by selecting appropriate modeling tools from the model base. The user knowledge base is then used to evaluate and interpret the model results.

*We are indebted to Professor Scott C. McIntyre of the University of Colorado, Colorado Springs for suggesting the concept of a Knowledge-Based Decision Support System and for many of the ideas contained in this section.

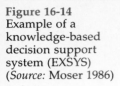

Figure 16-14
Example of a knowledge-based decision support system (EXSYS) (*Source:* Moser 1986)

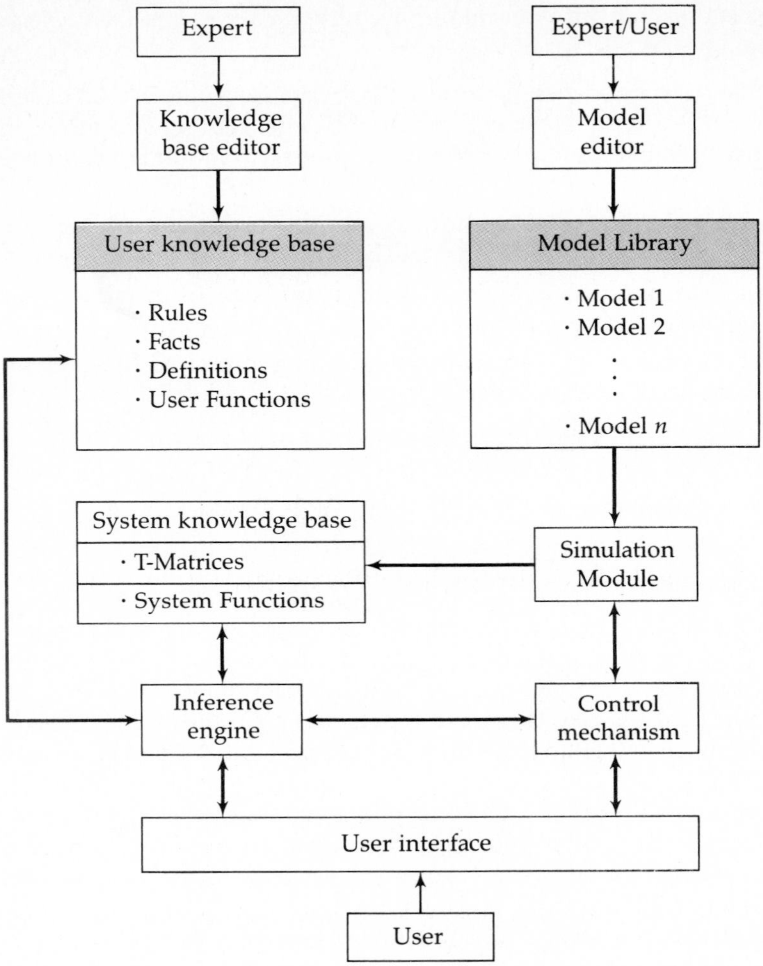

In this model, the user has access to a knowledge base that (in conjunction with the inference engine) consults with the user in using the DSS in solving a problem. The expert system can provide assistance in the following areas (among others):

1. Identifying and describing a problem in the real-world problem domain
2. Selecting appropriate models from the model base and appropriate data from the data base
3. Suggesting decision alternatives and appropriate methods of analysis
4. Interpreting results and suggesting new queries and problem formulations
5. Providing rules for terminating the analysis and recommending a course of action

SUMMARY

Many authors, futurists, and management thinkers believe that we are now a part of an information society. Estimates have been made that from 10% to 50% of payroll costs are being spent to collect, distribute, and maintain the organizational information resource. There is even discussion in the accounting profession on how to value the *information asset* of a business and how to include this in financial statements.

Data base management will play an important role in such an information society. Systems analysts, designers, programmers, and users alike will define, administer, protect, account for, and guarantee the accuracy of the information resource. DBMS technology will permit a variety of data organizations that will facilitate cost-effective storage and access of this valuable resource. It is becoming increasingly more important for managers to be able to effectively use technology to manage data.

Computer industry analysts predict that the number of DBMSs will increase significantly in the future, in part because vendors of other management support software products (e.g., electronic spreadsheets, statistical analysis, graphics presentation, and text processing) are expanding to include DBMS functionality. Further, PC-DBMSs are growing in power as the power of PCs expands, and some PC product vendors are introducing mainframe versions (as mainframe vendors are introducing PC versions). The Macintosh desktop metaphor is significantly influencing DBMS technology to provide highly nonprocedural, user-friendly front-ends to relational DBMSs. And the rapidly developing trends reviewed in this chapter (distributed data bases, data base computers, and expert data base systems) add to the picture of a field under constant and, at times, concept-shaking change.

To become an information systems professional in general and a data base specialist in particular requires a commitment to continued learning, acceptance of new ideas and technologies, and a humble attitude that comes from recognizing that you can never know enough. To be involved in the development of data bases in organizations places one in the center of an evolution of management practice. Best wishes on putting the principles of data management into practice!

Chapter Review

REVIEW QUESTIONS

1. Define each of the following terms:
   a. centralized data base
   b. distributed data base
   c. decentralized data base
   d. partitioned distributed data base
   e. data base computer
   f. logic-per-track

g. mainframe link PC-DBMS
h. location transparency
i. artificial intelligence
j. knowledge engineer

2. Explain the relative advantages of centralized, decentralized, and distributed data bases.
3. Explain how distributed data bases help to achieve both centralized and decentralized data processing.
4. What are the disadvantages of replicated data in a distributed data base?
5. Describe a situation in which a vertical partitioning of the Pine Valley Furniture data base would be of benefit.
6. Explain how deadlock can occur in a distributed data base.
7. Explain the benefits of a special-purpose data base computer.
8. Why do you think that data base computers are not standard equipment in a modern data center?
9. Why might a natural language processor not always answer the question the user wanted to ask?
10. What can an expert system do?
11. Match the most appropriate definition with each of the following terms.

_____ star network
_____ array processor
_____ horizontal partition
_____ backtracking
_____ gateway
_____ transaction manager

a. fragmentation of a row from a table across many sites in network
b. access mechanism to communicate with devices outside a LAN
c. inference strategy
d. distributed computers with a central hub node
e. multiple, parallel processors
f. component of a distributed DBMS responsible for concurrency control and logging

REFERENCES

Andriole, Stephen J., ed. 1985. *Applications in Artificial Intelligence.* Princeton, N.J.: Petrocelli Books (in particular p. 48).

Banerjee, Jayanta, Richard I. Baum, and David K. Hsiao. 1978. "Concepts and Capabilities of a Database Computer." *ACM-TODS* 3 (December): 347–384.

Bernstein, Philip A., Nathan Goodman, Eugene Wong, Christopher L. Reeve, and James B. Rothnie, Jr. 1981. "Query Processing in a System for Distributed Databases (SDD-1)." *ACM-TODS* 6 (December): 602–625.

Champine, G. A. 1977. "Six Approaches to Distributed Data Bases." *Datamation* 23 (May): 69–72.

Curtice, Robert M., and William Casey. 1985. "Database: What's in Store." *Datamation* (December 1): 83–88.

Date, C. J. 1983. *An Introduction to Database Systems.* Vol. 2. Reading, Mass.: Addison-Wesley.

Epstein, Robert. 1983. "Why Database Machines?" *Datamation* (July): 139,140,144.

Hawthorn, Paula. 1981. "The Effect of Target Applications on the Design of Database Machines." In *Proceedings ACM SIGMOD 1981*, available from Association for Computing Machinery.

Kerschberg, Larry, ed. 1986. *Expert Database Systems.* Menlo Park, Calif.: Benjamin/Cummings (in particular p. 7).

Korth, Henry F., and Abraham Silberschatz. 1986. *Database System Concepts.* New York: McGraw-Hill.

Maryanski, Fred J. 1980. "Backend Database Systems." *ACM-Computing Surveys* 12 (March): 3–25.

Moser, Jorge G. 1986. "Integration of Artificial Intelligence and Simulation in a Comprehensive Decision Support System." *Simulation* 47 (December): 223–229.

Sprague, Ralph H., and Barbara C. McNurlin. 1986. *Information Systems in Practice.* Englewood Cliffs, N.J.: Prentice-Hall.

Zloof, M. M. 1977. "Query-by-Example: A Data Base Language." *IBM Systems Journal* 16(4): 324–343.

Glossary of Acronyms

ACM Association for Computing Machinery.

AD Action Diagram.

ADF Application Development Facility.

ANSI/SPARC American National Standards Institute/Standards Planning and Requirements Committee.

ASCII American Standards Code for Information Interchange.

BCNF Boyce-Codd Normal Form.

BSP Business Systems Planning

CAD/CAM Computer-Aided Design/Computer-Aided Manufacturing.

CDC Control Data Corporation.

CD–ROM Compact Disk–Read-Only Memory.

COBOL COmmon Business Oriented Language.

CODASYL Committee On DAta SYstem Languages.

CPU Central Processing Unit.

DA Data Administrator

DASD Direct-Access Storage Device.

DBA Data Base Administrator.

DBACP Data Base Administrator Control Program.

DBC Data Base Computer.

DBCS Data Base Control System.

DBD Data Base Description.

DBMS Data Base Management System.

DBSS Data Base Storage System.

DBTG Data Base Task Group (part of CODASYL).

DCB Data Control Block.

DD/D Data Dictionary/Directory.

DD/DS Data Dictionary/Directory System.

DDL Data Definition Language. *Also* Data Description Language.

DEC Digital Equipment Corporation.

DK/NF Domain Key Normal Form.

DL/I Data Language/I (part of IMS).

DMCL Device Media Control Language.

DML Data Manipulation Language.

DSDL Data Storage Description Language.

DSS Decision Support System.

E/R Entity-Relationship.

ES Expert System.

FIFO First-In-First-Out.

FORTRAN FORmula TRANslator.

GBF Graph-By-Forms.

HDA Head-Disk Assembly.

HDAM Hierarchical Data Access Method.

HIDAM Hierarchical Indexed Direct Access Method.

HISAM Hierarchical Indexed Sequential Access Method.

HSAM Hierarchical Sequential Access Method.

IBM International Business Machines Corporation.

IDD Integrated Data Dictionary.

IDM Intelligent Database Machine.

IDMS Integrated Database Management System.

IDMS/R Integrated Database Management System/Relational.

IDS Integrated Data System.

IMS Information Management System.

I/O Input/Output.

IS Information System.

ISAM Indexed Sequential Access Method.

ISN Internal Sequence Number.

ISO International Standards Organization.

KBDSS Knowledge-Based Decision Support System.

LAM Logical Access Map.

LAN Local Area Network.

LDB Logical Data Base.

LDBR Logical Data Base Record.

LIFO Last-In-First-Out.

MB Million Bytes.

MIPS Millions of Instructions Per Second.

MIS Management Information System.

N/A Not Available.

OLE OnLine English.

OLQ OnLine Query.

OSAM Overflow Sequential Access Method.

PC Personal Computer.

PCB Program Communication Block.

PC-DBMS Personal Computer—Data Base Management System.

PC-RDBMS Personal Computer—Relational Data Base Management System.

PDBR Physical Data Base Record.

PL/I Program Language/I.

PSB Program Specification Block.

QBE Query-By-Example.

QBF Query-By-Forms.

QLP Query Language Processor.

RDBMS Relational Data Base Management System.

SAM Sequential Access Method.

SDM Semantic Data Model

SQL Structured Query Language.

SQL/DS Structured Query Language/Data System.

TODS Transactions on Database Systems.

TP TeleProcessing.

VIFRED VIsual FoRms EDitor.

VSAM Virtual Sequential Access Method.

1NF First Normal Form.

2NF Second Normal Form.

3NF Third Normal Form.

4GL Fourth-Generation Language.

4NF Fourth Normal Form.

5NF Fifth Normal Form.

Glossary of Terms

Abstraction An entity class that contains subclasses of specialized entity classes—for example, customer that might have specialized subclasses of Business Customer and Residential Customer.

Access Method A file management subprogram provided by the operating system; used for moving data between computer main memory and peripheral devices.

Access Time The elapsed time between an instruction being given to retrieve a block of data from secondary storage, and that data being made available in primary storage.

Action A step or operation that is applied to one instance of a normalized record in a data base.

Action Diagram A map or diagram that shows a sequence of actions to be performed on a data base.

Active Data Dictionary/Directory A data dictionary/directory approach in which the DD/D is the sole source of metadata in the data management system.

Activity The lowest level unit or function on a business chart. Indicates a specific action required to carry out a business process.

Activity Ratio The proportion of records in a file that are accessed or updated during a given computer run.

Address A label or identification of a location in storage. A *physical address* is a technology-dependent and specific label; a *logical address* is some form of indirect reference to a physical address.

After Image A copy of a data base record or page after it has been modified or updated.

Aggregation A collection of entities that form an entity. For example, a Work Order entity composed of Raw Material, Tool, Work Center, and Factory Worker entities.

Alternate Key A candidate key in a relation that is not selected or used as a primary key.

ANSI/SPARC The Standards Planning and Requirements Committee of the American National Standards Institute.

Application Program Software that supports a task or end user activity, such as a payroll program.

Area See *Realm.*

Artificial Intelligence The use of computers to carry out tasks that, if performed by humans, would be considered intelligent.

Association A relationship between two data entities in a data model.

Attribute A named characteristic or property of an entity.

Attribute Synthesis A bottom-up or detailed approach to data base design.

Average Search Length In hashed files, the average number of disk accesses to retrieve a specified record.

Backward Recovery A recovery technique that restores a data base to an earlier state by applying before images. Also called *rollback* or UNDO.

Before Image A copy of a data base record or page before it has been updated or modified.

Bidirectional Chain A list structure in which each record has both "forward" and "backward" pointers.

Binary Tree A tree data structure that permits at most two branches (or paths) coming out of each node or element.

Binding The process of linking an application program to its external schema or data description.

Binding Time That time at which binding occurs.

Block The smallest addressable unit of data on a disk. Also called a *physical record.*

Block Header Data that allow the storage subsystem to locate and identify a block of data.

Block Index An index in which each entry refers to a block of records rather than a single record. Used in indexed sequential organizations.

Blocking Factor The number of data records contained in a block.

Bond Energy Algorithm An algorithm for clustering data items into stored records.

Boyce-Codd Normal Form (BCNF) Describes a relational normal form in which every determinant is a candidate key.

B-tree A tree data structure in which all leaves are the same distance from the root (B stands for "balanced").

B^+-tree A B-tree in which the leaves are connected by means of a linked list.

Bucket A conceptual addressable storage location that may contain one or more physical records.

Buffer An area of memory that is used to receive a block of stored records from a storage device or used to transmit a block of records to that device.

Business Activities Specific actions required to carry out a business process.

Business Functions Broad groups of closely related activities and decisions that contribute to a product or service life cycle.

Business Processes Decision-related activities that occur within a business function.

Candidate Key One or more attributes in a relation that uniquely identify an instance of an entity, and therefore may serve as a primary key in that relation.

Catalog A directory of all data in a data base. In a distributed data base, the catalog will contain the locations of each data base fragment.

CD/ROM Compact disk/read-only memory. A form of optical disk storage that provides read-only access to the data stored on a compact disk.

Chain See *Linked List.*

Checkerboard Effect A problem in memory management where there are blocks of both used and unused memory cells.

Checkpoint A DBMS facility that allows programs to be restarted at an intermediate point, rather than at the beginning, when some abnormal condition is encountered.

Clustered Data Base For a distributed data base, each node may have unique subsets of the data base as well as selected redundant copies of some files or subsets of files.

Clustering The process of dividing a logical record into distinct, noncontiguous physical parts. If the parts do not have any of the same attributes, then the process is called *partitioning.*

CODASYL Conference on Data Systems Languages. An organization of computer vendors and users that developed the specifications for the COBOL language and for the DBTG network data base model.

Collision In hashed files, the situation that results when the hashing routine computes the same address for two records with unequal primary key values.

Commit Protocol An algorithm to ensure that a transaction is successfully completed, or else it is aborted.

Concatenated Key A primary key that is comprised of two or more attributes or data items.

Conceptual Schema The overall logical model of an organization's data base, which is independent of a particular DBMS. Also called *Conceptual Data Model.*

Concurrency Control DBMS function that prevents interference between transactions when several users are updating a data base concurrently.

Control Area In VSAM, a group of control intervals.

Control Interval An indexed group of records in VSAM.

Cylinder The set of tracks on a secondary storage device that can be read without moving the read/write mechanism.

Data Facts concerning entities such as people, objects, or events.

Data Administrator A person who is responsible for the overall information resources of an organization.

Data Base A shared collection of logically related

data, designed to meet the information needs of multiple users.

Data Base Administrator A person who is responsible for controlling the design and use of computer data bases.

Data Base Machine An attached processor that has been especially configured to handle the processing of data base access and manipulation.

Data Base Management System (DBMS) A generalized software system that is used to create, manage, and protect data bases.

Data Base Server In a local area network, a dedicated microcomputer that manages a local data base.

Data Definition Language (DDL) The language component of a DBMS that is used to describe the logical (and sometimes physical) structure of a data base.

Data Dictionary/Directory *(DD/D)* The repository of all metadata (or data definitions) for an organization.

Data Dictionary/Directory Manager A software module that is used to manage the Data Dictionary/Directory.

Data Independence The property of being able to change the logical or physical structure of data without requiring changes to application programs that manipulate that data.

Data Item A unit fact concerning some entity. A data item is the smallest named unit of data in an information system. Also called an *attribute* or *data element*.

Data Manipulation Language (DML) A language component of a DBMS that is used by a programmer to access and modify the contents of a data base.

Data Model An abstract description (or map) of the data in an organization. See also *Conceptual Schema*, *External Schema*, and *Internal Schema*.

Data Structure Diagram A graphic data model that uses arrows to portray the associations between entities.

Deadly Embrace Impasse that may result when two users lock certain resources, then request resources locked by the other user. Also called *deadlock*.

Decision Support System A system that supports managerial decision making by providing information and modeling tools.

Delimiter Special symbol used to indicate the end of a field or other piece of data.

Determinant Any attribute on which some other attribute is fully functionally dependent.

Direct Access The ability to retrieve or store a record by reference to its location on a storage volume, and without having to reference previous records on the volume.

Direct Access Storage Device (DASD) A secondary storage device (such as magnetic disk) that supports direct access.

Disk Directory An index to the contents of a disk volume.

Distributed Data Base A single logical data base that is spread across computers in multiple locations that are connected by a data communications network.

Distributed Free Space In VSAM, reserved space for the insertion of new records at the end of each control interval.

Division/Remainder Method A commonly used hashing algorithm in which a primary key value is divided by a prime number, and the remainder is used as the relative bucket address.

Domain The valid set of values for an attribute in a relation.

Domain-Key Normal Form (DK/NF) A conceptual normal form in which every constraint on the relation is a logical consequence of key constraints and domain constraints.

Encryption The process of coding (or scrambling) data so that they cannot be read by humans.

End User Computing An approach to data processing where users who are not computer experts provide their own computing needs through the use of high-level software and languages such as electronic spreadsheets.

Enterprise Model A high-level conceptual data model for an organization.

Entity A person, place, object, or concept about which an organization chooses to store data.

Entity Class A collection of entities that possess similar properties or characteristics.

Entity-Relationship Data Model A type of network data model that uses a special symbol (the diamond) to represent associations between entities.

Existence Dependency A semantic control that indicates that an instance of one entity cannot exist unless an instance of a related entity also exists.

Expert Data Base System See *Intelligent Data Base*.

Expert System A system that captures the knowledge and experience of a human expert, in the form of facts and rules, so as to aid others in decision making.

Extensibility Feature of a data dictionary/directory that allows users to define new entities, attributes, and relationships.

Extent A collection of contiguous physical storage blocks in secondary storage.

External Schema A description of a user's or application program's view of data in a data base. Also called *user view* or *subschema*.

Fifth Normal Form (5NF) A property of a relation that has no join dependency.

File A collection of logically related records. These records are often (but not always) of the same type.

First Normal Form (1NF) A relation in which the intersection of each row and column contains only atomic (or single) values.

Flat File A two-dimensional array of attributes or data items.

Foreign Key A non-key attribute in one relation that appears as the primary key (or part of the primary key) in another relation.

Fourth-Generation Language A high-level nonprocedural language that allows users to write programs much faster than with COBOL or other third-generation languages.

Fourth Normal Form (4NF) Describes a relation that is in Boyce-Codd Normal Form and contains no multivalued dependencies.

Full Functional Dependence Indicates that an attribute in a relation is functionally dependent on the whole of a concatenated key, but not on any subset of that key.

Functional Dependence A relationship between two attributes in a relation. Attribute B is functionally dependent on attribute A if attribute A identifies B (that is, each value of A has exactly one value of B at any given time).

Global Deadlock In a distributed data base, a deadlock (or deadly embrace) involving two or more sites.

Global Transaction In a distributed data base, a transaction that requires reference to data at one or more nonlocal sites to satisfy the request.

Granularity Size or scope of an object to be protected by a system.

Hashed File Organization A file organization that permits direct access to records through the use of a hashing routine.

Hashing Routine An algorithm that converts a primary key value into a relative disk address.

Hierarchical Model A data model in which data are represented as a set of nested 1:*M* relationships. Each record in a hierarchical model may have several offspring, but only one parent record.

Homonym A single word that is used with different meanings in different contexts. Also, two words that are pronounced the same but have different meanings.

Horizontal Positioning Distributing the rows of a table into several separate tables.

Host Language A programming language, like COBOL and PL/I, with which Data Manipulation Language commands can be combined to write a program to perform data base processing.

Identifier An attribute in an entity that distinguishes it from other entities. Also called a *primary key.*

ID Dependency A semantic control or constraint that states that the primary key of one entity must include an attribute that is also the primary key of a related entity.

Index A table or other data structure that is used to determine the location of records in a file or data base.

Indexed Sequential Organization A file organization that permits both sequential and direct access to records in a file. This organization is supported by the indexed sequential access method (ISAM).

Inference Engine In an expert system, a program that processes and interprets the facts and rules in the knowledge base.

Information Data that have been organized or prepared in a form that is suitable for decision making.

Information Resource Management The concept that information is an important organizational resource and must be planned, managed, and protected like other resources such as people, materials, and financial resources.

Instance An occurrence of an entity or data type. For example, a personnel record is a record type; the record for Sally Jones is an instance of that record type.

Intelligent Data Base A data base that contains or is interfaced with a knowledge base, or shared logic for assisting users in accessing and using the data base.

Internal Schema A description of the physical structure of data, or the way data are represented on secondary storage media. Also called *internal data model.*

Interrecord Data Structures Data structures (such as lists) that are used to connect different but related records in the same file or in separate files.

Intersection Record A record that lies at the conjunction of two or more record types and contains data common to those record types.

Intrarecord Data Structures Data structures used to connect fields within a single record.

Inverted List A table or list that is organized by secondary key values.

Join A relational algebra command that causes two tables with a common domain to be combined into a single table.

Join Dependency A relation that cannot be decomposed by projection into smaller relations, and then rejoined into the original relation without spurious results.

Key An attribute or data item that uniquely identifies a record instance or tuple in a relation. See *Secondary Key.*

Knowledge-Based Decision Support System An extension of a decision support system to include an expert system that assists the user in using the DSS and interpreting its results.

Leaf In a tree data structure, a leaf is a node that has no children.

Linked List A data structure in which the logical order of records is maintained by pointers rather than by physical sequence of the records.

Local Transaction In a distributed data base, a transaction that requires reference only to data that are stored at the site where the transaction is originated.

Location Transparency A design goal for a distributed data base, which says that a user (or user program) requesting data need not know at which site those data are located.

Logical Access Map (LAM) A chart or graph showing the sequence of accesses to the records in a data model for a particular application.

Logical Data Model A mapping of the conceptual model into a DBMS-processible data model. Most contemporary DBMSs support either the hierarchical, network, or relational logical models.

Logical Record A collection of data items that describes an object or entity.

Maintenance Modifying or rewriting application programs in response to new requirements, new data formats, and so on.

Mapping (1) An association or correspondence between data entities. (2) Rules that govern the transformation from one form or structure to another form or structure.

Metadata Data descriptors; information about an organization's data.

Multilist Organization A data structure in which there are multiple paths or linked lists connecting the records.

Multiprogramming Process by which several programs are executed concurrently in primary storage.

Multivalued Dependency A dependence that exists when there are three attributes (A, B, and C) in a relation, and for each value of A there is a well-defined set of values for B and a well-defined set of values for C. However, the set of values for B and C are independent of each other.

Natural Language System An artificial intelligence-based language subsystem that allows the user to carry on a dialogue with the computer in an unstructured version of English or other language.

Network Data Model A data model consisting of records, data items, and associations between records. Each record type in the network may have 1:*M* associations with any other record type in that network.

Nonkey Attribute An attribute in a relation that is not part of the primary key of that relation.

Normalization The process of decomposing complex data structures into simple relations according to a set of dependency rules.

Null Pointer A pointer that is empty or contains a special character to indicate the end of a list or data structure.

Null Suppression A data compression technique that suppresses blanks and zeros in data items.

Operating System The overall supervisory and control program of a computer. The operating system allocates memory, controls the execution of tasks, and provides a variety of utility and support functions.

Owner Record Type In a CODASYL data base, a record type that is declared as the "owner" in a set relationship. The set may contain one or more member record types.

Partitioned Data Base In a distributed data base, each node is allocated disjoint subsets of the organization's data base.

Pattern Substitution A data compression technique in which recurring sequences of characters are replaced by shorter codes.

Physical Child In an IMS data base, a child or subordinate segment.

Physical Data Base A representation of the form in which a data base is stored on secondary storage. Generally, the physical data base is represented as a collection of one or more types of stored records.

Physical Disk Address The combination of cylinder, track, and block numbers required to locate a specific data block on a rotating storage volume.

Physical Record See *Block.*

Pointer A field in a record that contains data that can be used to locate another related record. A *physical pointer* contains the actual address. A *relative pointer* contains the relative position. A *logical pointer* contains the primary key of the related record.

Primary Key See *Key.*

Primary Key Attribute An attribute in a relation that is a component of the primary key for that relation.

Primary Storage Computer random access memory. Also called main memory.

Query Languages An end user–oriented language for specifying data retrievals.

Queue A data structure in which all record insertions occur at one end and all deletions occur at the other end of the structure.

Random Access See *Direct Access.*

Realm In a CODASYL data base, a named, contiguous area of secondary storage. Also called *area.*

Record A named collection of related data items.

Recovery The process of restoring a data base and data base operations to a normal state after an error has occurred.

Recursive Association An association between entities in the same entity class.

Referential Integrity An integrity constraint that specifies that the value (or existence) of an attribute in one relation depends on the value (or existence) of the same attribute in another relation.

Relation A named collection of attributes. Data in a relation are represented as a flat file or two-dimensional array of data items.

Relational Algebra A data manipulation language that provides a set of operators for manipulating one or two relations. The most commonly used operators are SELECT, PROJECT, and JOIN.

Relational Calculus A data manipulation language that provides the user with a standard command structure for manipulation relations. The command structure is based on the key words SELECT . . . FROM . . . WHERE.

Relational Model A logical data model in which all data are represented as a collection of normalized relations.

Relationship See *Association.*

Relative Disk Address On a disk storage device, the address of a data block relative to the start of the file.

Replicated Data Base In a distributed data base, each node retains a complete copy of the organization's data base.

Ring A closed-loop list structure in which the last element points to the first element in the structure.

Rollback See *Backward Recovery.*

Rollforward See *Forward Recovery.*

Root In a tree data structure, the node at the top of the tree. The root has no parent.

Rotational Delay On a rotating storage device, the time required for a given data block to rotate to a position under the read/write head.

Schema A representation of the logical structure of a data base. A schema may be expressed in graphic form or in a data definition language.

Search Strategy A technique used to define an access path and locate a specific stored record.

Second Normal Form A relation that is in first normal form and in which each nonkey attribute is fully functionally dependent on the primary key.

Secondary Key A data item that is used to identify the records in a set that share the same property (attribute value). For each value, potentially more than one record may have that value.

Secondary Storage A storage device that is less expensive than primary storage. The primary types of secondary storage are magnetic disk and magnetic tape.

Sector A fixed-length subdivision of a track on a disk storage device.

Security Procedures for protecting a data base against accidental or intentional misuse or destruction.

Seek Time The time required to position the access mechanism in a direct access storage device.

Segment A named record or record component in an IMS data base.

Select A relational algebra command that extracts selected rows of a relation according to a search criterion.

Semantic Data Model A data model that focuses on documenting the meaning of data. It is appropriate for defining a data base at the external and conceptual levels.

Semantic Rules In a data model, rules concerning the usage and meaning of data.

Sequential File Organization A file organization in which the logical order of records is the same as the physical order. A given record in the file can ordinarily be accessed only by first accessing all records that physically precede it.

Set In a CODASYL data base, a named relationship between an owner record type and one or more member record types.

Siblings In a tree data structure, the nodes with a common parent.

SQL Structured Query Language. A standard data definition and manipulation language for relational data bases.

Stack Data structure in which record insertions and deletions are both made at the same end of the list.

Subschema See *External Schema*.

Synonyms Two different names that refer to the same data item or attribute. In a hashed file organization, two keys that are translated into the same block address.

Teleprocessing Monitor A software module that provides a shared interface between application programs and remote communications devices.

Third Normal Form A relation that is in second normal form, and in which no nonkey attribute is functionally dependent on another nonkey attribute. Thus, there are no transitive dependencies.

Three-Schema Architecture A data base architecture that provides three levels or views of data: the conceptual level, the external level, and the internal level.

Track Circular recording positions on a magnetic disk surface.

Transaction A sequence of steps that constitute some well-defined business activity. A transaction may specify a query or it may result in the creation, deletion, or modification of data base records.

Transaction Boundary The logical beginning and end of a transaction.

Transaction Manager In a distributed data base, a software module that maintains a log of all transactions and maintains an appropriate concurrency control schema.

Transfer Rate A measure of the speed with which data are moved between peripheral devices and primary storage.

Transitive Dependency Condition where a nonkey attribute in a relation is fully dependent on another nonkey attribute.

Tree Structure See *Hierarchical Model*.

Tuple A row in a table or relation.

Two-Phase Commit Protocol An algorithm for coordinating updates in a distributed data base.

User View See *External Schema*.

View Integration In conceptual data base design, the process of merging the relations for each user view into a single set of relations in third normal form.

Virtual Storage A memory management technique that permits primary storage to appear much larger to programs than it actually is, since blocks of data and/or programs are moved rapidly between primary and secondary storage.

Volume A demountable storage unit such as a magnetic disk cartridge or magnetic tape.

VSAM Virtual sequential access method. An updated version of the indexed sequential access method, which is device-independent.

Index

Page numbers for definitions are in italics.